how not to say what you mean

A DICTIONARY OF EUPHEMISMS

Reviews of previous editions

'A most valuable and splendidly presented collection; at once scholarly, tasteful, and witty.' *Lord Quirk*

'Euphemists are a lively, inventive, self-regarding and bumptious bunch. Holder goes among them with an etymological glint in his eye.' *Iain Finlayson, Financial Times*

'this fascinating book...don't put this dictionary in the loo—there's another euphemism for you—or else guests will never come out. It's unputdownable once you open it.' *Peter Mullen, Yorkshire Post*

'Concise, well-organized entries' *Library Journal* (USA)

'I am astonished at its depth and wit' Sam Allen (American lawyer and philologist)

'This bran tub of linguistic gems...A delight for browsers who love the vivid oddities of language...a valuable collection.' *City Limits*

'A very funny collection' *Financial Times*

'Many printable gems' *Daily Telegraph*

'Good bedside reading' *Sunday Telegraph*

'It will surely take its place...as a browser's delight and it will entertain book lovers for many hours, whilst at the same time providing useful background information, as well as instruction and clarification to many.' *Reference Review*

'An informative, amusing collection' *The Observer*

'Hugely enjoyable and cherishable' *Times Educational Supplement*

'Lovers of word play will have a field day' *Herald Express, Torquay*

'Excellent, informative, entertaining.' *Wilson Literary Bulletin* (USA)

'Great fun, but not for the maiden aunt.' *Sunday Telegraph*

how not to say what you mean

A DICTIONARY OF EUPHEMISMS

R. W. HOLDER

OXFORD
UNIVERSITY PRESS

OXFORD

UNIVERSITY PRESS

Great Clarendon Street, Oxford OX2 6DP

Oxford University Press is a department of the University of Oxford.
It furthers the University's objective of excellence in research, scholarship,
and education by publishing worldwide in

Oxford New York

Auckland Cape Town Dar es Salaam Hong Kong Karachi
Kuala Lumpur Madrid Melbourne Mexico City Nairobi
New Delhi Shanghai Taipei Toronto

With offices in

Argentina Austria Brazil Chile Czech Republic France Greece
Guatemala Hungary Italy Japan Poland Portugal Singapore
South Korea Switzerland Thailand Turkey Ukraine Vietnam

Oxford is a registered trade mark of Oxford University Press
in the UK and in certain other countries

Published in the United States
by Oxford University Press Inc., New York

First published as *A Dictionary of American and British Euphemisms* by Bath University Press 1987
Revised edition published by Faber and Faber Limited 1989
Second edition published as *A Dictionary of Euphemisms* by Oxford University Press 1995,
and in paperback 1996
Third edition published as *How Not to Say What You Mean:
A Dictionary of Euphemisms* in 2002, and in paperback 2003
This fourth edition published 2007

British Library Cataloguing in Publication Data
Data available

Library of Congress Cataloging in Publication Data
Data available

Typeset by SPI Publisher Services, Pondicherry, India
Printed in Great Britain
on acid-free paper by Clays Ltd, St Ives plc

ISBN 978-0-19-920839-5

1

Contents

An Explanation

In selecting euphemistic words and phrases I have accepted Fowler's definition: 'Euphemism means the use of a mild or vague or periphrastic expression as a substitute for blunt precision or disagreeable use.' (*Modern English Usage*, 1957). A second test is that the euphemistic word or phrase once meant, or prima facie still means, something else. If that were not so, it would be no more than a synonym. Because many euphemisms have become such a part of standard English that we think only of the current usage, I sometimes remind the reader of what the word means literally, or used to mean.

In speech or writing, we use euphemism for dealing with taboo or sensitive subjects. It is therefore the language of evasion, hypocrisy, prudery, and deceit. My selection is of necessity subjective. I reject anything which appears only in another dictionary but I include many obsolete literary entries. For the sake of brevity, I stay with the old rule that the use of the masculine pronoun may, where appropriate, include the feminine.

In previous editions I have given citations which do no more than confirm that the euphemism has been used in literature. This time I choose a citation only when it helps to explain a usage or where I find the context interesting. Although I include no entry which I have not seen in print somewhere, readers may have to refer to a previous edition if they want to trace when and where the euphemism was used, or get in touch with me direct.

The derivation of many euphemisms from association is common, such as death with sleeping or urination with washing. Some circumlocutions and abbreviations I have thought to be euphemistic. Others take the form of hyperbole or understatement. Servicemen especially have brought back foreign words which change their meaning when used in English speech. Euphemism can also be found in rhyming or black slang. Just as the Romans attributed unworthy characteristics to the Carthaginians, and vice versa, so the British continue to use euphemisms to belittle or insult their traditional enemies, particularly the Dutch and the French, and are joined by the Americans in their verbal denigration of the Irish. Whatever the imagery, I try not to patronize the reader when it is obvious but offer a suggestion about the etymology when it may be less so.

Labels such as *Irish* or *Australian* indicate that the usage may be restricted to that country. *American* refers normally to the United States.

It seemed a denial of what I was trying to achieve if I had to define one euphemism by the use of another. With certain words this is unavoidable. In the case of *lavatory*, for example, there is no synonym which is not, like lavatory itself, a euphemism. I also use *mistress* for a woman who regularly copulates with a man out of wedlock, without any qualifying prefix, and *promiscuous* as a definition in a sexual rather than a general sense. Because *fuck* and *shit* are ugly words which jar with constant repetition, I use the euphemistic *copulate* and *defecate* in their stead. I also avoid definitions such as *cripple*, *bastard*, *spinster*, and *whore*, which have unpleasant connotations.

I have reduced the headings in the Thematic Index to fourteen, covering the major subjects of taboo with one for Miscellaneous entries. Each of these sections has an introduction. Those who have heard me talk on euphemisms may find this material familiar. Where a word in the introduction is in italics, you will find it in the text. If it is not a headword, you will be able to locate it through the Thematic Index.

Dr Michael Allen of Bath University published the first edition in 1987 when it seemed unlikely to find a sponsor. Since then I have been indebted to many lexicographers at the Oxford University Press whose suggestions and criticism have improved each edition, and on this occasion especially to Ben Harris and Sarah O'Connor. I am also grateful to the many scholars and lovers of the English language who have taken the trouble to write to me. Any errors or mistakes are mine, not theirs. No edition can, however, be entirely up to date. The language continues to evolve. Meanings change. What was, not long ago, an evasion becomes standard English. Once again I liken my task to that of Sisyphus. The stone never rests at the top of the hill.

West Monkton
2007

Bibliography

Quotations have been included in the text to show how words and phrases were or are used, and when. The date given for each title refers to the first publication or to the edition which I have used. Where an author has deliberately used archaic language, I mention this in the text.

The following dictionaries and reference books are referred to by abbreviations:

DAS	*Dictionary of American Slang* (Wentworth and Flexner, 1975)
DSUE	*A Dictionary of Slang and Unconventional English* (Partridge, 1970)
EDD	*The English Dialect Dictionary* (Wright, 1898–1905)
F&H	*Slang and its Analogues* (Farmer and Henley, 1890–94)
Grose	*Dictionary of the Vulgar Tongue* (Grose, 1811)
Johnson	*A Dictionary of the English Language* (Johnson, 1775)
N&Q	*Notes & Queries*
ODEP	*The Oxford Dictionary of English Proverbs* (Smith and Wilson, 1970)
OED	*The Oxford English Dictionary* (1989)
SOED	*The Shorter Oxford English Dictionary* (1993)
WNCD	*Webster's New Collegiate Dictionary* (1977)

Ainslie, Hew (1892) *A Pilgrimage to the Land of Burns*
Allbeury, Ted
  (1976) *The Only Good German*
  (1981) *The Secret Whispers*
Allen, Charles (1975) *Plain Tales from the Raj*
  (1979) *Tales from the Dark Continent*
Amis, Kingsley (1978) *Jake's Thing*
  (1980) *Russian Hide-and-Seek*
  (1986) *The Old Devils*
  (1988) *Difficulties with Girls*
Andrews, William (1899) *Bygone Church Life in Scotland*
Anonymous (1996) *Primary Colors*
Applebaum, Anne (2003) *Gulag*
Archer, Jeffrey (1979) *Kane and Abel*
  (2004) *A Prison Diary: Part III Heaven*
Armstrong, Louis (1955) *Satchmo*
Atkinson, Rick (2003) *An Army at Dawn*
Attenborough, David (2002) *Life on Air*
Atwood, Margaret (1988) *Cat's Eye*
  (1996) *Alias Grace*
  (2003) *Onyx and Crake*

Bacon, Francis (1627) *Essays*
Banim, John (1825) *O'Hara Tales*
Barber, Noel (1971) *The War of the Running Dogs*
  (1981) *Tamara*
Beevor, Antony (1998) *Stalingrad*
  (2002) *Berlin the Downfall 1945*
Bence-Jones, Mark (1987) *Twilight of the Ascendancy*
Binchy, Maeve (1985) *Echoes*
Blanch, Leslie (1954) *The Wilder Shores of Love*

Block, Thomas (1979) *Mayday*
Bogarde, Dirk (1978) *Snakes and Ladders*
  (1981) *Voices in the Garden*
  (1983) *An Orderly Man*
Boldrewood, Rolf (1890) *A Colonial Reformer*
Boswell, James (1785) *The Journal of a Tour to the Hebrides with Samuel Johnson*
  (1791) *The Life of Samuel Johnson*
  (1792–3) *London Journal*
Boyd, William (1981) *A Good Man in Africa*
  (1982) *An Ice-Cream War*
  (1998) *Armadillo*
Boyle, Andrew (1979) *The Climate of Treason*
Bradbury, Malcolm (1975) *The History Man*
  (1976) *Who Do You Think You Are?*
Brown, Harry (1944) *A Walk in the Sun*
Bryson, Bill (1989) *The Lost Continent*
  (1991) *Neither Here Nor There*
  (1994) *Made in America*
  (2000) *Down Under*
  (2003) *A Short History of Nearly Everything*
Buckman, S. S. (1870) *John Darke's Sojourn in the Cotswolds*
Bullock, Alan, and Stallybrass, Oliver (1977) *The Fontana Dictionary of Modern Thought*
Burleigh, Michael (2000) *The Third Reich*
Burnet, Gilbert (1714) *History of the Reformation of the Church of England*
Burns, Robert (1786) *Poems in the Scottish Dialect*
Burton, Robert (1621) *The Anatomy of Melancholy*
Bush, Robin (1997) *Somerset Bedside Book*
Butler, Samuel (1903) *The Way of All Flesh*

Cahill, Thomas (1995) *How the Irish Saved Civilization*
Carter, V. Bonham (1965) *Winston Churchill as I Knew Him*
Cawthorne, Nigel (1996) *Sex Lives of the Popes*
Chandler, Raymond (1939) *Trouble Is My Business*
(1943) *The High Window*
(1953) *The Long Goodbye*
(1958) *Playback*
Channon, Henry (1993) *Henry Channon-Chips: The Diaries of Sir Henry Channon*
Cheng, Nien (1984) *Life and Death in Shanghai*
Cherry-Gerrard, Apsley (1932) *The Worst Journey in the World*
Christie, Agatha (1939) *Evil Under the Sun*
(1940) *Ten Little Niggers*
Clancy, Tom (1987) *Patriot Games*
(1988) *The Cardinal in the Kremlin*
(1989) *Clear and Present Danger*
(1991) *The Sum of All Our Fears*
Clare, John (1827) *The Shepherd's Calendar*
Clark, Alan (1993) *Diaries*
(1995) *Barbarossa*
(1998) *Diaries*
(1998) *The Tories*
(2002) *The Last Diaries*
Clark, Miles (1991) *High Endeavours*
Cleland, John (1749) *Memoirs of a Woman of Pleasure (Fanny Hill)*
Clover, Charles (2004) *The End of the Line*
Cobbett, William (1830) *Rural Rides*
Cole, John (1995) *As it Seemed to Me*
Collins, Jackie (1981) *Chances*
Collins, Wilkie (1860) *The Woman in White*
(1868) *The Moonstone*
Colodny, Lee, and Gettlin, Robert (1991) *Silent Coup*
Colville, John (1976) *Footprints in Time*
Commager, Henry (1972) *The Defeat of America*
Condon, Richard (1966) *Any God Will Do*
Cookson, Catherine (1967) *Slinky Jane*
(1969) *Our Kate*
Coren, Michael (1995) *Conan Doyle*
Cork, Kenneth (1988) *Cork on Cork*
Corley, T. A. B. (1961) *Democratic Despot*
Cornwell, Bernard (1997) *Sharpe's Tiger*
Cornwell, Patricia (2000) *The Last Precinct*
Cosgrave, Patrick (1989) *The Lives of Enoch Powell*
Coyle, Harold (1987) *Team Yankee*
Cromwell, Oliver (1643) *Letter*
Crossman, Richard (1981) *Backbench Diaries*

Dalrymple, William (1989) *In Xanadu*
(1993) *City of Djinns*
(1997) *From the Holy Mountain*
(1998) *The Age of Kali*
(2002) *White Moguls*
David, Saul (2002) *The Indian Mutiny*
Davidson, Lionel (1978) *The Chelsea Murders*
Davies, Norman (2003) *Rising '44*
de Bernières, Louis (1994) *Captain Corelli's Mandolin*
de la Billière, Peter (1992) *Storm Command*
de Mille, Nelson (1988) *Charm School*

Deedes, W. F. (1997) *Dear Bill*
Defoe, Daniel (1719) *Robinson Crusoe*
(1721) *Moll Flanders*
Deighton, Len (1972) *Close-up*
(1978) *SS-GB*
(1982) *Goodbye Mickey Mouse*
(1985) *London Match*
(1988) *Sky Hook*
(1991) *City of Gold*
(1993/1) *Blood, Tears and Folly*
(1993/2) *Violent Ward*
Dickens, Charles (1840) *The Old Curiosity Shop*
(1841) *Barnaby Rudge*
(1843) *The Life and Adventures of Martin Chuzzlewit*
(1859) *A Tale of Two Cities*
(1861) *Great Expectations*
Dickinson, William (1866) *Scallow Beck Boggle*
Dickson, Paul (1978) *The Official Rules*
Diehl, William (1978) *Sharky's Machine*
Dills, Lattie (1976) *The 'Official' CB Slanguage Language Dictionary*
Diski, Jenny (2002) *Stranger on a Train*
Donaldson, Frances (1990) *Yours Plum: The Letters of P. G. Wodehouse*
Donnelly, Jennifer (2003) *A Gathering Light*
Douglas, George (1901) *The House with the Green Shutters*
Doyle, Roddy (1987) *The Commitments*
(1990) *The Snapper*
(1991) *The Van*
(1993) *Paddy Clarke Ha Ha Ha*
(1996) *The Woman who Walked into Doors*
Dryden, John (1668–98) *Poetical Works*

Ellis, William (1750) *The Modern Husbandman*
Ellman, Lucy (1988) *Sweet Desserts*
Emblen, D. L. (1970) *Peter Mark Roget: The Word and the Man*
Enright, D. J. (editor) (1985) *Fair of Speech*
Enright, Dominique (2002) *The Wit and Wisdom of Winston Churchill*
Erdman, Paul (1986) *The Panic of '89*
(1987) *The Palace*
Evans, Nicholas (1995) *The Horse Whisperer*
(1998) *The Loop*
Evans-Pritchard, Ambrose (1997) *The Secret Life of Bill Clinton*
Evelyn, John (published in 1818 posthumously) *Diary*

Faith, Nicholas (1990) *The World the Railways Made*
Farmer, J. S. and Henley, W. J. (1890–94) *Slang and its Analogues*
Farran, Roy (1948) *Winged Dagger*
Faulks, Sebastian (1993) *Birdsong*
(1998) *Charlotte Gray*
(2001) *Green Dolphin Street*
Fielding, Helen (1996) *Bridget Jones's Diary*
Fielding, Henry (1729) *The Author's Face*
(1742) *The History and Adventures of Joseph Andrews*
Fiennes, Ranulph (1996) *The Sett*

(2003) *Captain Scott*

Fingall, Elizabeth (Countess of) (1977) *Seventy Years Young*

Flanagan, Thomas (1988) *The Tenants of Time*
    (1995) *The End of the Game*

Fleming, Lionel (1965) *Head or Harp*

Fletcher, John (1618) *Valentinian*

Follett, Ken (1978) *The Eye of the Needle*
    (1979) *Triple*
    (1991) *Night over Water*
    (1996) *The Hammer of Eden*

Forbes, Brian (1972) *The Distant Laughter*
    (1983) *The Rewrite Man*

Forbes, Colin (1992) *By Stealth*

Foreman, Amanda (1998) *Georgiana, Duchess of Devonshire*

Forster, Margaret (1997) *Rich Desserts and Captain's Thin*

Forsyth, Frederick (1984) *The Fourth Protocol*
    (1994) *The Fist of God*
    (1996) *Icon*

Foster, R. F. (1993) *Paddy and Mr Punch*

Francis, Dick (1988) *The Edge*
    (1998) *Field of 13*
    (2002) *Shattered*

Francis, M. E. (1901) *Pastorals of Dorset*

Fraser, George MacDonald (1969) *Flashman*
    (1970) *Royal Flash*
    (1973) *Flashman at the Charge*
    (1975) *Flashman in the Great Game*
    (1977) *Flashman's Lady*
    (1992) *Quartered Safe Out Here*
    (1994) *Flashman and the Angel of the Lord*

French, Patrick (1995) *Younghusband*
    (1997) *Liberty or Death*

Gabriel, Marius (1992) *The Original Sin*

Garfield, Simon (2004) *Our Hidden Lives*

Garve, Andrew (1963) *The Sea Monks*
    (1969) *Boomerang*

Gentles, Ian (1992) *The New Model Army in England, Ireland and Scotland, 1645–1653*

Goebbels, Josef (1945) *Diaries* (translated by Richard Barry)

Golden, Arthur (1997) *Memoirs of a Geisha*

Goldman, William (1986) *Brothers*

Gorbachev, Mikhail (1995) *Memoirs* (translated by Georges Peronansky and Tatjana Varsavsky)

Graham, Dougal (1883) *The Collected Writings*

Graves, Robert (1941) *Proceed Sergeant Lamb*

Green, Jonathon (1996) *Chasing the Sun*

Green, Shirley (1979) *Rachman*

Greene, G. A. (1599) *Works*

Greene, Graham (1932) *Stamboul Train*
    (1978) *The Human Factor*

Grisham, John (1992) *The Pelican Brief*
    (1999) *The Testament*
    (2002) *The Summons*

Grose, Francis (1811 edition) *Dictionary of the Vulgar Tongue*

Hailey, Arthur (1979) *Overlord*

Hall, Adam (1988) *Quiller's Run*

Hardy, Thomas (1874) *Far from the Madding Crowd*
    (1886) *The Mayor of Casterbridge*
    (1888) *Wessex Tales*
    (1891) *Tess of the D'Urbervilles*

Harland, John and Wilkinson, T. T. (1867) *Folk Lore*

Harris, Frank (1925) *My Life and Loves*

Harris, Robert (1992) *Fatherland*
    (1995) *Enigma*
    (1998) *Archangel*

Hartley, John (1870) *Heart Broken*

Harvey, William (1628) *Anatomica de Motu Cardis* etc.

Hastings, Max (1987) *The Korean War*

Hastings, Selina (1994) *Evelyn Waugh*

Hattersley, Roy (1995) *Who Goes Home*

Hawks, Tony (2002) *One Hit Wonderland*

Heath, Robert (1650) *Clarastella together with poems occasional* etc.

Heffer, Simon (1998) *Like the Roman: The Life of Enoch Powell*

Henderson, George (1856) *The Popular Rhymes, Sayings and Proverbs of the County of Berwick*

Henderson, William (1879) *Notes on the Folk Lore of the Northern Counties* etc.

Herd, David (1771) *Ancient and Modern Scottish Songs*

Herr, Michael (1977) *Dispatches*

Herriot, James (1981) *The Good Lord Made Them All*

Higgins, Jack (1989) *A Season in Hell*

Holland, James (2003) *Fortress Malta*

Holt, Alfred (1961) *Phrase and Word Origins*

Horne, Alastair (1969) *To Lose a Battle*
    (with D. Montgomery) (1994) *The Lonely Leader: Montgomery 1944–1945*

Horrocks, Brian (1960) *A Full Life*

Housman A. E. (1896) *A Shropshire Lad*

Hosseini, Khaled (2003) *The Kite Runner*

Howard, Anthony (1977) *New Words for Old*
    (1978) *Weasel Words*
    (1993) *Lives Remembered*

Hughes, Robert (1987) *The Fatal Shore*

Hunt, Robert (1865–96 edition) *Popular Romances of the West of England*

Irvine, Lucy (1986) *Runaway*

James, Lawrence (2001) *Warrior Race*

James, P. D. (1972) *An Unsuitable Job for a Woman*
    (1994) *Original Sin*
    (2001) *Death in Holy Orders*

Jennings, Gary (1965) *Personalities of Language*

Johnson, Paul (1997) *A History of the American People*

Johnson, Samuel (1755) *A Dictionary of the English Language*
Joliffe, Gray, and Mayle, Peter (1984) *Man's Best Friend*
Jolly, Rick (1988) *Jackspeak: The Pusser's Rum Guide*
Jones, R. V. (1978) *Most Secret War*
Jonson, Ben (1598–1633) *Works* (edited by Herford and Simpson, 1925–52)

Katzenbach, John (1995) *The Shadow Man*
Kee, Robert (1984) *The World We Left Behind*
(1985) *The World We Fought For*
(1993) *The Laurel and the Ivy*
Keegan, John (1989) *The Second World War*
(1991) *Churchill's Generals*
(1998) *The First World War*
Keneally, Thomas (1982) *Schindler's Ark*
(1985) *A Family Madness*
King, Stephen (1990) *I Shall Bear Witness*
(1996) *The Green Mile*
Kirkton, James (1817) *The Secret and True History of the Church of Scotland* etc.
Klemperer, Victor (1998) *I Shall Bear Witness* (translated by Martin Chalmers)
(1999) *To the Bitter End* (translated by Martin Chalmers)
Koontz, Dean (1997) *Sole Survivor*
Kramarae, Cheris, and Treichler, Panla (1985) *A Feminist Dictionary*
Kuper, Simon (2003) *Ajax*
Kyle, Duncan (1975) *The Semenov Impulse*

Lacey, Robert (1986) *Ford*
Lambert, Derek (2000) *Spanish Lessons*
Lauderdale, John (1796) *A Collection of Poems*
Lavine, Emanuel (1930) *The Third Degree*
le Carré, John (1986) *A Perfect Spy*
(1995) *Our Game*
(1996) *The Tailor of Panama*
(2001) *The Constant Gardener*
Lee, Joseph J. (1989) *Ireland 1912–1985*
Lewis, Nigel (1989) *Channel Firing*
Liddle, William (1821) *Poems on Different Occasions*
Lodge, David (2001) *Thinks*
(2004) *Author, Author*
Lomax, Eric (1995) *The Railway Man*
Londres, Albert (1928) *The Road to Buenos Ayres* (translated by Eric Sutton)
Longstreet, Stephen (1956) *The Real Jazz Old and New*
Ludlum, Robert (1984) *The Aquitaine Progression*
Lukacs, John (2000) *Five Days in London*
Lyall, Gavin (1972) *Blame the Dead*
(1982) *The Conduct of Major Maxim*
(1985) *The Crocus List*
Lyman, Raymond (2004) *Slim, Master of War*
Lynd, Robert (1946) *Dr Johnson and Company*
Lynn, Jonathan and Jay, Antony (1981) *Yes Minister*
(1986) *Yes Prime Minister*

Maas, Peter (1986) *Man Hunt*
McBain, Ed (1994) *There Was a Little Girl*

McCall Smith, Alexander (1998) *The No. 1 Ladies' Detective Agency*
McCarthy, Mary (1963) *The Group*
(1967) *Vietnam*
McCarthy, Pete (2000) *McCarthy's Bar*
(2002) *The Road to McCarthy*
McCourt, Frank (1997) *Angela's Ashes*
(1999) *'Tis*
McCrum, Robert (1991) *Mainland*
(2004) *Wodehouse*
McCrum, Robert, Cran, William, and McNeil, Robert (1986) *The Story of English*
McEwan, Ian (2000) *Atonement*
Macdonald, Ross (1971) *The Doomsters*
(1976) *The Blue Hammer*
Macintyre, Ben (2001) *A Foreign Field*
McNab, Andy (1993) *Bravo Two Zero*
(1995) *Immediate Action*
(1997) *Remote Control*
Mailer, Norman (1965) *An American Dream*
Major, John (1999) *The Autobiography*
Mandela, Nelson (1994) *Long Walk to Freedom*
Manning, Olivia (1960) *The Great Fortune*
(1977) *The Danger Tree*
(1978) *The Battle Lost and Won*
Mantle, Jonathan (1988) *In for a Penny*
Marvell, Andrew (*c*.1670) *Poems*
Massie, Allan (1986) *Augustus*
Massie, Robert (1992) *Dreadnought*
Mayhew, Henry (1851) *London Labour and the London Poor*
(1862) *London's Underground*
Mazower, Mark (1993) *Inside Hitler's Greece*
Mitchell, David (1982) *The Spanish Civil War*
Mitchell, David (2004) *Cloud Atlas*
Mitford, Jessica (1963) *The American Way of Death*
Mitford, Nancy (1945) *The Pursuit of Love*
(1956) *Noblesse Oblige*
(1960) *Don't Tell Alfred*
Mockler, Anthony (1984) *Haile Selassie's War*
Monkhouse, Bob (1993) *Crying with Laughter*
Monsarrat, Nicholas (1978) *The Master Mariner*
Moran, (Lord) (1966) *Winston Churchill: The Struggle for Survival*
Morison, David (1790) *Poems*
Moss, Robert (1987) *Carnival of Space*
Moynahan, Brian (1983) *Airport International*
(1994) *The Russian Century*
Muir, Frank (1990) *The Oxford Book of Humorous Prose*
(1997) *A Kentish Lad*
Murdoch, Iris (1978) *The Sea, the Sea*
(1983) *The Philosopher's Pupil*
Murray, D. Christie (1886) *Rainbow Gold*
Murray, Elisabeth (1977) *Caught in the Web of Words*

Nabokov, Vladimir (1968) *King, Queen, Knave*
Naipaul, V. S. (1964) *An Area of Darkness*
(1989) *A Turn in the South*
(1990) *India: A Million Mutinies Now*
Norfolk, Lawrence (1991) *Lemprière's Dictionary*

O'Brian, Patrick (1970) *Master and Commander*
Olivier, Laurence (1982) *Confessions of an Actor*
Ollard, Richard (1974) *Pepys*
Ousby, Ian (1997) *Occupation: The Ordeal of France 1940–1944*
Oxford English Dictionary (1989 edition)

Palin, Michael (2004) *Himalaya*
Parris, Matthew (1995) *Great Parliamentary Scandals*
Partridge, Eric (1969) *A Dictionary of Slang and Unconventional English*
Paterson, R. C. (1998) *A Land Afflicted*
Patten, Chris (1998) *East and West*
Patterson, James (2002) *The Beach House*
   (2003) *The Big Bad Wolf*
Patterson, Richard North (1996) *Silent Witness*
Paxman, Jeremy (1998) *The English*
Payn, James (1878) *By Proxy*
Pearsall, Ronald (1969) *The Worm in the Bud*
Pegge, Samuel (1803) *Anecdotes of the English Language*
Pepys, Samuel (1660–69) *Diary*
Pierre, D. B. C. (2003) *Vernon God Little*
Pope, Alexander (1735) *Poetical Works*
Price, Anthony (1971) *The Alamut Ambush*
   (1974) *Other Paths to Glory*
   (1978) *The '44 Vintage*
   (1979) *War Games*
Proulx, Annie (1993) *The Shipping News*
   (2002) *That Old Ace in the Hole*

Quiller-Couch, Arthur (1890) *I Saw Three Ships*

Ramsay, Allan (1800 edition) *Poems*
Ranfurly, Hermione (Countess of) (1994) *To War with Whitaker*
Rankin, Ian (1993) *The Black Book*
   (1998) *The Hanging Garden*
   (1999) *Dark Souls*
   (2000) *Set in Darkness*
   (2003) *A Question of Blood*
   (2004) *Fleshmarket Close*
Rendell, Ruth (1991) *Kissing the Gunner's Daughter*
Richards, Frank (1933) *Old Soldiers Never Die*
   (1936) *Old Soldier Sahib*
Ritchie, A. I. (1883) *The Churches of St Baldred*
Robbins, Harold (1981) *Goodbye Janette*
Roberts, Andrew (1999) *Salisbury*
Roberts, Michael (1951) *The Estate of Man*
Ross, Alan (1956) *Noblesse Oblige*
Rowe, Nicholas (1703) *The Fair Penitent*
Rowlands, Alan (1990) *Trautmann: the Biography*
Rushdie, Salman (1995) *The Moor's Last Sigh*

Sanders, Laurence (1970) *The Anderson Tapes*
   (1973) *The First Deadly Sin*
   (1977) *The Second Deadly Sin*
   (1977) *The Tangent Objective*
   (1980) *The Tenth Commandment*
   (1980) *Caper*
   (1981) *The Third Deadly Sin*
   (1982) *The Case of Lucy Bending*
   (1985) *The Fourth Deadly Sin*
   (1992) *McNally's Luck*
   (1994) *McNally's Caper*
Sayers, Dorothy (1937) *Busman's Honeymoon*
Scott, Paul (1968) *The Day of the Scorpion*
   (1973) *The Jewel in the Crown*
   (1975) *A Division of the Spoils*
   (1977) *Staying On*
Scott, Walter (1816) *The Antiquary*
   (1817) *Rob Roy*
Seitz, Raymond (1998) *Over Here*
Service, John (1887) *The Life and Recollections of Dr Duguid of Kilwinning*
Seymour, Gerald (1977) *Kingfisher*
   (1980) *The Contract*
   (1995) *The Heart of Danger*
   (1998) *The Waiting Time*
   (2002) *The Untouchable*
   (2003) *A Traitor's Kiss*
Shakespeare, William *Plays and Sonnets* (as noted)
Sharpe, Tom (1974) *Porterhouse Blue*
   (1975) *Blot on the Landscape*
   (1978) *The Throwback*
   (1979) *The Wilt Alternative*
   (1982) *Vintage Stuff*
   (2004) *Wilt in Nowhere*
Shirer, William (1984) *The Nightmare Years 1930–1940*
   (1999) *This is Berlin*
Simon, Ted (1979) *Jupiter's Travels*
Simpson, John (1998) *Strange Places, Questionable People*
Sinclair, Keith (1991) *A History of New Zealand*
Slang Dictionary (The) (1874)
Smith, Michael (1999) *Foley: The Spy who Saved 10,000 Jews*
Smith, Wilbur (1979) *Wild Justice*
Smith, William G., and Wilson, F. P. (1970) *The Oxford Dictionary of English Proverbs*
Smollett, Tobias (1748) *Roderick Random*
Sohmer, Steve (1988) *Favourite Son*
Somerville, A. E., and Ross, Martin (1894) *The Real Charlotte*
   (1897) *Some Experiences of an Irish RM*
Stamp, Terence (1994) *The Night*
Stewart, Graham (1999) *Burying Caesar*
Stevenson, Robert Louis (1882) *The Pavilion of the Links*
Stoker, Bram (1895) *The Watter's Mou'*
Strachey, Lytton (1918) *Eminent Victorians*
Strain, E. H. (1900) *Elmslie's Drag-Net*
Strong, Terence (1997) *Rogue Element*
   (1998) *Deadwater Deep*
Styron, William (1976) *Sophie's Choice*
Swift, Jonathan (1723–38) *Works*
Szpilman, Wladyslaw (1998) *The Pianist* (translated by Anthea Bell)

Taraporevala, Soomi (2000) *Pursis*
Taylor, William (1787) *Scots Poems*
Thackeray, W. M. (1848) *Vanity Fair*

Theroux, Paul (1976) *The Family Arsenal*
(1977) *The Consul's File*
(1978) *Picture Palace*
(1979) *The Old Patagonian Express*
(1982) *The London Embassy*
(1983) *The Kingdom by the Sea*
(1988) *Riding the Red Rooster*
(1992) *The Happy Isles of Oceania*
(1993) *Millroy the Magician*
(1995) *The Pillars of Hercules*
(2002) *Dark Safari*
Thomas, Hugh (1986) *Armed Truce*
Thomas, Michael (1980) *Green Monday*
(1982) *Someone Else's Money*
(1987) *The Ropespinner Conspiracy*
Thompson, Rupert (1996) *The Insult*
Thwaite, Anthony (1992) *Selected Letters of Philip Larkin 1940–1985*
Tomalin, Claire (1997) *Jane Austen*
(2002) *Pepys*
Tombs, Robert, and Tombs, Isabelle (2006) *The Sweet Enemy*
Torriano, Giovanni (1642) *A Common Place of Italian Proverbs and Proverbial Phrases*
Train, John (1983) *Preserving Capital and Making it Grow*
Tremain, Rose (2003) *The Colour*

Tuchman, Barbara (1962) *August 1914*
Turner, E. S. (1952) *The Shocking History of Advertising*
Turow, Scott (1987) *Presumed Innocent*
(1990) *The Burden of Proof*
(1993) *Pleading Guilty*
(1996) *The Laws of our Fathers*
(1999) *Personal Injuries*
Twain, Mark (1884) *The Adventures of Huckleberry Finn*
Tweeddale, John (1896) *Maff*
Tyrrell, Syd (1973) *A Countryman's Tale*

Ustinov, Peter (1971) *Krumnagel*

Vanderhaeghe, Guy (1997) *The Englishman's Boy*

Ward, Geoffrey C. (1990) *The Civil War*
Waugh, Evelyn (1932) *Remote People*
Webster, John (1623) *The Duchess of Malfi*
West, Morris (1979) *Proteus*
Whicker, Alan (1982) *Within Whicker's World*
Winchester, Simon (1998) *The Surgeon of Crowthorne*
Wodehouse, P. G. (1934) *Right Ho, Jeeves!*
Wolfe, Tom (1987) *The Bonfire of the Vanities*
Wright, Elizabeth Mary (1932) *The Life of Joseph Wright*

Addictions

This section includes alcohol, drugs, and gambling, but not tobacco, the smoking of which has been, until recently, so socially accepted and common since Victorian days as not to require evasive language, except among prisoners where *snout* is currency. At various times, it has not been illegal in Britain and America to drink intoxicants, ingest opiates and other drugs, or make bets. When any of these activities is taken to excess, the damage is not just to health and wealth. The fabric of family life can be destroyed and much unhappiness created for the addict and for other people. It is not surprising that we, and those addicted, choose to allude to these matters with euphemism.

If your host at a party asks you 'What would you like to drink?' you are not expected to request a glass of water or a cup of tea. The word *drink* is commonly used for alcohol and *drunk* is standard English for what happens to you if you take too much of it. If we probe deeper, we see that *alcohol* is a shortened form of *alcohol of wine*, meaning a condensed spirit, and so that word is also euphemistic. In turn, a *spirit* is literally any liquid in the form of a distillation, or the essence of something. In modern use, a *beverage* is literally any kind of potable liquid although, as with the slang *bevvy*, the word is used of intoxicants. But again, we have run into difficulty with the word *liquid*, a *liquid lunch* not being a meal where the main items are soup and water.

Apart from the words for intoxicants which have become standard English, we use a plethora of evasions when we refer to our consumption of intoxicants. A glance at the letter S indicates the breadth and ingenuity of our use of language. The *sauce* is usually drunk by others to excess, *on the sauce* indicating alcoholism. *Sea-food* was what Americans drank during Prohibition, referring to its mode of importation. A *scoop, sharpener, short, shot, slug, snifter, stiffener,* or *stimulant* usually refer to spirits. We may fill the *social glass* with *something moist* or, if we are leaving, with *something for the road.* If abstemious, we may confine ourselves to a *sip* or a *spot,* avoiding *strong waters* for which, if we are Irish, we are liable to confess to a

strong weakness. Equally undesirable is *stump liquor,* even in a *sundowner.*

We are also evasive about the places where we choose to consume alcohol. The British *local* is no more local than any other nearby establishment and the *public house* is private property. The only handicap you receive at the *nineteenth hole* is to your sense of balance. Discreet tradesmen used to refer to *groceries' sundries* and intoxicants may still be bought in an American *package store.* The *bottle* is assumed to contain alcohol and the *bottle shop* does not sell empty containers. We expect our *glass* to be filled with wine or spirits, and order a *pint* or *half* when we drink beer in a *bar.*

We select the evasions we use for intoxication according to who happens to be the drunkard. If we ourselves have *enjoyed a drink,* we may be *indisposed, mellow,* or suffering from a *migraine.* Other people are treated less charitably. We may suggest that their condition is only *half* as bad as it might be, but here the half equals the whole, whether they are *half-canned, corned, cooked, cut,* or on through the alphabet. Only with *half-seas over* do we find another etymology. Some of our evasions come from rhyming slang, such as *cop an elephant's* (trunk), or the choice of composers between *Brahms* or *Mozart* (and Liszt).

In a society where abstinence is taboo, euphemism may be used to describe the teetotaller. He can be a *pioneer* in Ireland or, in America, have worn a *blue ribbon.* British soldiers stationed in India referred to an abstainer as a *bun-puncher, charwallah,* or *wad-shifter* who might, if he no longer wished to *sign the pledge,* decide to *smash the teapot.*

In my definitions I use *narcotics* in the knowledge that many of the drugs which are illegally ingested have other effects than narcosis, there being insufficient space to enlarge on specific scientific characteristics of the various substances. Many of the evasions associated with narcotics are addict jargon. Among the myriad euphemisms, none is more misleading than *controlled substance,* suggesting that the authorities have the ability to manage an evil and illegal multi-billion dollar business.

A browse through the letter H gives us an idea of the language involved. *H* is heroin, a *hard drug,* also known as *horse,* ingested by those who have the *habit*. *Hash* and *hemp* are marijuana which may turn you into a *hash-head* if you become *hooked*. A home-grown opiate in England was the *headache*, made from the native poppy into something called *headache-wine*. *Hop* was opium and an addict would *hit the pipe* containing a *hop-joint* before becoming *hopped* and turning into a *hophead*. Cocaine is *happy dust* or *heavenly dust* which will give you a *high* but is dangerous to *hold* if you are liable to be searched. To obtain these, and other substances such as LSD or ecstasy, you will have to *hustle*, especially if you want a *highball*, or concoction of illegal substances.

Some of the euphemisms refer to the source of the narcotic, such as *Colombian gold*, *Eastern substances* or *Mexican brown*. Others pun on the characteristics of the powder or crystal. For example, from *snow*, cocaine, come *snowball*, *snowbird*, *snow-blind*, *snowed in*, *snowed under*, *snowed up*, *snow-head*, *snow-man*, *snowstorm*, and *sleighride*.

Gamble comes from the Middle English word meaning to play, sharing its root with *gamester* and *gaming*. The imagery of *playing* is one which those who take our bets seek to nourish. They are called *bookmakers* (although not authors, publishers, or printers), *commission agents*, or *turf accountants*, while we, who fill their pockets, may be termed *investors*. We may also visit the *casino* or the *fruit machine*, and few sights are as melancholy as rows of addicts sitting hour after hour before vast banks of *one-armed bandits* hoping that one day they will hit the jackpot.

abuse
acid
   acid freak *at* freak
action[1]
aerated
afloat
alcohol
Alderman Lushington *at* Lush
ambrosia
amusement with prizes
anti-freeze
ardent spirits
auld kirk (the)
Aunt Cissed
awful experiment (the)

bacchanalian
back teeth floating
bagged
bamboozled
bar
barley
   barley-cap
   barley-king
basted
bat
battered
beat the gong
befuddled
belt
bend
bend the elbow *at* crook the
   elbow
beverage
   beverage host/hostess
   beverage room
   bevvied
   bevy
binge
bird dog

black smoke
black stuff (the)
   black velvet
bladdered
blast[3]
   blasted
blind
   blind drunk
   blind-fou
   blind pig
   blitzed
blow[6]
   blow a stick
   blow Charlie
   blow horse
   blow snow
blow one
blue ribbon
blue ruin
   blue devils
   blue flags
   blue heaven
   blue joy
   blue stone
   blue velvet
boiled
bombed out
   bomb
   bomber
   bombita
bookmaker
bookie's runner *at* runner[3]
bother the bottle *at* bottle[1]
bottle[1]
   bottled
bottle club
   bottle party
   bottle shop
bracer
Brahms

branch water
brew[2] (a)
brown tea
bug-eyed
bun on (a)
bun-puncher
bung[1]
burn with a (low) blue flame
burra peg *at* chota peg
bush-house
bust[3]
   bust a cap
butler's perks
buy
   buy a brewery
   buyer
buzz on (a)
   buzzed

C
camel
can on (a)
   canned
candy
   candy man
   candy store
   nose candy
carry[2]
carry[4]
   carry a (heavy) load
celebrate
charge[2]
Charlie
   Charlie girl
chase the dragon
chaser
chemical
   chemically affected
   chemically inconvenienced
China white

Chinese tobacco
chippy[2]
chota pegchuck horrors
chuck up
    chucked
clear up
clobbered
club[2]
cock-eyed
cock the little finger
cocktail[2]
    cocktail bar
    cocktail hour
    cocktail lounge
coke
    coke-hound
    coked
    cokie
cold turkey
cold-water man
Colombian gold
come down
comfortable[1]
    comforting beverages
commission agent
commune with Toby
concerned *at* concern
confused
connect[2]
controlled substance
convivial
cook[3]
cool[2]
cool a turkey *at* cold turkey
cooler[2]
cop an elephant's
cordial[2]
corked
corn[1]
    corn juice
    corn mule
    corned
cough medicine
cousin Cis
crack[3]
    crackhead
crack a bottle
crash
creature (the)
crocked
    crock
crook the elbow
cruise[2]
crystal
cup too many *at* in your cups
cut[3]

damaged[1]
damp

damp the sawdust
dash[1]
dead soldier
deal
    dealer
debt of honour
deceived in liquor *at*
    deceived
deck
decks awash
dependency[2]
dip[2]
disciple of
    disciple of Bacchus
disco biscuit
disguised
dive[2]
do a line
doll[2]
dope
down among the dead men
downs
    downers
dragon (the)
dram
draw a blank
dream
    dream dust
    dream stick
drink[1]
    drink a lot
    drink at Freeman's Quay
    drink some
    drink taken
    drink too much
drink problem *at* problem
drop[2]
    drop of blood
    drop on
    drop taken
drop anchor
drown the miller
drown your sorrows
drunk *at* drink[1]
dry[1]
    dry canteen
    dry county
    dry out
Dutch cheer
Dutch courage
Dutch feast
Dutch headache

Eastern substances
ecstasy
edged
elbow-bending
    elbow-bender
elephant's

elevated
embalmed
emotional;
enjoy a drink
enjoy a jar *at* jar
excited by wine
eye-opener

fall among friends
far gone
feed your nose
feel no pain
fellow commoner
firewater
fix
    fixer
flawed
floating
flutter
fly[2]
    fly-by-night
    fly one wing low
foggy
fond of
    fond of a glass
foot
    footing
footless
forward
four sheets in the wind *at*
    sheet in the wind
foxed
fractured
fragile
freak
    freak out
French article
    French cream
    French elixir
    French lace
    Frenchman
fresh[1]
    fresh in drink
    freshen a drink
fricasseed
fried
fruit machine
fruit salad
fuddled
full
full of liquor *at* liquor

G-nose *at* G
gamester
gargle
gas-house *at* gas
gassed *at* gas
gear
    geared

get off[3]
   get on
girl[3]
given to the drink
   at drink[1]
glass[1]
   glass too many
glow on *at* glow
go up[2]
God's own medicine
   gom
gone[2]
gone junkyard *at* junk
good lunch (a)
goof
   goof ball
grape (the)
grass[2]
gravy
greased *at* grease
green grass *at* grass[2]
groceries sundries
groggy
   grog-hound
   grog on board
gypsy's warning (a)

H
habit
hair of the dog
half[1]
   half a can
   half and half
   half-pint
half[2]
   half and half
   half canned
   half-cut
   half-foxed
   half-gone
   half in the bag
half-on *at* on[1]
half-seas over
   half-sea
half-screwed *at* screwed
half-slewed *at* slewed
half-sloshed *at* sloshed
half-stewed *at* stewed
half under *at* under the
   influence
hang a few on
hangover
happy dust
happy hour
hard drink *at* hard
hard drugs *at* hard
hard stuff *at* hard
harden a drink *at* hard
hardware

have a few
have a load on *at* load[1]
have a nose *at* nose job
head[3]
headache wine *at* headache[1]
heaven
   heaven dust
heel-tap
hemp
herb
high
highball
hit[1]
hit the bottle
hoist a few *at* hoist
hold
hold your liquor
hollow legs
hop
   hop-joint
   hophead
   hopped
horn of the ox (that gored
   you) *at* hair of the dog
hospitality
hung
hunt the brass rail
   at hunt
hustle
   hustler

ice[2]
ill[3]
illuminated
imbibe
in bits
in drink *at* drink[1]
in liquor
in the bag[2]
in the rats
in the tank
in your cups
incapable
Indian hemp
indisposed[2]
indulge
intemperance
investor
Irish thing (the)

jab a vein
jagged
jar
jerk off
jet lag
John Barleycorn
joint[1]
jolly[1]
jolt (a)

joy[2]
   joy flakes
   joy popper
   joy rider
   joysmoke
joy-stick *at* stick[2]
jug[2]
juice[1] (the)
   juice head
   juice joint
   juiced
juniper juice *at*
   juice[1] (the)
junk
   junked up
   junker
   junkie

keelhauled
kick the habit
knock back

laid out
legless
libation
lid
lift[2]
lift your little finger
lightning
like a drink
line[2]
liquid
   liquid dinner
   liquid lunch
   liquid supper
   liquid restaurant
   liquid refreshment
liquor
   liquored
lit
   lit up
little something
livener
load[1]
   loaded
local
locked
look on the wine when it was
   red
looped
lotion
lubricate
   lubricate your tonsils
   lubrication
Lucy in the sky with
   diamonds
lush
   lushed
   lushy

M
mainline
make use of
Mary
medicated
medicine
mellow
merry
Mexican brown
Mickey (Finn)
migraine
Moll Thompson's mark *at* moll
monkey[1] (the)
mood freshener
moonlight[1]
morning after (the)
mother-in-law
mother's blessing
mother's ruin
  mother's milk
mountain dew
Mozart
muddy
muggy
mule
muzzy

nasty
native elixir (the)
near beer *at* near[2]
needle
Nelson's blood
nightcap
nineteenth (hole)
nip[2]
no heeltaps
noggin
non-drinker *at* drink
not known for his temperance
    at not known for
nose habit *at* habit

O
off the wagon
off your face
oiled
  oil of malt
  oil the wig
on[1]
on[3]
  on a cloud
  on cloud nine
  on the needle
on the bottle *at* bottle[1]
on the piss
on the roof
  on the tiles

on the sauce *at* sauce (the)
on the sniff *at* sniff
on the town
one-armed bandit
one for the road
one over the eight
one too many
over-fond of the bottle
over-refreshed
overdo the Dionysian rites
overdose
  OD
overindulge
overtired
  overtiredness

package on (a)
package store
paint the town red
panther sweat
  panther piss
paralysed
  paralytic
parboiled
parliament[2]
partake
peg
people's lottery
petrified
pharmaceuticals
  pharmacy
pick-me-up
pickled
pie-eyed
pioneer[2]
pipe
piran
pissed
plasma
plastered
play[2]
  play the dogs
  play the horses
pledge
poison
polluted *at* pollute
pooped
pop[1]
porchclimber
pot[2]
  pot-valour
  pot-walloper
  potted
pot[4]
potation
powder
  powder your nose
  powdered lunch
prairie oyster[2]

preserved
primed
psychologically disadvantaged
public house
punish the bottle
punk[2]
purge[1]
push[4]
  pusher
put (it) away[4]

queer[1]
quench your thirst
quick one
  quickie

racked
ragged
railroad bible
ran-dan *at* randy
rat-arsed
rattled
reading Geneva print
recreational drug
red cross
red eye
reefer
refresher
  refreshed
  refreshment
restorative
  restore the tissues
reviver
ripe
ripped
ripples on (have)
roach
rocky[2]
rollocked
rosy
runny nose
rush the growler

sauce
scoop
scorched
score[2]
Scotch mist
screwed
scuttered
sea food
see a man about a dog
sent
several sheets in the wind *at* sheet in the wind (a)
sewn up[2]
sharpener
sheet in the wind (a)

shellacked
shoot[3]
shoot the cat
short[1]
shot[1]
shot[2]
shout[2]
  shout a beer
  shout yourself hoarse
sign the pledge *at* pledge
sip
  siper
six o'clock swill
skinful
slang
slewed
sloshed
slug[2]
smack
smashed
  smash the teapot
smeared
smoke[1] (the)
snapper
sniff
snifter
snort[1]
snort[2]
snow[1]
  snow-blind
  snow-storm
  snowball
  snowed in
  snowed under
  snowed up
  snowman
soak
social glass *at* glass[1]
sodden
soft drink *at* soft[2]
something[1]
  something damp
  something for the thirst
  something for the throat
  something helpful
  something moist
  something short
sop
sot
souse
  soused
sozzle
  sozzled
spaced out
  space-head
speed[1]
spifflicated
spike[1]
splice the mainbrace

sponge
sportsman
spot[1]
sprung
spunkie *at* spunk
squashed *at* squash
squiffy
stash
  stash pad
stewed
stick[2]
  stick a drink
  stick of tea
sticky
stiff one
  stiff
  stiffener
stimulant (a)
stinking
stitched
stoned
street
  street bets
  street drugs
strong waters
  strong weakness
strung out
stuff[1]
stump liquor
stunned
stupid
  stupid-fou
substance
  substance abuse
suck the monkey
sugar[3]
sun has been hot today
sun is over the yardarm
Sunday traveller
sundowner
surf-freak *at* freak
suspect cigarette
sweet tooth
swill
swing[2]

take a drink
  take (a little) something
  take needle
  take too much
take a drop *at* take the drop
take the pledge *at* pledge
take to the bottle *at* bottle[1]
tanked (up)
tap[1]
taste for the bottle
  taste of something
tea
  tea-head

  tea party
  tea-sticks
ten two thousand *at*
  ten one hundred
Thai stick
the worse
thirst
  thirsty
three sheets in the wind *at*
  sheet in the wind
throat
tiddly
tie one on
tiger-sweat
  tiger juice
  tiger milk
  tiger piss
tight[1]
tincture[2]
tip[2] (the bottle)
  tiper
  tipped
  tipper
  tipsy
tipple
  tippler
  tippling-house
tired[2]
toot
top-heavy
toss down
  toss-pot
tot
touched[1]
  touched with liquor
tracks
transfusion
travel agent
trip
tumble[2] (down the sink)
turf accountant
turn up your little finger

under the influence
under the table[1]
unfortified
unwell[2]
up[2]
use[2]
  use some help
  user

wall-eyed
warm[2] (with wine)
wash the baby's head
wasted
water of life (the)
watering hole
way out

weakness
  weakness for the drink
  weakness for the horses
wee drop
  wee dram
  wee half
weed
well away
  well bottled
  well corned
  well in the way
  well oiled
  well sprung
wet[2]
  wet a bargain

wet canteen
wet the baby's head
wet your beard
wet your mouth
wet your quill
wet your whistle
wetting
whacked
whiffled
whip the cat
whistled
white girl
  white lady
  white lightning
  white line

  white powder
  white stuff
white satin
  white lightning
  white stuff
willie-waught
wired[1]
worship at the
    shrine of
wrecked

yak

zoned out
zonked

Affairs of State

Under this heading are euphemisms relating to government, politics, warfare, and espionage. These are subjects in which evasion and deceit are common, hypocrisy not unknown, and prudery rare. Survival for politicians, whether in a despotism or a democracy, involves securing control over your compatriots, and retaining it through convincing them of your fitness to rule. The least corrupt of governments have information which they are reluctant to disclose, perhaps obtained through espionage. In such cases, if the public has to be told anything, the communication must be shrouded in words or phrases more emollient than the naked truth.

The suggestion by a political appointee that 9/11 was a good day to bury bad news revealed more than crass insensitivity. The impact of all news, but bad news especially, must be managed so that the governed are deceived. *Presentation, positioning,* and *spin* become ends rather than means. This may then lead to a temptation to choose policy because of its short-term effect on public opinion rather than its long-term benefits on society as a whole.

In any climate of denial and deceit, euphemism is a potent tool. Public officials, no less than their masters or mistresses, must use emollient phrases. Often repeated, the evasions become recognized for what they are. What started as euphemism ceases to mislead. The word or phrase becomes standard English for what was sought to be avoided, demanding yet more linguistic contortions. The sequence has no end.

Taxation remains, as it always has been, unpopular among those who bear it. Under the *droit de seigneur,* the medieval peasant cannot have been happy with having to perform *boonwork,* and still less when it was called *love boonwork.* In the 17th century, Charles I sought to supplement his revenue by using the time-honoured method of forced loans, which were never repaid, or *benevolences.* John Hampden went to prison in 1627 when he refused to contribute. Seven years later he led the parliamentary opposition to Charles's latest scheme, a tax called *Ship Money.*

In modern times, we may note the British *post-war credit* of the Second World War, a tax which was actually refunded years later, albeit in a depreciated currency without interest. We still live with the impost called *National Insurance,* a supplementary tax levied on the income of those in employment and on their employers. By increasing the rate of contributions to *National Insurance,* a government is able to raise tax from income while denying that it is raising income tax. In any event, taxes are never increased but *revenue is enhanced.*

Despots, even one like Hitler who enjoyed popular acclaim, have proved masters of euphemism. For Communists, opponents were not just opponents; they were *anarchistic groups, anti-socialistic elements, class enemies, counter-revolutionaries,* and so on through the alphabet, people who needed to be confined to *camps* for *corrective training* until they thought *correctly* like the *comrades* who *carried a card.* (We're still only on C, you will notice.) The horrors and prejudices of Nazi Germany were equally obfuscated by language, and none more than methods employed in achieving their *final solution,* justified by the disciplines of *German science.* Klemperer called this linguistic abuse 'lingua tertii imperii'.

How then are we to know when our masters are using language to conceal the truth from us? Fortunately, there are a number of trigger words, such as *democratic* or *new,* which put us on guard. Any state describing itself as *democratic* is almost certainly a tyranny, such as the *German Democratic Republic* which had to erect its *anti-fascist barrier* in Berlin to stop its citizens fleeing. Hitler's regime was called the *New Order* and many socialists looked askance at Mr Blair's *New Labour.* The three most pervasive of these trigger words are *people's, special,* and *social.* Each of these deserves individual attention.

A government of the people by the people for the people and so on does not need to draw attention to the fact, because those involved know what their rights and duties are. If however you decide to call your state *The People's Republic of China,* for example, you can be quite sure that the words mask an autocracy of some kind. In such societies, you must be careful not to land yourself before a *people's court* to be accorded *people's justice* by a *people's judge* or *tribune*. The story of Hitler's *people's car* is well known, although that at least had a happy ending, of a sort, except for those unfortunates who paid their instalments to the Nazis prior to 1939 without ever taking delivery of their Volkswagen.

Social is a valuable word for those who seek imprecision or evasion when dealing with a taboo subject such as charity or race. Social scientists tell us of the advantages of *social inclusion* with its resulting *social cohesion*. We need to subsidize homes for the indigent, or *underprivileged*, in *social housing*. It is when politicians, start referring to *social justice* that we should feel for our handbag or wallet.

Special almost always has sinister overtones. Few *special police* are as benevolent as the British *special constabulary*, although even that proud record was sullied by the *B Specials* of Northern Ireland. The *special detachments* or *squads* in Germany who used *special action* to round up Jews did not even bother to bring them before *special courts*. If your child is in a *special class* or at a *special school*, it is not because of special cleverness. When in 1983 a British airline claimed to accord its German customers *special treatment*, or *Sonderbehandlung*, there were unfortunate connotations.

On the broader canvas, government prefers to deal with illness through a *Department of Health* or *National Health Service,* while the invasion of Iraq was overseen by a *Department of Defense* and a *Ministry of Defence*. Fortunately, we no longer have to rely on the *information* supplied by a Ministry of Information for news about the hostilities.

This brings us to the language of warfare, and especially of defeat, where *straightening the line* may involve *a movement to the rear* or a *withdrawal to prepared positions*. How lucky we are that wars are still fought with *conventional weapons*, despite the unfortunate casualties from *civilian impacting* and *friendly fire* on whom *incontinent ordnance* has fallen. A trigger word to look out for is *strategic*: anything so prefixed is almost certainly unplanned and carried out under compulsion.

War is a word which should be avoided. Harry Truman initiated a *police action* in Korea; at the time of the Suez invasion, Eden was able to reassure us we were 'not at war with Egypt but in a *state of armed conflict*'; and the destructive rampage by the Israeli Defense Force in the Palestinian districts of Ramallah and Jenin in 2002 was part of an invasion called *Operation Defensive Shield*. And so we now have very few wars—only *confrontations*, *conflicts*, *interventions*, *operations*, and similar less worrying *incidents*. People still seem to get killed and wounded however.

Espionage, being a form of deceit, has developed its own evasions, with special thanks to Richard Nixon and Watergate. I have known four people engaged in the business of spying, or *security* as they would call it, and their language has been disappointingly free of the euphemisms which pepper the pages of the thriller writers. Perhaps, knowing my obsession with words, they regarded me as an *extremely sensitive source* or suspected that I was wearing *electronic underwear*. On which note, we must *terminate* this introduction, but happily not *with extreme prejudice*.

absorption
Aktion *at* action[2]
activist
adventure[1]
adviser
agent
allow your name to go forward
alter the demographics
alternative defence *at* alternative
America First
annex
Anchluss
anti-
 anti-fascist
anti-personnel
appropriate technology *at* electric methods
armed struggle (the)
asset

assimilation
Austrian problem *at* problem

babysitting
bamboo curtain
banana
bederipe *at* droit de seigneur
benevolence
blocking detachment
blow the whistle on *at* blow[5]
Bluebellies *at* blue[1]
blue-on-blue
boat people
bobtail
body-bag *at* body
boonwork *at* droit de seigneur
box-ticking
 box-tickers
boys in the bush *at* boys[1]

boys upstairs *at* boys[1]
boy scout[2]
brew[1]
 brew-up
brief
brushfire war
bug out

camp *at* concentration camp
carry a card
ceasefire
change your jacket
Charlie
check
Civil Co-operation Bureau
civilian impacting
claim responsibility for
clean[1]
clean[2]
clean house

clean up[2]
cleanse[1]
co-belligerent
collaborator[1]
   collaborationist
collateral damage
colony
come into the public domain
come up with the rations
coming of peace
Committee (the)
   Committee for the Protec-
      tion of the Revolution
company[2] (the)
concentration camp
concession
concessional
   concessional financing
   concessional loan
confederation
conflict
confrontation
constructed
contact
controversial[1]
conventional
conversations
Cook County *at* Find Cook
   County
cool relations *at* cool[2]
cooperate
cordial[2]
correct
cosmopolitanism
counter-attack
counter-insurgency
counter-revolution
credibility gap
cross the floor
currency adjustment
curry colonel
cut[5]

day of action
defensive victory
degrade
deliver
democrat/democracy
demographic strain
demonstration
   demo
deniable
   deniably
   deniability
dependency[1]
detain
diplomatic
   diplomatic cold
   diplomatic gout

diplomatic illness
direct action
dirty (atomic)
   bomb *at* dirty
disengage
disinvestment
do[4]
do business with
document retention
doorstep[2]
dove
downward adjustment
draw the enemy into a trap
draw water
drill
drop your flag
dry clean
duration

ear
   earpiece
educate
elastic
   elasticity
electric methods
electronic underwear
   electronic counter-
      measures
   electronic penetration
emergency[1]
emergency[2]
encourage
enforcement officer *at*
   enforcer
enhance
   enhanced procedures
   enhanced radiation
      weapon
   enhanced revenue
equilibrium
exchange of views
   exchange of ideas
expendable device
   at device
extrajudicial killing
extraordinary
   extraordinary camps
extremely sensitive
   source

fact-finding
   fact-finding observer
fact sheet
fail to win
fair[2]
   fair rent
   fair trade
   fair trade arrangements
fair-haired boy

fellow-traveller
   fellow-travelling
fifth column
find Cook County
first strike
fish[3]
flexible[1]
   flexibility
floater
fold back
former person
frank[2]
fraternal assistance
fraternization
fratricide
free world
freedom fighters
freeze[1]
French leave
friendly
   friendly fire
front
frontier guards
full and frank *at* frank[2]

garden
general discharge
German
   German chemistry
   German maths
   German science
German Democratic
   Republic
Ginza cowboy
go native
gold-plating
granny farming
great and the good (the)
Great Game
Greybacks *at* blue[1]
greymail
guardian

hang out to dry
   hang-out
hardware
harmful elements
have your ticket
   punched
hawk
healthy
heightened interrogation
hillside men
holy wars
honours
hospital
house-trained
housecleaning
human intelligence

I must have notice of
   that question
ideological supervision
improvement[1]
in the bag[1]
incident
incontinent ordnance
incursion
indulgence flight
   at indulge
initiative
intelligence
internal security
interpret pragmatically
intervention[1]
intruder

joe

kick upstairs
king over the water
knight starvation

lack of governance
lame duck[1]
late disturbances
   late unpleasantness
lay pipes
leak[2]
   leaker
leakage
legal resident
liberal
   limousine liberal
liberate[1]
limited action
little gentleman in black velvet
little local difficulty
living space
log-rolling
lose[1]
lot

medium machine
migration
militant
military intelligence
militia
   milice
mistaken developments
modern
modernization[2]
mole
Molotov cocktail
mountain sickness
move to a more secure camp
   move to a more secure
      location
   move to a more secure place

nanny
   nanny state
national emergency
national savings
national service
nationalize
negative propaganda
negotiate
nerve agent
new economic zones
New Labour
New Order
   new state
   new times
new Soviet man
news management
nightingale[1]
no comment
non-aligned
non-person
normalization
nuclear device *at* device

occupied
off the reservation
on-message
Operation Defensive Shield
orderly progress *at* orderly
orphan-hugging
out of context
over-civilized
over there
overflight
overhear

pacify
   pacification
   pacification camp
   pacification center
parallel
   parallel justice
   parallel policeparty
party member
patriotic reticence
pause[2]
peace
   peace council
   peace-keeping action
   peace-keeping force
   peace offensive
penetrate[2]
people's
people's army
people's car
people's court
people's democracy
people's government
people's justice
people's palace

people's party
people's republic
people's tribunal
persona non grata
pioneer[1]
place-man
planning
   planner
play back
player
Plum Book
police action
political engineering
polygraph
population transfer
pork
   porkbarrel
   pork chopper
position
post-war credit
Potomac fever
pre-dawn vertical
   insertion
pre-emptive
   pre-emptive action
   pre-emptive self-defence
   pre-emptive strike
preparedness
press
   press gang
prime the pump
proletarian
protect
   protective reaction
   protectorate
public ownership
public-private partnership
public sector borrowing
   requirement
pull rank
purge[2]

Quaker gun
quarantine
question[2]

radical
   Radical Squad
rainbow fascist
realign
   realignment
reasonable
rebuilding costs
recent unpleasantness
reconstructed
   at constructed
rectification of frontiers
regroup
regularize

relocate
  relocation camp
renegotiate
  renegotiation
reshape
reshuffle
resistance
resources control *at* resources
restore order
restraint[1]
restraint[2]
return fire
returned to unit
  RTU
revenue enhancement
  revenue emolument
revolutionary
  revolutionary elections
  revolutionary firmness
run[2]

safe house
salami
  salami tactics
sanitized
second strike
  second strike capability
  second strike destruction
Second World *at* first world
secret agent *at* agent
secret (state) police
security
  security adviser
  security service
  security risk
selective
  selective ordnance
  selective response
  selective strike
self defence
send ashore
send in your papers
serious credibility gap *at*
  credibility gap
settle[2]
  settlement
  settler
shoo-in
shorten the front line[1]

show[2]
sick-out
sing a different tune
  sing from a different
    song-sheet
sit-in
sleep-in *at* sit-in
slight chill
slowdown[2]
social agenda
Social Area Council
social dimension
  at social agenda
social model
social ownership
soft target *at* soft[2]
softness in the economy
somewhere in...
source
special camp
  at extraordinary
special clinic
special duty
special investigation unit
special operations
special services and
  investigations
special weapons
  special stores
spin
  spin doctor
  spinner
squeeze[2]
stabilization
standstill
state protection
sterilize
sticky stranger
straighten the line
strategic
strategic differences
strategic movement to the
  rear
strategic targets
strategic withdrawal
stray off the reservation
struggle
  struggle for national
    existence

stunt
surgical strike
surrendered personnel

tactical
target of opportunity (a)
taskforce
team player
temporary
  temporary local difficulty
tongue
trail
transfer
treasonable activity
troubles (the)
turn[2] (round/around)
  turn your coat
twin-tracking

U-turn
uncoordinated
  withdrawal
undocumented
university
unofficial relations
unsound
useful fool

vacuum
voluntary withdrawal
  at voluntary
volunteer

ward off invasion
water gardener
wear a wire *at* wired[2] (up)
well-informed sources
whistleblower
Whitehall warrior
whitewash
wire-pulling
wired[2] (up)
withdrawal to prepared positions
workers' control
working party
workshop
World Peace Council

year of progress

Bodily Functions

We refer to most of our bodily functions in unequivocal speech. There are, for example, no taboos about breathing, digestion, or the circulation of the blood. Among our less favoured conditions, halitosis is not one we choose to talk much about even though it can be as offensive as the odour of stale sweat. A hundred years ago to say fart was not considered particularly vulgar, but now the word and the activity are taboo, at least in polite society. Belching is also frowned upon in public, although the word itself can be used without causing offence. An *erection* of the penis may be referred to allusively, if at all, as may be the ejaculation of semen and the orgasm. Menstruation is spoken of euphemistically both by the woman concerned and by third parties. None of these subjects has called for so many linguistic evasions as pissing, shitting, and the places where these activities take place, a *lavatory* being so much the subject of taboo that we do not have a non-euphemistic word for it.

Bad breath has not developed its lexicon of evasions, perhaps because it comes from the mouth. Malodorous sweat comes from the armpits and the crotch, both places the subject of taboo. While the *odorously challenged* may only *glow* or become *bedewed* if they are female, advertisers of deodorants aim their pitches at both sexes. We can thank a soap manufacturer for giving us the standard English *body odour*, and its initials BO. Underarm *wetness* may also prove a linguistic survivor.

The only evasion about belching which we commonly hear is *break wind*, the term, as Shakespeare reminded us, applying also to farting. The prude might choose to use the adjective *emunctory* instead of farting, although most of us would recognize a more common expression such as *bad powder* or, among children, a *rude noise*. While it may be *unsociable* to *pass air*, *gas*, or *wind* in public, it is only among friends that we might use such expressions as *cut a cheese* or *let fly*. We even have an evasion for the noise of a fart made with the lips, when we blow a *raspberry* (tart). A *Bronx cheer* can apply to oral or anal generation.

Penises become *tumescent* either through *arousal* or, on waking, as the *pride of the morning*. The *hard-on* or *horn* in a *man-root* may, with military imagery, *present arms* or *stand to attention*. If its owner suffers from *hair-trigger trouble*, he may *shoot over the stubble* or even *cream his jeans*. The accidental male soiling of nightwear and sheets may be put down to a *nocturnal emission* or a *wet dream*. But beware: we are moving on to dangerous ground. A male sufferer from *Irish toothache* may well pass the condition on to his female sexual partner.

In copulation, either participant may *bring off* the other, who will then *come off*, perhaps also in a literal sense. The process will be complete when either or both of those involved *dies*, *expires* or *finishes*, unless of course the male has been unable to *raise a beat* and lacks *lead in his pencil*. If that happens, his partner has obviously been unable to *pull his trigger*.

Menstruation, a phenomenon not explained medically until the middle of the 19th century, has its own taboos, such as the persistent myth that a menstruating woman touching meat will taint it. Mrs Pepys was *ill of those* when she had her *month's* upon her and the *curse (of Eve)* and *period* might now be described as standard English. Evasions mainly refer to the bleeding and the colour of blood, to the inconvenience, or to the regularity of the *visitor*, who may, in a combination of imagery, have come *from Redbank* or be *red-haired*. Other *(little) visitors* may include the punning *Aunt Flo*, *Charlie* or *Kit*, *old faithful*, or the *prince*. When a woman *has the painters in* at that *time of the month*, the *danger signal is up* and *baker flying* to indicate that she is *out of circulation* during *wallflower week*. My usually erudite correspondents have yet to tell me why an American female may *fall off (the roof)*.

When a visitor arrives at your house after a journey, you do not ask her if she wants a piss or even, more genteelly, does she wish to urinate. She may be *breaking her neck* to *ease her bladder* but decorum demands that you should invite her to *freshen up* or *wash her hands*. With so many evasions to choose from, let us look at the letter *P*, which also appears as *pee* or *pee-pee*. We *pass water* when we *pay a visit* to *perform a natural function*. We may excuse ourselves from company to *pick*, *pluck*, or *pull a daisy*, *a pea*, or *a rose*, the *pea* being a pun on the vegetable and the *rose* on a sprinkler. On watch at sea, the helmsman will urinate *in a pig's ear*. On land we may need a *pit-stop* when we wish to *point Percy at the porcelain* or *polish the mahogany*. While our female companion goes to *powder her nose*, we can *pump bilges* or *ship*, hoping our pet has not made a *puddle* in the house.

To *defecate* is to cleanse, but I use the verb, and *defecation*, both now being standard English, instead of shit and shitting, because the latter are such ugly words. The euphemisms can be divided into those relating to diarrhoea and those to normal *bowel movement*. The imagery in diarrhoea euphemisms comes either from the liquid nature of the *motion* or from the often alliterative location where the condition was acquired. There is none of us who has not suffered a *runny tummy* or the *threepenny bits*. On their vacation, many Americans are not sufficiently robust gastronomically to counter the *Aztec two-step*, the *Mexican fox-trot*, or *Montezuma's revenge*. *Cairo crud*, *Delhi belly*, the *Rangoon runs*, and *Spanish tummy* are among the hazards that await other travellers. We also have a wide choice of allusive terms for the *night soil* when we have *been* or done *big jobs*, of which *manure* is possibly the least offensive and of most interest to philologists. *Lavatory* meant somewhere where you might wash, as did *latrine*, and *lavabo*, while *ablutions* were a religious rite of washing. We still *wash and brush up* in the *water closet* or *WC*, the *washroom* or, for the Americans, the *bathroom*. The *house of commons, ease, lords,* or *office* might also be a *carsey*, from a corruption of *casa*, which Dr Johnson defined as 'a house unfurnished'. We still have the *little house* and the *little boys'* (or *girls'*) *room*, which is a little room for boys and girls (and adults) rather than a room for little boys and girls. In my own dwelling the *smallest room* happens to be the larder, which means we must choose our euphemisms with care when asked about the *geography* of the house, if we are to avoid misunderstanding.

ablutions	body odour *at* BO	chic sale
accident[1]	bog-house	clear
accommodate yourself	boom-boom[1]	climax
Ajax *at* jakes	bottle[2]	cloakroom
answer the call[2]	boys' (room)	cloaks
army form blank	break wind	close stool
article	break the sound barrier	closet[1]
aunt[2]	break your neck	cock the leg
Aunt Flo	bring off[1]	coffee-shop *at* coffee-housing
Aztec two-step	Bronx cheer	come
	brown stuff *at* brown	come off come aloft
BO	bucket[1]	come around
bad powder	bugle	come on[1]
baker flying	bulge	comfort[2]
bale out	bum-fodder *at* bum	comfort break
banana *at* peel a banana	bun[2]	comfort station
basement	bunny[2]	commit a nuisance
bathroom	burst	commode
be excused	bury a Quaker	common house
bedwetting		continent *at* incontinent[2]
been	Cairo crud *at* crud	contribution
bends (the)	call of nature	convenience
big jobs	caller (a)	corner[2]
biggies	can[1]	cottage *at* cottaging
bigs	captain is at home (the)	country cousins *at* relations
bind	carsey	have come (my)
blood	caught short	courses
bloody flag is up	CC pills *at* C	cover your boots
blow[1]	cement	cream for
blow off	chamber	cream
blow[2] (off)	change[1]	cream your jeans
blow a raspberry	chapel of ease[2]	crud
bodily functions	charge[1]	curse (the)
bodily wastes	Charlie's come *at* Charlie	curse of Eve

cut a cheese
    cut one
cycle of blood

defecate
    defecation
Delhi belly
demands of nature
deposit
detumescent
diddle[1]
die
dirt
    dirty your clothing
    dirty your pants
    dirty your trousers
    dirty yourself
discharge
do a bunk
    do a dike
    do a rural
    do a shift
domestic afflictions
doodoo
drain off
drop the crotte
    drop a log
    drop wax
drop your drawers
    drop your pants
    drop your trousers
droppings
duck
dump
dunny
Dutch clock
duty
    duties of life

EC *at* earth closet
earth closet
earth moved for you (the)
ease nature
    ease your bladder
    ease your bowels
    ease springs
    ease yourself
effluent
empty out
    empty your bladder
    empty your bowels
    empty yourself
emunctory
erection
    erect
essence
essential purposes
evacuate
    evacuate your bowels

evacuation
excrete
expire

facility[1]
fall off the roof
female physiology
feminine hygiene
fertilizer
    fertilize
fill your pants
find a tree
finish[2]
finish yourself off
fire a shot
flag is up (the)
flowers
flute
flux[1]
flux[2]
flying handicap
foul[1]
    foul yourself
fourth
freshen up
friend has come (my)

gather a daisy *at* pick a daisy
gentlemen
    gents
geography
get off[1]
get into trouble *at* trouble
gippy tummy
    gyppy tummy
girls' (room)
glow
go[3]
    go about your business
    go for a walk (with a spade)
    go on the coal
    go over the heap
    go places
    go round the corner
    go to the bathroom
    go to the lavatory
    go to the toilet
    go upstairs
    going
go off[1]
gold-digger
    gold-finder
    goldbrick
grunt

hair-trigger trouble
have the painters in
head(s)[2]
holy of holies

holy week
honey
    honey barge
    honey bucket
    honey cart
    honey-dipper
hooky
hopper
horn
hors de combat
horse apples
house[2]
    house of commons
    house of ease
    house of lords
    house of office
human waste
hygiene facilities
    hygiene break

ill[1]
    ill of those
impacted soilage *at* soil
in purdah
in season
incontinent[2]
    incontinency
indisposed[1]
Irish toothache[1]
Irish wedding
issue

jakes
jam rag
jane[2]
jerry
Jimmy
    Jimmy Britts
    Jimmy Riddle
job
john[1]
Jordan

kill a snake
Kit has come

ladies
    ladies' convenience
    ladies' room
land of Nod (the)
late[2]
latrine
lead in your pencil
leak[1]
leak[3]
leaky
leave before the gospel
leave the room
leavings

let off
  let fly
lift a gam
lift a leg[2]
little boys' room
  little girls' room
little house
little jobs
little visitor (a)
  little friend
loo
look at the garden
looking glass
loose[2]
  loose disease
  loose in the bowels
  loosen the bowels
lose your lunch

mail a letter
make a call
make a deposit *at* deposit
make a mess
make room for tea
make water
man root *at* root
manure
Maria Monk
men's convenience *at*
  convenience
men('s room)
menses
mess[2]
  mess your pants
Mexican foxtrot *at*
  Montezuma's revenge
Mexican toothache *at*
  Montezuma's revenge
Mexican two-step *at*
  Montezuma's revenge
minor function (the)
miss[2]
  mis(s)
mistake[2]
modern conveniences
  mod cons
Montezuma's revenge
monthly period
  month's
  monthlies
  monthly blues
  monthly courses
motion (a)
move your bowels
  movement
Mrs Chant
my word

Napoleon's revenge

nappy
natural functions
  natural necessities
  natural needs
nature stop
  nature's needs
necessary (house)
  necessary woman
need the bathroom
night bucket
night loss
  night emission
night stool
nip[3]
no man's land
nocturnal emission
number nine
number one(s)[1]
  number two(s)

odorously challenged
off duty
old faithful
on heat[1]
on the seat
on the trot
open your bowels
  opening medicine
ordure
others
out of circulation
outdoor plumbing
outhouse
  out the back
overdue[1]

P
painters are in (the)
pan
pancake
parliament[1]
pass air
pass water
pause[1]
pay a visit
pee
  pee-pee
perform
period[1]
personal hygiene
  personal hygiene station
petty house *at* little house
physic
pick a daisy
  pick a pea
  pick a rose
pig's ear
  pig
pit-stop

place
play Onan
pluck a daisy *at* pick a daisy
plumbing[1]
point Percy at the porcelain
pole
polish the mahogany
pony
poop[1]
  pooper-scooper
poop[2]
poorly[2]
post a letter
pot[3]
  po
  potty
  potty-training
powder room
powder your nose
  powder your puff
present arms
priapus
  priapism
pride
  pride and joy
  pride of the morning
  prides
prince has come (the)
private office
privy
  privy-stool
pro-pack *at* pro
problem days *at* problem
prophylactic
protected sex
  protector
public convenience
puddle
pull a daisy *at* pick a daisy
pull his trigger
purge[3]
purpose(s) of nature

Quaker's burial ground *at*
  bury a Quaker
quiescent

rag(s) on
raise a beat
Rangoon runs *at* Rangoon itch
raspberry[1]
rattle[2]
rear
rears
red
  red flag is up
  red rag
  Red Sea is in
  red-haired visitor

reds
regular[1]
regular[2]
relations have come (my)
relieve yourself
   relieve your bladder
   relieve your bowels
rest room
retire[1]
   retiring-room
Richard
ride the red horse
ripple
rise
road apples
road is up for repair (the)
roses
rude noise
run off
run on (a)
runny tummy (a)
   runs

safe sex
   safer sex
sample
sanitary man
sanitary stop
sanitary towel
   sanitary napkin
   ST
scour
   scour-the-gate
see a man about a dog
see the rosebed
   see the compost
      heap
   see the view
   see your aunt
seed
sewage
shake hands with the bishop
   shake hands with the
      unemployed
   shake hands with the
      unemployable
   shake hands with
      your best friend
   shake hands with
      your wife's best friend
   shake the lettuce
shift (a)
shoot a lion
shoot off
   shoot blanks
   shoot over the stubble
   shoot your load
   shoot your roe
show[1]

showercap *at* showers[1]
sick
sink[1]
siphon the python
skidmarks
skin[1]
slack
   slack off
slash
sluice[2]
smallest room (the)
smear[2]
snatch mouse *at* snatch[2]
snick *at* snip
snip
soil
   soil your pants
   soil yourself
solid waste
   solids
something for the weekend
Spanish tummy
specimen
spend (seed)
   spend his manly marrow
   spent
spend a penny
spirits[1]
splash your boots
spunk
squat[1]
   squatter
squirt
   squirts
   squit
   squitters
stale[2]
stand[1]
   stand to attention
stand[2]
start bleeding
state of excitement
stoppage[1]
strain your greens
stretch your legs
surge in the loins *at* loins

take care of
take the air
Tampax time
technicolor yawn (a)
ten one hundred
term
those days
threepennies (the)
throne
throw up
   throw a map
   throw up your tonsils

thunderbox
time of blood *at* time
time of the month *at* time
tinkle
toilet
   toilet paper
Tom[1] (Tit)
toot
touristas (the)
trots (the)
trouble
tumescent
turn up your tail

unsociable
unwell[1]
use[3] (in)
use paper
   use the bathroom

visiting card
visitor (a)
void water

W/WC *at* water closet
wallflower week
   at wallflower
wash[1]
wash and brush up
wash your hands
   washroom
waste[2]
   waste management
      compartment
water
   water the garden
   water the roses
water closet
waterworks[1]
wear a pad
wee(-wee)
wet[1] (the bed)
   wet your pants
   wet yourself
wet weekend
wetness
what you may call it
   whatsis
   whatzis
whizz
wind[1]
   windy
women
   women's room
women's things
wretched calendar (the)
wrong time of the month

you-know-what

Business and Commerce

Included in this section are such varied subjects as auctions and real estate, aircraft, banking, bankruptcy and indebtedness, commerce, dismissal, employment, and entertainment. The common factor is that, whatever their artistic or altruistic merits or pretensions, all of these activities have to do with, or result from, the process of supplying someone with goods or services in return for payment, or what is known generically as business. Although as anxious to conceal certain matters by the use of evasive language as are politicians or civil servants, those in business operate under constraints which are perhaps less stringent in the public sector. Financial reports, forecasts, and advertisements are monitored by a number of regulatory bodies. Journalists study them looking for good or bad portents. The language can then be picked over at leisure by lawyers whose mission to defend the world from greed and injustice knows no restraint, so long as there is the hint of a class action against a wealthy defendant.

Auctioneers are not meant to *boost* prices by accepting bids *off the chandelier* although it is permissible to *buy in* a lot which has not received its reserve. Estate agents, or realtors, have developed their own sets of evasions. Where a property in a neighbouring region may command a higher price, renaming is in order, such as *East Village* in New York or *South Chelsea* in London. Houses are never old, although they may be *ante-bellum*, without saying which war, *Georgian*, without identifying which of six monarchs, or *period*, which is not specific but means earlier than last week. Basements become *lower ground floors*, attics are described as *studios*, and so on. If you are considering the purchase of a *handyman special* or somewhere *ideal for modernization*, be sure to consult a surveyor first.

Air travel is an experience where the perceived risks of being conveyed in a complex machine through an inhospitable environment have to be minimized by the choice of language. *Operational difficulties* and *unscheduled* are words which the seasoned traveller prefers not to hear, especially in the air from the captain's microphone. Whatever names the airlines think up to describe differing fare structures and leg room, the reality of air travel remains the same. Your only fellow-member of the club in *Club class* is the captive in the next seat. For the avoidance of confusion, your *air hostess* has become a flight attendant who offers you nothing more titillating than a *bread roll*. A *Dutch roll* is something else, as is a *Chinese three-point landing*.

Banking and bankruptcy go together, linguistically, the 'banc' being the bench which was 'rupted', or turned over, if the Lombard money-lender became insolvent. Under modern conditions, a failed bank *closes its doors*, a fate achieved by holding an excess of *non-performing assets* or being too generous with its granting of a *facility*. Loss is a forbidden word, although you are allowed to talk about a *negative contribution*.

The degree of shame associated with bankruptcy has changed over the centuries. In the 18th century arrest for debt and the *sponging house* were accepted as hazards of urban life, rather as we might view speed cameras today, although the debtors' prison was best avoided. For the Victorians bankruptcy was a matter not just of personal hardship but of deep shame, and some of the euphemisms they used to describe it are the same as those for death. The stigma of insolvency, whether personal or corporate, has now diminished. A receivership has become *corporate recovery*, an insolvency is a *negative cash situation*, and the person who *does a phoenix* incurs small opprobrium, apart from among the unpaid suppliers of goods and services.

Our job title indicates to ourselves, our families, and those with whom we have dealings how important we are. In America we come across a great number of *agents*, few of whom appear to have delegated authority, and we may be surprised to learn that the Capital Market Division of an investment bank in New York needs 258 Managing Directors. It is only when a rat catcher becomes an *exterminating engineer* or a *rodent operator* that we stray from pomposity or exaggeration into euphemism.

In the world of advertising, it is tempting to confuse puff and exaggeration with euphemism. When you are told you can *save* money by buying a car without delay, you are facing an attempt to *bounce* you into spending money. The packet which the supermarket calls *large* may be small, and be subject to *slack fill*. If you see a shop advertising *rubber goods*, do not enter it if you are seeking a bouncy ball. In this world of make-believe, fat children are *chubby* and obese women have a *fuller figure*.

Mindful of public criticism or possible court proceedings, employers are selective in their language when announcing the dismissal either of a large number of staff or of a single senior employee. Discharge became the punning *fire*, and the *sack* in which the workman placed his tools when he left work for the last time is a distant memory. As each generation of euphemism moves into general use, if not standard English, so new usages emerge. When a lot of people are losing their jobs, the phrases are chosen to preserve the employer's image as a benevolent institution, *letting them go* rather than keeping them hard at work. Where an individual is being dismissed, no word or phrase should be used which might imply that the parting has been brought about through personal inadequacy or incompetence. Those who choose to *spend more time with their family* or *pursue other interests* must be allowed to enjoy their *gardening leave* with their self-esteem and reputation intact.

The wording of company reports may dismay the literary purist, or pedant, but can be rewarding to the euphemism-hunter prepared to overlook the clichés and able to decipher the coded messages. The future can never be predicted but if a Chairman tells us it is *unpredictable* he is saying more than a truism. So long as there are competitors, markets will be *challenging*, but this is another word which rings the alarm bells among investors. Anything *as planned* is unlikely to have been foreseen and has been as nasty a shock to the board as it is to the shareholders. While directors may, under pressure, admit to a *cash flow problem*, the word insolvency must be avoided at all costs. It is also dangerous to admit to having too much stock, although a *back-up of retail inventories* may be less alarming.

Financial analysts have their own conventions when it comes to writing corporate reports and advising investors. If they suggest that a holding might be *reduced*, you need to sell quickly. *Hold* or *underweight* are equally dire warnings that all may not be well and *neutral* does not mean that you can relax your guard. Before long the dividend will be passed, or at best *rebased*, and the market will have undergone a *correction*.

As you might expect, entertainment has developed its own euphemisms, there being no business like show business. Despite the precariousness of their profession, actors are never out of work, only *at liberty*, *between shows*, or *resting*. Theatre seats are not given away although the impresario may on occasion *paper the house* in the hope that the theatre will not go *dark*. The writer who brings out a *potboiler* may still hope for a *blockbuster*. which, I am sorry to record, is more likely to be a *bodice ripper* than a dictionary Among the plethora of *best sellers* greeting us in a bookshop, we may even find an *international best seller*, which is no guarantee that it will not be *remaindered*.. Professional games players are also meant to be entertainers, although a *professional foul* may displease the onlooker and you do not have to be a swimmer to take a *dive*. In the fullness of time, relegated to a *bench-warmer*, they too are obliged to *hang up their boots*.

above your ceiling	back-end loaded	bestseller
accumulate	back up in retail inventories	bet the farm
acknowledgement (of services)	backroom boys *at* boy[1]	between shows
	bag[2] (the)	between jobs
adjustment[1]	bait and switch	bijou
adjustment[2]	bandwagon	bite the bullet
affordable	bank	black up
agent	banker	blackbird
aggressive	bazaar gains	blind copy
air (the)	bean counter	blockbuster[1]
airport novel	belly up	blockbuster[2]
ambulance-chaser	below stairs[1]	bodice-ripper
apportion	Beltway Bandit *at* belt	boiler room
as planned	bench	boiler house
ask for your papers	bench-warmer	boiler shop
at liberty	bet the farm	boilerplate
axe[2]	Best Brian	bolt

bolt the moon *at* moonlight
   flit
bombed-out
boost[2]
boot (the)
boot money
bottom fishing
  bottom feeders
  bottom line
bought in
bounce[2]
bounce[3]
bounce[4]
bowler hat
boys in the backroom
   at boy[1]
boys upstairs *at* upstairs[3]
brass (the)
brother
  brother of the bung
bucket shop
budget
bug
Buggins' turn
bullet (the)
bump[1] (the)
bump[5]
bust[1]

California kiss-off *at* kiss-off
cameo
can[2]
cards (your)
career change
  career transition center
carpet[1]
carpetbagger
cash flow problem
cash in hand
catch a cold[3]
category killer
celebrity
challenging
channel stuffing
chant
  chanter
Chapter Eleven *at* go[2]
character
cherry-pick
Chinese bookkeeping
Chinese copy
Chinese paper
Chinese rejection
Chinese (three-point) landing
Chinese wall
chop[2] (the)
circular file
claims farmer
clear your desk

clock-watcher
close its doors
club[1]
collaborator[2]
colonial
colt[2]
come-on[3]
come to a sticky end
commodious
complimentary
concert party
concoct
conference (in)
confident pricing
consistent with plan
consultant[1]
consultant[2]
contingent
controversial[2]
convenient[2]
cook[2]
  cook the books
cookie pusher *at* cookie
corner[1]
corporate recovery
corpse
correction
cost growth
couldn't be reached
country
country pay
courtesy
creative
  creative accounting
critical power excursion
cross-firing
crumbling edge
cuff[2]
cut[2]
cut[4]
cut-and-paste job
cut numbers

DCM
daily
daisy chain
dark[1]
dawn raid
de-accession
dead cat bounce
deadhead
decommission
deconnect
decrease in footfall
dehire
delayering
delinquency
  delinquent balance
demanding

demanning
demonstrator
designer
dime out
direct mail
directional selling
disappointing
dispense with assistance
dispute
ditch
do a phoenix *at* phoenix
dollar shop
domestic
dose of P45 medicine
down population
downsize
downstairs[1]
drop-dead list
drown the miller
dry[2]
Dutch auction
Dutch bargain
Dutch reckoning
Dutch roll
duvet day

early release
  early retirement
East Village
easy terms
eat-in kitchen
eat stale dog
economically inactive
economy
efficiency
employment
energy release
equity release
  equity equivalent contin-
    gent participation
  equity withdrawal
excess[1]
excess[2]
exclusive
expand your balance sheet
expenses
  expense-account living
experienced[2]
expert
exterminating engineer
extra

facility[2]
fall on your sword
fall out of bed
  fall off the wire
fallout
fan club
fast buck (a)

fat cat
fat finger
   fat-fingered
fat-cutting exec rise
fee note
file Chapter Eleven *at* go[2]
file thirteen
filler[1]
filler[2]
financial services
   financial irregularities
financially challenged *at*
     challenged
fire
fireman[2]
fishing expedition
   fishing trip
float paper
fly a kite[1]
fly the blue pigeon[2]
flying on empty
flying picket
fold
   fold your hand
for reasons of health
for the chop *at* chop[2] (the)
for your convenience
fractional ownership
free
freeze out
front running
fudge
   fudge figures
furlough
further your career

gardening leave
garnish
gate[2] (the)
gender
   gender analysis
   gender-norming
gentleman
   gentleman of the cloth
Georgian
get a result
get on your bike
get the sack *at*
     sack (the)
get the shaft
   get the push
   get the shove
ghost[1]
ghost[2]
give a P45
give (someone) the air
given new responsibilities
glass ceiling
go[2]

go at staves
go Chapter Eleven
go crash
go for a Burton
go smash
go under
go west
go-around
go down[3]
go down the tube(s)
go off[2]
go on the box
   go on the club
go slow
go south
go to the wall
gold-brick
golden
golden cheerio
   golden goodbye
   golden handshake
   golden hallo
   golden handcuffs
   golden parachute
   golden retriever
golden boy
good voyage
goodbye
grannies
gravy train (the)
greenmailer
grey[1]
   grey goods
   grey market
   grey marketeer
gross height excursion
guest[2]
   guest fee
   guest house
guest worker
guidance to the market

haircut
halve the footprint
hammer[1]
hand[1]
handout[2]
handshake
handyman special
hang a red light on
hang up your boots
hatchet (man)
   hatchet job
haute cuisine
headcount management
   headcount reduction
heave (the)
heavy landing
help[1]

help[2]
hike
   hike off
historic
hit the bricks
hit the silk *at* silk
holiday ownership
home equity loan
horse-chanter *at* chant
hospital
hospital job
hospital pass
hot[4]
hot seat
   hot-desking
   hot-seating
human resources
human sacrifice

ideal for modernization
identification
imaginative journalism
immaculate
impaired credit
impairment
   impairment charge
improvement[2]
in Carey Street
in need of modernization
in the barrel
in the cart
in the departure lounge
in the glue
in the red
in the ring
income protection
industrial action
informal
   informal market
insider
interim
intermission
inventory adjustment
investment in prices
involuntary conversion
involuntary separation
Irish promotion
Irishman's rise

jawbone
job action
job turning
jolly[2]
junket

keep the pot boiling *at*
     potboiler
kick[2] (the)
   kicked into touch

kick the tyres
kiss-off
kitchen-sinking
kite
    kiteman
knight of the Golden Fleece
    at knight
knock-out
Korean tartan

labor optimization
labour[2]
lack of visibility
lame duck[2]
landscaped
lard the books
large[2]
late booking
    late trading
lay off
lay paper
leave of absence
less enjoyable at less
let go
letterhead
leveraged
libel chill
liberate[4]
limited edition
line your pocket
    line your coat
    line your vest
link prices
liquidity
    liquidity crisis
load[3]
load-shedding
long-term buy
look after (your)
        other interests
lose[2]
lose your shirt
    lose your pants
    lose your vest
loss of separation
loss-shopping
    loss-trafficking
low-budget
lower the boom on

maid
manage the attrition rate
marching orders
margin compression
mark a card
market timing
market value adjuster
massage[3]
me-too

measure for the drop
medium
meeting (at/in a)
men in suits
merger accounting
message
Mexican raise
mirror operation
modernization[1]
mole
money house
monkey[2]
moonlight[3]
moonlight flit
    moonlight flight
    moonlight touch
    moonlight walk

natural break
near[2]
need help
negative cash
    negative cash flow
negative containment
negative contribution
    negative profit contribution
negative employee situation
negative equity
negative growth
negative investment return
negative pricing
negative stock-holding
negatively impacted
negotiable
networking
neutral
never-never (the)
New York kiss-off at kiss off
no show
non-performing
    non-performing asset
    non-performing loan
non-profit
non-strategic
not rocket science
not available (to comment)
not invented here
    NIH
not return calls
notice
nouvelle cuisine

oblige
off the chandelier
    off the ceiling
    off the wall
off the payroll
off the peg
old-fashioned

on health grounds
on jawbone at jawbone
on the beach
on the black
on the cuff at cuff [2]
on the fly
on the labour at labour [3]
on the skids
operational difficulties
    operating difficulties
order of the boot
orderly
    orderly market
organic
organize
out of a position
outplace
outsourcing
over-invoicing
overdue[2]
overhaul
owned

pad
paid off at payoff
paint the tape
pancake
paper aeroplane
paper-hanger[2]
paper the house
parallel
    parallel importer
    parallel pricing
    parallel trader
parity
park
pay with the roll of a drum
paying guest at guest[2]
payroll adjustment
pear-shaped
pencil[2]
people cuts
period[2]
personality
personnel ceiling reduction
phantom
phoenix
    phoenix company
piggyback
pink slip
planned
plant[3]
plastic chicken circuit (the)
ploughman's (a)
plug[3]
point-shaving
poison pill
poke[1] (the)
posted

posting
potboiler
prairie-dogging
pre-driven
　pre-used
premium
pressure of work
prestige
　prestigious
price crowding
prime
private enterprise
　private sale
product
product placement
product shrinkage
production difficulties
proposition selling
provision
pull a Benedict Arnold
pull out of a hat
pull the pin
pull the rug
pump
　pump and dump
pursue other interests
　pursue another career
　pursue other opportunities
push[2] (the)
push the envelope
put in the mobility pool
put on file
put out to grass
　put out to pasture
put the skids under

qualify accounts
quota

R-word (the)
RD *at* refer to drawer
railroad
rainmaker
rationalize
reasons of health *at* for
　reasons of health
rebalance
　rebalance stock
rebase
red card
red ink
redlining
reduce the headcount
reduce your
　commitments
reduction in force
　riff
redundant
reengineer

refer to drawer
regular[3]
release[1]
relieve
relinquish
relocate
remainder
removal[2]
remunerated
　balances
repositioning
reshuffle
resign
resources
　resources director
resting
restructure
restructured
restructuring
result
retire[2]
retrenched
reverse engineering
revolving-door[2]
richness of stock
right-sizing
rights at work
ring[2]
Rio trade
roller-coaster
Roman candle
round-trip
　round-trip trade
rubber cheque
run[3]
run[4] (the)
runner[3]

sack (the)
salami
　salami tactics
save
say goodbye to
scandal sheet
scissor-and-paste job
scope for modernization
scorch eliminator
seasonal ownership
secluded
seek fresh challenges
seepage
select
selected out
selective distribution *at*
　selective
semi-detached
send down the road *at* send
　down
separate[1]

service[2]
service lawyer
services no longer
　required
set back
severance
　severance pay
shade[1]
shake the pagoda tree
shared freehold
sharpen your pencil
　sharp with the pen
　sharp with the pencil
shelved
shift expenses
ship
shoot[2] (the)
shoot the moon *at* moonlight
　flit
shop[1]
short-shipped
shortism
shout[1] (the)
shove (the)
show the door
sickie
silk (the)
sitting by the window
slack fill
slash and burn
slowdown[1]
slowdown[2]
small print
smell of the counting-house
　at smell of
smoke and mirrors
smooth
snow[2]
　snow-job
snug
social dumping
solidarity
sought after
south[3] (going or moving)
South Chelsea
spam[2]
Spanish practices
spectral
spend more time with your
　family
spike[2]
splash
sponsor
spring-loading
stale pricestand down
stand down
stand-up[2]
standard
starter home
　starter house

statutory
steer
step down
sticky floor
stoppage[2]
strategic
strategic differences
strategic premium
strategic review
streamline
stretch[2]
structured
studio
stuff the channel
sub-prime
subsidy publishing
suggestion
suits (the)
supplier discount
supporters' club
surplus[1]
surplus[2]
swallow the anchor
swaps
sweet equity
sweeten[2]
sweetheart
swing around the buoy
swing the lead
switch-selling
synergy benefit

tail-pulling
take a bath
take a break
take a hike
  take a powder
take a walk
take a wheel off the cart
  take the wheels
    off the wagon
take the air abroad *at*
    take the air
take the pants off
  take the shirt off
take the wind
  take the breeze
take to the hills

Tartans (the)
technical adjustment
  technical correction
  technical reaction
teflon
  teflon man
temporary
  temporary liquidity
    problem
terminate[2]
testing
thin out the team
tie a can on
tin handshake
token
  tokenism
too busy to take/return
    calls
top brass *at* brass (the)
top floor (the)
top line visibility
top up
toss[2]
touch signature
tourist
transfer pricing
triple entry
turf accountant
turkey shoot
  turkey farmer
turn away
turn off[3]
twenty-four-hour service

unaddressed
unassigned
unavailable
  unavailable for comment
uncertain
under-invoicing
under the counter
under the table[2]
under water
undisciplined
uneven
unfair
unheard presence
unofficial action

unpredictable
unwaged
up-and-coming
upstairs[3]
used
useful girl

valentine
vanity publishing
visiting fireman
voice risk analysis

walk[2]
  walking papers
walk out
walk the golden gangplank *at*
    walk the plank
warehouse
warning
wash[2]
wash out
  wash its face
  washed up
water stock
wear lead boots
weekend
weigh the thumb
well rewarded
what the traffic will bear
white knight
white-knuckler
white sale
white tail
white van man
wind[2] (the)
window dressing
withdraw your labour
word from our sponsor (a)
work both sides of the street
  work a street
work to rule
work with writers
working capital shortfall
working people

yellow page

zero grazing

Childbirth

No other human event embraces so many topics about which we choose to speak indirectly as childbirth. From the method of conception to the delivery of the baby, we are treading linguistically on uncertain ground. We use contraception to avoid unwanted impregnation and then hope that the identity of the father is as certain as is that of the mother. Pregnancy involves the cessation of menstruation and the possibility of miscarriage or abortion. Taboo parts of female anatomy are affected during the period of *carrying the child* and in the *accouchement*. Pregnancy is accompanied by sickness, discomfort, and lassitude, apart from the physical indications. Giving birth is a painful and potentially dangerous event. It is no wonder that we choose to refer to these issues allusively. We will look at contraception, cuckoldry, illegitimacy, abortion, miscarriage, pregnancy, and birth in this section. Menstruation, copulation, and human bodies are dealt with elsewhere.

Contraception is not a modern phenomenon. Boswell told us that, in his encounters with prostitutes, he *fought in armour*, although when he chose to be a *bareback rider* he had cause to regret it The non-use of a *circular protector*, *collapsible container*, *French letter* or *tickler*, *froggie*, *johnny*, *raincoat*, *rubber*, *safety*, or *sheath* meant that he was engaging in *unprotected sex*. He could not have worn a *welly*, because the Iron Duke had yet to appear on the stage, to give his name first to an item of rubber footwear and so allusively to a condom. *Family planning* was more difficult in the days when it was not possible for women to go *on the pill* although *Vatican roulette* was a game that Protestants also were allowed to play, unless they preferred to *leave before the Gospel*. Today *birth control* is managed by so many *devices* that it is a wonder any babies are conceived in western societies.

Cuckoldry used to be a matter of great male concern, especially for those with a landed estate to pass down to their eldest son. The husband might not wish to *wear horns* or suffer the *forked plague* himself, although he might perhaps be ready to *abuse the bed* of another, but he was determined that his own offspring should not be illegitimate, *by-begot* or *chance-born*, a *child of sin* which had *come in at the window* or though any other place than the front door. Blackstone disagreed with Dr Johnson when the latter maintained that *Borough English* entailed the disinheriting of the eldest son because he might have been conceived in the exercise of the jus prima noctis under the *droit de signeur*, but the very fact that there was a debate showed how serious was the issue of illegitimacy.

In the days when it was illegal to *bring off* an unwanted foetus by means of a *criminal operation*, the pregnant woman finding herself *in trouble* might resort to *female pills* such as *French renovating pills* to achieve a *planned termination* or *pregnancy interruption*. She might even persuade her physician that she needed a *D and C*, which would achieve the same result. Today *planned parenthood* gives us *reproductive freedom*, a situation which is welcomed by the *pro-choice* lobby but opposed, sometimes violently, by *pro-life* campaigners. While an Englishwoman south of the Border, having a miscarriage might *part with her child*, her Scottish neighbour would possibly *part with Patrick*.

When we talk about pregnancy, we use words and phrases which range from the demure through the polite to the coarse and scatological. The American woman who announces that she is *anticipating* does not have to detail what it is she expects to happen any more than does someone who is *expectant*. She may be described as being in a *certain*, *delicate*, or *interesting condition* while she awaits the *little stranger*, the standard English *with child* being less often heard today, as is *enceinte*, which was a double euphemism being one in French before its adoption in English. Having *fallen for a child*, she should not be called a *fallen woman* unless she was unmarried at the time and had *cheated the starter*. In that case, before these permissive times, she would hope that the putative father would *make an honest woman* of her, even if it were a *costume*, *off-white*, or *shotgun wedding*, or, as they might say in Ireland, one *arranged by circumstances*.

Pregnancy is described less formally by those who refer to being *in the family way*, having a *bun in the oven*, or *joining the club*, which is not an association giving pre-natal companionship but the *plum* or *plump pudding club*. Having been *knocked up*, she may be *in for it* or *in* various situations chosen from the mammalian world, from *in foal* to *in pup*. She may also be described as being *up the pole*, *stick*, or *spout*, the imagery coming from where monkeys are said to find themselves, or from the location of a round in the barrel of a gun. Other vulgarisms we need not particularize.

If the pregnancy were a *mistake* and the baby an *accident*, the *afterthought* will almost

be certainly be welcomed by parents and siblings alike, because, as they say, they bring their love with them.

When at last the pregnant woman is *confined* and *brought to bed*, these days she will not have the attention at home of a *lying-in wife* when she had gone *upstairs*. Nor will anyone suggest to brothers and sisters that the *happy event* had any connection with the *parsley bed* or *gooseberry bush*. Let us hope that the mother does not decide to *doorstep* the baby or the father take his *steg month*.

absent parent
abuse a bed *at* abuse
accident[2]
accouchement
Actaeon
afterthought
anticipating
antlers
armour
arranged by circumstances
    at arrange

bareback
base born
bear[1]
bed[1]
belly plea
bend sinister
beyond the blanket
big
birth control
born in the vestry *at* born in
Borough English
break your elbow
    break you knee
    break you leg
    break your leg above the
        knee
bring off[2]
bulge
bun in the oven (a)
by(e)
    by(e)-begot
    by(e)-blow
    by(e)-chap
    by(e)-come
    by(e)-scape

cardigan
care *at* in care
carry[1]
cast[1]
    cast a girth
    cast a laggin (or leglin)
        girth
caught[1]

certain condition (a) *at*
        condition[2]
chance
    chance bairn
    chance begot
    chance born
    chance child
    chance come
    chanceling
change[2]
child of sin
    child of grief
child-bed (in)
circular protector
cleanliness training
cleanse[2]
click[2]
co-respondent
collapsible container
colt[1]
come-by-chance *at* chance
come in at the window
    come o' will
come to a sticky end
condition[2]
confinement
    confined
costume wedding
criminal operation
cut[1]

D and C
delicate condition *at*
        condition[2]
device
difficult
do the right thing
do your duty by
doorstep[1]
drop[3]

eat for two
empty nesters
enceinte
expectant
expose

facts (of life)
fall[2]
fall[5]
family planning
family way *at* in the family way
feed
female pills
fiddle
fight in armour
flyblow
forked plague (the)
free of Fumbler's Hall
Freeman of Bucks
French letter
    FL
    Frenchie
    French tickler
French renovating pills
froggie
from both sides of the
    blanket *at* wrong side of
    the blanket
full in the belly
fumbler *at* fumble

gander month *at* gander-
    mooner
gander moon *at* gander-
    mooner
get with child
give to God
gone[1]
gooseberry bush
graft
great
    great-bellied
    great with child

happy event
hatch
heavy of foot
have a full belly *at* full
    in the belly
horn
    horn-maker
how's your father

illegal operation
illegitimate
impotent
in calf
  in foal
  in pig
  in pod
  in pup
in for it
in the club
in the family way
in trouble[1]
indiscretion
interesting condition *at*
    condition[2]
Irish toothache[1]

Johhny
join the club *at* in the club

knight of Hornsey *at* knight
knock up

labour[1]
ladies' medicine
lady- in-waiting[2]
  lady in the straw
large[1]
latchkey
left-handed
lie in
  lying-in wife
lined *at* line[1]
little stranger
lone parent
love-begotten *at* love
love bird *at* love
love-born *at* love
love child *at* love
lover child *at* love

magic word (the)
make an honest woman of
  make a decent woman of
merry-begot
midnight baby
midwives' mercy
misfortune
  misbegot
  mishap

mistake[1]
mixed heritage

natural[2]
nephew
niece[1]
nurse
  nurse-child

off-white wedding
on[2]
on her way
on the nest
on the path
on the pill at pill[2]
one-parent family

parentally challenged *at*
    challenged
parsley bed
part with patrick
  part with child
pill[2]
planned parenthood
  planned termination
plum(p) pudding club *at*
  in the club
precautions
precocious
pregnancy interruption
premature
pro-choice
  pro-life
pup

quality time
quick (with child)

raincoat[1]
reproductive freedom
ring the bell
rubber
  rubber cookie
  rubber johnny
rush job

sewn up[1]
sheath
shot in the tail
shotgun marriage

shotgun wedding
single parent
  single mother
  single mum
slink a (great) belly away *at*
  belly plea
slip[1]
  slip a foot
  slip a girth
son of a bitch
son of a gun *at* gunner's
    daughter
souvenir
spurious
  spurious issue
steg month
  steg-widow
stung by a serpent
swell

tender a fool
termination
that way[2]
throw[1]
time
top and tail

unknown to men
unlawful
untrimmed
up the pole
  up the duff
  up the spout
  up the stick
upstairs[1]

Vatican roulette
voluntary pregnancy
    interruption *at* voluntary

watermelon
wear a fork
welly
wet nurse
whelp
wind the horn
  at horn
with child
wooden hill
wrong side of the blanket

Crime and Punishment

The crimes we deal with in this section exclude homicide, which is more closely associated with the euphemisms surrounding death. Lying and cheating are not always criminal acts, but they are included here, along with pornography. Punishment embraces the officers of the law concerned with the apprehension of felons and the places in which they are confined if they are caught.

Nobody likes to be accused of being a *stranger to the truth* or *stretcher-case* although there are few of us who do not on occasion tell a *tall story* or *porky pies*. Politicians and administrators are sensitive to any imputation that they are being *economical with the truth*, which is why a newspaper described Harold Wilson as a *martyr to selective amnesia* rather than calling him a liar. Where there is a *credibility gap*, we may find that a *deniable* statement has been made, a method adopted by Richard Nixon when he decided to *misspeak*. While we may have to put up with *news management* as a tool in *psychological warfare*, that is not an excuse for *creative* journalism. The safest line to take if we find ourselves in a spot of bother is to say '*no comment*'.

When we are *taken for a ride* by a *con man*, it is our own fault that we have been *ripped off* or *caught a cold*. Playing cards, we should be able to detect a *leaner* indulging in what used to be called *coffee-housing*, but that is difficult if he is an *operator*. Today the used car salesman has assumed the mantle of the *horse-chanter*, although we may hope that, in a society where blame can always be placed on another for a loss resulting from our own stupidity or misfortune, it is the cheat and not ourselves who is *taken to the cleaners*.

We deplore pornography in others and may be ashamed if it is our own secret vice. The Victorian who read a *French novel* might today prefer to see an *adult* movie in a *smut-house* or on a *girlie-video*. What some call *amusing* others find *blue* or *off-colour* and are glad that *hard core* material which is *less edited* and appears in *men's magazines* is kept on the *top shelf* of the bookshop.

Our attitude to, and speech about, crime depends on whether or not we consider the offence reprehensible. In my youth I *liberated* an SS staff car, which I sold profitably, and

later *won* various *souvenirs* from Japanese *surrendered personnel*, without losing any sleep at night, or my liberty. Many otherwise law-abiding citizens may have acquired from an *informal dealer* or on the *black market* an item which had *fallen off the back of a lorry*. But they would not refer to a thief as a *tea-leaf* or use any of the other euphemistic words and phrases in which the *light-fingered* or a *penman* would describe his behaviour. Uncertainty about what language means can arise when lawyers start talking about a *crime against nature*, which is not cutting down a rain forest; or a *criminal assault*, because most of us would consider all assaults are criminal. We must not forget the unfortunate Daisy Hopkins who, in 1891, was charged in Cambridge with *walking with* a member of the university and given 14 days in prison. As the Lord Chief Justice commented when quashing the conviction, other females such as a mother, sister, wife, or friend might also walk with an undergraduate.

If we have no personal or family involvement with the courts, we are unlikely to resort to euphemism when talking about trials, sentences, and prisons, although we will be familiar with such terms as *attendance centre* or *approved school*. The lawyers, or *knights of the golden fleece*, have their own courtroom flummery and counsel may be less than sincere when he says that he 'is obliged' to a judge who has contradicted his interpretation of the law or facts. It is only when he addresses the bench, prefixing his remarks with the phrase *with respect*, that we hear him stray into euphemism. If the prisoner has been *sent down* or *up*, what we might call five years becomes a *fistful*, *five fingers*, or a *handful* for someone about to *do bird*, the prisoner's family explaining the absence by saying that the person in the *slammer* is *on vacation*, without adding that he is *enjoying Her Majesty's hospitality* or staying at the *sheriff's hotel*.

Just as we law-abiding citizens would not dream of referring to a prison warder as a *screw*, so, unless we are *ethically challenged*, we would not choose an allusive or abusive expression when talking to, or about, a police constable or officer, unless of course we meet a *badge bandit* operating a *bear trap* from a *blue-and-white*. Staying with the letter B, there are other varieties of *bear*, some of them otherwise described as *boy scouts*, from their hats. A *blue lamp* indicated a British police station and *blue* was the colour of the uniform, giving us on both sides of the water *blue-bellies*, *blue jeans*, *blue suits*, *bluebirds*, *bluebottles*, and *bluecoats*. American *bird dogs* acquired a better reputation than Irish *B-specials*. The *bill* or *bobby* remain more popular figures than the *bogy*, while the *bent copper* deserves to be sent to *Bridewell*.

accommodation collar
    at collar[2]
accost
acquire
action[1]
administrative detention
adult[1]
amusing
anoint (a palm)
anti-social
appropriate[1]
approved school
around the Horn *at* run
    (a)round the Horn
arrange
art
aryanize *at* Aryan
Asian levy
assembly area
assimilation
assist the police (with their
    inquiries)
assistance[2]
associate with
    association
at government expense
at Her Majesty's pleasure
at it
attendance centre
away[2]

backdoor[2]
backhander
bad-mouth
badge bandit
bag[1]
    bag job
bag[4]
bagman
ball money *at* bell money
bang up
barker
bear[2]
    bear bait
    bear bite
    bear cage
    bear in the air
    bear trap
beard
beer money *at* tea money
bell money

ball money
bend the rules
    bend the regulations
bent[1]
big house
    big pasture
    big school
bill
bin-raiding *at* bin
biographic leverage
bird[2]
black
    black dollars
    black euros
    black economy
    black fish
    black market
    black marks
    black money
    black pounds
black-and-white
    black-and-tans
black bag
black hole
blackball
blackbird
    black cattle
    black hides
    black pigs
    black sheep
blackmail
bleed
    bleed the monkey
blood money
blow[5]
    blow the gaff
blue[1]
    blue-and-white
    blue-belly
    blue jeans
    blue lamp
    blue police
    blue suit
bluebird
bluebottle
bluecoat
blue[2]
bobby
bogy
bone[1]
book

boom-passenger
boost[1]
 - booster
    booster bag
    booster bloomers
bootleg
    bootlegger
    bootlegger turn
borrow
bottle[3]
bounce[4]
boy scout
break the news
bred in the moonlight *at*
    moonlight[1]
Bridewell
brig
brown envelope
browse
bubble
bucket[2]
bug
bull[3]
    bull-pen
bunch of fives
bung[2]
burn[2]
bushwhack
business
bust[2]
busy
button[1] (man)
button[2]

cabbage
cadge
can[3]
canary[1]
canary[2]
    canary trap
cannon
captain
card[1]
careless of integrity
carousel
carry[3]
carry the can
carrying piece *at* piece[2]
chat
check into Crowbar
    hotel

cheese eater
Chicago typewriter
chirp
chisel
  chiseller
chokey
chopper[1]
clean[1]
clean up[1]
  cleaners
click[1]
  clicker
  Clickem Fair
  Clickem Inn
clink
clip[1]
  clip artist
  clip joint
clock
clout
cobbler
cockchafer
coffee-housing
collar[1]
collar[2]
collect
come across[1]
come through
come to a sticky end
come to the attention
  of the police
commission
community alienation
community safety unit
compliments
con
  con artist
  con man
contract
control unit
convey
  conveyance
  conveyancing
coop
cooperate
cop[1]
cop[2]
  cop house
  cop shop
cop out
copper
corner[1]
corporate entertainment
  corporate hospitality
correctional
  correctional facility
  correctional officer
  correctional training
  correctional training camp

cough[1]
county farm
crack[1]
  cracksman
crib man *at* crib
Cross-bar hotel
  Crowbar hotel
cross your palm
cuff[1]
cumshaw
curio
custody suite

damaged[3]
dance[2]
Davy Jones's natural children
  at Davy Jones's locker
deal from the bottom of the
  deck
  deal from the bottom of
  the pack
decontaminate[2]
deep freeze
dick[2]
  Dickless Tracy
dip[1]
  dip squad
disappear[1]
disinformation *at*
  information
distribution
dive[1]
  diver
dive[3]
do[2]
do[3]
  do down
  do over
do[5]
do a number
do a runner
doctor
dodgy
  dodgy car
  dodgy night
donation
double-dipper
double entry
douceur
down
  down the line
draw the king's picture
drink[2]
drink tank *at* tanked (up)
drip gas
drive-away
drop the hook on
duty not paid
  DNP

earn
eat porridge
eat the Bible
economical with the truth
end up with Her Majesty
energetic
enforcer
enjoy Her Majesty's
  hospitality
enlightenment
entertain[2]
ethically challenged
  at challenged
evasion
everlasting staircase
extra-judicial killing

facilitation payment
  facilitator
failure of memory
fair trader
fall[4]
fall off the back of a lorry
family[1]
family[2]
Fanny Hill *at* fanny
feather your nest
federal camp
feed the bears
feed the meter
feel a collar
fence
fetch[2]
fiddle
field associate
fill in
fillet
financial irregularities *at*
  financial services
find[1]
  finder
find[2]
finger
  finger-man
finger-blight
fireman[1]
firm (the)
fisherman's tale
  fish story
fishing expedition
  fishing trip
fistful
fit up
five-fingered discount
five fingers
fix
  fixer
fizzer
flash tin *at* flash

fleece
flowery[1]
flutterer *at* flutter
fly[1]
fly the blue pigeon[1]
flying squad
footpad *at* highwayman
forage
form
frame[1]
  frame-up
free trade
freeloader
  freebie
Freemans
freeze on to
freezer
French novel
frightener
front
frosting
funny money
fuzz

G-man *at* G
gain
gang-bang *at* bang
gear
gentleman of fortune
  at gentleman
gentleman of the road
  at gentleman
get your collar
  felt *at* collar[2]
gild
girlie DVDs *at* girl[1]
girlie flicks *at* girl[1]
girlie magazines *at* girl[1]
girlie videos *at* girl[1]
give a line
Glasgow kiss
glass[2]
glass house
glean
glove money
glue
go down[2]
go for a walk *at* walk[3]
go over
  go over the hill
  go over the wall
go state
go to the Bay
go up the river
go walkabout
gold shot
goods (the)
  green goods
goon squad

gooseberry lay
governmental relations
grab
graft
grass[1]
gratify
graze
grease
  grease hands
  grease palms
  grease paws
  grease the skids
  grease the system
grind the wind *at* grind (a)
guest[1]
  guest of Her Majesty
  guest of Uncle Sam
guest-fee *at* guest[2]
gumshoe
gunner's daughter
gunrunner *at* run[1]

half-inch
handful
handout[1]
  hand-out
  hand-pay
hang paper
Hanoi Hilton
hard
  hard case
  hard core
hard room
headhunter
heat[1]
heat[2]
heavy
heeled
heist
helmet
help the police
  (with their inquiries)
help yourself
hide
highgrade
  highgrader
highwayman
  high law
  high lawyer
  high pad
hijack
hit[2]
hit the bricks
  hit the lump
hit the wall
hoist
hold paper on
hold the bag
hold-up

hole *at* black hole
holiday
honey trap
hook[1]
hook[2]
hooker
hoosegow
horn-emporium *at* horn
horse
hose
hot[2]
  hot market
  hot money
hot-wire
house man
house of correction
hulk
hush money
hustle
  hustlerice box
  ice-house

in
in protection *at* protection
in trouble[2]
incentive
  incentive travel
individual behavior
   adjustment unit
inducement
informal dealer *at* informal
information
  Information Research Unit
inoperative
inside
inside track
insurance
internal affairs
interrogation with
   prejudice
introducer's fee
inventory leakage
Irish evidence
Irish vacation
iron[1]
irregularity *at* irregular
itching palm *at* palm[1]

jack[2]
jacket
job
john[2]
joint[3]
jolt (a)
joyride
jug[1]
juice[2]
  juice dealer
  juice man

jump[1]
junior jumper *at* jump[2]
jump[3]
   jump a check
   jump bail
   jump ship

kangaroo
   kangaroo club
kickback
kindness
kitty
kneecap
knight of the road *at* knight
knock off
   knock-off market
   knock-off variety
known to the police
knuckle sandwich

laddish
   laddish magazine
lady bear
last shame (the)
lavender
lay hands on
lean on
leaner
length
less edited *at* less
liberate[2]
life preserver
lift[1]
   lifter
lift[3]
lift a hand *at* lift
     a leg[1]
light-fingered
limb of the law
local bear
   local
   local boy
   local yokel
lose your (good)
     character
lubricate
lunchtime engineering
Lydford law

made at one heat
make[2]
make a purse for yourself
make away with[2]
make off with
make tracks
man[2]
man in blue *at* blue[1]
mark[2]

martyr to selective amnesia
   at martyr to (a)
massage[1]
massage[2]
mattress extortion *at*
   mattress
meat[3]
   meat wagon
men of respect
men's magazine
Mickey Mouse
militant
milk
Ministry of Information *at*
   information
missing trader
misspeak
mob
mooch
moonlight[1]
   moonraker
moonlight[2]
Mr Big
mudlark
mug
   mugger
municipal farm
muscle
   muscle man
mush

nab
   nab the snow
   nab the stoop
Newgate
nibble[2]
nick[2]
nick[3]
   nicked
nickel and dime
nightingale[1]
nip[1]
nobble
noddy
North

oat opera *at* oats
obtain
off the rails
oil
old Bill *at* Bill
old oil *at* oil
on ice
on the chisel *at* chisel
on the gallop
on the lam
on the left
on the out *at* inside
on the outside *at* inside

on the pad
on the run
   on the trot
on the take
on the wall *at* on
     vacation
on vacation
open palm *at* palm[1]
operator
organization *at* organize
out of town
over the wall

paddy wagon
paint a picture *at*
     paint the tape
palm[1]
   palm grease
   palm oil
   palm soap
   palmistry
palm[2]
   palm off with
paper-hanger[1]
past (your)
payoff
peeler
peeper
persuade
   persuader
pick
   pick a pocket
   pickle
   pickpocket
piece[2]
piece off
pigeon
   pigeon-drop
pike *at* pick
pinch[1]
pinch[2]
place of safety
plod
pluck the pigeon
   at pigeon
pocket
poetic truth
poke[3]
pork pies
   porkie pies
   porkies
porridge
Potsdam
pouch
pourboire
present
pressure
preventive detention
procedure

protective custody
pull in (for a chat)
pull off
punter
put the arm on
   put the black on
   put the burn on
   put the muscle on
   put the scissors on
   put the squeeze on
put the boot in
put the clock back
put the clog in
put to the question

Queen's evidence
queer[4] (the)
question[1]
quod

racy
railroad
raincoat[2]
ramp
rap
   rap sheet
razor
re-educate
   re-education
receiver
record
redistribution of property
refresh your memory
requisition
retainer
revolving-door[1]
ride-by
ringer
rinse[2]
rip off
rod
   rodded
roll[2]
roll over
room and board with Uncle
     Sam
rubber heel
rumble
   rumbler
run[1]
run[5]
run (a)round the Horn
runner[1]
runner[2]
running rumbler *at* rumble

safety camera
salvage
Sam

scandalous event *at* scandal
     sheet
school
score[2]
screw[2]
screw[3]
see[2]
segregation unit *at* segregation
selective facts *at* selective
sell out
send away
send down
send up
sensitive payment
set up[2]
sexual assault
shade[2]
shaft[2]
shake[1]
   shake down
shake[2]
shanghai
sheriff's hotel
shield
shop[2]
shoplift
shoplifter *at* lift[1]
short[2]
shrinkage
siphon off
skim
skin[2]
   skin business
   skin house
   skin magazine
slammer
   slam
slice
   slice the gentry
slice of the action *at* action
slippery palm *at* palm[1]
slops
slush
   slush fund
smear[1]
   schmear
smokey
   smokey beaver
   smokey on four legs
   smokey on rubber
   smokey with camera
   smokey with ears
smoking gun (a)
smut house
snaffle
snag
snatch[3]
snatch[4]
   snatch squad

sneak
   sneak thief
sneezer
snout[1]
snout[2]
snowdrop
social education
socialist justice
soft commission
   softing
something on you
speak with forked tongue
Special Branch
special camp
special constable
special court
special detachment
special operations
special police
special regime
special task force
speed[2]
speed money
spicy
spill
   spill the beans
sports medicine
spring
squeal
squeeze[1]
stag
stake-out
stalk
state farm
   state home
   state hospital
   state training school
statutory offense
stick it into
stick up
sticky-fingered
stiff[2] (out)
stiff-arm
sting
stink on *at* stinking
stir
   stir-wise
stitch up
stockade
stool pigeon
   stool
story
straighten out
strain credulity
stranger to the truth
strangle
strap
street
   street bets

street drugs
street money
street tax
stretch[1]
stretcher
  stretch credibility
  stretch the truth
  stretcher case
stripper
strong-arm
stuck
sugar[1]
surprising
  surprising change of form
  surprising staying power
swallow the Bible
sweat it out of
  sweat-box
Sweeney *at* Flying Squad
sweeten[1]
swipe
switch the primer
syndicate

tagged[2]
tail[2]
take[1]
take a walk
take care of
take the can back
take the Fifth
take to the cleaners
take your end
talk to
tank
  tank fight
  tanking
tax

tea money
term
terminological
  inexactitude
thank
third degree
third party payment
three-letter man[1]
throw[2]
throw the book at
tick
time
tip over[1]
tip over[2]
to one side of the truth
tolbooth
top shelf
torch
toss[1]
touch a palm *at* palm[1]
tout
transported
travel expenses
traveller
treat
treatment
tribute
trouser
trunk
trustee
  trusty
truth-shader
tub of grease
turn in
  turn up
turn over

unavailable

uniform
upon the panel *at*
  on the panel
upturned palm
  at palm[1]
useful expenditure

vacation
velvet
  velvet-lined drawer
  velvet-lined pocket
verbal
voluntary statement
  at voluntary

walk[3]
walk[5]
wankery *at* wank
warn off
wash[3]
water cure
wet job
  wet operations
  wet work
whiff of
whip
white van man
win[1]
windfall
wire
women in blue *at*
  blue[1]
word to the wise
work on[1]

yardbird
youth (guidance)
  center

Death

My interest in euphemisms began in 1978 when I pondered on the evasions people use about dying. I made some notes and sent them to a publisher who told me that his firm had been considering a dictionary of euphemisms, of which none had then appeared. I have lived with them ever since.

It is an act of kindness to present to the bereaved and to children the reality of death in as acceptable words as possible, although the young can be remarkably realistic and aware of mortality, as was demonstrated when a 6-year-old granddaughter told me recently that she was glad I was older than Granny because I would die first. She later modified this statement by saying that Granny and I would not, for the same reason, go to heaven together, which illustrated a further point. We soften the reality of our mortality by believing, or suggesting, that there is some form of life beyond death, and of course, if we believe that at our last conscious moment, then we will pass into eternity with that comfort, whether it happens or not.

We use for death a class of euphemism which relies on an assumption of our being *called to higher service* when we will *meet our Maker* or *the Prophet* in *another state* after *crossing the River Jordan*, *gathered to our fathers* (but not our mothers, it would seem) and enjoying or suffering *eternal life*. There is a wide choice of destinations to which we may *go*. We might be gratified to *go aloft* or *go to heaven*, although apprehensive if we have to *go to our reward*. To *go home* or *go into the ground* indicates a more gloomy prognosis. To suggest, however, that a corpse is *not dead but gone before* may stretch our credulity.

More pessimistic or realistic, but still offering comfortable evasions, is the imagery which comes from *passing*, *reposing*, or *resting*. To say that a dead person has *fallen asleep* is more comforting than that he has *fallen off the perch*. The tombstone may tell us that the occupant is *at rest*, and *peace at last* is not indicative of prior domestic strife. A stroll round somewhere like Bath Abbey reveals the verbal dexterity of those who penned the memorials of the *departed*, as well as providing a potted history of the British Empire.

More severe are expressions such as *call off all bets*, *cardiac arrest*, *cash in your checks* or *chips*, *cast for death*, *catch a packet*, *cease to be*, *check out*, *chuck seven*, *close your eyes*, *combat ineffective*, *come home feet first*, *conk out*, *cool out*, *cop a packet*, *cough*, *count the daisies*, *croak*, or *cut the painter* when it is *curtains*. And that is only the letter C. The dividing line between euphemism and avoidance of the truth is narrow, as was illustrated by the message sent to the relatives of those who had been shot for what was thought to be cowardice in the First World War, saying that they had 'Died of wounds'. That was true, but not the whole tragic truth.

Judicial killing breeds its own evasions among perpetrators and victims alike, with the imagery of *dancing* and *hemp* referring to the role of the *topping fellow*. When you were *in the cart* taking the *ride up Holborn Hill* on the way to meet the *King of Tyburn*, you would end up doing the *Tyburn dance*, *hornpipe*, or *jig* on the *Tyburn tree*. In America the unfortunate may still go to the *chair*, *get the gas pipe*, or be injected with the *green needle*. It is to be regretted that Israeli *extrajudicial killing* of Palestinians with missiles fired from aircraft kills and wounds so many people other than the intended target.

Most of us have no contact with homicide and no qualms about using the words murder or manslaughter, although the police may prefer to talk of *foul play*. Criminals, and crime writers, are less direct. Thus the victim may have a *bellyful of lead*, *be filled with lead*, *eat lead pills*, be loaded with *lead ballast*, *wear lead buttons*, and *suffer from lead poisoning*, as an alternative to *dropping down the chute* or wearing a *concrete overcoat*. Other words and phrases allude to the violence involved, such as *bagging*, *baking*, *blanking*, *blasting*, and so on.

Suicide may be a cause of shame as well as, for some, proscribed by their religion. For others *self-deliverance* is altogether different from *self-violence*, and a *mercy death* is a *release* rather than a crime. The deceased may have *done the Dutch* but to *die queer* did not carry any implication of sexual aberration. While it is sad that people should *OD themselves*, we have no compunction in *putting to sleep* old or ill domestic pets although we may be more squeamish about *bucketing* kittens. If an American obituarist amends a *prepared biography* to say that someone has died of a *short illness*, it is likely that the subject has committed suicide.

An *undertaker* who plies the *dismal trade* has every justification for cloaking his operations on the *loved one* with allusive language. The *restorative art* and *hygienic treatment* which is carried out in the *preparation room* enhances the appearance of the *late* person, (or, in South Africa, someone who is *late*), before the *remains* are placed in a *slumber-box* and taken in a *professional car* to a *memorial park*, where, in a *garden crypt*, the pleasant view can be enjoyed into eternity. Nor can we forget that a *ground sweat cures all disorders*.

above ground *at* remain
    above ground
account for
adverse event (an)
all night man
all over with
  all up with
anointed *at* anoint (a palm)
another state (in a)
answer the call[1]
asleep *at* fall asleep
at rest
at the last day
at your last
auction of kit
auto-da-fé
away[1]
axe[1]

back-gate parole
bag[3]
bake
bath-house *at* bathroom
bellyful of lead *at* lead
better country (a)
  better state
  better world
beyond help
big D (the)
bite the dust
black job
blank[2]
blast[2]
blip off
block out
blot (out)
blow away
body
  body bag
bonds of life being gradually
    dissolved
bone[2]
  bone-house
  bone hugging
  bone-orchard
  bone-yard
box[1]
brace
breathe your last
  breathing problem
Bridport dagger

bring down
bump[4] (off)
  bump-man
Burke
bury
buy it
  buy the farm

call (the)
  call a soul
  call away
  called home
  called to higher service
call off all bets
capital
  capital charge
  capital crime
  capital punishment
  capital sentences unit
carry off
cash in your checks
cast for death *at* cast[2]
catch a packet[1]
cease to be
cement shoes
chair (the)
chapel of ease[1]
  chapel of rest
check out
chew a gun
chill
chop[1]
  chop shot
chuck seven
church triumphant
climb the ladder
clink off
clip his wick
clipped *at* clip[2]
close an account
close your eyes
clunk
cold[1]
  cold-box
  cold cart
  cold cook
  cold-meat
  cold storage
comb out
combat ineffective
come again

come back
come home feet first
come to a sticky end
come to your resting place
commit suicide
compromise
concrete shoes (in)
  concrete boots
  concrete overcoat
conk (out)
contract
cook[1]
cool[1]
  cool one
cop a packet
cough[2]
count (the)
  count the daisies
country sports
  country pursuits
crack[2]
crap
crease
croak
  croak yourself
cross the Styx
  cross the River Jordan
cull
curtains
cut[6]
  cut down on
  cut off
cut the painter
  cut adrift
  cut your cable

dance[1]
  dance a two-step to an-
    other world
  dance at the end of a rope
  dance on air
  dance off
  dance the Tyburn jig
  dance upon nothing
Davy Jones's locker
daylight
dead meat
decontaminate[1]
deep six
demise
demote maximally

Death

depart (this life)
  departed
  departure
destroy
die queer
die with your knees bent
diet of worms
disappear[1]
disinfection
dismal trade
  dismal trader
  dismals
dispatch
dispose of
  disposal
dissolution[1]
do[2]
  do yourself in
do away with
dole-meats *at* dole
draw
  draw a bead on
  draw upon
drill
  drill full of holes
drop[1]
  drop down the chute
  drop in their tracks
  drop off
dust
  dustbin
  dustman
Dutch (do the)
  Dutch act

earn a passport
earth
  earth-dole
East (go or be sent)
easy way out (the)
eat a gun
eat lead pills *at* lead
eliminate
emigrated
empty a saddle
end
  end of the road
enter the next world
erase
eternal life
  eternal home
evacuee
  evacuation
everlasting life
exchange this life for a better
execute
executive measure
  executive action
expedient demise

expended
  expendable
expire
extrajudicial killing
extremely ill

fade away
  fade
fall[3]
fallen (the)
feed a slug
  feed a pill
feet first
fill full of holes
  fill with daylight
  fill with lead
final solution
finish[1]
flit[1]
floater
floral tribute
fog away
fold
follow
food for worms
foul play
frag
  fragmentation device
fry[1]

game[1]
gang
garden of remembrance
  garden crypt
  Garden of Honor
gas
gathered to God
  gathered to his ancestors
  gathered to his fathers
  gathered to Jesus
  gathered to Mohammed
ga(u)ge
get a slug *at* slug[1]
get away
get it
get the chop *at* chop[1]
get the gas pipe *at* gas
get the needle
give the good news
  give (someone) the works
give up the ghost
  give up the spoon
give your life
go[1]
  go aloft
  go away
  go corbie
  go down the nick
  go for a Burton

go forth in his cerements
go forward
go home
go into the ground
go off
go off the hooks
go on
go out
go over
go right
go round land
go the wrong way
go to a better place
go to grass
go to heaven
go to our rest
go to our long home
go to ourselves
go to the wall
go together
go under
go west
go again
go down[1]
go for your tea
go to heaven in a string
go up[1]
goner
  gonner
Grace of Wapping (the)
grassed down
grave (the)
  gravestone gentry
grease
great certainty (the)
Grim Reaper (the)
ground
  ground-lair
  ground-mail
  ground-sweat

had it
hand in your dinner pail
  hand in
hang
  hang-fair
  hanging judge
hang up your hat[2]
  hang up your dinner pail
  hang up your mug
  hang up your spoon
happen to
happy release
harvest
have your neck stretched *at*
  necktie party
head[1]
  heading
  heading-hill

head[1] (*cont.*)
  heading-man
heels foremost
hemp
  hemp quinsy
  hempen fever
  hempen widow
  Hempshire gentleman
hereafter (the)
high dive *at* dive[3]
higher state (of existence) (a)
hit[2]
  hitman
hole
  hole in the head
hop off
 hop the living
  hop the twig
hot seat
hot shot
human remains pouch *at* body
hygienic treatment

ice[1]
ice box[2]
if (or in case) anything should
    happen (to me)
in Abraham's bosom
in eternity *at* eternal life
in heaven
  in the arms of Jesus
in the churchyard
in the soil
invalid coach
iron out
  iron off
irreversible coma

jack it in
join[2]
  join the (great) majority
jump the last hurdle
justify

keel over
keep sheep by moonlight
kick[1]
  kick in
  kick it
  kick off
  kick the bucket
  kick the wind
  kick up
  kick your heels
King of Tyburn at Tyburn
kingdom come
kiss off
kiss St Giles' cup
kiss the ground

kissed by the maiden
knock down
konk off
  konk out

ladder
laid to rest
lamping
land of forgetfulness (the)
last call (the)
  last bow
  last debt
  last end
  last journey
  last resting-place
  last round-up
  last trump
  last voyage
last drop *at* drop[1]
last waltz
late[1]
latter end[2]
lay down your life
lay out
lead
  lead ballast
  lead buttons
  lead poisoning
leap in the dark (a)
leave the building
  leave the land of the living
  leave this life
  leave town
lick the dust
life[2]
  life assurance
  life cover
  life everlasting
  life office
liquidate
long count *at* count (the)
long drop *at* drop[1]
long home (your)
  long journey
long walk off a short
    pier (a)
loop
Lord sends for you (the)
  Lord has you
lose[3]
lose the vital signs
  lose the number
    of the mess
  lose the wind
lost[2]
  lost at sea
loved one
lump
  lump of meat

make a hole in the water
make away with[1]
make dead meat of *at* dead
    meat
make for the exit
make the supreme sacrifice
make use of
make your bones
mausoleum crypt
maximum demote *at* demote
    maximally
measured for a necktie *at*
    necktie party
meet your Maker
  meet the Prophet
memorial
  memorial counsellor
  memorial house
  memorial society
mercy death
  mercy killing
mop up
move on

narrow bed
  narrow passageway to the
    unknown
necklace
necktie party
  necktie sociable
negative patient care
    outcome
neutralize
night (the)
no longer with us
  no longer in service
  no more
  no right to correspondence
nobble
non-heart beating donor
not long for this world
not dead but gone before
nullification
number is up (your)
NYR
  not yet returned

off[1]
  off yourself
off-line
off the voting list
Old Sparky
on your shield
one-way ride
other side (the)
over the Jordan

pack it in
packet[1]

Paddington
paper (out) on
part
pass[1]
  pass away
  pass beyond the veil
  pass in your checks
  pass into the next world
  pass over
  pass to the other side of
    the Great Divide
  pass to the other side of
    the Jordan
  pass to the other side of
    the Styx
  passing
pay nature's (last) debt
  pay the price
  pay the supreme sacrifice
  pay your debt to society
peace at last
peg out
personal representatives
pick off
pine overcoat
planned termination *at*
    planned parenthood
plant[1]
plough under *at* plow under
plow under
plug[1]
pop[4]
pop off
  pop your clogs
  popping up the daisies
pot[1]
  pot-shot
pre-arrangement
  pre-need
preach at Tyburn Cross *at*
    Tyburn
prepare
  preparation room
prepared biography
procedure
professional car
promoted to Glory
pronounce
pull the plug on
purification of the race
push the button on
push up the daisies
  push up the weeds
put (a person's) lights out
put against a wall
put away[1]
  put yourself away
put daylight through
put away[2]

put down
  put off
put in your ticket
put on ice *at* ice[1]
put on the spot
put out of your troubles
  put out of your misery
put the juice to
put to rest
put to sleep
put to the sword
put under the sod
  put underground

quietus
quit

Reaper (the)
release[2]
relieved of your sufferings
remain above ground
remains
removal[1]
removal[3]
  removed
repose
  reposing room
resettle
  resettlement
resign your spirit
restorative art
resurrection man
  resurrection cove
  resurrectionist
return to
  return to ashes
  return to dust
ride backwards
  ride up Holborn Hill
ring eight bells
roll[3]
rope (the)
rub out

scalp
scrag
scratch[3]
screwed down
self deliverance
  self-destruction
  self-execution
  self-immolation
  self-violence
send to heaven
  send home
  send to his happy hunting
    grounds
  send to his last account
  send to his long account

send to the happy land
  send to the land of the
    lotus blossom
separation
settle[1]
shoot[1]
short illness (a)
shot while trying to escape
shove over
shovelled under
showers[2]
  shower baths
shuffle off this mortal coil
six feet of earth
  six feet underground
sizzle
sleep
  sleep away
  sleep in Davy Jones's locker
  sleep in your leaden
    hammock
  sleep in your shoes
slip[2]
  slip away
  slip off
  slip your breath
  slip your cable
  slip your grip
  slip your wind
slot
slug[1]
  slugged
slumber
  slumber box
  slumber cot
  slumber robe
  slumber room
smear out
smoke[2]
  smoke it
snatched from us
  snatched away
sniff out
space
  space and bronze deal
spared
special action
special education
special treatment
spot[2]
squash
stabbed with a Bridport
    dagger *at* stab
stake (the)
stand before your
    Maker
step away
  step off
step on

stick[1]
stiff[1]
  stiffy
stiff and stark *at* stark
stop a mouth
stop one
  stop a slug
  stop the big one
stretch the hemp
  stretch the neck
strike out
string up
succumb[1]
suffer
  suffer the supreme penalty
supreme measure of
    punishment
  supreme penalty
swing[1]
  swing off

tagged
take[3]
  take away
  take home
  take leave of life
  take off
  take someone with you
  take to God's bosom
  take your life
take a long (deep) sniff *at*
    sniff out
take a leap
take electricity
  take the walk
take for a ride
take out[2]
take refuge in a better world
    by your own hand
take the drop

  take the high walk
taken (hence)
  taking (a)
  taking hence (a)
taps (the)
terminate[1]
  terminate with extreme
    prejudice
three-legged stool
tip off
top[2]
  topping fellow
triple stool *at* three-legged
    stool
tuck away
  tuck under
turn off[1]
turn up your toes
  turn your face to the wall
twisted
Tyburn
  Tyburn blossom
  Tyburn dance
  Tybrun hornpipe
  Tyburn jig
  Tyburn scragging
  Tyburn tippet
  Tyburn ticket
  Tyburn top
  Tyburn triple tree

ultimate intentions
under the daisies
  under the grass
  under the sod
  underground
  undersod
undertaker
undiscovered country (the)
united

upstairs[2]
useless eaters

vault[2]
ventilate

wages of sin (the)
wake
  wake the
    churchyard
walk the plank
want out
waste[1]
watch
wax[2]
way of all flesh (the)
wear a bullet
  wear lead buttons
wear away
whack
  whack out
win home
  win to rest
  win your way
wipe off
  wipe out
with your Maker
  with us no more
withdraw from life
withdrawn from the roll
    of the living
without baggage
  without the right to
    correspondence
wooden box
  wooden breeches
  wooden breeks
  wooden coat
  wooden overcoat
work off

Education

Euphemisms occasionally prove helpful, as when consoling the bereaved, and in other contexts they are at worst harmless, smoothing the rough edges of direct speech and cushioning us against harsh reality. There are occasions however where their use can confuse what might be better explained in explicit language, affecting important decisions and, in the world of education, in the opinion of some, potentially blighting young lives.

Where the state has taken upon itself the laudable duty and burden of providing free education for all, with a further target that half the youth of the country should attend tertiary education, it is inevitable that politicians will demand a leading role in how the industry is managed and what is taught. It is in the nature of politics, as we have already noted, that failure should be glossed over and language chosen to lessen the impact of any inadequacy, mistake, or error of judgement. If the politician is an egalitarian, it can become an article of faith to establish that there are no stupid, naughty, or idle children from backgrounds where learning is not respected. In such cases, the *learning disabled* must be educated with those of average ability, and potentially more talented children should not permitted to receive instruction at a level which might lead to faster learning and thus discourage their less intelligent or motivated classmates. If language were the only casualty of this philosophy, philologists would be alone in feeling the pain. It appears to many, however, that the children, and society as a whole, may suffer the consequences.

In Britain the majority of selective grammar schools, which had for generations provided a ladder for the able poor into the full development of their talents and subsequent careers, were replaced by *comprehensive* schools and the disappointment or stigma of failing an examination at the age of eleven no longer faced a majority of children.. Splitting pupils into categories, or streams, where they could be taught in what was considered the manner best suited to their ability gave way to the *convoy concept*. Some disciplinary sanctions whereby teachers might persuade or compel lazy or unruly children to temper their behaviour became proscribed by practice as by law. At the same time, lazy or unruly children ceased to exist in a world where *backward* gave way to such conditions as *attention deficit disorder* to describe the *less academic* who might be *disturbed*, *maladjusted*, or have a *concentration problem*, despite which they remained in classes where their fellow-pupils were not labouring under any such *handicap*. For *verbally deficient underachievers* with *special needs*, the best hope became that they would eventually be sent to a *special class* in a *special school* where they might benefit from *special education*. Most clever children could expect no such discriminatory and costly favours.

Where parents have opted to pay for their children's education, the teacher's language does not need to be modified by *political correctness* to the same extent as in the public sector and there remains the ultimate sanction of expulsion. A child, described by parents as a *late developer* or *not a great reader*, may be faced with a more direct assessment in the end-of-term report, however satisfactory the *soft skills* which have been displayed. Tuition may take place in an environment where the blackboard has not been replaced by a *chalkboard*.

Parents paying for their children's education see truancy as a waste of their own money, rather than that of taxpayers as a whole, and are likely to stamp on any delinquency. The same constraint does not apply in state schools and those pupils suffering from the *school phobia syndrome* may in the fullness of time come to the attention of the *educational welfare manager*, although for them the sanction of *academic dismissal* is not a significant deterrent.

Because politicians need to show, and often believe, that, under their direction, things continually get better despite *comprehension*, *literacy*, and *numeracy* having replaced reading, writing, and arithmetic as core subjects, sceptics suggest that examinations have been *dumbed down* to ensure almost every candidate passes and that very few have to suffer the disappointment or humiliation of failure. They draw attention to the statistics which say that, in the Britain of 2006, 98% of the candidates were successful in the intermediate public examinations and a mark of 47% in a mathematics paper in the higher examination entitled the examinee to an A grade. Critics then point out that, despite such qualifications, a minority of those proceeding to university need to attend *foundation* or other *remedial* courses before they can pursue more advanced studies, despite which a high proportion of them are likely to be *plowed*, *shipped*, or *sent down*. At least on graduation they will not find themselves *plucked* for non-payment of their student loans.

We are looking at language, not policy, but if the euphemistic use of language makes it harder for teachers to teach and for children to learn, more difficult for admission tutors to decide which applicants to accept and which to reject, then words have become accessory to an injustice. We are told by organizations representing employers that many of their members have so scant confidence in certain examination results that the years of study and expense by students can count for little when it comes to applying for a job. Some academics go further and predict that many intelligent young people may decide that the time devoted to tertiary education will be wasted and that the burden of debt incurred at a university is best avoided. If either of these propositions were valid, our continued refusal to use plain language when we assess achievement in the classroom would be both craven and unfair.

academically subnormal *at* subnormal
alternative education *at* alternative
attention deficit disorder ADD

backward[1]
Blue Peter

chalk-board
chuck (the)
comprehension comprehensive
concentration problem (a)
conduct disorder
convoy concept
creative freedom *at* creative

deconstruction
developmental
disparate impact
dumb down

educable
education welfare manager

fair[1]
foundation
foundation course
foundation degree place
foundation language arts

gap year
gate[1]

home economics

jerk

language arts *at* language
late developer
learner
learning difficulties learning disabled learning disability
less less academic less gifted
limited
literacy *at* comprehension

mature student *at* mature

negative peer pressure
no Einstein no genius no scholar
no-fly zone
not a great reader
numeracy *at* comprehension

open access
Oppositional Defiant Disorder ODD

personal correction
play hooky *at* hooky
plough[2]
plucked

race-norming
rather naughty child *at* rather
referred
remedial
retarded *at* retard
rusticate

School Phobia Syndrome *at* syndrome
score adjustment
send down
ship
slow
soft skills
special class special education special school
special needs
status deprivation

tenure

underachiever

verbally deficient

widening access
within-group norming

Human Bodies

I place under this heading parts of the body, nakedness, and obesity. Because we are all vain about ourselves, to varying degrees, I also include clothing and cosmetics.

Reticence about mentioning parts of the body has changed over time, as with so much of our language. The Victorian prudery about legs, which gave humans *benders* and poultry *dark meat* and *drumsticks*, has vanished. Today the stomach is seldom referred to as *little Mary*. Bottoms are no longer considered vulgar, although *backside* and *derrière* may still be heard, along with *Khyber*, which is rhyming slang on *Khyber Pass*. There are a number of homosexual euphemisms for the anus, among which *bronze* or *second eye* are the less offensive. The British *arse* is only a euphemism when it describes a person's sexuality, unlike the American *ass* which once led prudes to call a jackass as a Johnny-bum.

Moving up the sensitivity scale, we come to female breasts or, for poultry, *white meat*. Here the dividing line between euphemism and vulgarity is narrow. For example, *boobs*, as a shortened form of the slang *boobies*, has no other meaning but it gave us the punning, if ephemeral, garment, the *booby-trap*. When men describe a comely female as *endowed*, they are not talking of a marriage settlement just as *bristols* does not refer to the west-country conurbation or to its soccer team, Bristol City.

The parts of the body of which mention is cloaked in evasive language are the male and female genitalia. Reluctance to use the word *cock* has given us the American *rooster* and *roach*, while the imagery of *balls*, *nuts*, and *stones* for the testicles appears in various forms. The euphemisms for the penis can be divided into those which relate to it in its flaccid state, and to *erections*. With no sexual implications, it may acquire a variety of male names, so that *Percy*, a corruption of *person*, is in the company of *Cecil*, *John Thomas*, *Willy*, and sundry foreign friends such as *Fritz*, *Giorgio*, and *Jean-Claude*. The *meat* imagery can be applied to the penis whatever its condition, the accompanying *two veg* being the testicles. When erect, it may assume an aggressive image, the *instrument* becoming a *pork sword* or *split-mutton*, among other

vulgarisms. However a speaker of British English may be misunderstood if he advises an American to 'keep his *pecker* up'. Male sportsmen are protected from injury to their *family jewels* by wearing an *abdominal protector* or *box*, despite which a blow to the *lower abdomen* can be very painful.

The vagina, also called the taboo cunt or *monosyllable*, is usually referred to allusively whether or not it is being viewed sexually. Thus the *intimate part* may become *Cupid's arbour*, *cave*, *cloister*, *corner*, or *cupboard*. The only female name which it is commonly given is *fanny*, which means something different on either side of the Atlantic. Feline imagery, probably from the hirsute nature of the *beaver* or *bush*, gives us both *cat* and *pussy*, the latter being also generic of nubile females. The taboo against saying cunt, or cunny, is venerable and explains why we have *rabbits* in our fields instead of coneys and use *Charlie uncle* as an insult.

We were all born wearing our *birthday suit*, *attire*, *finery*, or *gear* but are not expected to flaunt it in public later in life. Of course, *nature's garb* is acceptable if you are a *naturist*, and the weather not inclement. While in a remote place, we might decide to *skinny-dip* and, in summer, sleep *in the buff*, but for most of us the adult human body is better clothed than naked, except when we decide to *streak*.

It is unfortunate that obesity should affect so many Britons and Americans, not just for those starving elsewhere in the world but also because of the stigma which it brings on the person involved, which is why we use allusive language when we refer to it. The *bay window* which protrudes ahead of you is not because you are *big-boned* but indicates that you have a *bit if a stomach*, possibly caused by *brewer's goitre*. And so through the alphabet, remaining *well-fleshed* to the last. We may be *corn-fed* but we are not fat.

Few of the euphemisms about clothing show the humour of the *abandoned habits* once worn by the prostitutes in London's Hyde Park. Some men are careless about their appearance, and remain *sartorially challenged*. The taboo about trousers, or pants for the Americans, has vanished along with the *continuations*, *don't-name-'ems*, *indescribables*, *ineffables*, *sit-upons*, *unexpressables*, *unmentionables*, *unspeakables*, and *unwhisperables*, the sole survivor being *bags*, a shortened form of *leg bags*. We males must still *adjust our dress* after urination or we will find ourselves *at half mast*, *catch a cold*, be told that we are wearing a *canteen* or *Turkish medal*, learn that *Charlie's dead*, *fly a flag* or *low*, let *Johnny out of jail*, have a *medal showing*, hear that it is *one o'clock at the waterworks*, be warned that *the shop door is open*, or see a *star in the east*. The warning to a woman that her slip was showing below her skirt might be that it was *snowing down south*.

Happily, women choose attractive clothing to enhance their girth and stature. A man is not necessarily of *restricted growth* if he chooses to wear *Cuban heels*, *lifts*, or *risers* but, for women, they are no more than high heels. Most adult females prefer to have support for their breasts, a *brassière* or *bust*

bodice, while others call in aid from a *body shaper*, a *foundation garment*, or even *cheaters*, *falsies*, or *sides*. Those who prefer *sensible* shoes are also likely to eschew *enhanced contouring*. If you have a medical abnormality, you may wear an *appliance*, apart from the usual sportsman's *athletic supporter* or *jock strap*.

And so to cosmetics, where we will stick to hair, or at least to those who are not *follicularly challenged* with a *high forehead* or a *receding hairline* calling for the use of a *sky-piece* or *syrup* (of figs). *Blue hair* may be out of fashion but the *rinse* is still with us along with the *colour-tinting* and other devices to keep the years at bay. Be on your guard, however, if your coiffeur asks you if you would like a *touch up*.

abdominal protector
Abyssinian medal *at* medal
   showing
acorns
active
Adam's arsenal
adjust your dress
aesthetic procedure *at*
   aesthete
after-shave
ample
  amply endowed
appendage
apples
appliance
arrange yourself *at* arrange
as Allah made him
at half mast
athletic supporter
au naturel

back door[1]
back passage
backside
bags
balls
banana
basket[2]
bay window
BB *at* bust bodice
beaver
beef
behind
below medium height
below stairs[2]
benders
between the legs
big-boned
bikini wax
  bikini line

bird[1]
  bird's nest
birthday suit (your)
  birthday attire
  birthday finery
  birthday gear
blue rinse *at* rinse[1]
body image
body shaper
  body briefer
  body hugger
  body outline
bone *at* bone-ache
booby
  boobies
  boobs
booby-trap
bottle blond(e)
bottom
box[2]
boy[2]
  boys
brassière
brewer's goitre
  at brew[2] (a)
bristols
bronze eye
buff (the)
bum
bush
bust bodice

calorie counter
canteen medal
carpet[2]
catch a cold[2]
Cecil
Charlie
  Charlie's dead
  Charlies

cheaters
cherry
chestnuts
chopper[2]
Christmas crackers
chubby
classic proportions (of)
cleft *at* cleavage
cleavage
cobblers
cobs
cock
  cockpit
cojones
conditioner
continuations
contour
co-respondent's shoes
  at co-respondent
corn-fed
corner[3]
couch potato
crown jewels *at* jewels
Cuban heels
Cupid's arbour
  Cupid's cave
  Cupid's cloister
  Cupid's corner
  Cupid's cupboard

decent
décolletage
derrière
designer stubble *at* designer
devoted to the table
dick[1]
differently weighted *at*
  differently
ding-a-ling
don't name 'ems

down below
  down there
downstairs[2]
duff
dummy[2]

elephant and castle
eliminate manhood *at*
  manhood
endowed
enhance
  enhanced contouring
enlist the aid of science
Eve's custom-house *at*
  Adam's arsenal
exhibit yourself
expose yourself

face between her forks *at*
  fork
falsies
family jewels *at* jewels
fanny
feed the ducks
feminine gender
flash
  flasher
flesh
fleshy part of the thigh
fly a flag
follicularly challenged *at*
  challenged
fond of
  fond of food
foundation garment
front door (the) *at*
  back door
fry[2]
full figure (a)
  full-figured
  fuller figure

gear
generously built
  generous girth
  generously proportioned
  generously sized
glands
go to the fat farm
goolies
  goolie chits
goose[2]
groin

hairpiece
hampton
heaviness
  heavily built
high forehead (a)

hindside
hole
  holy of holies
homely
honk
hot meat *at* meat[2] (and
  two veg)
hung like

improving knife (the)
in his naturals *at* nature's
  garb
in the altogether
  in the buff
  in the raw
  in the skin
  in your nip
indescribables
  inexpressibles
ineffables *at*
  unmentionables[1]
innocence
instrument
intact
intimate
  intimate part(s)
  intimate person
inviolate
it

jack[1]
jewels
jock
  jock rash
  jock-strap
John Thomas
  John Peter
  John Willie
  JP
  JT
  Johnson
Johnnie's out of jail
joint[2]
jugs

Khyber
knackers
knob
knobs
knocker
knockers

large endowment *at* well
  endowed
larger
latter end[1]
  latter part
lead apes in hell
less attractive *at* less

lift[4]
limb
little Mary
load[2]
loins
long-arm inspection
long pig
love muscle *at* love
lower abdomen
  lower stomach
lower limbs
lower part
lunch box
lungs

male parts
man-root *at* root
many pounds heavier
marbles
marriage tackle
  at tackle
masculinity
maturer
meat[2] (and two veg)
medal showing
melons
member
mickey
middle-aged spread
monosyllable
moon
most precious part
mousehole *at* mouse
muff

nasty complaint
nature's garb
naturist
nest
nether parts
  nether regions
  Netherlands
nick[4]
non-self material
nose job (a)
nuts

old man
one o'clock at the
  waterworks
optically challenged
  optically handicapped
  optically inconvenienced
  optically marginalized
orchestras
organ
  organ of bliss
  organ of sex
oval office

partially sighted
parts
pecker
peculiar members *at* peculiar
pencil[1]
people of/with
   people of size
   people with differing
     abilities
   people with impaired
     hearing
personal
personal parts *at* person
peter
petite
pill[1]
pills
pin
pistol
plumbing[2]
pork sword *at* pork[2]
posterior(s)
pride
   pride and joy
   prides
private parts
   privates
   privities
   privy parts
puppy fat
pussy
   pussy lift

quantitively challenged

raw
rear end
   rear
receding (hairline)
restricted growth
ring[1]
rinse[1]
riser
rocks
root
rubber tire *at* spare tyre
rug

sartorially challenged
seat

second eye
   at bronze eye
secret parts
sensible
serpent
sex[2]
sexual organ *at* organ
shop door is open (the)
short-arm *at* short-arm
   inspection
short hairs
   short and curlies
shorten the front line[2]
sides
sit-upon
   sit-down-upon
   sit-upons
   sitting
skinny-dip
sky-piece
smalls
snatch[2]
snowing down south
south[2]
   south pole
spam[1]
   spam alley
   spam chasm
   spam javelin
   spam sceptre
spare tyre
stacked
star in the east (a)
stark
state of nature (a)
step-ins
stern
stick *at* stick it into
stomach (a)
stones
streak
   streaker
surgical appliance at
   appliance
sword
syrup

tackle
thing
ticker

tint
Tommy
to the buff
   at buff (the)
tool
   tools
topless
   topless bar
touch up[2]
traditionally built
tube of meat *at* tube
tuck

uncut *at* cut[1]
under the knife
unmentionables[1]
   unexpressables
   unspeakables
   unwhisperables

vertically challenged
   at challenged
vital statistics
vitals

wank
wardrobe malfunction
warpaint
waterworks[1]
wax[1]
wedding tackle *at*
   tackle
weenie
weight watcher
   weight problem
well built
   well fleshed
well endowed
   well hung
what you may call it
   whatsit
   whatzis
whistle
wick
wiener
willy
winkle
   winkie

yard

Illness

We reserve the use of euphemism for the more unpleasant, painful, or life-threatening illnesses which may affect us. If we have a cold or a bad back, there is no need for evasion in conveying the information to others, however unwilling they are to hear about it. A sufferer from diarrhoea will, however, resort to allusive language, as we noted when looking at **Bodily Functions**. More serious ailments, such as those affecting the heart, may be wrapped up in such terms as a *cardiac incident*, as though every beat of that organ were not, a *coronary inefficiency*, or a *dicky ticker*, *dicky* being rhyming slang for sick. Until the identification of the tubercle bacillus in 1882, *consumption* was not so much a euphemism as a description of the effect of the disease, with the *white plague* causing an inexplicable *decline*. *Consumption* was, however, to remain the preferred evasion, preferable to the more technical *TB*, until the advent of penicillin removed much of the dread associated with the complaint. Moving to the higher end of the scale, *stroke* is standard English for a cerebral haemorrhage, and then we come to the *mitotic disease*, when we have a potentially fatal *growth*, *neoplasm*, *tumour*, or the *big C*.

Language used between medical staff and patients owes a great deal to prudery. There may be references from both parties to *plumbing* when there are problems *down there* with the *waterworks*. A woman may suffer from a *feminine complaint* if she has a *woman's problem*. A taboo condition such as haemorrhoids may call in aid rhyming slang, such as the *Chalfonts (St Giles)* or *Farmer Giles*. A youth who tells his doctor that he has been *caught* is not referring to apprehension by an officer of the law. The infection of which he speaks is one which in the past would have been attributed to dirty foreigners, as a *Neopolitan favour*, *Spanish gout*, or, nearer to home, the *French ache*, *compliment*, *disease*, *fever*, *measles*, or *pox*, causing the sufferer to be *Frenchified*. If not the fault of those beyond Calais, then a man had to blame the *ladies' fever* from which he had contracted his *affliction of the loins* or *social infection*.

There are a number of taboo conditions for which the medical profession provides less frightening alternatives, such as Hansen's disease for leprosy, and this is where *syndrome* becomes such a useful word,

appearing in phrases such as *Down's syndrome*, *Kraepelin's syndrome*, and *Korsakoff's syndrome* to avoid using emotive definitions such as mongolism, schizophrenia, and delirium tremens. The *syndrome* which has passed into standard English is AIDS or, to give its full title *Acquired Immune Deficiency Syndrome*, also known in the godly American mid-west as the Wrath of God Syndrome, or WOGS, because of the lifestyle of a those with the greatest risk of contracting it. A sufferer is likely to be referred to as a *PWA*, the acronym for *person with AIDS*.

Doctors have another argot whereby they seek to exchange information between themselves in a code which they hope the patient cannot understand. Some of the expressions are not euphemistic, such as plumbo-oscillosis for a malingerer who *swings the lead*, or multiple-diplomatosis for a perpetual student fearful of life outside academe. Others, such as *sigma-phi*, play on the presumption that the person described is not familiar with the Greek alphabet and so will remain ignorant that he is syphilitic, while an *eating disorder* on a medical report does not refer to an untidy breakfast table.

When you go into hospital, you are usually requested to bring a *sample* with you. While recuperating, you may asked if you have *used paper*, which is not an enquiry into your reading habits. If your condition is said to be *comfortable* after a *procedure* or *intervention* you may well actually feel *under the weather* and the nurse with a hypodermic needle in her hands who tells you that you may feel a small *prick* is giving you a warning, not an insult. *Discomfort* is another word to watch out for, especially in the dentist's chair. You can only hope that nobody has written on the medical sheets at the foot of your bed *no i/v access*, *no active treatment*, *no mayday*, *routine nursing care only*, *TLC*, or any other intimation that you are a *goner*. Even if the nursing staff say no more than that you are *poorly*, beware the arrival at your bedside of the mortician with a tape measure.

It is no longer permissible to use the word cripple about a lame person, although crippled does not yet seem to have incurred the same opprobrium. Your *handicap* may be such that you are no longer *active*, being *mobility impaired*, and *use a wheelchair*. If any other of your senses is defective, you will discover that you are *challenged*, although fortunately not to a duel. Those who are *inconvenienced* or *differently abled* tend to be more direct about their *disability* than third parties and a *sight deprived* or *unsighted* person usually makes no bones about the blindness.

In the case of mental illness, sympathetic evasion in the use of language can cause misunderstanding. No other area of definition gave me so much pause because the use of words such as mad or lunatic can be misleading as well as offensive. For example, we use the word mad to describe conditions of the mind ranging from mild annoyance or folly to acute dementia, and many of the euphemisms we use about mental illness cover the same wide spectrum. Consider the phrases starting with *off*—*off at the side*, *off the wall*, *off your chump*, *off your gourd*, *off your head*, *off your napper*, *off your nut*, *off your rocker*, *off your tree*, *off your trolley*, and *off your turnip*. Without knowing a person whom you hear so described, it is impossible to tell if they are occasionally slightly eccentric or permanently suffering from a severe mental illness. And so it is with other *headbangers* who are said to have *bats in the belfry* and *march to a different drummer*.

Medical talk about *diminished responsibility*, or the *disability* of someone who is *disturbed*, makes it equally difficult for the listener to gauge the seriousness or duration of the illness. It is, for example, a matter of guesswork to evaluate the *condition* of someone described as having *learning difficulties*. Is there any one of us who doesn't, on occasion? And yet the phrase has become standard English, although whether it refers to an imbecile, an idiot, a moron, or to someone suffering from autism, mongolism, or dyslexia is a matter of conjecture. Only when the patient is *certified* or *sectioned* can the gravity be understood and you know why they have to remain in a *residential home* or *sent away* to a *state farm*, *home*, *hospital*, or *training school*, also known as an *asylum* and with less charity as an *acorn academy*, *bin*, *booby hutch*, and other unkind phrases.

Euphemisms about injury are mainly employed by the military. A minor wound may be described as a *scratch*. If more serious, the soldier who *stops one* may say that he has *caught a packet* and his commander will record him as *combat ineffective*. At least, if these days he gets a *blighty* on a distant shore, he will not run the risk of contracting the *do-lally-tap* while he waits for homeward-bound transport.

ableism
acorn academy
afflicted
    affliction of the loins
    affliction of venery
alternative medicine *at*
    alternative
ape
around the bend *at* round the
    bend
asylum
aurally challenged *at*
    challenged
aurally handicapped *at*
    handicap

balance of mind disturbed
bananas
bang and biff *at* bang
barking
bats in the belfry
    bats
    batty
battle fatigue
big C (the)
bin
bit missing (a)
black dog (the)
blighty

blood disease
blow a gasket
bone-ache
booby
    booby hatch
    booby hutch
born in a mill *at* born in
both oars in the water
break your shins against
    Covent Garden rails
    at Covent Garden
brick short of a load (a)
bughouse
burn¹
    burn his poker
    burner
bust a string
by yourself

card short of a full deck (a)
cardiac incident
    cardiac arrest
catch a cold¹
catch a packet²
catch the boat up
caught²
cerebrally challenged *at*
    challenged
Chalfonts

change your bulbs
Clapham
claret
clean¹
clip²
    clipped
coco
cold³
come home by Clapham *at*
    Clapham
comfortable²
commit
communicable disease
complications
condition¹
consumption
contagious and disgraceful
    disease
    Contagious Diseases Act
content
coronary inefficiency
    coronary
    coronary adjustment
Covent Garden gout *at*
    Covent Garden
cracked
    crack-brained
    crackers
    crackpot

critical incident
croaker *at* croak
cuckoo[2]
Cupid's measles
    Cupid's itch

dateless
decline
delicate
derailed
Derbyshire neck
developmentally challenged
    at challenged
devil's mark (the)
dicky
differently abled *at* differently
diminished responsibility
disability
discomfort
disease of love
distressed
disturbed
do-lally (tap)
dope
dose
dotty
Down's syndrome
Drury Lane ague
dry pox (the)
dummy[1]
Dutchman
    Dutchy

East Ham *at* barking
eating disorder
eccentric
elevator does not go to the
    top floor (the)
Emmas
    Emma Freuds

face your maker
falling sickness (the)
    falling evil
Farmer Giles
fatigue
feed the fishes
feminine complaint
fifty cards in the pack
flake
flip your lid
fly the yellow flag
for the birds
French ache
    French compliment
    French disease
    French fever
    French gout
    French measles

French pox
    frenchified
fruitcake
    fruit
funny[1]
    funny tummy
funny[3]
    funny farm
    funny home
    funny place

garden gout/house *at*
    Covent Garden
gears have slipped *at* gear
go bush *at* go native
God's child
growth

half deck
handicap
hard of hearing
harpic
headshrinker
    headbanger
    head case
health
    health care
    health clinic
    health farm
    health insurance
heart condition
heart problem
    at problem
hopping-Giles
hospice
hospital
hot[3]
human difference

ill[2]
ill[4]
    ill-adjusted
impaired hearing
in left field
inconvenienced
incurable bone-ache
institutionalize
intellectually challenged
    at challenged
intervention[2]
Irish beauty
Irish fever (the)

Korsakoff's syndrome *at*
    syndrome
Kraepelin's syndrome *at*
    Down's syndrome

ladies' fever

ladies' troubles
laughing academy
lay a child
learning difficulties
    learning disabled
    learning disability
left field
less
    less abled
    less gifted
light in the head
long illness (a)
loopy
loose in the attic
    loose in the head
loose connection *at* connect[1]
lose hold
    lose it
    lose the plot
    lose your grip

maladjustment
malady of France
Malta dog
march to a different
    drummer
medical correctness
medical intervention *at*
    intervention[2]
mental
    mentally challenged
    mentally deficient
mental disease
mentally handicapped *at*
    handicap
meshugga
minus
    minus buttons
    minus screws
misadventure
mitotic disease
mobility impaired
moon people
motion discomfort
    motion discomfort bag
muster your bag
mutt

nasty complaint
natural[1]
neoplasm
nervous breakdown
nil by mouth
no active treatment
    NAT
    no mayday
not all there
not sixteen annas in the
    rupee

not very well
not with it
nothing intrusive
nut
  nutcase
  nut college
  nut farm
  nut hatch
  nut house
  nutter
  nutty
  nuts

off[2]
  off at the side
  off the rails off your chump
  off your gourd
  off your head
  off your napper
  off your nut
  off your onion
  off your rocker
  off your turnip
  off your tree
  off your trolley
off-colour[2]
off the wall
old man's friend
on the box
on the club
on the panel
one bubble left of level
  one brick short of a load
one foot in the grave
operation (an)
out of your skull
  out of your gourd
  out of your head
  out of your senses
  out of your tree
out to lunch

packet[2]
panel[1] (the)
penny short of a pound
person with AIDS *at* person
  of/with
  PWA
physically challenged *at*
  challenged
physically handicapped *at*
  handicapped
pick up a nail
piled with French velvet
ping-ponging
piss pins and needles
  piss pure cream
play with a full deck *at* play
  a card

poorly[1]
potentially ineffective care
  PIC
potty
pox (the)
preventable diseases
private patient
problem
procedure
put away[3]
put out for the count *at* count
  (the)

queer[2]
  queer in the head

Rangoon itch
  Rangoon runs
raspberry[2]
rest home
retard
right Charlie *at* Charlie
rocky[1]
round the bend
  round the twist
routine (nursing) care only

Sandy McNabs
scald
scratch[2]
screw loose (a)
section
self-abuse[2]
shoot between wind and
  water *at* shoot off
short-arm inspection
shrink *at* headshrinker
shroud waving
  shroud waver
sick through negligence
sight-deprived
sigma phi
simple
slate-off
slippage
smear[2]
snake pit
so-so
social disease
soft[1]
sore
Spanish gout
special care
  special care unit
  special home
  special hospital
spot[3]
squirrel
staining

statement
structural changes
subnormal
syndrome

take in your coals
tap[4] *at* do-lally tap
tap the claret *at* claret
ten commandments (the)
tender loving care
  TLC
thick of hearing
throw the switches
tip off your trolley
  at tip off
touched[2] (in the head)
translocation
tumour (a)
turn[3]
twelve annas to
  the rupee

unbalanced
under the weather
unglued
unhinged
uniquely
  uniquely abled
  uniquely coordinated
unmentionables[2]
unplugged
unscrewed
unsighted
unslated
untoward incident
unwired
up the loop
use a wheelchair

visually challenged
visually impaired
visually handicapped
  at handicap
voluntary patient
  at voluntary

wandered
want[1] (a)
  want some pence in the
    shilling
white plague (the)
wholesome
winded
winged
without the highest IQ
  in the world
women's problem *at*
  problem
wooden log

Miscellaneous

There are relatively few euphemisms which cannot be linked with a particular taboo. Some in this category relate to prudery about the sexuality of animals. People tend to refer allusively to boasting or flattery and are reluctant to accuse another of cowardice. We need also to consider swearing and vulgarisms.

Apart from the *French pigeon* or the *Irish horse*, which was not a quadruped, most animal euphemisms exist to avoid using words such as bitch, bull, cock, or stallion. The bitch might be referred to as a *lady dog*. The bull, which enjoys the greatest linguistic variety, could be anything through the alphabet from a *big animal* to a *stock beast*, *animal*, *brute*, or *cow*. The cock became a *crower* or *rooster*, with *dark meat*, *drumsticks*, and *white meat* replacing its legs and breast, while the American cockroach lost its *cock*. The stallion was a *stable horse*, taken to *cover* a mare *in season* by a *stoned horse man*.

There were few solecisms less tolerated among our recent ancestors than boasting and in this context the word *bull* may be used without impropriety, although the common *bullshit*, the American *bull-rinky*, or simply *BS* are less polite. The *bull* might also be *shot*, although it is more usual to *shoot a line* or *the breeze* and we no longer *shoot among the doves*. Others may *blow*, or *blow smoke*, *their own horn*, or *their own trumpet*. Only a bounder would *angle with a silver hook* or *shoot with a silver gun*. We hesitate to accuse another directly of seeking to win *brownie points*, even if they are *brown-nosed* or have a tendency to *grandstand*. English speakers may envy the Germans their delightful *Pantoffelheld* and no longer *ride abroad with St George but at home with St Michael*, but some men may still be *hen-pecked*, especially by a *house-proud* wife or *partner*.

Attitudes have changed to such an extent that, some ninety years after the event, all those British soldiers shot for cowardice in the First World War have received posthumous pardons, to be followed perhaps by claims for compensation by their remote descendants. Many of the men accused of having a *yellow streak* or presented with a *white feather* may indeed have had an *acute environmental reaction* arising from *battle fatigue* and thus proved *far from staunch* in the face of the enemy. In the Second World War some of us proved *allergic to lead* and showed a *lack of moral fibre*. A better understanding of the effect of prolonged exposure to peril has made us more sympathetic to those with *cold feet* or a tendency to get the *wind up* although, remarkably, mental illness was almost unknown among the British civilian population between 1940 and 1945 despite the horrors of bombing, the hardships of rationing, and the absence of those in the forces. People were too busy to expend time and energy on worrying about trivia.

The evasions, such as *expletive deleted*, used by Rose Mary Woods when transcribing the Nixon tapes, have enriched the language. We ourselves may use *Anglo-Saxon* or *four-letter words* if we have a penchant for *flowery language* and have to ask the hearer to *excuse our French*. It is immaterial to which of three *Gordon Bennet(t)s* we allude when we seek to invoke the name of our deity and questionable whether corruptions of the word god, such as *golly* or *gum*, should be rated as euphemistic. Perhaps it would be better just to leave a *blank*.

The nature of the relatively few entries which defy classification can best be illustrated by picking one letter. We may describe someone as *difficult* when we mean thoroughly objectionable and unreasonable. We do not admire a *do-gooder* for the good that is done. Household servants used to live, and be referred to, as *downstairs*. Among the *Dutch* entries emanating from our 17th-century antagonism, we have failed to find a place elsewhere for *Dutch comfort*, a *Dutch fuck*, or a *Dutch uncle*. And a *Dutch consolation* is an appropriate way of bringing this, or any other, interlude to a close.

bar steward *at* bar
barrack-room lawyer
  barracks lawyer
basket[1]
battle fatigue
behind the eight ball
berk *at* Burke
big animal
Billingsgate
blank[1]
  blanking
  blankety-blank
blast[1]
bleeding
bleep
blooming
blow[3]
  blow smoke
  blow your own horn
  blow your own trumpet
  blowhard
blow[4]
born in
  born in a barn
Boston marriage
break your elbow in the
  church *at* break your
  elbow
bromide job
brown-nose
  brown-noser
brownie points
brute *at* big animal
bug-out fever
  at bug out
bull[2]
  bull-rinky
  bullshit
  bullshitter
bunk flying
bunny-hugger

C-word *at* C
California blankets *at*
  California widow
call out
characterization deleted *at*
  expletive deleted
Charlie uncle *at* Charlie
Chelsea tractor
chicken[2]
clean[1]
clotheshorse
cold feet
combat fatigue
communication problem *at*
  problem
cow brute
  at big animal

D
dark meat[1]
darn
dash[2]
dirty
dog and pony show
draw the long bow
Dutch comfort
Dutch concert
Dutch consolation
Dutch fuck
Dutch uncle
Dutch wife

early bath
earthy
effing
embroidery
enhance
excuse my French *at* French[2]
expletive deleted

F
  F word
Fanny Adams
  FA
far from staunch
feather-bed
filth
  filthy
  filthy language
  filthy joke
flapper
favoured
flowery[2]
forget yourself
four-letter man
four-letter word
foxtrot oscar
French[2]
French drive
French pigeon
friend[1]
frigging *at* frig
fringe
  fringe theatre

G
gaffe
gentleman cow/ox *at* big
  animal
get out the onion
get your feet under the table
give the finger to
go abroad
golly
Gordon Bennet(t)
grandstand
  grandstand play

Greek Calends (the)
Greek gift
guardhouse lawyer
gum at golly

H
Hail Columbia
hard
he-cow *at* big animal
he-thing *at* big animal
head for the hills
house-proud

I hear what you say
in a pig's ear
in Dutch
in your brown *at* brown
invigorating
Irish confetti
Irish hoist
Irish horse
Irish hurricane
Irish local
Irish pennant

joiner

kangaroo court *at* kangaroo
kick over the traces

lack of moral fibre
  LMF
lady dog
language
lend
live it up
load of old cobblers *at*
  cobblers
loose cannon
lose your bottle *at* bottle[1]
low flying
low profile

male beast *at* big animal
male cow *at* big animal
man cow *at* big animal
martyr to (a)
meet
  meeting
merchant banker
micky *at* take the mick(e)y
miss the bus
  miss the boat
mother[2]
mountain chicken
Mrs Duckett

N-word
naff off

negative
negative aspect(s)
negative incident
never modest
new
new man
next door to
no
not
not at home
   not innot known for

off-colour[1]
out[3]
out of the envelope
own goal

p off *at* P
party-goer *at* goer
past its sell-by date
pay lip service
pick up a knife
poodle
poor-mouth
pot hunter
pound salt
   pound sand
prairie oyster[1]
prey to (a)
professional

rabbit
ram-riding (a)
rather
redneck
reluctant to depart
ride abroad with St George
     but at home with St
     Michael *at* ride
riding *at* ram-riding (a)
roach
roof rabbit
rooster

rooster-roach *at* roach
ruddy

saddle soap
satisfaction
say a few words
sea lawyer *at* barrack-room
    lawyer
seed-ox *at* big animal
send to the showers
set up shop on Goodwin
    Sands
sex and travel
sheep buck
ship's lawyer *at* barrack-
    room lawyer
shoot a line
   shoot among the doves
   shoot the breeze
   shoot the bull
shoot with a silver gun
sledge
smear[3]
smell of
so-and-so
social
soft[2]
soft-shoe
soft soap
something[2]
   something-something
sow your wild oats
special
spin a line
squat[2]
   squatter
stable horse
stand up[1]
stock beast *at* big animal
stoned horse man *at* stones
stroke
   stroke job
suffer fools gladly

sugar[2]
Sunday
   Sunday driver
sweet Fanny Adams *at* Fanny
    Adams
sweetbreads
swing the lamp

take an early bath
take the mick(e)y
talking
   talking cardigan
   talking head
tell me about it
tin ear (a)
tinpot
toot your own whistle
    at toot
touchy-feely
tree-hugger
trophy
   trophy home
   trophy model
   trophy wife
tuft-hunter

uncle[2]

variety meats
vehicle incident
vicar of Bray

white elephant
white feather
white meat[1]
white rabbit scut
wind up (the)
with respect

yellow[1]
   yellow belly
   yellow streak
   yellow stripe

Prostitution

Even if it is not the *oldest profession*, prostitution has been around for a long time. As the word 'whore' has unacceptable overtones for some, I use prostitute as a definition knowing that, in Latin at least, it was a euphemism, meaning a woman exposed for sale. The exposure is understandable but hire or licence might seem a better description of the subsequent transaction. Prostitute is not a euphemism because it has had only one meaning in standard English. It has, however, given rise to a great number of euphemisms because of the nature and illegality of the *life* and the desire for concealment or secrecy of many who become involved with it. Before looking closer at how *working girls* spend their time, let us see what usages we can find under the letter C .

A *call girl* or *call-button girl* was not originally someone whose attendance was requested over the telephone but a prostitute who lived in a *call house*, which was a brothel where men might visit or call. For male homosexuals, modern society also provides *call boys*. While *in circulation*, a *camp follower*, *cat*, *cavalry*, *chick*, *child of Venus*, *chippy*, *cockatrice*, *cockchafer*, *cocktail*, *coffee grinder*, *commercial sex worker*, *convenient*, *country-club girl*, *courtesan*, *Covent Garden goddess*, *creature of sale*, *Cressida*, *crib girl*, *cross girl*, *cruiser*, *currency girl*, or *Cyprian* may *call the tricks* or *crawl the kerb*. Shakespeare talks of a *common customer*, although she would seem to have been selling rather than buying. We also had *common jacks*, *maids*, *sewers*, and *tarts*, as well as the *commoner o' th' camp*, who performed the same duties as the *comfort girls* did for Japanese soldiers, after the rape of Nanking had caused the victors heavy casualties through venereal disease. Their German allies stationed in France had to rely on *collabos horizontales*. These days, as a civilian, a Japanese man may, if so minded, resort to *compensated dating*.

Given the antiquity of their *trade*, we should not be surprised that someone who *sells herself* might like to be called a *professional woman*. Others might say less respectfully that those who *hawk their mutton* are *on the game*. If *walking the streets*, she may be also described as *on the street*, *stroll*, or *town where*

she may *flutter a skirt* or *show her charms* to attract the attention of a man who looking for an *available indigenous female companion*. Whatever we may think of the *social evil*, we can be sure that the *sinful commerce* will continue, although perhaps with fewer *naughty ladies* than Mayhew reported regularly *hustling* in Victorian London, when men tended to marry late and women without the *pill* were wary of premarital sex and, after marriage, of repeated pregnancies. The plot of *Bleak House*, based on the dishonour of an unmarried woman giving birth, seems today so implausible as to be ridiculous, but it cannot have been so for its audience, despite being the weakest Dickens novel.

Servicemen in foreign stations tend not to meet respectable girls and the converse was, and probably still is, equally true. For many soldiers the local word for girl became synonymous with prostitute, which has added *bibi*, *bidi*, *bint*, and *moose* to the language and suggested an alternative occupation for the *tree-rat* of the Indian subcontinent. Not every *Dutch widow* resided in the Netherlands.

It was a conceit of our ancestors to suppose that women with a religious vocation were *abandoned* and that *nunneries* were *abodes of love*. A brothel might also be called a *case*, *casa*, or *casita*, the domestic imagery persisting in the terms based on *house*. Many useful phrases such as *house of civil reception* or *house in the suburbs* are obsolete, although we may still talk about a *house of ill fame*, which may in fact have an excellent reputation for the comeliness of its occupants, or a *disorderly house*, which may be a pristine example of domestic economy. *Knocking-house* is not heard today, although the *knocking shop* remains in constant use, linguistically. Some men expect to receive more than therapeutic treatment when they go to a *massage parlour* for a *body rub*, especially if they are paying for *extras*. Those after a *quickie* may prefer the comfort offered by a *hot-pillow joint* or *hourly hotel* as an alternative to a *knee trembler* in a dark alley or a *quick time* with a *park woman*.

The area of town in which a *pavement princess* offers *personal services* or where *talent-spotters* may find a *girlie bar* or *pick-up joint* is usually in the *red-light district* or *precinct*, where there are *red lamps* among the *rap clubs* and *sporting houses*. In such a location you may be disappointed if you drive into a *service station* hoping to fill your tank with gasoline. Nor should you expect to see quadrupeds or reptiles if, in that part of town, you visit a *zoo*, although you may discover multi-coloured *birds* for your delectation.

So widespread and lucrative a *business* needs managers while the *sex care providers* are being *nice to* their customers. The appellation *abbess* was taken from the religious imagery, while *governess*, or the common *madam*, for a *bawd*, suggest the authority of the schoolroom. Many ponces appear to have been named *Charlie* or *Joe (Ronce)* and a *procurer*, even if not a *white slaver*, might be called a *husband*. Please remember that the *solicitor* in this *trade* is not the person sitting in the comfort of a remote office, shuffling the paperwork and banking the profits.

abandon yourself (to)
    abandoned
    abandoned habits
abbess *at* nun
academy
accost
accommodation house *at*
    accommodate yourself
actress
all-nighter *at* all night man
alley cat
angel of the night
at the game *at* game[2]
aunt[1]
available casual indigenous
    female companion *at*
    available[1]

bad
badger
    badger game
baggage
bang-tail *at* bang
bar girl
barrel-house
bash (the)
bawd
belter *at* belt
bibi
    bidi
bicycle *at* town bike
bint
bird[1]
    bird-cage
bitch
black velvet
board lodger
bobtail
body rub (a)
bottom woman *at* bottom
brasser
break luck
brother of the gusset
    at brother
business woman
    at business
buy love *at* buy

call girl
    call-button girl
    call boy
call the tricks
canhouse
    can
case[1]
    casita
cat
    cat-house
cavalry
chick
    chickie house
child of Venus
chippy[1]
    chippie-joint
cockchafer
cocktail[1]
    cockatrice
    coffee grinder
comfort therapy *at* comfort[1]
comfort women
    comfort girls
    comfort houses
commercial sex worker
common customer
    common jack
    common maid
    common sewer
    common tart
commoner o' the camp
common house
compensated dating
convenient[1]
country-club girls
coupling house *at* couple
courtesan
Covent Garden
    Covent Garden abbess
    Covent Garden goddess
crawl a kerb *at* kerbcrawling
creature of sale
creep-joint
Cressida
crib
    crib girl
cross girl *at* cross

cruiser *at* cruise[1]
currency girl
Cyprian
Cythera

dance the Haymarket
    hornpipe *at* dance at
dasher
daughter of the game
    daughter of joy
degradation *at* degrade
demi-mondaine
    demi-rep
disorderly house
doe
dog
dolly-common *at* dolly
dolly-mop *at* dolly
doxy
dress for sale

erring sister *at* err
escort
    escort agency

fancy bit *at* fancy
fancy piece *at* fancy
filth
fish[2]
fishmonger's daughter
    fish market
fix up *at* fix
flash-girl *at* flash
flash-ken *at* flash
flash-tail *at* flash
flash-woman *at* flash
flat-backer
fleshpot
flutter a skirt *at* flutter
forty-four
frail sister *at* frail
fresh meat *at* meat[1]
fun-house *at* fun
game[2] (the)

gamester
garden house *at* Covent Garden

gay girl *at* gay
gay life *at* gay
girl[1]
   girl of the streets
   girlie
   girlie bar
   girlie house
   girlie parlor
go case
go into the streets
good time
   good time (bar) girl
goose[1]
governess
grande horizontale *at*
    horizontal
grass bibi *at* bibi

hawk your mutton
   hawk your meat
   hawk your pearly
hold-door trade *at* hold
hooker
   hook-shop
hostess
   hostess bar
   hostess club
hot-house *at* hot[1]
house[1]
   house in the suburbs
   house of accommodation
   house of assignation
   house of evil repute
   house of ill fame
   house of ill repute
   house of pleasure
   house of profession
   house of resort
   house of sale
   house of sin
   house of tolerance
hustle
   hustler

immoral
   immoral earnings
   immoral girls
   immoral house
ill-famed house *at* house[1]
importune
improper house *at* improper
in the game *at* game[2] (the)
in the trade
infamy
introducing house

jag house
Jane[1]
Jezebel

joe
john[2]
joy-boy *at* joy[1]
joy-girl *at* joy[1]
joy-house *at* joy[1]
Judy

kerb-crawling
knocking-shop
   knocker's shop
   knocking-house
   knocking-joint

lady
   lady-boarder
   lady of a certain
    description
   lady of easy virtue
   lady of intrigue
   lady of negotiable
    affections
   lady of no virtue
   lady of pleasure
   lady of the night
   lady of the sisterhood
   lady of the stage
   lady of the streets
   ladybird
lady in waiting[1]
leaping academy *at* leap on
leaping house *at* leap on
less respectable *at* less
life[1] (the)
life of infamy
light skirts *at* light-footed
light the lamp
live by trade
live off *at* live on
live on
live on immoral earnings *at*
    immoral
loose[1]
   loose house
   loose in the hilts
   loose woman
lost[1]
low girls

madam
Magdalene
massage parlour
   masseuse

naughty lady *at* naughty
naughty-house *at* naughty
nautch girl
nice time
night girl
   night job

nightclub hostess
nightingale[3]
nocturne
nun
   nunnery
nymph
   nymph of darkness
   nymph of delight
   nymph of the pavement

oldest profession (the)
on the bash *at* bash (the)
on the cross
on the game
   on the grind
   on the loose
   on the street
   on the stroll
   on the town
one of those
owl

pagan
painted woman
panel[2]
   panel-house
   panel-joint
Paphian
park women
parlor house
party girl
pavement girl
   pavement princess
peddle your arse
personal services *at* personal
    relations
piece of trade *at* piece[1]
place of ill fame
play house
pleasure house *at* pleasure
prima donna
princess
pro
   professional woman
procure
   procurer
   procuress
profession (the)
punk[1]
pushing academy *at* push[1]
pushing shop *at* push[1]

quail
queen[1]
   queen-house
quick time

rag (the)
ramps (the)

rap club
  rap parlour
  rap studio
receiver-general
red lamp
  red light
  red light district
  red light precinct
  red-lighted number
rent boy
  renter
rib joint
riding academy *at* ride

sand rat
sauna
scalding house *at* house[1]
scarlet woman
scrubber
sell yourself
  sell your back
  sell your body
  sell your desires
seraglio
service station *at* service[1]
services *at* service[1]
sex care provider *at* sex[1]
sex worker *at* sex[1]
short time

sister
  sister of charity
  sister of mercy
skivvy
  skivvie-house
sleck-trough *at* slake your lust
slapper
  slapper sweep
snake ranch *at* snake pit
social evil (the)
soiled dove
solicit
sport-trap *at* sport (the)
sports bar *at* sport (the)
sporting-house *at* sport (the)
sporting section *at* sport (the)
stale[1]
  stale meat
stepney
stews (the)
street
  street girl
  street tricking
  streetwalker
succubus

tenderloin district
    at tenderloin
tomboy

totty
trade (the)
tramp
tree rat
trick
trollop
trot
two-by-four

unfortunate

vaulting-school *at* vault[1]
victualler
  victualling-house

walk[1](the streets)
wang-house
warm one *at* warm[1]
warm shop *at* warm[1]
wench
white slave
Winchester goose
    at goose[1]
woman of the town
  woman of the world
work the streets
working girl

zoo

Religion and Prejudice

Gathered into this broad spectrum, along with religion, are what some consider its concomitant, superstition, and various subjects about which people show prejudice, in behaviour as well as language, such as age, charity, race, parsimony, and poverty.

The scholars who produced King James's version of the Bible, and those who have subsequently sought in vain to improve on their translation, have been resourceful in their search for euphemisms when dealing with sexual and lavatorial matters. I have chosen to include only those few examples which a modern churchgoer is likely to hear. I have, however, omitted all the convoluted evasions with which worshippers seek through prayer to placate, or ingratiate themselves with, their God. For these errors I run the risk of being *read out of* the congregation but, even in Scotland, I will not be landed with a *game fee*. I no longer have the option of changing my ecclesiastical allegiance by *lifting my lines*, although, for Irish Roman Catholics, *souper* remains a term of abuse to this day. It is of course unthinkable that men of the cloth should take issue with me, despite their being permitted *creative* conflict between themselves.

It has long been human practice to seek to limit an evil influence by flattery. The Greek name for the Furies was the Kindly Ones, or *Eumenides*, while the Black Sea became the gentle *Euxine*, despite its dire reputation. For our recent ancestors, the malevolent fairies became the *good folk*, *neighbours*, or *people* and the hawthorns on which fairies placed their spells were the *gentle thorns*. I have noted over 30 names for the devil which start with *auld* or *old*, some of which survive in modern speech, such as *old Harry* and *old Nick*. He may not have been so pleased to hear himself described as the *black lad*, *gentleman*, *man*, *prince*, or *spy*, even though he was the *Prince of Darkness*. He might have been mollified when he received *Clootie's croft* or the *given rig*, which was land the farmer left uncultivated for his use. His successors in Brussels call it set-aside.

You had to be equally discreet when talking about witches and wizards, the *cunning men* and the *wise women*. If there were any doubt about their status, it was always possible to check them out. You could *wake a* *witch* through torture or make a warlock *swim for a wizard*, the latter being a particularly effective form of trial because the victim drowned if he was not guilty and confirmed his guilt if he survived. Modern ladies may sleep more soundly in the knowledge that they are never going to be asked to drink out of the *horn of fidelity*.

When seafarers' lives were even more hazardous than they are now, there were several superstitions to be observed, which have survived to this day. Some related to salt beef, which a chandler might replace with rabbit, which soon rotted, or to bad pork. The pig had to be referred to in allusive terms, such as a *grunter*, while the rabbit became a *furry thing* or *stunted hare*. The seaman had to touch a hare before embarkation, although it seems that to touch hair would do at a pinch, so long as it was female, on the head or pubis. Or that was his excuse.

As the German adage reminds us, everyone wants to live long but nobody wishes to grow old. For that reason a *girl* or *boy* may not necessarily be a juvenile and, although we are *not as young as we were*, our *middle age* can extend until we become *senior citizens*. At best we can hope to remain *active* during the *golden years* until we are sent to a *convalescent home* or *somewhere where we can be looked after*, by a stranger rather than our relatives. Despite being *forward at the knees*, we will have achieved an *honurable age* during our stay in *God's waiting room*.

There was a time when, for most people, it was so shameful to be in receipt of charity that both they, and the benefactors who provided for them, cloaked the activity in allusive language. Those who were, in Victorian times, *on the parish*, in later years found themselves *on the dole* or *on the labour*, while the *workhouse* remained a dread institution rather than a normal place of business. The modern *claimant* who is in receipt of *public assistance*, *social security*, or *welfare* may have less inhibitions when receiving an *entitlement* and will be understandably miffed if found to be *out of benefit*. Many accept that society should provide *income support* to all those on a low wage, possibly through a system of *negative tax*. Even those who cherish their financial independence, and would reject a *handout*, are ready to take advantage of any *concessional fares* to which they may be entitled.

Race is for many such a sensitive issue that an attempt at rational discussion or analysis may be excoriated as *racist*, while the failure to examine openly the very real issues leads to injustice and unrest which harm a *minority* as well as the population at large. The methods used by the Nazis as they moved towards their *final solution* spawned much evasive language which I have sought to record in translation. Nor have I omitted euphemisms used by the Israeli state to justify certain actions towards non-Jewish Palestinians. Within living memory Americans and Britons of Caucasian descent considered themselves genetically superior to their *non-white* fellow citizens, either within their community or their Empire, and spoke and acted accordingly. Some of the words or phrases then commonly used are offensive and I have excluded them, and especially the *N-word*. Even now it is necessary to tread carefully when looking at language relating to *community relations* in a *multicultural society* without incurring the wrath of a *community affairs officer* or being prosecuted by the *Race Relations Board*.

Prejudice is not shown only against *persons of colour*, *visible minorities*, or *new Australians*. *Female-Americans* and their counterparts elsewhere may complain that their advancement is blocked by a *glass ceiling* or a *sticky floor* which no amount of *tokenism* can offset. Nor will *women's liberation* be achieved by *obligatory* or *statutory* appointments. Let us hope that the day will come when the *West Briton* is as unknown in Dublin as *NINA* has become in Boston.

None of us likes to be accused of parsimony: *careful*, possibly, but not a *tightwad* who *fumbles for a check* or invites others to a *Dutch treat*. We may from time to time admit that we are *boracic* but it is others whom we describe as *economically disadvantaged*, especially those who live in an *industrializing* or *less developed* country. *Vulnerable* we may be, but not yet to be numbered among the *pavement people*.

advantaged
affirmative action
African
    African-American
    African-descended
afterlife
ageful
aid
Annie Oakley
anti-diversity
apartheid *at* separate
    development
appropriate[2]
article
Aryan
    aryanize
assistance[1]
auld *at* old

B
backhander
backward[2]
bad man
    bad fire
    bad lad
    bad place
banana republic
basket case
BCE
    Before Common Era
benefit
black hole
black lad

black gentleman
black man
black prince
black Sam
black spy
blazes
bleeding heart
blockbuster[1]
blow-in
blue-eyed brother *at* brother
blue hair
    blue rinse
boracic
boy[1]

Cape coloured *at* coloured[1]
card[2]
careful
caring
    carer
carry the banner
    carry the balloon
    carry the stick
case[2]
cash problem *at* problem
cast[2]
casual
cattle[1]
certain age (a)
chair-days
challenged
changeling *at* change[2]
Charlie

charm
    charmer
chi-chi
child of God
Chinese
    Chinese fire-drill (a)
    Chinese parliament
    Chinese whisper
claimant
    Claimants' Union
cloot
    clootie
    clootie's croft
close[1]
colour
    colour-blind
    colour problem
coloured
colourful
committed
community relations
    community affairs officer
    community relations cor-
        respondent
connections
convalescent home
country blood
    country-born
country in transition
creative
    creative conflict
    creative tension
crinkly

crumbly
cult
cultural
  cultural deprivation
cunning man

dark[2]
  dark-complected
  dark-skinned
dark man
dark meat[1]
decadent
demographically correct
depleted
deprived
  deprivation
developing
  Development Areas
dickens
dietary difficulties
differently
  differently advantaged
disadvantaged
discrimination
dispossessed
diversity
  diversity awareness
  diversity content
  diversity training
do-gooder
  do-gooding
dole
  dole-bread
  dole-money
don the turban
drop the boom on
Dutch
Dutch dinner
Dutch treat

economically disadvantaged
  economically abused
  economically exploited
  economically margina-
    lized
emergent
  emerging
entitlement
estuary
ethical investment
ethnic
ethnic cleansing
    at clean[2]
ethnic loading
Eumenides
Euxine at Eumenides
evening of your days
  eventide home
excluded (the)

fail
father of lies
feel a draft
female-Americans
fetch[1]
financial assistance
financially excluded
  financially constrained
first people
first world
flit[2] (do a)
floater
fly a kite[2]
fly-by-night
forward at the knees
foul[2]
  foul ane
  foul may care
  foul skelp ye
  foul thief
French
fumble for a check
furry thing

gentle
  gentle bushes
  gentle thorns
  gentle place
  gentle people
gentleman
  gentleman of the road
  gentleman of color
gentry
get along
get on
get the shorts
girl[2]
giro day
given rig
go Dutch at Dutch treat
go over
God's waiting room
golden ager
golden years (the)
good folk
  good neighbours
  good people
greying
Grundyism at Mrs Grundy
grunter
guest[1]
gypsy's warning (a)

handout[1]
hard up
Harry
hearts (of oak)
high-fly (the)
high-yellow at yellow[2]

home
homelands
honourable age (of)
horn of fidelity
horny
hot place (the)
house[3]
  house of industry
human rights

ill-wished
immigrant
in trade at in the trade
in years
inclusive language
income support
indigenous
industrializing country
inner city
Inquiry and Control Section
inquisition
integrated casting
involved
  involvement
Irish
irregular
itinerant

Jim Crow

kid

left-footer
less developed at less
libber at women's liberation
lift the books
  lift your lines
little people
  little folk
living Harry at Harry
long in the tooth
long day at long home (your)
longer-living
look in a cup
lord Harry at Harry
Lord of the Flies

mainstreaming
make old bones
marginalized
mark[1]
mature
maturer
men in sandals
middle age
minority
  minority issues
mixed heritage
mom-and-pop

Monday morning
    quarterback
moth in your wallet
Mrs Grundy
multicultural
    multiculturalism
mutton dressed as lamb

N-word
narrow
    narrowness
national assistance
native
Native American
near[1]
negative (income) tax
negatively privileged
new age
    new age travellers
new Australian
New Commonwealth
Nick[1]
    Nicker
    Nickie
NINA
no (spring) chicken
no pot to piss in
non-Aryan
non-industrial
non-traditional (casting)
non-white
North Britain
    North Briton
not as young as I was
number one[2]
nursing home

obligatory
of mature years
old
    old bendy
    old blazes
    old bogey
    old boots
    old boy
    old chap
    old child
    old cloot
    old clootie
    old dad
    old Davy
    old driver
    old gentleman
    old gooseberry
    old hornie
    old lad
    old mahoon
    old man
    old Nick

old one
old poger
old poker
old Roger
old ruffin
old Sandy
old scratch
old serpent
old smoker
old sooty
old thief
old toast
old Harry *at* Harry
older woman (the)
on assistance *at* assistance[1]
on the dole *at* dole
on the parish
on the ribs
    on your bones
one of us
open housing
other side of the tracks
over-privileged
oversee
    overlook
    overshadow

PC *at* politically correct
panhandle
    panhandler
pavement people
peculiar institution (the)
people of/with
    people of color
permissive
person of/with
    person of colour
person of the coloured
    persuasion *at* coloured[1]
pigment
pigmentation problem
    at problem
pill[3]
play a card
playboy
plotcock
politically correct
    political correctness
pop[3]
preliterate
Prince of Darkness
privileged
pro bono
progressive
public assistance

race defilement
race card at play a card
race-norming

race relations
    race relations officer
racial
    racial purity
    racial science
    racial war
racism
    racialism
rational
re-emigration
read out of
relief[1]
remittance man
reservation
resettlement
residential home *at* home
rest home
retirement home *at* home
reverse discrimination
right-on
rootless

scheduled classes
scratch[1]
seen better days
segregation
senior citizen
    seniors
senior moment (a)
separate but equal
separate development
servant
sexual discrimination card
    at play a card
shame
sharp elbows
sheltered
shorts (the)
smoker (the)
snow-capping
social
social agenda
social cohesion
social dimension *at* social
    agenda
social fairness
social housing
social inclusion
social justice
social landlord *at* social
    housing
social rented home
social security
social services
social worker
socially excluded
somewhere where he (or she)
    can be looked after
souper

south[1] (the)
special area
sponging-house
 at sponge
stain[2] (the)
step on
stroller
stunted hare
sunset years
supportive
swim for a wizard
sympathetic ear

take the soup
take the wall
tarbrush (the)
thief (of the world)
thing
third age (the)
third world
three-point play
tied aid *at* aid
tight[2]
tincture[1]
tinker
to the knuckle
Tom[2]

toot
touch[2]
trains potter
traveller
 travelling community
 travelling people
triangular trade (the)
trouser test
Turkish ally
turn[4]
twilight home

un-American
uncle[1]
Uncle Tom
underdeveloped
underground railroad
underprivileged
union[2]
up along
up the creek

visible
 visible community
 visible minority ethnic
  groups
vulnerable

wake a witch
weaker half (the)
wear down *at*
 wear away
wee folk
 wee people
welfare
west Briton
 west British
wet-back
white flight
white top
wise woman
 wise man
women's liberation
 women's lib
 women's libber
women's movement
women's rights
workhouse
wrinkly

yellow[2]
young
younger brother

Sex

Some sexual matters have been referred to in the note preceding **Childbirth**. In this area of human activity, infested with prudery, evasion, and deceit in both word and deed, we now have to consider euphemisms associated with copulation, courtship, masturbation, and sexual variations such as homosexuality.

One of the words most often heard in coarse speech is 'fuck', used as a redundant expletive adjective or as in the expression 'Fuck me', an injunction seldom to be taken literally. It is an ugly word and one I have chosen not to give as a definition because its constant repetition would jar on me as much as on the reader. And constant repetition would be required, because I have recorded over a thousand evasive phrases alluding to *copulation*, from the demure, such as the *act of generation*, to the ribald and coarse. Some have entered standard English. To say, for example, that one adult is *sleeping with* another implies wakeful activity rather than slumber, nor need it be taking place in a bedroom. Other common phrases have changed their meaning, so that *make love* no longer means to flirt with or court. A glance through the relatively few entries under the letter T gives us a cross-section of what we come up against.

When Shakespeare uses *take* in *Richard III*, he relies on the common male imagery of *possessing*. To *take a bit from* a female implies a single act of extramarital copulation. To *take a turn in the stubble* alludes to the female pubic hair and either premature, or withdrawal before, ejaculation. The female might *take a turn on her back*, from the position adopted, unless she were *tired*. A man could also take several geographically punning *turns, in Cupid's Corner, Love Lane, Mount Pleasant*, and so on. He might *take advantage of* the woman with whom he *took pleasure*, which would involve *taking her dear* or *good name away*. If she were *taken to bed* and he *took his trousers off*, it was not for repose. The common violent imagery in *throw, throw down, throw a leg over, thump*, or *tip*. The Shakespearean *top* is obsolete but the *torch of Hymen* still burns in the presence of the *two-backed beast*. A *toss in the hay* suggests that the female may have take a *tumble* with someone

truant to his bed and *'twixt her sheets*. To *touch*, or for Shakespeare, *touch forbiddenly*, is what the male does. Only birds *tread* but *tupping* may be a human as well as an ovine activity.

Readers of the great Victorian novels learn of courtship rituals as remote to modern practice as are the rites performed by the druids to evensong in a parish church. We are reminded of the limited opportunities for gainful employment which convention allowed single women, who preferred marriage to being an *old maid* after being *left on the shelf* or, in Scotland, *without a head*. Even if she were allowed a *follower* who would *walk out with her*, a girl was more likely to suffer from the *green sickness* than wear a *green gown*. It was preferable perhaps to *hang on the bough* rather than *hang in the bell-ropes*, until such time as she might decide to *hang out the broomstick*. Single young women from richer homes might have the opportunity of joining the *fishing fleet*, although even they faced the humiliation of being *returned empty*.

In modern use, to inquire if a person is *seeing* anyone has nothing to do with vision. A man may *like the ladies* but girls *go on the pull* and both parties may enjoy *fun and games*. In this context *bit* and *piece* are synonyms and a run through phrases starting with *bit* reveals linguistic nuances. A *bit* is a young woman viewed sexually by a male. She may be particularized as a *bit of crumpet, fluff, goods, muslin, skirt*, or *stuff*. A *bit of all right* may suggest all round social graces as well as sexual attraction. A *bit of arse* or *ass* is a sexually attractive male or female. A *bit of hot stuff* or *bit of jam* is, in male eyes, a promiscuous female. A *bit of how's your father* or *bit of you know what* is copulation, usually extramaritally. A *bit of meat* may describe a promiscuous but not particularly attractive female. A *bit on the side* is a mistress.

Within living memory marriage was accepted as the natural state of those who wished to *cohabit* and raise a family. There were no words for third parties with whom a man or woman regularly copulated extramaritally, and, to rectify the omission, *lover* and *mistress* became standard English. Any euphemisms related principally to unions which took place unconventionally, such as the *hop-pole marriage* or *broomstick match*, although reference might be made to an *open marriage* or a *free relationship*. Evasion was also useful when you wanted to suggest that a man had *hung up his hat* and we can but admire the resource of Mrs Van Butchell's widower who continued to enjoy her wealth so long as she *remained above ground*. These days we no longer look askance at *cuckolding the parson* and take it for granted that he who seeks a *trophy wife* may first go *forum shopping*.

The *secret vice* or *solitary sin* involving *auto-erotic practices* and *self-abuse* persists despite Shakespeare's condemnation of those who *traffic with themselves*. *Lone love* may be something whereby males rather than females *fool with themselves* and a woman who *touches* or *caresses herself* or *thrills* to a vibrator has a more restricted vocabulary than a man who may obtain *easement* from the *five-fingered widow* as he *pumps his pickle*. It may however be inaccurate as well as offensive to describe another as a *jerk* or a *tosser* without knowing whether he actually *bashes the bishop*.

Sexual variation is an area in which judgement and opinion vary widely. There are those, usually among the young, whose *permissive* beliefs permit no censure of others whose sexual practices differ from heterosexual exchanges between a man and a woman. There are others who, through religious conviction or confidence in the social benefits engendered by the institution of marriage, deplore homosexuality and other sexual variations, and condemn those who are *same gender oriented* or commit *crimes against nature*. Female homosexuality has long been referred to by reference to the poetess Sappho and her island home, so that *Sapphic* and *Lesbian* have become standard English. We can run through the letter P to note words and phrases which owe less to the Ancients.

A *pansy*, *pooftah*, *pouff*, or *punk* is a male homosexual. He may be described as *peculiar* because of his *predilection*, *preference*, or *proclivity*. He can *peddle his arse* or *ass*, or *plug* another male, although a *plater* is more likely to be a prostitute. He may have *personal relations* with a *petit ami* with whom he *plays the pink oboe*, or be involved in a *posterior assault*, although unlikely to be *pogey bait*. Females rather than males tend to become involved in *pashes* but only males haunt a *pink district* where they can spend the *pink pound*. *Peeping Toms* are almost always men.

The use of euphemism is not always harmless. The referee who told the British Admiralty that Vassall *took very little interest in the opposite sex* bore part of the blame for the ensuing spy scandal when he had been entrapped and blackmailed by the KGB.

We like to attribute our failings to others, and especially to foreigners. The *Aussie kiss* is performed *down below*. To *French* is to indulge in oral sex, or the *French vice*. For the British the *English vice*, flagellation, differs from what Americans may describe as *English arts*, *discipline*, *guidance*, or *treatment* and few Englishmen admit to suffering from the *English disease*. The *Greek way* persists, as does *Roman culture* or the *Roman way*, but an *Irish wedding* is different altogether.

beastliness
beat the gun
beat the mattress *at* mattress
beat your meat
  beat off
  beat on
  beat your dummy
beau
bed²
  bed and breakfast
  bed-hopping
  bed with
  beddable
  bedfellow
  bedroom eyes
  bedtime business
  bedwork
  bedworthy
beefcake
belt
bent²
bestiality
bestow your enthusiasm on
betray
between the thighs *at*
    between the legs
between the sheets
big prize (the)
bimbo
bird¹
  bird circuit
bisexual
  bi
bit¹
  bit of all right
  bit of arse
  bit of ass
  bit of crumpet
  bit of fluff
  bit of goods
  bit of hot stuff
  bit of how's your father
  bit of jam
  bit of meat
  bit of muslin
  bit of skirt
  bit of you-know-what
  bit on the side
bit² (a)
  bit of the other
bit of crackling
    at crackling
bit of leg-over *at* get
bit of spare *at* spare
bit of tail *at* tail¹
bit on the side *at* on the side
bitch
blind date *at* date
blow¹

blow job
board
  board a train
boff¹
bolt
  bolter
bondage
bonk
boom-boom²
boondock
both-way
bother
bounce¹
  bouncy-bouncy
bout
boyfriend
break a commandment
break the pale
Brighton pier
broad
broken home
broomstick match *at* jump
    the broomstick
brother starling *at* brother
brown
  brown-hatter
brown shower *at* shower¹
buff (the)
bull¹
  bull-dyke
bum-bandit *at* bum
bum-boy *at* bum
bum-fighting *at* bum
bump³
  bump bones
bundle with
bung up and bilge free
bunny¹
bush marriage
  bush patrol
butch
by(e)-courting *at* by(e)
by(e)-shot *at* by(e)

California widow
call down
camp
camp down with
canned goods
canoe
capon
caress yourself
carnal
  carnal act
  carnal appetite
  carnal knowledge
  carnal necessities
  carnal relations
carry a torch for

carry on with
carry out a sex act
casting couch (the)
cat about *at* cat
catch
cattle²
chambering
change your luck
chap
charity girl
charms
chase
  chase around
  chase hump
  chase skirt
  chase tail
chat up
chavver
cheat
cheat the starter
cheesecake
chère amie
cherry-picker *at* cherry
chicken¹
  chickenhawk
child of Uranus *at* Uranian
chichevache *at* prey to (a)
choke your chicken
cissy
click with *at* click²
clicket
climb (into)
  climb aboard
  climb in with
  climb into bed with
climb the ladder on her back
    at climb the ladder
close
  close companion
  close friend
  close relationship
close the bedroom door
closet²
cock
  cock a led across
  cock a leg athwart
  cock a leg over
  cocksman
cohabit
coition
cold²
come across²
come hither
  come-hither look
  come-hither register
come-on²
come out
  come out of the closet
come to

come to see
come together
come your mutton
comfort[1]
commerce
commit indecency *at*
   indecency
commit misconduct
  commit infamy
  commit the seventh
community of wives
companion
company[1]
compound with
compromise
  compromising position
  compromising situation
concede to
confirmed bachelor
congress
conjugal rights
connect[1]
  connection
connubial pleasures
conquer a bed
consenting adults
console
  consolation
consort with
constant companion *at*
  companion
consummate (a relationship)
  consummate your desires
contact with
  contact sex
continent
conversation
cookie
cop[3]
  cop a cherry
  cop a feel
copulate
  copulation
corn[2]
corridor creeping
corrupt
cottaging
couple
  couple with
cover
crack a Jane
  crack a doll
  crack a Judy
  crack a pipkin
  crack a pitcher
crackling
cradle-snatcher
  cradle robber
cream for

creamer
creep around *at* creep-joint
crime against nature (a)
criminal assault
  criminally used
criminal connection
criminal conversation
  crim con
cross
cross-dress
  cross-dresser
cruise[1]
crumpet
crush
cuckoo[1]
  cuckold the parson
cupcake
cut the mustard
  cut it

daddy *at* sugar daddy
daisy chain
  daisy-chaining
dally
  dalliance
damaged[2]
  damaged goods
dance at
  dance barefoot
  dance in the half-peck
dangerous to women
dark meat[2]
dark moon
date
dead to honour *at* dead to
dead to propriety *at* dead to
dear friend
dear John
debauch
deceive
deed (the)
defend your virtue
defile
  defile a bed
  defile yourself
  defiler
deflower
  defloration
degenerate
degraded *at* degrade
deny yourself to
  deny a bed
designs on (have)
desire
despoil
  despoiler
destruction
dick[1]
  dick around

Dick's hatband
diddle[2]
dip your wick
dirty
  dirty deed
  dirty joke
  dirty old man
  dirty weekend
disciple of Oscar Wilde *at*
  disciple of
discipline
disgrace
dish
dishonoured
display your charms *at*
  charms
disport amorously
dissolution[2]
distracted by
divergence
do[1]
  do it
  do it with yourself
  do something to yourself
  do yourself
do a favour to *at* favour
do the business
do what comes naturally
do wrong
dock
dodgy deacon *at* dodgy
doll[1]
dolly
dominance
Don Juan
  donjuanism
double-gaited
double-header
  double in stud
double time
doubtful sexuality
down on
drag
dress to/on the left
droit de seigneur
drop beads
drop your drawers
  drop your pants
dry bob
  dry run
duality
duff

early treatment room
earnest
easement
East African activities
easy woman
  easy affections

eat flesh
  eat
  eat out
  eat a pussy
écouteur
effeminate
elevator eyes
embraces
emotionally close to
employ
en flagrant délit *at* in
    flagrante delicto
English
  English arts
  English discipline
  English guidance
  English treatment
English disease (the)[1]
English vice
enjoy
  enjoy favours
  enjoy her person
  enjoy hospitality
  enjoy yourself
  enjoyed
entanglement
entertain[1]
err
  errant
eternal triangle
    at triangular
Eve
  Eve-teasing
excitement (the)
exercise
exercise your marital rights
    at marital rights
experienced[1]
extra-curricular
extramarital excursion
extramural
eye-candy

fag
faggot
fairy
faithful
fall[1]
fallen woman
false
familiar
  familiarity of marriage
fancy
  fancy man
  fancy woman
fast
fate worse than death
favour
  favours

feather-bed soldier *at* feather-
      bed
feather your nest
feed from home
feel
  feel up
fell design
female oriented
  female identified
femme fatale
fidelity
filly
finger[2]
  finger yourself
fish[1]
  fishwife
fishing fleet
fishy
five-fingered widow (the)
flamboyant
flesh your will *at* flesh
flexible[2]
fling
flirty fishing
flit[3]
flog off
  flog your beef
  flog your donkey
  flog your dummy
  flog your mutton
flop
flower[2]
fluff your duff
fluter *at* flute
flutter
fly[3]
follower
  follow
fond of
  fond of the women
fondle
fool (about with/around with)
  fool about with yourself
force yourself on
  force favours from
fork
forum shopping
foul desire
  foul way with
foxy
frail
  frailty
frame[2]
frank[1]
free love
free relationship
free samples
freelance
freeze[2]

French[1]
French kiss
French vice (the)
fresh[2]
friend[2]
frig
frippet
frottage
fruit
fudge-packer *at* fudge
full treatment (the)
fumble
fun
  fun and games
  fun-loving
funny[2]

gallant
  gallantry
gallop
game-fee *at* game[2]
gander-mooner
gang-bang *at* bang
gash
gay
gender-bending *at* gender
gentleman friend
get
  get a leg over
  get busy with
  get in/into her bloomers
  get in/into her girdle
  get in/into her knickers
  get in/into her pants
  get into bed with
  get it
  get it in
  get it off with
  get it on
  get it together
  get it up
  get laid
  get lucky
  get round
  get there
  get through
  get your end away
  get your end in
  get your greens
  get your hook into
  get your muttons
  get your rocks off
  get your share
  get your way with
  get your will(s) of
get a hand up a skirt *at* hand
    trouble
get in the saddle *at* saddle up
    with

get off[2]
  get off our hands
get your corner in *at* corner[3]
gift of your body (the)
ginger
  ginger beer
girler *at* girl[1]
girlfriend
give
  give a little
  give access to your body
  give head
  give her one
  give it to
  give the ferret a run
  give time to
  give (up) your treasure
  give way
  give your all
  give your body
  give yourself
give green stockings *at*
    green gown
give the eye
go all the way
  go any further
go at yourself
go beyond friendship
go down on *at* down on
go into
go out with
go steady (with)
go the whole way
  go through
go to bed with
go to it
go with
goat
goer
gold-digger
  goal-digger
golden shower *at* showers[1]
good friend(s)
good time
graft
grass widow
gratify your passions
  gratify your amorous de-
    sires
  gratify your (amorous) will
  gratify your (amorous)
    works
  gratification
Greek way (the)
green gown
  green sickness
grind (a)
groom
  groomer

grope
  groper
gross indecency
group sex
  groupie

hammer[2]
  hammer away
hand[2]
  hand-fasting
hand job
hand trouble
handle[1]
hang in the bell-ropes
hang on the bough
hang out with
hang up your hat[1]
hanky-panky
haul your ashes
have
  have a bit
  have a man/woman
  have at
  have intercourse (with)
  have it
  have it off
  have (sexual) relations
    (with)
  have (something) to do
    with
  have your (wicked) way
    with
  have your (wicked) will of
have the hots *at* hot[1]
have two left legs *at* left-
    footer
head job (a)
headache[2]
heart's desire
heavy
  heavy breathing
  heavy date
  heavy involvement
  heavy necking
hen
  hen brass
  hen-drinking
  hen silver
history
hit-and-run
hit on
hit the sack with
  hit the hay
hochle
hoist her skirt *at* hoist
hole
honest
honour
hop into bed

hop-pole marriage
horizontal
  horizontal aerobics
  horizontal collaboration
  horizontal conquest
  horizontal life
  horizontal jogging
horn
  horny
hot[1]
  hot backs
  hot for
  hot pants
  hot-pillow
  shot-sheet
  hot-tailing
  hot stuff
hourly hotel
housemate
how's your father
human relations
hump
hunt

ice queen
idiosyncrasy
illicit
  illicit embraces
  illicit commerce
  illicit connection
  illicit intercourse
improper
  improper connection
  improper suggestion
in drag *at* drag
in flagrante (delicto)
in full fling
in full venery *at* in flagrante
  (delicto)
in my knickers
  in my pants
in name only
in relation with
in the box
in the closet *at* closet
in the hay
  in the sack
  in the saddle
in the heat *at* on heat[2]
inamorata
inconstancy
incontinent[1]
indecency
  indecent assault
  indecent exposure
  indecent offence
indiscretions *at* indiscretion
initiation
  initiation into womanhood

insatiable
inseparable
insult
   insult worse than death
intentions
intercourse
interfere with
intimacy
   intimate
intimate association *at*
     associate with
intrigue
introduce yourself to a bed
invert
   inverted
   inversion
involved with
iron[2]
irregular
   irregular conduct
   irregular situation
   irregularities
irregular intercourse *at*
     intercourse
it
Italian vice (the)
itch
   itchy feet
item

jab
jack of both sides
jail bait
jam *at* jam rag
jasper
jazz bunny *at* bunny
jerk off
jig-a-jig
   jig
   jig-jig
   jiggy-jig
jiggle
job jocker *at* jock
john[2]
   John and Joan
join[1]
joy[1]
   joy-ride
juiced up
jump[2]
jump the broomstick

keep
   kept mistress
   kept wench
keep
   kept woman
   keeping
keep company with

keep your legs crossed
   keep her legs together
keep his pants on
   keep his pants zipped
kind
King Lear
kinky
kiss
kiss-and-tell
   kiss money
knee-trembler
knees up
knight
knock
   knock off
knot

lad
ladies' man
lady of intrigue *at* lady
lady of pleasure *at* lady
ladybird *at* lady
lady friend
lady-killer
lance
lass
last favour (the)
lavender
lay[1]
   lay down
lay[2]
lay a leg on
   lay a leg across
   lay a leg over
leap on
   leap into bed
leap the broomstick
learn on the pillow
leather
   leather bar
   leather queen
leave
   leave alone
left-footer
   left-handed
left-handed wife
leg-over
lesbian
   lesbianism
   lesbic
   lezzer
   lizzie
liaison
lie with
   lie on
   lie together
lifestyle
lift a leg[1]
light

light-footed
   light-heeled
   light-housekeeping
light on his toes
like that
lily
limp-wrist
   limp-wristed
line[1]
linked with
little woman
live as man and wife
   live in mortal sin
   live in sin
   live tally
   live together
   live with
live-in girlfriend
lone love
long-term relationship
   long-term friend
loose[1]
lose your (good) character
   lose her good name
   lose her innocence
   lose her reputation
lose your cherry
   lose your snood
Lothario
love
   love affair
   love nest
   love that durst not
     speak its name
   lovemaking
love-in *at* sit-in
lover

main thing (the)
make[1]
   make it with
make a play for
make a (an improper)
   suggestion
make babies together
make happy
make little of
make love to
   make love to yourself
make out with
make sheep's eyes at
make the beast with two
   backs *at* beast
make the (bed) springs creak
make the chick scene
make time with
make up to
make way with
make whoopee

make yourself available
male
   male identified
   male oriented
man[1]
man about town
man friend *at* man[1]
man of pleasure
management privileges
marital aid
marital rights
marriage joys
   marriage act
Mary Fivefingers
massage *at* massage
    parlour
mate
   mating
mattress
   mattress drill
maul
meat[1]
meat rack
meddle with
ménage à trois
mess[1]
   mess about
   mess about with
   mess with yourself
migraine
minor wife
misbehave
misconduct
miss[1]
Miss Nancy *at* nancy
missionary position (the)
mistress
misuse
molest
monkey business
more than a (good) friend
   more than just friends
mother[1]
mount
   mounting drill
mount a corporal and four
mouse
move in on
   move in with
muff-diver *at* muff
musical
mutton
   mutton-monger

nail
nameless crime (the)
nancy
   nancy boy
national indoor game (the)

natural vigours *at* natural
    functions (the)
naughty
neck
nelly
new cookie *at* cookie
nibble[1]
niece[2]
night games
night physic *at* night loss
nightwork
no better than she should be
   no better than she ought
    to be
noble game *at* game[2] (the)
nocturnal exercise *at*
    nocturnal emission
nonsense
nose open
not all she should be
   not all she ought to be
not inconsolable
not interested in the opposite
    sex
not seeing anybody

oats
oblique
occupation wife *at* occupied
odd
offer yourself
old Adam
old maid
on[4]
on heat[2]
on the couch
on the job
on the make
on the pull *at* pull[2]
on the shelf
on the side
on your back
onanism
one-night stand
   one-nighter
one of those
one thing
open legged
open marriage
   open relationship
oral sex
   oral service
orientation
Oscar
other (the)
   other thing
   other woman
other way (the)
out[1]

out[2]
   outing
outrage
over-familiar
over-gallant *at* gallant
over the broomstick
overfriendly

pansy
parallel parking
paramour
partner
pash
pass[2]
patron
paw
peculiar
peel a banana
Peeping Tom
penetrate[1]
   penetration
personal relations
pet[1]
pet[2]
petite amie
petticoat
   petticoat government
petting-stone
physical involvement
pick up
   pick-up joint
piece[1]
   piece of arse
   piece of ass
   piece of buttered bun
   piece of crackling
   piece of crumpet
   piece of gash
   piece of goods
   piece of muslin
   piece on a fork
   piece of rump
   piece of spare
   piece of trade
   piece of work
   piece on the side
piece of skirt *at* skirt
piece of tail *at* tail[1]
pillow partner
pin-up
pink
   pink district
   pink pound
play[1]
   play about
   play around
   play at hot cockles
   play away (from home)
   play-fellow

play games play hookie
play in the hay
play mothers and fathers
play on your back
play Onan
play the beast with two backs
play the field
play the goat
play the organ
play the pink oboe
play tricks
play with
pleasure
  pleasure yourself on
  pleasuring
plough[1]
pluck a rose
  pluck
plug[2]
plumb
  plumber
pocket job (a)
pogey bait *at* poke[2]
poke[2]
pollute
  pollute yourself
poontang
pop[2]
popsy
possess
posterior assault *at* posterior(s)
pouff
  pooftah
predilection (a)
preference (a)
press your attentions on
  press conjugal rights on
prey to the bicorn *at* prey to (a)
probe
promised
proper
proposition
pull[2]
pull the pud(ding)
  pull your rod
  pull yourself off
pump up
pump your shaft
  pump your pickle
punk[1]
push[1]
pussy
  pussy hound
  pussy-whipped
put
  put it about
  pit it in
  put it up
  put out

put a move on
put to
put yourself about

queen[2]
queer[3]

quickie *at* quick time

raisin
ram
randy
rattle[1]
raunchy
ravish
ream
recreational sex
refuse nothing
relationship
release[3]
relief[3]
répos de guerrier
retread
returned empty
rich friend
ride
  ride St George
  riding master
rip off a piece of arse *at* rip off
rip off a piece of ass *at* rip off
rivet
roast
rob the cradle
roger
roll[1]
  roll in the hay
  roll over
Roman
  Roman culture
  Roman way
Roman spring (a)
romance
  romantic affair
  romantic attachment
  romantic indiscretion
  romantic relationship
  romantically linked
root
  root about
  root rat
rough trade
roundheels
roving eye
  rover
rub off
  rub the bacon
  rub the pork
  rub up
  rub yourself
ruin

  ruined in character
rum-johnny
run around with
run away
  run off

sacrifice your honour
saddle up with
St Colman's girdle has lost its
  virtue
same gender oriented
Sappho
  Sapphic
Sarah
save it *at* save
scarlet fever *at* scarlet
  woman
score[1]
screw[1]
  screw around
season (the)
seat cover *at* seat
seduce
see[1]
self-abuse[1]
  self-gratification
  self-indulgence
  self-love
  self-manipulation
  self-pleasuring
  self-pollution
separate[2]
serve
  serve your lust
service[1]
set up[1]
settled
seven-year itch
sex[1]
  sex love
sexual ambiguity
sexual act *at* act (the)
sexual intercourse
  sexual commerce
  sexual congress
  sexual conjunction
  sexual knowledge
  sexual liaison
  sexual relations
  sexual relief
sexual preference
  sexual irregularity
  sexual orientation
  sexual proclivity
  sexual tropism
  sexual variety
shack up (with)
shaft[1]
shag[1]

shag[2]
shame
share someone's affections
   share someone's bed
sheep's eyes (make)
sheets
shirtlifter
   shirtlifting
shoot over the stubble *at* take
   a turn in the stubble
shoot the agate
show your charms *at* charms
showers[1]
ski bunny *at* bunny[1]
side orders
significant other
sin
sinful commerce *at*
   commerce
singles
   singles bar
   singles joint
   singles night
sissy
sixty-nine *at* soixante-neuf
skin off all dead horses
skippy
skirt
slag
slake your lust
slap and tickle
sleep around
sleep over
sleep together
sleep with
   sleeping dictionary
   sleeping partner
   sleepy time girl
sluice[1]
Smithfield bargain
snatch[1]
so
soil your reputation *at* soiled
   dove
soixante-neuf
   six-à-neuf
solace
solitary sex
   solitary sin
   solitary vice
spare
speak to
   speak for
   speak till
special friend
spend the night with
spoken for
spoon
sport (the)

sport for Jove
sports bar
sprain your ankle
spread for
   spread your legs
spur of the moment passion
stab
stain[1]
stand by
steady company
steal privately to
steg *at* steg month
step out on
   step out with
   step out together
stir the porridge *at* stir
stoat
Stoke-on-Trent
stoop your body to pollution
straddle
stray
   stray from the hearth
   stray your affection
stroke off
strop your beak
stuck on
stud
   stud farm
stuff[2]
subdue to your will
submit to
   submit to pleasure
   submit to will
succumb[2]
suck off
sugar daddy
sure thing
surf bunny *at* bunny[1]
surrender to
sweet man
   sweet boy
   sweet woman
swing[2]
   swing both ways
   swing together
swish
switch-hitter
sword-swallower
   at sword
swordsman *at* sword

tail[1]
take[2]
   take a bit from
   take a liberty with
   take advantage of
   take pleasure with
take a turn in the stubble
   take a turn in Cupid's Corner

take a turn in Love Lane
take a turn in Mount
   Pleasant
take a turn on her back
take a walk
take little interest in the
   opposite sex
take out[1]
take someone's (good or
   dear) name away
take to bed
take up with
take your trousers off
talent
   talent-spotting
tanquem sororem
tart
tearoom
   teahouse
tenderloin
that side of marriage
that way[1]
thing about *at* thing
thing going *at* thing
three-letter man[2]
throw down
thump
tickle
tip[1]
tired[1]
together
tomcatting
top[1]
torch of Hymen (the)
toss in the hay
toss off
   tosser
touch[1]
   touch up
   touch yourself
touch up[1]
town bike
toy boy
triangular
trim (your wick)
triple
troll
trophy
   trophy model
   trophy wife
trouble
   trouble with his flies
truant with your bed
true
tube
tumble[1]
turn off[2]
turn on
turn to

twixt the sheets *at* between
    the sheets
two-backed beast
two-backed game *at* beast
two-on-one
two-time

Uganda
ultimate (the)
    ultimate connection
unbiblical sex
uncertain sexual preferences
uncontaminated
uncover nakedness
undo
unfaithful
unhealthy
union[1]
unlawfulness *at* unlawful
unmarried
unmentionable crime (the)
unnatural
    unnatural crime
    unnatural practice
    unnatural vice
unprotected sex
    unsafe sex
untrue
up[1]
up for it
Uranian
    Uranist
use 1

vault[1]
Venus
    venerous act
vigorous
violate
virtue

virtuous
voyeur
Vulcan's badge

walk out with
    walk along with
    walk with
wallflower
wander
wandering eye
wank
    wank off
want[2]
warm[1]
warm a bed
warm up old porridge
weakness
    weakness for boys
    weakness for men
    weakness for women
wear Dick's hatband *at* dick
wear green garters
wear the breeches
    wear the breech
    wear the pants
    wear the trousers
wear your heart upon your
    sleeve
wet[3]
    wet hen
    wet deck
    wet for
    wet your drawers
    wet your knickers
    wet your pants
    wet yourself
wet dream
wet your wick *at* wick
whack off
wham

wham, bang, and thank
    you ma'am
white marriage
whore-hopping *at* hop into bed
wicked way (your)
    wicked design
    wicked purposes
will
willie-puller *at* willy
win[2]
without a head
without domestic bliss
woman
    womanizer
woman friend
woman of intrigue
woman in a gilded cage
woman named
woman's thing (the)
work on[2]
working dictionary
worry
wrack
    wrack of maidenhead
wreak your passion on
wrist job (a)
wrong[1]
wrong[2]

yield
    yield her body
    yield her person
    yield her virginity
    yield to ardour
    yield to desire
    yield to solicitation
young lady
    young woman

zipper

A

AC/DC indulging in both heterosexual and homosexual practices
The reference is to the incompatible direct and alternating current in electricity supply. Also spelt phonetically as *acey-deecy*:
> Young attractive housewife, AC/DC, would like to meet married AC/DC people to join well-endowed husband for threesomes or moresomes. (*Daily Telegraph*, May 1980)
> So, he was acey-deecy...Lots of old altar boys play hide-the-weenie when they shouldn't. (Sohmer, 1988)

à outrance involving extramarital copulation
Literally, to the utmost:
> I think if anyone read *carefully* they would say it was an affair *à outrance*. (Fiennes, 2003)

abandon yourself (to) (of a woman) to copulate promiscuously (with)
Literally, to hand yourself into the custody of:
> ...the very few women [in occupied France] who abandoned themselves to the Germans would uniformly have preferred to give pleasure to a French man.
> (Macintyre, 2001—the 'very few' must have been prolific breeders to have given birth to 50,000 babies between them)
In obsolete use, an *abandoned* woman was a prostitute and the punning *abandoned habits* were the flashy clothes she wore when riding in London's Hyde Park.

abbess see NUN

abdominal protector a shield for the male genitalia
The *abdomen* is the lower cavity of the trunk, which the shield, commonly called a box, does not cover. If you hear a commentator suggest a player writhing in agony on the ground has been hit 'in the lower abdomen', it means he has had a disabling blow in his genitalia. See also WINDED.

aberration a sexual act or preference which is not heterosexual
Literally, a deviation from the norm.

ableism *American* insensitivity towards lame or injured people
The expression may be used by those who, having decided that the word *disabled* is discriminatory, describe the fit as *temporarily abled* and the lame as *differently abled*.

ablutions lavatories
Originally, the rite of cleaning, from which washing and then the place where you wash. Mainly army usage.

abnormal *obsolete* homosexual
In the days when heterosexuality was the only accepted norm.
Whence *abnormality*, homosexuality.

above ground see REMAIN ABOVE GROUND

above your ceiling promoted to a level beyond your abilities
Not merely rummaging about in the attic:
> L. M. is a very nice chap...but he is definitely above his ceiling. (Horne, 1994—Montgomery was speaking of Leigh-Mallory, the senior allied airman during the 1944 invasion of Europe)

absent parent a parent who does not live with his or her infant child or children
Usually, the father, who is not just away on a business trip.
See also LONE PARENT and SINGLE PARENT.

absorption a military conquest
Literally, the chemical or physical process of assimilation:
> These measures, together with the 'absorption' of the Baltic states in the north, advanced the western frontiers of the Soviet Union by hundreds of miles. (A. Clark, 1995, writing about the Russian seizure of eastern Poland in 1939)

abuse the use of a person or object for a taboo or illegal purpose
Literally, any kind of maltreatment or abuse. It may refer to illegal ingestion of drugs or excessive drinking of alcohol, or to taboo sexual activity, especially by adults towards children. To *abuse a bed* was to make its usual occupant a cuckold and to *abuse yourself*, to masturbate, of either sex.

academically subnormal see SUBNORMAL

academy *obsolete* a brothel
Literally, a school, from the original garden where Plato taught.
Continuing the joke, if such it was, the prostitutes were termed *academicians*.

accident[1] involuntary urination or defecation
Literally, anything which happens, whence, in common use, anything undesirable:
> I've never punished him, the way our mothers and nurses did, when he has an 'accident'. (M. McCarthy, 1963)

accident² an unplanned pregnancy
To treat impregnation as though it were an unforeseeable happening may seem unduly innocent or cavalier.
A child born under these circumstances may also be called an *accident*.

accommodate yourself to urinate
At some distance from the Latin root, meaning 'to make fit or suitable'.
The obsolete *accommodation house* was not a lavatory but a brothel.

accommodation with appeasement of
Not making a fair agreement but involving craven or unworthy conduct:
By 1970 the long process of concealed 'accommodation' with trade unions... the insidious creep of inflationary pressure and certain chronic industrial weaknesses were omnipresent. (A. Clark, 1998)

accost to approach a stranger with a taboo request or suggestion
Originally, it meant to lie alongside, which presumably is what the prostitute who *accosts* a man has in mind:
Gladstone refers to being 'accosted', i.e. the initiative was the prostitute's, not, as in the past, his. (Parris, 1995—the Liberal Prime Minister habitually sought out prostitutes in the streets, to reform them, so he averred, his efforts sometimes requiring prolonged discussion with them at No. 10 Downing Street)
Accosting people is what an aggressive beggar does in a public place.

accouchement the period of childbirth
What was a euphemism in French becomes doubly so in standard English use.

account for to kill
Used of animals by humans and of humans by soldiers. The usage might imply a reckoning of the number slain but it may equally refer to a single victim:
A more suitable way of describing such an event, the Foxhunters' Society suggested delicately, might be a casual 'the animal was accounted for'. (Whicker, 1982)

accumulate (of securities) do not sell
Jargon of the financial analyst whose job is to promote activity among investors rather than pass them bad news.

acid lysergic acid diethylamide
Better known as LSD. To *drop acid* is to ingest it illegally. An *acid-head* or *acid freak* is someone addicted to LSD.

acknowledgement (of services) the payment of a bribe
I marked this usage as obsolete until Saddam Hussein's relationship with corrupt politicians and officials saw its reappearance in their explanations as to how it was that they had received his bounty:
Pepys explained that he was not to be bribed but was prepared to accept 'acknowledgement of his services'. (Tomalin, 2002)

acorn academy *American* an institution for the mentally ill
Where you consign a NUT.

acorns *American* the testicles
A variant of NUTS.

acquire to steal
Literally, to gain possession of, as by purchase. Whence *acquisition*, obtaining by stealing or subterfuge.

act (the) copulation
Sometimes *tout court* but more often as the *act of shame* (if outside marriage); *of generation*, *of intercourse*, *of love*; or *the sexual act*. Note however that *a sexual act* may imply no more than a pinched bottom. A man who *acts like a husband* is not the breadwinner or idle and slovenly about the house but is having a sexual relationship with a female to whom he is not married:

Actaeon *literary* one who cuckolds another
In the legend Actaeon was no more than a casual observer of Artemis's nakedness, and she had no husband to take offence. Nevertheless she turned him into a stag and set his own pack on him.

action¹ vice or illegal activity, or its proceeds
Usually illegal gambling, narcotics, or prostitution.
A *slice of the action* is a share in the activity or proceeds.
See also PIECE OF THE ACTION.

action² the brutal harassment of supposed opponents
The *Aktion* of the Nazis, normally directed at Jewish citizens.

action³ a chance of casual copulation
Someone going out for an evening looking for the *action* is visiting places where like-minded individuals may be congregating:
Then he stared around [the bar] to check the action. (Sanders, 1982—he was trying to pick out and up an unaccompanied woman)

active not physically impaired by age or illness

Descriptive of geriatrics who have retained mobility:

> Active Adult Golf Community.
> (advertisement in Gainesville, Florida, November 1987, for houses adjacent to a golf course)

or of those who continue to engage in sexual activity:

> They say Willie Maugham had [youth pills], too, and he was still active, if you know what I mean, the day he died. (B. Forbes, 1972)

activist a political zealot
No longer merely a supporter of the philosophy of *activism* but someone willing to break the law in pursuit of strongly held beliefs.

actress *obsolete* a prostitute
Until a liberating decree of Charles II female roles on stage were played by males. Thereafter, for some three centuries, acting was not considered a respectable profession for a woman.

acute environmental reaction *American* an inability to continue fighting
Vietnam jargon, for a condition where it is hard to tell mental illness from self-preservation or cowardice:

> Most Americans would rather be told that their son is undergoing acute environmental reaction than to hear he is suffering from shell shock. (Herr, 1977)

Adam's arsenal the male genitalia
The source from which the human race was first engendered, so we are led to believe. Of the same tendency is, or was, *Eve's customhouse*, where Adam was supposed to have 'made his first entry'. (Grose)

ADD see ATTENTION DEFICIT DISORDER

adjust your dress to do up the fasteners on your trousers
Once fly-buttons, now zips. Still sometimes seen in the admonition in public lavatories for males: 'Please adjust your dress before leaving.'

adjustment¹ an adverse price movement
If you are a buyer, the price will go up. On the stock market, an *adjustment* denotes a fall, either in an individual security or generally. A *currency adjustment* is a devaluation.

adjustment² the subjective alteration of published accounts
With publicly owned corporations, usually showing increased profits or assets, and with those privately owned, attempting to reduce profit and so avoid paying tax:

> The purpose of the 'adjustments' was to

put the bank in the best possible light when the year-end figures ultimately appeared in the annual report. (Erdman, 1986)

administrative detention imprisonment without trial
Administration means management. The phrase is used by the Israeli government for the indefinite incarceration of Palestinians.

administrative leave *American* suspension from duty for alleged malpractice
A usage by a cautious employer anxious to appear not to have prejudged the issue:

> Administrative leave is the same thing as being suspended... the first step to being fired. (P. Cornwell, 2000)

admirer a woman's regular sexual partner outside marriage
In Jane Austen's day and writing, an *admirer* indulged in formal courtship. Half a century later the euphemistic use had developed:

> ... met her admirer at a house in Bolton Row that she was in the habit of frequenting. (Mayhew, 1862)

Still occasionally used humorously.

adult¹ pornographic
Used in connection with literature, films, stage shows, and erotica deemed unsuitable for children but, by implication, in accord with the tastes of fully grown people. However the American *adult trailer park* merely bars residents with children.

adult² adulterous
The way grown-ups supposedly behave:

> The Duchess had never made any secret of her adult relationships in the years before she married. She had affairs with... (*Daily Telegraph*, 14 January 1994)

advantaged rich
Political jargon of those who believe that much poverty stems from injustice and exclusion:

> By constantly devoting attention and resources to the least advantageous section of the community, deprivation will be eliminated altogether. (Hattersley, 1995—it might appear that well-meaning politician was not familiar with *John 12:8*)

adventure¹ a war
Originally, a chance happening. Normally a description of a conflict in which the aggressor expects easy gains.

adventure² a sexual relationship with other than your regular sexual partner
Another chance or exciting event, perhaps.

An *adventuress* does not travel the world or do exciting deeds but takes lovers, being also described as *adventurous*.

adverse event (an) a death
Medical jargon but not of losing your wallet.

adviser the representative of an imperial power in a client state
They do much more than merely give *advice*. In the British Empire they were called Residents.

aerated drunk
Literally, describing a liquid charged with gas, rather than a body charged with liquid.
Aerated, of a person, may also mean angry or agitated.

aesthete *obsolete* a male homosexual
Literally, one who affects a higher apprecia-tion of beauty than others. *Aestheticism* was male homosexuality.
An *aesthetic procedure* is not some homosexual activity but cosmetic surgery.

affair(e) an ongoing sexual relationship with other than your regular sexual partner
The English version is now more common. An *affaire* may also refer to the third party involved:
    He comes to see the singer Floriana. He's her latest *affaire*. (Manning, 1960)
A *man of affairs* is not a philanderer but a businessman.

affair of honour *obsolete* a duel
From the days when insults were taken seriously.

affirmative action preferential treatment for particular classes of people when making appointments
Originally, in America, denoting attempts to promote black people. Now used of similar preference given to those who are not dominant white, fit, heterosexual males.

afflicted subject to physical or mental ill-ness or abnormality
Not just labouring under the effects of a tempor-ary disability. For the Victorians an *affliction of the loins* or *of venery* was a venereal disease.

affordable cheap
Used to describe household equipment or small newly built houses. An estate in Beverley Hills is, however, affordable to a pop star and a Ferrari to a professional soccer player.

afloat drunk
From the sensation at one stage of intoxica-tion, and not just confined to the cliché about your *back teeth*:
    ... dear scatty Marigold, often afloat before breakfast and regularly before lunch.
    (D. Francis, 2002—Marigold was not a yachtswoman)

African *American* black
In phrases such as *African-American* and *African-descended*, the euphemisms only being used about those whose ancestors came from sub-Saharan regions (and were not Boers).

after-shave a perfume used by males
The original justification for its use, in the days when men did not use perfume, was the alleviation of smarting after using a razor blade. The continuing choice of macho names for these products indicates that the taboo against male use of cosmetics is not quite dead.

afterlife death
Used especially by Quakers, spiritualists, and others who have confidence that death is not the end:
    'It is the smell of afterlife.' 'It smells more like that of afterdeath,' said Jessica.
    (Sharpe, 1978)

afterthought a child born in wedlock fol-lowing an unplanned conception
Among the processes connected with the event, premeditation is not prominent.

ageful *American* old or geriatric
Coined by the POLITICALLY CORRECT, among whom any mention that people grow old, and therefore often infirm, is taboo. In British legal jargon, to be *of full age* is to be eighteen years or older.

agent a participant in a taboo employ-ment
In espionage, a spy, and specifically a *secret agent*. *Agent* is also used in job descriptions to enhance status, without necessarily being euphemistic. Thus the British *estate agent* (the American *realtor* or *real estate agent*) is at law the agent of neither the buyer nor the seller. There is an infinite variety of American *agents*, most of whom have no delegated responsibility other than to drive a train or punch a ticket. An *agent* may also be a noxious substance, such as the *agent orange* used by the Americans for defoliation in Vietnam.

agreeable to prepared to consort and co-pulate with
Not just showing good manners:
    When one mayor [in occupied France] dared to complain about such immoral behaviour,

Evers [the German commandant] issued an order—'I forbid you to reprimand women who wish to be agreeable to the [German] officers.' (Macintyre, 2001)

aggressive recklessly optimistic or dishonest

An extension of the commercial meaning, keenly seeking new business:

Enron had been very aggressive in its accounting—most notably in the Raptor transaction and the Condor vehicle. (*Sunday Telegraph*, 20 January 2002—and we know what became of Enron)

aid a gift from a rich to a poor country

Or, as Lord Bauer pointed out, a gift from the poor in a rich country to the rich in a poor country:

MPs are to launch an enquiry into allegations that British aid was used to buy a fleet of 35 Mercedes limousines for the government of Malawi. (*Sunday Telegraph*, 29 October 2000)

Tied aid means that the donor is arranging credits or spending cash to assist its exporters.

aided by making surreptitious use of

It may mean anything from the use of a ghost writer by a public figure to a cosmetic procedure:

[Virginia Mayo had] ash-blonde hair which, if occasionally aided by the peroxide bottle, lacked the brashness of some of her companions. (*Daily Telegraph*, 19 January 2005)

air (the) peremptory dismissal from employment or courtship

Referring to the figurative or actual ejection from the premises in which the work or courting took place. The *air*, it would seem, is given but not received.

airport novel a book written for a person who does not read regularly

For the captive traveller market and considered by the literati to be unworthy of their attention.

Ajax see JAKES

alcohol an intoxicant

The standard English is a shortened form of *alcohol of wine*, from the meaning, a condensed spirit. This in turn was derived from *kohl*, 'a fine powder produced by grinding or esp. by sublimation' (*SOED*).

Alderman Lushington see LUSH

all night man *obsolete British* a dealer in corpses

He exhumed newly buried corpses for sale to teaching hospitals, especially in Scotland where Edinburgh hosted a celebrated medical school at a time when Oxford and Cambridge were more concerned with spiritual enlightenment, producing Doctors of Divinity rather than of Medicine. There was no property, or right to ownership, in a corpse and the lack of refrigeration made it important to maintain a steady supply for dissection. The paucity of voluntary donors was because they were fearful of a piecemeal return to earth by themselves or their relatives at the Resurrection of the Dead. The same phenomenon was observed in 19th-century America where a hobo, or hick, might be killed to satisfy demand.

Today an *all-nighter* is no more than a contract with a prostitute to enjoy her services overnight.

all over with death for

From the meaning, finished but showing little faith in the life hereafter:

All up with means about to die or dead.

all-rounder a person of both heterosexual and homosexual tastes

In a sport it describes someone with ability in various aspects of a game.

See also BATTING AND BOWLING.

all the way (of sexual activity) with full penetration

As different from intermediate stages of caressing.

allergic to lead see LEAD

alley cat a prostitute

Both are reputed to frequent narrow lanes. As a verb, of a male, it means to be promiscuous:

...couldn't stand the thought of the guy alley-catting around. (Sanders, 1977)

allow your name to go forward to seek election to a public office

With a due show of modesty:

Quite a friendly piece in today's *Independent* 'allowed his name to go forward'. That's more like it. Just the phrase. (A. Clark, 2002—he was seeking a safe constituency)

alter the demographics to practise genocide

A practice of Saddam Hussein and others:

It was...a Kurdish region, although the Iraqi government had tried to 'alter the demographics of the area'. (*Daily Telegraph*, 26 March 2003)

alternative differing from existing social arrangement, practicality, or convention

Those who pursue *alternative* policies or methods believe them to be more efficacious than normal arrangements. Thus *alternative medicine* may reject drugs and surgery in favour of acupuncture and similar treatment, *alternative nutrition* may mean being a vegan, *alternative education* rejects conventional schooling, an *alternative lifestyle* may be spent in a caravan, *alternative sexuality* or an *alternative proclivity* is homosexuality, *alternative defence* is the rejection of nuclear weapons etc.:

> ...an 'alternative defence workshop' led by Mrs Joan Ruddock, CND Chairman. (*Daily Telegraph*, November 1983)

ambidextrous having both heterosexual and homosexual tastes

Of men or women, from the ability to use either hand with equal precision.

Also as *ambiguous* or *ambivalent*.

ambrosia an intoxicant

Originally, the food, and less often the drink, of the gods.

ambulance-chaser someone who greedily touts for business

Referring to the practice, supposedly originated by American lawyers, of following an ambulance to hospital in the hope of being retained by the victim to sue someone. Now also prevalent in the British legal profession. Also as *ambulance-chasing* and in figurative contexts:

> During the summer months we were constantly being associated with potential bidders but we are quite clear that we want to remain independent. We want all ambulance-chasing merchant banks to understand that. (*Daily Telegraph*, 17 November 1997)

America First isolationism

It was the name of an organization campaigning for neutrality in the Second World War. This stance was supported by 67% of a sample in a poll conducted in 1939. Of the same sample, 12% wanted aid sent to those fighting Nazism and 2% were prepared to agree to providing military assistance. (Deighton, 1993)

amorous favours copulation

Usually granted by a female rather than a male, but not always:

> It had become embarrassingly and sickeningly plain that the fickle Kim was bestowing amorous favours simultaneously

on Melinda. (Boyle, 1979—Kim was the traitor Philby and Melinda the wife of his fellow traitor, Maclean)

For *amorous sport*, see SPORT (THE).

He who displays *amorous propensities* has lewd thoughts:

> I'll come no more behind your scenes, David; for the silk stockings and white bosoms of your actresses excite my amorous propensities. (J. Boswell, 1791—Dr Johnson was speaking to Garrick)

An *amorous tie* is a sexual commitment to another person.

amour a sexual partner outside marriage

Literally, love or affection, but now standard English. An *amour* may also mean copulation, especially in the plural:

> Those women who live in apartments and maintain themselves by the product of their vagrant amours. (Mayhew, 1862—they had strangers as partners, not hobos)

ample (of a woman) fat

Literally, wide and commodious.

If *amply endowed*, she comes not with a generous marriage settlement but with large breasts. An *amply endowed* male has large genitalia.

amusement with prizes gambling

Amusing, we may assume, for the owner of the automatic machines programmed to take a percentage off those who put money into them.

amusing (of art) pornographic

Jargon from a milieu where overt vulgarity is deplored:

> Pictures medium only, but some amusing. ('amusing' means 'erotic', doesn't it, in an auctioneer's catalogue description). (A. Clark, 1993)

angel of the night a prostitute

With no halo.

angle with a silver hook *obsolete* to pretend to have caught a fish which you have bought

Not the behaviour of a sportsman or a gentleman. There followed some figurative use, to indicate willingness to accept a bribe.

Anglo-Saxon (of language) crude or vulgar

The supposition is that many obscenities in English have that ancestry.

animal confinement operator *American* a farmer

The circumlocution might be better applied to a zookeeper:

> Manure Management Plans, which all the state's 'animal confinement operators'—

pig farmers to you and me—are required to file periodically. (Bryson, 2003)

animal rights the attribution to selected animals of human characteristics
The fanaticism of some in a cause which has overtones of anthropomorphism can be distasteful to many who also abhor cruelty to animals.

annex to conquer and occupy
Literally, to attach:
Nobo had been severely injured in a bombing outside Seoul in 1910, at the time Korea was being annexed to Japan. (Golden, 1997)

Annie Oakley *obsolete? American* a free meal ticket
It was punched each time you used it at the designated eating place, thus eventually resembling the playing card the celebrated gunslinger filled with holes after flinging it in the air at the circus.

anoint (a palm) to bribe
Obsolete as *anoint* on its own and see PALM. Described in Farmer & Henley as 'To flatter. To bribe: grease the palm: creech the hoof.' If in Ireland you were *anointed*, it meant you were on your death bed, from the practice of so treating those who were mortally ill.

anorak an enthusiast for an unintellectual pastime
Thought boring by those who use the word and may think themselves superior and avantgarde. The usage comes from the article of clothing favoured by those who take their pleasures in the open.

another state (in a) dead
Not just on a day trip to France or Mexico. See also BETTER COUNTRY.

Anschluss a military conquest
Literally, the German word means connection. This was how Germany described its occupation of Austria in 1938, becoming a euphemism in both German and English.

answer the call[1] to die
Usually of those killed in war, called to arms and then, it might be hoped, to life eternal.

answer the call[2] to urinate
In this case, answering a CALL OF NATURE.

anti- avoiding a statement of your allegiance
When the cause being promoted is likely to have few adherents, you declare yourself to be against something which sensible, well-meaning, or gullible persons are likely to abhor. Thus in the 5th century, Athanasius set himself up as *anti-Arian*, and millions since have repeated his doctrinal niceties each Sunday. Many of us are *anti-fascist* but not Communists:
The anti-fascist protection barrier is particularly deep and formidable where the railway crosses the Alexander Ufer. (Deighton, 1988—most of us called it the 'Berlin Wall')

anti-diversity *American* racist
Or perceived as such by those with a heightened awareness of skin pigmentation and gender:
Mayor Fernandez is going to come down hard on anyone operating in this area espousing a racist or anti-diversity message. (Patterson and Gross, 2002)

anti-freeze a spirituous intoxicant
Some humorous use, because it may warm you in cold weather.

anti-personnel designed to kill or maim
It could mean no more than opposed to people.

anti-social criminal or offensive
Literally, reclusive or self-centred. Used of dropping litter or obstreperous behaviour in public. For the IRA *anti-social behaviour* meant petty crimes in a Nationalist district, for which the perpetrator might be 'jointed', or shot in the knees or ankles. For autocrats it describes any conduct which might question their rule. An *anti-social noise* is a fart.

anticipating *American* pregnant
Another way of saying EXPECTANT.

antlers an indication of cuckoldry
Formerly given as a pair, to be worn by the cuckold.

apartheid see SEPARATE DEVELOPMENT

ape *mainly American* mad
Usually of a temporary condition, from the supposed simian behaviour.

appendage the penis
Literally, something attached or hung on:
... her mean little hand ready to perform its spiritless operation on my equally jaded appendage. (Styron, 1976—it can't have been that jaded)

appetites an obsession with sex
In the singular, an *appetite* is a craving for anything, normally for food:
... consigned to an early grave by his wife's various appetites. (Sharpe, 1974)

apple-polish *American* to seek favour or advancement by flattery
You rub the skins to make them look more palatable.
Whence an *apple-polisher*, who so behaves.

apples *obsolete* the testicles
Victorian humour or exaggeration.

appliance an item of medical equipment worn on the body
Literally, anything which is applied for a specific purpose. A shortening of *surgical appliance*, which might describe a scalpel. An *appliance* may be a truss, a hearing aid, a wooden leg, or anything else you don't want to be precise about—but not spectacles.

apportion to allocate components of a purchase price in a single transaction so as to evade tax
There is a narrow and ill-defined line between tax evasion (which is illegal) and tax avoidance (which isn't):
    If...he officially paid a lower price which was beneath the higher rate threshold, and made up the difference by appearing to buy 'fixtures and fittings' for cash, then he would have been guilty of 'apportioning'. (*Daily Telegraph*, 17 August 1999, reporting on the British minister Peter Mandelson's dealings in real estate)

appropriate[1] to steal
Originally, it meant to take for your own use, without any taint of impropriety:
    All old *mali* had actually done, though, was appropriate his half share of what he had hoed and sweated to grow. (P. Scott, 1977—the *mali*, or gardener, had been dismissed for theft)

appropriate[2] in line with your dogmatic prejudices
Appropriate and *appropriately* are described (by R. Harris, 1992) as 'the favourite words in the bureaucrat's lexicon, the grease for sliding round unpleasantness, the funk-hole for avoiding specifics'. They are also beloved by the POLITICALLY CORRECT:
    Freedom of speech is still guaranteed by the Constitution, but it can be exercised only so long as it is 'appropriate'. (A. Waugh in *Daily Telegraph*, 13 August 1994, commenting on the refusal of an American publisher to publish writings by the Pope because they were considered anti-feminine)
and also beloved by tyrants:
    In the House of Assembly, Harare's Commons, [Ushekowokunza, Home Affairs Minister] called it 'appropriate technology', a euphemism for electric shock treatment

that drew appreciative nods from his colleagues. (*Daily Telegraph*, September 1983, reporting on the torture of white officers in the Zimbabwe air force)

approved school *British* a penal institution for children
The *approval* was by the Home Office as being suitable for the incarceration of young criminals. You would be wrong to assume that educational establishments not so described lacked the blessing of society.

ardent spirits spirituous intoxicants
Referring to the burning of the throat, not from the DUTCH COURAGE which may follow.

arm candy a good-looking female companion
Escorted by a man in public:
    Hurley, then seen merely as Grant's arm-candy, became famous when she wore a dress by Gianni Versace. (*Daily Telegraph*, 24 May 2000)

armed struggle (the) terrorism
The language of Irish dissidents, among others.

armour *obsolete* a contraceptive sheath
As worn, or not, by Boswell:
    I took out my armour, but she begged that I might not put it on, as the sport was much pleasanter without it. (J. Boswell, *c*.1792)

army form blank *British* lavatory paper
The only bits of paper in the army without an identifying number.

around the Horn see RUN (A)ROUND THE HORN

arouse to cause sexual excitement in another
Literally, to awaken from sleep. It is used of either sex, heterosexually or homosexually:
    ...he aroused her in a way that her husband had never done. (Allbeury, 1976—and not by a new alarm clock)
Whence *arousal*, such sexual excitement:
    ...the muted talk of women made him excited and he had to roll onto his stomach to conceal his arousal. (Boyd, 1982)

arrange to do something underhand, shameful, or taboo
Accounts which are prepared in a misleading manner are *arranged*. The word is also used of bribing officials or castrating tomcats.
To *arrange yourself* is to put your clothing straight after a taboo activity, such as urination or extramarital copulation:
    She was...arranging herself. She seemed a bit dazed. She whacked her shoulder on

the bedroom door, trying to squeeze by him. (Anonymous, 1996)

An *arrangement* is what ensues, whether it be a pot for urine in a bedroom, a bribe, a settlement with your creditors (or *Deed of Arrangement*), regular extramarital sexual activity, etc.:

> The majority of diplomats and businessmen away from home for long periods made 'arrangements' for themselves. (Faulks, 1993)

The Irish phrase *arranged by circumstances* does not refer to an arranged marriage in which the bride takes a husband chosen for her by her parents, but to one necessitated by her unplanned pregnancy.

arse a person viewed sexually
Literally, the buttocks but, because they were the subject of taboo while a donkey wasn't, it was changed to *ass*, which quickly acquired similar connotations and persists in America. Thus in obsolete British use, a jackass became a *Johnny Bum*, *Jack* and *ass* being vulgar, while *bum* was still respectable. The commonest use, of male or female, is when they are described as a *bit* or *piece of arse* or *ass*.
An *arse* or *ass man* is a promiscuous person.
An *arse-bandit*, sometimes shortened to *bandit*, is a male homosexual.
An *arse peddler* is a prostitute, heterosexual or homosexual.

art pornographic
A survival from the days when pornographers were liable to prosecution, and a favoured defence was that the matter in question was artistic rather than titillating:

> She finally makes it in 'art' (that is French soft-porn) movies before tragedy strikes. (*Sunday Telegraph*, 3 May 1998)

article an object which is the subject of taboo
Such as a chamber pot for urine, or *article of furniture*, as it was once called.

Aryan without Jewish ancestry
Originally, 'a native or inhabitant of Ariana, the eastern part of ancient Iran' or 'a member of the peoples who spoke the parent language of the Indo-European (or esp. Indo-Iranian) family' (*SOED*). This was a Nazi classification in their anti-Jewish obsession, of inanimate objects as well as people:

> *Coffee* Eva's Aryan 60 grammes a constant source of envy on the part of Frau Voss. We give her 5 grams as a present. Bliss. We invite the Reichenbachs for genuine Aryan coffee. (Klemperer, 1998, in translation—diary entry 26 November 1940: Klemperer's wife, Eva, was not Jewish)

To *aryanize* was to remove any Jewish link of involvement, which turned into seizing property without compensation:

> Reka, the most reputable, the best department store in Dresden, was aryanised last year. (ibid.—diary entry of 9 October 1937)

as Allah made him naked
The way he was born.
In the same sense others attribute the manufacture to God.

as planned regrettably
Corporate-speak when managers wish to suggest that failure is not due to their incompetence:

> As planned, losses for the period were less than the corresponding period last year. (United Utilities Interim Report, 2001/2002)

Asian levy *British* a bribe
This was paid by ship-owners to the National Union of Seamen at £30 a head annually for each lowly paid Asian crew member employed on a British-registered ship in return for the union raising no objection.

ask for your papers to resign from employment
Usually from an official position in a huff, the *papers* being the supposed commission which you were handed on appointment:

> ... his plumbing is done and he has asked for his papers. (Sayers, 1937—he was a diplomat, not an artisan)

asleep see FALL ASLEEP

ass see ARSE

assault to attack sexually
Literally, to use any force against another:

> If I'd been assaulted by men of my own race I would have been an object of pity. (P. Scott, 1973—a white woman had been raped by Indians)

And as a noun:

> ... the main proceedings, which happened to be a rape trial (in the papers of the *Intelligencer* the crime would be referred to as 'assault on a woman'). (King, 1996)

or with adjectival embellishment, as an *indecent assault*—see also INDECENCY.

assembly area *American* an internment camp
Second World War term for the place of long-term incarceration of Americans of Japanese descent.

asset a spy
Literally, anything useful or valuable. Common espionage jargon, according to the novelists.

assignation a meeting for extramarital copulation
Literally, the allotment of something, whence a tryst.
Also of the act itself:
  Palmerston died there on the billiard table, reputedly after an assignation with one of the maids. (*Daily Telegraph*, 11 February 1995, referring to Brocket Hall)

assimilation theft
The expropriation in Nazi Germany of property owned by Jews:
  [Civilians who had been ready to steal Jewish assets but were being castigated for turning against the Nazis] took part in the so-called assimilation of Jewish properties. (Kee, 1985—translation of report in *Schwartze Korps*, February, 1945)

assist the police (with their inquiries) see
HELP THE POLICE (WITH THEIR INQUIRIES)

assistance¹ a regular payment to those entitled to make a claim from state funds
Literally, help of any kind. To be *on (the) assistance* is to be receiving such payments. See also PUBLIC ASSISTANCE.

assistance² a bribe
Helping someone to do what you want:
  G-Tech, the gaming company, had approached the governor with an offer of 'assistance' over Lincoln Park. (*Sunday Telegraph*, 12 October 2003)

associate with to meet in an illegal or taboo capacity
It describes those with criminal connections. An *association* may refer to an illegal relationship and, if *close* or *intimate*, to an extramarital sexual relationship.
  Poor old Alan Stewart [resigned] today as PPS because of his 'association' with a woman he met in an alcohol-dependency clinic. (A. Clark, 2002—wine and women, even without the song, can indeed lead to impoverishment and premature ageing, especially for a Member of Parliament)

asylum an institution for the mentally ill
Originally, a place where pillage was sacrilegious, which is why there was so much fuss about Henry II's murder of Becket. Then it became a safe place or benevolent institution. Now a shortened form of *lunatic asylum*.

at government expense in prison
The expression is not used for the provision for politicians, public employees, soldiers, and others maintained from the public purse.

at half mast with trouser zip undone
Referring to a flag incorrectly hoisted, except in mourning. The phrase is used as a coded message from one male to another in mixed company.

at Her Majesty's pleasure *British* indefinitely
The wording is used when a judge chooses not to place any term on the confinement of the prisoner due to madness or other factors.

at it engaged in a taboo activity
In appropriate circumstances, the phrase can apply to anything from picking your nose to bestiality. In the East End of London, it usually refers to being a villain. Elsewhere is may indicate sexual activity. *At yourself* means masturbating:
  Do you know what he's doing in there? At himself... Every time a new American magazine comes in with the women's underwear he goes in. (McCourt, 1997)
At a person may indicate hostile, bullying, or demanding behaviour:
  Oh, don't be dense, Mattie! I mean *at me*. I'm so sore down there. (Donneley, 2003—she had just given birth but had an importunate husband)

at liberty involuntarily unemployed
Actor's jargon in a profession where it does not do to say you are out of work.

at rest dead
A tombstone favourite which might seem to suggest a torpid AFTERLIFE, although playing a harp and singing hymns could be quite restful, I suppose. Also as *at peace*.

at the last day when you are dead
The *last day* is, for devout Christians, the Day of Judgement, although the numbers of those in the dock might seem to merit a longer sitting.

at your last about to die
Not just of cobblers. See also LAST CALL.

athletic supporter a brief tight undergarment worn by males to hold the genitalia
Not a football fan.

attendance centre *British* a place to which young criminals are required to report for disciplinary training
Taken literally, the term might equally apply, for example, to a theatre or a skating rink.

attendance management persuading employees to turn up for work
Especially when they expect to be paid for absence:

Rod Eddington said one of the issues he would discuss with the unions was 'attendance management' or sick leave. (*Daily Telegraph*, 29 January 2004—female staff at British Airways appeared especially vulnerable to illness during the Wimbledon tournament or at school half-terms, while males tended to be similarly afflicted on Mondays)

attention deficit disorder idleness, stupidity, or indiscipline
The medical condition affecting some pupils is also more widely applied, allowing an issue to be raised without using educationally taboo words such as lazy, backward, or naughty. Often as *ADD* and occasionally in even more convoluted phraseology.

attentions sexual activities with someone other than a regular partner
What in the singular may be no more than a mark of respect, interest, or good manners assumes sexual overtones in the plural:

Jack Profumo... had become involved with a young lady who was also enjoying the attentions of the Soviet Military Attaché. (A. Clark, 1993—the community of interest would have been less noteworthy if Profumo had not also been Minister of Defence)

attractive to the opposite sex (of a male) promiscuous
Few people are not attractive to the opposite sex at some time or on some occasion in their existence:

Ever-attractive to the opposite sex, with a taste for the good things of life...(*Daily Telegraph*, 18 June 2002, in the obituary of a libertine)

au naturel naked
Borrowed from the French by the Americans more than by the British, who have fewer taboos about nakedness.

auction of kit *British* one of the consequences of death
Naval usage. Shipmates pay inflated prices in the knowledge that the proceeds will go to the dependants of the dead person. The practice was formerly referred to as the punning *sale before the mast*.

auld kirk (the) *Scottish* whisky
The ecclesiastical derivation is unclear, except perhaps for those of us who have sat through a sermon in an unheated Scottish church in winter.

aunt[1] a promiscuous woman or prostitute
The modern American use for an elderly prostitute was anticipated by Shakespeare:

...summer songs for me and my aunts,
While we lie tumbling in the hay.
(*Shakespeare, The Winter's Tale*)

aunt[2] a lavatory
To whom many women say they are paying a visit. In Victorian days it was their *Aunt Jones*.

aunt[3] an elderly male homosexual
Those so described are generally a generation older than those whose company they seek. Less often as *auntie*.

Aunt Cissed drunk
Rhyming slang.

Aunt Flo menstruation
The lady who comes regularly to visit you, and a pretty awful pun.

auto-da-fé killing by burning
Literally (translated from the Portuguese) the *act of faith* of the Inquisition, itself in its own eyes no more than an inquiry. The Spanish *auto de fé* was no less palatable. However, before the Anglo-Saxons start preening themselves, they should recall that the English contemporary foul-mouthed Lord Chancellor, Thomas More, reintroduced and rejoiced in the burning of Protestants. On 5 November 2000 Pope John Paul II in Rome proclaimed him to be the patron saint of politicians.

auto-erotic practices masturbation
By either sex, and not just thinking evil thoughts or watching pornographic videos. Also as *auto-erotic habits*.

available[1] willing to start a sexual relationship
Mainly of females and not usually on a permanent basis, with or without payment. A male might be said to *avail himself* of her. The US State Department combined circumlocution with euphemism when describing a prostitute as an *available casual indigenous female companion*. (Bryson, 1994)

available[2] involuntarily unemployed
Used by those who still are ashamed of not having a job:

'I'm, as they say, "between jobs".'
'Available.' 'That too.' (N. Evans, 1998)

away[1] *obsolete* dead
With an implication of a temporary parting,

perhaps:
> Rachel mournynge for hir children and
> wolde not be comforted, because they were
> awaye. (Coverdale Bible, *Jeremiah* 31:15—
> the Authorized Version says 'because they
> were not')

away² in prison
The use was more common when the stigma
of incarceration was greater:
> Apart from six months spent 'on the gallop',
> mostly in Eire, he's been away for eighteen
> years. (Stamp, 1994—he was an Irish
> terrorist)

awful experiment (the) the prohibition
of sale and consumption of intoxicants
in the USA from 1920 to 1933
Awful for those denied intoxicants or faced
with illegality to obtain them: much more
awful for the impetus it gave to organized
crime.

axe¹ to kill after judicial process
Originally by beheading, then by any other
form of killing:
> They were brought to Berlin and axed.
> (Shirer, 1984, referring to two German
> Socialist leaders handed over to the Nazis
> by Pétain's Vichy government in 1940)
Some figurative use:
> You were out to ax me. (Turow, 1987—an
> attorney had tried to discredit a hostile
> witness)

axe² to dismiss summarily from employ-
ment
Invaluable to sub-editors short of space.
Occasionally too of a broken courtship.

Aztec two-step (the) diarrhoea
An affliction of visitors to Mexico—you have
to keep dancing to the lavatory. Also as the
Aztec hop; and see also MONTEZUMA'S REVENGE.

B

B anything taboo beginning with the letter B

Specifically for *bloody* as in the expression *B fool*; for *bugger* in the expression *B off*; for *bitch* in the insulting *silly B*, of a woman; for *benzedrine* in the expression *B-pill*; etc.

BO the smell of stale sweat

The initial letters of the advertising slogan of the makers of Lifebuoy Soap, which claimed to correct the condition which they termed *body odour*.

babysitting undisclosed telephone monitoring

Espionage jargon for the watchful third party in the house.

baby-snatcher a person with a much younger regular sexual partner

Usually heterosexual, with the woman older than the man.

Rarely the older person is referred to as a *baby-farmer*. See also CRADLE-SNATCHER.

bacchanalian drunken

Literally, anything to do with Bacchus, or Dionysus, who was the god of wine and debauchery:

Burgess fell from grace at the Foreign Office as a result of another bacchanalian holiday trip. (Boyle, 1979—the authorities were less vigilant about Burgess's treachery)

A *devotee*, *son*, or *priest of Bacchus* is a drunkard. *Bacchanals*, a carouse, lives on in the English pub sign *Bag o' Nails*.

back door[1] the anus

Mainly homosexual use. In vulgar slang the *front door* or *front parlour* is the vagina. A *back-door man* might also be heterosexual, leaving the house by that route after an assignation with the wife when the husband returned. The *back-door trot* was not a description of his exit but diarrhoea, in the days when the lavatory was outside the house.

backdoor[2] involving bribery or impropriety

Open transactions can be done through the front door. It may refer to bribery:

Hoo-men or 'backdoor business' was what oiled the wheels of the new entrepreneurial China. (Strong, 1998)

or to improperly revealing information:

Don't backdoor me. I'll hear it from the DA in court. (Turow, 1996)

back-end loaded coming later rather than sooner

An explanation for a delay caused by management error:

I am confident [Shell] can achieve [100% replacement of resources by 2009] but we know that it will be back-end loaded. (*Daily Telegraph*, 4 February 2005, quoting a company statement after a period of overstating reserves and resulting financial scandal)

back-gate parole *American* the natural death of a prisoner

The portal through which the coffin is carried.

back passage the anus

Medical jargon.

back teeth floating having drunk too much alcohol and wishing to urinate

The liquid in your body has supposedly risen that high.

back-up in retail inventories holding excess stock

Literally, an accumulation due to a jam:

Chairman and chief executive Paul Fireman said the softer demand for athletic apparel and footwear had resulted in a 'back-up in retail inventories'. (*Daily Telegraph*, 12 December 1997— the sub-editor was not deceived: his headline was 'Sales of Reeboks have run out of puff')

backhander a bribe

Literally, a blow with the back of the hand. The giver of the bribe figuratively rotates his palm to conceal the passing of the money:

Last year, a special adviser alleged in a video recording that Mr Chirac had sanctioned and witnessed a £500,000 backhander to a colleague. (*Sunday Telegraph*, 15 July 2001—M. Chirac was the president of France)

In obsolete use a *backhander* showed bad manners as 'A glass of wine out of turn, the bottle being passed back or retained for a second glass instead of following the sun round the table.' (Farmer & Henley, 1905)

backside the buttocks

This standard English use ignores the other parts of the body similarly situated, from the back of the head to the heels. Some figurative use:

But then it was just my...backside was at risk. (Price, 1978)

backward[1] very stupid

Educational jargon which indicates more than doing poorly in a class of normal children.

Lay people use *backward* of adults who are slow-witted or illiterate.

backward² poor or uncivilized
It is used of sovereign states. The first of a series of patronizing post-colonial euphemisms:
    ...countries which have progressively and with increasing euphemism been termed backward, underdeveloped, less-developed, and developing. (Bullock and Stallybrass, 1977)

backward³ through the anus
Describing sexual activity, from the Great Diarist onwards:
    ...and so to Mrs Martin and then did what je voudrai avec her, both devante and backward, which is also muy bon plazer. (Pepys, 1660–69)

bad working as a prostitute
A judgement on morals rather than job proficiency:
    ...lost her place for staying out one night with the man who seduced her; he afterwards deserted her and then she became bad. (Mayhew, 1862)

bad man the devil
Although, if you didn't want to upset him, you might call him the *good man*. He was also the *bad lad* in Scotland.
For the devout, the *bad fire* or *bad place* was hell.

bad-mouth to denigrate
It applies to personal comment or commercial skulduggery.

bad powder a fart
Like the slow and smelly combustion of a faulty charge in a firearm, which is why men, who use this phrase, say it has been burnt or let off.

badge bandit *American* a highway police officer
Badge is slang for police and the *banditry* because the fine you hand over may or may not be passed on to the authorities.

badger a prostitute
Formerly, a licensed huckster who had to wear a badge, from which the standard English meaning, to importune excessively, and so to the prostitute who accosts men in the street. The usage survives in the *badger game*, in which the victim is led by a prostitute into a sexually compromising situation, and then blackmailed.

bag¹ to steal

Referring to the method of concealing and taking away the loot. Still common use among schoolchildren. An American *bag job* is the unauthorized taking of documents by a government agency.

bag² (the) dismissal from employment or courtship
A synonym of SACK.

bag³ to kill by hunting
Standard English, referring to the birds and small mammals which are put into the hunter's *bag*. You can only speak figuratively if you claim to have *bagged* a rhinoceros or lion. A *bag* of partridges etc. indicates how many were killed by the hunter in a day. Some allusive military use of killing humans:
    We've bagged quite a few snipers. (J. Major, 1999—explaining that British soldiers in Bosnia were not fired on because they shot those who targeted them)

bag⁴ a prison for those captured in war
Perhaps from BAG³, and usually in the phrase, *in the bag*, confined in a camp for prisoners-of-war.

baggage *obsolete* a prostitute
Formerly in standard English, a worthless person, male or female. Shakespeare uses the euphemism in one of his more complex sexual puns:
    No barricado for a belly know't;
    It will let in and out the enemy,
    With bag and baggage. (*The Winter's Tale*)

bagged *American* drunk
From BAG³? You certainly may feel like death later.

bagman someone employed in a taboo activity
Originally a tramp, with his bag of belongings over his shoulder. Now a passer of bribes, a person who distributes narcotics illegally, etc.:
    'Shri Adam Zogoiby', who had allegedly been the 'bagman' in the affair, carrying suitcases containing huge sums of used, out-of-sequence banknotes to the private residences of several of the nation's most prominent men, and then, as he subtly put it in his evidence, 'accidentally forgetting' them there. (Rushdie, 1995—in Indira Gandhi's India, not all those bribed were men)

bagnio *obsolete* a brothel
The common bathing imagery, because that was where prostitutes were available.

bags trousers
An abbreviation of *leg-bags* and a survival from the 19th-century taboo on trousers.

bait and switch obtaining investment funds by deceit
Financial jargon:
> The phenomenon has been described by some market participants as 'bait and switch' where banks win mandates offering certain terms which are subsequently changed because they are unachievable. (*Daily Telegraph*, 6 July 2001—but normally not after just one month, as in the case reported)

bake to kill
The culinary imagery seems inappropriate:
> All he had left to hope for was the governor, who as a rule didn't issue clemency to folks who had baked half a dozen of his constituents. (King, 1996)

baker flying *American* menstruating
The red quartermaster (or baker) flag is flown when a ship is loading fuel or ammunition, warning other craft to stand clear.

balance of mind disturbed temporarily insane
Legal jargon, especially of suicides where people want to bury the corpse in consecrated ground, or merely to reject the probability that someone had been driven to suicide as a rational choice:
> The verdict of the coroner was that he took his life while the balance of his mind was disturbed. I know little of my son's mind but I reject the comfortable euphemism. (P. D. James, 1972)

bale out (of a male) to urinate
Like the removal of water from small boats.

ball to copulate with
Of either sex, probably punning on the slang meaning, an orgy.

balls the testicles
Common male usage. Also used of courage, of either sex despite the physiological inaccuracy.

bamboo curtain the censorship and other restrictions in China to limit knowledge of and contacts with foreigners
The Russian *Iron Curtain* in eastern form:
> I had always understood that Western films were kept well away from the People's Republic to make sure no one ever got a hint of the life enjoyed on the affluent side of the bamboo curtain. (Dalrymple, 1989, after watching *Dr No* with Tibetan, Chinese, and Ulgar subtitles in Kashgar)

bamboozled *American* drunk
Literally, hoaxed, and perhaps suggesting that you have been deceived in liquor.

banana *American* do not allow any development here
The acronym of *Build Absolutely Nothing Anywhere Near Anyone*, and equivalent to the British Nimby—*Not In My Backyard*.
In American slang, a *banana* is also a penis, and may be said to have been *peeled* by copulation.

banana republic a poor and possibly corrupt country
A derogatory expression to describe those whose economies may appear to depend on the fruit as a main crop.

banana skin a potentially embarrassing or dangerous situation
Alluding to the supposed tendency of pedestrians to fall over after slipping on those discarded in the street. Journalistic jargon, mainly used of politicians but sometimes of other threatened species:
> Townsend, the Irish captain, is aware of the potential banana skin that awaits his side. (*Daily Telegraph*, 24 June 1994—it had to be a large specimen to threaten the entire soccer team, which did indeed slip, losing its match against the Mexicans)

bananas mentally disturbed
Probably because the fruit is favoured by monkeys. The phrase is often used to refer to mild hysteria.

bandwagon a cause or chance for profit which attracts opportunists
Literally, a vehicle carrying musicians in a circus parade.
A *band-wagoner* is an opportunist:
> ... sufficiently politically confused to rank either as a bandwagoner or a half-baked pain in the neck. (P. Scott, 1973, writing of Ghandi in 1943)

bang a taboo activity
The imagery is from the violence. Thus to *bang*, of a male, is to copulate, a *bang* is a single act of copulation, a *gang-bang* is a rape committed by more than one man at the same time, and a *bang-tail* was at one time a prostitute.
A *bang* may also be an ingestion of narcotics illegally, a pun perhaps on HIT[4]. *Bang and biff*, syphilis, is rhyming slang.

bang up to imprison
From the slamming of the door:
> Bang me up again, he thinks. Prison's the place where you go when you don't want to make decisions. (le Carré, 1996)

bank *obsolete* to fail in business
The *bank* was the bench on which Lombard money-lenders conducted their business.

It was turned over—*rupted*—if they failed to meet their commitments. In the late 19th century banks were failing regularly and the phrase was still in use.

A *banker* was a bankrupt, which seems odd to us today when it is the bankers who do most of the bankrupting of others.

bar a place for the sale and consumption of alcohol

A plank was used both as a counter and a barrier, giving the world perhaps its most multinational word. A *bar-fly* is a drunkard. However, *bar steward* is a term of personal abuse, for *bastard*.

bar girl *American* a prostitute

She seeks custom in bars. The shortened form, *B girl*, may allude to the fact that she may not merit an 'A' rating in her profession.

Barclays *British* an act of masturbation by a male

Rhyming slang on *Barclays Bank*, WANK. Noteworthy, among many similar vulgarisms, because it was used by the comedian Kenneth Williams in his diaries.

bareback copulating without a contraceptive

The common equestrian imagery, but this time without a saddle.

Men or women can be *bareback riders*.

barker *American* a handgun

Neither a fairground tout nor a dog, but from the noise.

barking mad

From canine behaviour.

A cockney may in similar fashion describe another as *East Ham*, which is *one stop before Barking* on the London tube railway network.

barley associated with drunkenness

From the grain used in making Scotch whisky. In obsolete use a *barley-cap* or *barley-king* was a drunkard and *barley-fever* intoxication. *John Barleycorn*, sometimes knighted, is still whisky:

I turn myself over to a higher power, LNU, who'll keep me safe from John Barleycorn. (Turow, 1993—*LNU* is an imaginary person, *Last Name Unknown* in police jargon)

barrack-room lawyer an opinionated but well-informed know-all

Usually an old soldier who combines knowledge of army regulations with experience and bloody-mindedness. In America also as *barracks lawyer* and in the navy as *ship's lawyer* or *sea-lawyer*.

barrel-house *American* a brothel

Originally a cheap saloon, especially in New Orleans, where the intoxicants were served from barrels.

base born *obsolete* illegitimate

Nor merely of humble parentage in the days when primogeniture was paramount:

One Sarah Gore came to me this morning and brought me an Instrument from the Court of Wells to perform publick penance next Sunday at C. Cary Church for having a base born child, which I am to administer to her publickly next Sunday after divine Service. (Bush, 1997, quoting James Woodforde, 3 January 1768: had the practice continued, modern churchgoers would sit down late to luncheon of a Sunday)

basement *American* a lavatory

It is frequently located there in shopping malls, public rooms, etc. Usually in the query 'Where's the basement?', which may be made in a building manifestly devoid of a lower level.

baser needs the desire to copulate

The dated assumption was that regular sexual activity is good for a man's health but is morally reprehensible:

What you need is a sensible wife to take care of your baser needs. (Sharpe, 1982)

bash (the) working as a prostitute

Usually in the phrase *on the bash*. From the slang meaning of *to bash*, to walk or march, as in the army *square-bashing*.

To *bash the bishop* was not to grant ecclesiastical sexual favours but to masturbate, of a male, from the likeness of the flaccid penis to a chessman.

basket¹ a term of vulgar abuse

It sounds like the taboo *bastard*. Used only between males figuratively and often jocularly. In obsolete British use, the punning *basket-making* was extramarital copulation by a male.

basket² the male genitalia seen through tight trousers:

Homosexual jargon.

basket case a person, institution, or society incapable of self-reliance

The *basket* is the container from which food might be charitably distributed to the hungry. The phrase is applied to indigent people, to failing companies, and to poverty-stricken nations.

basted *American* drunk

Literally, being roasted and periodically

covered with molten fat. The common culinary imagery.

bat a drunken carouse
A *bat* was a drunkard some time before we though of him as a player of cricket or baseball. The use survives in the phrases *on the bat*, on a carouse, and *over the bat*, drunk.

bathroom *American* a lavatory
Among the most enduring of the many euphemisms which associate washing with urination and defecation:
> ...asked where the bathroom was. The restroom was filthy. (Diehl, 1978—and what was the lavatory like?)

For the Nazis, the *bath-house* was the chamber into which they drove naked victims for mass murder on the pretext that they were being deloused.

bats in the belfry mental abnormality
The phrase covers anything from absent-mindedness through eccentricity to madness, when the wild ideas may circle in your head like the mammals in the church tower at twilight. *Bats* and *batty* are used as adjectives.

battered *American* drunk
Covered with *batter* before being fried, or feeling roughly handled? Probably a bit of both, with the culinary imagery uppermost.

batting and bowling *British* having both heterosexual and homosexual tastes
The imagery is from the game of cricket, in which most players tend to specialize in one or the other. See also ALL-ROUNDER.

battle fatigue the inability to continue fighting
Not just tiredness from missed sleep or overexertion.
In wartime it is difficult to distinguish between psychological illness, idleness, and cowardice.

bawd the keeper of a brothel
Standard English, from the original meaning, dirt.
Bawdy has many of the meanings of DIRTY. A *bawdy house* is a brothel.

bay window a fat person's stomach
Literally, the architectural feature of a house which protrudes from the lower floor only:
> The big man folds his arms protectively over a bay window girded in a filthy apron. (Vanderhaeghe, 1997)

bazaar gains *obsolete* riches improperly acquired by British officials of the East India Company

It was fortunate for the predators that the Indians kept their wealth in portable items such as jewels and precious metals:
> ...requiring him to send me a monthly *nerak* (tariff rate) in order to set some bounds on his enormous and undue bazaar gains. (Dalrymple, 2002, quoting from a report of 1801)

BCE *British* prior to the year zero
The letters stand for *Before Common Era* and seek to avoid giving offence to those professing other than the Christian faith.

be excused to go to the lavatory
No more than politely to obtain release from the company of others. Perhaps the first thing we learned when we started school.

be nice to to copulate with
Prostitutes' jargon and see NICE TIME:
> Wouldn't you like to be nice to Dasha? (Amis, 1980—Dasha was not what we would call a *nice girl*)

be with to copulate with
Of either sex, usually extramaritally and in the past tense.
> The girl talked. We know you've been with her. (Mailer, 1965)

Also, of males, as *be into*. *Been there* is a claim by a male to have copulated with a specified female.

bean counter an accountant
Hardly a euphemism but more a term of disparagement of those in a profession which, like the law, is regarded by others with a mixture of fear, envy, and derision.

bear[1] to be pregnant or to give birth
The standard English use makes us forget that anyone who lifts up a baby *bears* a child and is of *child-bearing* age.

bear[2] *American* a policeman
Threat and violence are characteristics which the quadruped and the officer of the law are thought to have in common. Among the many derivatives, we may note the following: *bear bait*, a speeding motorist; *bear cage*, a police station; *bear in the air*, a police helicopter, especially one on traffic duty; *bear bite*, a ticket for speeding; *bear trap*, a police radar operation (in which illogically the *bears* do the trapping); *lady bear*, a policewoman.

beard a person acting as a decoy
The derivation is from the false *beard* worn as a disguise, despite which the use is of both sexes:
> 'He's the beard.' That's what they call the other man who pretends to be the lover. (Sanders, 1981)

She was a beard for Mark, to keep Robbie unsuspecting about who was really informing on him. (Turow, 1999)

beast to copulate with
When the male approaches a kneeling female as would a quadruped. The *beast with two backs*, which may be *made* or *played*, is copulation with the parties facing each other, forming the *two-backed beast* and engaged in the *two-backed game*. *Beastliness* in the 19th century meant copulation, at a time when it was not thought proper for a woman to relish the activity. Now it means masturbation, which is hardly fair, as most animals don't masturbate.

beat the gong *American* to smoke opium
From the oriental association of ideas. A *beat pad* is where communal smoking takes place, now usually of marijuana.

beat the gun to copulate with a proposed spouse before marriage
The *gun* is the starter's pistol. Used specifically of conception before marriage even if only evident afterwards. Also as *beat the starter*; and see CHEAT THE STARTER.

beat your meat (of a male) to masturbate
Also as *beat your dummy* or *beat off*. However to have a *beat on* is merely to have an erection of the penis.

beau a woman's male sexual partner
Not necessarily beautiful, but paying court to her and, especially if she is married to another, implying that she has a sexual relationship with him.

beaver the female genitals viewed sexually
From the slang meaning, a beard, whence the pubic hair.

bed¹ childbirth
The *bed* is the symbol of birth, marriage, and copulation. To be *brought to bed* is standard English for the delivery of a child.

bed² to copulate with
As in Shakespeare's 'Woo her, wed her and bed her'. (*Taming of the Shrew*). In modern use to *bed* may apply to either sex although men tend to *bed* women and women to *bed with* men.
Bedtime business is not sleep but copulation, as is *bedwork*. *Bed-hopping* is promiscuity and *bed and breakfast* may indicate overnight extra-marital copulation.
A sexually attractive woman may be described by men as *beddable* or *bedworthy* and, if she is thought to be seeking a male's attention, to have *bedroom eyes*.

A *bedfellow*, literally someone with whom you share a bed, whence a close companion or comrade, is a partner in copulation.

bedewed (of a female) sweating
A lady is not supposed to sweat in public or, in some circles, at all.

bedwetting involuntarily urinating in a bed
This standard English makes us forget that there are many other ways of making a bed damp.

beef a person or the genitalia of a male viewed sexually
Beef has most of the sexual meanings of MEAT¹ and MEAT². Thus it may mean a prostitute, the penis, or copulation.

beefcake a male seen as a sexual object
The derivation is from the former meaning, a picture of a male for erotic female gratification, the converse of CHEESECAKE. Both heterosexual and homosexual use:
... the bellboys were choice beefcake—dressed as native bearers, bare-chested, in loincloths and sandals. (Anonymous, 1996)

been having urinated
Polite usage and effectively the past tense of GO³:
Hari's realization that I hadn't 'been' rather cast a blight on the evening. (P. Scott, 1973)
Occasionally also of defecation.

befuddled slightly drunk
Literally, confused:
I drank a little and became befuddled but no more. (Channon, 1993—diary entry of 11 November 1936)

behind the buttocks
It could be any part of you, from your head to your heels.
Occasionally used for the anus, in a non-sexual sense or homosexually.

behind the eight ball *American* in serious difficulty
From a potentially losing position in the game of pool.

bell money *obsolete Scottish* a levy on a bridegroom at a wedding
Not a corruption of the more common *ball money*, which was demanded by spectators at weddings ostensibly so that they could buy a ball, but payment demanded by the ringers. In either case the donation was spent in the inn. This is an example of several ways in which onlookers preyed on bridegrooms long before the advent of the photographer and the outside caterer.

belly plea a claim that the accused is pregnant

A pregnant woman could not be hanged and therefore so advised the judge if she were convicted on a capital charge:

My mother pleaded her belly, and being found quick with child ... (Defoe, 1721)

To *slink a (great) belly away* was to have an induced abortion:

Lady Castelmayne, who he believes hath lately slunk a great belly away ... (Pepys, 1664—at least it saved Charles II lumbering the British with another dukedom)

belly up bankrupt

The phrase is used of companies, with piscine imagery.

bellyful of lead see LEAD

below medium height short

Of male stature, where tallness may be equated with manliness, and a favourite among the writers of obituaries.

below stairs[1] *British* employed as a domestic servant

The construction of town houses afforded day accommodation for the servants in cellars or semi-basements and sleeping space in the attics, communication taking place through the *back stairs* of gossip fame:

To have one affair might be manageable: but to bed so many, and to stoop below the stairs, and then get caught, was a bed too far. (Parris, 1995, writing of the Victorian literary figure Charles Dilke)

below stairs[2] the genitalia

A variant of DOWN BELOW:

The wretched bitch was halfway down my throat and rummaging below stairs with an expert hand. (Fraser, 1994)

below the salt socially inferior

The salt, being then a scarce commodity needed by all, was put in the middle of the dining table in medieval times. The diners were seated in descending social order from the head of the table:

... in comparison with other professions— the Church, Education, the Law, the higher levels of journalism, and the BBC—I am afraid it must be admitted that advertising sits rather below the salt. (E. S. Turner, 1952)

The saline distinction usually only works against you but:

... it's a big dinner and you'll be well above the salt. (N. Mitford, 1960)

belt a taboo article or activity

From the slang meaning, a blow. It may refer to copulation, illegal narcotics, alcohol, etc. Thus a *belt* may be a portion of spirits and a *belter* a prostitute.

The *Washington Beltway*, or ring road, is used for 'government' because of the area which it surrounds, as *Westminster* and *Whitehall* are in Britain, but without any suggestion that those working within it are addicted to drink or narcotics, or sexually promiscuous. A *Beltway Bandit* is not a highwayman but a former government employee engaged as a lobbyist.

bench to cause to withdraw from active participation

It is where the reserve players sit waiting for the coach to send them on to the field of play and where they end up if substituted. Some figurative use:

... if I say you're benched, you're benched. (Deighton, 1982—a commander was grounding a pilot)

A *bench-warmer* is a less competent performer.

bend *obsolete* to drink intoxicants to excess

Probably a shortened form of *bend the elbow*.

A *bender* is still a drunken carouse and *bent* means drunk.

bend sinister an imputation of illegitimacy

The heraldic *bend sinister* runs from the upper right to the lower left corner of a coat of arms. To suggest that someone, whether or not entitled to a coat of arms, has a *bend sinister*, is to imply that he is actually or figuratively a bastard.

bend the rules to act illegally

The implication is that the *rules* were unfair and the infringement insignificant. Less often as *bend the regulations*.

benders *obsolete* the legs

From one of the 19th-century taboos, especially in New England, where even tables had *benders*.

bends (the) menstruation

Literally, decompression sickness and its painful symptoms:

She was having her monthly period, she said, a real bastard, cramps, the bends, you name it. (le Carré, 1986)

benefit state aid paid to the needy

Literally, an advantage. *Benefit* was formerly the specific advantage of being a member of a fund from which you could draw if you were ill. If the illness lasted too long, or you failed to keep up your subscriptions to the fund, you went *out of benefit*. The modern use is of regular or ad hoc payments:

Jobless CSE candidates 'should be given £13 benefit'. (*Daily Telegraph*, December 1980)

benevolence *obsolete* an arbitrary tax
Literally, generosity. English monarchs extracted such taxation from their rich subjects under the guise of loans which were described as *benevolences* but never repaid. The 1689 Bill of Rights brought this method of taxation to an end, until revived in the Second World War with a tax called the *Post-War Credit*, which was eventually repaid in a depreciated currency without interest.

bent¹ dishonest
Not straight, as in the punning *bent copper*. It may also refer to something stolen:
Having sold a stolen or *bent* car to a complainant...(Lavine, 1930)

bent² (of a male) homosexual
As different from *straight*, heterosexual.

Best Brian a devoted, industrious, and uncritical servant
Doing the donkey work for his master:
Branson regarded his finance director as Best Brian, a reliable acolyte. (*Sunday Telegraph*, 24 September 2000—his name was in fact Trevor)

bestiality copulation of a human with an animal
Literally, qualities or behaviour appertaining to a beast. Legal jargon for such a relationship with a mammal quadruped of either sex. In the case of *Rex v. Brown*, where the accused's amorous attentions were directed towards a duck, he was convicted of an attempt at bestiality only, despite achieving his desires, and left to reflect on the axiom that hard cases make bad law.

bestow your enthusiasm on (of a female) to copulate with promiscuously
So acting without payment:
Swiftly, concealed from the puritan gaze of 'Master', several of them acquired girlfriends there, eager to bestow their enthusiasm on the liberating British. (Horne, 1994, writing of staff officers in Belgium in 1945—*Master* was Montgomery)

bestseller a book of which the first impression is not remaindered
Publishers' puff—there could only be one *best* in any given period. An *international bestseller* is a novel set with American spelling. *Instant bestseller* indicates an expensive pre-release advertising campaign.

bet the farm *American* to make a risky decision or investment

From the possibility of losing your property and your livelihood. See BUY IT for *buy the farm*.

betray to copulate with a third party while married
Literally, to prove false:
He swiftly confessed, saying that he 'betrayed the covenants of marriage'. (*Daily Telegraph*, 29 September 1998—the adultery of a pastor who was a spiritual adviser to Clinton had been publicized)
In modern use, one spouse *betrays* the other. Formerly a male might *betray* a single woman by copulating with her with her consent.

better country (a) life after death
The belief or hope of those who profess certain religions. Also as a *better state* (which here is not synonymous with *country*) or a *better world*.

between **shows** involuntarily unemployed
Theatrical jargon, not used of those rehearsing for a new part. Also as *between jobs*, especially for those who do not tread the boards:
'What do you do?'...'I'm between jobs.'
'Are you an actor?'...'No.' (Hall, 1988)

between the legs on or around the genitalia
The term may be used to denote the location in male or female of anything from prickly heat to amorous fondling.
Between the thighs means copulating with a female:
A man can learn more between the thighs of a good woman than he ever needs to know. (Sharpe, 1974—academically and anatomically incorrect for all its vivid imagery)

between the sheets copulating
Or, for Shakespeare, '...twixt my sheets, Has done my office'. (*Othello*)

beverage an intoxicant
Originally, any kind of drink, and then standard American English for any alcoholic drink served in a bar or *beverage room* by a waiter or *beverage host* (or *hostess*). In Britain, shortened to *bevvy* (with *bevvied* meaning well supplied with intoxicants) or *bevy*.

beyond help dead
Not just out of reach:
I was with him in moments, but he was beyond all help. He had suffered a massive coronary. (Major, 1999—a member died while speaking in the House of Commons)

beyond the blanket conceived outside marriage
This reference to bedclothes is less common than WRONG SIDE OF THE BLANKET and may be used of someone conceived outside, but born within, wedlock.

bibi a prostitute
In Hindi *bibi* means lady, and was used in 19th-century India to describe a white woman married to a white man:
    The *bibi*, or white wife, was a great rarity; but the *bubu*, or native wife, was an accepted institution. (Blanch, 1954)
In later British army use, a *bibi*, *grass bibi*, or *bidi*, was an Indian prostitute.

bicycle see TOWN BIKE

biddy a sexually complaisant woman
In 19th-century England *biddy* meant a young prostitute, in Ireland a chicken, and everywhere, including America, it was a short form of the Irish name *Bridget*, at a time when many maidservants were Irish:
    ... for a pound of sausages you could find a biddy who would actually chuck her old man out of bed and send him to sit downstairs till you'd finished. (Seymour, 1980, writing of Germany immediately after the Second World War)

big pregnant
A shortened form of *big with child*, but also used before the swelling is visible. A *big belly* indicated pregnancy.

big animal *American* a bull
The word *bull* was taboo in polite society, from its sexual overtones. The fastidious had a plentiful choice of euphemisms, including *brute*, *cow brute*, *gentleman cow*, *gentleman ox*, *he-cow*, *he-thing*, *male cow*, *man cow*, *seed-ox*, and *stock beast*.

big-boned fat
The phrase is used of children and adults, seeking to suggest that their frame needs the extra padding.
    ... in his beefy adolescence his mother had tactfully described him as 'big-boned', though 'burly' was how he now liked to see himself. (Boyd, 1981)

big C (the) *American* cancer
The dread affliction which may lead to the BIG D.

big D (the) death
Also as the *big jump*, or, for military men, the *big stand-easy*.

big house *American* a prison
Usually, as with *big pasture* or *big school*, for male convicts.

The *little school* is usually for women or children prisoners.

big jobs defecation
Nursery usage, sometimes shortened to *bigs* or *biggies*.
LITTLE JOBS is urination.

big prize (the) copulation
A male may hope to win it after lesser awards during courtship:
    ... allowing moist liberties but with steel-trap relentlessness withholding the big prize. (Styron, 1976)

bijou inconveniently small
Estate agents' jargon which seeks to persuade you that a minute dwelling is a jewel.

bikini wax a procedure for the removal of women's pubic hair
It is the skin which is waxed, not the bathing costume. The *bikini line* is the lower extremity of the garment below which hair should not protrude:
    Removes extremely short hair ... and is gentle enough to use on the bikini line. (*Daily Telegraph*, 28 June 2003—advertisement for an electric razor)

bill a policeman
Derived perhaps from the weapon once carried by constables, but there is probably a simpler etymology.
Also as *old Bill*, which may refer to an individual or to the force generally:
    He was in Borstal for robbery, involved in many fights, acquitted of a stabbing murder in '79 and of knifing Ol' Bill in '83. (Fiennes, 1996)

Billingsgate foul language
The language was once used by the women sellers of fish, rather than by the male porters, in the London market which was closed in 1982. According to Dryden, 'Parnassus spoke the cant of Billingsgate', and in modern use:
    ... his ears had surely overflowed with such billingsgate. (Styron, 1976)

bimbo a sexually complaisant female
From the Italian, meaning little (male) child. She is not a prostitute but may be prepared to exploit her youth and good looks:
    But why should a bimbo file cause such alarm? (Evans-Pritchard, 1997—the list was of women supposed to have caught the eye of Governor Clinton)

bin an institution for the insane
Literally, a container and a shortened form of the slang *loony bin*.

Bin-raiding is not what bears do in American parks or foxes in English suburbia but searching by criminals through garbage for discarded vouchers or other documents containing confidential financial information.

bind to cause to suffer from constipation
Literally, to tie fast:

Up and took phisique … only to loose me, for I am bound. (Pepys, 1662)

A *bind* is not a period of constipation but a nuisance or tedious obligation.

binge to go on a drunken carouse
Literally, to soak.
In modern use, mainly as a noun, which can cover overeating as well as drunken excess.

bint a prostitute
The British army picked up the Arabic word for young woman and carried it across the world.

biographic leverage blackmail
The jargon of espionage and American politics.

biological clock referring to the increasing difficulty of women conceiving due to ageing
A phenomenon caused by delayed marriage and female careers:

'But if you want babies, Francesca …' Again the brave laugh. 'Sure, the biological clock is ticking away.' (Read, 1995—Francesca was unmarried and in her midthirties)

bird¹ a young female companion
The common and venerable avian imagery. *Bird* used to mean a girl in Middle English but this sense fell out of use until revived in modern times. In America, a *bird* may be a prostitute, working in a *bird-cage*, or brothel.
In male vulgar use the *bird* may also be the vagina, and the *bird's nest*, pubic hair.
Confusingly, the American *bird circuit* is an area containing saloons frequented by homosexuals, where the game is the cock rather than the hen.

bird² imprisonment
Derived from the caging. Usually in the phrase to *do bird*, to be imprisoned.

bird dog *American* someone working for a criminal
Literally, the retriever of game. Some figurative use:

Your bird dog, the Senator. (Chandler, 1939—of a dishonest politician)

To *bird-dog* is so to act, and specifically to retrieve stolen goods or information:

So he would be bird-dogging occasionally and bring you things? (Colodny & Gettlin, 1991—a Yeoman copied secret documents and passed them to his superior)

To confuse matters, in horse-racing jargon, a *bird dog* follows the betting pattern of a professional or dishonest gambler, who may have inside knowledge or have arranged for interference with the runners.
It may also refer to a police detective who tracks his quarry down.

birth control the prevention of conception
Standard English, although the phrase would better describe stratagems by midwives to prevent the arrival of babies at weekends or other times inconvenient to themselves.

birthday suit (your) nakedness
What you were born in. Also as *birthday attire*, *gear*, or the obsolete *finery*.

bisexual having both homosexual and heterosexual tastes
In biology, it means having both sexes in the same plant or animal. Often shortened to *bi*.

bit¹ a woman viewed sexually by a male
A synonym of PIECE¹ but not used of a spouse. Seldom of a prostitute.
Normally in a phrase such as *a bit of all right* (or *alright* for the less literate), *arse*, *ass*, *crumpet*, *fluff*, *goods*, *hot stuff*, *how's your father*, *jam*, *meat*, *muslin*, *skirt*, *stuff*, *you-know-what*, etc., most of which are elaborated under those headings.
A *bit on the side* is a regular sexual partner other than your spouse, adverting to the *side*, or additional, plate served with a formal meal.

bit² (a) copulation
It can refer to either sex:

… taking a little bit now and then from her husband's valet. (Condon, 1966)

Also as a *bit of you know what*. A *bit of the other* is not a homosexual encounter but copulation, usually with other than a normal partner.

bit missing (a) of low intelligence
Not an absent girlfriend.

bitch *American* a male homosexual
The word is used in homosexual jargon of someone thought to be as spiteful or vindictive as a woman so offensively described. In obsolete use, a *bitch* was a prostitute and to *bitch* was to visit brothels.

bite the bullet to take a difficult or costly decision
A soldier being flogged was given a bullet to bite to prevent his crying out in pain. Today only metaphorical *bullets* are bitten.

bite the dust to die
A synonym of LICK THE DUST, and usually of
violent death, although not necessarily after
falling from your horse in a Western movie.
Also in figurative use:
> ...Jerry will unleash some devil's device
> and another brilliant novelist will bite the
> dust. (Thwaite, 1992, quoting a letter from
> Philip Larkin written in 1944)

black associated with illegality
Describing things better kept concealed. Thus
the *black economy* is the sum of goods and
services provided without official cognizance
or the payment of tax; *black fish* are those
landed commercially additional to any permitted quota; the *black market* deals in goods
which are in short supply, rationed, or stolen;
black money is the proceeds of vice, especially
the sale of illegal narcotics and prostitution,
and may be specified as *black dollars, pounds,
euros*, etc., although we no longer enjoy the
punning *black marks*.

black-and-white *American* a police car
From the distinctive paintwork.
The *black-and-tans* were the inexperienced,
ineffective, and detested police recruited by
the British-controlled Dublin government to
augment or replace the Irish constabulary
which, through sympathy and intimidation,
was unable or unwilling to maintain order
and suppress dissent in provinces other than
Ulster during the uprising against British rule.

black bag (associated with) an illicit inquiry
Usually relating to telephone tapping or the
robbery of documents, from the holdall in
which tools are carried.

black dog (the) melancholia
Black for the negative aspect, but the canine
seems to be unfairly impugned:
> But what will you do to keep away the *black
> dog* that worries you at home? (J. Boswell,
> 1791, quoting from a letter by Dr Johnson
> dated 1779)

black hole *obsolete* a prison
So called because it was unlit, insanitary, and
below ground. Sometimes shortened to *hole*.
Many British towns had one, although in the
days when British children were taught
imperial history, the only *black hole* they were
told about was the Calcutta version of 1756.
For Farmer & Henley in 1905, the *black hole*
was 'Cheltenham, from the number of Anglo-
Indians who live there'. These 'Anglo-Indians'
were not of mixed race but white people,
often with ruddy complexions, who had
served or worked in India.

black job a funeral
The darkness of death.

black lad the devil
The Prince of Darkness entered a house by the
chimney in the days of coal fires and soot.
Also as the *black gentleman, man, prince, Sam,
spy*, etc.

black smoke opium
Also as *black pills* or *stuff*.

black stuff (the) *Irish* stout
Usually Guinness, but people also relish
porter produced by Messrs Murphy and
Beamish. If mixed with champagne it becomes *black velvet*.

black up (of a white actor) to take the role
of a non-white character by applying
dark make-up
Unacceptable today on several counts, especially as being seen to mitigate against the
employment of black actors:
> This means that actors should be cast
> because of their talent. But this policy has
> been refined. We do not believe that white
> actors should black up. (*Daily Telegraph*, 12
> August 1996, quoting Martin Brown, a
> union official)

black velvet a dark-skinned prostitute
Originally used by white British soldiers in
India, but the pun became more widely
accepted:
> In sophisticated circles *Black Velvet* is a mix
> of champagne and Guinness. But in the
> outback the phrase has a different meaning
> derived from an obscure Ugandan dialect.
> (*Private Eye*, January 1982—see UGANDA for
> the obscure in-joke)

blackball *obsolete* to steal
Not from the rejection of a candidate for
membership but from the *Black Ball* line of
steamers between New York and Liverpool
'known all over the world for the cruelty of
the officers and the thieving propensities of
its sailors.' (Farmer & Henley, 1905)

blackbird *obsolete* a black African slave
conveyed to America
The jargon of those engaged in the TRIANGU-
LAR TRADE.
To *blackbird* was to be a slave-trader. A *black-
birder* was a ship carrying slaves or someone
who transported or dealt in them. The victims
might also be referred to as *black cattle, hides,
pigs*, or *sheep*. In Polynesia, a *blackbird* was an
indigenous indentured labourer whence, as a
verb, to kidnap, that being a customary form
of recruitment.

blackmail extortion by threats
Mail was a tribute or tax, becoming *black* when
paid by a Lowland Scot to a Highlander.
Standard English. A century ago Dr Wright in
EDD was so rash or naïve as to say the use was
obsolete.

bladdered drunk
And still retaining the fluid ingested, it would
appear.

blank[1] a mild oath
A blank space may be left in print for the
taboo word.
Also, adjectivally, as *blanking* and *blankety-
blank*.

blank[2] *American* to kill
The victim is sent into a void:
    ...none of whom seemed particularly
    distressed by the sudden blanking of Victor
    Maitland. (Sanders, 1977)

blast[1] a mild oath
Perhaps from the obsolete meaning, lightning, as with the German *blitz(en)*.

blast[2] *American* to kill by shooting
Referring to the discharge of the weapon or
the blowing away.

blast[3] an intoxicant or illegal narcotic
From the sensation induced.
The verbal form is only used of the ingestion
of narcotics but *blasted* can refer to drunkenness or narcosis.

blazes hell
The eternal fires burn sinners, without consuming the body or making it insensible to
pain.

bleed to extort money from on a regular
basis
Like a 19th-century surgeon, but not for the
good of the victim. The obsolete British *bleed
the monkey* was to steal rum from the *monkey*,
or mess tub.

bleeding a mild oath
For the once taboo *bloody*.

bleeding heart a person who ostenta-
tiously expresses concern about or
seeks to relieve the suffering of others
The dividing line between a *bleeding heart* and
a DO-GOODER is not wide or distinctly marked:
    I'm not a bleeding heart racially, believing
    in universal brotherhood. (Naipaul, 1989)

bleep an obscenity or a taboo word or expression
An electronic note is introduced by broad-

casters etc. to replace obscene or offensive
matter in a recording.

blighty a serious but not fatal wound
Blighty, from the Hindi *bilayati* meaning
foreign, became their home country for
British servicemen abroad, and not just those
serving in India.
In the First World War a wound which caused
repatriation was thought by some to be preferable to remaining to be killed in the trenches.

blind a drunken carouse
The use seems to pre-date the cliché *blind
drunk* or its Scottish form *blind-fou*.

blind copy a document of which a copy is
given to a third party without the person
to whom it is addressed being informed
Good manners suggest that the addressee
should be told of other recipients. Less often
as *silent copy*.

blind pig *American* an unlicensed place
for the consumption of intoxicants
Hidden from the *pigs*, or police, perhaps?

blindside *American* to rob, cheat, or catch
at a disadvantage
From the jargon of basketball and not just
approaching from beyond peripheral vision.

blip off *American* to kill
Blips indicate that an oscilloscope or other
monitoring equipment is working. They vanish if the instrument malfunctions or is
switched off.

blitzed drunk
The victim is devastated, as was England
during the German Blitz.
Despite escaping the attentions of the Luft-
waffe, more Americans than British use the
expression.

block out to kill
The imagery is from the word-processor or
computer, where matter can be made in-
stantly to disappear from the screen or file,
sometimes inadvertently:
    I'm aware of his CV...That's why I wanted
    him blocked out. (Strong, 1997)

blockbuster[1] *American* a real-estate dealer
who induces whites to sell their homes
through threat of other racial groups
moving into the area
The use puns on the Second World War
bomb. In this case, the *block* of real estate
occupied mainly by white families may be
more valuable if redeveloped.

blockbuster² a novel which is expected to sell well
Publishers' jargon. See also BESTSELLER.

blocking detachment a unit positioned to stop retreat or desertion
A characteristic of the Red Army between 1942 and 1945 and of the Wehrmacht in the closing stages of the Second World War.

blood menstruation
Or the first onset:
My blood, for instance, it came late, as if worried it might upset things.
(R. Thompson, 1996, of a tomboy)
Bloody may mean menstruating, either *tout court* and in various phrases such as *the bloody flag is up*.

blood disease *obsolete* syphilis
The condition was doubly taboo as being incurable and contracted in a shameful manner. Less often as *blood poison*.

blood money extortion
In standard usage, a reward for bringing about another's death or compensation paid to surviving relatives in respect of a killing:
...collecting 'blood money', that is, shaking down prostitutes, poor peddlers, &c. (Lavine, 1930)

blooming a mild oath
Used for the taboo *bloody*.

blot (out) to kill
Literally, to eradicate:
The Emperor left here for Ethiopia today, flying to the frontier, and then in by ground. I hope he doesn't get blotted. (Mockler, 1984—in January 1941 Haile Selassie was as much at risk from his subjects as from the Italians who were being defeated)

blow¹ orally to excite the genitals of another
Homosexually or heterosexually, the operation being described as a *blow job*.
In America a *blow* may still be a prostitute, perhaps a shortened form of the obsolete *blowen* rather than one offering non-vaginal sex, and to *blow* or *blow off* was to ejaculate semen.

blow² (off) to fart
A common vulgarism. To *blow a raspberry* is to make a farting noise through the lips, being rhyming slang on *raspberry tart*.

blow³ to boast
Seldom in modern use *tout court* but found in phrases such as *blow your own horn*, or *blow your*

own trumpet.
To *blow smoke* can indicate boasting or giving irrelevant or misleading information, like a ship seeking to cover its withdrawal from an enemy.
A *blowhard* is a braggart or someone who cannot keep a secret:
In a business that attracts pompous blowhards, senators are the crème de la crème. (Mark Steyn in *Daily Telegraph*, 27 July 2004)

blow⁴ a mild oath
Of the same tendency as BLAST¹.

blow⁵ to betray or inform against
Probably a shortened form of *blow cover*, to reveal what was intended to be kept hidden, or of *blow the gaff*, to betray a confidence or secret, the *gaff* being gossip.
To *blow the whistle on* is to reveal embarrassing information about another, often a superior or an official, with imagery from what a referee does after a player commits a foul.

blow⁶ an illegal narcotic
The normal *hitting* imagery but perhaps also alluding to the emission of smoke, as in *blow a stick, Charlie, horse, snow*, etc.

blow a gasket to become mentally deranged
Usually describing a temporary condition, capable of simple repair.

blow away *American* to kill
Usually by gunfire at short range, although the corpse is left for disposal by others:
He got blown away. I went to his funeral. (Sanders, 1977)

blow-in *Irish* a foreigner who meddles in domestic affairs
Used in the South rather than the North:
[Cosgrave] fumed against 'blow-ins'—a jibe apparently aimed at Bruce Arnold, the English-born reporter of the Irish *Independent*. (J. J. Lee, 1989—it was through lying about the tapping of Arnold's telephone that Charles Haughey eventually fell from power)

blow one *American* to serve a glass of draught beer
The bartender either scoops, or very occasionally, *blows off* the froth which results from decanting beer from a pressurized container.

blow the whistle on see BLOW⁵

blue¹ *American* a police officer or prison warder
From the normal colour of the uniform. Also

as a *bluebottle*, *bluebird*, *blue-belly*, *blue jeans*, *blue suit*, or *blue-and-white*. And as an adjective:

> The famous blue wall of silence...Every cop is taught in the academy, keep your mouth shut. (J. Patterson, 2002)

In Britain a *man* (or occasionally *woman*) *in blue* or *bluecoat* is a police officer working out of a *blue lamp*, or police station, named after the standard exterior lit sign.

For the Nazis the *blue police* were thugs enforcing their rule in the occupied territories under the control of the SS. Confederate troops in the Civil War called Northerners *Bluebellies*, again from the colour of their uniform. In return they were called *Greybacks*.

blue² erotic

Probably from the French *bibliothèque bleue*, a collection of seamy works of literature, rather than from the colour of the brimstone which awaits evil-doers.

blue-eyed boy someone favoured by his superiors

He may also be described as FAIR-HAIRED, without actually boasting either of these physiological distinctions.

blue hair an old woman

From the dye.

Blue rinse, in the same sense, is more often used adjectivally.

blue-on-blue shelling or bombing your own troops

The derivation is from the colour marked on military chinagraph maps to indicate your own positions.

Blue Peter British (of education) undisciplined or ineffective

The derivation is from a television programme for children in which, among other activities, they were shown how to construct models out of waste materials. The use is derogatory of primary education where formal instruction in the 'three Rs' may be neglected in favour of letting the children express their personalities through unstructured activities:

> ...marginalised and often trivialised into the so-called *Blue Peter* technology and cardboard engineering. (*Daily Telegraph*, 7 September 1995)

blue ribbon teetotal

It was the favour worn by those who had foresworn the demon drink:

> One minor victory was won by the 'blue ribbon' brigade; in 1917 all bars closed nightly at 6 o'clock. (Sinclair, 1991—when America entered the First World War the brothels were also shut down)

blue ruin obsolete gin

From the colour and the effect on addicts in the 19th century.

Also known as MOTHER'S RUIN.

Blue stone was whisky, and in modern addict slang *blue* is a prefix for a variety of illegal narcotics from the colour of the pills, including *blue devils*, *flags*, *heaven*, *joy*, and *velvet*.

board obsolete (of a male) to copulate with

Allowing Shakespeare to introduce another of his vulgar puns:

> I am sure he is in the fleet. I wish he had boarded me. (*Much Ado About Nothing*)

The American vulgarism to *board a train* was to copulate with a woman in succession to other men.

board lodger obsolete a prostitute

The definition covered two categories: those who obtained their finery in addition to their accommodation from a pimp, and those who worked on their own, paying commission to the bawd of the brothel which they frequented.

boat people political or economic refugees fleeing a country by sea

A phenomenon first noted in Vietnam after the communist victory and now common among those without entry visas sailing from Indonesia for Australia or Africa for Europe.

bobby a policeman

The derivation is from the pet form of the Christian name of Sir Robert Peel, who reorganized first the Dublin police and subsequently, in 1828, those in London.

bobtail American a dishonourable discharge from the army.

The bit about 'honorable and faithful service' was clipped off the bottom of the standard certificate of discharge.

In obsolete use, a *bobtail* was a prostitute, perhaps from her pelvic motion.

bodice-ripper a novel containing pornographic scenes

Usually written by women, and featuring an aggressive male attitude to casual copulation.

bodily functions urination and defecation

The equally important breathing, eating, sweating, etc. do not count.

Bodily wastes are urine and faeces.

body a corpse

It is assumed that life is extinct.

The American *body bag* is a container for the transfer of a corpse, especially of a serviceman who has been killed overseas.

body image physical beauty
Not a portrait, photograph, X-ray, or scan but
the jargon of the beauty parlour or cosmetic
surgeon which avoids saying that the person
paying them is ugly or ageing.

body odour see BO

body rub (a) masturbation by a prostitute
One of the services which may be offered,
usually to males, in a MASSAGE PARLOUR by a
body worker.

body shaper a corset
An invention of advertisers to persuade the
buyer that she (normally) is neither fat nor
buying a corset. Also as *body briefer*, *hugger*,
and *outline*.

boff¹ (of a male) to copulate with
The common violent imagery, from the slang
meaning to hit, rather than a corruption of
buff, to rub.

boff² to fart
Common usage. The etymology is obscure.

bog a lavatory
A shortened form of *bog-house*, from the
marshy ground which might surround it in
the days before modern drainage, the septic
tank, or the cesspit:

At the court held in October 1753…
Edward Clanvill was charged with a 'public
nuisance in emptying a bogg house (privy)
in the street'. (Tyrrell, 1973)

And in modern use:

… been in the bog a long while… What do
you suppose he's doing there? (Theroux,
1979—what indeed?)

bog(e)y an enemy
Literally, a devil, from the apparition which
could frighten you in the nursery and which
might make your horse rear, or *boggle*, by
suddenly appearing in its path. For the Irish
and British, a *bogy* was a policeman. In
modern military jargon a *bog(e)y* is an enemy
aircraft. For children, it's a piece of snot.

boiled *American* drunk
The common culinary imagery.

boiler room an operation for the unscru-
pulous selling of securities
Punning on the intense heat applied. Also as
boiler house or *shop*.

boilerplate excessive disclaimers or provisions
As used in a warship to protect from incoming fire, but here designed to cover lawyers,
accountants, and bankers rather than the

client who pays their fees. *Boilerplate* can also
describe any action where undue caution has
been shown:

… firms should deploy their analysts more
imaginatively than simply producing
another piece of boiler-plate work on BP.
(*Daily Telegraph*, 4 June 2004)

bollocks the testicles
The old variant *ballocks* suggest derivation
from BALLS, of which it is a synonym both
anatomically and figuratively, as a vulgar
denial or riposte.

bolt suddenly leave home, desert a
spouse, or bilk your creditors
Like a runaway horse. In marriage, the *bolter* is
the wife:

Frances [Shand Kydd] was branded a
'bolter', and in a court action in June 1968
lost care and custody of her children. (*Daily
Telegraph*, 4 June 2004)

For *bolt the moon* see MOONLIGHT FLIT.

bombed (out) under the influence of narcotics or alcohol
Either or both.
A *bomb*, *bomber*, or *bombita* is usually a
marijuana cigarette or a dose of cocaine. For
financiers, a *bombed-out* security is one of
doubtful worth.

bondage sexual activity involving physical restraints or abasement
Literally, a condition of slavery or of being
tied up.

bonds of life being gradually dissolved
dying slowly
Bath Abbey, from which this example comes,
offers many delightful morbid evasions in its
epitaphs:

The Bonds of Life being gradually dissolved
She Winged her Flight from this World in
expectation of a better, the 15th January,
1810.

bone¹ *American* to enrich by deceit
In obsolete use, to *bone* was to steal, with the
imagery perhaps of FINGER-BLIGHT or alluding
to the ossivorous delectation of dogs. The
usage may owe something to improving the
edible weight of meat by removing the bone
before sale.

bone² associated with human death
What is eventually left after burial, along with
the teeth, if any. Many obsolete uses such as
bone-house, a coffin; *bone hugging*, carrying a
corpse to a grave; *bone-orchard* or *bone-yard*, a
burial ground; etc.
See also MAKE YOUR BONES.

bone-ache *obsolete* syphilis
Punning perhaps on the symptoms and the *bone*, the penis in old vulgar use.

bonk to copulate
The usual violent imagery. Also as a noun.

booby a mentally ill person
Literally, a fool. A *booby hatch* or *hutch* is an institution for the insane.
The punning American *booby-trap* was, perhaps only ephemerally, a brassiere, punning on the slang *boobies* or *boobs*, the breasts.

book *American* a sentence in prison
Normally for a year. The derivation might be from a criminal *record*, which is entered for future reference. If the judge *threw the book at you*, you would expect a longer period of confinement than twelve months.

bookmaker a person who accepts bets for a living
Not an author but from a shortened form of the 19th-century *betting-book maker*. Now standard English.

boom-boom[1] *American* defecation
Nursery usage, from the firing of ordnance.

boom-boom[2] copulation
Again from the firing of a gun? That would imply only male activity, but it is used of either sex:
'No more boom-boom for that mammasan,' the Marine said, that same tired remark you heard every time the dead turned out to be women. (Herr, 1977)

boom-passenger *obsolete British* a convict sentenced to transportation
Not a libidinous passenger on a cruise but a prisoner chained to the boom on deck while being taken to a penal colony.

boondock *American* to court sexually
Supposedly from the Tagalog *bundok*, a mountain, whence the isolated place where a car might be parked, and carried home by servicemen serving in the Philippines. *Boondagger*, a female homosexual taking the male role, may be a punning corruption of *boondocker*.

boost[1] *American* to steal
Literally, to give a lift to. Whence *booster*, a casual thief. The articles stolen are concealed in a *booster bag* or *bloomers*.

boost[2] to importune or badger in selling
Pushing too hard. An American auctioneer who *boosts* makes or accepts fraudulent bids to raise the price.

boot (the) summary dismissal from employment
From the kick to speed the departing servant, which today would land you in court if not in hospital.
The British *Order of the Boot* is such dismissal.

boot money a wrongful payment to an amateur in sport
A relic from the days when talented people played sport for fun rather than money and the respective status of amateurs and professionals was strictly regulated. Supposedly the money was left in the player's *boot*, with a suggestion that it was to help pay for his sporting footwear.

bootleg smuggled or stolen
Originally it referred to intoxicants, supposedly from the bottles concealed on the legs when transporting supplies illegally to American Indians. Standard English of smuggled intoxicants during Prohibition.
Now of anything stolen. Also as a verb:
Do you think...that he might come back and bootleg a copy and give it to you? (Colodny & Gettlin, 1991, reporting the cross-examination of Admiral Welander in 1971)
A *bootlegger* is a smuggler or thief and a *bootlegger turn* is a rapid manoeuvre rotating a car through 180 degrees using the handbrake, to avoid a pursuing vehicle.

boracic *British* indigent
Rhyming slang, *boracic lint*, skint. Usually denoting a temporary embarrassment, when the sufferer may describe himself as *brassic*.

born in having an imperfection associated with
Someone accused of having been *born in a barn* has omitted to close a door. *Born in a mill* indicates inattention rather than deafness.
In obsolete use, those *born in the vestry* were illegitimate, their parents not having been married in the body of the church.

Borough English *obsolete* a form of disinheriting the eldest son
The subject came up in a discussion on 16 October 1773, concerning *Marcheta Mulierum*, a custom whereby the Lord of the Manor was entitled to *jus primae noctis*:
Dr Johnson said, the belief that such a custom having existed was also held in England, where there is a tenure called *Borough English*, by which the eldest child does not inherit, from a doubt of his being the son of the tenant. (J. Boswell, 1773— Blackstone in his *Commentaries* disagreed with the omniscient Doctor)

borrow to steal, take, or plagiarize
The loan may be involuntary and the object will be consumed or not returned.
> In the Army it is always considered more excusable to 'win' or 'borrow' things belonging to men from other companies. (F. Richards, 1936)
> Mr B.... has made his name in the art world by 'borrowing' from the paintings and sculptures of others. (*Daily Telegraph*, 24 November 2000)

Boston marriage *American* two women sharing a home
But not a homosexual arrangement. Owing something, perhaps, to the legendary propriety of the ancient city.

both oars in the water *American* mentally normal
Euphemistic in the negative, from the uneven progress of a boat propelled with one lateral oar.

both-way having both heterosexual and homosexual inclinations
When you *swing both ways*—see SWING[2]:
> Maybe he wasn't a fag. One of those both-way people you were always reading about. (Goldman, 1986)

bother to make unwelcome approaches to
Usually sexual, by a male:
> ...grandma whispering hoarsely, 'Leave me alone, will you?'...I only knew he was bothering her. (Cookson, 1969—as a child she shared her grandparents' bedroom)

bottle[1] associated with drinking intoxicants
Usually of intemperance in drinking wines or spirits. To *be on the bottle*, *bother the bottle*, or *take to the bottle* is to be an alcoholic and *bottled* means drunk.
The slang meaning 'bravery' may be only euphemistic when you *lose your bottle*, and appears to have no connection with DUTCH COURAGE.

bottle[2] to sodomize
Rhyming slang on *bottle and glass*, arse:
> I want to bottle you, mate, Tom says. Kim has never heard the expression but he immediately understands it. (Burroughs, 1984)

bottle[3] to injure with a broken bottle
The jargon of drunken youths.

bottle blond(e) a woman with hair dyed yellow
The dye or bleach comes in a glass container.

bottle club an unlicensed establishment where alcohol is drunk
To comply with regulations, the customers brought their own alcohol or, more often, the proprietor purported to obtain it from licensed premises on their behalf.
A *bottle party* is one where those invited are expected to bring alcohol for general consumption.
A *bottle shop* is a store selling liquor, usually in a country where the sale of alcohol is only permitted in dedicated outlets.

bottom the buttocks
Literally or physically, the soles of your feet.
An American *bottom woman* is a pimp's favourite prostitute, which seems illogical until you consider why he should be attracted to her.

bottom fishing buying a security whose price has fallen
Stock market jargon, showing little knowledge of commercial fishing in which beam trawlers, or beamers, destroy the seabed by dragging it to disturb flatfish. Those seeking supposed bargains are known as *bottom feeders*.
The *bottom line* is not used on a rod to catch fish but a cliché for a sticking point in terms of policy or price, from the arrangement of a financial statement where the lowest figure shows the final result.

bought in failing to sell at auction
Trade jargon. People may be less inclined to bid if lots have been seen not to reach their reserve price.

bounce[1] to copulate
From the motion, especially on a sprung mattress.
A *bounce*, or *bouncy-bouncy*, is an act of copulation.

bounce[2] to be dishonoured by non-payment
Referring to cheques, returned to the person who drew them, like a rubber ball dropped to the ground and caught again.

bounce[3] to dismiss peremptorily from employment or courtship
From the notional rebounding after hitting another surface, such as the sidewalk.
A *bouncer* performs the same function at a public gathering, forcibly excluding the unwanted or unruly.

bounce[4] to induce or persuade another through importunity or violence
Criminal jargon for extortion or blackmail; police jargon for obtaining a confession; for salesmen and hucksters, it means to obtain

a binding commitment from someone who has not been given the time or opportunity to make a considered judgement.

bout an act of copulation

The imagery is from wrestling:

> I was sorry to hear that Sir W. Penn's maid Betty was gone away yesterday, for I was in hope to have had a bout with her before she had gone, she being very pretty. (Pepys, 1662, who added 'I have also a mind to my own wench, but I dare not, for fear she prove honest and refuse and then tell my wife')

bowel movement (a) defecation

Medical jargon when the result is a MOTION.

bowler hat the discharge, especially prematurely, of an officer from the armed services

What was once the standard business headgear replaces the uniform cap.

Now also of civilian premature discharge, and as a verb.

Those who receive a *golden bowler* are paid well for being retired or leaving early.

box[1] a coffin

Still heard in sayings such as *When I'm in my box*, meaning when the speaker is dead. In obsolete use, to *box* was to place the corpse into the coffin prior to interment.

box[2] a shield for the male genitalia

Mainly sporting use but also of riot protection gear.

box-ticking purposeless compliance with excessive regulation

Supervising authorities, especially those imposing imported legislation in addition to domestic laws, seek to justify their existence or perform their duty by issuing questionnaires which are answered by the respondents *ticking* appropriate *boxes*. Those who perform this tedious function, or do their job without any lateral thinking, are known as *box-tickers*, as also, it would seem, are the advisers who insist on meticulous compliance with the system:

> He blames the 'box-tickers' for the continuing delay in any announcement. (*Sunday Telegraph*, 27 February 2005)

boy[1] an adult male

Used by and of men until their middle years to perpetuate an illusion of youthfulness and, in a derogatory sense, by white people of adult black servants.

The *boys*, equally of full age, are a group of men engaged in a common enterprise such as American politicians (the *boys upstairs*), servicemen, members of a sporting team (*the boys* get a

result when they have won a match), insurgents (such as the Rhodesian *boys in the bush*), managers (the *boys in the backroom*), or development engineers (the *backroom boys*), etc.

boy[2] the penis

A vulgarism. The *boys* are the male genitalia:

> Carrie hadn't provided any socks or underpants, so I just had to let my boys hang free. (McNab, 2001)

boy scout[1] *American* a state police officer

They wear clothes reminiscent of a Baden-Powell scoutmaster and are seen as enjoying a lower status than other police officers.

boy scout[2] a petty or insincere person

Usually of public figures who are anxious to be seen doing their good deed every day:

> [Politicians are] only interested in getting votes and occasionally making some Boy Scout points for themselves by proposing a big cut in our foreign aid budget. (Lederer & Burdick, 1958)

boyfriend a male sexual partner

Of almost any age over puberty. Heterosexual or homosexual.

See also GIRLFRIEND.

boys' (room) a lavatory for exclusive male use

Not just for juveniles.

brace *American* to kill

Literally, to fasten tightly or strengthen. There is also a slang meaning, to waylay, none of which gives us a satisfactory etymology.

bracer a spirituous intoxicant

Something to strengthen you, you hope, and much favoured by Wodehouse characters.

Brahms *British* drunk

Rhyming slang on *Brahms and Liszt*, pissed. See also MOZART, which is rarer.

branch water *American* water which is offered from a bottle

It is supposed to come from an unpolluted tributary, or *branch*, of a stream, and therefore not to spoil the taste of your whisky with the taint of chlorine. Many bartenders depend on a closer, less costly source.

brass (the) senior management

Not necessarily used in a derogatory sense:

> ...too many dinners at evening functions with the brass. (Rankin, 2003)

Perhaps from the ornamentation on the uniforms of senior army officers, or *top brass*. (In the Royal Air Force the gold braid on the headgear of senior officers is known as *scrambled egg*.)

brasser *obsolete*? a prostitute
Rhyming slang from *brass-nail*, for TAIL[1], which is kept alive by the cliché *as bold as brass*.
Brass rags were not the prostitute's finery but clothes worn by sailors when scrubbing the deck, and to *part brass rags* means to quarrel and break off a friendship.

brassière a garment to contain women's breasts
Originally in French a sleeved garment, thus becoming euphemistic there before the English accepted it to cover the taboo *breasts* with a double evasion. Now standard English, often shortened to *bra*, pronounced as the French *bras*, thus completing the circle.

break a commandment to copulate outside marriage
Yes, the one proscribing adultery:
    Look, there is a pretty man. I could be contracted to break a commandment with him. (Pepys, 1666—the speaker was the 'bonny lass' Lady Robinson)

break luck *American* as a prostitute to obtain the first customer of the day
Owing nothing to the slang *break a lance*, to copulate, but probably because her *bad luck* has ended with the arrival of a customer.

break the news *American* to obtain a confession or other information through violence
The victim is made aware of the extent of his predicament.

break the pale *obsolete* to be promiscuous
The *pale*, as in *paling*, was a piece of wood, then a fence, then a fenced-in curtilage, and finally a district under the control of a centre with hostile natives prowling outside. If you *broke the pale*, you were somewhere where you should not have been:
    ...he breaks the pale,
    And feeds from home. (Shakespeare, *The Comedy of Errors*)

break wind to fart
The taboo about saying 'fart' in polite company is comparatively recent.
The American punning *break the sound barrier* means the same thing.
Also used of belching.

break your elbow *obsolete* to give birth to a child outside marriage
The fracture was sometimes caused by a figurative bed:
    And so she broke her elboe against the bed. (Heath, 1650—of a single woman who had a child)
If a woman *broke her elbow in the church*, she was judged not immoral but a bad housekeeper after marriage. A woman who copulated outside marriage was said to *break her knee*, in a direct translation from a French euphemism. If she *broke her leg above the knee*, referring to a ruined horse and the position of her genitals, she gave birth while unmarried, the putative father also being said to have *broken his leg*:
    If her foot slip and down fall she,
    And break her leg above the knee.
    (Fletcher, 1618)

break your neck to have an urgent desire to urinate
Normally of a male, without suicidal tendencies. It indicates that *break-neck* speed is required.

break your shins against Covent Garden rails see COVENT GARDEN

breathe your last to die
Circumlocution and evasion rather than euphemism, as you cannot expect to live more than two or three minutes after the event.
For the Nazis, a *breathing problem* was a routine cause of death given to the family of a murdered person:
    He received notification...of her death in Brandenburg from 'breathing problems'. (Burleigh, 2000—an epileptic woman was killed as a matter of policy, along with others who had chronic illnesses, in 1940)

brew[1] *British* to burn
Referring to an armoured vehicle in wartime, from the brewing of tea by soldiers over an open fire, often raised by pouring petrol into sand.
A *brew-up* was the infusion of the tea or, in sardonic humour, the combustion of a tank.

brew[2] **(a)** *American* beer
For the British, a *brew* or *brew-up* is tea. *Brewer's goitre* is obesity in a male despite the thyroid gland, the swelling of which gives you a *goitre*, being situated in the neck not around your waist:
    —the crenellated face, the brewer's goitre slung under his belt...(Keneally, 1985—in practice the belt normally rides under the protuberance)

brick short of a load (a) of low intelligence
Of the same tendency as many similar expressions denoting a shortage from the norm.

Bridewell *obsolete British* a police station
The original in London was a holy well with supposed medicinal properties, then a hospital for the poor, then a prison.

Bridport dagger *obsolete* a hangman's rope
There was apparently an inn of this name at Tyburn, where public hangings were held. The Dorset town of Bridport, with a climate suited to growing flax, was noted for its rope-walks, long pieces of ground where ropes were made. If you were *stabbed by a Bridport dagger*, you were hanged.

brief to disclose information which is misleading or incomplete
Literally, to inform another of the relevant facts:
> Washington and London share the same problem between 'briefing' and 'leaking'; the rule of thumb is that a 'leak' is when someone else does it. (Seitz, 1998)

brig a prison
Shortened form of *brigantine*, a ship often used as a naval prison.
Civilian as well as military use.

Brighton pier *British* homosexual
Rhyming slang for QUEER³, and perhaps alluding to the presence of many homosexual men in the resort.

bring down to kill by shooting
Military and sporting jargon:
> Since 1998. 15,638 partridges and 20,233 pheasants have been brought down. (*Sunday Telegraph*, 9 June 2001)

bring off¹ to cause to achieve a sexual orgasm
Of either sex, by whatever means.

bring off² to cause the abortion of a foetus
It is physically removed from the mother:
> I was left in the club... like any tiresome little skivvy, but unlike her we were able to arrange to have it brought off. (P. Scott, 1975)

bristols the breasts of an adult female
Rhyming slang on *Bristol City*, titty, after the soccer team rather than the conurbation:
> Laidback, funloving author, 44, is anxious to meet respectable bit of stuff with big bristols and own teeth. (advertisement in *Private Eye*, November 1988)

broad a sexually complaisant female
A corruption of BAWD, or from the American term for a woman, or from the meaning vulgar, as a shortened form of *broad woman*, which referred to moral laxity, not girth. The implication of promiscuity is less common in modern usage.
Broads were playing cards, in the days when they were, for many, the devil's pictures.
The *Norfolk Broads* are neither complaisant East Anglian maidens nor playing cards but waterways resulting from medieval digging for peat.

broken home a family with young children whose parents have parted
Not a building struck by some natural disaster.

bromide job a superficial excuse or explanation
Bromide, either as *sodium bromide* or *potassium bromide*, is given medicinally as a sedative and, by popular myth, to soldiers in their tea to reduce their libido.

Bronx cheer a fart
Simulated orally or generated anally.

bronze eye the anus
A male homosexual use.
Also as *second eye*, and not just of the Cyclopes.

broomstick match see JUMP THE BROOM-STICK

brother a man in a taboo occupation
Thus a *brother of the bung* was a brewer or publican; a *brother of the gusset* was a pimp; a *brother starling* was someone with whom you shared your mistress; etc.
For a person of African descent, a *brother* is someone of the same ancestry, and a *blue-eyed brother* is a white man sympathetic to the black population or espousing black racial militancy.

brown associated with the anus
As in the vulgar male riposte *in your brown*.
To *brown* is to sodomize and a *brown-hatter* is a sodomite. The *brown stuff* is faeces. See also *dick's hatband* under DICK¹.

brown envelope a bribe
The cover in which it is handed over is unidentifiable.

brown-nose to flatter
Not from exposure to the sun but from the figurative proximity of your proboscis to the anal area of the object of your sycophancy.
A *brown-noser* or *brown-nose* so acts.
> Unit Two, a cadre of teacher's pets captained by the infamous brownnose Iovescu, sat firmly atop the heap. (Furst, 1988)

A toady may figuratively replace his *nose* with his *tongue*:

> Also his tongue was busy and almost perfectly brown. (de Bernières, 1994, describing an obsequious officer)

brown tea an intoxicant
A usage by expatriates in Saudi Arabia where it is illegal to consume alcohol.
A *brownie* in America may be whisky or brandy, or no more than a roast potato.
In addict use, *brown sugar* is heroin.

brownie points the supposed rewards of currying favour with your superiors
Baden-Powell's *Brownies*, whose name puns on the colour of the uniform and the benevolence of the creatures who perform good deeds around the home by night, win promotion, to the exalted position of sixer or beyond, through the award of points for good works or achievement.

browse to steal and consume food within a store
The thief adopts the feeding habits of a ruminant, carrying his booty past the checkout desk in his stomach.

brushfire war a conflict in which a major power is not directly involved
It involves figuratively the undergrowth rather than the standing timber:

> The language of the mad foments violence ... 'Brushfire wars', 'limited actions', 'clean atom bombs'. (West, 1979)

brute see BIG ANIMAL

bubble to inform against
Rhyming slang for *sneak*, from *bubble and squeak*, the fried dish of cabbage and potato.

bucket¹ a place for defecation
A male usage, especially where a smaller receptacle is provided for urination inside communal living quarters. Some figurative usage:

> Get off the bucket. I'm serious. (Theroux, 1978)

bucket² *British* a prison
Rhyming slang on *bucket and pail*, jail.

bucket³ to kill by drowning
A way of disposing of an excess of kittens.

bucket shop an insubstantial vendor of overvalued securities or cut-price services
Not an ironmonger, but selling bombed-out shares or empty airline seats.

budget cheap

Advertising jargon. The implication is that the cost will not exceed the amount which you have allocated for the purpose.

buff (the) nakedness
A shortened form of *buffalo* (from the colour of its hide) and normally as *in the buff* or *to the buff*. In Victorian times to *buff it* was to strip. The obsolete meaning, to copulate, may have come from the association with nudity or from the associated rubbing.

bug to conceal or use an apparatus for eavesdropping
From the colour and shape of the device.
In America a *bug* may also be a mark on a label indicating the use of union labour in manufacture.

bug-eyed drunk
Referring to the protrusion of the eyeballs.

bug out *American* to retreat
From the slang meaning, to quit rapidly. *Bug-out fever*, in the Korean War, was cowardice:

> 'Bug-out fever', the urge to withdraw precipitately in the face of the slightest threat from the flank ... (M. Hastings, 1987)

Buggins' turn *British* promotion on the grounds of seniority rather than merit
The mythical *Buggins* is an incompetent or unambitious employee who remains in the same job for a long time. The expression may also be used of providing sinecures for failed politicians.

> [The appointment] deserves to be more than a prize in the game of Euro-Buggins turn. (*Daily Telegraph*, 5 April 2004)

bughouse mentally unbalanced
Perhaps from the insects figuratively buzzing round in the head.
The noun in America denotes an institution for the mentally ill.

bugle *Irish* an erection of the penis
Male vulgar slang, from the rigidity and playing an instrument.

bulge to reveal pregnancy
A usage in the days when society was less tolerant of pregnant brides:

> He married his childhood sweetheart, whose stomach bulged at the ceremony. (Seymour, 2003)

A *bulge* may also refer to sexual arousal in a male seen in an outer garment, but not a pot belly.

bull¹ (of a male) to copulate with
The function for which the animal is kept. Whence, as a noun, a promiscuous male or a

female homosexual taking the male role, when it is a shortened form of *bull-dyke*.

bull² egocentric boasting, irrelevant information, or slavish adherence to protocol

A shortened form of *bullshit* or, in America, *bull-rinky*. A *bullshitter* is a braggart or someone who acts officiously, the letters BS being used for *bullshit* and *bullshitter* in all senses as noun and verb. The 19th-century *bull-scutter* was 'anything worthless or nasty' (*EDD*).

bull³ *American* a policeman

Originally a detective, presumably from his aggressive behaviour and now also of any armed protector of property.

A *bull-pen* is a prison, but not for the confinement of police officers.

bullet (the) peremptory discharge from employment

What happens when they FIRE you. Only in spy fiction is the gun loaded.

bum *obsolete* a cheap prostitute

Origin unknown but possibly from the meaning, worthless. In Scotland a *bum* was any coarse female.

The phrases deriving from *bum* as a shortened form of *behind* include *bum-fodder*, toilet paper; *bum-fighting*, copulation; *bum-bandit*, a male homosexual; and *bum-boy*, a catamite, (not someone working on a *bum-boat*, that *bum* coming from the Dutch *boom*, as in *boom-schip*). The American *bum*, or vagrant, comes from the German *bummeln*, to stroll or idle, whence to tramp.

bump¹ (the) peremptory dismissal from employment

The displacement is sudden. In America to *bump* an employee is to induce or encourage a resignation by allocating unpleasant or demeaning tasks, thus avoiding having to pay compensation for dismissal.

bump² (the) pregnancy

Literally, any swelling of the body, usually caused by a blow. A *bumper* is not the putative father but a stripper in a stage show.

bump³ to copulate

From the pushing of the bodies against each other:

> One could imagine brother and sister bumping like frogs in broad daylight. (Theroux, 1978—they committed incest)

Occasionally also as *bump bones*.

bump⁴ (off) to kill

The blow is fatal.

A *bump* is such a killing, possibly by a *bump-man*, a professional assassin.

bump⁵ to cause a pre-booked passenger to travel by a later aircraft

Airlines routinely overbook seats if they can, to allow for the frequent NO-SHOW. If too many passengers turn up, the last arrivals or the most docile are left off the flight.

bun¹ a prostitute

The still current mariner's fetish about mentioning the word *rabbit* before a voyage to ward off ill luck dates from the time when fraudulent chandlers supplied cheap rabbit meat, which doesn't keep when salted, for pork, which does. The superstitious had, before a trip, to touch the tail of a hare or, if none were to hand, the pubic hair of a woman, including one who might for a fee allow hers to be touched. Thus the *bun*, a shortened form of *bunny* (the diminutive for the rabbit), came to mean the hair and the prostitute.

bun² a lump of faeces

From the shape in the highway:

> ...the crunchy snow which is spread here and there with cinders from people's furnaces and dotted here and there with frozen horse buns. (Atwood, 1988)

bun in the oven (a) pregnancy

Punning on the rising of cake mixture and the growth of the foetus.

bun on (a) drunkenness

Usually *tied* but occasionally *got* or *had*, being a shortened form of *bundle*, a large amount.

bun-puncher *British* a person who never drinks intoxicants

Army usage, in a society where abstention from intoxicants can be as taboo as drunkenness in civilian life:

> If a teetotaller he was known as a 'char-wallah', 'bun-puncher' or 'wad-shifter'. (Richards, 1933)

bunch of fives a fist used as a weapon

Less often it means an open hand used for chastisement:

> Wright did not hesitate to call his pupils' attention to his 'bunch of fives', a term he was specially fond of using to denote his powerful hand, which might now and again come into palpable contact with a pupil's cheek. (E. M. Wright, 1934, writing about her husband, Joseph, who edited the *EDD*)

bundle with to copulate with

From the proximity. In Northern England it also implied an engagement to marry. In Scotland and New England courting couples were allowed to *bundle*, which was supposedly the chaste sharing of a bed to save fuel and provide companionship. At least it prevented marriages between those who were sexually incompatible.

bung¹ *obsolete* a drunkard
Literally, a stopper for a cask.
A drunkard might be said to have been to *Bungay Fair*, punning on the Suffolk market town.

bung² a bribe
The notes are literally or figuratively *bunged* into a pocket. *Bung* is used specifically in Britain for illegal cash payments made when a footballer transfers to a new club.

bung up and bilge free copulating
Naval usage, from the way a cask of rum should be stored aboard ship, whence anything in good order. The derivation may involve some vulgar wordplay but does not involve a pun on *bung* in its slang meaning, a female fitted contraceptive device.

bunk flying *American* boasting
Air force usage. The daring exploits which you relate are dreamed or otherwise invented in bed.

bunny¹ an unmarried sexual companion
Homosexual or heterosexual, in the former case taking the female role. The use comes from the pet name given to someone who may share the timid character of the rabbit. Also descriptive of females, in many phrases denoting the venue, such as *beach,·jazz, ski,* or *surf bunny.*

bunny² a towel worn during menstruation
Possibly from the shape and softness. Whence the Australian *buns on,* menstruating.

bunny-hugger a person obsessed with the welfare of a selective choice of non-human mammals
Foxes, rabbits, and badgers score more highly than rats and mice. A dysphemism, especially among the practitioners of country sports:
Judging from letters sent to the Press, many bunny-huggers believe that the average mink lives the life of a fur-clad Buddhist monk. (Robin Page in *Daily Telegraph,* 6 September 1998—those describing themselves as animal lovers had released some 6,000 mink from captivity in the unfulfilled hope or expectation that the predators would live a vegetarian life of self-denial and peaceful coexistence among the native fauna)
Tree-hugger is used pejoratively of an environmentalist, especially one with an arboreal fixation.

Burke *obsolete* to murder
The celebrated Irishman killed people to replenish his stock of corpses which he sold for medical research until he was hanged in Edinburgh in 1829. The modern usage as a mild insult, usually spelt *berk,* comes via rhyming slang from the *Berkshire* or *Berkeley Hunt,* viewed figuratively and not anatomically.

burn¹ *American* to kill
Originally, by electrocution, from the singeing of the corpse by the contacts. Latterly, of any death, especially by shooting.
In obsolete use, a man who had *burnt his poker* suffered no more than being infected with a venereal disease, or *burner,* from the sensation which resulted.

burn² to extort from or to cheat
Probably a shortened form of *put the burn on,* to compel, through figurative application of HEAT¹ or by physically contra-rotating the skin at the wrist.
In narcotic jargon, it may mean to take money for illicit supplies and fail to deliver, or to give information to the authorities about another's addiction.

burn with a (low) blue flame *American* to be very drunk
The imagery is from a dying fire, about to go out.

burra peg see CHOTA PEG

burst to have an urgent need to urinate
With a full bladder; a shortened form of the phrase *bursting for a pee.* Occasionally as *bust.*

bury to inter (a corpse)
So long standard English that we assume the thing buried is a dead body, unless we elaborate by saying *buried alive.* So too with *burial,* with its assumption of prior death.

bury a Quaker *obsolete* to defecate
A *Quaker* for the Irish was a turd, perhaps from their brown clothing. A *Quaker's burial ground* was a lavatory, and a tasteless pun.

bush the pubic hair
Of male or female, with obvious imagery.

bush-house *obsolete British* a house selling intoxicants
Often opening on fair or market days, it signalled its availability by hanging a bush outside.
Whence the proverb *Good wine needs no bush.*

bush marriage a marriage performed without due ceremony

In a remote place the registrar or priest may not be available.

The American *bush patrol* may be no more than an al fresco sexual encounter, punning on the pubic hair.

bushwhack to ambush
Literally, to hack a path through woods or to propel a craft by pulling on overhanging foliage.

business any taboo or criminal act
It can refer to defecation or, less often, urination, by humans or domestic pets; to sexual activity, including prostitution; to killing; to illegal narcotic use; etc.
To *do the business* may mean to copulate:
> This was the first time they'd done the business in a good while, two months nearly. Made love. (Doyle, 1991)
In the jargon of prostitution, a *business woman* is not a Soroptimist but a prostitute.

bust¹ financially ruined
Literally, broken. Standard English.

bust² to arrest during a police raid
Again from the concept of breaking.
A *bust* is such a raid.

bust³ a drunken carouse
Either broken or broke after it.
To *bust a cap* is to ingest narcotics illegally, from breaking the seal on the container.

bust a string to become mentally unbalanced
Probably alluding to tennis rather than playing a fiddle.

bust bodice a garment for holding women's breasts
A *bodice* is a garment which covers the upper parts of the body. Barely euphemistic, except when shortened to *BB*.
The usage lapsed rather when Brigitte Bardot appeared on the scene.

busy *British* a policeman
Probably a shortened form of *busybody*, a nosy or interfering person.

butch (of a female) masculine
A shortened form of *butcher* and not from an old Manx word meaning witch. A woman so described may also be a homosexual playing the male role. Rarely of homosexual men.

butler's perks opened but unfinished bottles of wine

Not always decanted and kept for future use by the master.

button¹ (man) *American* a professional killer
Presumably you press him for action.

button² *American* a policeman
He wears them on his uniform.

buy to purchase narcotics illegally
The nature of the goods is not mentioned between the dealer and the addict, or *buyer*.
To *buy a brewery* is to be an alcoholic.
To *buy love* is, of a male, to copulate with a prostitute.

buy it to be killed or wounded in action
Military jargon, from acquiring the missile which hits you. The American *buy the farm*, to be killed, probably referred to the $10,000 payment which the US government made on the death of a serviceman in the Second World War. As most were unmarried, this huge sum went to their parents and enabled them to achieve a common ambition of buying their farm.

buzz on (a) drunk or under the influence of narcotics
From the ringing in the ears or general air of excitement.
Whence *buzzed*, drunk.

by(e) *obsolete* an indication of illegitimacy
Literally, ancillary. A *by(e)-blow*, *chap-*, *-scape*, etc. indicated illegitimate birth of one who was *by(e)-come*, *-begot*, etc.
By(e)-courting, by a male, was done deceitfully without any intention of marriage.
In Scotland a *by(e)-shot* was an elderly unmarried woman, not always as a result of Cupid's bad marksmanship.

by mutual consent without litigation
Corporate speak when a senior manager is dismissed and damages are agreed between the parties:
> Quest's chief executive...has gone with the usual cheque and 'by mutual consent' euphemism. (*Daily Telegraph*, 25 March 2002)

by yourself mad
In a world of your own, perhaps:
> But monie a day he was by himself, He was so sairly frighted. (Burns, 1786)
We retain the usage in the expression *by* (or *beside*) *himself with rage*.

C

C anything taboo beginning with the letter C

Cancer, or the BIG C, cocaine, or CRACK[3]. The *C-word* is cunt, used as an insult:

The sort of people who read these books or articles would never dream of addressing the C-word to a bus driver. (*Daily Telegraph*, 10 February 2006)

US army laxatives in the Second World War were called *CC pills*.

cabbage to steal

Cabbages were odd snippets or spare lengths of cloth which were traditionally the perquisite of tailors, who sometimes consigned good material into that category. The term than passed into, and has stayed in, general use, mainly of pilfering.

cadge *obsolete* to steal

The linguistic progression appears to have been from selling as an itinerant vendor to stealing, then to our modern meaning, to sponge or beg.

cage a prison

Dangerous convicts in the 19th century wore yellow clothes, at a time when a canary was a popular pet. The imagery also comes, as with CHOKEY and other slang words for prison, from reference to a confined space.

California widow *obsolete American* a deserted wife

Her husband might literally or metaphorically have left her to strike gold elsewhere. *California blankets* in the Great Depression were newspapers used to pad clothing for warmth, as they are still used by those sleeping rough.

call (the) death

Your God demands your presence elsewhere. As with a sporting contest, the deceased may also be *called home* or *away*. Anyone *called to higher service* is not just summoned by a deity but has the expectation that good works performed on earth will be replicated in heaven.

In former times to *call a soul* was to announce the death of a parishioner, which was done after matins on Sunday from a flat tombstone in the churchyard.

call down *obsolete* to announce publicly that you will not pay your wife's debts

A relic from the days when the wife's possessions passed to her husband on marriage and all she retained was the right to pledge his credit for food and clothing for the home. The *calling down* was done by the town crier and from then on, in theory at least, the husband had no responsibility for paying further debts contracted by his wife. Failing the town crier, a notice might be inserted to the same effect in a local newspaper, as sometimes happened in Britain within living memory.

call girl a prostitute

Originally operating from a call house, or brothel, rather than being summoned by telephone. Also rarely as a *call-button girl*. A *call boy*, who once ensured that actors did not miss their cue, is a male prostitute.

call of nature the need to urinate or defecate

The visit demanded by your bodily functions.

call off all bets to die

When, under certain conditions, a horse is withdrawn from a race, all wagers are invalid.

call out to challenge to a duel

The contest took place in the open air, and those who pick a quarrel still invite their opponent to 'come outside'.

call the tricks to solicit as a prostitute

A TRICK is the customer:

They weren't allowed to call the tricks like the girls in Storeyville. (Armstrong, 1955)

caller (a) menstruation

A usage which uses the same imagery of interruption as the more common VISITOR.

calorie counter a fat person

Advertising jargon, suggesting that the physical condition is not due to gluttony, the lack of exercise, and so on.

camel a smuggler of illegal narcotics

It describes those operating from Africa, where you are unlikely to find a MULE, into Europe.

cameo a minor screen appearance by a well-known performer

The usage suggests that one who normally takes a leading part has not lost status through accepting a minor role. The imagery comes from the profile head carved in relief.

camp homosexual

Originally it described male homosexuality, but now refers to either sex. The origin is obscure, which gives free rein to speculation among etymologists. Ware suggests that it is 'probably from the French' who are naturally blamed for things of which we may disapprove. Partridge urged us to consult the *EDD*, but which of Dr Wright's definitions caught his fancy is hard to decide: 'gyrating in the air', 'gossiping', 'a heap of potatoes or turnips earthed up in order to be kept throughout the winter': we can only guess. The progression from using exaggerated gestures to male homosexuality is well documented in the *OED*:

> The red shadow is at large. Did you ever see anything quite so camp? (P. Scott, 1975—the dialogue about a male homosexual in 1946 was probably anachronistic, especially when placed in India)

To *camp it up* in Britain means no more than to accentuate or display male homosexual characteristics; in America it may imply participation in group male homosexual activity. To *camp about* can mean no more than to act jokingly.

camp down with to live with as a sexual partner
Permanence is implied in the arrangement without any suggestion that it is under canvas or homosexual.

campaign wife a mistress
But for senior officers only:
> Eisenhower later invited Zhukov and his 'campaign wife'... to visit the United States. (Beevor, 2002—to meet Mamie, no doubt, rather than Kay Summers)

can[1] *American* a lavatory
Originally, a bucket. Now used of any kind of plumbing sophistication.

can[2] *American* to dismiss from place or employment
Figuratively, being put in the *ash-can* rather than flushed down the CAN[1].
Also used of dismissal from academia for misconduct or underachievement.

can[3] *American* a prison
Literally, a container. Usually of a short-stay lock-up or a confined cell.

can on (a) drunkenness
The phrase antedates the drinking of beer out of aluminium cans and refers to intoxication from any cause.
Canned or *half-canned* mean drunk.

canary[1] *obsolete* a convict
Some were obliged to wear yellow clothes and lived in figurative cages.
A canary was also a female accomplice to a crime in 19th-century London.

canary[2] a person who gives information clandestinely
Formerly, an informer to the police who might SING. Now also of someone who gives information without authority to third parties such as journalists, whence the *canary trap*, a small alteration to each copy of a confidential document so that the source of any additional copy made for improper distribution can be identified.

candy illegal narcotics
At one time *candy* was cocaine, and then embraced marijuana or LSD on a sugar lump. *Nose candy* is a narcotic in powdered form.
The punning *candy man* or *candy store* is a dealer in illegal drugs.

canhouse *American* a brothel
The derivation may be from the slang *can*, the buttocks.
The use of *can* to mean a prostitute may be a back derivation from *canhouse*, or vice versa.

canned goods *American* a virgin
Describing an adult female, untainted (or free of disease) and unopened (with maidenhead intact). Occasionally of a male.

cannon a pickpocket
We are faced with two tributaries to this etymological stream. Some maintain that the derivation comes from the thief bumping into his victim, causing him to stumble, which enables the thief to take the wallet or watch in the confusion, with imagery from the billiards or pool table. The older general meaning, a thief, comes from the Yiddish *gonif*, whence the shortened *gon*, whence *gun*, whence *cannon*.

canoe *American* to copulate with
If a young man took a woman for a trip in such a craft, there was no room for a chaperone, which gave them unwonted seclusion when they went ashore:
> Her Old Man... had been hearing about me and Daisy canoeing from the first night we'd got together. (Armstrong, 1955—they were not into aquatic sports)
Canoodle, to fondle sexually, dates from the mid-19th century, which means it is not a compound of *canoe* and *cuddle*.

canteen medal an exposed trouser fly button
Originally, a wine cellar, a *canteen* acquired its general use as a public place of refreshment, and especially for British servicemen who expressed disdain for any medal awarded other than for an act of bravery.

capital involving killing
Literally, of the head but now seldom referring

to beheading. A *capital crime* is one which
involves a killing, leading to a *capital charge*
before the court and, upon conviction in some
parts of the world, to *capital punishment*, death,
which in some American states will take place
in a *capital sentences unit*.

capon *American* a male homosexual
Literally, a castrated cock. In obsolete use it
meant a eunuch.

captain *obsolete* highwayman
He who ruled a section of the road:
   ... every posting house and ale-house could
   produce someone in the Captain's pay.
   (Dickens, 1859)

captain is at home (the) I am menstruating
A red coat was once worn by British officers.

card[1] *obsolete Irish* to punish by laceration
A 19th-century toothed tool for combing wool
was a weapon used to harm those who
assisted unpopular or absentee landlords.

card[2] an argument supported by preju-
dice or favouritism
The *card*, with a suitable prefix such as *race* or
Welsh, is *played* to win a trick unfairly:
   When Peter Walker played the 'Welsh'
   card yet again, I dictated him a note and
   Carys translated it into Welsh before we
   dispatched it. (Major, 1999—Walker, the
   Secretary of State for Wales, could not
   speak Welsh)

card short of a full deck (a) stupid
A variant of FIFTY CARDS IN THE PACK.

cardiac incident a malfunction of the
heart
Medical jargon, but every heartbeat might be
so described. With a *cardiac arrest*, the heart
stops beating.

cardigan *American* a contraceptive sheath
The use is at two removes from the Crimea,
where the pugnacious earl gave his name to
an article of clothing.

cardinal is at home (the) I am menstruating
Princes of the Church wear a red biretta and
robes of office.

cards (your) *British* dismissal from employment
At one time, revenue stamps were affixed
weekly to cards, originally to provide basic
insurance and pension rights but latterly as a
tax on employment paid by both the employer and the employee. It was necessary to show

a properly stamped card either to a new
employer or to the authorities when claiming
money while unemployed.
An employee wishing to leave employment
might *ask for his cards*.

care see IN CARE

career change dismissal from employment
True as far as it goes, but unlikely to be the
whole story:
   The company's claim that its trading
   director had suddenly decided it is time for
   a career change after 23 years with
   Sainsbury's was a surprise to the rest of us
   ... but a £270,000 pay-off rather gives the
   game away. (*Daily Telegraph*, 29 October
   1998—it transpired that the recipient had
   not arranged another career to change
   into)
If you dismiss a lot of people, you may set up a
career transition center, as a clearing house.

careful stingy
From the concept that thrift is praiseworthy
but avarice is a deadly sin.

careless of integrity *British* lying
A parliamentary evasion following the convention that members always tell the truth:
   When further evidence came to light of
   officials turning a blind eye, it became
   clear that Miss Hughes had been a little
   careless of her integrity. (*Daily Telegraph*, 2
   April 2004)

caress yourself to masturbate
Of a female, from the literal meaning, to
touch gently.

caring the ostentatious display of social
conscience
Originally used in this derogatory sense by
those critical of hypocrisy or self-advertise-
ment in others:
Now standard English of nurses, home helps,
and the like, or *carers* in the jargon, a pun
perhaps on their being concerned for, and
their looking after, other people. *Uncaring*
means cruel, selfish or insensitive, often in a
double negative:
   Ulyatt, who was not a cruel man, or an
   uncaring one, simply shut his eyes.
   (Kyle, 1975)

carnal pertaining to copulation
Literally, of the flesh. Legal jargon and
standard English in phrases such as *carnal
act*, *appetite*, *knowledge*, *necessities*, or *relations*.
Also as an adverb:
   'Know you this woman?' 'Carnally, she
   says.' (Shakespeare, *Measure for Measure*)

carousel *British* a fraud involving tax repayment
The goods are imported without being declared, sold to an exporter charging British
value added tax, and then re-exported, when
the exporter reclaims the tax from the
Revenue. The importer then disappears and
fails to reimburse the Revenue.

carpet[1] to reprimand
Unlike the workshop or servants' quarters,
the master's room had a floor covering on
which the defaulter had to stand.
Beware the French *sur le tapis*, which means
only up for consideration.

carpet[2] a wig
A variant of the RUG worn by an American
male.

carpet bombing delivering to recipients
multiple unsolicited advertising circulars
Jargon of the advertising industry. The imagery is from the military technique of
saturating defences in the Second World
War. It is thought that 1% of recipients
respond to the first communication, a further
2% to the second, and a further 4% to the
third. Thereafter the circulars are ignored.

carpetbagger a seeker of short-term gain
Originally, an absconding American banker,
who so carried away the bank's reserves when
he left. Then widely used of Northerners who
sought easy pickings in the South after the
Civil War. In modern use it refers to a tout
who seeks to put together a deal without any
personal investment or risk, as by seeking a
buyer for a property which does not belong to
him.
The term is also used in Britain of those who
place small deposits with mutual building
societies, in the hope of profit if the societies
abandon their mutual status; and of politicians seeking a safer constituency.

carry[1] to be pregnant (with)
Of the same tendency as BEAR[1] but sometimes
without stating the burden:
    She was in the seventh month of
    pregnancy and carrying big.
    (J. Collins, 1981)
To *carry a child* is specific:
    Mrs Thrale is big, and fancies that she
    carries a boy. (Johnson)

carry[2] to have an illegal narcotic on you
A shortened form of *carry drugs*. Because of
the risk of detection in a body search, a rule
among drug users says *Never carry when you can
stash.*

carry[3] *American* to be in possession of a
handgun
Again a shortened form, and used of both
legal and illegal sidearms.

carry[4] to drink too much intoxicant without appearing drunk
Such a gift was supposed to be an indication
of good breeding:
    ...as gentlemen should, carried their two
    bottles of an evening. (Strachey, 1918)
To *carry a (heavy) load* means to be drunk,
usually on beer.

carry a card to be a member of the Communist party
The use was developed in the 1920s when
such membership was not flaunted in polite
circles because it might lead to ostracism.

carry a torch for to desire sexually
The imagery is from a religious processional
light. Usually of unrequited love.

carry off to cause the death of
It is used of dying from an epidemic or sudden
illness.

carry on with to have an extramarital sexual relationship with
The 19th-century use implied no more than
companionship or courtship:
    I carry on with him now and he likes me
    very much. (Mayhew, 1862)
In modern use, of either sex, the relationship
is explicit and often censurable:
    ...administered a public wigging to
    Princess Margaret when she was carrying
    on with that nancy-boy pop singer. (*Private
    Eye*, April 1981)

carry out a sex act to masturbate
The phrase is not used of copulation:
    He was accused by a masseuse at the Old
    Course Hotel, in St Andrews, of carrying
    out a sex act on himself after removing a
    towel. (*Daily Telegraph*, 26 April 2006)

carry the banner *American* to be destitute
Perhaps from the activities of the Salvation
Army, who provide food and shelter for
the homeless, among their many good
works. Other phrases used of and by hobos
are *carry the balloon*, from the rolled bedroll,
and *carry the stick*, as used in walking.

carry the can to receive undeserved punishment while the culprit goes free
Some authorities suggest that the can contained
beer. Common use in the First World War
suggests that it was more likely to have carried
food prepared behind the lines for those in the
trenches. The full version *carry the can back* may

have referred rather to the unpleasant and dangerous duty of taking the CAN¹, with its malodorous cargo of urine and faeces, back to the rear from the trenches; and see also REARS. The phrase is also used of a guilty person singled out or available for punishment among several miscreants.

See also TAKE THE CAN BACK.

carsey a lavatory
From the Italian *casa*, a house, and defined by Dr Johnson as 'A building unfurnished'.
Also as *carsy*, *karsey*, *karzey*, and *karzy*.

case¹ *obsolete* a brothel
Again from the Italian (or Spanish) *casa*, a house, and occasionally so spelt. Also as *casita*, presumably a smaller establishment. F&H say a *case* was a lavatory (1905).

case² a person the subject of a taboo
Tout court of an eccentric or unconventional person. Medical jargon for a patient whose identity should remain confidential. Funeral jargon of a corpse. A *hard case* is a recidivist.

cash flow problem an insolvency
Cash flow, the money we receive against what we have to pay, is always a problem, needing constant attention. This usage is of corporate trading when insolvent.
Also used of temporary personal indigence.

cash in hand payment for goods or services avoiding taxation
The buyer does not pay sales or value added tax and the seller does not declare the income.
    Could have been cash in hand. Plenty of cowboys out there who'll lay a floor, no questions asked. (Rankin, 2004)

cash in your checks to die
Equally common as *cash* (or *pass*) *in your chips*, from turning your counters into money when you quit the gambling table.

cast¹ to give birth prematurely
Standard English of quadrupeds, from the meaning to cause to fall.
Whence two obsolete punning phrases of bipeds, both meaning 'to give birth while unmarried'. To *cast a girth* used equestrian imagery, and to *cast a laggin* (or *leglin*) *girth* came from the spilling of the staves of a tub when the hoop round them is displaced.

cast² *obsolete* to use magical powers of divination
If you were *cast for death*, you had not been selected to play Julius Caesar but were terminally ill.

casting couch (the) sexual activity between a female seeking a favour and a male in a position to grant it
Originally used of aspiring actresses.
This particular piece of furniture is found less often outside the theatrical profession:
    Young lady, I do not need a casting couch. I can have any woman I want. (*Private Eye*, May 1981, quoting a journalist)

casual an institution which housed the destitute
A shortened form of the British *casual ward*, accommodation available for tramps arriving on foot without reservation at uncertain intervals. Those who tramped the road and slept in such places were known as *casuals*, a word which now applies to people in temporary employment.

cat a prostitute
Male or female, from the feline rather than the slang word for vagina, a variant of PUSSY¹. A *cat* does not necessarily work in a *cat-house* or brothel.
A male *cat* may be no more than a snappy dresser who may or may not *cat about*, be promiscuous:
    I had on a brand new Stetson ... fine black suit and new patent leather shoes ... I was a sharp cat. (Armstrong, 1955)

catch a rich marriageable adult
The imagery comes from angling. In former times a (*good*) *catch* might be either male or female so long as he or she was rich.

catch a cold¹ *British* to contract gonorrhoea
Army use, punning on the meaning, to get yourself into trouble. Shakespeare may have had the same thing in mind when he wrote:
    A maid, and stuff'd. There's goodly catching of cold. (*Much Ado About Nothing*)

catch a cold² to have a trouser zip undone
An oblique warning from one male to another, received by me on the quay at Destin, Florida, on a mild day in November 1987.

catch a cold³ to suffer a loss
Normally as a speculator or gambler:
    The 1960s speculative bubble burst and while the rest of the world caught a cold, Japan got pneumonia. (*Daily Telegraph*, 5 December 1994)

catch a packet¹ to be killed or severely wounded
Usually after being struck by something solid, like shrapnel. The common use from the First

World War changed to mean getting into trouble until the Second World War, when the phrase reverted to its former meaning, and also came to embrace the ordeal of a town which was severely bombed or of a unit which was subjected to a heavy attack.

catch a packet² to contract venereal disease
A common use among servicemen in the Second World War.

catch fish with a silver hook *obsolete* to pretend to have caught fish which you have bought
An expression among anglers, where such behaviour is opprobrious, as was that of the man who liked to SHOOT WITH A SILVER GUN. See also ANGLE WITH A SILVER HOOK, which was an even less gentlemanly activity.

catch the boat up *British* to have contracted venereal disease
Naval usage. Jolly (1988) suggests a derivation from the days of pressing, when seamen were not allowed ashore for fear that they would desert. A *sick boat* would circulate among the fleet and take patients, with or without venereal disease, to a naval hospital ashore. On discharge from hospital, the sailor would be required to rejoin his ship wherever it was.

category killer a cut-price store in a shopping precinct
Articles are sold at prices which deter competition, until there is no competition for those specific products, when the prices may rise.

cattle¹ a category of despised persons
More dysphemism than euphemism. Evelyn used the word of prostitutes:
Nelly... concubines and cattell of that sort.
A similar derogatory use was of slaves in the Southern States.

cattle² an act of copulation
Rhyming slang on *cattle truck*, and used figuratively, if at all:
I don't give a flying cattle if you give me fifteen thousand pounds a week. (Kersh, 1936)

caught¹ pregnant
Mainly female use of unwanted pregnancy, with obvious imagery.

caught² infected with venereal disease
Medical practitioners report that this is the commonest way in which their diseased and embarrassed young patients introduce the subject of their visit.

caught short having an urgent desire in an inconvenient place to urinate or defecate
Of both sexes, from the days when coaches or trains stopped at regular intervals but offered no lavatory accommodation between one stage or station and the next.

cavalry prostitutes who solicit from motor vehicles
The usage, if not the practice, is peculiar to the Far East, leaving the INFANTRY, as usual, to slog it out on foot.

cease to be to die
Hardly euphemistic for an atheist. Of more interest perhaps is the biblical use for the menopause:
It ceased to be with Sarah after the manner of women. (*Genesis* 18:11)

ceasefire a continuation of fighting
A usage when the opponents are operating under different rules, and especially if politicians wish to give the impression that hostilities are coming to an end:
Lord Carrington will negotiate no more ceasefires in Bosnia until the warlords there have reached stalemate or exhaustion, he announced yesterday. (*Daily Telegraph*, 24 July 1992)

Cecil the penis
One of the many male forenames by which the appendage is known. To *dip Cecil in the hot grease* is to copulate.

celebrate to drink intoxicants to excess
Literally, to mark a happy or festive occasion, when intoxicants may be drunk. When a drunken person is said to have been *celebrating*, there is no suggestion of prior festivities:
No, I haven't been celebrating. I can drive. (Seymour, 1998)

celebrity a person employed as an entertainer
Literally, deserving fame. Jargon of the entertainment industry.

cement to prevent defecation
Used of medicine taken after an attack of diarrhoea, although concrete might seem more appropriate.
And in various compound uses, such as:
The water came from a communal tap down by the road, so it was cement-sandwich country as far as I was concerned. (Lyall, 1972)

cement shoes weights attached to a corpse
For those murdered, especially in Chicago, and dumped in deep water.

certain age (a) old
The precise figure is often uncertain, although none of us is not of a certain age, unless we cannot trace a certificate of birth:
> They were a certain age, they had bumps and braces and wooden legs. (Theroux, 1979)

certain condition (a) see CONDITION²

certain eventuality the possible defeat of France
An evasion used by British planners ahead of the event in 1940:
> Entitled 'British strategy in a Certain Eventuality', it was a long paper. It assumed...the French making peace with Germany, Italy entering the war...and the loss of most of the British Expeditionary force—a euphemistic wording regularly used in such papers in place of a direct reference to a French collapse. (Lukacs, 2000)

certifiable mentally unstable but still at liberty
Medical experts and a magistrate had at one time to certify that a mentally ill person could be involuntarily incarcerated.

chair (the) judicial death by electrocution
From the furniture to which the victim is strapped.

chair-days *obsolete* old age
Before the advent of hip replacements:
> ...in thy reverence and thy chair-days, thus
> To die in ruffian battle. (Shakespeare, *2 Henry VI*)

Chalfonts *British* haemorrhoids
Rhyming slang for piles, from the town Chalfont St Giles.

chalk-board a blackboard
A usage originally in the classroom, to avoid offence to black people.

challenged differing from the norm in a taboo fashion
Not faced with a duel, but of those thought to be or actually facing life at a disadvantage. Thus the bald may be *follicularly challenged*, the deaf *aurally challenged*, the blind *visually challenged* (and not by 'Halt! Who goes there?'), the mentally ill *cerebrally challenged*, the stupid *developmentally* or *intellectually challenged*, a dwarf *vertically challenged*, a lame person *physically challenged*, a pauper *financially challenged*, etc. An *ethically challenged* person is a crook, the phrase being used on 18 June 1996 by the chairman of the committee investigating, inter alia, Hillary Clinton's deals in Arkansas.
To describe someone as *parentally challenged* is an insult (the non-euphemistic term would be *bastard*).

challenging unprofitable
One of the code words used by company chairmen when things are going badly, disregarding the fact that the firm is *challenged* by its competition every day.

chamber a receptacle for urine
A shortened form of *chamber-pot*, which was formerly kept for nocturnal urination under the bed or in a small cupboard in the bedroom. The urine, or *chamber-lye*, might be collected, fermented, and put to various good uses, like the washing of clothes or the dressing of wheat.

chambering copulation
The activity normally takes place in an upstairs room:
> Harriet heard more than she wanted of the chambering next door. (Manning, 1978)

chance illegitimate
From the unplanned nature of the pregnancy in the days when it was considered appropriate for children to be born in wedlock. In many standard English and dialect phrases such as *chance bairn*, *begot*, *born*, *child*, and *come*. A *chanceling* or *come-by-chance* child was illegitimate:
> [He used to] stand godfather to poor little come-by-chance children that had not father at all in the eye of matrimony. (Hardy, 1874)

change¹ the menopause
A shortened form of the standard English *change of life*.

change² *obsolete* to grow into a difficult or stupid child
Babies born wise and beautiful grew up stupid, ugly, and mischievous if the fairies did a switch in the cradle.
Thus a *changeling*, such a child, resulting from the malevolence of the fairies and not from incest and other inbreeding which was endemic in rural areas before the Railway Age.

change³ to replace by a clean one a soiled napkin on a baby
The baby in fact remains unchanged, albeit cleaner and sweeter-smelling for a while.

change your bulbs to become subject to mental abnormality
Presumably from the difference in light emitted when those of different wattage are selected.

change your jacket to desert an old allegiance
A modern variant of *turn your coat*:
> This was made possible because there were those in the new Socialist Order who had 'changed their jackets' following Franco's death. (letter in *Daily Telegraph*, 17 December 1998)

change your luck *American* to copulate with a black woman
By a white male, from switching from red to black in roulette after a losing streak.

channel stuffing fraudulently recording excess sales
The *channel* is the retail chain through which the manufacturer distributes the goods. By taking into the figures the profit on fictitious sales, misleading accounts can be issued:
> A grand jury is scheduled to gather this month to examine whether Coke took part in so-called 'channel stuffing' to inflate profits. (*Daily Telegraph*, 4 May 2004)

chant *obsolete* falsely to describe a horse for sale
Literally, singing, but singing the nag's praises dishonestly. A *chanter* or *horse-chanter* was the equine equivalent of a second-hand car salesman, except that for age, temper, hooves, soundness, teeth, coat, etc. you must read mileage, roadworthiness, tyres, compression, fuel consumption, bodywork, etc.

chap *obsolete* a male suitor
Originally, a buyer, then in colloquial use any man, and in the 19th century specifically a suitor. *Chapping* was courtship for a female, but not with the *old chap*, the devil.

chapel of ease¹ a mortuary
Originally, a place of worship for the convenience of parishioners residing a long way from their parish church. Also as *chapel of rest*.

chapel of ease² a lavatory
A punning British use, of the place where you might *ease yourself*, and especially of an ornate public urinal for men, such as used to grace the streets of London.

Chapter Eleven see GO²

character saleable
Literally distinctive, the derivation coming from the Greek instrument for marking and engraving. This is real-estate jargon for any property about which the selling agent cannot think of anything better to say.

charge¹ *American* an erection of the penis
DAS suggests derivation from 'activation from an electric charge and/or the sensation of electric shock', an etymology with which most males would find themselves uncomfortable. Likening the phenomenon to the loading (or *charging*) of a piece of ordnance in preparation for a discharge is more acceptable.

charge² an illegal injection of narcotics
The imagery is again from loading, or revitalizing, as in the cliché *a shot in the arm*, the use of which does not imply wrongdoing or illegality. (You may read a report that a troop of Brownies received a shot in the arm after some gift or other good fortune, as though the small girls and Brown Owl—or Tawny—were about to behave in an animated fashion after being injected with heroin.)

charity girl *obsolete American* a sexually complaisant young female
A Second World War usage: patriotism was an excuse for promiscuity with servicemen. A *charity dame* was her mother, acting with the same abandon.

Charlie a substitute word for a taboo subject or expression
In some instances the usage derives from the letter C in the phonetic alphabet, as when *Charlie* means cocaine—also as *Charlie girl*—or a stupid person, a *right Charlie* or *Charlie uncle*, the latter being the first two phonetic letters of the taboo word 'cunt'. For Americans in Vietnam, *Charlie* was the Viet Cong. It may also mean the police, a homosexual male, the male or female genitalia, a prostitute, or menstruation, in the phrase *Charlie's come*.
If a man is told *Charlie's dead* it means that his trouser zip is unfastened while for a woman it used to mean that her petticoat was showing under her skirt.
Charlies, a woman's breasts, is obsolete.

Charlie Ronce a pimp
A brother to JOE in rhyming slang, for *ponce*.

charm *obsolete* to effect a magical cure
A *charm* was originally the singing of a song, whence an incantation, and the medical virtuosity of a *charmer*, or white witch:
> Soom folk says it's hall bosh about charmin' yer cock... Mah feyther took a feather o' his cock to t'old witch an' she charmed un. (*Good Words*, 1869, quoted in *EDD*—an avian remedy was supplied, not an aphrodisiac)

Thus to be *charming* was to be in good health:
> An' how's Coden Rachel?—She's charmin', thankee. (Quiller-Couch, 1890)

charms the sexual allure of a female
The arts or physical attributes which work

magic with men. She who *displays* or *shows her charms* does more than wear an amulet.

chase to seek to copulate with extra-maritally
Usually of the male, from the hunting, but women also *chase* men. In general terms, men *chase hump, skirt,* or *tail.* Those who *chase around* are promiscuous:

> There is a certain kind of woman...who would rather have their man a eunuch than have him 'chasing around'. (A. Clark, 2002)

chase the dragon to smoke a narcotic
Formerly of opium, with the traditional Chinese association, but now of heroin.

chaser an intoxicant of a different kind from that just taken
It follows the previous libation down the throat. Usually of beer after spirits or vice versa. Less often of a further portion of what you have been drinking.

chat *British* an interview in which the police may seek to make a suspect incriminate himself
Literally, an informal or light-hearted conversation. The British police use the word when they want to obtain evidence without the inconvenience of a caution or a defence lawyer in attendance.

chat up to seek to engage sexually
From the conversational approach. Usually a male does it to a female stranger.

chavver *Irish* to copulate
From the Romany *charver,* to touch. Also as *chauver.*

cheat to copulate with someone other than your regular sexual partner
Of either party, within or outside marriage, from the deception usually involved.

cheat the starter to conceive a child before marriage
Sporting imagery, from starting a race before the signal to go. As with BEAT THE GUN, the phrase was also formerly used of premarital copulation without impregnation between an engaged couple.

cheaters *American* cosmetic padding
The attempt is to deceive by enhancing the size of thighs, buttocks, and breasts.

check a defeat
Military use, where bad news must be gift-wrapped:

> Within twenty-four hours of the débâcle, without taking time to assess what was

officially called a 'check' to the French armies...Joffre issued on August 26 [1914] a new General Order. (Tuchman, 1962)

check into Crowbar hotel *American* to send to prison
Or other suitably named penal establishments.

check out *American* to die
The imagery is said to have come from the medical examination on demobilization, but leaving a hotel or cashing in when you quit gambling are just as likely.

cheese eater *American* a cheat
A figurative use. *DAS* says 'Euphem. for rat'.

cheesecake an erotic picture of a female
The word puns on the sweet confection and the smile-inducing cheese demanded by photographers. Mainly Second World War use.

Chelsea tractor *British* a vehicle designed for off-road driving
A derisive use describing expensive four-wheel drive vehicles bought by rich urban dwellers, very few of whom actually live in Chelsea or leave a paved highway.

chemical involving the use of illegal drugs
Many of the agents ingested are indeed produced through chemistry, although the term is also applied to those of biological origin.
To be *chemically inconvenienced* or *affected* means that you are incapacitated by illegal drugs or, less often, by alcohol.

chère amie a sexual mistress
The French euphemism is carried into English.
Occasionally translated as *dear friend.*

cherry a woman's virginity
In vulgar use, the hymen from the colour and appearance.
A *cherry-picker* is a libertine.

cherry-pick fraudulently to select bargains
You select only the best of the fruit. Financial jargon of trades done in the morning on discretionary accounts where the gains or losses can be allocated fraudulently when the paperwork is completed later or at the close of business:

> Since rules for designating customer accounts are lax, the broker can do blank trades in the morning, then 'cherry-pick' the profitable ones at lunchtime, and allocate them to the intended beneficiary.

(*Sunday Telegraph*, 27 March 1994—suggesting that an American politician had so enjoyed good fortune in the market)

chestnuts the testicles
A variant of the NUTS theme.

chew a gun to kill yourself
You put the barrel in your mouth and aim upwards.

chi-chi of mixed white and Indian ancestry
A derogatory use. It means dirty in Hindi.

chic sale *American* a primitive outdoor lavatory
The American humorist Chic (Charles) Sale had a stage act on the construction of privies, and wrote *The Specialist* in order to establish his copyright in the material.

Chicago typewriter a sub-machine gun
A combination of the staccato noise of the machine and the city's reputation for lawlessness.

chick a prostitute
The common avian imagery of any young female. Also as *chickie*.
A *chickie house* is a brothel.

chicken[1] a youth attractive to homosexuals
A variant of CHICK. A *chickenhawk* is a homosexual adult who seeks out boys for sexual purposes, punning on *sparrowhawk*.
If however someone describes you as *no (spring) chicken*, it means you are showing your age.

chicken[2] cowardly
From the supposed nature of the domestic fowl. To *chicken out* is to behave in a craven way.
An American *chicken colonel* is not being accused of cowardice but is wearing the ordained badge of rank on his shoulders.

child of God *Indian* a member of the former untouchable class in Hindu society
A *Harijan*, whose lot is to collect human excreta among other menial tasks, to touch whom is to be defiled.

child of sin *obsolete* an illegitimate child
The *sin* was its conception, at least so far as the mother was concerned. Also as *child of grief* or *love child*.

child of Venus a prostitute
Supposedly mothered by the goddess of love. The term is also used of a woman who relishes sexual activity:

...a merry little grig and born child of Venus. (F. Harris, 1925—a *grig* was originally a dwarf before becoming a cheerful person)

child-bed (in) giving birth
Not a cot but standard English for parturition.

chill to kill
The common cooling imagery.

China white heroin
From the colour, the origin, and the porcelain, perhaps.

Chinese is used in phrases to indicate dishonesty, wiliness, duplicity, or muddle, some of which follow.

Chinese bookkeeping false accounting

Chinese copy a production model stolen from another's design
Used as a noun or verb.

Chinese fire-drill (a) pandemonium

Chinese paper *American* a security of doubtful value
Commercial jargon but not referring to the currency linked to the dollar.

Chinese parliament a disorganized discussion group
It would seem the converse of what happens in Beijing, where mute and subservient nominees appear only to be harangued at length by their masters.

Chinese rejection a decision not to publish a book because it is too literary
Publishers' jargon for well-written manuscripts which might not appeal to a mass audience.

Chinese (three-point) landing a crash on the runway
Punning on the mythical Oriental Wun Wing Lo. Tricycle undercarriages came later.

Chinese tobacco opium

Chinese wall the pretence that price-sensitive information will not be used by an adviser or his associates to their own advantage
Said to have been first used in this context by F. D. Roosevelt in 1927. The paper-thin nature of such a wall may prevent sight but is unlikely to affect hearing.

Chinese whisper an unsubstantiated rumour

chippy¹ *American* a prostitute
Usually at the lower end of the profession, from *chip*, a BIT¹ or PIECE¹.
A *chippie-joint* is a brothel.

chippy² *American* to ingest illegal narcotics on an irregular basis
Where using illegal drugs is the norm, non-addiction may be taboo (as in FISH¹ for homosexual females). In such a culture a non-addict may wish to avoid being thought stuffy by not entirely eschewing narcotics, as it were merely *chipping* at a mass. This may be inferred from *chippy-user*, 'one who uses narcotics infrequently' (Lingemann, 1969). To confuse matters, a *chippy* in black slang is a regular taker of strong narcotics, although in Britain he is merely a carpenter.

chirp *American* to be an informer to the police
Underworld slang using the common *singing* imagery (Chandler, 1950). Whence *chirper*, an informer.

chisel to steal or cheat
The imagery is from the removal of slivers from wood with a sharp instrument. The thefts so described may be minor and repetitious, and the cheating mean. *On the chisel* is so to behave.
A *chiseller* steals or cheats, or, in America, saves expense by avoiding compliance with a law or regulation of which he disapproves.

choke your chicken (of a male) to masturbate
The derivation is from the likeness of the penis to a chicken's plucked neck.
Whence *chicken-choker*, a masturbator, which is also said to be 'a friendly term truckers use for each other' (Dills, 1976.).
I have what may be a rogue example of the meaning to urinate:
    Whenever Walker was about to go and answer a call of nature, he would announce 'Well, I'm gonna choke my chicken'. (de la Billière, 1992—we must assume the gallant general was not mistaken in his assumption of his colleague's intentions)

chokey a prison
The Hindi *chauki*, originally meaning four-sided, became a space surrounded by walls, whence a police station or customs house and then a prison.

chop¹ to kill
Originally standard English, meaning to kill an animal by a blow from the hand. When killing humans, the blow is with a sharp instrument.
To *get the chop* was to be killed in battle. The newspaper jargon *chop shot* is a picture of the corpse of someone who has been killed.

chop² (the) sudden dismissal from employment
The metaphorical blow with a sharp instrument, of individual rather than multiple dismissals. The employer does the *chopping*.
For the chop describes the status of a candidate for dismissal.

chopper¹ a sub-machine gun
Underworld jargon referring to its ability to chop down its targets.

chopper² the penis
Perhaps from its divisive sexual function and common slang. Of the same tendency as the obsolete *cleave*. My daughter, whose job included editing crossword puzzles, erred by allowing 'a butcher's chopper' as a clue for 'cleaver', which calls to mind Dr Wright's definition:
    Broach—a butcher's prick. (*EDD*)

chota peg a spirituous intoxicant
Chota is small in Hindi, although the measure may not be.
A *burra peg* is an even larger measure of spirits. These British Indian phrases are now passing out of use as those who lived or served in India die off.

Christmas crackers the testicles
Rhyming slang on KNACKERS.

chubby fat
Literally, like the thick, coarse-fleshed fish, whence agreeably plump, especially of babies. You meet the adjective in advertisements calculated to avoid upsetting mothers who have to select capacious clothes for an obese child.

chuck (the) peremptory dismissal from employment, school, or courtship
You would be wrong to infer that the ejection was forcible. Also as a verb:
    [Eddie Shah] was chucked as well [from Gordonstoun]. (*Daily Telegraph*, 18 March 2006)

chuck horrors *American* acute withdrawal symptoms
Used of drug addicts denied access to a supply to which the body has become accustomed. The phrase is used of those under medical supervision, and of those displaying the same symptoms in prison, being similarly deprived of narcotics. Whence perhaps the further

meaning, a claustrophobic fear of being imprisoned.

chuck seven *Australian* to die
The single dice has no seven on it.

chuck up to vomit
Not playing catch with a ball. Usually associated with drunkenness, and *chucked* means drunk.

church triumphant the dead
A Christian use, especially of those who are considered to have well served the *church militant here on earth*, while the less devoted or martial among us are doomed to languish among the vanquished.

churn to deal unnecessarily in a client's securities in order to generate commission
The imagery is from constantly turning the milk to obtain butter or cream. In this case, the investor is milked and the advisers get the cream.

circular error probability the extent to which ordnance will miss the target
A Gulf War usage, from the illustration by concentric rings on a chart.

circular file *American* a waste-paper basket
Most of them are round; see also FILE THIRTEEN.

circular protector *obsolete* a contraceptive sheath
This was what they used to be called in advertisements, although the description could have meant anything from sheep fencing to an envelope for junk mail.

cissy a male homosexual
Literally, an effeminate man, probably a corruption of *sister* via *sissy* or *sis*.

Civil Co-operation Bureau *obsolete South African* an extralegal governmental agency
This organization was established by the white South African government to harass and generally discomfort its critics and opponents.

civilian impacting the inadvertent killing or wounding of non-combatants
A Gulf War neologism.

claim responsibility for to admit to
A usage of terrorists, especially in Northern Ireland, who saw murder and arson as creditworthy.

claimant a poor person supported in part or whole by the state
They *claim* money to which they are entitled from public agencies etc.:
> Reductions for Students, OAPs and Claimants. (Theatre Wales poster, October, 1981—despite the standard English use of *claimant* as anyone who makes a claim, no self-sufficient person would be so unwise as to ask if he might pay a lesser price for his ticket)

There is also an organization called the *Claimants' Union* which seeks to maximize the receipts of its members from public funds.

claimed dead
Your deity has asserted ownership:
> Perhaps, too, fate would intrude, ficklely, and have me 'claimed'... (A. Clark, 2002)

claims farmer a person seeking to profit from the misfortune of others
Either a lawyer touting for business or someone seeking to act as agent for those whom the compensation culture has turned into victims, often of their own greed, ignorance, or folly:
> Lord Falconer, the Constitutional Affairs Secretary, will tell so-called 'claims farmers' that they must either agree on a voluntary code or face regulation by law. (*Daily Telegraph*, 10 November 2004—the English Common Law misdemeanours of maintenance, champerty, and barratry already exist to prevent these abuses but are not enforced)

Clapham an allusion to gonorrhoea
In the 19th century *to come home by Clapham* was to have been infected with clap, or gonorrhoea, Clapham Common being a haunt of prostitutes. Today male homosexuals use the Common for the same purpose, which may explain the embarrassment and immediate resignation of a government minister who went wandering there on his own and suffered what he later described as 'a moment of madness'. Pope's prognosis was invalid when he wrote: 'Time, that at last matures a clap to pox.'

claret blood
Boxing jargon, of blood from the nose. To *tap the claret* was to make your opponent's nose bleed.

classic proportions (of) fat
Originally, *classic* meant belonging to the literature of Greek or Latin antiquity when that was considered the only stuff worth reading, less taxing literature being written in the vernacular, or Romance, whence our modern romantic novels. The female models chosen by Rubens

and other old masters, or *classic* painters, were nearly always on the plump side.

clean¹ free from unpleasantness, danger, illegality, or addiction
The opposite in many uses of DIRTY. *Clean* may refer to a casual sexual partner who is free from venereal disease, to a location without any enemy infiltration, to a person who is unarmed, to the fact that narcotics are not being carried or used, etc.
A *clean* atom bomb distributes less radioactive fall-out than a *dirty* one.

clean² to kill or evict indigenous inhabitants of a different race or religion to your own
The practice is age-old but the language more recent:
> The displacement of the Arab majority had been achieved only by a process which Yigal Allon, the commander of the Jewish military forces in Galilee (and later Deputy Prime Minister of Israel), himself described as a 'cleansing'. 'We saw a need to clean the Inner Galilee', he wrote in his memoirs, 'and to create a Jewish territorial succession in the entire region of Upper Galilee. We therefore looked for means to cause tens of thousands of sulky Arabs who remained in Galilee to flee... Wide areas were cleaned.' (Dalrymple, 1997)
The world paid more attention to the *ethnic cleansing* in Bosnia and Croatia, perhaps because there were more television channels than half a century earlier, and no networks controlled by Serbian or Croat sympathizers.

clean house to remove incriminating evidence
By destroying either documents or witnesses or both:
> Once he muttered darkly that Bill Clinton's people were 'cleaning house', and he was 'next on the list'. (Evans-Pritchard, 1997—he was murdered soon after and his file on Clinton was stolen)

clean up¹ to bring the proceeds of vice into open circulation
A variant of LAUNDER, with the same imagery and alluding perhaps to the meaning, to achieve a success.
Whence *cleaners*, or money-launderers and the punning *take to the cleaners*, to bring the proceeds of crime into open circulation.

clean up² illegally to destroy evidence
More than just dusting the files and sweeping the floor:
> Mr Quattrone, 47, is accused of obstructing justice by sending an e-mail to colleagues advising them to 'clean up' old files just

after he was told that his firm, Credit Suisse First Boston, was under criminal investigation. (Daily Telegraph, 29 September 2003)

cleanliness training *American* teaching young children controlled urination and defecation
Not just learning to wash your neck and keep nits out of your hair. The British talk of *potty training*, which is explicit (see POT³).

cleanse¹ to free from enemy occupation or sympathizers
Military jargon for an infantry operation.
Also, as a variant of CLEAN², of killing or forcibly evicting indigenous inhabitants of a different race or religion to your own.

cleanse² to remove the placenta from domestic cattle
Veterinary jargon:
> I was 'cleansing' a cow (removing the afterbirth). (Herriot, 1981)

clear not menstruating
Some ancient taboos relating to menstruating women still persist in India and elsewhere:
> I could only visit them on my 'clear' days. (Taraporevala, 2000, referring to her Parsee relatives)

clear up *American* to desist from the regular use of illegal narcotics
Literally, to tidy up or redress any situation. Drug abusers' jargon.

clear your desk to be summarily dismissed from employment
The instruction is given to prevent an employee compiling and stealing a dossier of useful documents or otherwise causing disruption.
> Last February Derek Linton and a fellow director were given the fabled five minutes to clear their desks at the advertising agency they themselves had founded 18 years earlier. (*Telegraph Magazine*, 1 June 1995)

cleavage the division between a woman's breasts
Literally, the act of splitting apart, and often partially displayed, or flaunted, by immodest dressing. A *cleft* in male vulgar speech is a vagina.

click¹ *obsolete* to steal
Literally, to snatch or seize hold of.
A *clicker* was a thief, a body-snatcher, or a pestering touting shopkeeper. (Body-snatchers were not thieves as there was no property in a corpse.) Stolen goods might be taken from

Clickem Inn to be sold at *Clickem Fair* (the forerunner of the car-boot sale).

click² to conceive a child
From the commonplace sound of a successful connection having been made. To *click with* another is merely to form a romantic attachment.

clicket to copulate
From the French *cliqueter*, to make a clicking noise and using the same imagery as CLICK². It is used properly of foxes, less often of deer and hares, and almost never of humans.

climax a sexual orgasm
Literally the culmination of anything.

climb (into) to copulate with
Of a male, form the position atop the female perhaps. Also as *climb aboard*, *in with*, or *into bed with*. Some phrases suggest further athleticism:
> You practically had to let them climb into your underpants before they'd let you fly anywhere. (Atwood, 2003)

climb the ladder *obsolete* to be hanged
Either from the ascent to the scaffold or because the *ladder* itself was used for the drop. However a woman who is said to *climb the ladder on her back* does no more than seek to turn male advances to advantage and advancement.
For *climb the wooden hill*, see WOODEN HILL.

clink a prison
Originally the jail in Southwark, but then used generally, helped no doubt by the onomatopoeic attractions of keys in locks and heavy doors shutting.

clink off *obsolete* to die
From a Scottish meaning, to depart.

clip¹ to swindle or rob
The association is with the shearing or the venerable practice of cutting the edges off silver coins. Now often it is used of picking pockets. A *clip artist* is a swindler and a *clip joint* a night club or similar establishment where customers are overcharged and otherwise cheated.

clip² to hit with a bullet
Literally, to cut or shear, whence to mark as by removing cardboard from a ticket, which is what a *clippie* used to do on a bus. In America the person *clipped* is usually killed, but in British use he would only be slightly wounded, without being incapacitated.

clip his wick to kill
Like putting out a candle by cutting the wick below where it was burning:
> Maitland found out. So they clipped his

wick. (Sanders, 1977—writing of killing, not circumcising)

cloakroom a lavatory
Coats are often stored in or near lavatories. The shortened British form *cloaks* normally refers only to the place where outer garments are stored in a public place.

clobbered *American* drunk
The common beating imagery. It was used by Thurber in the *New Yorker* in 1951, but may now be obsolete.

clock fraudulently to alter the reading of a milometer
A motor trade device to increase the apparent value of a second-hand car. Some figurative use of falsely changing other statistics:
> 'The revenue and cost trends ... are still not meeting our expectations,' he declared, which was a polite way of saying load was clocked. (*Daily Telegraph*, 3 May 2001)

clock-watcher a disinterested employee
Usually in a menial or boring job and waiting for the shift to end, even if no timepiece is in view. The phrase is also used of those approaching retirement age who have lost enthusiasm for their work:
> ... the ones biding their time until pension day. The clock-watchers. (Rankin, 1999)

cloot the devil
Literally, one of the divisions of a cloven hoof, a physical characteristic shared by Satan and cattle. Also as *clootie*.
Clootie's croft was land set aside by a farmer and left untilled so that the devil would be content to leave the rest of the farm in peace:
> The moss is soft on Clootie's craft.
> (G. Henderson, 1856—with its 'set aside' programmes, the bureaucracy in Brussels now performs the same function)

close¹ stingy
A shortened form of close-fisted. See also NEAR¹.

close² having an extramarital sexual relationship with
From the requisite proximity.
A *close relationship* with a *close companion* or *friend* may be heterosexual or homosexual.
> Di was having a close relationship with the muscular Tommy Yeardye. (Monkhouse, 1993—of the actress Diana Dors)

close an account to kill
With imagery from banking or story-telling?

close its doors to fail
Used of a bank, although it will prudently

close its doors every day at the close of business, in the hope of reopening them on the morrow.

close stool a portable lavatory
Originally for use in the CLOSET[1], but now usually found in the sickroom, if at all:
> Your lion, that holds his poll-axe sitting on a close-stool, will be given to Ajax.
> (Shakespeare, *Love's Labour's Lost*—see JAKES for the punning *Ajax*)

close the bedroom door to refuse to copulate with your spouse
Not just to keep the children out. The female usually does the metaphorical *closing*, even if the spouses continue to occupy the same room.

close your eyes to die
Or explicitly, *close your eyes for the last time*. If you close another's eyes, that person is already dead:
> I trust that I shall be able to close your eyes in peace. (Hughes, 1987, quoting a letter from a 19th-century convict in Australia to his parents in England)

closet[1] a lavatory
Literally, a small or private room. The word usually comes with the descriptive prefixes *earth* or *water*, whence the initials EC and WC, and the charming French noun *le water*.

closet[2] concealing in public your homosexuality
Again from the small or private room where you act according to your inclinations. Usually of a male, as in the phrases *closet queen* or *closet queer*, but occasionally of a female.
Whence *in the closet* for a homosexual who so acts.
To *come out of the closet* or COME OUT is to cease to hide your homosexuality from the public.
In occasional and convoluted use, a *closet homosexual* may be a heterosexual male who affects homosexuality, as for example to avert the suspicions of a cuckolded husband:
> Dexter Dempster, New York's leading closet homosexual...(M. Thomas, 1980—Dexter was cuckolding someone)

clothes horse an expensively dressed woman
For display, not drying:
> Who will say a kindly word about... Barbara Amiel, the well-preserved clotheshorse who put the chic into the chicanery of which Black stands accused? (*Daily Telegraph*, 2 December 2005—Barbara was the wife of Conrad Black, the former proprietor of the *Daily Telegraph*)

clout *American* to steal

Probably from the meaning, to hit, whence perhaps by transference from the American HIT[3], to rob, and often referring to thefts from cars.

club[1] an agency promoting the sale of a specific product
Customers, styled as members, usually have a continuing obligation to buy despite not forming an association of like-minded people.

club[2] a business operating illegally or evading regulations
Usually engaged in the sale of alcohol, the showing or distribution of pornographic material, or prostitution. The *members*, almost always men, may avoid criminality because the general public is not admitted.
For a woman, to be *in the club* suggests pregnancy rather than voyeurism.

clunk *American* a corpse
Literally, the sound of a blow or a dull person, neither of which explains the etymology.

co-belligerent a former enemy helping a conqueror in continuing war
By 1943, when Italy tried to change sides, COLLABORATOR[1] had become pejorative, and so
> ...the word 'co-belligerent' was invented to proclaim the new status. (Jennings, 1965)
The wise Italians had shown little belligerence between 1940 and 1943, and had no reason to show any more thereafter.

cobbler a forger
Criminal and espionage jargon, of someone who forges credit cards, passports or other documents. To 'cobble' was literally to repair in a slipshod manner, although we expect more of our shoemakers.

cobblers the testicles
Rhyming slang on *cobblers' awls*, balls, which may or may not be a shortened form of balderdash. Mainly figurative use, with a *load of old cobblers*, meaning nonsense.

cobs the testicles
Literally, small stones, and either a shortened form of COBBLERS or a variant of the American NUTS, a variety being the hazel or *cob* nut

cock *obsolete* to copulate with
Cock, the penis, is a venerable use, as in Shakespeare's lewd pun 'Pistol's cock is up' (*2 Henry IV*). In modern speech a male might *cock a leg across*, *athwart*, or *over* a female. A *cocksman* is a philanderer and the *cockpit*, the vagina, punning on the site of avian contest. For 19th-century Americans particularly *cock*

was an unmentionable word, whence the ROOSTER. To confuse matters, in 20th-century American black slang a *cock* might be a vagina. I offer no explanation for a *cock* as 'A horse not intended to win in the race for which it is put down, but kept in the lists to deceive the public'. (*F&H*)

cock-eyed drunk
Literally, askew. In former times *cocked* also meant drunk, probably from a firearm about to go off. *Half-cocked* is no less inebriated although here the firearm imagery is less cogent.

cock the leg to urinate
Normally of a dog, but not of a bitch.
Sometimes used humorously by and of men.

cock the little finger to be addicted to alcohol
From the manner in which some hold a cup.

cockchafer *obsolete* a prostitute
Punning on the beetle, the maybug *Melolontha vulgaris*, and the soreness which a man might experience after an encounter with her.
For convicts, the *cockchafer* was the treadmill, from the discomfort caused by the *chafing* on the genitalia of rough prison clothes.

cocktail¹ *obsolete* a prostitute
Possibly a pun, also referring to *cockatrice*, a prostitute, from the fabulous serpent which killed by its glare.

cocktail² a mixture of alcohol or illegal narcotics
We have a choice of derivations, some more far-fetched than others. We can rule out the 'six-oared boat used by Kentish smugglers' and derivation from the Krio *koktel*, meaning a scorpion. In Yorkshire it once meant a flaming tankard of ale, which is getting closer. The obvious candidate is the French *coquetel*, from the feather used to stir the drink, but I still stay with the Aztec *xoc-tl*, named from the maiden Hochitl who introduced to the king a concoction devised by her father, thereby winning his heart and immortality. Commoner in America than in Britain, where it tends to refer specifically to a drink based on a spirit without a generic meaning of intoxicants.
Whence *cocktail bars*, *hours*, *lounges*, and the like.

coco mad
A Second World War military use, sometimes as *cocoa*. Not from the drink or the famous clown but from a shortened form of *coconut*, slang for the head.

coffee grinder *American* a prostitute
She may also be a belly dancer or stripper, and the three professions are not mutually exclusive.

coffee-housing cheating at cards
Referring to the behaviour of whist players in 18th-century London coffee houses.
The 1874 *Slang Dictionary* gives *coffee-shop* as a 'watercloset, or house of office', presumably because, as today, passers-by used their lavatories.

cohabit to have a regular sexual relationship with
Literally, merely to live in the same abode, as do parents and children.

coition copulation
It started by meaning mutual attraction, as of planets.

cojones *American* the testicles
A borrowing from the Spanish:
> But Burton spoke fluent Arabic, and he would have learned Maghrebi Arabic for such a venture, and his *cojones* were of legendary size. (Theroux 1995—of Burton's visit to Mecca, although what the testicular idiosyncrasy had to do with that exploit is unclear)

Cojones is also 'often used to indicate machismo. Offensive.' (*Dictionary of Cautionary Words and Phrases*, 1989—however any document prepared for a 'Multicultural Management Program' is likely to take offence easily)

coke cocaine ingested illegally
A shortened form, without reference to the carbonated beverage.
A *cokie* or *coke-hound* is an addict, thereby becoming *coked*.

cold¹ dead
Usually but not exclusively used of hot-blooded creatures, although *knocked out cold* refers to unconsciousness only. Whence several morbidly humorous 19th-century phrases, of which the most common was *cold meat*, a corpse.
A *cold-meat party* was a funeral; a *cold-box* a coffin; a *cold cart* a hearse; a *cold cook* an undertaker; and *cold storage* the grave.

cold² not easily susceptible to sexual excitement
The opposite of HOT¹ but also of someone who fails to be sexually excited on a specific occasion:
> I have often been asked why on my African travels I was cold in regard to the native women. (F. Harris, 1925—what strange interlocutors he must have met)

Despite Mr Harris's unwonted abstinence, more of women than of men, as in Shakespeare's *cold chastity*.

cold³ an evasion to explain an absence
As with the *diplomatic cold* under DIPLOMATIC. Also used by those wishing to conceal infirmity of prominent people, such as Andropov, the Soviet leader, who spent months on a dialysis machine dying from kidney failure and diabetes, but was reported to the suffering from a *cold*.
A Chinese Communist official who has a *cold* is one who has lost his job.
In the Second World War, a serviceman who said he had *caught a cold* had contracted gonorrhoea.

cold feet cowardice or fear
There is a physical justification for this standard English use. We do experience the symptoms of coldness when we are frightened.

cold turkey the effect of sudden and sustained deprivation of narcotics
The sufferer resembles a bird which has been plucked. Usually of withdrawal from drugtaking, drinking alcohol, or smoking tobacco. To help a person shake off an addiction is to *cool a turkey*.
In America other fowls may replace the turkey.

cold-water man *Scottish* a person who drinks no alcohol
A usage in a society where, among many men, abstinence is taboo, especially if the abstainer eschews the comfort of whisky.

collaborator¹ a traitor
Literally, working with another like-minded person. Descriptive of those living in occupied countries in the Second World War who assisted their conqueror. Also as *collaborationist* and to *collaborate* was so to act.

collaborator² a ghost writer
The labour is mostly done by the ghost.

collapsible container *American* a contraceptive sheath
Police jargon which transfers the male postcoital collapsing to the contraceptive.

collar¹ to steal
Either from putting a collar on a dog in the days when they were taken for ransom (although in English Common Law they could not be the subject of theft) or, more probably, from securing possession of anything.

collar² an arrest

From the act of grabbing the miscreant by the *collar*, whence to *get your collar felt*, to be arrested.
In America an *accommodation collar* is an arrest to fill a quota and prove dedication to the work, whence also a *collar*, a police officer.

collateral damage killing or wounding civilians by mistake
Literally, damage running alongside.

collect *American* to accept a bribe
Usually it refers to taking bribes on a regular basis:
> Woe to the cop who collects anything...
> and doesn't 'see the sergeant'. (Lavine, 1930)
Of the same tendency was the British *collector*, the highwayman who ordered you to stand and deliver.

Colombian gold high-quality marijuana
From the source, the colour, and the profits.

colonial *American* old
Real estate jargon of buildings which were not always there before the 1780s. *Antebellum*, referring to the Civil War, is more likely to be authentic, but don't count on it.

colony a distant territory ruled by expatriates
Literally, a place to which people emigrate in order to live but most British, French, German, and Italian *colonies* retained their majority of indigenous inhabitants. Immediately before the British Crown Colony of Hong Kong was returned to China, 98% of its population were people of Chinese extraction.

colour relating to racial descent
Literally, the universal human characteristic of skin pigmentation. A *colour problem* is tension between different racial groups:
> It was now accepted that some form of control was unavoidable if we were not to have a colour problem in [Britain] on a similar scale to that in the USA. (Heffer, 1998, quoting Rab Butler in 1961)
To be *colour-blind* is to be unprejudiced concerning the skin pigmentation of others.

colour-tinted dyed
Describing hair, where it is not just circumlocution because the process involves more than changing a shade. To *colour correct* hair is to dye it, the new appearance being incorrect with regard to its natural state, and dyed hair is said to be *coloured*, although hair is never colourless, whether dyed or not.

coloured not exclusively of white Caucasian ancestry

Oscar Wilde correctly described himself on entering the United States as pink.

In South Africa *coloured* or *Cape coloured* was used of those of mixed ancestry.

An America you may also meet a *person of the colored persuasion* or a *person of color.*

colourful amoral or defying convention
A catch-all word for journalists wary of defamation. Obituarists can be more outspoken.

colt¹ *obsolete* to impregnate a woman
Punning perhaps on an old meaning, to cheat, because it was used of extramarital impregnation:

She hath been colted by him. (Shakespeare, *Cymbeline*)

colt² *obsolete British* a fine extracted from a recruit by other employees
The money was spent on intoxicants as part of a ritual called *shoeing the colt*, which tells us the etymology. This was one of many similar expressions relating to initiation ceremonies for apprentices.

comb out to massacre
How the Germans described their treatment of Soviet citizens:

. . . anti-partisan operations resulted in the deaths of a quarter of a million Russian civilians in a given area was encircled and then 'combed out', a euphemism for lining up the inhabitants of villages and shooting them. (Burleigh, 2000)

combat fatigue an unwillingness or inability to continue fighting
Not just weariness from broken nights, poor shelter, irregular food, unchanged clothing, lice, ulcers, and the other discomforts of active service but a reaction to prolonged exposure to danger and seeing the death and mutilation of comrades.

As with BATTLE FATIGUE, it was difficult for those undergoing the same dangers and privations to distinguish between psychological disturbance and cowardice.

combat ineffective dead, seriously ill, or badly wounded
Not describing a gun which doesn't shoot straight but how a commander assesses his troops.

come to achieve a sexual orgasm
Of both sexes.

Come off is less common and seems to be used of the male rather than the female experience. *Come* is used also to describe the fluid secreted by the male and by the female during copulation.

come across¹ to do something unwillingly under coercion
It refers to extortion, bribery, or making a confession.

come across² to have a casual sexual relationship with
Again acceding to a suggestion, usually from a man, but without any coercion.

come again to resume your living physical state after death
An eagerly awaited expectation by some devout people despite the manifest problems such a happening might pose:

He shall come again in His glory, to judge both the quick and the dead. (*Book of Common Prayer*, 1662)

Come back in the same sense is obsolete.

come aloft to have an erection of the penis
Punning perhaps on the duties of deck-hands on sailing ships:

I cannot come aloft to an old woman. (Dryden, 1668)

come around to menstruate
Regularity is hoped for, except for those wishing to become pregnant.

come-by-chance see CHANCE

come down to cease to be under the influence of illegal narcotics
After a feeling of levitation and implying the unpleasantness and ill-temper of one so affected.

come hither inviting a sexual approach
Descriptive of female conduct, either on a single occasion, as with a *come-hither look* or *register*; or habitually:

She was through and through a police officer, not primarily a come-hither female. (D. Francis, 2000)

come home by Clapham see CLAPHAM

come home feet first to be killed
Corpses are usually carried that way, although the opposite happens with coffins.

come in at the window *obsolete* to be illegitimate
The newcomer was figuratively introduced into the household by any aperture other than the front door. Following the window in popularity were the side door, the back door, the wicket, and the hatch. Also as *come o' will*:

In at the window or else o'er the hatch
. . . I am I howe'er I was begot.
(Shakespeare, *King John*)

come into the public domain to cease being a secret
No more than pompous circumlocution, it might seem, except that the phrase is used when something which politicians or officials wish to keep quiet becomes, or threatens to become, public knowledge, to their discomfort or embarrassment.

come off see COME

come on[1] to menstruate
Obvious derivation and wide female use.

come on[2] an invitation to another to make a sexual approach
Either sex may so encourage the other, although it is mainly done by a female.
To *come on* means that a female is so signalling a male.

come-on[3] a deceptive inducement to enter into a long-term commitment
Advertising jargon for the offer intended to tempt or trap the unwary.

come out to announce your availability as a sexual partner
Until the 1950s this was social jargon for the parade of marriageable girls of wealthy parents, in London especially, before supposedly eligible bachelors; see also OUT[1].
The phrase is now used specifically of homosexuals who make public their sexual preference for the first time, being a shortened form of *come out of the closet*.

come through to act under duress
From the meaning, to achieve a desired result. It is used of the payment of a bribe or of giving information under duress.

come to to copulate with
Particularly in a marriage where the spouses occupy separate beds:
   I have come very seldom to you in the last few years. (Bogarde, 1981—a husband was speaking to his wife)

come to a sticky end to fail disastrously but deservedly
The fate of a fly on flypaper. It may describe an untimely death of a dissolute or criminal person, the incarceration of a rogue, an unwanted pregnancy of a flighty girl, or any other unpleasant upshot which allows third parties the satisfaction of saying 'I told you so'.

come to see to court
Literally, to visit, but a man who *comes to see your sister* is unlikely to content himself merely with a visual inspection. See also SEE[1].

come to the attention of the police to be a habitual criminal
The constabulary do not so refer to their law-abiding citizens.

come to your resting place to die
Not reaching your overnight hotel but the common imagery of likening death to resting while you await resurrection or whatever may be in store. Also as *come to the end of the road*.
I like the Shetland *come to yourself*, with its Buddhist overtones.

come together to copulate
Without necessarily reaching simultaneous orgasms:
   When his mother Mary was espoused to Joseph, before they came together, she was found with child by the Holy Ghost.
   (*Matthew* 1:18)

come up with the rations *British* to be awarded as a matter of routine
An army use where campaign medals were not valued highly and those for bravery appeared to be awarded at random.
Now used of routine awards to British functionaries and time-servers.

come your mutton (of a male) to masturbate
The common MEAT[2] imagery. See also MUTTON.

comfort[1] copulation
Sought by the male, as when Bothwell *sought comfort* with his divorced wife Jean because of the frigidity of his current wife, Mary Queen of Scots. (Linklater, 1964); or *provided* by the female, as Harriet Howard did to Louis Napoleon when exiled in England. (Tombs & Tombs, 2006)
Comfort therapy is prostitution.

comfort[2] urination
As in the *comfort break* at meetings.
An American *comfort station* is a public lavatory.

comfort women Japanese army prostitutes
Providing COMFORT[1] to the troops. Following high rates of venereal disease in the 1930s among their soldiers in China, the army established *ianjo*, or *comfort houses*, staffed by *inafu*, or *comfort girls*, prostitutes recruited or conscripted in Japan, China, and Korea. The ration was one prostitute for every 40 soldiers, or in total 80,000 women in 1945, paid two yen by each customer and, in theory at least, free to leave the army when they had earned 1,000 yen. (Louis, 1984)

comfortable¹ *American* drunk
A feeling of well-being may be experienced at some stage. For the Victorians, *comforting beverages* were alcoholic drinks. (Hardy, 1886)

comfortable² not in mortal danger
Hospital jargon, although a patient so described would seldom admit to being 'free from pain and trouble' (*OED*) unless deeply sedated. Thus we can sympathize with 'Mr Steve Wickwar, 27' who:

> sustained severe cuts after being attacked
> by a two-year-old male leopard...His
> condition at Northampton general hospital
> was said to be comfortable. (*Daily Telegraph*,
> April 1982—but why not 'a leopard, 2'?)

coming of peace a military defeat
The words used by Hirohito in his broadcast of 15 August 1945, when he announced Japan's capitulation in such evasive and formal language that some of the military misunderstood his message and carried on fighting. He also asserted, with considerable understatement, that the war 'had turned out not necessarily to Japan's advantage'. (Keegan, 1989)

commerce copulation
Literally, exchange or dealings between people, but long used of copulation, especially if it is outside marriage. *Sexual commerce* is explicit. *Sinful commerce* is not thieving or receiving stolen goods but copulating with a prostitute.

commercial sex worker a prostitute
Neither a salaried nurse running a VD clinic nor even someone employed to categorize day-old chicks:

> A St John Ambulance worker...tells me
> that she is only allowed to describe
> [prostitutes] as CSWs—short for
> Commercial Sex Workers. (*Daily Telegraph*,
> 5 January 1994)

commission a bribe
Not the warrant to do something for another but from the reward in percentage terms for doing it. Commercial usage where a gloss of legality is used to conceal bribery.

commission agent a person who accepted bets for a living
Neither an agent of those who place the bets nor rewarded by commission. In former times, some opprobrium used to attach to gambling and those who facilitated it.

commit to consign to an institution for the insane
Literally, to give in charge, and clearly the shorter form of a longer phrase.

commit a nuisance to urinate in public

Usually of a male, where *commit* meant perform and *nuisance* is legal jargon for an offensive act.
You may still see some of the old signs enjoining us to 'Commit no nuisance'—don't urinate here.

commit misconduct to indulge in extramarital sexual activity
Used of either sex and also as *commit infamy* or *commit the seventh*, breaking a commandment. *Commit adultery* is standard English and not euphemistic, being the first use of the phrase, and is defined in the *OED* as 'Violation of the marriage bed', a euphemistic evasion worthy of Dr Wright's *EDD*.

commit suicide to be murdered
One of the Nazi evasions when explaining the death of a prisoner:

> The Hamburg Gestapo chief Bruno
> Streckenbach came to a local arrangement
> in 1934 with the courts, whereby those
> who 'committed suicide' after he had
> smashed their kidneys with a
> knuckleduster were cremated to prevent
> autopsy. (Burleigh, 2000)

committed dogmatic as to political or social views
Literally, devoted, although people who use the phrase are not likely to elaborate on the cause which is the object of their devotion. Whence, *commitment*, such dogmatism:

> He believed the best journalism was not the
> balanced, objective kind...but the
> 'journalism of commitment'. (Simpson,
> 1998)

Committee (the) an instrument of state repression
A common abbreviation in totalitarian states like the former Soviet Union. Thus the *Komitet Gosudarstvennoi Bezopasnosti*, or KGB, became the *Komitet*, or Committee.
In Cuba you may still find the *Committee for the Protection of the Revolution*, which involves neighbours spying on each other in the manner of the Nazi *Blockwächter* organization.

commode a portable lavatory
Originally, a woman's tall headdress, whence a tall chest of drawers, and then any wooden bedroom cupboard, which many of these lavatories, disguised as furniture, came to resemble.

commodious too large
Literally, convenient, but in real estate jargon, where we might have expected elegant spaciousness, all we find is a place too big to heat or keep in repair.

common customer *obsolete* a prostitute

Supplier might have seemed more appropriate. Shakespeare also uses *commoner o' the camp*. And as *common jack*, *maid*, or *sewer*, not necessarily working in a *common house*, or brothel. *Common tart* may still be heard.

common house a lavatory
From the sharing and a feature of 19th-century urban development. Not to be confused with the Shakespearean *common house*, or brothel. (*Measure for Measure*)

commune with Toby to drink intoxicants to excess
Normally beer, drawn from a *Toby jug* or *mug*.

communicable disease a venereal disease
For medical practitioners the phrase has two meanings. It can be either a disease like meningitis, which must be reported (communicated) immediately to the authorities, or a disease which can be transferred by contact from one sufferer to another. Lay use is normally only in the second sense.

community alienation lawlessness
Social-service jargon which seeks to avoid blaming thugs for anti-social behaviour. It does not mean the place has been taken over by foreigners.

community of wives polyandry
Nothing so tame as the Women's Institute, Mothers' Union, or Ladies' Circle. The practice seems to have been last sanctioned in England during the religious blossoming of the Commonwealth, when it was common among the Ranters, a religious sect which has proved less enduring, if more lively, than the Quakers.

community relations social tension between those of a different racial background
The use seeks to avoid reference to COLOUR and can be found in various phrases relating to problems which may occur through the distrust, ignorance, jealousy, fear, or other factors which may be present when those of different racial backgrounds move into territory formerly occupied mainly by another ethnic grouping. Thus a *community affairs officer* is concerned to prevent, and a *community relations correspondent* to report on, discord between such groups, not to arrange or write about church fêtes and the like.

community safety unit *British* a police squad devoted to investigating and recording high profile cases
Although nominally supposed to investigate serious crime, the agenda is usually set by tabloid newspapers, committing the officers to concentration on racial or sexual issues rather than the safety of the community at large.

community treatment center *American* a prison
Not a doctor's surgery, hospital, or operating theatre.

companion a person with whom you have a regular extramarital sexual relationship
Originally in this sense, an employee who lived with and attended to another person. Of either sex, and heterosexual or homosexual:
    Princess Stephanie of Monaco and her companion, Daniel Ducruet, her former bodyguard, pose with their second child Pauline. (*Daily Telegraph*, 7 June 1994)
A *constant companion* is journalese to describe such a relationship where one of the parties might sue for defamation.

company[1] a person with whom you have an extramarital sexual relationship
Literally, companionship. Often of a transient relationship, except when you KEEP COMPANY WITH someone who is STEADY COMPANY.

company[2] **(the)** the main US organization for espionage and foreign subversion
A pun on the initial letters of *Central Intelligence Agency* and the Spanish *Cia*, an abbreviation for *compañía*, company.

compensated dating prostitution
As practised by some schoolgirls in Japan where copulation with females over the age of 13 is legal.

complications the swelling of an adult's testicles during mumps
This symptom, additional in some cases to swollen glands in the neck, is very painful and may lead to infertility.

complimentary included in the price
The usage often seeks to mask an inferior or unwanted substitution for a discontinued service, such as a paper strip with which to clean your shoes in place of a night porter. However, there are exceptions:
    We will shortly take your beverage order. The wine in your basket is complimentary. (Republic Airlines Flight RC 207 Greenville–New York, May 1981)

compliments the subjection to rape
Literally, congratulation or commendation, neither of which is likely to have been felt by those left behind in territory overrun by the Red Army in 1945:
    [The Moscow apologist Ehrenburg's] only reference to rape, however, was to say that Soviet soldiers 'were not refusing "the

compliments" of German women'.
(Beevor, 2002)

compound with *obsolete* to copulate with
Literally, to mingle with:
> My father compounded with my mother
> under the dragon's tail. (Shakespeare, *King
> Lear*)

comprehension the ability to read
Literally, understanding. Educational jargon,
along with *literacy* and *numeracy*, to avoid
having to mention the three r's, which used
to be the foundation of every child's education in the days when teachers were not
obliged to attend teacher training colleges:
> MID-GLAMORGAN ADULT LITERACY/
> NUMERACY SERVICE for help with:
> READING SPELLING ARITHMETIC.
> (Advertisement in *Rhymney Valley Express*,
> noted in *Private Eye*, October 1981,
> addressed to those who had failed to
> acquire these skills at school)

A British *comprehensive* school is one financed
by the state which offers non-selective entry
and is not necessarily characterized by comprehension.

compromise to expose to embarrassment or danger
Literally, to accept a lowering of standards.
Sexually, it means involving someone in, or
revealing, adultery. Anyone found in a *compromising position* or *situation* is unlikely to be
fully clothed.
In American use, to *compromise* may also mean
to murder or destroy.

con to trick
Not relating to the path of a ship or 'set in a
notebook, learned, and conned by rote' but a
shortened form of *confidence*, which was first
used in this sense in 1866 of the advisers of
the Confederate President Davis.
Whence the *confidence trick, or fraud*, practised
by the *con man* (are there no 'con women'?) or
con artist.

concede to to copulate under duress
The female is forced into the concession:
> Many other [German] women also
> 'conceded' to one [Russian] soldier in the
> hope of protecting themselves from gang
> rape. (Beevor, 2002)

concentration camp a place for arbitrary
imprisonment of political and other opponents
They were originally the areas in which
civilians were concentrated by the Spanish
in Cuba and the British in South Africa to
prevent the feeding and hiding of men
engaged in fighting against them. The Nazis

adopted the tactic and the terminology—
Konzentrationslager. Their prisons, which
started as places for extortion, ransom, and
humiliation, became depots for slave labour
and genocide.
Sometimes abbreviated to *camp*:
> ...three-fifths of [Polish Jews] had
> disappeared into camps that used the new
> scientific methods... They had an official
> name... Vernitchtungslager,
> extermination camp. (Keneally, 1982)

concentration problem (a) idleness or
inattention
Educational jargon in a world where there are
no lazy or stupid children.

concern political dogmatism
Literally, care or interest but used by and of
pressure groups and extremists to justify their
obsession with single issues.
Concerned, which once meant drunk as a
shortened form of *concerned in liquor*, now
indicates dogmatism.

concert party the concerted buying of
shares in a company using different
names
Stock Exchange jargon for an attempt to build
up a key or large holding without putting on
notice the board of the company or the Stock
Exchange. There is also a more innocent use,
where individuals have banded together to
acquire a large holding which remains sep-
arately owned.

concession a reduction in an inflated demand
The jargon and practice of politics:
> The bids... are invariably padded so that
> the minister can be seen to make
> 'concessions' in head-to-head negotiations
> with the Treasury. (Major, 1999)

concessional free or subsidized
The use seeks to mask the granting of charity
or privilege to individuals who receive *concessional fares* on public transport and to countries which receive *concessional loans* or
financing:
> Most big companies that work in the
> regions where concessional financing is
> used believe that the countries other than
> their own twist and bend and creatively
> interpret these rules. (Patten, 1998)

concoct to falsify
Originally, to form from different ingredients.
Now used of inflating claims for expenses,
publishing inaccurate figures, telling lies, and
the like.

concrete shoes (in) murdered and hidden

A more accurate description of CEMENT SHOES, and also as *concrete boots* or *overcoat*.

condition¹ an illness

Literally, any prevailing circumstance, but in matters of health any *condition* is bad, be it of the heart, liver, bladder, or whatever.

condition² a pregnancy

This usage is not reserved for unwanted or difficult pregnancies and merely avoids direct reference to the taboo surrounding pregnancy.

The *condition* may be adjectivally enhanced, as by *delicate*, *interesting*, or *certain*.

conditioner a mild acid liquid

Sold to neutralize the alkaline effect of soap after washing hair. In former times people used vinegar to this end. A product which says it combines shampoo and conditioner is one which has been formulated with a pH of 7 and costs more.

conduct disorder habitual disobedience, selfishness, and incivility

The phrase might refer to a number of things other than naughty children, the majority of whom are the product or victims of the absence of any sanction for bad behaviour:

A study for the Office of National Statistics, however, found that about three percent of five- to 10-year-olds and about four percent of 11- to 15-year-olds have 'conduct disorders'. (*Sunday Telegraph*, 11 April 2004)

confederation a pressure group

Literally, an alliance or union of states for joint action. Thus the *British Confederation for the Advancement of State Education* sought not so much to improve the quality of teaching in state schools as to close down those which achieved higher standards through the selection of pupils.

conference (in) unwilling to see or talk to callers

A standard excuse, which sounds grander than TIED UP.

The 'formal meeting for consultation and discussion' (*SOED*) is where we go when we are *at a conference*, unless were are in medical or academic employment, when a *conference* may be a paid holiday to be enjoyed with our peers and a chosen companion in a congenial place at the expense of a third party.

confident pricing charging more for the same product

The circumstances are that you expect the buyers not to make a fuss about it or stop buying.

confinement the period of childbirth

Literally, no more than be cooped up, as in prison. Standard English.

Thus to be *confined*, which might be taken as being unable to leave a sickroom, is to be giving birth, this usage having superseded the 19th-century meaning, constipated.

confirmed bachelor a homosexual

Literally, a man who has eschewed marriage. Much used in obituaries.

conflict a war

Literally, a strong disagreement or a single battle. It sounded better than war, especially when the Korean *conflict* burst upon us so soon after the Second World War.

confrontation a war

Literally, a meeting face-to-face. Indonesia's 1963 *confrontation* with the fledgling state of Malaysia included subversion and armed incursions, the latter being repulsed with the help of the British (a debt now forgotten). The word is also used by terrorists of indiscriminate violence against society.

confused drunk

It certainly can take you that way.

congress copulation

Literally, a coming together, as in the *Indian Congress Party*, which restricts its activities in the main to politics. Also as *sexual congress*.

conjugal rights copulation with your spouse

Legal jargon, from the parties being yoked together, and indeed in some societies a symbolic yoke formed part of the marriage ceremony. A woman is unlikely to seek these rights from her husband except in satire.

If a wife goes to court for the *restoration of conjugal rights*, she seeks pecuniary rather than sexual gratification.

conk (out) to die

From the unplanned stoppage of an engine and the consequent immobility.

connect¹ to copulate

The imagery is from joining or fastening together. *Connection* implies promiscuous copulation, but the *ultimate connection* may take place in or out of the marriage bed. A *loose connection* implies mental rather than sexual incapacity, with imagery from electric wiring.

connect² a source of illegal narcotics

The *connection*, in the jargon of drug usage, runs from the manufacturer to the retailer.

connections people liable to favour or assist you unfairly

Literally, those to whom you are related or whom you know well, but also used of those susceptible to bribery.

connubial pleasures copulation

Although *connubial* means to do with marriage, the *pleasures* to which the phrase alludes can be taken within or without that institution.

conquer a bed *obsolete* to copulate with a female extramaritally

The common BED² imagery, its occupant being the vanquished.

> When you have conquer'd my yet maiden bed. (Shakespeare, *All's Well that Ends Well*)

consenting   adults male homosexuals over the age of 18 who engage in sexual acts with each other

British law concerns itself less with female homosexuality:

> Two consenting adults had been ejected from the gents. (Sharpe, 1975—they were not consenting to their ejection)

consistent with plan due to management incompetence

A more elaborate edition of AS PLANNED and a warning to investors that something is amiss:

> [On 16 May 2006] EADS reported a rise in R&D expenses...which was 'consistent with plan'. (*Daily Telegraph*, 25 June 2006—on 13 June 2006 the company announced costly and potentially calamitous delays in delivery of a new aircraft. In March 2006, M. Forgeard, EADS' Chief Executive, had wisely cashed in options worth €6.7m. His German counterpart, even wiser perhaps, had declined to do so)

console to copulate with

Literally, to alleviate sorrow. It is used of either sex, especially when a regular sexual partner is absent.

Consolation is such copulation.

consort with to have an extramarital sexual relationship with

A consort is someone who keeps you company:

> Some of them consorted with—with the worst type of native woman. (Fraser, 1975)

constructed *American* conquered or recaptured

The language of Vietnam:

> A 'constructed' hamlet meant not a newly built one but a former Viet Cong hamlet that had been worked over politically. (M. McCarthy, 1967)

If it was taken by the Vietcong and recaptured, it became, in the jargon, *reconstructed*.

consultant¹ a senior employee who has been dismissed

A usage by and of those who seek to conceal the loss of face arising from dismissal.

consultant² a salesperson

The suggestion is that they give the customer impartial advice:

> Virgin Associates Direct has a network of 6,000 consultants demonstrating products in people's homes. (*Daily Telegraph*, 5 April 2000)

consummate (a relationship) to copulate

Originally, to accomplish to the full.

Consummation is one of the essential ingredients of Christian marriage, in default of which a British or Vatican court, among others, may grant an annulment. To *consummate your desires* implies copulation, usually of men but:

> ...there is a house in Regent Street, I am told, where ladies, both married and unmarried, go in order to...consummate their libidinous desires. (Mayhew, 1862)

consumption pulmonary tuberculosis

Prior to penicillin, this was the dread disease which wasted away, or consumed, the sufferer.

Also known as *the white plague*, both phrases were replaced latterly by *TB*, for *tubercule bacillus*.

contact a military engagement

Army jargon for engaging opponents whom they do not in fact touch:

> ...men from the Parachute regiment spoke uninterrupted about their recent experience of 'contact' (army-speak for fighting) with the Taliban in Afghanistan. (*Daily Telegraph*, 10 June 2006)

contact with sexual activity with

From the touching. In heterosexual encounters, it appears to apply only to the male, despite the mutuality of the transaction.

Contact sex involves more than kissing, voyeurism, and the like:

> Reynolds denied ever having had 'contact sex' with Miss Heard. He said the taped telephone conversations were simply manifestations of an embarrassing craving for 'phone sex'. (*Daily Telegraph*, 24 August 1995—even more embarrassing was the fact that Reynolds was a US Congressman and Miss Heard was a 16-year-old girl)

contagious and disgraceful disease a
venereal disease
Legal jargon in the English law of defamation
whereby, if you wrongly imputed it when
speaking about a woman, she did not need to
prove special damage to succeed in an action
for slander. The Slander of Women Act 1891
also made an imputation of unchastity in a
woman actionable without proof of special
damage. Josephine Butler and other feminists
campaigned against the British *Contagious
Diseases Act*, which gave the police powers to
compel suspected prostitutes to submit to
medical examination.

content kept involuntarily under heavy
sedation
Medical jargon for the treatment of those
whose mental illness makes them violent.

continent see INCONTINENT[12]

contingent not bearing interest
Jargon of the insurance industry where loans
are made which will only earn interest if
there is sufficient capital in the funds of the
borrower.

continuations *obsolete* trousers
They continued a Victorian male's upper
garments in a direction too delicate to mention. See also UNMENTIONABLES[1] for more of
these quaint usages.

contour a fat shape
Literally, the outline of any figure, but
promising to *reduce your contour* is how
advertisers try to sell you health foods,
exercise equipment, and the like.

contract a promise of payment to murder
(someone)
Underworld jargon for a murder treated as a
commercial transaction with payment or a
reward to the killer.
The *contract* may also be the proposed victim.

contribution a quantity of urine
Medical coyness when asking a patient to
provide urine for analysis:
'The usual contribution, please,' she said
motioning towards the lavatory door.
(Sanders, 1981)

control unit *American* a cell for solitary
confinement
There is no inference that the other prisoners
are out of control.

controlled substance a narcotic
So called because its legal manufacture and
distribution are regulated and supervised.

controversial[1] politically damaging
Bureaucratic jargon of a policy which may
offend populist susceptibilities:
'Controversial' only means 'this will
lose you votes'. 'Courageous' means 'this
will lose you the election.' (Lynn & Jay,
1981)

controversial[2] disreputable or untrustworthy
Journalistic jargon, especially of businessmen
and politicians who might sue for defamation
if the truth were spelt out.

convalescent home an institution for geriatrics
The inmates are sent there to die, not to get
better.
An official or minister in China, said to be
convalescing, has been banished to a remote
region of the country.

convenience a lavatory for public use
Literally, anything which accommodates.
Often specifically described as *public*, *men's*,
or *ladies'*, or merely in the plural.

convenient[1] *obsolete* a prostitute
She restricted her clientele to one regular
customer.

convenient[2] tiny
Real-estate jargon, describing a garden which
is manifestly inconvenient for drying washing, privacy, lighting bonfires, growing produce, and all the other uses to which a garden
should be put.

conventional not involving nuclear or
germ warfare
There is something bizarre in the notion that
any weapons for killing or maiming are
sanctioned by general agreement or established by social custom.

conversation *obsolete* copulation
The use survives, just, in the legal jargon
CRIMINAL CONVERSATION. The usage must
have led on occasion to embarrassment and
misunderstanding, as with Shakespeare's reference to 'His conversation with Shaw's
wife'. (*Richard III*)

conversations the preparation of military plans
One of the euphemisms agreed between the
British and French prior to the First World War
in an attempt to avoid further deranging the
paranoiac Kaiser Wilhelm II. (Tuchman, 1962)

convey *obsolete* to steal
The article taken is carried off. A *conveyor* was
a thief:

...conveyors are you all,
That rise thus nimbly by a true king's fall.
(Shakespeare, *Richard II*)

Conveyance was theft and *conveyancing* swindling, the usage pre-dating, and not alluding to, the fees charged by lawyers for transferring title to real estate.

convivial habitually drunken

A journalistic evasion:
...obituaries are simply eulogies of the great and the good, any of whose peccadillos (unusual sexual tastes, drunkenness and so on) are tactfully powdered over with euphemism ('flamboyant', 'convivial' etc.) (Lewis Jones in *Daily Telegraph*, 1 December 1994)

Whence *conviviality*, drunkenness.

convoy concept an educational theory whereby the rate of instruction is lowered to the rate of the most stupid or least able to learn

A theory once espoused by teacher training institutions and practised by their products, thereby threatening to condemn some able children to a lifetime of menial work or unemployment.

cook¹ to kill

Perhaps not from the usual culinary imagery, despite the attractions of derivation from *cook your goose*, to cause to fail. Possibly from execution by electricity.

Also of stock in a dry country:
A drought...would cook half the stock in the country. (Boldrewood, 1890)

cook² fraudulently to alter

As in the common *cook the books*, to prepare accounts falsely, from the culinary art of re-arranging ingredients to make a more acceptable dish. Sometimes also of records of events.

The phrase was first used of the 'Railway King', George Hudson, who, after overreaching himself, falsified accounts so as to pay dividends out of capital. Among other achievements, he devised the now universal 'clearing' system for shared public services.

cook³ an addict who ingests heated illegal narcotics

Formerly of opium only, when heated over a flame.

Cook County see FIND COOK COUNTY

cookie a promiscuous female

Supposedly warm, sweet, and fresh. A *new cookie* is a younger female consorting with a man who has abandoned his wife.

A *cookie-pusher* is not a pimp but a junior male

employee who curries favour with his boss, the imagery coming from the menial task of handing round the cakes or biscuits at a function.

cool¹ dead

It alludes to the loss of body heat.

In rare American use, to *cool* is to kill. A *cool one* is a corpse.

cool² not carrying illegal narcotics

The reverse of *hot*, meaning illegal, and perhaps owing a little to the meaning, posed or unruffled.

Cool relations between diplomats indicate total disagreement.

Cool is also an overused adjective among younger people, implying social acceptability.

cooler¹ a prison

Common imagery of the place where miscreants are sent to cool down.

cooler² an intoxicant which is diluted and served in a large glass

Normally with ice, to cool you down.

coop *American* a prison

In this case for humans, not for hens and rabbits.

cooperate to assist another through fear or duress

Literally, to work with. It is what the police suggest criminals ought to do when being interviewed. The word was also used of those among the indigenous population in Vietnam who assisted the American forces.

The USSR used *Comecon*, its European Cooperation Council, to control and economically exploit its vassal states in Eastern Europe.

cop¹ to steal

Literally, to catch or seize. Whence to obtain illegal narcotics, through buying, stealing, or howsoever.

The American *cop the drop* is to accept a bribe.

cop² a policeman

Usually thought to be a shortened form of COPPER but also because he *cops* or seizes you. A *cop shop* or *house* is a police station.

Cop, prison is obsolete.

cop³ to experience sexually

As in *cop a feel*, to fondle a female sexually, or *cop a cherry*, to copulate. Less often of homosexual activity.

cop a packet to be killed or severely wounded

A variant of CATCH A PACKET in all its meanings, including contracting a venereal

disease. Sometimes also as *cop it*.
Cop out, in this sense, is rare.

cop an elephant's to become intoxicated
Rhyming slang on *elephant's trunk*, drunk.
Occasionally a drunkard may be described as
elephant's.

cop out *American* to plead guilty to a
minor offence in return for the prosecution dropping a more serious charge
A part of the process of plea-bargaining.

copper a policeman
Probably from the metal buttons on their
19th-century uniforms, but COP[2] offers an
alternative etymology.

copulate to fuck
Originally, to link together, whence to become joined together. As it is explicit in
standard English and less jarring than *fuck*,
I use the word, along with *copulation*, throughout this dictionary.

cordial[1] *obsolete* an intoxicant
Originally, any food or drink which comforted
the person who ingested it.
In modern use a drink so described, for
example lime juice, is likely to please but
not to intoxicate.

cordial[2] cold and unfriendly
Diplomatic jargon which indicates the opposite of the correct meaning, warm and
friendly.

co-respondent a male accused at law of
having cuckolded another
Legal jargon for the man who has to *respond*
jointly with the wife to a husband's petition
on the grounds of adultery.
Whence articles of clothing, such as *co-respondent's shoes*, of suede or two-toned leather,
thought to be affected by philanderers.
In America a woman may also be a *correspondent*, being in Britain no more than a *party
cited*.

corked *American* drunk
Of people: the converse of wine, which should
not be drunk when it is corked. The imagery
is unclear.

corn[1] low-grade whisky
From the material, and often distilled privately and illegally. In many compounds such
as *corn juice*, *corn mule* (with a special kick), and
the obsolete *corn waters*.
Corned means drunk.

corn[2] copulation with a woman
A less common version of OATS, from the food

a horse likes best and often.
The obsolete *cornification*, lust, comes from the
Latin *cornus*, a horn.

corn-fed *American* plump
A description of a young female, from the
fattening of livestock through an augmented
diet.

corner[1] to establish a monopoly in an essential product
Probably from driving cattle into the corner of
a yard rather than from storing goods in a
hidden place.
To *corner* is British criminal jargon for selling
shoddy goods at more than their worth by
persuading greedy buyers that they are in
short supply or have been stolen.

corner[2] a urinal
Male use, from the facility of urinating in an
open space so long as the penis is concealed:
   Oh, I'm so sorry, I was looking for a corner.
   (Olivier, 1982, quoting Winston Churchill
   who entered a theatre dressing room in
   1951)

corner[3] a penis
The etymology is unclear. Usually in the
phrase, *get your corner in*, to copulate with.

coronary inefficiency an abnormal functioning of the heart
Medical jargon verging on circumlocution and
pomposity rather than euphemism.
A *coronary adjustment* is a medical procedure to
improve the functioning of the heart.
Those who have suffered a *coronary* have had a
heart attack.

corporate entertainment bribery
When customers are given treats at the firm's
expense. Also as *corporate hospitality*:
   The boxes [at Covent Garden opera house]
   are largely used for corporate
   entertainment, that is to say buttering up
   clients. (H. Porter, *Daily Telegraph*, 22
   October 1994—he also noted *business
   entertainment*, *freebie*, *conference*, JOLLY[2], *jaunt*,
   concessionary fare, *facility trip*, *sale preview*, and
   HOSPITALITY as being indicative of bribery)

corporate recovery the management or
winding-up of insolvent companies
Accountants' jargon which seeks to draw
attention to the often slim hope of revival
rather than the probability of demise.

corpse (of a performer) to be unable to
continue to act
Forgetting your lines or through uncontrol-
lable laughter.

correct in line with received opinion or enforced dogma
Not adhering to high moral standards but following the party line slavishly in thought and deed in Nazi and other totalitarian regimes. See also POLITICALLY CORRECT.

correction a serious fall (in value)
Stock exchange jargon for a collapse after heavy selling, which seeks to imply that prices had previously risen too high.

correctional of or pertaining to prison
The theory is that convicts are there to be taught better ways.
An American *correctional facility* is a prison and a *correctional officer* is a jailer. For the Soviet communists, *correctional training* included political imprisonment in *corrective training camps*.
See also HOUSE OF CORRECTION.

corridor creeping extramarital copulation
From the days when individual lavatories in large houses were not attached to bedrooms:
   Hatfield was tacitly barred to [the Prince of Wales] because of his habit of corridor creeping, unless Princess Alexandra was also of the party. (A. Roberts, 1999)

corrupt to copulate with outside marriage
Literally, to spoil or lead astray. It is the male who usually did this kind of spoiling:
   Angelo had never the purpose to corrupt her. (Shakespeare, *Measure for Measure*)

cosmopolitanism treachery
Literally, interest in and familiarity with many parts of the world.
Stalin distrusted Jews in particular and accused them of *cosmopolitanism*, plotting against the Soviet state.

cost growth an unbudgeted escalation of expense
A phrase used in an attempt to avoid attributing blame to the mistakes of government officials, the incompetence of a contractor, and the dishonesty of politicians:
   The Ministry of Defence said it had 'mutually agreed' with Swan Hunter to close the contract to build two logistic ships 'which had experienced considerable cost growth'. (*Daily Telegraph*, 14 July 2006—an additional £84m had previously been paid to the company without publicity prior to a general election so as not to damage the prospects of government candidates in five nearby constituencies)

cost reductions involving people the enforced dismissal of employees
Any cost reduction involves people, whether they retain their jobs or not. Another example of corporate evasion.

costume wedding the marriage of a pregnant bride
Her physical indications rather than her remorse at her premarital behaviour may inhibit the wearing of the traditional white dress.

cottaging seeking a male homosexual partner in a public urinal
Cottage is a slang name for urinal.

couch potato a person who habitually spends leisure time watching television
Not a vegetable related to the pernicious couch-grass, or *Triticum repens*, but a person vegetating on a sofa.

cough[1] to give information to the police
Of a criminal, and a variant of the *singing* theme. It may include an admission of guilt. *Cough medicine* or *syrup* is a payment or other inducement by the police to an informer.

cough[2] to die
The terminally ill suffer from laboured breathing and catarrh.

cough medicine a spirituous intoxicant
Mainly humorous by men with disapproving wives, usually of whisky, from the colour and supposed medicinal value.

couldn't be reached was avoiding being questioned
A journalistic evasion when the suspected perpetrator of a sin of omission or commission, usually a politician or a person in business, decides to avoid the media for a while.

count (the) death
Boxing imagery. The *long count*, though rarer, shows greater knowledge of the sport. To *put out for the count*, again from boxing, is to make unconscious rather than to kill. To *count the daisies* is to be dead, the sums being done from the roots upwards, it would seem.

counter-attack an unprovoked aggression
The Nazis, and some who emulate their example in the modern world, do not need an *attack* to counter before staring a war. Hitler so described his invasion of Poland in August, 1939.

counter-insurgency waging war in another country
The insurgents are usually the native inhabi-

tants who seek to establish their own administration in place of that imposed by those
who use this expression, such as the French in
Algeria, the British in various places, and the
Americans in Vietnam.

counter-revolution any internal opposition to a totalitarian regime
The only permitted *revolution* is the one which
brought the government to power.

country *American* not reconstituted
The language of the coffee shop(pe):
> Your choice of three crisp slices of bacon
> . . . served with one large country egg.
> (Holiday Inn menu, May 1981—in the
> event, the chef chose the slices for me)

country blood *obsolete* having in part
black ancestry
The term was used by the British in India to
describe those of mixed race. Also as *country-
born*. It was supplanted in part by the term
Anglo-Indian, which had formerly referred to
British people serving or working in India.

country-club girls *American* prostitutes operating out of town
When the law closed New Orleans brothels in
1917 to remove temptation from servicemen,
many of the prostitutes moved into the
countryside.

country in transition a poor and backward country
The phrase fails to specify in which direction
it is moving:
> . . . those thrilling economies known to the
> IMF as Less Developed Countries or (a new
> euphemism) countries in transition. (*Daily
> Telegraph*, 15 September 1994)

country pay *obsolete American* payment in
kind
During the War of Independence, currency
issued by various states, in dispute about
federal powers, was rightly distrusted and, if
pounds, shillings, and pence were not available, barter was preferred to local banknotes.
The wise George Washington kept his savings
safely in sterling in the Bank of England in
London.

country sports killing wild animals for
pleasure
The trio hunting, shooting, and fishing. Also
as *country pursuits*, which do not seem to
include hiking, gardening, or simply watching the grass grow.

county farm *American* an institution where
people are detained involuntarily

Either through mental illness or as convicts.

couple to copulate
The standard meanings are to marry (of
humans) and to copulate (of animals). *Couple
with* may be explicit of human copulation.
A *coupling house* was a brothel.
If a male and a female are described as a
couple, they have an exclusive sexual friendship with each other.

courses *obsolete* menstruation
From the meaning, a period of time.

courtesan a prostitute
In the 15th century, it referred to someone at
court. The derivation is more likely to be from
the Italian *cortigiana*, despite the morals of
Tudor courtiers.

courtesy included in the price
From the meaning, given freely; but the
courtesy coach takes you to an inaccessible
hotel which you would not have patronized
without it.

cousin Cis a drunken carouse
Rhyming slang for piss which, in the expression
piss-up, has the same meaning. *DAS* says *sis*.

Covent Garden *obsolete* engaged in or
ancillary to prostitution
The London district, with the neighbouring
Drury Lane, was a 17th-century haunt of
prostitutes (see also DRURY LANE AGUE). As
Covent is a corruption of *convent*, there were
many ecclesiastical puns and witticisms. Thus
a *Covent Garden abbess* kept a brothel, or *garden
house*, which contained *Covent Garden goddesses*.
They often infected their customers with
Covent Garden gout, or *garden gout*, venereal
disease, the customers then being said *to have
broken their shins against Covent Garden rails*.

cover to copulate with
Standard English of stallions, from the mounting of the mare.
Also of other mammals, but rarely used of
humans.

cover your boots to urinate
A literal translation from the Hebrew in the
Coverdale and the Geneva Bibles.

cow brute see BIG ANIMAL

crack[1] to rob
By forcible entry of a building or specifically
by *cracking* a safe, an art in which a *cracksman*
specializes.

crack[2] *American* to hit or kill
Not necessarily with a blow that damages the

skull. Criminal argot, or of those who write crime novels.

crack³ an illegal compound narcotic
The compound is notorious for the immediate onset of addiction after use.
A *crackhead* is one so addicted.

crack⁴ *American* to arrest
From *cracking*, or solving a case, perhaps.

crack a bottle to drink wine
Perhaps the more impatient among us might break a neck to get at the contents more quickly, but the phrase is also used when the cork is withdrawn by conventional means.

crack a Jane to copulate extramaritally with a female virgin
From CRACK¹ or from *cracking a problem*? To *crack a doll* or *crack a Judy* means the same thing. The obsolete British phrases for the same achievement, to *crack a pitcher* or a *pipkin*, showed more imagination: both these pieces of pottery remain serviceable after the *cracking*, but not as desirable as those without blemish.

cracked mentally unstable
The article is usable but flawed. There are various similar words using the same imagery.
A *crackpot* may be no more than eccentric, although the adjectival use may imply greater mental instability.
Crack-brained means slightly dotty. *Crackers* can mean anything from mildly eccentric to raving mad.

crackling a woman viewed sexually by a man
Literally, the crisp and tasty outside of roast pork. She is usually described as a *bit* or *piece of crackling*.

cradle-snatcher an older person marrying one much younger
In everyday English, someone who steals a baby, not its bed. Usually of a man and sometimes as a verb. Also as *cradle robber*.

crap associated with hanging people
The meaning to defecate is venerable and not euphemistic; nor is *crapper*, a lavatory or a person who defecates. Death by hanging, with the muscular relaxation and the fear, caused a loss of urine and faeces:
> The hangman was Jack Ketch...the crap merchant, the crapping cull, the switcher, the cramper, the sheriff's journeyman, the gaggler, the topping-cove, the roper or scragger. (Hughes, 1987—describing 19th-century criminal argot)

crash to return to normality after taking an illegal narcotic
To descend from a HIGH.

cream for to desire sexually
Of a female, from a symptom of sexual arousal, whence the American *creamer*, a promiscuous young woman.
In vulgar male use, to *cream* is to ejaculate semen and to *cream your jeans*, to experience premature ejaculation through sexual excitement.

crease to kill by violence
Mainly in America, from the collapse of the victim. In British use it means to hit with a bullet without severely wounding.

creative disputatious or dishonest
Thus for churchmen *creative conflict* is a bitter doctrinal argument. For a businessman *creative accounting* is false bookkeeping.
Creative tension means violent disagreement.
Creative freedom for artists and academics can mean anything they want it to, other than something conventional.

creature (the) spirituous intoxicant
Literally, something created, and perhaps only a shortened form of *creature comfort*.
The use, which survives in Ireland, often spelt *cratur*, *crathur*, or *crater*, was common in 19th-century England too:
> Never a drop of the crater passed down Chancy Emm's lips. (Mayhew, 1862)

creature of sale *obsolete* a prostitute
For sale might have been nearer the mark:
> The house you dwell in proclaims you to be a creature of sale. (Shakespeare, *Pericles*)

credibility gap the extent to which you are thought to be lying
Or, which is more honourable, reluctant to come to terms with unpalatable truth. The phrase comes from US strategic analysis in the 1950s and was used in this sense by Gerald Ford in 1966 when questioning President Johnson's statements about the extent of American involvement in Vietnam.
A *serious credibility gap* means that everyone thinks that you are a liar.

creep-joint *American* a brothel
Originally, an illegal gambling operation without a liquor licence which moved from place to place to avoid detection by, or paying off, the police.
To *creep around* was not to frequent such haunts but, of a man, to act promiscuously, although not necessarily in suede shoes, or *brothel-creepers*.

Cressida a prostitute

She was the lady who gave Troilus a bad time and Chaucer, Shakespeare, and others a plot.

crib *American* a brothel

Literally, a poor sort of house:

> Miserable naked girls in the twenty-five and fifty cent cribs. (Longstreet, 1956—and who wouldn't be miserable on that money?)

A *crib girl* is a low-grade prostitute.

A *crib man* is not a male prostitute but a thief who robs from private houses.

crime against nature (a) *American* sodomy or bestiality

As proscribed in the laws of many states:

> Most states have laws against fornication and even masturbation lying somewhere on their books... One of the most popular phrases is 'crime against nature'... but almost never do they specify what a *crime against nature* is. (Bryson, 1994—as he concludes, it could be anything from walking on grass to chopping down trees)

criminal assault the rape of a female

Any force offered against another intentionally (other than *in loco parentis*) is a crime, whether or not sexually inspired:

> ...leading a criminal assault by several Indians on an English girl. (P. Scott, 1975, describing a rape)

The woman may be said to have been *criminally used*.

criminal connection *obsolete* extramarital copulation

The *connection* is as in CONNECT[1], although adultery was never a crime in the British Isles if the other party were above a prescribed age and consented:

> These [prostitutes] seldom or never allow drunken men to have criminal connection with them. (Mayhew, 1862)

criminal conversation adultery

Legal jargon, often shortened to *crim. con.* The offence, which was not a crime under English law, was usually described as such if committed by the wife.

criminal operation an illegal abortion

Not a planned robbery or cutting off a hostage's ear but aborting a foetus in the days when it was forbidden by law.

crinkly old or an old person

As wrinkled as a WRINKLY.

critical incident an unexpected deterioration in a patient's condition

Medical jargon for a potentially mortal event:

> It would be, thus, not at all surprising to

find that this 'failure of overall care' is quite common, as the cause of about a third of 'adverse events' or 'critical incidents' in hospital. (James le Fanu in *Sunday Telegraph*, 22 May 2005)

critical power excursion a nuclear meltdown

Jargon of the nuclear power industry which hoped it would never happen, until Chernobyl.

croak to die

A dying person unable to clear mucus in the throat makes such a sound. Less often *croak* means to kill and to *croak yourself* means to commit suicide.

A Victorian *croaker* was not a dying man but a doctor, a reflection perhaps on his professional competence.

From the 17th century to the Second World War, to *croak* also meant to whinge.

crocked drunk

From drinking out of too many crocks, or from being injured by the excesses.

Rarely, a *crock* is a drunkard.

crook the elbow *Scottish* to be a drunkard

A variant of *bend the elbow*, which may imply no more than having a drink.

cross (of a male) to copulate with

From the attitude adopted on the female.

A *cross girl* at one time was a cheating prostitute, who *crossed* or *double-crossed* her customers.

Cross-bar hotel *American* a prison

The criminal fraternity, or those who write about it, refer to jails as *hotels* with mordant humour, this being but one example, from the *cross-bar* which secures a gate. Also as a *Crowbar hotel*, in which case the imagery is even more obscure.

cross-dress to be a transvestite

Usually of a male homosexual playing the female role. Whence *cross-dresser*, who so behaves:

> W. C. Blaquiere, the startling effeminate police magistrate [in Calcutta]... being a noted cross-dresser who used to leap at any opportunity to adopt female disguises. (Dalrymple, 2002)

cross-firing a commercial fraud to secure increased borrowings

The imagery is from what happens on the battlefield:

> It appears the alleged fraudulent activity at Versailles could have involved a system called cross-firing. This involves setting up a fictitious company as a trading client,

then approaching a bank for finance to support the deal with the phantom company. (*Daily Telegraph*, 4 March 2000)

cross the floor *British* to change political allegiance

The seating arrangements in Westminster have the opponents facing each other across the floor of the House. If you change parties, you sit on the other side.

Sir Hartley Shawcross, thought to be increasingly disenchanted with the Labour Party of which he was a member, acquired the nickname 'Sir Shortly Floorcross'.

cross the Styx to die

In classical mythology, you were ferried to the other side of the Styx by Charon, so long as your relatives had remembered to put the fare in your mouth when they buried you. A dead Christian might figuratively *cross the River Jordan*, which is toll-free.

cross the threshold into adult life to start copulating

Of a female, who is not necessarily carried across the *threshold* of the marital home by a bridegroom.

cross your palm to bribe

The derivation is probably from the request of a gypsy to have her palm *crossed with silver*, after which she will tell you your fortune. Divination falls within the sphere of influence of the devil, whose powers can be negated only by the use of the Christian cross. The gypsy keeps the silver.

crower *obsolete American* a cock

Another evasion from the days when it was thought indelicate to talk about cocks, bulls, stallions, and asses.

crown jewels see JEWELS

crud human excreta

Originally, curdled milk. Mainly American army use, as in the expression *Cairo crud* for diarrhoea induced by Egyptian culinary experience. Civilians tend to prefer the adjectival form used figuratively:

This Reape was a cruddy character. (Sanders, 1980)

cruise¹ to seek a sexual partner at random

Usually of a male, seeking someone of either sex according to his predilection, on foot or in a car, on the street, in a bar, or at a party.

A *cruise* is such a foray.

In Victorian London and elsewhere a *cruiser* was a prostitute who solicited custom from a hansom cab.

cruise² to be under the influence of illegal drugs

The imagery is from flying or freewheeling.

crumbling edge an inexorable slow downward movement

Jargon of the stock market, when dealers are uncertain when the sea of troubles will no longer erode the cliff:

But we could be in for a 'crumbling edge' with violent movements up and down, albeit on a downward trend. (*Sunday Telegraph*, 23 August 1998—the imagery fits ill with movements 'up')

crumbly an old person

Presumably about to disintegrate. The expression is used only by the young.

crumpet a person or persons of the opposite sex viewed sexually

Literally, a cake made of flower and yeast, and usually of females.

Usually in the phases a *bit* or *piece of crumpet*.

crush a sexual attraction towards another person

Is it from the wish to embrace the object of your affection? American *crushes* are heterosexual for the most part while British schoolgirls in single-sex schools have them homosexually, usually on an older female.

crystal cocaine

In concentrated form, from the appearance.

Cuban heels thick soles and heels on footwear to enhance height

As worn by the shorter Caribbean male at one time, and by the vain still.

cuckoo¹ a male profligate

Despite the derivation from the bird which makes use of nests built by other birds, he does not necessarily cuckold anyone:

The cuckoo then on every tree
Mocks married men. (Shakespeare, *Love's Labour's Lost*)

To *cuckold the parson* was to copulate not with his wife but with your betrothed before the wedding.

cuckoo² mentally unbalanced

The cuckoo has the reputation of being a silly bird.

cuff¹ to arrest

The handcuffs are placed on the victim rather than hitting him about the ear.

cuff² *American* to obtain on credit

Eating *on the cuff* occurred when the waiter noted the amount on a starched shirt *cuff*.

Some customers paid later but others, who did not, were said to *cuff* the restaurant or grill.

cull to kill
Originally, to select for rejection, as deer, seals, etc. The standard English use is never of killing humans.

cult appealing only to a minority
From esoteric religions, we move to *cult* movies, books, art, or even radio or television shows.

cultural having characteristics differing from the norm
Originally, relating to good taste, manners, etc. but:
> 'Cultural'... is the sociologists' jargon for saying as Lewis Carroll once put it 'the word means what I choose it to mean'. (Shankland, 1980)

Cultural deprivation may be what an immigrant to a land with a different tradition to his homeland may be said to suffer and for which the natives of the host country are sometimes castigated as being blameworthy.
A *cultural bias* is anything which may be thought to favour one section of the community over another.
Mao's *Cultural Revolution* was correctly named, creating anarchy to preserve the autocracy of the unbalanced tyrant.

cumshaw a bribe
The derivation is from the Mandarin used by beggars, although a normally reliable authority thought otherwise:
> The expression was originally 'come ashore money', a sailor's tip to the launch's boatman. (Jennings, 1965)

I am indebted to Mr John Black, who tells me that his father, when Accountant-General of Hong Kong, was a prime target for *cumshaws*, which he refused or passed on to worthy recipients as the case might be. The word still means a windfall or something for nothing in British naval slang.

cunning man *obsolete* a wizard
Cunning meant knowing and, as most wizards were in league with the devil, you had to talk nicely about them.

cup too many see IN YOUR CUPS

cupcake a homosexual
Why the inoffensive confection was chosen for this use is unclear. For an American, it may also mean an ineffective male.

Cupid's arbour *obsolete* the vagina
As the God of Love, he provided the Victorians

with many similar phrases—*Cupid's cave*, *cloister*, *corner*, *cupboard*, and so through the alphabet. In his Greek name, *Eros*, he also gave us *eroticism*.

Cupid's measles *obsolete* syphilis
The symptoms are similar at one stage.
In America also as *Cupid's itch*.

curio a piece of loot
Literally, a collector's item:
> He was periodically concerned to acquire what he euphemistically called 'curios', more straightforwardly 'loot'. (Keegan, 1991, writing of Field Marshal Sir John Dill as a young officer in the Boer War)

curious *obsolete* homosexual
Literally, unusual, from the days when it really was unusual to acknowledge or display homosexuality.

currency adjustment a devaluation
Political use, to disguise the failure of the policies which led to its necessity. See also ADJUSTMENT[1].

currency girl a prostitute who copulates only with foreign visitors
A feature of hotels in Communist capitals prior to the collapse of the Soviet empire, when roubles or other local currencies were not acceptable.

curry colonel a British staff officer in the Indian army
From their preferred dish and enjoying a reactionary reputation:
> [Wingate's] opponents were [not necessarily] 'curry colonels' who had not an ounce of offensive spirit in their bodies. (Lyman, 2004—the spirit in their bodies was more likely to have been gin)

curse (the) menstruation
A shortened form of *the curse of Eve*, who thus burdened all females:
> You've probably got the curse or something. (Bogarde, 1978)

curtains death
The derivation is from the end of a play or the darkening of a room.
Some figurative use for dismissal from employment.

custody suite *British* a prison cell
Usually in a police station. In 1986 the police were told to use this term instead of 'cell', I suppose because they must not upset the linguistic susceptibilities of malefactors or infringe their civil rights.

cut¹ to render sexually impotent
Of tomcats by castration, of male humans by vasectomy. An Indian report of 1794 refers to 'Hindoos' as *uncut* fellows of 'Musselmens', meaning that they had not been circumcised. (Dalrymple, 2003)

cut² to dilute in order to cheat customers
Mainly of intoxicants and drugs sold illegally, from the practice of dividing before adulteration.

cut³ drunk
Literally, in dialect, tacking or weaving. Often as *half-cut*.

cut⁴ an illegal or concealed commission payment
Common criminal and commercial use, again from the dividing. Whence as a verb, to take such a payment.

cut⁵ a reduction in the size of the increase desired or expected by the recipient
Normally of spending in the public sector:
So, too has [grown] the number of welfare lobbyists raised in that public-sector culture who protest that every reform is a 'cut' while spending continues to climb. (*Daily Telegraph*, 5 December 1995)

cut⁶ to kill
Mainly American use, and not necessarily with a knife. Also as *cut down on*.
Cut off, meaning dead, is a common use of those who meet an untimely end, often happening in their *prime*, it would appear.

cut a cheese to fart
The smell may be rich and unpleasant. In Somerset you may say that you have *cut a leg* in the same sense. The more general use is merely to *cut one*.
Grose (1811) gives 'Cheeser. A strong smelling fart.'

cut-and-paste job a report sloppily prepared from various sources
The script might be thus edited prior to word processors, which have however retained the terminology.
The same term is disparagingly used of a non-fiction book where a hurried author has undertaken little original research.

cut numbers to make employees redundant
The evasion is in the imprecision about the commodity being counted. Business jargon.

cut out to deprive (someone) of something valuable
Said formerly by sailors, from singling out a ship in the opposing fleet for concerted attack and capture. The term is also used about displacing a female's partner, especially on the dance floor.

cut the mustard to be able to copulate
Cut means to have a share in. The involvement of the condiment is perplexing unless it is a literal translation of *senf*, meaning pizzazz in German slang, which may have come through Wisconsin German/American English. Shortened to *cut it*, and normally used in the negative of an impotent male.

cut the painter to die
Like a boat cast loose on the water and used of old seafarers. *Cut adrift*, of the same tendency, is probably obsolete. *Cut your cable* should logically imply suicide but it is used of natural death, usually in old age.

cut the pigtail to leave your employment
The imagery comes from bullfighting, when the matador who retires no longer affects the traditional hairstyle.

cycle of blood the onset of menstruation
In standard English, the *menstrual cycle*.

Cyprian *literary* a prostitute
Aphrodite, the Greek Venus and goddess of love, was associated with Cyprus.

Cythera *literary* associated with copulation
Again from Aphrodite, this time with her Cretan connections.

D

D anything taboo beginning with the letter D

Usually *damn, damned, damnable*, and the like which used to be less socially acceptable in polite speech than they are today:

> And at last he flung out in his violent way, and said, with a D, 'Then do as you like.' (Dickens, 1861)

The BIG D is death.

D and C the abortion of a foetus

The medical abbreviation of *dilation and curettage*, a common operation for older women but, in the young adult, perhaps involving the removal of a foetus:

> ...a pro-choice ad that sold the Crackers on the notion that the founding fathers fought and died for the right to a D & C. (Anonymous, 1996)

DCM a notice of dismissal from employment

The initial letters of 'Don't come Monday' punning on the Distinguished Conduct Medal. Mainly American use: among British railway employees it denoted suspension for one day only.

daily a non-resident domestic servant

Almost always a female, from the time of rather than the frequency of her attendance:

> Relieved of all chores by the excellent 'daily' we found. (Garve, 1961)

daisy chain a gathering or association to carry out a taboo activity

In America, professional investors who collaborate in order to make short-term gains. Sexually the term describes an orgy, or *daisy-chaining*, with each of the participants joined to another.

dally to copulate with extramaritally

Originally, to talk idly, but in this usage men do it more than women.
Dalliance is such behaviour.

damaged¹ drunk

Mainly American use, from the temporary incapacitation.

damaged² having copulated before marriage

Such a woman, under former convention, would have become less desirable as a bride, and hence was described as *damaged goods*.

damaged³ of criminal habits

Those who use the adjective in this sense see villains' actions as a result of the harm society is thought to have done to them, rather than something that harms society:

> No one can be bad, only 'damaged'. (*Daily Telegraph*, 3 October 1995—reporting on the treatment of young criminals)

damp an alcoholic drink

Often in the phrase *something damp*. In obsolete use, as *damp the sawdust*.

dance¹ *obsolete* to be killed by hanging

Alluding to the kicking of the victim and the gyration of the corpse.
You might also be said to *dance on air, at the end of a rope, off, the Tyburn jig, upon nothing*, etc.
The *dance-hall* was the condemned cell and the *dancing master* the hangman.
To *dance a two-step to another world* is to be killed, but not necessarily by hanging.

dance² to be involuntarily under another's control

You have to move when another tells you to, and not necessarily because a gunman is shooting at your feet. Much figurative use.

dance at *obsolete* to court

Not like the activities of Salome nor probably from the courtship of birds:

> I should have no opinion of you, Biddy,
> if he danced at you with your consent.
> (Dickens, 1861)

To *dance the Haymarket hornpipe* was to copulate with a prostitute, the *Haymarket* in London being a haunt of prostitutes and their clients, while the *hornpipe* introduced two vulgar puns.
To *dance barefoot* was to remain unmarried after a younger sister had married, probably because it would affect the size of your dowry. If a man remained single after his younger brother had married, he was said to *dance in the half-peck*, a *peck* being a liquid measure of two gallons, and it may be that this was a reference to the amount of intoxicant with which the elder brother consoled himself. In rural society, the need to keep labour in the family business or on the farm meant that it was desirable that brothers and sisters respectively married in descending age order.

dangerous to women adept at seduction

The expression does not necessarily imply rape. Lady Caroline Lamb implied as much of Lord Byron when she confided to her journal that he was 'Mad, bad, and dangerous to know'.

Darby and Joan *obsolete British* two male homosexuals in a permanent relationship

Army usage when a posting to India lasted five

or seven years without home leave. The usage is taken from Woodfall's 18th-century ballad about the married couple who grew old together.

dark¹ closed
Theatrical jargon, from the absence of foot-lights etc., when a play has flopped or a theatre management has failed.

dark² (of people) having non-white ancestry
A usage by white people and not necessarily offensive. Also as *dark-skinned* or *dark-com-plected*.
The noun *darky* to describe a non-white is objectionable.

dark man the devil
The colour came from his evil night-time deeds and the soot which adhered to him as he made his way down the chimney.

dark meat¹ the flesh of poultry other than the breast
A survival from the days when prudery forbade the mention of breasts and legs, which also became BENDERS or *lower limbs*. See also WHITE MEAT¹.

dark meat² *American* a black woman viewed sexually by a white male
The usual MEAT¹ imagery:
    Bill, you better try some dark meat and change your luck. (Sanders, 1982—Bill was not averse to the breast of poultry but unable to copulate with his white wife)

dark moon *obsolete* a wife's secret savings
A 19th-century expression, from the days when a married woman was not allowed independent assets and had to hide any savings away without telling her husband, to provide against future disaster.

darn a mild oath
A shortened form of the obsolete *tarnation*, which was a blend of 'damnation' and by the 'tarnal' (Jennings, 1965—'tarnal' meant eter-nal). Still widely used for *damn*, which itself is now mild when less people believe in hell.

dash¹ to adulterate a drink
Literally, to mix or dilute, as in a culinary recipe:
    This beer's dashed an' 'er aulus do dash it.
    (*EDD*)

dash² a mild oath
A literary convention replacing a taboo word like *damn* with a dash.

dasher *obsolete* a prostitute
Not because she sprinted but, because she *cut a dash*, was smartly turned out.

date a heterosexual companion
You specified the time of meeting:
    ...theories as to the girl's possible date. (Davidson, 1978—they were speculating about her companion, not her age)
On a *blind date* you take pot luck.
In America a *date* may describe a prostitute:
    ...pictures and other materials about the women...were given to Bailey's DNC contact, so that prospective clients could choose among possible dates. (Colodny & Gettlin, 1991, describing facilities for obtaining prostitutes for Democratic visitors to Washington)
To *date* is to take out such a companion.

dateless *obsolete* senile
Not leading a celibate life but unable to recall the passage of time.

daughter of the game a prostitute
Working ON THE GAME.
A *daughter of joy* was also a prostitute, not a female whose mother was so named.

Davy Jones's locker a grave at sea
David Jones was 'the devil, the spirit of the sea' (Grose) and his *locker* was the chest where he stored the corpses. Derivation from the biblical *Jonah* seems improbable.
Davy Jones's natural children were pirates, or 'maritime bastards' to other seafarers.

dawn raid the unannounced and rapid accumulation of a large block of shares
City jargon, from the surprise military attack. The manoeuvre is used to avoid having to disclose a gradual accumulation or pay the price increase which would follow sustained demand.

day of action a politically motivated strike
For many, a day of inaction:
    In 1982, we ran into a new sort of dispute over the Health Service workers' strike. The print unions demanded that we print statements in support of the strike. The TUC staged a 'Day of Action' which printers were required to support. (Deedes, 1997)
See also INDUSTRIAL ACTION.

daylight associated with killing by shooting
What is improbably supposed to be seen through the body after the passage of a bullet.

de-accession to dismiss from employment
Denying people access to the former place of work:

Not much help here from Morgan, which is currently de-accessioning 1,500 staff. (*Daily Telegraph*, 12 June 2001)

dead cat bounce a temporary increase in the value of a security or currency of which the price has been falling but which remains overvalued
Like a rebound of a corpse dropped on a hard surface.

dead meat a human corpse
Criminal jargon beloved of writers of detective stories. To *make dead meat of* is to kill a human being.

dead soldier an empty bottle of wine or spirits
The imagery is from the military appearance of a line of bottles.

dead to recklessly ignoring
A Victorian survival, which used to refer mainly to sexual behaviour, when a person might be *dead to honour* or *propriety*.
Dead to the world means asleep.

deadhead *American* a successful scrounger or non-payer
You can't include his cash when you count the takings. Of a non-paying spectator at a ball game, a fare-evader on a train, etc. The word is also used of a cadger in a bar who doesn't stand his round.

deal to sell illegal narcotics
The language of commerce is used to conceal criminality.
Whence a *dealer*, who so behaves.

deal from the bottom of the deck *American* to lie or cheat
The imagery is from card-sharping. The British equivalent using the word *pack* is less common.

deal with to kill
Literally, to manage or take care of a situation: They knew that, in the East, Soviet Jews were already being 'dealt with'. (L. Rees, 2005)

dear friend an extramarital sexual partner
Male or female, but in the latter case less explicit than CHÈRE AMIE.

dear John the ending by a woman of an engagement or marriage
In the Second World War, the missive of dismissal received by so many men serving abroad started formally rather than by using warmer appellations.

The phrase is now used of such a decision communicated by any medium.

debauch to copulate with extramaritally
Literally, to corrupt.
Boswell, who expressed the view that 'a man may debauch his friend's wife genteely' (J. Boswell, 1791), was clearly less moral than his hero:
Take care of me; don't let me into your houses without suspicion. I once debauched a friend's daughter: I may debauch yours. (ibid., quoting Dr Johnson who was speaking hypothetically—*take care* means beware)
Debauch, a drunken revel, is standard English.

debt of honour unpaid money lost at gambling
Under English law gambling debts are not recoverable, but a defaulter would lose his good name, especially if the wager was with a social equal.

decadent not conforming to accepted tastes
Literally, in a state of decline from past standards. Much used by autocrats about anything of which they disapprove, from homosexuality to artistic style:
Shetland had accepted eight 'decadent' surrealist paintings that Goering had confiscated. (Deighton, 1978)

deceive to copulate with another than your regular sexual partner
Literally, to mislead as to the truth in any respect. In former times, it meant to seduce:
[He] courted a young woman over at Mellstock, and deceived her as he had deceived many before. (Hardy, 1891)
If you were *deceived in liquor*, you were not seduced while your defences were down, but drunk.

decent wearing clothes which hide any suggestion of nakedness
You do not have to be fully clothed to be adjudged *decent*, but your attire must not suggest immodesty:
... since I could see she was clothed—'decent', as girls used to say. (Styron, 1976—and they still do)

deck *American* a packet of illicit narcotics
Usually heroin, from being wrapped in paper like a pack of cards. To *deck up* is to pack heroin for retail sale.

decks awash *American* drunk
Applied not only to sailors and owing much to HALF-SEAS OVER.

decline an irreversible physical or mental condition
Literally, a downward slope, but in this use, of pulmonary tuberculosis in the 19th century or mental health in the 20th, there is no prospect of the condition being improved and the slope turning upwards.

décolletage the breasts of an adult female
Literally in French, the cutting out of the neckline of a dress whence, in English, what may be revealed by excessive cutting out.

decommission to dismiss an employee
Literally, to take an inanimate object out of use:
> So many companies are laying off that this issue has become more and more apparent. It's about commissioning and decommissioning. (*Daily Telegraph*, 10 January 2002)

deconnect to dismiss from employment
Correct as far as it goes, we might assume, but not the whole story:
> We cover the life cycle of an employee. When they need to be disconnected immediately, we do that. (*Daily Telegraph*, 10 January 2002)

deconstruction analysis
Literally, pulling to pieces. Jargon of those who teach or study English in academe for looking for hidden meanings in texts, counting the colons in classics, and so on.

decontaminate[1] *American* to embalm
The majority of corpses are no more *contaminated* than a leg of mutton, a side of bacon, or a flitch of beef:
> The incentive to select quality merchandise would be materially lessened if the body of the deceased were not decontaminated and made presentable. (J. Mitford, 1963—the survivors will spend more if the corpse is spruced up)

decontaminate[2] to destroy evidence
You wipe a disk or destroy a file ahead of an investigation.

decrease in footfall (a) less customers
Jargon of the retail trade used as an excuse for falling sales:
> The retailer 'had suffered from the general decrease in High Street footfall' over recent months. (*Daily Telegraph*, 4 January 2007)

deed (the) copulation
Usually extramarital and always so if it is *dirty* or *vile*:
> ... one that will do the deed
> Though Argus were her eunuch.
> (Shakespeare, *Love's Labour's Lost*)

deep freeze *American* a prison
The common imagery of the cooler[1].

deep six to kill or destroy
The original meaning was merely to dispose of, not from the traditional depth in feet of a grave but from the lowest mark on a naval heaving line in fathoms, below which all vanished. Used of destruction, death, or figuratively.

defecate to shit
The original meaning was to purify or cleanse. Thus William Harvey could write in the 17th century:
> The blood is not sufficiently defecated or clarified, but remains cloudy. (Harvey, 1628)
Now *defecate* and *defecation* are used in medical and polite standard English.

defence aggression
As in a government department concerned with waging war which calls itself a *Ministry of Defence*:
> The war cabinet, which will be called the Ministerial Council for the Defense of the Reich, was given sweeping powers by Herr Hitler. (Shirer, 1999, writing of 31 August 1939, when Germany attacked Poland)
The British *D Notice*, short for *Defence Notice*, is an instruction to the media to suppress news, ostensibly on the grounds of state security.

defend your virtue to refuse to have a sexual relationship
Usually of a female and indeed:
> A male defending his virtue is always a farcical figure. (M. McCarthy, 1963)

defensive victory a defeat
The debacle at Dunkirk was so presented to the British in 1940. The same phrase was used by Goebbels in his efforts to keep the *Wehrmacht* fighting in 1945.

defile to copulate with extramaritally
Literally, to make filthy. The *defilement* is usually done by men in the face of female reluctance, passivity, or resistance.
To *defile yourself* is to engage in such activity.
To *defile a bed* does not imply involuntary urination:
> My bed he hath defiled. (Shakespeare, *All's Well That Ends Well*)
and he who so copulates is a *defiler*:
> ... thou bright defiler
> Of Hymen's purest bed. (Shakespeare, *Timon of Athens*)

deflower to copulate with (a female virgin)

OED gives a 14th-century quotation from Wyclif in this sense and Shakespeare speaks of 'A deflower'd maid' (*Measure for Measure*). The imagery of plucking a bloom can refer to the loss of the maidenhead other than by copulation:

> His female admirers had a model made of it in pure gold and organized a ceremony in which several virgins deflowered
> themselves on this object. (Manning, 1977)

Defloration is such copulation.

degenerate a homosexual
To *degenerate* means to cease to be able to function as before, and as the function of sex is the propagation of the species, there might be some logic in so describing those who do not breed. However, the imagery comes from the meaning degraded or corrupt.

degrade to damage or render of less value
Literally, to reduce a substance in strength or purity. Military jargon:
> ... an air assault to 'degrade' by 50 per cent the strength of the Iraqi forces arranged north of the border. (Forsyth, 1994)

A *degraded* woman used to be one who had been detected in extramarital copulation, and *degradation* is prostitution.
> ... the hiring of stage-struck girls by foreign impresarios who took them abroad and sold them into degradation. (Paxman, 1998)

dehire *American* to dismiss from employment
Barely euphemistic in a country when to *hire* has become synonymous with to employ.

delayering dismissing employees
Literally, dispensing with a layer of management in a hierarchical organization.

Delhi belly diarrhoea
An alliterative use not confined to India or its capital.

delicate *obsolete* suffering from pulmonary tuberculosis
One of the 19th-century euphemisms for the common disease.
Today a *delicate condition* indicates pregnancy.

delinquency a bad debt
Banking jargon in a milieu where the word *loss* is taboo. Also as a *delinquent balance*:
> Impairment losses rose significantly reflecting delinquent balances and security rates in the UK card business and changes in recognition methodology. (*Daily Telegraph*, 9 August 2005—Barclays Bank might have said 'We checked and found we had higher bad debts on credit cards'.)

deliver to drop (an explosive) on an enemy
Military jargon of bombs or ordnance, thus a *delivery vehicle* is not a milk float but a missile which carries a bomb.

demanding awful
Business jargon when trade is bad, but not suggesting other customers don't *demand* attention and service:
> Furthermore, the outlook for the Logistics business is satisfactory, whereas conditions in the French courier market are demanding. (Hays PLC Annual Report, 8 September 2003)

demands of nature urination and defecation
You might think gravity came first, followed by breathing.

demanning the dismissal of employees
Not an operation to change masculinity:
> It is imperative the process of demanning continues. (*Daily Telegraph*, 8 March 1994— a chairman was announcing the dismissal of 2,000 employees)

demi-mondaine a prostitute
Married people who 'went to the world' in the French Second Empire were the *monde* and women on the fringes of that society unaccompanied by men were the *demi-monde*. The obsolete English *demi-rep*, a shortened form of *demi-reputation*, meant the same thing.

demise a death
Originally, a lease or the transfer of an estate on a death which became standard English for the death itself.

democrat/democracy have always meant different things to different people and seldom, outside the parish meeting, 'rule by the people'. An example was the *German Democratic Republic*, Soviet Russia's totalitarian satellite. We are wise to look for a flaw in any concept or political argument claimed to be based on the principles of *democracy*.

demographic strain too many people
Demography is the study of population statistics, but this phrase does not mean that your eyes ache from reading too many censuses. It is taboo, as well as being simplistic and offensive, to suggest that poor countries face starvation because ignorant people breed too fast and medical science allows too many to survive.

demographically correct containing a proportionate ratio of blacks, whites, Hispanics, etc.
Not merely counting or classifying them without error:
> ... sitting on a school desk in a dark suit, a demographically-correct display of acne-free teenagers in front of him. (Anonymous, 1996—a politician was doing a commercial in an election campaign)

demonstration a mass assembly to protest about a specific isssue
Literally, a showing, illustration, or proof.
The shortened form *demo* has no non-euphemistic use.

demonstrator a used item of equipment offered for sale
Jargon of the motor trade, where a vehicle driven from new by a member of the firm for their personal use is put up for sale suggesting it has only been used to show its performance to prospective customers. The term is also used where other equipment or machinery is sold by the original supplier at a reduced price.

demote maximally to kill one of your associates
Espionage jargon. The victim's career as a spy certainly can fall no lower.
A *maximum demote* is such a killing.

deniable describing something for which responsibility can be plausibly refuted
Usually of a statement made off the record or an act done by a third party on your behalf. Whence also *deniably*, describing such conduct, and *deniability*, the chances of getting away with it.

deny yourself to to refuse to copulate with
Usually within marriage.
A spouse may also, if so minded, *deny a bed*.

depart (this life) to die
Sometimes *tout court*:
> Her spoken wishes were to depart, to stop bothering them. (Faulks, 2001)
The *departed* are the dead and *departure* is death.

dependency¹ a subject territory
British imperial use for those distant parts of the globe ruled from London which were not dominions, colonies, or protectorates.

dependency² an addiction to narcotics or alcohol
The victim *depends* on regular ingestion.

depleted *American* poor

Literally, emptied or reduced in quantity:
> Claratwiceaweekdroveher Sevilletothecity's depleted neighbourhoods for the morning. (Turow, 1990—she went slumming)

deposit a turd
Of humans and domestic pets. Usually in the punning *make a deposit*, to defecate.

deprived poor
Literally, having lost something, which is not so for most paupers:
> Deprived Families on Increase (headline in *Daily Telegraph*, 4 October 1983—meaning that there were more poor families rather than the other constructions which might be put upon the four words)
Whence *deprivation*, poverty.

derailed mad
The common transport imagery.

Derbyshire neck a goitre
The water in the county is high in fluoride which means that those brought up there usually have fine teeth but may show a swollen thyroid gland.

derrière the buttocks
The French too have behinds and use the same euphemism, although without our salacious overtones.

deselect to dismiss (a political incumbent)
The action is taken by a caucus rather than the electorate.

designer more expensive
Descriptive of clothing or accessories where a much-advertised name is attached. Other products without such endorsement or provenance also have to be *designed* by someone. *Designer stubble* is modish unshaven facial hair.

designs on (have) to wish to seduce
Not just wearing a patterned dress or carrying plans:
> ... they contain no mention of his having had designs on the local girls. (Bence-Jones, 1987, writing about the dissolute Earl of Leitrim who was murdered in Donegal in 1878)

desire to want a sexual relationship with
Not just any old longing:
> ... he was desiring her more and more—she could certainly tell when a man got like that. (J. Patterson, 2003)

despoil to copulate with
Literally, to plunder, and it was what men were said to do to virgins. A man can be a *despoiler* even if the woman is unlikely to have been a virgin:
> It's his duty ... to try to like the father of his

grandchild. The despoiler of his daughter. (McEwan, 2000)

destroy to kill
Venerable standard English of killing and, in modern use, specifically of domestic pets:
   If [the dog] makes another mess... I'll have him destroyed. (N. Mitford, 1945)

destruction *obsolete* the seduction (of a female)
Especially if there was no prospect of subsequent marriage:
   I gather from [a remark] that you are one of those who go through life seeking the destruction of servants. (Bence-Jones, 1987—a young member of the Kildare Street Club in pre-1914 Dublin had drawn the attention of an older member to a pretty girl cleaning the windows of a house across the street)

detain to imprison for political purposes
Each of us is detained when our train is held up at a signal.

detumescent not having an erection of the penis
Literally, not having any swollen glands:
   All the talk [with prostitutes] of AIDS kept me detumescent. (Theroux, 2002)

developing relatively poor
The direction in which the *development* is happening, if at all, may not be particularized:
   ...countries which have successively and with increasing euphemism been termed backward, under-developed, less developed and developing. (Bullock & Stallybrass, 1977)
The British *Development Areas* were those parts of the country faced with industrial decline, higher unemployment, and lower wage levels, partly due to remoteness and partly because of technological and industrial changes.
The *development industry* consists of those whose profession it is to succour the poor, especially in sub-Saharan Africa, usually managing to remain in better health, better paid, better housed, better clothed, and better fed than those among whom they work:
   The so-called development industry—the name itself is an insult to the genuinely poor—has become one of the most distorted and corrupt arrangements on the planet. (*Daily Telegraph*, 13 October 2004)

developmental associated with ignorance, idleness, or the lack of ability
Educational jargon, as in the *developmental class* for the unruly or stupid, and the *developmental course*, which used to be called cramming.

device any object which is the subject of a taboo
Literally, a mechanical contrivance.
For the military a *nuclear device* is an atom bomb and an *expendable device* a missile.
A woman fitted with a *device* uses a permanent method of contraception.

devil's mark (the) *obsolete British* congenital idiocy
Mainly in rural use.
God, Satan, and the fairies seem to have been equally to blame for the results of inbreeding—see also GOD'S CHILD and CHANGE².

devoted to the table gluttonous
Not merely fond of a piece of furniture:
   Heavily overweight, [Joffre] was devoted to the table and allowed nothing, even at the height of the crisis in 1914, to interrupt lunch. (Keegan, 1998)

dick¹ the penis
Possibly rhyming slang from PRICK although the penis is given many other male names in English, as in other languages.
To *dick* is to sodomize or to copulate with:
   Six bad [years] in San Quentin getting' dicked by the residents. (J. Collins, 1981)
To *dick around* is to be promiscuous, of a male, although there is a figurative use meaning merely to mess about.
Dick's hatband was an indication of homosexuality and a double pun, on the discoloration induced by sodomy and on Richard Cromwell, who was a homosexual and unfit to wear the *hatband*, or crown, of his mighty father, Oliver. Thus, to *wear Dick's hatband* was to be a homosexual male.

dick² *American* a policeman
Usually a detective.
A policewoman may be described as a *Dickless Tracy*, punning on the cartoon character and her femininity, but not, I suggest, in her presence.

dickens the devil
The origin is unclear, despite the notorious marital behaviour of the novelist.

dicky unwell
Rhyming slang on *Uncle Dick*, sick. Widely used to refer to our own indispositions; in others, it signifies a chronic state of ill-health.

diddle¹ to urinate
Literally, to jerk from side to side, which a male may do with his penis after urination to eliminate drips. *Dicky Diddle* was also rhyming slang for piddle.

diddle² to masturbate
Of both sexes, again from the jerking movement.

diddle³ *American* to copulate
Literally, in this sense, to CHEAT:
> I play golf with the insurance industry, a
> sin apparently even more troublesome to
> Americans than diddling a hairdresser.
> (Anonymous, 1996—a presidential
> candidate had been accused of copulating
> with his wife's hairdresser)

die to achieve a sexual orgasm
Of male or female:
> I will live in thy heart, die in thy lap, and be
> buried in thy eyes. (Shakespeare, *Much Ado*
> *About Nothing*)
> These lovers cry—Oh! Oh! they die.
> (Shakespeare, *Troilus and Cressida*)

die queer *obsolete Kent* to kill yourself
A use which might be misunderstood today.

die with your knees bent *American* to be
killed in an electric chair
Sitting down at the time.
To *die in a horse's nightcap* or *die in your shoes*
meant to be killed by hanging.

diet of worms a corpse
Modern scientists tell us that the process of
corporal dissolution is fungal, with worms
obtaining little sustenance. Happily in 1670 or
thereabouts Marvell knew better:
> ... then worms shall try
> That long preserved virginity,
> And your quaint honour turn to dust,
> And into ashes all my lust.
The *Diet*, or assembly, was held in the Rhine-
land city of Worms in 1521 and is remembered by generations of schoolchildren for the
pun in English rather than for Luther's
courage in attending.

dietary difficulties the barring of Jews
from service in the German Imperial navy
Prior to 1914 anti-Semitism was not a
uniquely German phenomenon but, unlike
the Kaiser, some did not bother to find an
excuse. Jewish applicants were allowed to
enlist in his navy if they consented to be
baptized and subsequently ate pork.

differently affected by a taboo condition
In a series of phrases such as *differently abled*,
crippled or of low intelligence; *differently*
advantaged, poor; *differently weighted*, obese:
> It can only be a matter of time before the
> differently-weighted push for job quotas in
> the fire departments and the police.
> (*Sunday Telegraph*, 6 March 1994)

difficult particularly objectionable
You may say this about other peoples'
children, but it is wise to keep out of earshot
of their parents if you do so.

dime out *American* to cheat, betray, or
short-change
A shortened form, perhaps, of NICKEL AND DIME.

diminished responsibility a suggestion
of temporary insanity
A defence seized on by lawyers when the
accused has no other.

dine well to be a drunkard and a glutton
The goodness lies in the excess of food and
wine.

ding-a-ling a penis
Referring to the pendent position of a bell
clapper.
Some figurative use as an insult.

dip¹ to steal
Literally, to put into liquid, which involves a
downward movement, and so a *dip* or *dipper* is
a pickpocket:
> Twenty years of muggers and dips, safe
> men and junkies. (Mailer, 1965—but don't
> place reliance on the *safe man* unless you
> wish him to open a safe for you)
The *dip squad* consists of police charged with
apprehending pickpockets:
> He was not happy about being taken off the
> dip squad. (*Daily Telegraph*, 27 April 1996—a
> policeman returning to normal duty, after
> the investigation of an allegation of
> dishonesty, sported a pigtail: when given
> new duties less to his liking he claimed to
> be a victim of sexual discrimination)

dip² a drunkard
A shortened form of *dipsomaniac*. To *dip your*
beak or *your bill* means to drink intoxicants to
excess.

dip your wick to copulate
Common male punning use—see also WICK—
on its immersion in an oil lamp.

diplomatic pretended to avoid an obligation
The *diplomatic cold* was first contracted by
Mr Gladstone, as being preferable to a direct
refusal of a social invitation. Neville Chamberlain contracted *diplomatic gout* in May 1938
and Boris Yeltsin absented himself from the
public eye for a while with a *diplomatic illness*
in 1994 when the campaign in Chechnya was
launched.

direct action unlawful violence or trespass
It describes acts of a minority group opposed
to a legal pursuit enjoyed by others.

direct mail unsolicited enquiries sent by
post

The communication seeks an order, a sub-scription, a donation, political support, etc. but the delivery is not more or less direct than the rest of your mail, most of which you actually want to read.

Junk mail is accurate but not euphemistic.

directional selling promoting the product of an associated company without disclosing the financial link

Either the subsidiary of a supplier is trading under another name or a supposedly independent adviser is recommending a purchase in respect of which he will obtain an undisclosed commission or other benefit.

dirt faeces

As with CRAP and other synonyms, we cannot be sure which meaning precedes the other:

There was a stink [in an abandoned camp in the jungle] of putrescent food, human dirt, rottenness, piles of refuse ... (Barber, 1971)

Whence the figurative meaning, information which may be damaging to another, especially in the phrase *have the dirt on*.

To *dirty yourself, your pants, trousers, clothing*, etc. is to urinate or defecate without removing your dress.

dirty pertaining to anything harmful or damaging or which may be the subject of a taboo

A *dirty (atomic) bomb* will go on killing people longer and more unpleasantly than a *clean* one. A *dirty joke* is one which concerns itself with sex. A *dirty book* may be pristine but contains salacious material. A *dirty deed* may be extra-marital copulation, especially by a male and, if he seeks such with a much younger partner, he is a *dirty old man*. If the partners leave together for clandestine copulation, they will be said to have passed a *dirty weekend*, however clement the weather. For Moslems, the left hand is the *dirty hand*, being the one used to wash themselves after defecation. Among young boys, *dirty* implies masturbation:

Here communities [receiving wartime evacuees] complained about 'verminous' and incontinent children, 'loud' expectant mothers, unruly youngsters and boys with 'dirty' or 'filthy' habits. (L. James, 2001)

disability a limiting mental or physical condition

Literally, the fact of being rendered incapable, or *disabled*, but the two words have for so long been standard English that we forget there is normally no suggestion that the condition has been wilfully brought about:

The passage of the Americans with Disabilities Act in 1990 extended the same legal protections ... to an estimated 43 million disabled Americans. (*Chicago Tribune*, 20 May 1991)

Since the term 'disability' can include a former addiction to cocaine, marijuana etc., this means that an employer cannot enquire into past use of drugs, even for jobs such as airline pilots. (*Sunday Telegraph*, 6 March 1994)

The [Olympic Committee] suspended all events for the mentally handicapped and spent six months assessing the rest of the mentally disabled athletes who had competed in Sydney before allowing them to keep their medals. (*Sunday Telegraph*, 9 February 2003)

She worked for an educational group which lobbied for special schools for the developmentally disabled. (Diski, 2002)

disabled see DISABILITY

disadvantaged poor

Sociological jargon which has passed into standard English, suggesting that those so described have lost an advantage which they once enjoyed, such as having rich parents or good schooling:

I do want to help him—because he's black and probably grew up disadvantaged. (Theroux, 1982)

A 1965 Jules Feiffer cartoon tracks the progression from 'poor' to 'needy' to 'deprived' to 'disadvantaged'.

disappear¹ to be imprisoned or murdered

The language of espionage and crime, or of novelists specializing in the genre.

disappear² to urinate

Mainly female use. Women do not in fact vanish after telling you that they are going to *disappear*, but they pay a fleeting visit to a lavatory.

disappointing poor

Business jargon in public announcements when trade has been terrible and profits have fallen.

discharge to ejaculate semen

As from Pistol's gun:

I will discharge upon her, Sir John, with two bullets. (Shakespeare, *2 Henry IV*—the 'bullets' were his testicles)

Discharge, meaning to dismiss from employment, comes from the literal meaning to free or to rid; but see also FIRE.

disciple of a person addicted to participating in the activities of someone associated with something taboo

Thus a *disciple of Bacchus* is a drunkard, a *disciple of Oscar Wilde* is a male homosexual, etc.

discipline a male sexual perversion
The prostitute is paid to subject her client to forms of humiliation.

disco biscuit an ecstasy tablet
The location where the illegal drug is ingested.

discomfort agony
Mainly the language of dentistry. When the dentist tells you that you may feel a *little discomfort*, it is time to grip the arms of the chair. The word was also used to conceal sickness from the public:
   [Macmillan, who had an illness affecting his bladder,] was sixty-nine and experiencing, more acutely than in previous months, what in medical parlance is termed 'discomfort'. (A. Clark, 1998)

discrimination selective and unfair treatment of others
Literally, the exercise of any choice or taste, but standard English in this use for over a century.

disease of love a venereal infection
Where *love* indicates no more than copulation.

disengage to retreat
The language of defeat:
   But they cannot impose a decisive battle on us before our lines are on the terrain we have chosen; we are disengaging with great skill. (Klemperer, 1999, in translation)
A *disengagement* is such a retreat:
   'Disengagement proceeds according to plan.' 'According to plan' has been much in favour recently. (ibid.—diary entry of 24 September 1943)

disgrace *obsolete* to copulate with a woman outside marriage
Literally, to bring into disrepute. It was *her disgrace* if others got to know about it, and especially if she had been impregnated.

disguised drunk
Not showing your true face perhaps? Probably not.

dish a sexually attractive woman
A male use, with common culinary imagery.

dishonoured *obsolete* (of a female) copulated with outside marriage
She has thus lost her HONOUR:
   ...he could think of a number of ways for a dishonoured woman to spend the rest of her life. (Farrell, 1973)

disinfection mass killing
The Nazi pretence was that Jews, gypsies, and others killed by gassing were being put into a confined place for the purpose of eliminating lice etc.:
   The underground chambers were named 'disinfection cellars', the above-ground chambers 'bath-houses'. (Keneally, 1982—writing of Auschwitz)

disinvestment the disposal of shares etc. as a political gesture
Not just a normal sale for economic reasons but because of opposition to an activity in which the corporation participates. The rare alternative, *divestiture*, literally means dispossession and has clerical overtones, because that is what can happen to naughty parsons.

dismal trade the arranging of funerals for payment
Literally, *dismal* means dreary.
A *dismal trader* is not necessarily gloomy about business, and *dismals* were once mourning clothes.

disorderly house a brothel
Originally 19th-century legal jargon and still in use, even of the most tidy and well-conducted brothel.

disparate impact *American* a difference in intelligence, education, or ability
Sociological jargon to explain away the result of any examination or test where one group consistently achieves better results than another:
   Wherever there is 'disparate impact'—one race getting more marks than another—the Government assumes bias in the methodology of testing. (*Sunday Telegraph*, 20 November 1994—for ten years the NYPD had failed to evolve tests which resulted in whites and blacks achieving equal results)

dispatch to kill
Literally, to send. It has long been used for the killing of humans and other animals.
Also as a noun, it still implies efficient and unspectacular killing.

dispense with assistance to dismiss from employment
The phrase is normally used to describe the peremptory dismissal of a senior employee who has proved a failure.

disport amorously to copulate
Literally, no more than frolicking with sexual overtones:
   Same old rut. A Richmond resident tells me that it is once again that time of the year when the deer in Richmond Park are disporting themselves amorously. Notices in the park are models of tact. They read demurely: 'Warning, Excessive Deer Activity'. (*Daily Telegraph*, October 1987)

dispose of to kill
Literally, to deal with, whence to discard. Of animals and humans:
> [The communist leader's] dominance of the resident population was almost total and reinforced every time he felt it necessary to 'dispose' of a suspected agent or informer. (Leng, 1998)

A *disposal* is such a killing.

dispossessed indigent
Those so described are unlikely to have owned valuable possessions in the first place:
> There the spit-and-polish troops are immigration police; the hordes, the Mexicans, Haitians, and other dispossessed people seeking illegal entry. (Cahill, 1995)

dispute a strike
Shortened form of *industrial dispute*. Used twice in three minutes by BBC Radio 4 on 15 June 1983:
> A dispute among Southern Region guards has led to the cancelling of trains. (They were not arguing with each other, as might have been supposed.)
> A dispute among camera and technical staff has prevented the televising of sporting events. (Again, the difference of opinion was with the employer, not with the fellow workers.)

dissolution¹ death
Literally, the splitting up into constituent parts, as the corpse into bones, or the body from the soul:
> A fetch... come to assure... a happy longevity or immediate dissolution. (Banim, 1825—a *fetch* was a ghostly figure)

dissolution² a persistent course of licentious behaviour
The word is used of casual copulation, homosexuality publicly flaunted, heavy gambling, drunkenness, the use of illegal narcotics, etc. In each case normal constraint is *dissolved* and he who so acts is *dissolute*.

distracted by having a sexual relationship with
Literally, having your attention drawn away from something, in this case your spouse:
> The couple had a wobbly time last year and even separated for a while briefly when Brian became momentarily distracted by his (married) secretary. (*Sunday Telegraph*, 27 February 2000)

distressed mentally ill
Medical and sociological jargon. Literally, it means sorely troubled but today you call such people distraught.

distribution the payment of a bribe

Usually where there are several recipients, or where the organizer of a corrupt deal hands on bribes to others, which may then be called a *secondary distribution*.

disturbed mentally abnormal
Medical jargon, referring to the unease of many patients.
The word is also used in sociological jargon for naughty children, which does not mean that the miscreants have been interrupted in their activities.

ditch to land an aircraft in water
Not of seaplanes. A *ditch* is a drain dug to receive water, whence the standard English meaning, to discard in such a drain, or elsewhere, any unwanted object. Originally a Second World War punning use but now of any aircraft making a forced landing, especially in the sea.

dive¹ *obsolete* to steal by picking pockets
From the movement of the hand:
> In using your nimbles, in diving in pockets. (Jonson)

Grose notes *diver* as a pickpocket.

dive² *American* a place for the sale and drinking of intoxicants
Often low-class, from the use of cellars, where the rent is less. In the same sense Grose gives *diver* as 'one who lives in a cellar'.

dive³ a pretence of having been knocked down
Made by a boxer who goes of his own volition to the canvas, a soccer player seeking to earn an undeserved free kick, or a pedestrian seeking compensation for a self-inflicted injury:
> ...there must be a chance that the crafty old bugger took a dive hoping to get a big payday. (P. McCarthy, 2000—commenting on the headline PRIEST SUES CORPORATION OVER KNEE)

To take a *high dive* is to kill yourself by jumping from a height without a parachute.

divergence homosexuality
Moving away from the norm.

diversity the presence of people from different ethnic groups
Literally, the condition of being different, whence, giving preference to a selected category. *Diversity awareness* is being careful not to say or do anything which might offend those not of the same gender, race, and colour as yourself, and *diversity training* is a process designed to eliminate or suppress emotions which others might regard as natural:
> At Cornell University, a student-employment 'diversity' training session included the

showing of X-rated gay porno movies to show if applicants showed any signs of discomfort or distaste. (*Sunday Telegraph*, 21 January 1996—Cornell had also stopped teaching European history because there wasn't sufficient *diversity content*, apart perhaps from the Black Death, we might assume)

The usage, and the thinking behind it, such as there may be, is not confined to one side of the ocean:

The Lord Chancellor explained at the launch [of a Faith Forum in the Department of Constitutional Affairs] that it would 'sit alongside a number of Staff networks that promote and protect diversity'—including 'the Proud Network, for black and ethnic minority issues; the Rainbow Network, looking at lesbian, gay, bisexual and transgender issues; the Disability Network; and the Network for Caring, for staff who are carers at home'. (*Daily Telegraph*, 23 February 2006)

divert to steal
Usually of embezzlement, where the funds are directed into the wrong channel, but sometimes of goods.

do¹ to copulate with
Mainly male usage, from his supposedly taking the initiative. Both sexes *do it*:
Doing a filthy pleasure is, and short. (Jonson)
To *do yourself*, *do it with yourself*, or *do something to yourself* is to masturbate, of either sex:
[Tom Pepys's maidservant talked] of his disquieting sexual practices—although sitting up all night 'doing something to himself' does not sound very bad. (Tomalin, 2002—but it did to the maid)

do² to kill or injure
Also as *do for*, *do down*, *do in*, *do over*, etc.:
Some of our chaps say that they had done their prisoners in whilst taking them back. (F. Richards, 1933)
. . . the thug swaggered off down the pavement, doubtless eager to tell his friends that he'd 'done' one of the visiting fans. (Paxman, 1998)
To *do yourself in* is to commit suicide.

do³ to cheat or steal from
Sometimes *tout court*, usually in the passive:
It has been a good thing for me to get 'done' like this [buying fake antiques] as it will make me more careful in future. (Garfield, 2004)
The perpetrator may *do down* or *do over* the victim.

do⁴ a battle
In standard usage, a party or function. Usually of a less successful and bloody encounter,

such as the British *Arnhem do*.

do⁵ to charge with an offence
Police jargon.
A person charged, especially with a motoring offence, will refer to having been *done*.

do a bunk to urinate
Literally, to depart quickly. There are numerous slang and dialect phrases meaning to urinate or to defecate which employ the verb *to do*. I have listed many, SLASH for example, under the noun, because slashes etc. are had, done, or gone for, and the noun imparts the sense. Phrases not noted elsewhere include *do a rural*, to defecate out of doors; *do a shift*, to urinate; and *do a dike*, to urinate or defecate.

do a line to ingest narcotics illegally through the nose
From the sprinkling of power in a line:
The only people present were Patty-Anne, Lasater, and Bill Clinton. 'He was doing a line. It was just there on the table.' (Evans-Pritchard, 1997)

do a number (of a criminal) to give information to the police
A variant of SING.

do a runner to leave without prior notice
Escaping, you know, from your spouse, creditors, jailers, or anyone else who might have an interest in your peremptory departure.

do away with to kill
So long standard English that it is hard to recall that the words mean something different.

do business with to cease to be confrontational with
Mrs Thatcher's often-quoted (and copied) assessment of Gorbachev.

do-gooder a self-righteous person who forces his concerns on others
Nearly always used derogatively.
Do-gooding, as different from doing good, is so acting:
What were her do-gooding parents but pious cheats? (Theroux, 1976)

do-lally-tap mad
The derivation is from the transit camp at Deolali near Bombay where time-expired British soldiers were sent to await repatriation. The heat and boredom were accentuated by the vagaries of intercontinental transport in the days of sail. If you arrived at the camp in the wrong season, you could be stuck there for six months, which would be additional to your contracted service:
In India he had a touch of the sun, which

we old soldiers called 'Deolalic Tap'.
(Richards, 1933)

The 'old soldier' also uses another spelling:
Oh, he's got the do-lally tap. (F. Richards, 1936)

In the Second World War sometimes shortened to *tap*.

do the business to copulate with
Often within marriage or a permanent relationship, and not to be confused with DO BUSINESS WITH:
This was the first time they had done the business in a good while; two months nearly. Made love. He'd never called it that; sounded thick. Riding your wife was more than just riding. (Doyle, 1991)

do the right thing to marry a woman you have impregnated
After you had been seen to DO WRONG.

do what comes naturally to copulate
Of either sex.

do wrong to copulate with someone other than your regular sexual partner
The *wrong* may consist of the betrayal of trust between regular partners or in a man seducing a woman:
One in 1943 admitted to being very much in love with a soldier who, just before embarkation overseas, 'asked me to do wrong'. (L. James, 2001)

do your duty by to impregnate (your wife) or to have a son by your husband
Much store was formerly set by both parties on a wife not copulating with other than her husband before they had jointly produced a son and heir.

dock to copulate with a female
The expression was at one time confined to copulation with a virgin, using the imagery of pruning.
This is a convenient place to note that etymologists do not always agree with each other. Farmer & Henley trace this meaning of *dock* to the Romany *dukker*. Partridge, in *DSUE*, looks to the standard English meaning, to curtail, which, in his judgement, 'is obviously operative'. Grose makes no suggestion as to the etymology but reports 'Docked smack smooth; one who has suffered an amputation of his penis for a venereal complaint'. *EDD* correctly reports that *dock* means to undress, as in 'mun dock this gound off'. *OED* reminds us that the *dock* in which a prisoner stands comes from the Dutch word for a rabbit hutch. The *New Oxford Dictionary of English* adds further to our understanding with the definition 'to attach (a piece of equipment) to another', which is one way of describing the copulatory process. My contribution to the debate is to draw attention to a marine *dock*, a long, narrow, moist space into which a ship moves and may fit snugly. I am sorry that we shall never know what Alfred Holt, the erudite author of *Phrase and Word Origins*, thought.

doctor to change through deception
By adulterating intoxicants, administering drugs to racehorses, falsely adjusting accounts, castrating tomcats, etc.:
They've doctored the tapes. (Colodny & Gettlin, 1991, of Watergate)

document retention the destruction of potentially damaging evidence
Not just keeping the papers in a safe place:
The controversial memo, written by [a lawyer] in 1990, gives advice about so-called 'document retention'. (*Daily Telegraph*, 3 June 2004)

dodgy indicating some characteristic that is taboo or of doubtful legality
Thus for a sailor a *dodgy deacon* is a homosexual priest and a *dodgy car* is one which has been stolen.
For a transport driver a *dodgy night* is one spent at home but entered on his time sheet as being passed with his vehicle.

doe *obsolete* a prostitute
The progression from this 17th-century use was to a woman student at Oxford University and, in modern America, to a woman who goes to a party unaccompanied, but not a *stag party*.

dog to frequent a haunt of prostitutes
Police jargon. Those stopped by the police often claim to be merely *walking their dog*.

dog and pony show *American* a bogus exhibition or insincere conduct calculated to deceive
Where you may put on a *dog and pony act*:
Well, my darling wife and I are having this sort of terrible argument, but I suppose we can do the dog and pony act. (Proulx, 1993—they could pretend to be on good terms)

dole a payment by the state to the involuntarily unemployed
Originally, a portion, whence a gift made regularly to the poor, as *dole-bread* or *dole-money*, and at funerals *dole-meats*:
She's on the dole, so hopefully we'll trace her soon enough when next time she claims benefit. (Strong, 1997)
Now largely replaced by new euphemisms—see RELIEF¹.

doll¹ a sexually attractive female

Dr Johnson reminds us that *Doll* was a contraction of *Dorothy* as well as being 'A little girl's puppet or baby'. A female so described may be beautiful though slow-witted, but a *real doll* implies beauty and brains.

doll² a narcotic in pill form
Formerly a barbiturate or amphetamine. The punning title of Jacqueline Susann's novel *Valley of the Dolls* started or sanctified this usage.

dollar shop a store which will not sell in the local currency
A feature of Communist regimes where luxuries, and even some necessities, were reserved for foreign tourists and party officials. The currency did not have to be the American dollar so long as it was not from any Communist country.

dolly a mistress
Certainly from DOLL¹ but also perhaps owing something to her smart dress—*dolled up*.
A Victorian *dolly-common* or *dolly-mop* was a prostitute.

domestic a servant in the home
A shortened form of domestic servant or domestic help:
   We used to call them servants. Now we call them domestic help. (Chandler, 1953—and now we call them *domestics*, but not to their face)

domestic afflictions menstruation
It could mean myriad other things which cause unhappiness in the home.

dominance a male sexual perversion
Literally, authority or control over another, which is what the client asks the prostitute to simulate with a whip or other apparatus.

Don Juan a male philanderer
The successful practitioner in seduction inspired the music of Mozart and the words of Molière, Byron, and Shaw, to name but a few. Whence *donjuanism*, such behaviour.

don the turban to become a Muslim
Certain Europeans, for reasons of conscience or expediency, changed religion while resident in a Muslim society.

donation a bribe
Not necessarily to a political party in return for being made a lord:
   He had been a probationer beat constable out of Caledonian Road and had taken the first small 'donation'. (Seymour, 2001)

don't name 'ems *obsolete* trousers
A 19th-century example of the great trouser taboo—see also UNMENTIONABLES¹.

doodoo faeces
From baby talk. Some figurative use:
   Only last month he told the annual meeting the same-store sales at Somerfield and Kwik Save were improving. Now he's found himself deep in the doo-doo. (*Daily Telegraph*, 15 October 2002)

doorstep¹ to abandon a baby
In the days when there was a stigma attached to unmarried woman having babies and little help for them if they did, the baby might be left on the doorstep of a prosperous house, the mother ringing a bell and then leaving. Some figurative use of the behaviour of parents towards unwanted children:
   When it became obvious... from the hour of my conception, that my parents intended to doorstep me... (N. Mitford, 1945)

doorstep² to conduct an unscheduled interview
From waiting for the person to appear from home or office, usually in circumstances when the victim would prefer to be neither seen nor heard:
   ... ministers and senior officials scuttling to and fro being 'doorstepped', alternatively blustering and wheedling on the television screen. (A. Clark, 1998)

dope a narcotic
Originally, a thick liquid, from the Dutch *doop*, sauce, as used once on the canvas fuselages of aircraft. Whence prepared opium, which has the same appearance.
Now it may refer to any illegal narcotics. To *dope* is to give such narcotics to horses, athletes, or greyhounds, whence the *dope*, inside information or, in this case, which runner has been drugged?
Dope, a simple person, comes from the drugged mien and behaviour.

dose a venereal infection
Literally, an amount of medicine, and the usage, normally of gonorrhoea, comes from the remedy formerly prescribed:
   And if I give that man a dose, that's my pleasure and he just gettin' what he's payin' for. (Simon, 1979—a prostitute was talking, not a medical practitioner)

dose of P45 medicine *British* the summary dismissal of employees
The tax form handed to those leaving employment is numbered P45.

dotty eccentric or mentally ill
Originally, of unsteady gait, whence feeble and then feeble-minded.

double dipper a person in receipt of bribery or a second source of income

Not taking the classic sauna, passing from the hot chamber to the cold. Also as a verbal noun and of corrupt institutions:

> A spokesman for the anti-fraud office [of the European Union] said that there had been a widespread practice of 'double-dipping' by aid agencies. (*Daily Telegraph*, 29 June 2005)

double entry dishonest
The development in Lombardy of *double-entry bookkeeping*, a self-balancing method of keeping accounts, was an important factor in making that region pre-eminent in European banking. The euphemistic use alludes to the keeping of two sets of books in parallel, one of which is intended to deceive.

double-gaited having both homosexual and heterosexual tastes
The imagery comes from equestrian sport.

double-header sexual activity by a male with two females in each other's presence
Prostitutes' jargon, from the use of two locomotives to pull a train and punning on *give head*, to engage in oral sex.
Also as *double in stud*.

double time copulation outside marriage
There is increased payment for overtime working, and see also TWO-TIME.

doubtful sexuality homosexuality
The choice is not really in doubt.

douceur a bribe
Literally, a gratuity, in French and English. I prefer the 19th-century spelling:
> Nobody is allowed to take dowzers. (*EDD* from 1885)

dove an appeaser or pacifist
The allusion is to the symbol of peace and the opposite of HAWK. The use is not necessarily pejorative and became hackneyed during the Cold War.

down to prison
The place where the judge sends you after sentencing, the cells often being situated in the cellar of the courthouse.
In the same sense, the tipstaff may be instructed to 'take the prisoner down', although the descent may be no greater than from the dock to the floor of the room. Prisoners of war were sent *down the line*.

down among the dead men drunk
The *dead men* are the skittles which have been knocked over in ninepins. Whence also the rarer *in the down-pins*.

down below the genitalia
Of either sex, despite that part of the body

being located above the legs. Also as *down there*.
> The first time she touched him 'down there' she thought she would die of mortification. (Forsyth, 1994)

down on providing oral sexual stimulation of another's genitalia
Homosexual and heterosexual use, from the posture adopted:
> 'When I'm up, Barbara's down,' says Howard ... 'When you're up who, Barbara's down on whom?' asks Flora. (Bradbury, 1975)

down population the compulsory dismissal of employees
Not the inhabitants of an Irish county. Jargon of management consultants who may leave the harder task of implementation to others.

Down's syndrome a congenital disorder due to a chromosome deficiency
This is an example of a phrase incorporating *syndrome* being used to avoid a taboo word—in this case what was formerly known as Mongolism. Here the stigma and the possible racial sneer are circumvented by naming the affliction after the English physician John Langdon Down (1828–1896).
In the same way we may prefer not to talk about schizophrenia:
> ... to rid the ailment of unpleasant associations, there are now moves to have it called Kraepelin's syndrome. (Winchester, 1998)

downs depressant narcotics
Addict jargon, always in the plural and the opposite of *ups*. Also as *downers*.

downsize to dismiss employees
The volume you wish to reduce is the size of the payroll:
> It was an unhappy time. We had to downsize the company substantially and we had quite a serious divergence of opinion between the management and the workforce. (*Sunday Express*, 12 February 1995—the *divergence* was not surprising as the workforce was suffering the job losses, not the managers)

downstairs[1] *obsolete* the house servants
Their normal location was in a semi-basement of a town house. Whence the British television series *Upstairs, Downstairs*.

downstairs[2] the genitalia
A genteel use by and of male and female without the possible sexual implication of DOWN BELOW.

downward adjustment a devaluation or an economic depression
The phrase attempts to lull fears by implying that events are still under control.

doxy *obsolete* a prostitute
As with TART, the original meaning was sweetheart, from the Dutch *dock*, a doll.

drag the clothing of the other sex worn by a homosexual
Originally theatrical use, referring to a male actor (not necessarily a homosexual) in female clothes, the long train being *dragged* on the floor. A homosexual so attired is said to be *in drag*.
A *drag* is also an American homosexual party for males.

dragon (the) habitual illegal use of narcotics
The association is of opium with China, dragons, and so on:
> You're standing between me and the big, bad dragon. (Gabriel, 1992—he was stopping an addict getting heroin, not intervening between man and wife)
In many phrases such as CHASE THE DRAGON, to be addicted to narcotics.

drain off to urinate
Usually of a male, with obvious imagery.

dram a drink of spirituous intoxicant
You used to buy spirits from apothecaries, who used their own measurements, in this case one eighth of a fluid ounce which was originally known as a drachm, corrupted to *dram*.

draw to aim a weapon at
Removing the handgun from a holster. Also as *draw upon*:
> I have been tempted, in these two short interviews, to draw upon that fellow, fifty times. (Dickens, 1841)
To *draw a bead on* means to shoot at, whence to wound or kill.

draw a blank *American* to be very drunk
Punning on the loss of awareness and an unsuccessful attempt in a lottery.

draw the enemy into a trap to retreat involuntarily
Military use when you want to disguise your predicament in order to keep up morale:
> Of course the officers knew, but they were telling us we were drawing the enemy into a trap. (Richards, 1933, describing a retreat in the First World War)

draw the king's picture to counterfeit bank notes
Or the queen's, or the president's, as the case may be, from forging the likeness.

draw the long bow to boast or exaggerate
The longer the bow, the further the potential range. Also as *pull the long bow*.
See also SHOOT A LINE.

draw water to have power or influence
Naval jargon, from the size of the ship.
The official or officer who *draws too much water* is not to be gainsaid.

dream associated with illegal narcotics
Especially heroin as in *dream dust*, although a *dream stick* was opium.

dress for sale *American* a prostitute
In this CB use, the *dress* is not what's on offer and the transaction contemplated is one of hire or licence. In 19th-century London a *dress lodger* was a prostitute clothed in suitable style by a pimp, working from a brothel called a *dress-house*.
Today an American pimp who decks out a prostitute is said to provide her with *bonds* or *threads*.

dress to/on the left to be a male homosexual
Literally, in the jargon of bespoke tailoring, having the penis naturally reposing on that side of your pants. The pun uses the common *left* homosexual imagery.

drill *Irish* to organize civilians in an illegal militia
From the rudimentary training.
To *drill* is also to kill by shooting, often in the cliché to *drill full of holes*, with imagery from carpentry or engineering.

drink¹ an intoxicant or to drink intoxicants
A euphemism which has become standard English. Thus, if a friend offers you a *drink*, you do not expect to be served water. To *like* or *enjoy a drink* may indicate a modest addiction to alcohol, whereas to *drink a lot* or *some* suggests excess. *Drink taken*, *in drink*, or the obsolete *drinky*, mean intoxicated and *drunk* is explicit of intoxication, while a *drunk* is a dipsomaniac. To *be a heavy drinker* does not mean that you are overweight and those *with a drink problem* have no restriction of the throat but, as with *drinkers* who *drink too much*, suffer from alcoholism. A *non-drinker* drinks no alcohol.
Those who *drink at Freeman's Quay* cadge intoxicants from others, *Freemans* being the mythical brand of cigarettes cadged by British servicemen in the Second World War.

drink² a bribe or tip
Given as such to save any embarrassment when handing over cash, but less explicit than the French *pourboire*.

drink³ the sea
Used by airmen when forced to put down on
water, or *in the drink*.

drip gas *American* stolen petroleum
It is collected from a small hole in the pipeline
from the refinery.

drive-away the theft of fuel
By those who *drive away* from a filling station
without paying:
> ...the garage surveillance cameras...
> were focused on the forecourt to catch
> drive-aways. (McNab, 1997)

droit de seigneur copulation by a male
employer with a female employee
Literally, a right of the lord of the manor,
which was said to include, fictitiously in most
cases, copulating with each virgin in his
domain. In modern times such a privilege
was claimed by other dominant males, especially in the entertainment industry:
> The droit de seigneur died with the
> Hollywood czars. (Deighton, 1972)
The feudal system functioned primarily on
the lord's ability to demand unpaid labour
from tenants or villeins, in return for protection. This practice coined euphemisms such
as *bederipe* (reaping by request) and *boonwork*
(granting a favour).
Another word for this forced labour, *love-
boonwork*, can only have been used ironically.

drop¹ to kill
By shooting, after which the victim falls. To
drop down the chute in gangland America was to
murder, with imagery from the disposal of
garbage in an apartment block.
To *drop dead* is not euphemistic of death,
although it is sometimes shortened to *drop*.
Those who *drop in their tracks* die suddenly.
Humans may also be said to *drop off* (to die, not
to doze), a shortened form of the avian *drop off
the perch*, which a bird does when it dies.
The *long* or *last drop* was death by hanging,
although the distance travelled by the
body was not far, and to *drop* was to kill by
hanging.

drop² a quantity of intoxicant
Usually of spirits and seeking to imply a
moderate consumption:
> The rum came up with the rations and was
> handed over by the Company-Sergeant-
> Major. If he liked his little drop, he took his
> little drop. (Richards, 1933)
Occasionally as a *drop of blood*.
A *drop on* or *drop taken* indicates intoxication:
> My father was always giving out about it
> when he had a drop taken. (Flanagan, 1979)

drop³ to give birth to

Usually of quadrupeds but, of women, to *drop
a bundle* meant to have an induced abortion.

drop⁴ a bribe
Literally, in criminal argot, a place where
stolen goods are left for collection by a third
party:
> Over the years Robbie had made 'drops' to
> many judges. (Turow, 1999)

drop anchor fraudulently to cause a horse
to run slowly in a race
The imagery is naval and the practice associated with crooked gambling.

drop beads *American* to identify yourself
esoterically to another homosexual
By speech or body language. The wearing of
beads by a male may imply effeminacy. If the
string breaks, the beads spread themselves
over a wide area.

drop-dead list a list of names of people to
be dismissed from employment
The offensive expression *drop dead* expresses
rejection.

drop the boom on to discriminate against
Literally, to activate a defensive obstruction to
navigation. Of the withdrawal of credit facilities, exclusion from confidence, or dismissal
from employment.

drop the crotte to defecate
From the French word for dung, *crotte*, rather
than from the obsolete English *crottels*, horse
dung. Also as *drop a log* or *wax*. Some
figurative use.
> Willie said, 'I almost dropped a log.'
> (Theroux, 1993—Willie had been taken by
> surprise)

drop the hook on *American* to arrest
The imagery is from fishing.

drop your drawers to copulate
Of women, usually promiscuously, and in
Britain as *drop your pants*.
Either sex may be said to *drop their pants* or
trousers, indicating defecation (and urination
in women).

drop your flag to surrender
Which a warship might do, by lowering it to
denote submission.

droppings the excreta of animals
Standard English since at least the 16th century.

drown the miller *obsolete* to be made
bankrupt
According to the Scottish proverb, 'o'er much
water drowned the miller', from the days

when most flour mills were powered by a leat and a flood might destroy the mill. Whence the derivative use, meaning to add too much water to a glass of whisky.

drown your sorrows to drink intoxicants to excess
Supposed solace is brought about through intoxication.

drumstick the thigh of a cooked bird
Another way of avoiding mention of the taboo leg. And see DARK MEAT[1].

drunk see DRINK[1]

Drury Lane ague *obsolete* venereal disease
The affliction might be caught from a *Drury Lane vestal*, a prostitute. Drury Lane, adjoining COVENT GARDEN, was a notorious brothel area in pre-20th century London.

dry[1] prohibiting or not offering the sale of intoxicants
It does not mean that in a *dry canteen* there are no liquid refreshments nor that a *dry county* in America is arid.
A person who professes to be *dry* is usually looking for something more than water.
To *dry out* is to abstain from alcohol after a period of excess.

dry[2] to forget your lines
Theatrical jargon, a shortened form of *dry up*, something which should not happen to a professional actor.

dry bob copulation without ejaculation
A vulgarism which puns on the term for an English schoolboy who eschewed rowing in favour of cricket. A *dry run* indicates copulation during which the male wears a contraceptive sheath, being a triple pun on the absence of a free seminal discharge, on the sensation, and on the meaning, a practice or rehearsal.

dry clean to check or destroy for reasons of security
Either legally, as by a governmental agency, or fraudulently when files are shredded and tapes erased to destroy evidence.

dry pox (the) *obsolete* syphilis
More usual as the *pox*, *tout court*:
> The disease communicated by the Malays, Lascars, and the Orientals generally...goes by the name of the Dry—. (Mayhew, 1862—he isn't always so squeamish)

duality a sexual aberration
Normally in a male, where it seems to refer more to homosexuality than to having both

homosexual and heterosexual tastes.

duck *American* a urine bottle for males
Hospital jargon, from its shape.

duff *American* the buttocks
Referring to the suety pudding or pastry. In Britain the *duff* is the penis, normally in the phrase, *fluff your duff*, to masturbate, which has the same etymology as *pull the pudding*. A *duff* is a homosexual.

dumb down to make simpler
The phrase refers to public examinations, which retain the former names and grades but are set or marked so that a greater proportion of examinees appears to pass or do well; or to broadcasting, where effort is being made to attract a less cerebral audience.

dummy[1] a stupid person
Literally, a representation of the human form, from the meaning, a dumb person. It may denote someone who is momentarily unthinking or distracted, or it may refer to the mentally ill.

dummy[2] the penis
The shape may be likened to the baby's comforter. Usually in the phrase, *flog the dummy*, to masturbate.

dump to defecate
An obvious and rather distasteful male usage as a verb or a noun.
Some figurative use:
> But maybe you also recall how your Service dumped all over us on that one? (Lyall, 1985)
It is to be hoped that the prevalent roadside sign 'No Dumping' indicates the absence of such euphemistic use in Ireland.

dunny a lavatory
Not just an Australian usage. Probably a corruption of *dung*.
The *dunnie van* in rural Somerset collected the NIGHT SOIL for manure.

duration the time occupied by the Second World War
Shortened form of *duration of the war*. Common British usage, especially at the time when the outcome was uncertain and there was a taboo about predicting the future:
> ...you'd never get back to England. You'd be stuck there for the duration. (Barber, 1981)

dust to kill
Probably from wiping off or out, with blackboard imagery.
Dustman, a corpse, and *dustbin*, a grave, punned on the eventual state of an unembalmed corpse.

Dutch[1] appears in many offensive and often euphemistic expressions dating from the 17th-century antagonism between England and the Low Countries. Thus anything qualified as being *Dutch* is considered bogus or inferior, from being IN DUTCH, in trouble, to speaking *double-dutch*, incomprehensibly.

Dutch[2] unpopular
Dorrell has dropped out [of the contest for leadership of the Conservative party], but is dutch in the [House of Commons] tea-room. (A. Clark, 2002)

Dutch (do the) to kill yourself
You're not going to do the dutch, are you?...Commit suicide? (Sanders, 1980) Whence the *Dutch act*, suicide.

Dutch auction an auction in which the auctioneer drops the price until a buyer makes a bid, being the reverse of a normal auction in which bidders raise the price until only one remains in the auction

Dutch bargain an unfair or unprofitable deal

Dutch cheer a drink of spirits—the Dutch are supposed to be gloomy when sober

Dutch clock a bed pan—from the shape and contents

Dutch comfort an assumption that things cannot get worse

Dutch concert a cacophony
Music played out of tune, drunken singing, or any other discordant noise:
In the evening, as we were walking the ramparts, we were serenaded by a Dutch concert. (Emblen, 1970, quoting Roget—the noise came from frogs, ducks, crows, grasshoppers, peacocks, and asses)

Dutch consolation an assurance that, although things are bad, they could have been worse

Dutch courage bravery induced by intoxicants, implying a Dutchman is a coward when he is sober

Dutch dinner a meal to which you are invited but have to pay

Dutch feast an occasion where the host becomes drunk while his guests are still sober

Dutch fuck lighting one cigarette from another
Perhaps because the action is soon over, costs nothing, and may leave you with a burning sensation.

Dutch headache a hangover
For such a drink-sodden people there could be no other medical cause.

Dutch reckoning an inflated bill without details
DUTCH RECKONING, or ALLE-MAL. A verbal of lump account, without particulars, as brought in spunging or bawdy houses. (Grose)

Dutch roll combined yaw and roll in an aircraft which behaves with the gait of a drunken sailor
This usage, first noted by Moynahan in 1983 as modern airline pilots' jargon, shows that, with English speakers, old prejudices die hard.

Dutch treat an entertainment or a meal to which you are invited but where you have to pay for yourself
Where such costs are shared by agreement, it is called *going Dutch*.

Dutch uncle someone who reproves you sharply or gives you solemn advice, unlike the supposed geniality of real uncles
I talked to him like a Dutch uncle. It doesn't seem to have done him any good. (Baron, 1948)

Dutch widow a prostitute

Dutch wife a bolster
Once the sole bedmate of many white bachelors serving in the Far East.

Dutchman a stupid person
You so describe yourself rather than others when you express surprise or disbelief in the phrase *I'm a Dutchman* which is sometimes shortened to *I'm a Dutchy*.

duty defecation
Perhaps from the requirement placed daily on children but also a shortened form of the archaic *duties of life*:
When we go out [from our Antarctic tent] to do the duties of life...(Cherry-Gerrard, 1932)

duty not paid smuggled
Official jargon, especially for tobacco and alcohol imported from countries with lower tax regimes. Shortened to *DNP*.

duvet day an unjustified absence from work tolerated by an employer
Also known as a *mental health day*. The employee can have a good lie-in.

E

EC see EARTH CLOSET

ear a clandestine microphone
The jargon of espionage and spy fiction. In the same genre an *earpiece* is an informant keeping a watching brief.

early bath dismissal from a team game
Taken by a player sent off for foul play or, less often, after performing badly.

early release dismissal from employment
Not just getting away from work before your usual time. The British Telecom *early release scheme* announced in 1993 involved the dismissal of 30,000 employees of the former state monopoly.
Early retirement is not a voluntary decision to take your pension before the normal time or going to bed at 10 o'clock but the dismissal of a single employee under a face-saving formula.

early treatment room a station to which a soldier might go after promiscuous copulation
As different, in the Second World War, from the medical establishments such as Casualty Clearing Stations, to which the wounded would be directed or taken.

earn to steal
Military usage, seeking to show entitlement perhaps.

earn a passport to be rewarded as an assassin
Another duty, it would seem, of the women in the harem, who might be lent by the sultan to a minister with orders to kill him:
> Her task accomplished, she was reintegrated into the Royal household and rewarded for her services. In the argot of the Seraglio, this was known as 'earning a passport'. (Blanch, 1954)

earnest *obsolete* homosexual
Victorian slang and possibly what inspired Wilde's choice of title for *The Importance of Being Earnest.*

earth *obsolete* to inter (a corpse)
Mainly Scottish and Yorkshire dialect. The burial space was the *earth-dole.*

earth closet a non-flush lavatory
Soil is used to cover the faeces. Commonly abbreviated to *EC.*

earth moved for you (the) you had a sexual orgasm
Especially of females, but also used of male sexual activity:
> But she plays to the camera, eyebrows raised and euphemisms to the fore: 'So, Clurr, what everyone at 'ome wants to know is, did the earth move for you?' (*Daily Telegraph*, 1996—commenting on Cilla Black's performance as television presenter of *Blind Date*)

earthy vulgar
A venerable usage:
> Certainly we know that [Abraham Lincoln] enjoyed an earthy story. (Bryson, 1994)

ease nature to urinate or defecate
Also as *ease yourself*. To *ease your bladder* is to urinate and to *ease your bowels*, to defecate, which might be done on a CHAPEL OF EASE or a *house of ease* (see HOUSE²) .
Easing springs, urination, is only done by a male, with imagery from the military order in which a rifle bolt is moved rapidly up and down the breech to ensure that there is no round left in the bore or magazine, a manoeuvre which has a tenuous similarity to the stroking of the penis to prevent a drip of urine. Jolly (1988) suggests that a sailor who excuses himself from company in order to urinate may pretend to be seeing to the *springs*, or mooring lines, of a ship, which may need *easing* according to current or tide.

easement self-masturbation
Not a right of way, turbary, venery, piscary, or cow pasture but the supposed *easing* of your desires or tensions.

East (go or be sent) to be killed
It was the direction in which Jews and others were sent to the places of extermination by the Nazis:
> 'Where has Herr Hirschmann gone?' I was able to ask. 'The Germans sent him east.' (Keneally, 1985—in fact this particular victim may have gone West, from Belorussia)

East African activities extramarital copulation
A *Private Eye* refinement of the in-joke, based on UGANDA.

East Village *American* a less fashionable area of New York
Used by realtors and others to exploit the cachet of *The Village*.
London has its SOUTH CHELSEA.

Eastern substances illegal narcotics

The association is between China, opium, and the geographical source of much cocaine etc.

easy terms hire purchase
The use is so widespread that we no longer address our minds to the reality that everything involved in such a transaction is more expensive and difficult, except the size of the initial payment.

easy way out (the) suicide
The use implies a lack of courage.

easy woman a female with no reservations about casual copulation
Not necessarily a prostitute.
Such a person may also be said to have *easy affections*.
See also *lady of easy virtue* under LADY.

eat a gun to commit suicide with a firearm
By shooting yourself upwards through the mouth.

eat flesh to copulate with a woman
A venerable Shakespearean pun:
  Suffering flesh to be eaten in thy house...
  contrary to the law. (*2 Henry IV*)
Today to *eat* or *eat out* refers to a form of oral sex, as in the punning vulgarism *eat a pussy*.

eat for two to be pregnant
The theory, unjustified in affluent families, is that a woman needs double rations during pregnancy.

eat-in kitchen *American* a kitchen incorporating a dining area
Real estate jargon for a small house or apartment in which there is no separate dining room.

eat porridge *British* to be in prison
A staple of the prison diet.
See also PORRIDGE.

eat stale dog *American* to take a deserved reprimand
I think this is analogous to *eat dirt*, with *dog* being a shortened form of *dog shit*.

eat the Bible *American* to perjure yourself
You lie after swearing on the Bible in court to tell the truth.

eating disorder anorexia nervosa or bulimia
Not spilling egg down your shirt:
  The Princess of Wales also suffered from an eating disorder, which is thought to have added to the strain of her marriage. (*Daily Telegraph*, 22 April 1995)

eccentric severely ill mentally
Literally, not moving on a centrally placed axis, whence, of human behaviour, whimsical or unusual:
  The poor man is crazy, the rich man is eccentric. (old saw quoted in Sanders, 1977)

economical with the truth lying
Famously said by the Secretary of the British Cabinet, Sir Robert Armstrong, in a legal action ill-advisedly brought by Mrs Thatcher in Australia to try to prevent the publication of confidential, inaccurate, and largely inconsequential allegations about the secret service, as a result of which she enriched the author, his lawyer, and the language. Also as *economical with the actualité*.

economically disadvantaged poor
Those so described have not been positively penalized, as were the Jews in Nazi Germany. Also as *economically abused*, *exploited*, or *marginalized*.

economically inactive unemployed
The actions of each of us impinge on the economy, whether or not we create wealth:
  Both men claimed there had been an unlawful interference with their rights as EU citizens when they became 'economically inactive'. (*Daily Telegraph*, 21 March 1995—an Italian and a Portuguese with three dependants had migrated to England where they had been kept at public expense without working. When it was suggested that they should return to their country of origin, they issued proceedings for damages)

economy cheap
Literally, the avoidance of waste. That does not mean necessarily that a traveller in other than an *economy* seat in an aircraft is feckless. In supermarket jargon *economy* may mean large.

écouteur a person who obtains aural gratification from the sexual activity of others
Literally, the French word means a person who listens, but has a specific meaning in English.

ecstasy an illegal stimulant
Easier to pronounce than methylene dioxymethamphetamine.

edged slightly drunk
The obsolete Suffolk use was probably not the direct parent of the modern American, but both must have come from being *on the edge of drunkenness*, or some such phrase.

educable *American* dim-witted
Yet still capable of learning something at school.

educate to suppress independent thought
The language and practice of totalitarianism:
'[Dissidents] pay a fine, some are even put
in prison. We educate them.' . . . I seldom
heard the word 'education' in China
without it sounding like a smack in the
face. (Theroux, 2000)

education welfare manager a truancy
officer
Language has had to evolve to mask the
reality that many of those offered free education by society spurn the privilege and those
who were once called truants are suffering
from a form of illness and need treatment for
their School Phobia Syndrome.

effeminate (of a male) homosexual
Literally, having the characteristics of a
woman.

efficiency *American* a single-roomed apartment
An *efficient* use of space, I suppose.

effing an oath
For *fucking*, used figuratively.
And see also F.

effluent a noxious discharge
Literally, anything which flows out, but now
understood to refer to sewage or untreated
industrial waste.

elastic subject to unprincipled retraction,
disregard of law, or withdrawal under
pressure
It may refer to a politician's principles, to a
judge's attitude to inconvenient laws, or to a
battle front during a retreat:
    Since Stalingrad the line in the east has been
    elastic, and the enemy never achieves a
    breakthrough. (Klemperer, 1999, in translation)
Whence *elasticity*, such conduct:
    There was a similar emphasis on judicial
    'elasticity', for which read 'revolutionary
    consciousness'. (Burleigh, 2000—of the
    courts in Nazi Germany)

elbow-bending drinking intoxicants
Usually to excess, from the movement of the
glass to the lips.
An *elbow-bender* is a drunkard. See also BEND.

electric methods torture
As used by the Nazis and other tyrannies.
Mugabe's Home Affairs Minister called it
appropriate technology in 1983 when the regime
used electric shocks on white prisoners in
Zimbabwe.

electronic underwear the use of a clandestine recording device
The microphone is hidden beneath outer
clothing.
Electronic counter-measures or *penetration* mean
spying through such clandestine means.

elephant and castle *British* the anus
Rhyming slang on arsehole, from the area
named after a public house which stood at the
start of the old road from London to Brighton.

elephant's drunk
Rhyming slang, for elephant's trunk. See also
COP AN ELEPHANT'S.

elevated drunk
From the feeling induced at a certain stage of
drunkenness:
    JOHNSON. (who, from drinking only water,
    supposed every body who drank wine to be
    elevated.) I won't argue any more with you,
    Sir. You are too far gone. (J. Boswell,
    1791—Sir Joshua Reynolds not unnaturally
    took offence at this sally)
If, in Britain, you are *elevated to the peerage*, it does
not necessarily mean you are drunk as a lord.
There is also a rare use of *elevation* for
drunkenness.

elevator does not go to the top floor
American there is mental deficiency
A use not replicated in the British *lift*.

elevator eyes an indication of male promiscuity
The perusal goes up and down the woman's
figure:
    [Clinton] has what American feminists call
    'elevator eyes': his gaze will scan
    appreciatively up and down a female form.
    (*Daily Telegraph*, 22 June 2002)

eliminate to kill
Usually of political or espionage killings.
Whence *elimination*, such killing.

embalmed very drunk
Based on the lifeless condition of the subject
and the intake of fluid which led to it.
Embalming fluid is cheap whisky.

embraces copulation
Literally, clasping in the arms with familial or
sexual affection.
The singular is rare:
    When a girl's lips grow hot, her sex is hot
    first and she is ready to give herself and
    ripe for the embrace. (F. Harris, 1925)
Illicit embraces means adultery.

embroidery exaggeration or lying
Literally, fancy needlework:

Albert's tongue...may have led him into the odd spot of embroidery. (Major, 1999—the Irish prime minister was reputed to have 'never walked past an open microphone in his life')

emergency¹ a war
The suggestion that the Malayan *emergency* continued to be so described because there would have been fiscal, commercial, and insurance penalties if it were called a war seems improbable. Used by de Valera of World War II.

emergency² a political suspension of civil rights
Usually as a *state of emergency* proclaimed by a ruler wanting to assume absolute power or retain office, as Mrs Gandhi did in 1975.

emergent poor and uncivilized
The use is mainly of former colonial territories in Africa, some of which appear to be retreating into greater poverty and tribal division rather than achieving greater freedom and prosperity. Also as *emerging*.

emigrated killed
How the Nazis explained the absence of those sent to extermination camps:
I replied to her on the 25th and the card came back today. Blue stamp on it 'returned', note in pencil 'emigrated'... 'Emigrated' for *been* emigrated. Innocuous word for 'robbery', 'expulsion', 'sent to one's death'. Now, of all times, one can no longer assume that any Jews will return from Poland alive. (Klemperer, 1999, in translation—diary entry 27 February 1943)

Emmas *British* haemorrhoids
Possibly only a shortened form, but also heard in full, of *Emma Freuds*, from a British public figure. The name of her celebrated relative, Clement Freud, has been also used to describe the same affliction, but the late and venerated Sigmund has yet to be used in this context.

emotional drunk
Excitable and sentimental behaviour is sometimes displayed.

emotionally close to having a sexual relationship with
The language of the White House:
President Clinton called it 'getting close to someone emotionally', when everyone else called it a 'blow job'. (Hawks, 2002)

employ *obsolete* (of a male) to copulate with
Master and mistress:
Your tale must be, how he employ'd my mother. (Shakespeare, *King Lear*)

employment unemployment
This is one of those evasive opposites, such as DEFENCE and HEALTH. Thus a government *Department of Employment* is concerned with finding jobs or providing for the unemployed.

empty a saddle to kill someone
Not just dismounting from a horse.

empty nesters a childless couple
Either because the children have grown up and left home or because the woman is continuing to take full-time paid employment during years of possible childbearing, thereby hoping to attain a higher standard of living:
Yesterday the euphemistic jargon ranged from 'open strategic stock' to 'lifestyle market segments'. The latter term translates as the observation that Bournemouth has more 'empty nesters' and fewer 'couples pre-children' than Kensington. (*Daily Telegraph*, 16 April 1997)

empty out to urinate or defecate
The matter discharged is not specified. Also as *empty yourself*. *Empty your bladder* or *empty your bowels* are explicit circumlocution.

emunctory associated with farting
Literally, no more than relating to a bodily duct or orifice having an excretory use, including sweat glands.

enceinte pregnant
It means surrounded and is also euphemistic in French. When we use the word, we are doubly evasive or prudish.

encourage to compel
The language of totalitarianism:
At Christmas [1940, French schoolchildren] were 'encouraged'—a euphemism for 'required'—to send cards, messages and drawings to their leader. (Ousby, 1997—the leader was Pétain)

end to kill
The common scepticism about reincarnation: The sword hath ended him. (Shakespeare, *1 Henry IV*)
The *end* or the *end of the road* mean death:
I should like you to know how splendid he was at the end. (Cherry-Gerrard, 1932, quoting Scott's letter of 1912)

end up with Her Majesty to be imprisoned
Not the destiny of Prince Philip.

endowed having large breasts or a large penis

The inheritance is physical rather than fiscal, and no less so than for those who are WELL ENDOWED.

energetic using violence
Literally, being very active:
> But the threat of being caught by Spain's sometimes energetic police force and being extradited has done little to deter British criminals from decamping to Spain. (*Daily Telegraph*, 9 January 2001)

energy release *American* an accidental release of radioactive material
An atomic power station should only release energy which is converted into electricity. Much nuclear jargon seeks to play down risks to health, real and imagined.

enforcer a criminal who terrorizes under orders
Usually working for an unpaid bookmaker, gang leader, etc.
Avoid confusion with the British *enforcement officer*, who performs much the same function, enforcing myriad regulations for a local authority but without violence or illegality.

English *American* denoting or pertaining to sexual deviation
As in the coded advertisements for *English arts, discipline, guidance, treatment*, etc., none of which have anything to do with elocution or any other kind of instruction in the most versatile of languages.

English disease (the)[1] male homosexuality
A usage not often heard in England.

English disease[2] a propensity to go on strike
This time the phrase was used both at home and abroad. See also FRENCH LEAVE and SPANISH PRACTICES.

English vice the obtaining of sexual gratification through pain
Not a piece of mechanical equipment secured to a bench but a predilection supposed to have developed from the experience of boys and their masters in 19th-century single-sex boarding schools.

enhance to alter or increase in a taboo or surreptitious way
Dye may be said to *enhance* real or imagined fairness of hair. Clothing is padded by *enhanced contouring* to display manly shoulders or shapely hips. Public bodies which put up taxes speak of *enhanced revenue*. An *enhanced radiation weapon* is a neutron bomb. A politician may improperly use *enhanced procedures* to do a favour to another:
> Fresh evidence emerged from Croydon that [Beverley Hughes, the Minister responsible for passports] had approved 'enhanced procedures' to waive checks [concerning another Minister's mistress's foreign nanny]. (*Daily Telegraph*, 2 April 2002)

enjoy to copulate with
Usually of the male, from the days when the pleasure was supposed to be his alone. Also as *enjoy favours, her person*, or *hospitality*.
An *enjoyed* female is one who is no longer a virgin, whether or not her previous partner or partners had a pleasurable experience.
To *enjoy yourself* is to masturbate yourself.

enjoy a drink to be a drunkard
You may also be said to *enjoy a cup, drop, glass, nip, the bottle*, etc.

enjoy Her Majesty's hospitality to be in prison
In jail you do not have to pay for your keep. The phrase has to be adjusted for kings, governors, and presidents.

enlightenment deception
In Nazi Germany and elsewhere, where effort is made to manage news, especially if something labelled NEW is on offer from politicians:
> Shortly after Hitler came to power in 1933, Goebbels and his new Ministry for Public Enlightenment and Propaganda built a bureaucracy that controlled every aspect of broadcasting. (Shirer, 1999)

enlist the aid of science to undergo cosmetic surgery
The *scientist* removes wrinkles, causes superfluous hair to vanish, implants it where it is scarce, etc.

entanglement an embarrassing or clandestine association
Literally, an ensnaring or enmeshing. It may refer to extramarital sexual relationships and other ill-advised adventures:
> Mr Hurd sought to extricate Lady Thatcher and other ministers from responsibility for the 'temporary and incorrect entanglement' of arms and aid in a protocol signed by Lord Younger. (*Daily Telegraph*, 3 March 1994—the British government was funding an engineering project in Malaya in exchange for a purchase of arms)

enter the next world to die
In various phrases, indicating devout belief or scepticism, including the *great perhaps* and the Bard's *undiscovered country*.

entertain¹ to copulate with
Another way of keeping a visitor occupied or amused, I suppose:
> She had 'entertained' him before and each time he had nearly ripped her in half.
> (J. Collins, 1981)

In China an *entertainment lady* is a prostitute.

entertain² to bribe
Commercial use, relating to excessive prodigality to a customer in return for business. *Entertainment* is such bribery.

entitlement state payment to the poor
A preferred usage, including by many who are not POLITICALLY CORRECT:
> I knew [Clinton] was a bounder, of course, but my hope was that he'd turn out to be the Carlos Menem of North America and slash entitlement spending. (Evans-Pritchard, 1997)

equilibrium surrender
Literally, a situation in which forces cancel each other out:
> [Halifax, the craven British Foreign Secretary] attached more importance than [Churchill] to the desirability of allowing France to try out the possibilities of European equilibrium. (Lukacs, 2000—in June 1940, Britain's quondam ally under Pétain was seeking a separate peace with Hitler)

equity release mortgaging a freehold property
Usually by way of a second charge to obtain more spending money or repay debt. Also as *equity withdrawal*. The American *equity equivalent contingent participation* is a loan whereby the lender illegally obtains an interest in the future profitability of a business venture.

erase to kill
Another way of saying RUB OUT.
If, in America, you are looking for something to rub out pencil marks on paper, you should ask for an eraser, not a RUBBER.

erection an enlargement of the penis due to sexual excitement
Literally, the condition of being upright. Standard English of both buildings and penises.
Whence *erect*, having such an enlargement:
> He had woken erect himself. (P. Scott, 1975—he had not been sleeping standing up)

err to copulate outside marriage
Literally, to stray or wander, whence to sin generally and then specifically of copulation. In the 19th century an *erring sister* was a prostitute.

Errant describes such behaviour and gave us the perfect crossword clue, 'Where to find errant pairs (5)'. (For those who don't try to solve cryptic crosswords, *errant* is an indication of an anagram of pairs—*Paris*.)

escort a paid heterosexual partner
Originally, a body of armed men, whence a person accompanying another. Usually in this sense a female who, on payment of a further fee, reveals herself as a prostitute.
An *escort agency* provides the services of such people.

essence semen
Literally, an 'essential being' and 'what is left after distillation'.

essential purposes urination or defecation
Not, in this instance, access to food, clothing, shelter, water, or air:
> The train rumbled up the west coast, with occasional stops for what we coyly termed 'essential purposes'. (Lomax, 1995)

estuary *British* common and inarticulate
The regional accent used mainly by unlettered people, and the BBC, in parts of the south-east of England:
> Only 39, he has a conspicuous estuary accent and supported Tottenham Hotspur. (*Sunday Telegraph*, 24 April 2005—perhaps it would have been different if he supported Arsenal)

eternal life death
A belief among the devout who may look to enjoy perpetual hymn-singing and other pleasures in their *eternal home* when dead, or *in eternity*.

ethical investment a policy of buying only stocks in companies which do not overtly offend the prejudices of dogmatists
The *ethics* are supposedly of those who invest their cash, which is not to suggest that those investing in other companies operating within the law are unethical.

ethnic not exclusively of white ancestry
Literally, 'pertaining to nations not Christian or Jewish' (*OED*), from which anyone who is not a Christian or a Jew. As the practice of those religions was largely confined to Europe or those of European descent, the word came to refer to those of other than white skin pigmentation.
An ethnic minority in America may include Hispanics as well as blacks, native Indians, or other non-white inhabitants. In Britain what was in the 1980s an acceptable euphemism is

now less so:

> Senior officers questioned by the enquiry used terms, including 'coloureds' and 'ethnics', that were offensive to black and Asian people. (*Sunday Telegraph*, 6 June 1999)

ethnic cleansing see CLEAN[2]

ethnic loading making appointments for reasons other than those of suitability or qualification

A way of achieving a quota, although not to be encouraged when choosing brain surgeons, airline pilots, sprinters, or those in similar occupations which call for special training or physical attributes:

> America's problem is that its 'intellectual elite' is now chosen by a system of positive discrimination and ethnic loading.
> (A. Waugh in *Daily Telegraph*, 10 April 1995)

Eumenides the Furies

The Greek word means 'kindly ones', and they were liable to get angry with you if you failed to flatter them, as would the GOOD FOLK with our recent ancestors. Similarly, the Greeks called the stormy and fearsome Black Sea the *Euxine*, 'the hospitable'. Some Christian prayers for an all-powerful and avenging God make strange reading too.

evacuate to defecate

A shortened form of *evacuate your bowels*. Whence *evacuation*, medical jargon for defecation.

evacuee a German citizen killed by the Nazis

Mainly Jews, who were forcibly driven from their homes:

> People have long been saying that many of the evacuees don't even arrive in Poland alive. They are being gassed in cattle trucks during the journey. (Klemperer, 1999, in translation—diary entry 27 February 1943)

The *evacuation* was to extermination camps:

> So deportation [from France] was labelled *Evakuierung* (evacuation)...(Ousby, 1997)

evasion a lie

More than merely an avoidance of the truth.

Eve *Indian* a female

Especially viewed sexually outside marriage:

> ...a local 'Eve-teasing' problem. The sexual harassment of women in public places, sometimes quite open, was a problem all over India. (Naipaul, 1990)

You may also see *Eve* as an indication of sex on a lavatory door, with the corresponding *Adam*. For *Eve's custom-house* see ADAM'S ARSENAL.

evening of your days old age

Not the period you spend at home after work. An *eventide home* is where geriatrics may reside and wait for death if their families will not or cannot look after them.

everlasting life death

The hope or expectation of the devout and a monumental variation of ETERNAL LIFE.

everlasting staircase *obsolete* a treadmill

The degree of arduousness was regulated by a jailor through a screw.

excess[1] *American* to dismiss from employment

When the employer wants to cut costs by getting rid of *excess* labour:

> Workers are never laid off; they're 'redundant', 'excessed', 'transitioned', or offered 'voluntary severance'. (*Wall Street Journal*, 13 April 1990, quoted in *English Today*, April 1991)

excess[2] to make a charge additional to the published tariff

As for an overweight package on an airline.

exchange of views a disagreement between dogmatically opposed parties

Diplomatic code for an argument, as used by Colin Powell who said he had had a 'candid and honest forthright exchange of views' with de Villepin, the French Foreign Minister, in January 2002. In a *cordial* or *helpful exchange of views*, the parties will have disagreed without coming to blows nor will they have made any concessions to each other in an *exchange of ideas*.

exchange this life for a better to die

Another monumental aspiration.

excited by wine having drunk alcohol

Not just being a wine buff:

> Addison and Thomson were equally dull until excited by wine. (J. Boswell, 1791)

excitement (the) *Irish* copulation

Perhaps a usage of the male rather than the female:

> I'll wear a shirt and tie...have the excitement with my wife, go to sleep...
> (McCourt, 1999)

excluded (the) poor people

Society denies them some of the advantages which come from being richer.

exclusive expensive

The places of business so described do not exclude people with the ability to pay:

> A year or so later I found myself in the

Crystal Room at London's exclusive
Grosvenor House Hotel. (Muir, 1997)

excrete to defecate
Literally, to discharge from a body. It could
therefore (but does not) refer to blood, sweat,
tears, snot, urine, etc.

excuse my French see FRENCH[2]

execute to murder
Literally, to carry out any task, whence to
effect the sentence of a court, especially a
death sentence. It became standard English
for beheading. Today terrorists have adopted
the word to try to cloak their killings with
legality.

executive measure a political murder
Another Nazi evasion of the Second World
War:

'Lohse, I recommend that your office
initiate an executive action aimed at
Oberfuhrer Willi Ganz'...
Executivmassnahme, a classic 'soft word'
whose intent can be convincingly denied
long after the corpses are counted.
(Keneally, 1985)

The CIA was said to describe an authorized
assassination by one of its operatives as an
executive action.

exemplary punishment death by hanging
Not being made an example by having to
stand in the corner for a few minutes:

Few people want to take direct
responsibility for hanging; understandably
they prefer abstractions—'course of
justice', 'debt to society', 'exemplary
punishment'—to the concrete fact of a
terrified stranger choking and pissing at
the end of a rope. (Hughes, 1987)

exercise copulation
Usually taken in a HORIZONTAL position:

The looks he gave me when he was talking
about faith and the Blessed Virgin. It isn't
only the bishops who like to get their
exercise. (Doyle, 1996—a woman had a
conversation with a priest shortly after
revelations about the fatherhood of the
Bishop of Galway)

For *exercise your marital rights* see MARITAL
RIGHTS.

exhibit yourself to show your penis to a
stranger in a public place
A form of male gratification, it would seem, the
display being mainly to women or children.
To *make an exhibition of yourself* is merely to
behave stupidly.

expand your balance sheet to borrow
more
Jargon of the business world, where the word
debt should be avoided. The *sheet* of paper
remains the same size:

The build-up [of debt] has not been uniform
across all industries. Financial services
companies in particular have sharply
expanded their balance sheets. (*Daily
Telegraph*, 3 January 2005)

expectant pregnant
A shortened form of *expectant mother*, who is
said to be *expecting*.
We take for granted that a person so
described is 'expecting' the birth of a baby
to herself, and not a birthday present or an
increase in salary.

expedient demise an unlawful killing by
a government agency
A *demise* is literally a failing or ending, whence
a death. The pretence is that a death so
described was natural but timely.

expended killed
Mainly military use, treating soldiers as
merely another resource like ammunition.
Expendable is the number of soldiers you can
afford to have killed or wounded in a battle,
or someone whose life may be sacrificed.

expenses an additional tax-free emolument
In standard usage, payment incurred by an
employee in the performance of duty and
reimbursed by the employer. Even those who
submit honest claims are unlikely to have
been as frugal in their expenditure as when
using their own cash and *expense-account living*
is synonymous with excess. In the sporting
world, especially among those who profess to
be amateurs, *expenses* are bribes:

There were allegations of payments—
'expenses'—being made in order to attract
the world's finest runners. (*Daily Telegraph*,
1 May 2003)

experienced[1] having copulated
Of either sex.
Whereas, in most disciplines, to gain experience you must practise often and become adept,
in this activity a single essay may be enough.

experienced[2] *American* not new
An evasion of the motor trade where dealers
reject terms such as second-hand and USED.

expert a person who makes a living by
professing knowledge
Others often find a claim of omniscience
spurious.
For *talking head* see TALKING.

expire to die
Breathing out for the last time. Dryden also used *expire* to mean have an orgasm, a double euphemism perhaps.

expletive deleted an obscenity
Part of our linguistic debt to Richard Nixon, and perhaps also to Rose Mary Woods, who transcribed the tapes.
The Nixon transcriptions (tape 13 February 1973) also used *adjective deleted* and *characterization deleted*, neither of which has passed into the language.

expose to leave in the open to die
Infanticide was once common, especially of female babies.

expose yourself to show your penis to a stranger in a public place
More common (etymologically) in Britain than in America.
See also *indecent exposure* under INDECENCY.

exterminating engineer *American* a controller of pests or vermin
This example illustrates the popular pastime of upgrading our job descriptions to gratify our self-esteem, and that of our spouses. Logically, this particular *engineer* might be in the process of personal dissolution, and even if we accept that he is *exterminating* something, the choice is large. The British *rodent operator* is no less pretentious and illogical—might he not provide performing shrews for a circus?

extinguish to kill
This possibly obsolete use seemed to be used more of kings than commoners. It is also used of genocide.

extra included in the price
A common commercial device on packaging or in advertisements to suggest that the buyer is getting a bargain.
Extras are sexual services provided in a MASSAGE PARLOUR, if you pay a supplement.

extra-curricular referring to taboo extramarital activity
Literally, anything at school, college, etc. which is done in addition to the prescribed course of study:
> Though industry pundits reckon Halpern—better known for his exuberant extra-curricular activities—itches to get back in the high street. (*Sunday Telegraph*, 5 June 2001—he had, when chairman of a multiple retailer, seen the details of his oft-repeated sexual activity with a young woman become public knowledge)

extrajudicial killing state-sponsored assassination
The expression is used by the Israeli government for the homicide of Palestinians who espouse violence in their campaign to destroy the state of Israel.

extramarital excursion a sexual relationship outside marriage
It might be, but is not, a skittles tour with the lads or a day at the seaside with the Mothers' Union.

extramural referring to taboo sexual behaviour outside marriage
Literally, outside the walls but jargon of something which has not taken place within academe. The word, as adjective or verb, is not used solely of academic sexual peccadillos.

extraordinary outside the law
The language of totalitarianism, and places so described were certainly out of the normal run of things. In Lenin's Soviet Russia, priests, former tsarist officers, and traders went to the SPECIAL CAMPS, while other, potentially more dangerous, opponents of the regime were sent to the *extraordinary camps*.

extremely ill under sentence of death
The coded public language of the rulers of Communist China:
> ...if a high official is said to have a cold he's likely to be fired, if he's 'convalescing' he has been exiled and if he is 'extremely ill' he is about to be murdered. (Theroux, 1988)

extremely sensitive source an illegal interception of messages
The usage does not refer to the quality of the equipment used:
> ...being careful not to mention the phrase wiretapping, but using instead the standard cover language, 'extremely sensitive source'. (Colodny & Gettlin, 1991, writing about Watergate)

eye-candy *American* a nubile young woman
Very pleasing to look at.

eye-opener an intoxicant or stimulant taken on waking
Punning on the meaning, a surprise.
The usage seems to have originated with British troops in France during the First World War, especially, albeit surprisingly, among airmen. Now generally used by people addicted to alcohol or drugs who need topping up before they can face another day.

F

F fuck

Nearly always for the verb as an expletive.
Also as the *F word*.
See also EFFING.

face your maker to be mortally ill

A prospect hoped for or feared by the devout.
It may also mean to die.

facilitation payment a bribe

Routinely demanded by officials in countries
where corruption is endemic.
A *facilitator* is not the recipient of the bribe but
a person who arranges illegal or shady
business deals, usually also dispensing bribes.

facility[1] a lavatory

Literally, anything which makes a performance easier.
Often seen in the plural, despite there being
only one:

> ...containing a washbasin, a folding table
> and two seats, one of which contained
> what the timetable coyly called 'facilities'.
> (D. Francis, 1988, describing a
> compartment in a railway carriage)

facility[2] an agreement to lend money by a
bank

Banking jargon for the limit to which you
may borrow. It makes life easier for the
borrower, for a while.

fact-finding taking a holiday at public
expense

One of the less onerous duties of local and
national politicians, and their employees,
who need to see things for themselves on
missions which require their travel at public
expense to distant and agreeable places.
F. D. Roosevelt sent *fact-finding observers* to
Britain before Pearl Harbor, not because
Ambassador Joseph Kennedy's anti-British
reports were unreliable but to liaise unoffi-
cially with British service chiefs.

fact sheet a selection of truths and un-
truths calculated to deceive

Literally, a summary of information issued to
confirm ephemeral publication, such as a
radio broadcast:

> Confidence in the claims of special interest
> groups was further undermined when the
> Commission of Racial Equality withdrew a
> 'fact sheet' on employment which wrongly
> said 'only one per cent of solicitors in

England' were from ethnic minorities.
(Sunday Telegraph, 27 August 1995—the
correct figure was over 3%)

facts (of life) the human process of repro-
duction

Thus breathing, eating, and growing old are
not the *facts of life*, while conception, pregnancy, menstruation, birth, etc. are.
Sometimes shortened to *the facts*.
A *fact of life* is an unpalatable truth.

fade away to die

What old soldiers are said to do.
In crime fiction, to *fade* is also to kill.

fag a male homosexual

Probably from the fact that male cigarette, or
fag, smokers were thought effeminate by pipe
or cigar smokers.

faggot a male homosexual

In obsolete British use, *faggot*, as a verb, meant
to copulate, and, as a noun, a prostitute. I
suspect the modern use comes from FAG, as
pouftah comes from POUFF:

> You made me out to be a drunk and a
> faggot. (Giles Brandreth in *Sunday Telegraph*,
> 8 July 2001—reporting a conversation with
> Lord Snowdon)

fail to display the symptoms of old age

Literally, not to succeed, or to discontinue.
The condition so described may long antecede
death, when a vital organ may really cease to
function, as with *heart failure*.

fail to win to lose

Not even to draw. This was the excuse of the
pusillanimous Unionist General McClellan in
the American Civil War:

> McClellan insisted that he had not lost; he
> had merely 'failed to win' only because
> overpowered by superior numbers. (Ward,
> 1990—in fact the numbers opposing him
> were inferior, but better led)

failure of memory (a) lying

A condition to which defendants in court and
government ministers easily fall victim:

> It was not the first time that [the Secretary
> of State responsible for the railway system]
> Byers had been accused by businessmen of
> a failure of memory. (*Daily Telegraph*, 29
> May 2002)

fair[1] poor

A classification denoting scholastic performance or the quality of goods and services
which is just above the lowest rating or
outright rejection. It should mean favourable,
or at least halfway between good and bad.

fair² unfair
One of the opposites favoured by politicians and pressure groups. Thus in Britain a rent restricted by law to a sum much lower than an open market or economic figure was described in a statute as a *fair rent*, resulting over many decades in a dearth of rented housing stock. The publicly-funded British Broadcasting Corporation, which competes in radio, television, and publishing with commercial businesses, describes its activities as *fair trade arrangements*. *Fair trade* may refer to attempts in the face of political opposition to allow less prosperous countries to create greater wealth by allowing them open access to European and American markets.
For the Victorians *fair trade* meant discrimination against imports to protect domestic producers:
> ... the NUCCA Conference [on 22 November 1887] meeting in Oxford voted by a thousand to twelve in favour of a resolution calling for Fair Trade, the established euphemism for retaliatory protectionism. (A. Roberts, 1999)

fair-haired boy someone unfairly favoured
He may be dark-haired, or bald, but he is being helped to political office or promotion beyond his deserts.
A *fair-haired girl* is a blonde.

fair trader *obsolete* a smuggler
Facing no excise duty, he charges his customer less.

fairy a homosexual
Usually denoting a male taking the female role, but also used collectively:
> A mob of howling fairies, frenzied because the best part went to younger stars who didn't lisp. (Theroux, 1976)

faithful not having a sexual relationship with anyone other than your regular sexual partner
Literally, true to your word or belief, but in this sense limited to one of the marriage vows.

fall¹ to commit adultery
The imagery is from *falling from grace*:
> It is their husband's faults,
> If wives do fall. (Shakespeare, *Othello*)
Less often as a noun, and of any promiscuity:
> The Queen was convinced that what she called 'Bertie's fall' was at least in part responsible for Prince Albert's death. (R. Massie, 1992—Bertie (later King Edward VII) had fallen in, with, on, and for Nellie Clifton, who had been introduced to his bed and embraces by fellow officers in camp in Ireland)

fall² to become pregnant
A common modern use, which does not imply illegitimacy. Also as *fall in the family way* or *fall pregnant*.
To *fall for a child* or *fall wrong to* are obsolete.

fall³ to die
Especially on military service but not neccessarily after being killed in action. The German government announced on 1 May 1945 that Hitler 'fell in his command post' after he had shot himself. You may also, when the time comes, take the avian path and *fall off the perch* or *off the hooks*. In America you might *fall out*, being no longer on parade. The *fallen* are those who die in the armed forces in wartime.

fall⁴ *American* an arrest
Against which possibility you may keep handy some *fall money*, to pay for an attorney, put up bail, bribe the police, etc.
In obsolete use to *fall* meant to be convicted of an offence, from the disgrace and reversal of fortune.

fall⁵ to be born
Of a quadruped which gives birth standing:
> The calf is lately fell. (Ellis, 1750)

fall among friends to be drunk
A variant of the biblical reference *fall among thieves*, which may be used to seek to explain to your wife what you imply is untypical and blameless behaviour (usually without success):
> ... 'the Fleetsh all lit up' commentary by Cdr Tommy Woodfruffe, who had lately fallen among friends. (*Daily Telegraph*, June 1990—in the obituary of the officer who had arranged the lighting for the Spithead Coronation Review of 1937, which is now remembered, if at all, for his drunken radio commentary)

fall asleep to die
The common sleeping imagery:
> ... fell asleep ... of enteric fever in Mesopotamia. (memorial in West Monkton church, Somerset)

fall off the back of a lorry to be stolen
In reality the days of insecure loads are long past.
Stolen goods similarly *fall off the back* of other goods vehicles such as vans and trucks.

fall off the roof *American* to start menstruating
My correspondents have failed to suggest a plausible etymology. Usually shortened in the past tense to 'I fell off'.

fall on your sword to resign after failure
The fate of defeated Roman generals:

Sources close to the company said that he had elected to 'fall on his sword' following a warning two weeks ago which forecast a loss of £2m. (*Daily Telegraph*, 7 May 1997, of a Chief Executive)

fall out of bed *American* to fail commercially or in a plea
An unplanned and usually painful experience. Less often as *fall off the wire*.

fallen (the) see FALL[3]

fallen woman a promiscuous female
Normally, but not necessarily, a prostitute. At one time you had to watch your words when a lady tripped over her skis or her shoelaces.

falling sickness (the) epilepsy
Falling over is one of the symptoms:
    To cure the falling illness wi' pills o' pouthered puddocks. (Service, 1887—*puddock* does not here have its normal meaning, a kite or buzzard, but is a corruption of *paddock*, a frog or toad)
Also as the *falling evil*.

fallout radioactive matter introduced into the atmosphere by human agency
Now standard English and no longer used of less noxious substances such as volcanic ash.

false committing adultery
The opposite of TRUE for either sex:
    False to his bed. (Shakespeare, *Cymbeline*)

falsies pads concealed under clothing for females
Mainly of devices to make breasts or thighs look more alluring. The padding of men's jackets at the shoulders, equally calculated to deceive, is not the subject of euphemism or derogatory comment.

familiar having a sexual relationship
Originally, relating to the family, whence a person with whom you associate freely:
    The intimation is that you have been indecorously familiar with his sister. (Jennings, 1965)
A *familiarity of marriage* is copulation. *Familiar* can also mean pushy, as in Oscar Wilde's put-down to a stranger who accosted him—'I don't know your face but your manner is familiar.'

family[1] not pornographic
Not as modern as we might think; Bowdler called his emasculation of the Bard *The Family Shakespeare*. Thus a *family show* is one in which the vulgarity is muted.

family[2] the Mafia
A society which had as its watchwords *Morte Alla Francia Italia Anela*.
(Theroux, 1995, points out that Mafia 'is identical to the obsolete Arabic word *mafya*, meaning "place of shade", shade in this case indicating refuge, and is almost certainly derived from it.' Although no longer dogmatic about derivations, I would be reluctant to let the 'death to the French in Italy' line of enquiry disappear.)
Nothing is new—in 18th-century England a *family* was an association of thieves.

family jewels see JEWELS

family planning contraception
This standard English use denotes the reversal of planning a family for most people most of the time. In many compounds, such as *family planning requisites*, contraceptives.

family way see IN THE FAMILY WAY

fan club people who clandestinely copy the actions of another
Stock-market jargon, where the one followed may be a successful manager or investor, especially if there is a suspicion that either enjoys inside knowledge:
    While there is a distinction between a legal 'fan club' and an illegal support operation, the black and white turns to grey when the 'fans' were selling Guinness short. (*Private Eye*, August 1989—they were not selling less stout than a full glass but shares in the company which brewed it)

fancy to lust after
Either sex may *fancy* the other.
In obsolete use a *fancy* was a suitor of a single woman or, in ante-bellum America, a comely young female slave.
A *fancy man* or *woman* is a person with whom a regular extramarital sexual relationship is maintained. A *fancy bit* or *piece* is a mistress.

fanny *American* the buttocks or *British* the vagina
Of the buttocks, it may refer to the male or female, as in the expression *sitting on your fanny*. Of the vagina, it is used both literally and figuratively.
Although derivation from a shortened form of fantail has its advocates, it probably comes from Cleland's *Memoirs of a Woman of Pleasure*, which relates the adventures of Frances (Fanny) Hill as a prostitute in 18th-century London. He would rejoice to know that the Sybil Brand Institute, a woman's prison on rising ground in Los Angeles, is popularly known as *Fanny Hill*.

Fanny Adams nothing
Sharing the initial letters of *fuck all*. She was murdered in 1810, her memory being kept alive in naval slang for tinned meat. Also as *sweet Fanny Adams*, *sweet FA*, or *FA*.

far from staunch cowardly
An example of the euphemistic use of understatement:
> I would inevitably learn later, that some Americans had been far from staunch. (M. Hastings, 1987—quoting the British General Mansergh on the Korean War)

far gone drunk
Despite physically remaining in the same place:
> I won't argue with you, Sir. You are too far gone. (J. Boswell, 1791)

Farmer Giles haemorrhoids
Rhyming slang for *piles*.

fast ready to copulate casually
Mainly of women, from the meaning 'high-living'.

fast buck (a) money obtained unscrupulously
The dollars come quickly and easily, although not necessarily dishonestly. Perhaps punning on the male deer which is fleet of foot. *Fast* is less often applied to other currencies in a similar way.
Fast money means funds held for a short-term gain:
> Most investors in GUS's £1.1bn of debt are 'fast money', such as hedge funds or proprietary trading desks. (*Daily Telegraph*, 3 April 2006)

fat cat a person who exploits a senior appointment for personal gain
Usually of politicians and company directors, who display greed and self-satisfaction, although they do not actually purr.

fat finger an erroneous commercial transaction
Banking jargon. The trader hits the wrong key when placing an order or hits two keys at once:
> We thought it was a fat finger because Citi has never had a reputation for being a big risk taker in these markets. (*Daily Telegraph*, 14 August 2004)
Whence *fat-fingered*, making such a mistake:
> ...there was widespread speculation that a 'fat-fingered' trader had actually lost his bank up to £120m. (*Daily Telegraph*, 21 September 2002)

fat-cutting exercise the dismissal of employees
Another form of butchery:

> BP said it could axe as many as 5,000 jobs in a 'fat-cutting' exercise. (*Daily Telegraph*, 3 December 2002)

fate worse than death unsought extramarital copulation by a woman
A pre-Second World War use, acknowledging the convention that women should be virgins when they married.
Still used humorously.

father of lies the devil
Dysphemism rather than euphemism, from Satan's being credited with the invention of lying.

fatigue mental illness
In medical jargon *mental fatigue* is synonymous with nervous breakdown. See also BATTLE FATIGUE.

favour to copulate with
Literally, to regard with kindness:
> He thanks our transport lady whom Mr Muspole claims to have favoured in the snooker room. (le Carré, 1986—and not by giving her an easy break)
Also as *do a favour to*.
Favours, extramarital copulation, are granted by women more than men and may be *shared* if the donor has more than one contemporaneous sexual partner. To *force favours from* or *on* is to rape.

feather-bed to grant excessive indulgence towards
The derivation possibly comes from the Rock Island Railroad whose train crews complained of hard bunks and were thereupon asked if they wanted feather beds (Holt, 1961).
A *feather-bed soldier* in obsolete British use was one who went whoring a lot.

feather your nest to provide for yourself at the expense of others
With avian imagery, through dishonesty, greed, or, in the olden days, through marrying a rich widow or heiress whose fortune by law passed under her husband's control.

federal camp *American* a prison
Not a weekend with the Boy Scouts.

fee note a request for payment
A precious usage of lawyers who wish to imply that their relationship with their customer (client) is not that of seller and buyer:
> My firm's Cost department has mentioned to me that it would be appropriate for fee notes to be submitted in connection with the winding up of your late father's estate. (letter dated 29 January 1998 to Mr Anthony Peter from his lawyers)

feed to suckle
You avoid mentioning the taboo *breasts*.
Not to feed a baby does not mean that you
starve it.

feed a slug to kill by shooting
The SLUG[1] is a bullet. Also as *feed a pill*.

feed from home to be promiscuous
Perhaps just another Shakespearean image:
        ... he breaks the pale,
        And feeds from home. (*The Comedy of Errors*)

feed the bears *American* to receive a
ticket for a traffic offence
The BEAR[2], or policeman, may or may not pass
the fine on to the local municipality.

feed the ducks to cut off a penis
The perpetrator, a wronged Thai wife, throws
the excision from the elevated living quarters
on to the ground below where the ducks
browse:
        The gruesome practice of penis disposal is
        referred to as 'feeding the ducks'. (*Sunday
        Telegraph*, 30 November 1997)

feed the fishes to be seasick
Old humorous use, but never funny to the
victim. You do not actually have to vomit over
the rail.

feed the meter illegally to extend a
period of parking
To prevent hogging parking space, you should
move on after the parking period for which
you have paid has expired.

feed your nose to inhale illicit narcotics
through the nose
Usually ingesting cocaine or heroin.

feel to excite sexually with the fingers
Either sex may *feel* the other, the same sex, or
themselves.
Males *feel up* females, and a *feel-up* is what he
does, has, or possibly enjoys.
A man who persuades a woman to permit this
activity is said to *cop a feel*.

feel a collar to arrest someone
The wearer has his clothing *felt* as he is
apprehended.

feel a draft *American* to sense prejudice
The *draft* (or British draught) is the invisible
but uncomfortable sensation felt by some
blacks in the presence of some whites, with
imagery from the household phenomenon.

feel no pain to be drunk
From the numbing effect of the intoxicant
rather than unconsciousness.

feet first dead
This is the way corpses tend to be carried.

fell design a male attempt at seduction
Fell means cruel or clever, this derivation being
from the former. Now only humorous use:
        'Are you a virgin?' he said suddenly,
        stopping right in the middle of his fell
        design. (M. McCarthy, 1963)

fellow commoner *British* an empty bottle
Originally, an 18th-century student at Cambridge or Oxford University who was wealthy
and thus supposedly empty-headed as he did
not need to work or become a parson. Still
heard in some academic circles.

fellow-traveller a Communist sympa-
thizer or apologist
Trotsky's *poputchnik* and Lenin's USEFUL FOOL
who may be described as *fellow-travelling*.

female-Americans adult women living in
the United States
The language of those who think that all
women are the subject of unfair discrimination, or worse.

female oriented *American* homosexual
Of women only: the phrase is not used of a
LADIES' MAN. Also as *female identified*.

female physiology menstruation
Physiology is literally the functioning of the
body.

female pills medication to abort a foetus
In 1950 a British Code of Standards was
introduced to ban misleading or dishonest
medical advertising and:
        ... the use in any advertisements for
        medicines or treatments of any phrases
        implying that the product could be
        effective in inducing miscarriage—for
        instance 'Female Pills', 'Not to be used in
        cases of pregnancy', and 'Never known to
        fail.' (Turner, 1952)

feminine complaint an illness which affects only adult females
Not just that her husband has been out late
drinking again.

feminine gender the vagina
Oddly, in languages where it is declined, it is
usually male, as for example *con* or *cunnus*:
        She went in to adjust her suspender.
        It got caught up in her feminine gender.
        (old vulgar song)

feminine hygiene associated with menstruation
Usually of the paraphernalia, such as towels,

tampons, and the like. See also PERSONAL HYGIENE.

femme fatale a woman considered by men to be irresistibly attractive
She only kills figuratively.

fence knowingly to deal in stolen property
Thus providing a screen between the thief and the eventual buyer.
A *fence* is someone who so acts.

fertilizer the excreta of cattle
It should mean anything which adds fertility to the soil, including compost or seaweed. *Artificial fertilizer*, a non-organic chemical nitrate-based substance, also *fertilizes*.
To *fertilize*, of an animal, may mean to urinate or defecate:
    [The horse] Truc is the first to fertilize the pitch. (Palin, 2004)

fetch[1] *obsolete* a ghost
Its appearance presaged imminent death—*fetching you away*—or long life. If the viewer did not die of fright, the alternative outcome was necessary, to avoid discrediting the phantom.

fetch[2] to abduct
What was once used of animal predators was also appropriate to the Gestapo:
    As long as they don't come to 'fetch' me, as long as I have halfway enough to eat. (Klemperer, 1999, in translation—diary entry of 2 July 1942)

fiddle to steal by cheating
Literally, to play a stringed instrument, as certain untrustworthy itinerants once did, whence embezzling cash or manipulating accounts.
A *fiddle* is any device, even within the law, whereby someone may be cheated or overcharged.
With the same etymology, an obsolete Scottish *fiddle* was a child abandoned by gypsies.

fidelity copulation only with a regular sexual partner
It means faithfulness, in all its senses:
    ... expecting complete fidelity from Christine. (S. Green, 1979—writing about the slum landlord Rachman and his mistress Keeler)

field associate *American* a police officer charged with detecting police corruption
An unpopular and taboo task for which the name changes from time to time.

fifth column traitors within your ranks
General Mola, investing Madrid in 1936 with four columns of soldiers, foolishly boasted that he already had a fifth column in the city, meaning covert supporters of the insurgents, of whom many fewer remained when Madrid eventually fell some three years later. The modern use usually implies treachery.

fifty cards in the pack of low intelligence
You need 52 cards, except for tarot.

fight in armour *obsolete* to copulate in a contraceptive sheath
Boswell used both the pun and the appliance, and had cause for regret when he omitted to do so. (J. Boswell, *c*.1792)

file Chapter Eleven see GO[2]

file thirteen a wastepaper basket
Where you dispose of unwanted or superfluous correspondence or printed matter.
In America, also known as *file seventeen*.

fill full of holes to kill by shooting
You may also, if so unfortunate, be *filled with lead* or *with daylight*.

fill in to maim or torture
The origin appears to be from British naval slang, meaning to beat.

fill your pants to defecate without removing your clothing
Not merely putting your body within the garment:
    The man beside me filled his pants...
    I could smell it. (Lodge, 2004)

filler[1] a trivial item included in a serious newspaper
Filling the empty space among the advertisements and features in the absence of hard news.

filler[2] a cheaper substitute surreptitiously introduced to increase apparent weight or volume
Either during manufacture, as china clay into cream chocolates, or during packaging, as coal dust into sacks of house coal.

fillet to steal
Literally, to remove the flesh from the bone:
    We did think some spare parts might be filleted, but luckily nothing's gone. (*Sunday Telegraph*, October 1981)

filly a young woman viewed sexually by a male
Literally, a female horse less than four years old:
    We pre-war soldiers always made enquiries as to what sort of a place it was for booze and fillies. (Richards, 1933)

filth a person in a taboo occupation
In obsolete use, a *filth* was a prostitute although, with the prevalent standards of personal hygiene, probably no dirtier than anyone else. In modern criminal slang, it is a police officer.
Filthy implies a taboo act, such as masturbation or rape.
Filthy language is swearing and a *filthy joke* involves obscenity.

final solution the killing of all Jews
The Nazi *Endlösung*:
Comprehension was not aided by the Nazis' deliberate carrying over of the same terms—Final Solution, evacuation, resettlement—as euphemisms for mass murder. (Burleigh, 2000)

financial assistance *American* state aid for the poor
True as far as it goes, but it could as well be a loan, gift, or subsidy to the rich:
'You're on welfare?' 'Financial assistance,' she said haughtily. (Sanders, 1985)

financial engineering accounting practices tending to distort or mislead
Not controlling a metal-working shop through the use of figures.
A *financial engineer* so behaves.

financial services moneylending
Language of those who offer credit, or *financial products*, to people who may be uncreditworthy. The words lending and usury are best avoided.
Financial irregularities are not wrong additions but theft or embezzlement:
There were also rumours that Ferguson's departure was prompted by the management consultant's report that had highlighted financial irregularities at the club. (*Daily Telegraph*, 18 March 2003—in the obituary of the father-in-law of a royal prince)

financially excluded unable to open a bank account
Not describing those unable to pay an entrance fee but because they are likely to default on any loan or overdraft.
Such people are also said to be *financially constrained*, although *poor* is a shorter description.

find¹ to steal
The pretence is as old as stealing, as in the obsolete Scottish phrase *find a thing where the Highlander found the tongs*, 'Spoken when boys have pick'd something and pretend they found it'. (Kelly, 1721—to Lowlanders the Highlander was an inveterate thief).
A 19th-century *finder* was a thief.

find² to fabricate (evidence)
The language of the Nixon White House:
There was no prior evidence of such a relationship between Rutherford and Anderson, and Stewart refused to try to 'find' one. (Colodny & Gettlin, 1991—Nixon was convinced that there was a homosexual relationship between the journalist and the naval yeoman)

find a tree to urinate
It may be said about humans as well as dogs:
The traffic was snarled on the George Washington Parkway...so Patrick pulled into Fort Marcy Park to find a tree. (Evans-Pritchard, 1997)

find Cook County to engage in electoral fraud
Cook County's votes were produced miraculously by the Democratic machine in Illinois to secure Kennedy's win over Nixon in 1960:
'They found Cook County,' was the jaundiced comment. (Major, 1999—writing of Mitterrand's decision in 1992 that the French had voted in a referendum in favour of the exchange rate mechanism)

finger¹ to indicate in a criminal context
The pointing is usually figurative.
The *fingering* may be naming a suspect to the police or suggesting a crime to accomplices. Either task can be performed by a *finger-man*, who may also be an assassin, from pulling the trigger of a gun.

finger² to excite sexually with a finger
Usually a male *fingers* the female. To *finger yourself* is to masturbate, of either sex.

finger-blight the reduction of a crop due to stealing
An occurrence once common in apple orchards, *blight* being a natural phenomenon, while scrumping by children is not.

finish¹ to kill
It is used of humans or animals. If they have been previously wounded or are sick, you *finish them off*. *Finished* may mean dead.

finish² to achieve a sexual orgasm
Very common use of either sex.

finish yourself off wipe your genitalia dry
An injunction after washing for children, invalids, or geriatrics which avoids mentioning the taboo parts of the body.

fire to dismiss peremptorily from employment
Punning on *discharge*, which is standard English, meaning, to dismiss from employment,

and on the rapidity with which the deed is usually done.

fire a shot *American* to ejaculate semen
Or more shots than one. The use of *ejaculate* and *ejaculation* in a sexual sense is now so pervasive that it can convey an unfortunate image to the reader of older literature:
> The vicar ejaculated from time to time and looked increasingly bewildered. (Sayers, 1937)

fireman[1] a motorist exceeding the speed limit
From the corny question asked by a traffic policeman, 'Where's the fire?'

fireman[2] a person to whom unpleasant duties are delegated
With obvious imagery:
> Since starting at the Pentagon, Buhardt had been a fireman...stave off or limit the fallout from a variety of scandalous episodes. (Colodny & Gettlin, 1991)

The Nazis called the Jews whom they used in death camps to enforce discipline over other prisoners, predominantly Jewish, *firemen*.
See also VISITING FIREMAN.

firewater whisky
As well as burning your throat and your guts, it is flammable.

firm (the) a clandestine, illegal, or bogus organization
A 19th-century usage of the Fenians in Ireland and much loved by espionage writers.
Also used by the Windsor family:
> ...masses of photographs of 'The Firm', as they somewhat affectedly style themselves. (A. Clark, 1993—reporting on the contents of British royal palaces)

first people *Canadian* the descendants of the indigenous population
Not Adam and Eve but the aboriginal population of the country:
> The constitution is filled with modish catchphrases of the late 20th century, affirmative action, first people (natives), collective human rights, and the equality of male and female persons. (*Daily Telegraph*, 23 October 1992—reporting a statutory innovation which the Canadian electorate rejected)

first strike unannounced aggression
A use referring to an attack before war has been declared; otherwise it would not be euphemistic. A *first-strike capability* is an ability to attack another with nuclear weapons without prior warning.
See also SECOND STRIKE.

first world rich
The language of those for whom talk of poverty and backwardness is offensive.
The *Second World* was inhabited by Soviet Russia and its satellites. See also THIRD WORLD.

fish[1] *American* a heterosexual woman
One caught by a male, as seen by female homosexuals among whom heterosexuality in females is taboo. A *fishwife* in the same argot is the wife of a male homosexual.

fish[2] a prostitute's customer
Jargon among prostitutes for the customers who are caught and gutted.

fish[3] a torpedo
Second World War jargon, seeking to make light of danger:
> We had a fish coming at our ship at about 265 degrees. (Lewis, 1989—it had been fired by a German E-boat)

fisherman's tale a lie or exaggeration
Anglers have a reputation for romancing about the size of their catch or the one that got away. Also as a *fish story*.

fishing expedition an attempt to obtain gratuitous information
Not knowing what you may catch, as cross-examining counsel, detective, journalist, or spy. Also as *fishing trip*.

fishing fleet *British* marriageable girls send abroad to find husbands
Single British girls were sent to Malta or India where single men on extended tours might be less discriminating in their choice of bride.

fishmonger's daughter *obsolete* a prostitute
As with *fish market*, a brothel, the allusion is olfactory:
> Excellent well, you are a fishmonger. (Shakespeare, *Hamlet*—Hamlet speaking to Polonius, implying that the latter's daughter, Ophelia, was a prostitute. Polonius misses the point, only to take another behind the arras in the third act)

fishy (of a male) homosexual
Punning on QUEER[3] and the meaning 'irregular'.

fistful a prison sentence of five years
Prison slang, a variant of FIVE FINGERS and HANDFUL.

fit up to incriminate falsely
Another way to FRAME[1].

five-fingered discount *American* a reduction in price due to theft
It refers to stolen goods sold below their market price.

five-fingered widow (the) *British* male masturbation
Army use among those long absent from the company of white women.

five fingers a prison sentence of five years
A variant of FISTFUL and HANDFUL.

fix to make an illegal arrangement or perform a taboo act
In standard usage, to adjust or mend. As a verb or noun, *fix* can relate to bribery, hurting a rival, arranging a gambling coup, castrating a tom cat, injecting illegal narcotics, or killing.
In America to *fix up* is to hire a prostitute for another's use. All these, and other similar clandestine functions, are performed by a *fixer*.

fizzer *British* an accusation of a military offence
An army pun on *charge*.

flag is up (the) I am menstruating
Punning on the redness of the danger flag and the blood. Also as *flag of defiance*, *fly the (red) flag*, and BAKER FLYING.

flake *American* an eccentric or strange person
Of uncertain derivation, although there are plenty of theories to choose from. Dr Johnson gives 'Any thing that appears loosely held together', and the imagery of disintegration is common in terms for mental illness.

flamboyant homosexual
Literally, colourful or showy, which is how some male homosexuals are thought to comport themselves:
     ...obituaries are simply eulogies of the great and the good, any of whose peccadillos (unusual sexual tastes, drunkenness and so on) are tactfully powdered over with euphemism ('flamboyant', 'convivial' etc.) (Leslie Jones in *Daily Telegraph*, 1 December 1994)

flapper *obsolete* a young woman who flouts convention
In northern English dialect, a young prostitute; in western England, a petticoat; in *OED* a 'young wild duck or partridge'; and in the 1920s a participant in the *flapper era*.

flash to display your genitalia in public to a stranger
Behaviour performed almost exclusively by men known as *flashers*.
The obsolete *flash-ken* was a brothel, where you might command the services of a *flash-tail*, *-girl*, or *-woman*, if that was your desire.
The American police officer who *flashes tin* does nothing more improper than revealing his status, the *tin* being his badge of office.

flat-backer *American* a prostitute
Mainly black speech, from her posture while at work.

flavoured scandalous or obscene
The smell that lingers is never sweet:
     [Churchill] told a highly-flavoured story, which he had retailed in the smoking-room of the House. (Moran, 1966)
The *flavour of the month* is not the current story in bad taste but a cliché describing something enjoying ephemeral popularity.

flawed drunk
Perhaps a pun on *floored*, from the tendency to fall over, and the common DAMAGED[1] imagery.

fleece to defraud
By robbery or overcharging, from the shearing of sheep.
And (for non-lawyers) see also *knight of the Golden Fleece* under KNIGHT.

flesh *obsolete* a penis
As used in the King James's version of *Ezekiel* 23:30 where 'she doted on their paramours whose flesh *is as* the flesh of asses and whose issue *is like* that of horses'.
Thus when Shakespeare used *flesh your will*, meaning to copulate, in *All's Well That Ends Well*, we cannot be certain what vulgar puns he had in mind.

fleshpot a brothel
Originally a vessel in which meat was cooked, whence a source of luxury and debauchery offering a variety of vicious attractions.

fleshy part of the thigh the buttocks
It was here that a military bulletin said Lord Methuen had been wounded in the Boer War. Apart from late 19th-century modesty, to be wounded in the buttocks might imply that you had not been facing the enemy.

flexible[1] unprincipled
In normal use, the opposite of dogmatic. *Flexibility* is a characteristic of politicians:
     Conservative MPs, impatient for the pre-election bribery to start, call for 'flexibility'. (*Financial Times*, December 1981)

flexible² condoning adultery
Literally, adaptable:
> Friends say their marriage falls short of
> being completely 'open' sexually. But they
> have a flexible arrangement. (*Sunday
> Telegraph*, 25 February 2001)

fling an extramarital sexual relationship
From the meaning, indulgence in any unac-
customed excess:
> I had my fling with the Tanglin wife.
> (Theroux, 1973)

flip your lid to lose your senses
The *lid* is slang for the head.
It describes temporary rather than permanent
derangement.

flirty fishing proselytization through the
promiscuity of young women
Females belonging to a cult established by
David Berg, an American evangelist, were
encouraged to recruit men through sexual
seduction. The use of condoms was forbidden,
resulting in numerous pregnancies.

flit¹ *obsolete* to die
Literally, to remove to another place.

flit² (do a) to leave accommodation without paying rent due
A shortened form of MOONLIGHT FLIT.

flit³ a male homosexual who usually
plays the female role
He affects female mannerisms by *flitting about*.

float paper to issue cheques or other securities unsecured by bank deposits or
assets
Before the computer, banks took even longer
than today to clear cheques, an interval which
could be used for taking unauthorized credit.

floater *American* a vagrant
A hobo with no fixed abode.
In the jargon of morticians, a *floater* is also the
corpse of someone who has drowned.
In British parliamentary elections a *floater* was
'A vending voter'. (*F&H*)

floating *American* drunk or under the influence of narcotics
Referring to the feeling of levitation and
mental detachment.

flog off (of a male) to masturbate yourself
The common beating imagery. Also as *flog
your beef, mutton, donkey, dummy*, etc.

flop (of a woman) to be promiscuous
She is thought readily to drop to a prone
position:

> Lois flops at the drop of a hat. (Chandler,
> 1943—he was not suggesting that she tired
> easily)

floral tribute a wreath presented at a funeral
TRIBUTE, protection money or rent paid on a
regular basis, has evolved in standard English
to mean a gesture of respect or praise on a
single occasion. Brides prefer to carry bou-
quets.

flower¹ *obsolete* the virginity of a woman
What you lose if a man chances to DEFLOWER
you:
> Threw my affections in his charmed
> power,
> Reserved the stalk and gave him all my
> flower. (Shakespeare, *A Lover's Complaint*)

flower² *American* a male homosexual
More widely dispersed than the PANSY, it
might seem.

flowers *obsolete* the menstrual flow
Normally expanded to *monthly flowers*, from
the flowing rather than the flowering.

flowery¹ a prison cell
Rhyming slang on *flowery dell* and sometimes
used to refer to the prison itself.

flowery² blasphemous or vulgar
Descriptive of language, although the concept
of blasphemy now seems to be out of date
except in Muslim communities.

fluff your duff (of a male) to masturbate
Probably likening the penis to a suety dish,
with the same imagery as PULL THE PUD(DING).

flute *Irish* an erect penis
As with BUGLE, a firm instrument which may
be played:
> But it's his fault as much as Sharon's.
> Whoever he is.—It was his flute tha'—
> (Doyle, 1987—they were discussing the
> cause of Sharon's pregnancy)
A *fluter* in America is a male homosexual.

flutter a wager
A 17th-century use which is still current, from
the excitement of gambling but seeking to
minimize the extent of the addiction.
A *flutter* may also be a short-term promiscuous
relationship.
To *flutter a skirt* was to be a prostitute, from
her seeking to attract a customer's attention.
A *flutterer* is nothing more exciting than a lie-
detecting machine, recording your temperature, pulse, and so on as you are being
questioned.

flux¹ menstruation
Literally, the condition of flowing or, as with solder, causing to flow.

flux² diarrhoea
Again from the flowing:
> Our bodies weakened with fluxes, our strength wasted with watchings, want of drink, wet and cold being our constant companions. (Gentles, 1992—quoting a soldier in the New Model Army before the Battle of Dunbar)

fly¹ *American* in plain clothes
It is used of a policeman assigned away from his normal precinct or uniformed duty, from the meaning 'knowing', but perhaps also referring to a *fly cab*, one plying for hire without a licence.

fly² to be under illegal narcotic influence
Usually the feeling induced by smoking marijuana. In rhyming slang a *fly-by-night* is drunk, or TIGHT¹.
In RAF slang in the Second World War, a drunkard might be said to be *flying one wing low*, like a damaged plane.

fly³ *obsolete* to elope
But not by air:
> It was as she said: the foolish young man has asked her to fly. (Thackeray, 1848)

fly a flag to have a trouser zip inadvertently undone
Whether or not a part of the shirt-tail is protruding. You may also, in this situation, be said to be *flying low*.

fly a kite¹ to tender a worthless negotiable instrument
Only the wind supports it. See also KITE.

fly a kite² *obsolete* to write a begging letter
A considerable industry and art in 19th-century England made possible by the advent of the penny post.

fly-by-night an absconding debtor
Not from a witch, on or off her broomstick, or from the ominous bird, also known as the whistler or gobbleratch, whose nocturnal flight presaged imminent death, nor even the tourist on a package holiday on the cheapest ticket, but the tenant with unpaid rent who took his goods with him to prevent distraint by the landlord. Now standard English for anyone who is financially unreliable. See also MOONLIGHT FLIT.

fly the blue pigeon¹ to steal lead
Usually from the roof of a church, where the birds might congregate, and from the colour of the metal, shortened in slang to *bluey*.

fly the blue pigeon² *British* to be a malingerer
A naval pun on SWING THE LEAD.

fly the yellow flag to have contagious fever aboard
The crew would not be allowed ashore. Now only figurative use:
> A ship that flies the yellow flag and cannot find a port. (Seymour, 1977)

flyblow an illegitimate child
Punning on the deposit of eggs left in meat by flies, and the taint.

flyer an unsolicited advertising leaflet
Most of them *fly* into the waste paper pile on receipt, but that is not the etymology.

flying handicap diarrhoea
The phrase puns on the celerity needed, the disability, and a typical name for a horse race.

flying on empty trading with insufficient capital
Aviation imagery:
> The carrier, which has been flying on empty after two years of soaring losses, is poised to change hands in a £30m rescue deal. (*Daily Telegraph*, 4 January 2007)

flying picket *British* a crowd from afar trying to stop others working
They travelled by road rather than by air. Perhaps obsolete since such intimidatory action has been made illegal.

flying squad a police detachment organized for rapid deployment
There have been earthbound *flying squadrons* from the 17th century. The London version formed in the 1920s is also known in rhyming slang as the *Sweeney*, from the demon barber, Sweeney Todd.

fog away *American* to kill
By shooting, perhaps also alluding to the smoke from the gun. Sometimes simply as *fog*.

fogbound of low intelligence
Unable to see things clearly.

foggy drunk
Your eyes may be and your memory becomes. Also as *fogged*.

fold to fail
The imagery is from collapsing. Mainly business jargon:

[The Japanese government] must let some of the banks fold to allow the financial sector to reconstruct. (*Daily Telegraph*, 15 January 1997)

In America, to *fold* is to die, another form of collapsing.

To *fold your hand* is to concede defeat, the imagery coming from poker, when a player drops out of the bidding.

fold back to retreat

A military usage to avoid implications of defeat or cowardice:

[On 16 May, 1940] Sir John Dill was handed a signal advising that the French left flank was being 'folded back' (i.e. withdrawn)... [opening] a corridor all the way to the Channel ports... for the advancing Panzers. (A. Clark, 1998)

follow to die after another named person

To be reunited elsewhere, it may be hoped.

follower *obsolete* a male who is courting a female

Specifically a man who courted a domestic servant girl. Then in upper-class use—those who had servants—of courting any girl.

To *follow* meant to court:

He followed his wife ten year afore they were wed. (*Leeds Mercury*, 1893, quoted in *EDD*)

fond of excessively addicted to

More than just being favourably disposed towards. Thus a man who is *fond of the women* is a profligate, and he who *is fond of a glass* drinks too much alcohol, or, if *fond of food*, is a glutton.

fondle to caress sexually

Literally, to handle something or someone fondly:

... she had learned to slide her hand into his slitted pocket and fondle him. (Sanders, 1973)

food for worms dead

Unless cremated. Also as *worm-food*.

See also DIET OF WORMS.

fool (about with/around with) to have a promiscuous relationship with

To *fool* is to behave in a frivolous or irresponsible way. Either sex can *fool about* or *fool around with* the other, although the male is usually considered more blameworthy.

To *fool about with yourself* is to masturbate.

foot *obsolete British* to take money from new employees to buy intoxicants

An initiation ceremony, perhaps a shortened form of *foot the bill*.

A *footing* was such a levy.

There are many euphemisms for the practice of older workers extorting money from new apprentices.

footless drunk

Neither better nor worse than LEGLESS.

for reasons of health in disgrace

After the dismissal of a senior employee:

Lord Hardinge resigned as Private Secretary to the King 'for reasons of health' a few nights later [after improperly writing to George VI in July, 1943 expressing his opposition to General Wavell receiving a higher award than a barony]. (Channon, 1993—Wavell had been blamed for a defeat in the Western Desert by Rommel, after sending British troops to resist the German invasion of Greece. This had caused Hitler to divert to Greece divisions poised for Barbarossa, delaying his attack on Russia by three weeks from the planned date. Whether the Germans would have taken Moscow or Leningrad with three more weeks of better weather is a question few historians ask.)

for the birds mentally unbalanced

With your head in the metaphorical clouds.

for the high jump in deep trouble

It originally meant to be sentenced to death by hanging, whence to be killed by any means.

for your convenience provided ostensibly as a special service

The pretence of giving you something extra when it is already in the price is mildly irritating.

However, all is forgiven when you meet an unconscious pun:

For your convenience—Sanitor tissue seat covers. (lavatory in Fall River, Massachusetts, May, 1981)

forage to steal

Originally as a noun, food for cattle. Such food was traditionally stolen for their horses by armies on the march, whence, as a soldier, to look for anything else to steal.

force yourself on to copulate with

The male usually does the forcing. Also as *force your ardour* or *force your attentions on*.

To *force favours from* may indicate a greater degree of female reluctance.

forget yourself to be guilty of a solecism

Not total amnesia but swearing when it is out of place, making a sexual approach to a woman who has not signalled that she would welcome it, and the like.

fork to copulate with
Of male promiscuity, punning on the pronging
and the place where the legs meet the trunk.
For Shakespeare the *face between her forks* is a
woman's frontal crotch. (*King Lear*)

forked plague (the) *obsolete* cuckoldry
Referring to the proverbial horns worn by the
cuckold, and see also HORN.

form a criminal record
Police jargon, probably from horse-racing,
punning on the special *form* on which these
details are recorded.

former person a perceived opponent of
the Communist state
Such people had already lost such rights as
were accorded to Soviet citizens.

forty-four *American* a prostitute
An unusual example of non-British rhyming
slang, for *whore*.

forum shopping choosing a jurisdiction
likely to favour your case
For those who have the choice:
    ... it was little wonder that 'forum
    shopping'—looking for the best country to
    start proceedings—has become such a
    popular sport among rich husbands in the
    international scene. (*Daily Telegraph*, 15 May
    2001)

forward *obsolete British* drunk
A use which may have referred to the
truculence associated with drunkenness:
    Twer querish tack—beer and reubub weind
    an' bacca juice a-mixed, but I knowed we
    could get furard on't. (Buckman, 1870—a
    mixture of tobacco juice, beer, and rhubarb
    wine was queerish tack indeed)

forward at the knees old
From the way some elderly people walk and
as depicted on British road signs.

foul[1] to defecate in an unacceptable place
Usually of dogs on carpets or pavements, but
occasionally of humans.
To *foul yourself* is to defecate or vomit in your
clothing.

foul[2] *obsolete Scottish* the devil
A shortened form of *foul ane* or *foul thief*,
still heard in expressions such as *foul skelp ye*,
the devil take you, and *foul may care*, devil-
may-care.

foul desire a wish to copulate
Where *foul* means disgusting it seems that
linguistically only males are thus taken:
    If foul desire has not conducted you.

(Shakespeare, *Titus Andronicus*)
A man may also have *foul designs* on a woman
who is not his normal sexual partner. If he *has
his foul way with her*, he will copulate with her,
not necessarily against her inclination. Still
used humorously.

foul play *British* murder
Police jargon, and not of the way professional
footballers behave on the pitch.

foundation bringing up to normal qualification standards
Educational jargon. A *foundation course*, or
instruction in *foundation language arts*, may
be taken by those accepted by a university but
unable adequately to express themselves on
paper. Such candidates on entering tertiary
education may be said to take up a *foundation
degree place*.

foundation garment a corset
The imagery comes from building, although
the word *buttress* comes more readily to mind.

four-letter man an unpleasant person
The letters are S, H, I, and T.

four-letter word an obscenity
Jennings (1965) demonstrated that there were
then only eight among the catalogue of
obscenities which contained four letters.
However the most hackneyed among them
do tend to have four letters.

four sheets in the wind see SHEET IN THE
WIND

fourth a lavatory
The use seems to have originated at Cambridge University, probably from the lowest
category of degree awarded on graduation,
rather than from the three Estates of the
Realm—the peers, the bishops, and the
commons. The literati in the 19th century
delighted in inventing candidates for the
fourth estate. Carlyle says Burke first suggested
the press, although Macaulay has a better
claim. The joke, if such it be, still lingers on.

foxed drunk
Literally, deceived, and so a variant of the
obsolete deceived in liquor, which seeks to
imply it was not your fault.
As usual, the half is the same as the whole:
    Here I was, half-foxed and croaking to
    myself in a draughty shack. (Fraser, 1971)
Both uses are now dated.

foxtrot oscar a vulgar rebuttal
The letters F and O in radio language, mean-
ing fuck off. This was the message sent by
Michael O'Leary to the European Commission

when in 2005, under French protectionist pressure, it ruled that airports at Gosselies and Strasbourg must renege on commercial contracts made with Ryanair, of which he was Chief Executive.

foxy (of a female) sexually attractive
Literally, like a fox and therefore cunning.

fractional ownership an entitlement to occupy property for a limited period
One of the phrases used to avoid mentioning the fell *timeshare*:
> Parque Share's Elite Fractional Ownership could provide the answer. (advertisement in *Daily Telegraph*, 25 October 2002—the question was not how to invest capital unwisely and commit yourself to an open-ended commitment)

The gullible may also be offered '1/6th ownership', or another named proportion of the liability for future unspecified charges.

fractured *American* drunk
The broken imagery again.

frag *American* to kill
A shortened form of *fragmentation device*, which is a long-winded way of saying 'hand grenade'. The use originated in Vietnam where the grenade was used to kill over-keen or unpopular officers, often white, by conscript GIs, often black. (Some rich white boys evaded conscription, which did not prove to be a bar to at least one, who obtained the appointment of Commander-in-Chief of the US forces. Most blacks had to serve.) Some general use of killing by any means.

fragile having a hangover
A word often chosen by the sufferer who may also be feeling *frail*.

frail *obsolete* copulating extramaritally
Of a female not strong enough, or unwilling, to resist male blandishments:
> ... to such as had been frail she showed no mercy. (Dickens, 1841)

A *frail sister* is a prostitute. In American slang, a *frail* was a young woman, a member of the weaker sex, we might hope, rather than promiscuous.
Frailty, in a female, was promiscuity, especially if she became pregnant.

frame[1] to incriminate falsely
Like mounting a picture, so that you can see it better.
The result is a *frame-up*.

frame[2] a male who is attractive sexually to homosexuals

Probably from the slang *frame*, a body. Not necessarily a homosexual himself, although dress and posture may send a signal to other homosexuals, in which case the *frame* takes the female role.

frank[1] *obsolete* copulating promiscuously
Dr Johnson gives 'licentious', from the early meaning, liberal or generous:
> Chaste to her Husband, frank to all beside A teaming mistress but a barren bride. (Pope, 1735)

frank[2] unfriendly and without consensus
It is used of political talks between fundamentally opposed parties:
> Mr Mugabe had agreed on the need for urgent and 'frank' talks. (*Daily Telegraph*, December 1980—note the inverted commas)

Full and frank in a communiqué tells you that the parties failed to agree on anything:
> These [talks] lasted an hour and a half and were described as having been full and frank. (Kee, 1984—Chamberlain and Mussolini met on 11 June 1939; Great Britain and Italy were shortly to be at war)

fraternal assistance an invasion
Those on the left politically are wont to address each other, and perhaps even think of each other, as brothers:
> But the decision to say 'counter-revolution' instead of 'uprising', 'people' instead of 'party', 'fraternal assistance' instead of 'invasion' are choices of the highest solemnity. For Communism exists by casting spells—change the language and the world itself will change. (*Sunday Telegraph*, March 1989)

fraternization copulation with enemy civilians in military occupied territories
Strictly, friendship with or treating as brothers, but to an occupying soldier the *frater* was of less interest than his sister(s).
Non-fraternization, not mingling with the natives, was the official policy of the winning side.

fratricide inflicting casualties by mistake on your own troops
Inadvertently or carelessly killing your brothers-in-arms.

freak a devotee of any taboo or unconventional activity
Literally, an irrational event or a monster. Usually in a compound noun, such as *acid-freak*, someone who uses LSD regularly, or *surf-freak*, who spends excessive time in, on, under, and around rollers.
An American *freak* may be a male homosexual and a *freak trick*, a prostitute's customer

requiring sexual activity other than copulation or masturbation.

In narcotic jargon, to *freak* is to ingest drugs illegally, as a result of which you may *freak out*, may behave in an uncontrolled manner.

free included in the price
An advertising gimmick seeking to persuade a buyer that more is being handed over than has been paid for. A prospective purchaser may also be offered a separate article which is described as being *free* as an inducement to buy what the seller is peddling.

free from infection not suffering from venereal disease
In the army, a soldier can have measles, and a heavy cold, but be so described. Usually abbreviated to *FFI*.

free love unrestricted copulation outside marriage
The use implies an absence of concealment and disregard of convention. It is used for either sex.

free of Fumbler's Hall *obsolete* (of a male) sexually impotent
The inference was that the husband so described might toy sexually with his wife without being able to do more.

free relationship licence within a heterosexual partnership to copulate with third parties
There is an implication perhaps that a normal union in which the parties copulate only with each other involves sexual servility.

free samples copulation permitted by a woman prior to marriage
The imagery is from a taster or trial quantity offered by a trader. The euphemism was much used of betrothed couples.

free trade *obsolete* smuggling
It was (and still is) a way of evading excise duty.

Today *free trade* in standard English describes commerce between states without tariff barriers, although international trade is seldom truly free because of non-tariff barriers, nationalism, and other factors.

free world those countries not under Communist control
A different kind of tyranny might be included under this heading, despite the imperfections of its political arrangements.

freed from earthly limitations dead
It is a kind of liberty to which few of us look forward with enthusiasm:
> That bright spirit was but freed from its

earthly limitations. (Wright, 1932—her young daughter had just died)

freedom fighters rebels
It is often unclear whether those who so describe themselves are *fighting freedom* or *fighting for freedom*. Where the rebellion succeeds, too often it leads to despotism.

freelance (of a woman) to be promiscuous
A complex pun on LANCE, to copulate (though normally of the male), being *free* from involvement with a pimp, or not demanding payment, and the *freelance* who works without being tied to a single employer. Also used as a noun to describe one who so behaves.

freeloader a systematic cadger
Showing greed where hospitality is provided by another, such an event being called a *freebie*:
> RAF crew on Blair's Queens Flight 'freebie' had a jolly good time too. (*Sunday Telegraph*, 16 January 2005)
Freeloader, meaning a thief, is rare.

freeman of Bucks *obsolete British* a cuckold
Punning on the distinction, the English county, and the horns of the stag.

Freemans cadged cigarettes
Army usage, referring to a fictional brand smoked by habitual cadgers.

freeze[1] an attempt to contain public expenditure by reducing wages or recruitment
In an inflationary economy, absence of an increase effectively reduces pay, and non-recruitment saves costs.

freeze[2] the refusal by a female to copulate with her regular sexual partner
First noted (etymologically) in Australia but now a widespread usage.

freeze on to to steal
Alluding to the adhesive quality of ice. It refers to minor peculation and stealing by finding.

freeze out to eliminate minority shareholders unfairly
Commercial jargon, from the meaning 'to exclude arbitrarily'. Minority shareholders in a British unquoted company have scant legal protection if their total interest amounts to less than 25% of the equity.

freezer *American* a prison
The imagery of the ICE BOX[1].

French is used by the English of anything which they consider bogus, over-rated, illegal, immoral, or otherwise undesirable, reflecting the mutual distrust between the countries which was not lessened by the events between 1940 and 1945. The following examples give a general flavour:

French¹ to indulge in oral sex
Using what the English call the FRENCH way.

French² an excuse for swearing
You pretend that the taboo word is foreign: ...not when some poor fucker...you'll excuse my French, Mr Carter...(Seymour, 1980)

French ache syphilis
Shakespeare refers to the baldness caused by this supposed import:
Some of your French crowns have no hair at all. (*A Midsummer Night's Dream*)
In former times you might be unfortunate enough to contract *French disease*, *fever*, *gout*, *measles*, or *pox*, or receive a *French compliment*, each of which would cause you to become *frenchified*, or syphilitic.

French article smuggled brandy
The euphemism passed into some general use to include imports which had been subject to excise duty. Also, in smuggling argot, as *French cream*, *elixir*, or *lace*.
A *Frenchman* was a single bottle of brandy.
I'm not sure why in Ireland *French cream* was whiskey.

French drive a miscued shot at cricket

French kiss a kiss during which the tongue is inserted into another's mouth
Such depravity has to be un-English.
An *Aussie kiss* is a *French kiss* performed *down under*.

French leave unauthorized absence
Originally of a soldier, implying a propensity in French soldiers for desertion. Some civilian and figurative use.

French letter a contraceptive sheath worn by a male
The term may come from their being packed in small envelopes, coupled with the supposed Gallic penchant for frequent copulation. I think any derivation from *letting*, or preventing, as in the phrase *let or hindrance*, is unlikely.
Also as *FL*, *Frenchie*, or *French tickler*.

French novel *obsolete* a salacious book

A 19th-century usage when pornographic literature was less likely to be published in Britain.

French pigeon a pheasant shot out of season
The action of a bounder.

French prints pornographic pictures
Obtainable in France when illegal in Britain or America and indicative of Gallic degeneracy. Farmer & Henley say merely 'indecent pictures'.

French renovating pills substances to induce abortion of a healthy foetus
Freely advertised in the 19th century, with a warning that pregnant women should not take them—in fact revealing their purpose.

French vice (the) cunnilingus or fellatio
And as the *French way*.

fresh¹ mildly drunk
Perhaps a shortened form of *fresh in drink*, or just in the lively state before becoming stupefied. When farmers' social life revolved around the weekly visit to the market, their intoxicated condition on the way home was *market-fresh*.
To *freshen a drink* is to add to that in a glass or serve more alcohol.
Just to confuse matters, in obsolete Scottish use, if a habitual drunkard had not been drinking alcohol, he was described as being *fresh*.

fresh² making unwelcome sexual approaches to another
Another form of liveliness.

freshen up *American* to urinate
A standard invitation to arriving visitors who are asked if they would like to *freshen up*.

fricasseed *American* drunk
The common cooking imagery. We may also marvel at the American-English conjugation of a French verb.

fried *American* drunk
More culinary imagery.

friend¹ *obsolete* a second in a duel
Part of the ritual:
When Rowdon told the Captain he wanted a friend, the latter knew perfectly well on what duty of friendship he was called to act. (Thackeray, 1848)

friend² an extramarital sexual partner
Sometime *tout court* but normally indicating the sex by a prefix such as *boy*, *gentleman*, *girl*, *lady*, *man*, or *woman*.

Friends, *good friends*, or *close friends* may also indicate the nature of the *friendship*, especially for journalists when libel lawyers are on the prowl. Also some homosexual use.

friend has come (my) I am menstruating
Punning on the arrival for a limited period and the relief at not being pregnant. Also as *my little friend*.

friendly lacking accord or sympathy
The language of diplomacy to describe discussions between mutually suspicious or antagonistic parties. This is one grade up the scale from FRANK[2].

friendly fire being bombed or shelled by your own side
The use seeks to play down one of the hazards of battle.

frig to copulate with
From the meaning to rub, despite the etymological attractions of the old Cornish *frig*, a married woman, and of *Frigga*, Odin's wife, the aptly named Norse goddess of married love whom we commemorate every Friday.
The vulgar *frigging* is a synonym for *fucking* as an obscenity.
Frig also means to masturbate, from the rubbing rather than the goddess.

frightener a person paid to intimidate illegally
Usually for the collection of usurious debt or to prevent the giving of evidence.

fringe unconventional, insubstantial, or fraudulent
Close to the edge of propriety or convention in the arts, as in the *fringe theatre*, or of honesty in commerce:
> The Bank of England's least favourite 'fringe' banker. (*Private Eye*, March 1981)

frippet a sexually available young woman
Usually unmarried. A *frip* was a scrap of cloth, whence something worthless. *Frippery* was clothing and the imagery is the same as SKIRT.

froggie *British* a contraceptive sheath
From the *French* in FRENCH LETTER and a derogatory name for a nation noted for the culinary delicacy, frogs' legs. Naval use.

front a deceptive stratagem
A *front* is an organization which masks its true intention and misleads the gullible, devised by the Communist propagandist Munzenberg, and used by extremist parties of every hue.
A *front* may also be a seemingly honest person or business masking, or *fronting*, a covert or illegal operation.

front door see BACK DOOR[1]

front-running dealing illegally as an insider
Market jargon. If a client places an order on the stock or commodity market the size of which will move the share price, the broker deals personally on a smaller scale before placing the client's order.

frontier guards troops used for invasion without a declaration of war
The Chinese Communists so described their armies which invaded India in the 1960s and Vietnam in the 1970s:
> Then a reference to 'Chinese Frontier Guards' alerted me. (Naipaul, 1964—he had thought he was listening to an Indian broadcast until the use of the euphemism told him the source was Chinese)

frosting stealing motor cars
Criminal argot for waiting on a cold morning for a motorist to start the engine and then leave the vehicle unattended and unlocked with the key in the ignition waiting for the heat to defrost the windows.

frottage sexual bodily contact between two people wearing clothing
Literally, touching or rubbing together.

fruit a male homosexual
Which came first, the RAISIN or the *fruit*? Probably the *raisin*, from the French meaning, 'lipstick'.

fruit machine a mechanical gambling device
The symbols on the rotating discs in the early versions are fruits.

fruit salad a mixture of illegal narcotics
Either of indiscriminate ingestion of whatever is to hand, or of the pooling of supplies by those who meet to ingest narcotics together.

fruitcake a mentally abnormal or eccentric person
A shortened form of the cliché *as nutty as a fruitcake*. Sometimes as a *fruit*.

fry[1] to die
In America, of judicial killing in the electric chair. Less often of being killed by other means.

fry[2] the testicles of lambs
It is how they are often cooked.

fuddled drunk
Literally, confused. We tend to use the term of others rather than ourselves.

fudge to attempt to deceive

Especially by making wrong entries in accounts, or *fudging figures*. A corruption of the standard English *fiddle*.

A *fudge-packer* does not work in a sweet factory, or figuratively make false entries in a ledger, but is a sodomite.

full drunk

It survives in the Scottish *fou*:

The cup that cheers, but makesna fou.
(Tester, 1865—he was referring to tea)

Now also heard in various clichés such as *full as a tick* or the less common *full as a boat*.

full figure (a) obesity

Not just possessing all your anatomical appendages:

Miss Lewinsky's already full figure appeared to have gained several more pounds in recent weeks. (*Daily Telegraph*, 20 August 1998)

A *fuller figure*, usually of a woman, is no *fuller* than *full*. *Full-figured* means obese, of either sex.

full in the belly pregnant

Not just having eaten a hearty meal. Also as *having a full belly*.

full treatment (the) copulation

The language of brothels which operate under the style of MASSAGE PARLOUR, and the like.

fumble a manual sexual approach to another

Literally, to use your hands awkwardly, whence to caress sexually:

The dish you was trying to fumble up the hall. (Chandler, 1958—and not describing a waiter)

Conversely, in the 18th century a *fumbler* was a sexually impotent man and see also FREE OF FUMBLER'S HALL.

fumble for a check *American* to seek to avoid payment for a shared meal etc.

You let the other person pick it up first.

fun promiscuous sexual activity

At some remove from the original meaning of *fun*, hoaxing or trickery, whence amusement or pleasure. When an advertiser in a Lonely Hearts feature says he is looking *for fun*, those who respond understand the code.

Fun and games means sexual promiscuity.
The American *fun house* is a brothel.
Fun-loving, a description cherished by journalists and obituarists, means licentious and hedonistic.

funny[1] unwell

Literally, strange or unusual. Thus when we *feel funny* we are unlikely to be in a humorous mood. A *funny tummy* may well be the result of drinking too much alcohol.

funny[2] (of a male) homosexual

Literally, odd.

funny[3] mad

Again from the oddness, and usually in the euphemisms of institutions for the insane such as *funny farm*, *home*, or *place*.

funny money cash which cannot be spent openly

Counterfeit notes or the proceeds of vice or crime.

furlough *American* involuntary dismissal from employment

Literally, paid leave of absence, whence suspension from duty without pay, and then dismissal. Airline pilots and cabin staff who were dismissed in the 1980s after striking were so etymologically described.

furry thing *British* a rabbit

Seamen must not mention rabbits before putting to sea under an old taboo based on the substitution by fraudulent chandlers of rabbit meat, which does not keep, for salt pork, which does.

further your career to be summarily dismissed

A face-saving phrase:

Mr Miller, 40, who will receive no compensation, will 'retire' from the board on September 10 after presenting the half-year results, 'to further his career in other fields'. (*Daily Telegraph*, 21 August 2002—Mr Miller was not a farmer)

fuzz the police

Perhaps a shortened form of *fuzzy bear*, which is noted under BEAR[2].

A *fuzz-buster* is a motor-borne radar detector.

G

G anything taboo beginning with the letter G
A mild expletive, usually spelt *gee*, a shortened form of *jeez*, from *Jesus*; in America, the leader of a *gang* of convicts, or a *gallon* of whisky.
A *G-man* is a federal agent, working for the US *government*.
A *G-nose* sniffs narcotics, and not necessarily glue.

gaffe an embarrassing statement of unpalatable truth
Literally, a tactless remark or action, via the French word for boathook:
> Indeed [the remarks by the Countess of Wessex] neatly bear out our favoured definition of a 'gaffe' as the statement of the obvious by a prominent person. (*Daily Telegraph*, 9 April 2001)

gain to steal
Literally, to acquire something desirable. In the 15th century, *gain* meant booty.

gallant *obsolete* a woman's extramarital sexual partner
Literally, as an adjective, chivalrous. To *be gallant to a woman* was to copulate with one who was not your wife and *gallantry* was licentious behaviour by either sex. In modern use *over-gallant* indicates an unwanted sexual approach to a woman.

gallop an act of copulation
Of a male, using the common equine imagery. The female partner may also be referred to as a *gallop*, invariably with a laudatory adjective.

game¹ wild animals killed primarily for human amusement
Standard English for animals hunted in the wild, birds conserved so that they can be shot, and certain large fish. *Big game* describes large mammals in Asia and Africa, in areas where they have not been hunted to extinction.

game² (the) female prostitution
The same imagery as SPORT but, for the women involved, business rather than pleasure. A prostitute may be described as being *at*, *in*, or *on the game*. For James Boswell it was the *noble game*. If however you were detected in adultery in his native Scotland, the kirk might demand a *game-fee* as penance.

A female who is *game* is one who is prepared to copulate promiscuously, from the slang meaning, willing, and often after a chance encounter:
> You had a few drinks, you told her she was beautiful. Sometimes she was game, sometimes not. (*Daily Telegraph*, 8 March 2004—obituary of Jorge Guinle whose mistresses included Marilyn Monroe, Jayne Mansfield, Rita Hayworth, Lana Turner, Ava Gardner, Hedy Lamarr, and Veronica Lake, to name a few)

gamester a gambler
Gaming has meant gambling since the 16th century because most wagers turn on the outcome of *games*:
> The credit of a race-horse, a gamester, and a whore lasteth but a short time. (Torriano, 1643)

In the ABC used by myself and my children:
> G was a Gamester who had but ill luck. (In those innocent days we saw no impropriety in 'U was an Usher who loved little boys')

In obsolete use, a *gamester* was also a prostitute, being employed in THE GAME².

gander-mooner *obsolete English* a husband copulating outside marriage
The month after the birth of a child was known as the *gander month* or *gander moon*, from 'the month during which the goose is sitting when the gander looks lost and wanders vacantly about' (*EDD*). During this period a husband was supposedly given licence to copulate with other than his wife.

gang *mainly Scottish* is used in many euphemistic phrases as an alternative to GO.

gap year a long period of inactivity between secondary and tertiary education
Formerly, the unavoidable delay (except during the Second World War) between being accepted in December as an undergraduate at Cambridge or Oxford and going up to university the following October.

garden *British* to sow mines in water from the air
Second World War usage which, by describing the operation horticulturally, avoided explicit lethal terms and adverted to the comparative safety of the operation:
> 'Gardening' was arranging for the RAF to lay mines in a particular naval grid square outside a German harbour. An hour later, you could guarantee the harbour master... would send a message using that day's Enigma settings, warning ships to beware mines in naval square such-and-such. (R. Harris, 1995—this was helpful to the code-breakers at Bletchley Park)

garden gout/house see COVENT GARDEN

garden of remembrance the curtilage of a crematorium

Usually a few seats, some roses, a path, stone slabs, and a lawn, all of which the mourners soon forget.

An American *Garden of Honor* is that part of the cemetery in which you can put up a plate naming a dead serviceman and a *garden crypt* is a drawer for a corpse facing outwards so that it can enjoy the view.

gardening leave suspension from office on full pay

The employee is told to keep away from his place of business, whether or not a horticulturist, either to enable an investigation into his conduct or to prevent his joining a competitor until his period of notice expires:

Kingfisher's chief executive insisted on lengthy 'gardening' leave which meant that Mr Holmes only joined M&S at the beginning of January. (*Daily Telegraph*, 8 March 2001)

gargle an alcoholic drink

Literally, a liquid suspended in the throat for medicinal purposes. The verbal use is perhaps obsolete.

garnish a redundant or token salad

In enables the publican to charge excessively for a sandwich or other snack to which a few leaves of lettuce and a slice of tomato have been gratuitously added.

gas deliberately kill or injure by poison gas

As suffered by soldiers in the First World War; by the chronically unfit, the gypsies, and the Jews in Nazi Germany; by civilians in Saddam Hussein's Iraq; and by convicted murderers in some American States, where they may also be said to *get the gas pipe*.

The American *gas-house* is not the execution chamber but a bar selling beer, on which you may first become bloated and then *gassed*, or drunk.

gash a woman viewed lecherously

Literally, in slang, an object obtained for nothing or something surplus to requirements.

gate¹ to confine to college as a punishment

Originally used with reference to those colleges in Cambridge and Oxford which had formidable barriers to prevent unobserved access and formidable porters in the gatehouse.

An American *gated community* is an area with high security to keep intruders out rather than inhabitants in.

gate² (the) *mainly American* peremptory dismissal from employment

The way out for the last time, *given* or *shown*: Amtrak board facing the gate. (*New York Post*, September 1981—they were threatened with dismissal en bloc, not about to board a train)

gathered to God dead

Seldom *tout court*:

Now all except me are 'gathered' as charladies would say. (Channon, 1993—diary entry on death of Ivor Novello)

The dead person is normally *gathered to his ancestors*, *his fathers* (but not his mothers), *God*, *Jesus*, *Mohammed*, or as the case may be.

ga(u)ge *American* to kill

Literally, to measure or, as a noun, an ancient token of defiance, which doesn't help us very much.

gay enjoying or doing something which is the subject of a taboo

Literally, happy or cheerful. In the 19th century a prostitute might be called a *gay girl* or *lady*, leading the *gay life*.

Until the 1960s, *gay* was synonymous with *merry* as an indication of intoxication.

Now standard English for homosexual.

gear anything which is the subject of secrecy or taboo

Literally, equipment. In obsolete Scottish use it meant smuggled spirits. It modern use it may mean the male or female genitalia, apparatus used to ingest narcotics illegally, housebreaking tools, etc.

In America *geared* means drunk.

If however your *gears have slipped* or *failed to mesh*, it means you are, in the opinion of those so describing you, mentally deranged, usually on a single occasion.

gender concerned with the advancement or protection of women in employment

The process is recorded in a *gender analysis*, which does not merely record the numbers of males and females. Public sector employers especially, for whom correct behaviour and sexual equality may be more important than efficiency or suitability for a specific job, may achieve their target by *gender-norming*—'the deliberate skewing of test results to make sure more women pass'. (*Sunday Telegraph*, 11 April 1993) Anything *gender-related* affects the well-being or status of women rather than men:

Mr Hartridge 'dishonestly suppressed information concerning a gender-related incident'. (*Daily Telegraph*, 2 April 2004—Hartridge was a juror on the Martha Stewart trial)

Gender-bending is no longer a pupil's struggles with Greek and Latin grammar but an effort by someone, usually someone who is homosexual, to adopt the characteristics of the opposite sex.

general discharge *American* dishonourable dismissal from the forces
Other people get *honorable discharge*.

generously built (of a woman) fat
Also as *generously proportioned* or *generously sized*, having *generous girth*:
> The generously proportioned diva...has had her contract cancelled after, she claims, being told she was too fat for the role. (*Sunday Telegraph*, 7 March 2004—her weight was not revealed but was estimated to have been in excess of 200 lbs)

gentle *obsolete Irish* bewitched
Unlike the Christmas pantomime variety, fairies were nasty creatures whom you called the *gentle people* because it was wise to speak kindly of them. Hawthorns were called *gentle bushes* or *thorns*, despite their pricks, because the fairies put spells on them. Land left uncultivated for occupation by the fairies was known as the *gentle place*.

gentleman someone in a situation or occupation the subject of vilification or taboo
In obsolete British use, he might be poor and involuntarily unemployed, a grim joke on the wealthy who did not need to work.
The *gentlemen* were smugglers.
And in many phrases such as *gentleman of fortune*, a pirate; *gentleman of the cloth*, a tailor, punning on the clergy; *gentleman of the road*, formerly a highway thief but in modern use, a tramp, etc.

gentleman cow/ox see BIG ANIMAL

gentleman friend a woman's sexual partner to whom she is not married
He does not have to be of gentle birth or indeed behave chivalrously towards her.

gentleman of color *American* a black man
Not (yet) considered offensive despite its inaccuracy in suggesting that other human skin pigmentation lacks colour.

gentlemen a lavatory exclusively for male use
Less often in a compound by the addition of *convenience* etc. than is the case with LADIES, and often shortened to *gents*.

gentlemen's club a venue not open to the public where gambling, drinking intoxicants, and prostitutes are available
The ladies found there are not ladies and the gentlemen do not behave like gentlemen.

gentry *obsolete Irish* the fairies
These malevolent creatures had to be flattered although the appellation may have been less of a compliment than they imagined, given Catholic Irish opinion of much of the Anglo-Irish Protestant *gentry*.

geography the location of a lavatory
A way of telling a visitor where the lavatory is to avoid a need for exploration or any reference to its purpose:
> Let me show you the geography of the house. (Ross, 1956)

Georgian *British* old
Estate agents' jargon for a house usually in poor repair. The implication is that the structure was built between 1714 and 1830, when the first four Georges reigned, rather than in the days of Kings George V and VI, from 1910 to 1952.

German distorted to fit Nazi dogma
In defence of their bizarre genetic theories, the Nazis were obliged to create new disciplines of *German chemistry, mathematics, science*, etc., especially where they felt a necessity to contradict the work of Jewish scientists. *Germanization* was the process of adapting anything foreign to their own use, including taking fair-haired children from conquered countries for adoption and rearing in Germany.

German Democratic Republic the totalitarian Soviet satellite state in eastern Germany
See also DEMOCRAT/DEMOCRACY. It is sad to recall that Victor Klemperer, whose *lingua tertii imperii* examined the abuse of language by the Nazis, should have ended his life condoning a regime as ruthless, unprincipled, and linguistically cynical as its predecessor. His life, along with that of the few other surviving Jews, was saved by the fire-bombing of Dresden which destroyed the Gestapo headquarters to which he had been ordered to report for deportation the next day.

get is used in many phrases associated with copulation, most of them vulgarisms. Among those relating to male copulation are *get a leg over, get it, it in, off, off with, on*, or *up*; *get in* or *into her bloomers, girdle, knickers*, or *pants*; *get lucky, round, there*, or *through*; *get your end in* or *away, hook into, muttons, rocks off, way with, will(s) of*, etc. Other phrases may refer to mutual copulation or to copulation by either partner, such as *get busy with, into bed with, it together, laid, your greens*, or *your share*. Some of the same phrases are used of sodomy, or bestiality:
> I know a pillar of the community who gets

it off with alligators. (Sanders, 1982—and more than once?)

As a less disagreeable footnote, we may record that in 1696 Aubrey wrote of Sir Walter Raleigh's 'getting up one of the mayds of honour'; and that, in obsolete use, to *get laid* meant no more than to drop off to sleep:

I couldn't get myself laid for the noise he mead. (*EDD*)

get a result *British* not to lose
The jargon of less literate soccer managers and players, who have problems in differentiating a draw or loss from an abandoned match.

(Soccerspeak has its own grammar, in which the past participle replaces the past tense and an adjective becomes an adverb. Thus *The boy done good* does not imply that the player is or has been a philanthropist, as becomes apparent when even better play elicits the comment *The boy done excellent.*)

get along to grow old
A shortened from of *get along in years* or some such phrase.

get away *obsolete Scottish* to die
The soul escapes from this Vale of Tears.

get it to be killed
Usually of violence in war.
Also of wounding:

Then I realised he had got it. He doubled up. I grabbed his right arm but he screamed, 'That's where I'm hit.' (Ranfurly, 1994—diary entry of 18 March 1943)

get off[1] to achieve an orgasm
It applies to either sex.

get off[2] to marry someone off
Usually of a woman, and a shortened form of *get off our hands* or some such phrase. However, to *get off with* implies no more than starting a sexual relationship with another.

get off[3] to ingest narcotics illegally
A feeling of floating is sometimes experienced. To *get on* is to become so addicted.

get on to grow old
Standard English, being a shortened form of *get on in years.*

get on your bike *obsolete* to be dismissed from employment
A reminder of the days when a majority of employees cycled to and from work. The phrase may also mean to make an effort to achieve something, from the locomotion of those seeking a job in the Depression.
In modern slang it can be no more than an

impolite injunction to someone to go away.

get out the onion to weep in order to gain sympathy
The etymology needs no explanation.

get the needle *American* to be judicially killed
By lethal injection rather than electrocution.

get the shaft *American* to receive harsh, precipitate, or unfair treatment
Specifically of summary dismissal from courtship or employment. There are several variants to the means of dismissal, such as *get the push* or *shove.*

The executives continue to take their pay and perks while the workers get the shaft. (*New York Times*, 17 March 1992)

get the shorts to be insolvent
Or temporarily without any money.

get with child to impregnate a female
Within or outside marriage, and not merely acquiring a stepchild as part of a new marital package.

get your collar felt see COLLAR[2]

get your feet under the table to achieve a comfortable and stable domestic situation
The phrase was in common use among servicemen stationed away from home in the Second World War when a local family offered frequent hospitality, which often led to courtship of a daughter. The phrase is now used of someone of either sex wanting to get married and settle down.

ghost[1] a fictitious employee
Either an invented name on the payroll or that of someone who exists but does not work for the organization:

As for the ghosts, some African governments have them on their payrolls. The Congo has just paid off 6,000 of them—fictitious employees...created to allow people to obtain five or ten salaries each month. (*Daily Telegraph*, 26 March 1994)

ghost[2] a writer whose work is published under another's name
Used by a public figure without literary expertise, and a shortened form of *ghost-writer.*

ghost does not walk (the) *?obsolete* the cast will not be paid
Theatrical jargon, the ghost being the cashier. The reference is to Hamlet.

gift of your body (the) *obsolete* extramarital copulation by a female
Loan or *licence* might better describe the nature of the transaction.

gild to tell a lie about
Literally, to cover thinly with gold, and perhaps alluding to that misquoted cliché *gild the lily*—Shakespeare actually wrote 'to gild refined gold, to paint the lily' (*King John*). In phrases such as *gild the facts, proposition, truth,* etc.

ginger homosexual
Of a male, and rhyming slang on *ginger beer,* queer. Sometimes written in full but now rare.

Ginza cowboy *American* an ineffectual soldier
Ginza from the shopping centre in Tokyo and *cowboy* meaning unprofessional and slipshod:
Most of the first American troops hopelessly attempting to stem the invasion [of South Korea] were 'Ginza cowboys'—young GIs from the occupation force in Japan, with little training and less discipline, unhappy and unready to fight. (Whicker, 1982)

gippy tummy diarrhoea
A corruption of *Egyptian tummy*, suffered by foreign visitors rather than the local inhabitants who have greater immunity to germs and bacteria in food and drink. Also as *gyppy tummy* and contracted elsewhere than in Egypt.

girl¹ a prostitute
Literally, a female child or servant, whence a sweetheart. Often in more specific phrases, such as *girl of the streets. Girlie* often indicates that the women involved are being exploited for, or engaged in, prostitution, as in *girlie houses, parlours,* etc. which are brothels, and *girlie bars,* where prostitutes solicit custom; or in pornography, where *girlie flicks, magazines, videos, DVDs,* etc. aim to titillate men.
The *girlie-trailer* seems to have been a wartime phenomenon:
Taxis became rolling brothels and fleets of 'girlie-trailers' served the concupiscent. (Atkinson, 2003, writing of Norfolk, Virginia in 1942)
A *girler* is a male profligate:
I hear this Frank Sinatra's a fearful girler. (Theroux, 1978—fearful or fearless?)

girl² any female less than 50 years old
The usage, often in the form of hyperbole, seeks to imply that the ageing process has been retarded or reversed:
I first met Winston Churchill in the early summer of 1906 at a dinner party to which

I went as a very young girl. (V. B. Carter, 1965—she was not in swaddling clothes but a woman of 19)
See also BOY.

girl³ *American* cocaine
Addict usage, the etymology being explained in the quotation:
Nobody called cocaine *white lady* any more, either. But the word *girl* had come to mean cocaine through a sort of perverse evolution. (McBain, 1994)

girlfriend a female extramarital sexual partner
Not just a *friend* who is a *girl*, but of a relationship which is generally exclusive, from courtship to cohabitation, heterosexual or homosexual.
See also BOYFRIEND.

girls' (room) a lavatory for exclusively female use
Usually adjacent to its male counterpart.

giro day *British* the day of the week on which recipients can draw pensions and other cash entitlements from the state
It is taboo to refer to the charitable nature of certain of the payments. Those wishing to visit a post office to carry out a normal commercial transaction learn to avoid this day.

give is used, occasionally *tout court*, but usually in a phrase, to mean copulation, as in *give a little, access to your body, (up) your treasure, way, your all, your body,* or *yourself* (where the donor is female) and *give her one, it to, to, the ferret a run,* or *time to* (where the male is supposedly dispensing generosity). The male seldom does the giving, linguistically:
Maybe Bill gives at the office. (Sanders, 1982—Bill was not a charitable benefactor nor did he copulate with his wife)
Some homosexual use. To *give head* is to practise fellatio.

give a line *American* to lie
The British prefer, if so minded, to SHOOT A LINE.

give a P45 *British* to dismiss peremptorily from employment
Referring to the number of the tax form given to the departing employee, including those who retire or leave of their own volition.

give (someone) the air to dismiss from employment

The employee may also, if so unfortunate, be *given* the BAG[2], the BOOT, the BULLET, the *breeze*, the SACK, NOTICE, WARNING, the WIND[2], *his running shoes*, etc. Also, apart from *the bag, the sack, notice*, or *warning*, the phrases may be used of the unilateral ending of courtship.

give the eye to look at a stranger in a manner denoting a sexual interest
Unless it is the *evil eye*, which may cast an unpleasant spell on the victim.

give the finger to to make an obscene gesture towards
The practice, of southern European origin, seems to be encroaching on the venerable Anglo-Saxon TWO-FINGERED message:
  'Goodbye, you ninny!' she called, giving him the finger. (L. Thomas, 1994—a wife was deserting the husband to whom she had previously given her hand)

give the good news to kill
Whatever might the bad news be?
  As the boy shouted, Mark gave him the good news. His body disintegrated in front of my eyes. (McNab, 1993)
Also, in slang, as *give (someone) the works*.

give time to other commitments to be peremptorily dismissed from employment
As with similar evasions, such as *give time to his other interests*, a face-saving form of words for senior employees.

give to God *Irish* to commit (a child) to a priestly or monastic life
The donors are the parents and family.

give up the ghost to die
The *ghost* is the spirit which you surrender to heaven, or as the case may be, when it leaves the body.
There are many obsolete dialect phrases indicating that the dead will make no further demand on terrestrial resources, such as the Lancashire *give up the spoon*—you will sup no more.

give your life to be killed fighting in a war
The donation is assumed on memorial tablets whether or not those who died volunteered for armed service.

given new responsibilities demoted
The *new responsibilities* are invariably less demanding or rewarding than those relinquished:
  ... the two existing top managers ... have been given new responsibilities. (*Daily Telegraph*, 2 September 1994, under the headline 'Simpson shakes up Lucas')

given rig *obsolete Scottish* a plot of land left uncultivated to placate the devil
An example of the common practice of seeking to mollify the devil by granting him his own land and discourage him from blighting the rest of the farm, although he was usually allotted a relatively infertile patch.

given to the drink see DRINK[1]

glands *American* taboo parts of the body
Especially the breasts of a female or the testicles of a male.

Glasgow kiss *Scottish* a headbutt
Parts of the conurbation have an unenviable reputation for violence.

glass[1] an intoxicant
The content, not the container, and usually of wine or spirits.
A *glass too many* indicates drunkenness and a *social glass* is alcohol drunk in the company of others.

glass[2] *British* to wound (someone) in the face with a broken glass
An unfortunate example of the antisocial behaviour of some young males whose income exceeds their manners, education, intelligence, or sobriety.

glass ceiling a level above which certain categories of people are unlikely to be promoted
It is there but cannot be seen. The phrase is mainly used, and the obstruction encountered by, women in a hierarchical structure.

glass house *British* an army prison
The derivation is from the glass roof of the one at Aldershot, and perhaps adverting to the figurative heat applied to the inmates.

glean to steal
Literally, to pick up ears of corn left by the reapers. Usually of pilfering small articles.

glove money *obsolete* a bribe
By ancient custom, you gave gloves to anyone who had done you a favour or might be persuaded to do so, concealing the bribe inside. Sir Thomas More, when Lord Chancellor of England, kept the gloves which Mrs Croaker gave him but returned the hidden £40. We should not then be surprised that, despite the uncouthness of his language, he was later beatified.

glow to sweat
A usage of horses from the visible sign on the skin, and of women in the days when perspiring was considered something a lady never did because of a taboo about secretions from the armpits and the crotch.
Having *a glow on* indicates a state of mild drunkenness, from the associated sweating and perhaps alluding to the feeling of exuberance.

glue *American* to pilfer
The object sticks to the hands of the thief.

go¹ to die
And in the northern British alternative, *gang, tout court*, or in many phrases. Thus a sailor, especially if retired, might *go aloft* even if he had never climbed the mast; a Scot might *go corbie*, from the crow, the messenger which brings bad tidings and does not return; cattle might *go down the nick*, to a slaughterhouse; an Egyptologist *might go forth in his cerements* (the waxed wrappings alluded to by Stringer in Powell's *Dance to the Music of Time*); and all of us will ultimately *go away, for a Burton* (even if teetotal), *forward, home, into the ground, off, off the hooks, on, out, over, round land, the wrong way, to a better place* (often identified in detail according to the delectations or aspirations of the deceased), *to grass, to heaven* (but not to hell), *to our rest, to our long home, to ourselves, to the wall, under, west*, etc.:
> ...leaving me to tell the story of his 'life's work' alone, while he went forward to receive the crown of righteousness laid up for him in another world. (Wright—the *life's work* was Joseph Wright's *English Dialect Dictionary*)
> I was assured yesterday that Lady Duncannon was gone off, surely it cannot be true...(Foreman, 1998, quoting a letter written in January 1785—her ladyship had died but not, so far as we know, deserted his lordship or putrefied)
> Hew had once said to Victoria that [Prince Albert] did not cling to life (as she did) and that, if he had a severe illness, he would go under. (Pearsall, 1969—Albert died of typhoid caught through the faulty drains at Windsor Castle, although Victoria preferred to believe that it was from mortification at the licentious behaviour of their son Bertie, of which more under FALL)

To *go together* is to die at the same time, and is one of the *go* euphemisms for death in the letters found with the body of the polar explorer Scott in his tent.
In obsolete use to *go right* was to die and go to heaven:
> I knowed 'e went right, for a says t'I, a says, 'I' a sin a angel. (*EDD*)

go² to become bankrupt
Alone, or in phrases, some of which are shared with death. *Go at staves* was what happened to a barrel when the hoops were removed; *go for a Burton* did not mean you had slipped out for a pint; the individual or firm might also *go crash, smash, to the wall, under, west*, etc.
The American Bankruptcy Reform Act of 1978 specified in successive chapters procedures for the protection of creditors or businesses, of which Chapter 11, which permitted continued trading under court protection during insolvency, is perhaps the most common. A corporation claiming such relief was said to *go* or *file Chapter Eleven* (or as the case may be), indicating that it is insolvent:
> The Lelands had first approached him in the summer of 1921, six months before they were driven to file Chapter Eleven. (Lacey, 1986—using the phrase anachronistically)

go³ to urinate or defecate
A shortened form of *go to the lavatory, bathroom*, etc. As with GO¹ and GO², it is used alone or in numerous phrases, such as *go about your business, for a walk (with a spade), on the coal* (for a blacksmith, to ammoniate it and make it burn hotter), *over the heap* (for a collier), *places, round the corner, to the toilet* (or whatever word is used for the lavatory), *upstairs*, etc. The use of euphemism can involve daunting imagery:
> ...he went to the toilet down a bit of hosepipe through Miss Kilmartin's car window. (Doyle, 1993—referring to a child urinating and not an escapologist)
The obsolete *going* was human excrement:
> No man shall bury any dung or going within the liberties of [London]. (Stowe, 1633)

go abroad *obsolete British* to accept a challenge to a duel
In the 19th century duelling was illegal in Britain but not in France. Not to accept a challenge made in Britain by fighting in France was considered cowardly by some:
> I have called frequently today and I find that you are not going abroad. (Kee, 1993, quoting a letter dated 13 July 1881 from O'Shea to Parnell, whom he had challenged to a duel in Lille. Parnell wisely ignored him)

go again *obsolete* to reappear after death
But not perhaps in the form we might choose, if consulted:
> ...but Vauther went agen, in the shape of a gurt voul theng. (*Exmoor Courtship*, 1746, quoted in *EDD*)

go all the way to copulate after previous sexual familiarity
Teenage use.

Those enjoined *not to go any further* are being requested not to copulate with the person whom they are caressing.

go-around an aborted aircraft landing
A pilot only aborts a landing when he is uncertain that he can land safely, the decision being often reached on the final approach due to obstruction on the runway, bad weather, or some other danger:
> An average of 10 go-arounds are necessary at Heathrow every week. (*Daily Telegraph*, 16 October 1998)

go at yourself to masturbate
Not self-criticism.

go beyond friendship to copulate with
The implication is that sexual partners cannot be friends:
> This was no more than a strong friendship but unfortunately, on one occasion, it went beyond friendship. (*Daily Telegraph*, 10 December 1999)

go case to work as a prostitute
From CASE[1], although the woman need not work in a brothel:
> I was green. It took me a week to realize that I was the only girl in the club not 'going case'. (Irvine, 1986—she was in a night club, not pregnant)

go down[1] to be killed or wounded
From the falling.
In obsolete use, to *go down* was to be hanged.

go down[2] to go to prison
See also DOWN. The usage may also refer to the descent to the cells from the dock.

go down[3] to crash
Not just ceasing to be airborne.
A plane crashing in the sea may be said to *go in*.

go down on see DOWN ON

go down the tube(s) to fail
Not a reference to a visit to the lamentable London subway system but from the mechanism through which carcasses were conveyed in the meat business, especially in Chicago.

go Dutch see DUTCH TREAT

go for your tea *Irish* to be murdered
A usage and practice of the IRA, of which the etymology is unclear.

go into (of a male) to copulate with
When Baroness Burdett-Coutts, a friend of Queen Victoria, married a man 40 years her junior, the *Pink 'Un* published the following announcement:

> AN ARITHMETICAL PROBLEM: How many times does twenty-seven go into sixty-eight and what is there over? (quoted by F. Harris, 1925)

go into the streets to become a prostitute
From the open soliciting.

go native to adopt the prevalent attitudes of an institution
The phrase was formerly used of British colonial officials who adopted the lifestyle of the indigenous population or were thought to incline too much towards its aspirations. Now usually referring to politicians who become ministers, their initial enthusiasm and fresh ideas being thwarted by bureaucrats with whose attitudes they identify themselves over time. The term may also refer to anyone surrendering to a prevailing dogmatism:
> [Bishop] Wienken went native to the extent of being sharply disowned by Cardinal Michael Faulhauber. (Burleigh, 2000—in 1940 the bishop had appeared to approve Nazi euthanasia and was later to become involved in negotiations with Eichmann)

The obsolete *go bush* meant to become mentally unbalanced, from the isolation of a white colonial official or planter in a remote region.

go off[1] to achieve a sexual orgasm
Of both sexes.

go off[2] to lose quality or putrefy
Standard English of food etc. and other figurative uses:
> But no shell had hit near Sergeant Porter. He had just gone off for no reason. (H. Brown, 1944—the sergeant had not deserted but had lost his nerve)

go on the box *obsolete British* to be absent from work through illness
Long before television, this *box* was a sick club, from the container into which the weekly subscriptions were placed. Also as *go on the club*, being a shortened form of *sick club*.

go out with to have an exclusive sexual friendship or relationship with
Standard English, even though the parties may remain indoors. The phrase is also used by children pre-puberty of playground preferences among the opposite sex.

go over to defect
The term describes the changing of one allegiance for another, whether in religion (usually from the Church of England to Roman Catholic), espionage, or politics.
To *go over the hill* or *wall* is to escape or desert, the use being normally figurative:

[Philby] didn't go over the wall until he had to. (Allbeury, 1981—Philby was a notorious British traitor)

go slow *British* a deliberate failure to complete the work allocated
A bargaining tactic which may in the short term cause an employer loss without corresponding hardship to his employees. See also SLOWDOWN[1].

go south to lose value or fail
From the direction of the line on a graph. Financial jargon and some general use:
They had bought it from an actor whose career had gone south. (Grisham, 1999)

go state *American* as a criminal to give evidence against an accomplice
It would never do to turn QUEEN'S EVIDENCE in a republic.

go steady (with) to court to the exclusion of others
A pleasing, if dated, usage.

go the whole way to copulate
After preliminary fondling or previous acquaintance.
The male vulgarism in the same sense, to *go through*, literally means to experience, use up, or transfix, giving etymologists a wide choice.

go to bed with to copulate with
Of either sex, and of homosexuality, although not necessarily in or on a *bed*:
Years ago she had gone to bed with him for a few weeks. (Amis, 1978—you might suppose they were a pair of invalids)

go to heaven in a string *obsolete* to be hanged
The fate of 16th-century English Roman Catholics when dynastic changes prevented their continued burning of Protestants.

go to it *obsolete* to copulate
Literally, to set about a task (as in its use as a slogan in 1940 urging the British populace to work harder):
The fitchew nor the soiled horse goes to't With a more riotous appetite.
(Shakespeare, *King Lear*)

go to the Bay *obsolete British* to be transported to Australia as a prisoner
The destination was Botany Bay in New South Wales.

go to the fat farm *American* to be obese
Not visiting a piggery:
[Monica Lewinsky was] an insecure girl, unfondly remembered to school mates as

having 'gone to the fat farm'. (*Daily Telegraph*, 27 January 1998)

go to the wall to fail or be destroyed
It may apply to corporate bankruptcy, to death, and to any enterprise which does not succeed.

go up[1] *obsolete* to be killed by hanging
Especially in 19th-century America. Occasionally also of natural death:
You'd better give it up if you don't want to go up. (Cookson, 1969—the thing to be given up was working with lead paint)

go up[2] to be under the influence of illegal narcotics
When you become UP[2], but may GO DOWN[2] if you are caught.

go up the river *American* to be sentenced to jail
Referring to the location of the penal institutions with relation to New York City, New Orleans, and elsewhere.

go walkabout to be stolen
Attributing to inanimate objects Antipodean characteristics.

go with to copulate with outside a permanent relationship
More often used of women than men despite the reciprocity:
[Keeler] hurt [Rachman] terribly when she went with other men. (S. Green, 1979)

goat a promiscuous male
From the Greek god Pan and the general reputation for fecundity of billy goats:
[Stanley Baldwin defaced] pictures of the Welshman in his photograph collection, ensuring his devilish resemblance to 'the Goat' nickname. (Stewart, 1999—we might have supposed a Conservative Prime Minister to have more important things to do than express in this manner his distaste for the promiscuous Liberal elder statesman)
To *play the goat* is to act lasciviously, although to *play the giddy goat* is merely to act foolishly. In the olden days, a *goat-house* was a brothel.

God's child *obsolete* an idiot
The defect was often attributed to divine agency rather than the consanguinity of the parents.

God's own medicine a narcotic or hallucinogen
Opium was so named in the 19th century, when it was freely available both for infants and for adult use. Now mainly referring to morphine when used illegally, and abbreviated to *gom*.

God's waiting room a retirement institution for geriatrics
Making a charitable assumption about posthumous selection.
Parts of Florida also share the appellation.

goer a sexually promiscuous woman
A male usage, perhaps adverting to an old car, or *banger*, which is still roadworthy and starts when needed:
> Babes were divided into those termed 'a goer'—a woman who looked as if she'd be sexually available and willing—and those known to be sexually active. (*Daily Telegraph*, 21 December 1995—a *babe* is a young female working in a male environment: there appeared to be no third category, chaste virgins)

A *party-goer*, whether male or female, is a gregarious hedonist.

gold-brick *American* a shirker
A common 19th-century trick was known as the *gold brick swindle*, whereby prospectors sought to sell base metal to the unwary by its colour. Whence trickery of any kind, and then specifically those who feigned illness in the army to avoid duty.

gold-digger a woman who consorts with a man because he is rich
Working a single, but often exhausted, vein, a large difference in age being a usual feature:
> This [case] was never about a gold digger seeking money. (*Daily Telegraph*, 29 September 2000—as the former stripper was 26 years old and the man owning a fortune of $1.6 billion was 89, it was clearly love at first sight)

In punning British use, a *goal-digger* is a young woman who seeks the company of a wealthy professional footballer:
> The allegations [of rape spawned] numerous interviews with other footballers who admitted sharing girls— 'goaldiggers' as football groupies are called by players taking part in orgies. (*Daily Telegraph*, 5 March 2004)

In perhaps obsolete American use a *gold-digger* or *gold-finder* was a lavatory cleaner and a *goldbrick* a turd, the word being used as a term of vulgar abuse.

gold-plating excessive bureaucratic regulation
Literally, no more than adding an attractive gloss to something. Under European legal practice and convention, which allows the citizen only to do what the law permits, unnecessary or intrusive laws and regulations emanating from the Commission in Brussels are ignored, the procedure being known as *tolérance*. In Britain, where under Common Law the citizen can do anything so long as the law does not forbid it, parliamentary draftsmen use their skills to ensure that these laws and regulations, often poorly or loosely drafted, are made as legally binding as possible before being incorporated in British law.

gold shot *obsolete* bribes
It is sad that so elegant a phrase is no longer in use:
> … 'the citadel of negotiation' might yet be taken 'by a well directed fire of gold-shot'. (Dalrymple, 2002, quoting from an Indian dispatch dated 1800)

golden large or excessive
In the financial jargon phrases, *golden goodbye* or *handshake*, a payment in lieu of damages when an employee is dismissed before the expiry of a contract; *golden hello*, to induce someone to join an employer and perhaps matching any accrued benefits from the previous job; *golden handcuffs*, to discourage an employee from leaving to join a competitor; *golden parachute*, to ensure a soft landing in the case of dismissal or a takeover; and less often, but with more wit, *golden retriever* to induce a former employee to return.
For *golden bowler* see BOWLER HAT.
A *golden cheerio* may mean no more than retirement after prescribed years of service with a gratuity and pension:
> Run-up to the golden cheerio and he gets landed with this. (Rankin, 2000—a policeman was nearing retirement)

golden ager *American* a geriatric
Not someone living in a mythical *golden age*, but an elderly person supposedly enjoying the GOLDEN YEARS.

golden boy someone unfairly favoured or marked for undue promotion
He is likely to be found in a large corporation or a political party. He may also be BLUE-EYED or FAIR-HAIRED.

golden years (the) old age
Referring not to the cost of increasing medical treatment but rather to ripened corn.

golly a mild oath
Perhaps the commonest corruption of *God*, a usage anticipating by some 40 years Florence Upton's *Golliwog* books, in which the black hero came to the rescue of the Dutch Dolls. Other such corruptions included *goles*, *golles*, *gollin*, *golls*, *gom*, *gommy*, *goms*, *gomz*, *goom*, *gull*, and *gum*, of which *by gum* is a lone survivor.

gone[1] pregnant
Usually indicating the period since conception:

'What's he going to do about our Doreen who is six months gone? (Tidy, in *Private Eye*, March 1981)

gone² drunk or under the influence of narcotics
Rational behaviour and comprehension have departed.
Gone about (someone) means no more than besotted with.

goner a person about to die or who has just died
Also spelt phonetically as *gonner*.

good folk *obsolete* the fairies
These malevolent creatures had to be flattered, especially in Ireland and Scotland where they were also called the *good neighbours* or *people*:
   ... so young that you were in girl's skirts lest you be carried away by the good people. (Flanagan, 1988—until the 19th-century Irish fairies, in search of baby boys, were thus duped)

good friend(s) having an ongoing extra-marital sexual relationship
A journalistic evasion when reporting such a condition might be considered defamatory:
   ... he mustn't say *good friends*, that was always taken as a euphemism for extreme intimacy. (Price, 1974)
See also FRIEND².

good lunch (a) a meal at which excessive alcohol is drunk
The food is less important:
   At Prime Minister's questions, the Speaker selected to ask a Supplementary Question a Tory backbencher, 'returning from a good lunch' (as it was put to me). (Cole, 1995)
See also DINE WELL.

good time a sexual experience with a stranger
A conventional invitation by a soliciting prostitute, or *good time (bar) girl*. The approach may also be made by a male prostitute.

good voyage *obsolete British* the use of a warship to carry commercial cargo
Until the beginning of the 20th century, Captains in the navy accepted civilian cargo, especially to remote destinations or where there was a risk of piracy, pocketing the payment. As Secretary to the Navy, Pepys disapproved.

goodbye peremptory dismissal from employment
It is the employer who initiates the farewell.

goods (the) an object which is the subject of taboo

The goods may be stolen property or illegal narcotics.
The American *green goods* are forged banknotes, from the colour of dollar bills.
To *have the goods on someone* is to know any information about them of a damaging nature which might be used to coerce or blackmail.
Also of the male genitalia:
   They say a man will generally keep his goods on the side he parts his hair. (Proulx, 2002)

goof *American* a habitual user of illegal narcotics
Literally, a stupid person, whence many uses to do with unsophistication and incompetence. A *goofball* is the addict or the narcotic and *goofed* means under narcotic influence.

goolies the testicles
The derivation both of the game of marbles, *gully*, and this euphemistic use, is from the Hindi *goli*, a ball.
To discourage Iraqis from castrating their British prisoners in the 1930s, the Royal Air Force issued *goolie chits* to pilots, documents printed in Arabic that promised a reward to anyone who brought a captured aviator back to British lines unharmed.

goon squad members of a police or military unit capable of acting violently or ruthlessly
A *goon* was, in dialect, a simpleton, whence a German guard in a prisoner-of-war camp.

goose¹ *obsolete* a prostitute
The common avian imagery.
If she were a *Winchester goose*, she had syphilis, from the insalubrious church-owned property in south London where the meaner prostitutes lived.

goose² to pinch the buttocks of
A male, or less often female, sexual approach, as delicate as a nip from the bird's beak, or as indelicate.

gooseberry the devil
Not obsolete because the use survives in the expression *play gooseberry*, to play the devil with a courting couple by keeping them company when they would rather be left alone.

gooseberry bush *obsolete* the place where new boy babies are found
In former times boy babies were explained to young siblings as having been found under a *gooseberry bush*, that being a part of the garden seldom dug over or hoed because the bush is shallow-rooted, allowing the weeds to remain

undisturbed and the stork to drop its bundle discreetly.

A baby girl might be found in a PARSLEY BED.

gooseberry lay *American* a risk-free crime
The practice of spreading clothes to dry on the prickly bushes from which they were not easily dislodged by the wind led to a *gooseberry* being a clothes line, from which garments might be stolen without much risk of detection.

Gordon Bennet(t) a mild oath
For *God*, from the American press proprietor who sponsored H. M. Stanley in his African travels and balloon races, not the London magistrate who came into prominence some decades later.

For an Australian, *Gordon Bennetts* were running shoes, in memory of their general who ran away in Malaya in 1942.

governess *obsolete* a female bawd
The 19th-century brothel she ran brought back memories of the schoolroom.

governmental relations *American* bribery or coercion
Not just voting, paying your taxes, and being told what to do by officials.

grab to steal
The common imagery which links seizing with theft.

In 19th-century Ireland to *grab* was to accept a tenancy after the eviction of the previous tenant by a protestant landlord, regarded as treachery by the Nationalists.

Grace of Wapping (the) *obsolete London* the killing of a pirate
Wapping lies on the north bank of the Thames where a port used to exist. The condemned man was tied to a pile at low water and left there until three tides had flowed over him. You can still get a drink in the eponymous pub.

graft bribery
Literally, hard work, from the original meaning, digging a grave. Now standard English for corruption.

In obsolete use, to *graft* was to cuckold, the figurative horns of cuckoldry being implanted on the victim's head.

grandstand *American* to accentuate a difficulty in order to win praise
Where the spectators whom you wish to impress are located, but the expression is not confined to sport.

A *grandstand play*, is such behaviour.

grannies *British* small private investors in public companies

In September 2001 the Transport Minister Stephen Byers decided to take Railtrack back into public ownership by a *coup de main* and without paying full compensation. The Prime Minister, however, was 'nervous about not bailing out shareholders'. An adviser, Shriti Vadera, assured the Minister that 'The grannies lose their shirts. It's the American investors we have to worry about.'

granny farming a form of vote rigging
Registering votes by proxy on behalf of muddled and deceived geriatrics.

grape (the) wine
Standard English since the 17th century. The obsolete punning *grape-shot* meant drunk but a *whiff of grapeshot* was something more debilitating—see also WHIFF OF.

grass¹ to inform against
Rhyming slang on *grass in the park*, coppers' nark.

A *grass* is an informer.

grass² marijuana
Shortened form of *grass-weed* in common use and occasionally as *green grass*.

grass widow a woman of marriageable age separated for an extended period from her husband
The derivation is from the *grass* of the hill stations to which wives were sent during the Indian hot season, or a corruption of *grace widow*? Originally it might mean a mistress or an unmarried woman who had had a child. If the husband was away for long periods, there might be an inference that the *grass widow* was promiscuous:

> ... her husband having run off on her, so that now she was no more than a grass widow. (Atwood, 1996—for which loss she found nightly consolation in the arms of her lodger)

Some humorous use of husbands who regularly absent themselves to play sport:

> When [Denis Thatcher] played cricket for the old boys, Margaret washed up the tea things in the clubhouse like any other grass widow of the period. (*Sunday Telegraph*, 7 May 1995)

grassed down dead
Under the sod rather than coloured chippings:

> ... they would all in a few years be as if they had never been and she herself grassed down and forgotten. (Hardy, 1891)

gratify your passion(s) to copulate
A venerable but perhaps obsolete usage. Also as *gratify your (amorous) desires, will*, or *works*. *Gratification* is also, it would appear, available to those who masturbate:

...he never let this feelings for his fellow passenger get the better of him, nor ever 'gratified himself in an unnatural way'. (Winchester, 1998)

In obsolete Scottish use, to *gratify* was to bribe, pleasing to the recipient no doubt.

grave (the) death
Standard English figurative use.
In obsolete Scottish use, the *gravestone gentry* were the dead:

My bed is owre amang yon gravestone gentry. (A. Murdoch, 1873)

gravy *American* an intoxicant
SAUCE is much more common.

gravy train (the) a situation in which supplemental benefits are received gratuitously
There is continuing excess of the pleasant but unnecessary complement to the main dish for those who ride this vehicle:

Kinnock's decade as a European Commissioner comes to an end in October, and his replacement as Britain's representative on the EC gravy train needs to be announced. (*Daily Telegraph*, 2 April 2004—the richness of the *gravy* served to commissioners in Brussels is enhanced by its accompanying exemption from all forms of taxation)

graze to steal and eat food in a supermarket
Like cattle in a pasture, you eat what you can pick up between the shelves and pass the checkout with empty hands and a full stomach. In obsolete use, to *graze on the plain* was to be dismissed from employment as a house servant and thus rendered homeless.

grease to bribe
The usage predates OIL, of which it is a euphemistic synonym. Either *tout court*, as a verb or noun, or in phrases such as *grease hands, palms, paws, the skids, the system*, etc.
In American slang, to *grease* means to kill, an allusion perhaps to converting the body into a fatty substance but more probably a crime writer's corruption of CREASE.
Greased may, in America, mean drunk, a condition in which things may seem to run more smoothly, for a while.

great *obsolete* pregnant
A shortened form of *great with child*:

O silly lassie, what wilt thou do,
If thou grow great they'll heez thee high.
(Herd, 1771—society would reward her not with a home of her own and a weekly stipend, but with death by hanging)

Also as *great-bellied*.

great and the good (the) *British* people comprising or approved by the political establishment
An often derogatory use by those who aspire to, but do not achieve, entry to the charmed circle.

great certainty (the) death
Also as the *great change, leveller, out, perhaps* or, for Charles II, *secret*, his dying words before or after expressing concern for 'poor Nellie's' future.
The *great majority of souls* are the dead, presumed to be in heaven, limbo, or a less favoured destination.

Great Game the 19th-century rivalry between Britain and Russia for empire and influence in Asia
In retrospect, the players were more amateur than professional:

...William Moorcroft, the self-appointed British spy who penetrated Central Asia to play some of the opening moves in the Great Game. (Dalrymple, 1993)

Greek Calends (the) never
The Romans were meant to settle their taxes and other accounts on the Calends, or first day, of each month, but the Greek calendar had no Calends.

Greek gift a present with dire consequences
A throwback to the Trojan Horse and Virgil's *timeo Daneos et dona ferentes*:

The control France was granted [by Hitler] over her navy also proved a Greek gift. (Ousby, 1997—on 2 and 6 July 1940 Churchill convinced the world that Britain would not surrender by ordering the destruction of major elements of the French fleet at Mers-el-Kébir after it had refused to continue the fight against Germany or take refuge in a neutral port)

Greek way (the) pederasty
The supposed sexual tastes of the ancient Greeks.

green gown *obsolete* an indication of unchastity in an unmarried woman
On the eve of May Day, convention allowed the lads and lassies to spend all night in the woods, supposedly gathering flowers. During the proceedings, many dresses were stained by the grass of the meadows:

...she had the salutation 'with a green gowne'...as if the priest had been at our backs, to have married us. (G. A. Greene, 1599, quoted in *ODEP*)

The *green sickness* was 'the disease of maids occasioned by celibacy' (Grose).

To *give green stockings* was to commit the solecism of getting married before your older sister had found a husband.

greenmailer *American* a corporate raider who seeks to get paid to go away
The *green* of the US dollar replaces the *black* of BLACKMAIL.

grey¹ (of merchandise) branded and authentic but sold at below the manufacturers' stated price
Especially of luxury goods and clothing where the manufacturer seeks to maintain higher prices in an affluent country than can be charged elsewhere. Thus the products are known as *grey goods*, the trade known as the *grey market*, and those involved are called *grey marketeers*.

grey² (of people) lacking personality or initiative
The adjective is used about subservient politicians and functionaries, who may also be described as *grey suits*, from their attire:
    The grey men in the home team were each
    speaking in turn about peace and unity.
    (Simpson, 1998, writing about politicians
    in Belgrade)

greying growing old
    Whiting or *balding* might be more apposite:
    [Increased leisure time] was helped by the
    'greying' of the population. (*Daily Telegraph*,
    14 July 2005)

greymail *American* a threat to tell state secrets if prosecuted
A type of BLACKMAIL, the shade variation indicating less criminality.

Grim Reaper (the) death
Grim for the death's head or skeleton in northern English dialect, and *Reaper* from the scythe he carries.

grind (a) copulation
Probably from the pelvic motion expected of the female participant, who is always referred to by her partner in flattering terms—where do all the *bad grinds* go?
An American *grind-mill* was a brothel and to *grind* means to copulate, of a male.
To *grind the wind*, in obsolete British use, was to be punished on a treadmill, introducing rotary power with no end product.

groceries sundries *obsolete* intoxicants
So described on the bill by the grocer so that the servants, and perhaps the husband, might not know the extent of the purchases of alcohol by the lady of the house.

groggy *obsolete* drunk
The celebrated British Admiral Vernon, who died in 1757, was known as *Grog*, because he wore a grogram cloak. He introduced to the navy a drink consisting of rum and water, which was called after his nickname. If you had *grog on board* or became *groggy*, you were drunk, and, if habitually so, a *grog-hound*. As drunkenness induces an unsteady gait, today you may say you are feeling *groggy* without having consumed any alcohol or incurring any opprobrium, merely feeling dizzy or unwell.

groin the genitalia
Literally, the place where the abdomen meets the thigh. Sports commentators talk of an injury to the *groin* when the player has suffered a more telling and painful blow. Non-sporting use is less common.

groom to cultivate a sexual relationship with a child in an Internet chatroom
From the sense, to train or prepare:
    The case [of abduction of a minor] again
    called into question the safety of internet
    chatrooms when used by children without
    supervision and their vulnerability to
    'grooming'. (*Daily Telegraph*, 10 October
    2001)
A *groomer* is a paedophile who so seeks to entrap a child.

grope to fondle another person sexually
Literally, to use the hands for feeling anything. Usually of a male whose activity may be inexpert or unwanted.
Whence a *groper*, an unattractive male suitor, replacing two more logical obsolete meanings, a blind person or a midwife.

gross height excursion a dangerous and unplanned loss of aircraft height
Civil aviation jargon in an environment where nothing must be acknowledged as dangerous or unplanned.

gross indecency bestiality or sodomy
Legal jargon when buggery was not considered a lawful activity.
See also INDECENCY.

ground associated with death
From the days when most corpses were buried rather than burned. *Ground-sweat* was the dampness arising from the soil, whence burial and the adage 'A ground sweat cures all disorders'. A *ground-lair* was a family burial plot and *ground-mail* the fee paid to the church for interment.

group sex a sexual orgy

It could mean no more than a meeting of the Mother's Union, all the *group* being of the same *sex*, so long as the vicar is male and stays away.

A *groupie* is a young person associating frequently with others who share an interest or participate in an activity, especially a young female, promiscuous perhaps but not necessarily into the polyandry of *group sex*.

growth a carcinoma
Literally, something which has grown and, even of human tissue, not necessarily malignant. A common usage to avoid reference to the dread cancer.

grunt *American* to defecate
The association is with the straining noise.

grunter a pig
Used among fisherman to avoid saying the word *pig*, there being a taboo arising from sickness on board caused by rotten pork.
See also FURRY THING.

guardhouse lawyer *American* an opinionated know-all and troublemaker
Also known as a BARRACK-ROOM LAWYER. Guard duty involves much tedium, providing fertile ground for bores and agitators. General as well as military use.

guardian an occupying conqueror
Literally, one who protects or manages the affairs of another:
    ... the indigenous Ughur inhabitants had shared a mutual hatred of the Chinese 'guardians' on and off for over a thousand years. (Strong, 1998)

guest[1] a prisoner
Seldom *tout court*; more often as *guest of Uncle Sam* or *of Her Majesty*.
The obsolete Scottish *guest* was a ghost, an unwelcome visitor or a linguistic corruption:
    Brownies, fays and fairies,
    And witches, guests. (Liddle, 1821)

guest[2] a customer
Literally, a recipient of free entertainment or hospitality, but not in the travel or, theme-park businesses, or in hotels where you may stay in a *guest house* or, if the accommodation is in a dwelling, be a *paying guest*.
A *guest fee* is a bribe or other inducement to a journalist, especially a leader writer, to promulgate or suppress information:
    They can eliminate awareness by ... paying 'guest fees' to leading writers. (D. Mitchell, 2004)

guest worker an alien employed without the right of permanent residence
Those so employed are paid, like the German *Gastarbeiter*, usually for menial work shunned by the indigenous population:
    A new development [in Israel] was that their dislike and fear of Palestinians had reached such a pitch that their answer now to Palestinian demands was the hiring of immigrant laborers and field hands from Thailand, the Philippines and Poland—desperate so-called 'guest workers'. (Theroux, 1995)

guidance to the market a profit warning
Financial jargon, from a world where it is important not to be detected in giving price-sensitive information to favoured individuals and an unambiguous profit warning will lead to a sharp fall in the share price:
    When is a profit warning not a profit warning? When it's just 'specific steady guidance to the market'. (*Daily Telegraph*, 9 February 2001)

gumshoe *American* an investigator in plain clothes
He has an ability to walk quietly on rubber soles. He may be a policeman or a private detective.

gun a criminal who carries a handgun
Criminal jargon. In America, a *gun* may also be an unarmed thief, from the Yiddish *gonif*.

gunner's daughter *obsolete* a flogging
Literally, the barrel of the gun over which the victim was strapped, thus *kissing* or *marrying* her.
A *son of a gun* was an illegitimate child, conceived on a long voyage and of doubtful paternity, although these connotations are forgotten in modern use.

gypsy's warning (a) an ambiguous or sinister message
Or, in some circumstances, no warning at all, all of which shows a surprising lack of confidence in Romany second sight. Before any soothsaying could take place, the gypsy's palm had to be crossed with silver (in the days when coins really did contain silver) which negated the influence of the devil, under whose jurisdiction necromancy falls.
In Ireland *gypsy's warning* was gin, which is also capable of leading to misfortune.

H

H anything taboo beginning with the letter H

Usually *hell*, in the expression *What the H?* In addict use, *heroin*.

habit an addiction to narcotics

Not used of the equally addictive alcohol or tobacco. Your preference may be indicated by a modifier as, for example, *nose habit*, and the degree of addiction in a phrase assessing the cost.

To *kick the habit* is not to treat your monastic attire roughly but to stop taking illegal narcotics.

had it dead or beyond repair

Of man, beast, clothes, household goods, or machinery.

Hail Columbia *American* an expression of annoyance

Hail from hell and *Columbia* from America. To *raise Hail Columbia* is to cause a fuss.

hair of the dog a morning drink of an intoxicant

Usually after too many the previous evening, the effects of which it is supposed to alleviate. A shortened form of *hair of the dog that bit you*. In America a *horn of the ox (that gored you)* means the same thing.

hair trigger trouble a tendency to premature ejaculation

Like a pistol where the trigger is set for too light a pull and goes off too soon:

The king, they said, suffered from a condition for which the medical name is 'hair trigger trouble'. (A. Waugh in *Daily Telegraph*, 29 April 1996)

haircut a severe financial loss

The locks are shorn. This kind of *haircut* is *taken*, rather than *got*, as in a barber's shop:

The rouble collapsed. Russia defaulted on $33 billion of bonds. And bank stocks finally 'took a haircut'. (*Daily Telegraph*, 29 August 1998)

hairpiece a wig

Literally, no more than a piece of hair, on or off the scalp.

half¹ a quantity of beer

Shortened form of *half a pint*. In obsolete use, to *half-pint* was to drink beer. In America as *half a can*:

'Bring me half a can.' A half-can meant a nickel's worth of beer. A whole can meant a dime's worth. (Longstreet, 1956—those were the days!)

Half and half is mild and bitter beer in the same glass.

half² wholly

Used of drunkenness in many phrases where the half is not a partial condition but usually equals the whole, as in *half and half*, *half-canned*, *cut*, *foxed*, *gone*, *in the bag*, *on*, etc. Although incapacity through ingesting alcohol or narcotics is often described by the same euphemism, only with alcohol does the spurious halving occur. HALF-SEAS OVER has a different etymology.

half-deck a mentally disturbed person

The partly open craft is less seaworthy than one fully decked:

But all those people on Dr Diana's list sound like half-decks. (Sanders, 1985—Diana was a psychiatrist)

half-inch to steal

Rhyming slang for PINCH¹, mainly of petty pilfering.

half-seas over drunk

All the other cases of drunkenness preceded by *half* indicate a condition of intoxication no less than the whole. In this case there is no *seas-over* to be *halved*, the phrase probably being a corruption of the Dutch *op-zee-zober*, strong imported beer. The suggestion that the decks are awash is more appropriate, we might feel. In obsolete use also as *half-sea*.

halve the footprint to implement multiple closures and dismissals

Financial jargon for what usually happens after a takeover or merger, where duplicated functions are identified, branches closed, and people lose their jobs:

Bank of Scotland said it planned to 'halve the footprint of the 1,700 NatWest branches. (*Daily Telegraph*, 15 September 1999)

hammer¹ to declare a defaulter

London Stock Exchange jargon, from the hammering to gain silence in which to make the announcement on the once noisy and crowded trading floor.

hammer² a philanderer

The common male violent imagery. To *hammer away*, a slang term for continuing an action, can also mean to copulate.

Do not confuse these uses with Thomas Cromwell, the *malleus monachroum*, or 'hammer of the monks' who proved more adept at dissolving monasteries than picking a wife for his sovereign.

Both sexes can, however, be *hammered*, meaning that they are drunk, the imagery coming from that awful throbbing sensation behind the eyeballs, no doubt.

hampton the penis
Rhyming slang on *Hampton Wick*, a district to the west of London, for PRICK, and the location of the palace to which Henry VIII may have taken Anne of Cleves, the 'Flanders Mare' chosen for him by Thomas Cromwell (see HAMMER²). Unusually both words in the phrase are commonly used as rhyming slang, but whereas *hampton* is only used literally, *wick* is also found in figurative use, in phrases such as 'it gets on my wick', expressing annoyance.

hand¹ an employee
Mainly American use, playing down any suggestion of servitude. Compound job descriptions are common, such as *cowhand*, *deckhand*, *farmhand*, etc.
However an *old China hand* (and they are always 'old', however young) does not work in a crockery store but is credited after residence in the Far East with understanding the intricacies of the geographical area mentioned.

hand² the giving of a woman in marriage
Either by her parents or herself and standard English. Of course the groom expects and receives much more than her hand:
> Nor could Clara doubt that her hand
> was stipulated as the price for the voyage.
> (Stevenson, 1882)
In obsolete Scottish use, *hand-fasting* meant a trial marriage:
> It was not until twenty years after the Reformation that the custom of 'hand-fasting', which had come down from Celtic times, fell into disrepute, and consequent disuse. By this term was understood cohabitation for a year, the couple being then free to separate, unless they agreed to make the union permanent. (Andrews, 1899—*plus ça change*)

hand in your dinner pail to die
The common imagery of making no more demand on terrestrial resources. *Hand in* is unusual:
> Will [Churchill] decide there is no purpose in living when he has nothing to do? Will he hand in? (Moran, 1966—Moran was Churchill's doctor)

hand job the masturbation of a male by someone else, especially a prostitute
Reference *tout court* to the *hand* may indicate male self-masturbation:
> I'm as well off [as copulating] with my hand and my imagination. (Doyle, 1996)

hand trouble *mainly American* unwelcome attempts by a male to fondle a woman sexually
She, not he, is experiencing the trouble with hands.
To *get a hand up a skirt* implies extramarital copulation by a male.

handful a prison sentence of five years
Criminal jargon of the same tendency as FISTFUL and FIVE FINGERS.
A *handful* may also be a badly behaved or troublesome person:
> Phyllis was a handful from the start, a wild, headstrong girl. (Proulx, 2002)

handicap a mental or physical defect
Standard English. Literally, a disadvantage imposed on a competitor to make an even contest. Those with mental illnesses are *mentally handicapped*; lame people are *physically handicapped*; those with poor sight or blind are *visually handicapped*; the deaf are *aurally handicapped*; etc.
See also CHALLENGED for another euphemism taken from sporting activity.

handle¹ to embrace a woman sexually
Literally, to hold with the hands.
The obsolete English dialect use was not euphemistic:
> In love making, where the swain may not have the flow of language, he may sometimes attempt to put his arm around the girl's waist; this is called 'handlin' on her' (*EDD*—as ever, Dr Wright uses *love making* for courtship)

handle² the power over another to coerce or extort
From the leverage.

handout¹ a payment for which nothing is given in return
Originally food and clothing given to the poor, whence money paid by the state to alleviate poverty or any payment made for which there appears to be no consideration. A *hand-out* or *hand-pay* may be a bribe:
> ... in Malawi it was another necessitous routine, not philanthropic but a permanent drip-feed, part of a system of hand-pays. (Theroux, 2002)

handout² a written or printed statement issued publicly containing tendentious information
In standard usage, a summary intended to record or amplify verbal information.

handshake a supplementary payment on leaving a job

Not necessarily GOLDEN and paid on summary dismissal or early retirement:

> Had he agreed to suppress his feelings for five months—thereby collecting a full pension and a brigadier's handshake over £8,000... (M. Clark, 1991)

handyman special *American* a derelict building

Real-estate jargon for a dilapidated house:

> * HANDYMAN SPECIAL * Huge house w/lots of potential. (*Chicago Tribune*, 30 July 1991—and lots of cockroaches, damp, dry rot, woodworm, etc.)

hang to kill by breaking the neck through suspension

Formerly, it meant death by crucifixion, but it is now standard English in the present sense, the past sense being *hanged* not *hung*.

A *hang-fair* was an execution by hanging in public and a *hanging judge* was one who readily sentenced people to death.

hang a few on to drink intoxicants

Mainly American and usually to excess. Also as *hang one on*, which is never limited to a single drink.

hang a red light on *American* to drive out of business

The imagery is from a closed road—for once the RED LAMP does not advertise a brothel.

hang in the bell-ropes *obsolete* to be jilted

Especially after banns had been called, thus denying the campanologists their reward for ringing the wedding bells.

hang on the bough *obsolete Scottish* (of a female) to remain unmarried

The imagery is from unplucked and wasted fruit, although for a woman forbidden to earn her living, remaining unmarried was once less attractive than it is now.

hang out the besom *obsolete* to live riotously during your wife's absence

A *besom* is a broom, once the preferred mode of transportation of witches, the aged menial who wielded it, and, in the 19th century, a prostitute because 'A girl described as "a besom" without a qualifying adj. would imply unchastity'. (*EDD*)

Inn signs were often poles with tufts on them, which looked like *besoms*. One way and another, a man *hanging out the besom* was consorting with unchaste women, or frequenting the pub, or both. However, a woman who was said to *hang out the broomstick* was no more than scheming to get herself a husband, the sign telling people that she was open for business.

hang out to dry *American* to expose a person publicly in an attempt to protect others

Someone is left on the washing line. Whence a *hang-out*, such a stratagem:

> Is it too late to go the hangout road? (Colodny & Gettlin, 1991, quoting Nixon who was asking if his accusers could be bought off by sacrificing a witness from the White House)

hang out with to enjoy an extramarital sexual relationship with

In slang, to keep company with:

> He thought about girls a lot...though Wakolla Price wouldn't hang out with him. (Atwood, 2003—Wakolla rebuffed his attempts to consort with her)

hang paper *American* to issue cheques or other securities fraudulently

Punning on house decoration. Those who so behave are known as PAPER HANGER[2].

hang up your boots to retire (from games or sporting activities)

Normally quitting an activity which requires special footwear but also some figurative use.

hang up your hat[1] *obsolete* to marry a woman much wealthier than yourself

Considered opportunistic and bad form, especially in the days when men controlled their wife's assets, and particularly reprehensible if he gave up work and moved into her house. Less often as *hang up your ladle*.

hang up your hat[2] *obsolete* to die

A reminder of the days when all adults wore headgear out of doors. Various other objects might also in similar fashion be *hung up* by those who would need them no more, such as a *dinner-pail*, *mug*, or *spoon*.

hangover symptoms of prior sub-acute alcoholic poisoning

Now standard English, from the *hanging over* of the ill effects until the next day.

hanky-panky extramarital sexual familiarity

Originally, trickery. It is what mothers used to tell their daughters to watch out for if spending an evening alone with a male.

Hanoi Hilton *American* a North Vietnamese camp for prisoners-of-war

In the First World War, British prisoners spoke of the Kaiser's home town POTSDAM in the same ironic way.

happen to to cause to die

Things *happen* to us every moment of our lives, but this particular *happening* old people especially prefer not to spell out, preferring the phrase *if anything happens to me . . .*

happy dust *American* cocaine
An addict usage:
> . . . that happy dust gonna take you a real great snow ride. (J. Collins, 1981)

happy event the birth of a child
Although:
> . . . an unhappy condition followed by a happy event, although the event is by no means always happy. (Atwood, 1996)

happy hour a period when a bar sells alcohol more cheaply
Its duration is not necessarily 60 minutes. The practice encourages those leaving work to drop in, relax, and relieve the tensions of the day but in reality to drink too much and arrive home drunk, broke, late, and in trouble domestically.

happy release the death of a terminally ill patient
We use it of others in pain, although they may feel otherwise. Less often as *happy dispatch*, a translation of the Japanese *hara-kiri* but without implying suicide.
The *happy hunting grounds* are said to be the post-mortem destination of American Indians, while Dr Johnson professed to believe that, when dead, he might sit in a *happier seat*:
> . . . although when in a celestial frame . . . he has supposed death to be 'kind Nature's signal for retreat', from this state of being to 'a happier seat', his thoughts upon this awful change were in general full of dismal apprehension. (J. Boswell, 1791—the Doctor was human after all)

hard denoting an extreme version of anything taboo or shameful
Thus *hard core* is explicit pornography: a *hard case* is a confirmed criminal; *hard drugs* are the more dangerous and addictive narcotics and hallucinogens; *hard drink*, the *hard*, or the *hard stuff* is spirits, and to *harden a drink* is to add more alcohol to it.

hard of hearing deaf
Not describing a noise which is indistinct. Deafness, when so described, is not, like blindness, understood to be an absolute condition, except where described as *stone deaf*:
> 'I'm hard of hearing, you know,' she said. 'Practically deaf.' (Sanders, 1980)

hard room a prison cell
It certainly has no feather bed and soft furnishings:
> . . . defacing the walls of some of the

subterranean 'hard-rooms'—a polite departmental euphemism for prison cells. (Deighton, 1985)

hard up poor
Usually of a temporary shortage of funds and perhaps a shortened form of the slang phrase *hard up against it*.

hardware any modern armaments
Military jargon for things made of metal such as tanks, bombs, planes, warships, guns, and missiles.
In 19th-century and Prohibition America, *hardware* was whisky, punning on HARD and using an evasion because of the taboo or illegality.

harmful elements those citizens opposed to a totalitarian regime
The jargon of Communism and Nazism which still persists in repressive societies.

harpic *British* mentally unbalanced
The brand name of a lavatory cleaner which claimed to clean the bowl 'right round the bend'.

Harry the devil
Usually as *old Harry*, the *Lord Harry*, or *the living Harry*.
We still *play old Harry* when something upsets us.

harvest *American* to kill for personal gratification
Fresh euphemisms are needed from time to time to describe or attempt to justify the activities of those who kill animals other than for self-protection or food:
> Trophy-hunters, or harvesters, as some prefer to be called, track and kill their prey . . . Mr O'Neill was glad that he had harvested his bear without unleashing the Inuit hunter's dogs on his prey. (*Daily Telegraph,* 29 April 1998—the intrepid hunter had paid for a licence to kill a single male polar bear; in error he and his two companions shot females)

hatch the birth of a child
Emergence from an egg is less taboo than the method of mammalian delivery:
> The female mind . . . takes an interest in the 'Hatch, Match and Despatch' of its fellow creatures. (Payn, 1878)

hatchet (man) someone entrusted with a job requiring ruthlessness or destructive criticism
The association is with the cutting tool, of anyone from a killer to those entrusted with introducing unpopular policies.

A *hatchet job* is such activity, especially applied to a piece of reportage:

> This series is going to be very sympathetic to the police...I'm not out to do a hatchet job. (Sanders, 1973)

haul your ashes *American* (of a male) to copulate

The imagery is from the extraction of residue from a furnace which is red and glowing, perhaps with an allusion to another meaning of *haul*, to harm another person physically, with the common violent imagery:

> I pop in a red, get a little shot, you get your ashes hauled. Same dif. (Diehl, 1978—or, in translation, 'I like self-induced narcosis while you prefer promiscuity—it's a matter of taste')

The American vulgarism, *haul your stick*, is to masturbate, of a male.

haute cuisine small portions of expensive food

Literally, high-quality cooking:

> When I'm away I live in hotels, where I get junk tricked out as haute cuisine. (Follett, 1979—and get charged accordingly)

have to copulate with

Of either sex, meaning to possess, however temporarily. *Have* is used in this sense *tout court* or in many phrases which are so common that we forget their intrinsic stupidity. Only hermaphrodites do not *have sex* and we *have relations with* everyone we meet.

Among common usages we find *have a bit, a man/woman, at, intercourse (with), it, it off, (sexual) relations (with), (something) to do with, your (wicked) way* or *will with*, and *your will of*. There are countless vulgarisms starting with *have*, many with vivid imagery, and some of the phrases are also used of homosexual activity.

have a few to drink intoxicants to excess

The noun—drinks, beers, or whatever—is not mentioned. It may refer to a single instance or to an addiction to alcohol.

have the painters in to be menstruating

Common female usage, with reference to the staining and colour, the protective sheeting, the temporary indisposition, and the inconvenience.

have your ticket punched *American* to do something or assume a position whereby you will attract favourable notice

Your presence on the bus has been recorded:

> He had come to Washington to have his ticket punched, that is, to hold down a Pentagon desk assignment, a pre-requisite in the modern Navy for being awarded the rank of admiral. (Colodny & Gettlin, 1991)

hawk *mainly American* a person who advocates aggression as a way of defence

The idea comes from Calhoun's War Hawks, a political party of 1812, and was revived during the Cold War. See also DOVE.

hawk your mutton to be a prostitute

Literally, to offer meat for general sale. Also as *hawk your meat* or *your pearly*.

In obsolete use, to *hawk your meat* might mean no more than to display an immodest amount of bosom.

he-biddy *obsolete American* a cock

An example of 19th-century prudery before ROOSTER took over.

A *he-cow* was a bull.

head[1] *obsolete* to kill by beheading

As in the modern use, where we *head* gooseberries etc. by taking the top off.

A *heading* was such an execution, carried out by a *heading-man* on a *heading-hill*, for the convenience of onlookers.

head(s)[2] a lavatory on a ship

Originally, in a warship, but now general.

head[3] a narcotics addict

Alluding to the effect on the mind. Usually in combination as, for example, *snow-head*, someone addicted to cocaine.

head for the hills to distance yourself from any threat in a craven manner

The *hills* are the traditional refuge of the escapee, whence much figurative use:

> Some business leaders headed for the hills, anxious to avoid the shellfire; others moved in quickly behind China's line. (Patten, 1998—the *shellfire* was Chinese bluster and bullying prior to the British handover of Hong Kong to China. Patten notes elsewhere that those Hong Kong Chinese most subservient to the Chinese policy appeared also the keenest to secure foreign passports for themselves and their families)

head job (a) fellatio

Not an appointment to manage a school or even what the barber does for you.

A *head chick* is a prostitute who offers such a service. See also *give head* under GIVE.

headache[1] *obsolete England/Ireland* a corn poppy used for narcotic purposes

The *Papaver rhoeas* may not have had the potency of its oriental cousins, but it was what was available. There was a fetish against unmarried girls touching the flowers, because the drowsiness and feeling of goodwill

induced by closer acquaintance might make them easier to seduce:
> Corn-poppies, that in crimson dwell,
> Call'd head-aches from their sickly smell.
> (Clare, 1827)

The narcotic made from the poppies was called *headache-wine*.

headache² a female excuse for not participating in a sexual activity
Normally declining copulation but also of refusing to go out with a male for the evening.

headcount management dismissing staff
No euphemism is needed when the firm is recruiting:
> Clifford Chance, the world's biggest law firm, in undergoing what it calls 'headcount management'. (*Financial Times*, 2 June 2003)

Headcount reduction also involves the dismissal of employees rather than its literal meaning, reducing the number of times you count them.

headhunter *American* a police internal disciplinary inspector
His quarry is any dishonest police officer, punning on the practice of primitive tribes.
In commercial use, a *headhunter* is a recruitment agent and the claim to have been *headhunted* on changing jobs, whether true or false, adds to be individual's self-esteem if nothing else.

headshrinker a psychiatrist
The evasion is needed because the need to consult a psychiatrist may be a status symbol for some but is a matter of shame for others. Also as a *shrink*.
A *headbanger* is no more than an irrational or confused person, from the supposed habit of the mentally ill of banging their heads against walls.
A *head case* may be thought to suffer from temporary or permanent mental aberration or illness.

health illness
As with DEFENCE and LIFE², the taboo subject is avoided by talking about the converse. Thus the pharmaceutical industry sells *health care products* to the sick; the British *National Health Service* provides, as best it can, for the ill and dying; and we refer to such things as *health clinics* or *farms*, *health insurance*, etc.

healthy in accordance with approved policy
One of the favoured evasions of the Nazis:
> They were to grasp the essence of a case, approaching it with a 'healthy prejudice' and in line with the main principles of the

Führer's government. (Burleigh, 2000—writing of instructions to German judges)

heart (condition) a malfunction of the heart
Medical jargon, in which all *conditions* are bad. Some patients survive, it might seem, in the absence of the vital organ:
> Now it appeared he didn't have a 'heart' after all. (Lodge, 2000)

heart's desire copulation
When the expression refers to some other aspiration, the object is usually named:
> ...the naked rector, blindfolded by the milkmaid and thinking he was about to have his heart's desire...(B. Cornwell, 1997—it is strange that milkmaids acquired a reputation for sexual impropriety; the chances of dalliance in the cowshed would seem to have been remote)

hearts (of oak) *British* penurious
Rhyming slang on *broke*, from a national savings and benefit society of the same name.

heat¹ an action which causes alarm or anxiety
The body temperature rises when we are in danger. The usage covers things like police activity against specific criminals, military attacks, enquiry into scandal, illegal coercion, etc.

heat² a handgun
The derivation is from the warmth of the barrel and perhaps punning on HEAT¹ and on firing. Also as *heater*.

heave (the) summary dismissal from employment
Literally, causing a heavy object to move:
> When the cuts came I fancy half the staff would have written in suggesting he was top target for the heave. (Seymour, 1998)

heaven associated with the ingestion of illegal narcotics
In various jargon uses by addicts, such a *heaven dust* for cocaine and *heavenly blue* for pills of that colour.

heaviness obesity
Literally, weight, without which attribute our gravity-bound existence on earth would cease. Fatness has joined the list of taboos associated with physical characteristics so that even describing an obese person as *heavily built* may no longer be POLITICALLY CORRECT:
> I recently came across a government pamphlet on fatness, or 'heaviness' as the

NHS describes it. (*Daily Telegraph*, 19 December 2002)

heavy indicating significant sexual activity

Heavy here means important. In various phrases such as a *heavy date* which may involve *heavy necking* and even result in a *heavy involvement*.

Heavy breathing is what a would-be seducer may do, especially over the telephone, and has a figurative meaning 'pornographic':

> ... at the back of the shop is the heavy breathing section. (Bryson, 2000—the front of the shop was devoted to household pet supplies)

A *heavy* is someone who is prepared to threaten or carry out violence on behalf of a criminal employer, from his build.

heavy landing an aircraft crash on the runway

All *landings* of a machine heavier than air are of necessity *heavy*. Aviation jargon for an accident which is not calamitous.

heavy of foot *obsolete* in a late stage of pregnancy

How sad it is that many of these useful phrases are no longer used:

> James cam to me ae morning when she was heavy o' fit. (Service, 1887)

heel-tap a small volume of alcohol left in a glass

A *tap* was the sole or heel of a shoe, whence the liquid at the bottom of the glass.

The expression survives in *no heel-taps*—everyone must drain his glass.

heeled carrying a gun

Literally, armed and equipped.

Well heeled does not mean it is a good gun, but that the person so described is wealthy.

heels foremost dead

You will almost certainly be carried that way as a patient on a stretcher on the way to hospital, but if so described, you are a corpse.

heightened interrogation torture

As authorized by the Nazis and other authoritarian regimes:

> Down in the cellar the Gestapo was licensed to practise what the Ministry of Justice called 'heightened interrogation'. (R. Harris, 1992)

heist *mainly American* a theft

A variant of HOIST, referring to taking a truckload of goods or to an armed robbery.

helmet a police officer in uniform

The derogatory jargon of those colleagues who do their duty in plain clothes. Now largely superseded by UNIFORM.

help¹ *mainly American* a domestic servant

In standard use, any employee and a shortened form of *hired help*. In the home it implies voluntary assistance rather than servitude.

help² the services of a ghost writer

Publishing jargon, which ignores the invaluable assistance given to all authors by their editors (especially mine):

> The odd thing about this kind of collaboration is that the celebrity... in seeking 'help' with a novel, inevitably appears dimmer than if she had never done a book at all. (*Daily Telegraph*, 9 September 1994)

help the police (with their inquiries) *British* to be in custody and presumed guilty of an offence with which you have not been charged

The purpose of the wording is not to prejudge guilt and so avoid the possibility of a subsequent conviction being quashed or an action for defamation.

To *assist the police* means the same thing, although to *help the police* in some parts of the globe can mean something quite different:

> 'He is helping us with our inquiries.'
> 'What a pompous name for torture.'
> (Theroux, 1977)

help yourself to steal

Literally, not to await service by another. Usually of pilfering, especially where the goods are unguarded.

hemp pertaining to hanging

The material of the rope. The *hemp string* was a noose, the *hemp quinsy* or *hempen fever*, death by hanging, and a *hempen widow* someone whose husband, a *Hempshire gentleman* (from whichever county he came), had been hanged.

Today *hemp* is no more than addict slang for marijuana.

hen associated with a bride

The usage, which survives in *hen party*, a meeting between the bride and her female friends immediately prior to a wedding, and in *hen night*, a social gathering limited to females, once occurred in northern English phrases more to do with extortion than with celebration. *Hen brass* or *hen silver* was demanded by onlookers for *hen-drinking*, ostensibly to toast the bride, and in a refined form firearms were used:

Formerly a gun was fired over the house of a newly married couple, to secure a plentiful issue of the marriage (probably to dispel the evil spirits that bring bad luck). The firing party had a present given them... and this was termed hen-silver.
(*Penrith Observer*, September 1896)

The male equivalent is not *cock* but STAG.

herb marijuana
Addict slang. At one time the *herb* was tobacco.

hereafter (the) death
Religious use, anticipating some sort of continuing existence.

hide to conceal illegally
Especially of the proceeds of crime or when associated with tax evasion:
> He said he is sure people buy these things to 'hide' their questionable gains. (Garfield, 2004)

high drunk or under the influence of narcotics
Referring to the feeling of elevation or elation, but not describing those who have lapsed into torpidity or unconsciousness.

high-fly (the) *obsolete British* sending out begging letters
The career was made economically viable by the introduction of the penny post. Today we have a more descriptive title in *junk mail*, which also includes general advertising matter.

high forehead (a) baldness
Hair on the scalp is a sensitive subject for most men:
> 'And the receding hairline?' 'Receding what?'... 'High forehead,' he said. (Lynn & Jay, 1986)

highball *American* to ingest a taboo substance
For railroad engineers, a *highball* was a clear track; for drinkers, an alcoholic mixture in a tall glass; for drug addicts, an amalgam of narcotics.

higher state (of existence) (a) death
Not necessarily frequenting the realm above the clouds guarded by St Peter but in a spiritual situation more blessed than our sinful life on earth:
> ... unite in the praise and prayer to our heavenly Father, from whom daily we receive so much good and may hope for more in a higher state of existence. (J. Boswell, 1791)

See also *called to higher service* under CALL.

highgrade *American* to steal
The derivation is from the meaning, to take the easiest pickings, of timber from a forest, ore from a mine, etc. A *highgrader* is a discriminating thief who goes for items of the highest value.

highwayman a thief on the highway
Not just any wayfarer. He was usually on horseback, when he was a *high pad*, as distinct from the *footpad*, who robbed on the *pad*, or path, on foot. His robbery was known as the *high law* and he was the *high lawyer*.

hijack to take illegal possession of (a vehicle)
Standard English and doubtfully euphemistic, despite its interesting etymology. Originally, American Prohibition use, when it became easier to steal liquor from smugglers than to smuggle on your own account, and the command to raise the hands from the *hijacker* was a laconic 'High, Jack'.
Now used of the theft of all types of motor vehicles, of aircraft piracy, and also figuratively:
> But the environmentalists are the main group to have figured out that science can be hijacked for ideological purposes. (*American Spectator*, February 1994)

hike an unwelcome increase in selling price
Literally, a raise of anything but used pejoratively when the price increase appears to be excessive and concerns a household necessity. In obsolete use to *hike* or *hike off* meant to dismiss from employment.

hillside men *obsolete Irish* outlaws
A 19th-century use when most of the population wished to be freed from English control but abhorred violence:
> He was no bog-trotter... but ranged on the side of the moonlighters and the hillside men. (Flanagan, 1988—a *bog-trotter* was either an outlaw or a dispossessed tenant; see also *moonlighter* under MOONLIGHT²)

hindside the buttocks
BACKSIDE is more common. Perhaps obsolete but for some figurative use:
> Although Richard had a tendency to look after his bureaucratic hindside, Barcella knew him and trusted him. (Maas, 1986)

historic old
A usage of estate agents which sometimes traps them in tautology:
> Historic Saxon barn. (*Sunday Telegraph*, May 1981, implying construction before 1066)

history a reputation for sexual impropriety

The historians who use this word are selective in their choice of material:

> ...she an unwed woman. One with a history no less. (Hosseini, 2003)

hit¹ a drunken carouse

From the effect of the alcohol and rhyming slang on *hit and miss*, which is sometimes given in full:

> Sorry about my breath—I've been out on the hit and miss. (*Daily Telegraph Magazine*, August 1990)

A *hit* in current use is more likely to be the ingestion of illegal narcotics and to *hit the pipe* is to smoke opium or marijuana.

hit² to kill

Usually describing assassination by a bullet, the *hit* being performed by a *hitman*.

In American criminal slang a *hit* may be no more than a robbery, whether or not accompanied by violence.

It may also mean to beg in a public place using menaces.

hit-and-run a single promiscuous encounter

Punning in Britain on the version of cricket and in America on baseball.

Hit in this sexual sense has a venerable ancestry:

> She'll find a white that shall her blackness hit. (Shakespeare, *Othello*)

hit on to attempt or achieve a sexual relationship with a female

Either trying to *make a hit with*, make a good impression on, her, or the usual violent imagery.

hit the bottle to drink intoxicants to excess

Of a single debauch or sustained drunkenness. Also as *hit the hooch* or *hit it*.

hit the bricks *American* to escape or desert

The imagery is from the materials once used on the sidewalk. Also as *hit the lump*, from the hill over which the fugitive disappears.

Those going on strike may also be said to *hit the bricks*, although most of them will have driven to and from their place of work.

hit the sack with to copulate with

To *hit the sack* or *hay* means no more than to go to bed on your own:

> ...blame a Colonel for hitting the sack with a hooker. (Ustinov, 1971)

hit the silk see SILK (THE)

hit the wall *American* to become a fugitive

Climb over the wall would seem more appropriate.

hochle *obsolete Scottish* to flaunt promiscuity

Literally, to sprawl about. Dr Wright gives as definition 'To tumble lewdly with women in open day.' (*EDD*—do not be misled into thinking that there was an 'open day' for tumbling lewdly with women)

hoist to rob

In 19th-century Britain it implied shoplifting. In modern America it is used as a noun to describe robbery from the person by a pickpocket.

The slang *hoist a few* does not mean multiple thefts but the drinking of intoxicants, from lifting the glass to the mouth.

A woman who *hoists her skirt* copulates promiscuously.

hold to possess narcotics illegally

For your own use or resale.

The obsolete *hold-door trade* was not drug-dealing but prostitution, from the practice of leaning on a partly opened door while awaiting custom.

hold paper on *American* to have a warrant for the arrest of

Criminal and police jargon:

> 'You holding paper on him?' I still wanted to know what it was for, what Kam, whoever he was, was supposed to have done. (Turow, 1993)

hold the bag *American* to accept the blame or the consequences

Rather like the game of pass the parcel, with the loser being the person holding it when the music stops.

hold-up a robbery

Literally, a delay of any kind, and I suppose a considerate thief may still *hold up* his hand to stop you before taking your valuables. Formerly, of stopping stagecoaches and robbing the occupants, but now of any robbery, especially where violence is threatened.

hold your liquor to drink a lot of alcohol without appearing drunk

Intermediate urination does not disqualify you but vomiting does.

hole *obsolete* to kill

I am unsure whether the derivation is from the entry of the bullet or the excavation of the grave. The modern cliché *a hole in the head* suggests the former.

In vulgar use to *hole* is to copulate, the *hole* being the vagina and, for a libertine like Frank Harris, the *holy of holies*.

holiday a term in prison
It is one way of explaining the absence.

holiday ownership a compounded annual rent paid in advance
When victims became aware of the scams and other disadvantages of *time-sharing*, another phrase had to be coined to ensure that the gullible would continue to part with their money:
    So you must agree that buying a holiday ownership apartment at the Lanzarote Beach Club will actually SAVE YOU £20,000. (*Daily Telegraph*, August 1989—see also SAVE for this kind of frugality)

hollow legs the ability to drink a lot of beer, wine, or spirits
The volume has to be stored somewhere, it seems. Sometimes in the singular.
The cliché is also applied to gluttony.

holy of holies a lavatory
A tasteless double pun on what should be a quiet and secret place. In obsolete use among classicists the Latin version, *sanctum sanctorum*, might be heard, losing all in translation.

holy wars the expansion into the Middle East in the Middle Ages by western adventurers
We know them better as the Crusades. Although the pretext, and motive for some, was religious, a major cause for the aggression and attempted conquest was the pressure on resources caused by the rising population in western Europe prior to the fortuitous onset of the Black Death. After humanity had been culled for a century, the problem was starting to recur when the Age of Discovery revealed softer victims in the Americas, Africa, and the East.

holy week the period of menstruation
You can take your pick from a variety of tasteless puns and allusions.

home a residential institution
Literally, the individual house in which you live with your family. A *nursing home*, *retirement home*, *residential home*, or any *home* with a similar prefix is a place to accommodate geriatrics away from their families.
Builders and real estate agents describe newly constructed houses as *homes* to induce a warm feeling in their potential customers.

home economics cooking and housekeeping

The tuition needs a name which avoids sexual stereotyping:
    In Home Economics, which really means cooking and sewing, I've learned how to install a zipper and make a flat-fell seam. (Atwood, 1988)

home equity loan a second mortgage
The security being deferred to the first mortgagee, the terms are onerous and only accepted by those in dire financial straits:
    'Home equity loan' sounded ever so much more palatable than 'second mortgage'. (M. Thomas, 1987)

homelands *South African* areas into which black people were forcibly resettled
The pretence was that these were the places from which urban and other black people originated. Nominally independent, they remained politically and economically under the control of the white government in Pretoria. See also SEPARATE DEVELOPMENT.

homely *American* plain-looking (used of women)
Literally, unaffectedly natural:
    It was the homeliest members of your class who became teachers. (M. McCarthy, 1963)

honest chaste
Not necessarily truthful or trustworthy in other respects:
    I do not think but Desdemona's honest. (Shakespeare, *Othello*)
A man may still *make an honest woman* of someone by marrying her after impregnating, or openly cohabiting with, her.

honey *American* associated with human excrement
Referring to the colour and texture rather than the smell or sweetness. A *honey bucket* is a portable lavatory for the army; a *honey barge* carries away lavatory waste for the navy; a *honey cart* does the same function for airlines; and a *honey-dipper* is not a bee but a person who empties lavatories.

honey trap an attempt to seduce for subsequent blackmail or exposure
The sweet experience ensnares the victim, usually a male. There is also a verbal use, to *honey-trap* rather than to *trap with honey*.

honk *American* to feel the genitals of a male
Like squeezing an old-style bulb horn, although probably more painful. Prostitutes' and police jargon, indicating a sexual approach.

honour chastity in a woman
Literally, maintaining moral standards and

formerly something jealously preserved by upright women.

honourable age (of) geriatric

It was dangerous under Communism to suggest that the sick and senile old men who clung to office until death, or even a few days after, were unfit to govern:

> We had in recent years a true gerontocracy, with the average age of the members of the leadership over seventy. Even though many new faces had joined the Central Committee since I had taken over, people of an 'honourable age' still predominated. (Gorbachev, 1995, in translation)

honours rewards

Given by British politicians in the name of the sovereign to those whom they wish allegedly to reward, bribe, or silence or from whom their party organization has received money.

hook[1] to steal

The imagery is from angling. In East Africa it still applies to the technique of introducing a pole with a *hook* on the end through the shutters of your bedroom, with razor blades let into the shaft to stop you grabbing it.

In obsolete British use a *hooker* was such a thief.

hook[2] a threat or enticement

The 'fish' is already on the line and can be influenced or blackmailed, or else is about to be caught.

Those who are described as *hooked* are subject to a compulsive addiction, usually to a harmful activity such as ingesting tobacco smoke or narcotics.

hooker a prostitute

From catching, *hooking*, a customer rather than General Hooker's exploits in Washington brothels or prostitutes in the *Corlears Hook* or *Caesar's Hook* districts of New York.

A *hook-shop* was a brothel where prostitutes took those they had *hooked*:

> Some nights we go about and don't hook a soul. (Mayhew, 1862—they were prostitutes, not Salvationists)

hooky *American* human excrement

Perhaps from the shape. It is used for *shit* in the literal, allusive, figurative, and expletive senses of that overworked word.

To *play hook(e)y* is to play truant.

hoosegow a prison

From the Spanish *juzgado*, a court, and from being judged in court and sent to jail.

hop a narcotic

Originally, opium, from the twisting vine rather than a corruption of some Chinese

word. A *hophead* is an addict, who may resort to a *hop-joint* where he may become *hopped*, or under illegal narcosis.

hop into bed to copulate promiscuously

Usually on a single occasion and not propelling yourself on one leg only.

The American *whore-hopping* is not leapfrog played in a brothel but copulation with two or more prostitutes in immediate succession.

The obsolete Kentish *hop-pole marriage* described a couple living together and possibly conceiving a child extramaritally while gathering hops as migrant workers, their resolve being publicly shown by together jumping over a stick of *hop-pole* without the formality of a ceremony in church. See also JUMP THE BROOMSTICK

hop off to die

Avian imagery. Formerly as *hop the living* and also, in modern use, as *hop the twig*.

hopper *American* a lavatory

Literally, an inverted cone through which solids are discharged into a container.

hopping-Giles *obsolete British* a lame person

St Giles was the patron saint of cripples in the days when they were accepted as a common and unremarkable feature of society, and before the word *cripple* was considered derogatory and it became taboo to allude in direct terms to any physical abnormality. A crippled person would also respond to the name *Hopkins*.

horizontal pertaining to copulation

From the normal posture of the parties. In many phrases such as *horizontal aerobics*, in which both participants take exercise; *horizontal collaboration*, or how some Frenchwomen greeted the German invader, earning the sobriquet *collabos horizontales*; *horizontal conquest*, where the victor takes the spoils; the *horizontal life*, or prostitution; *horizontal jogging*, the *horizontal position*, or copulation; etc. A *grande horizontale* is a well-known prostitute or unchaste woman.

horn the erect penis

Common enough in the 16th century for Shakespeare's punning vulgarism:

> I can find no rhyme for 'lady' but 'baby—an innocent rhyme; for 'scorn', 'horn', a hard rhyme. (*Much Ado About Nothing*)

Also as the *horn of plenty*, punning on the cornucopia which, before brimming over with good things, was no more than the capital adornment of the goat which suckled Zeus.

A *horn-emporium* was, for Kingsley Amis at least, a bookshop selling erotic literature for males. *Horny* means sexually excited and is used of both sexes despite, or perhaps because of, the masculinity of a *horn*.

Horns were also associated with cuckoldry, antlers being figuratively placed on the head of the deceived husband. To *wind the horn* was to acknowledge that you had been cuckolded, or *horned* by a *horn-maker*:

Our horn'd master (waes for him)
Believes that sly boots does adore him.
(Morison, 1790—but she wasn't sly enough to take in the servants)

horn of fidelity *obsolete* a magic drinking cup

Morgan le Fay sent it to King Arthur to enable him to test the chastity of the ladies of his court. Legend records that only four out of the hundred managed to *drink cleane*, thus preserving the liquid and their honour.

horn of the ox (that gored you) see HAIR OF THE DOG

horny the devil

He has horns on his head. Usually as *old horny*, *hornie*, *horney*, or *hoorney*. In 19th-century Ireland *horny* was an abusive name used by Nationalists for a policeman working for the Protestant government.

hors de combat menstruating

Literally, out of action. A male usage.

horse *American* a corrupt prison warder

A variant of the more common MULE, he carries contraband such as drugs and messages in and out of prison.

Horse is also a slang corruption of heroin, whence Deighton's punning title for a novel, *Horse under Water*.

horse apples *American* the turds dropped by a horse

Especially in a street, where they might pile up like apples on a fruiterer's shelf:

... 'horse apples', 'cowpats', 'prairie chips', 'muck', 'dung', etc. (Jennings, 1965, listing common euphemistic synonyms)

hose *American* to seek to confuse or cheat

Spraying with confusing and irrelevant detail. To *hose* may also mean to flatter, laying it on thick.

hospice an institution for the incurable or dying

Originally, a resting place for travellers, especially pilgrims, and often run by members of a religious order. The current use first emerged in Dublin at the end of the 19th century.

hospital a place of illegal confinement

Jargon of totalitarian regimes and the American Central Intelligence Agency.

hospital job a contract which can be loaded with excessive charges

In normal manufacturing use, it is a contract to which you can divert resources when business is slack, delivery not being urgent because the patient is unable to walk away while awaiting treatment. The dishonesty starts when such a contract is loaded with waiting time and scrap because the customer, usually a public body spending other people's money, is too inefficient or indifferent to detect malpractice.

hospital pass in football, a pass which is difficult to collect or exploit

Some figurative use:

When it became too much of a headache Granada lobbed a load of business to Compass. It was the biggest hospital pass... (*Daily Telegraph*, 9 September 2005)

hospitality free intoxicants

In standard usage, the provision of a welcome and entertainment to a visitor. In broadcasting, a *hospitality room* is the place where the tongues of amateur broadcasters are loosened prior to going on air and to which the staff repair for free drinks.

hostess a prostitute

As located in a *hostess bar* or *club*, where the provision of food or drink may be a secondary function. Those who were once called *air hostesses* now understandably prefer to be called cabin flight attendants, and when they ask if you wish to select bread from a basket they are always careful to put the word *bread* before the ROLL¹.

hot¹ sexually aroused

From the increased bodily temperature and flushing caused by the excitement, and also used of other emotions such as anger, which display the same symptoms.

Being *hot for* or *having the hots for* is to lust after someone of either sex, although only females are said, under that condition, to be *hot-tailing*. Someone who is *hot stuff* will induce sexual arousal in others.

For Shakespeare, the gods had *hot backs* and having *hot pants* is an indication of sexual arousal, either on a specific occasion or frequently, the British use being confined to females because their menfolk wear trousers.

The American *hot-pillow* or *hot-sheet motel*, *joint*, or *hotel* is one to which people may resort for promiscuous copulation, the bedlinen being

given insufficient time in which to cool down between customers.
Hot-house, a brothel, is obsolete.

hot² obtained or held illegally
Used of stolen goods to be disposed of on the *hot market*, or the proceeds of vice—*hot money*. Both of these commodities are likely figuratively to burn you if you touch them.

hot³ infected with venereal disease
Normally of a male, from the burning sensation when urinating if infected with gonorrhoea, and also perhaps from the risk of infecting another.

hot⁴ radioactive
Nuclear jargon, perhaps taken from a *hot spot* on a bearing, where heat indicates potential malfunction and possible danger.

hot place (the) hell
Where the fires for ever burn. Now rare, even among evangelical Christians.

hot seat *American* an electric chair used for execution
More figurative than direct use. Someone in the *hot seat* is liable to take the blame for other people's actions.
Hot-seating refers to shift-working in offices, where one employee moves into a predecessor's chair before it has had time to cool down. Also as *hot-desking*, although the occupants presumably still find chairs more comfortable.

hot shot *American* a fatal dose of illegal narcotics
Punning perhaps on the meaning, a lively person. The impurities of illegal narcotics, often adulterated in the distribution chain, constitute an additional risk to addicts.

hot-wire to steal a vehicle by bypassing the ignition switch
A mixture of HOT² and modification of the electrical circuitry.

hourly hotel *American* an establishment which lets rooms for casual copulation
Day or night, but not necessarily a brothel.

house¹ a brothel
Literally, a dwelling or any other building given over to a special purpose, such as a theatre or debating chamber. The use of *house* for a brothel *tout court* is obsolete:
    Some of the girls about here live in houses. (Mayhew, 1862—but not chastely with their families)
Brothels were also known as a *house of accommodation* or *assignation* (the equivalent

of the modern HOURLY HOTEL), *house in the suburbs*, *of profession*, *of resort*, *of sale*, *of sin*, *of tolerance*, etc.
Other obsolete uses are *common house*, *ill-famed house*, *scalding house* (where you were likely to contract disease), and *introducing house*.
We may still, if so inclined, visit a *house of evil* or *ill repute* (however proficient the residents), *house of pleasure*, or *house of ill fame*.

house² *obsolete* a lavatory
Again, the building given over to a particular purpose. Although Dr Johnson defines lavatories as *houses*, he does not so define a *house*. In varying compounds such as *house of commons*, *of ease*, *of lords*, and *of office*:
    I had like to have shit in a skimmer that day over the house of office. (Pepys, 1660)

house³ *obsolete* an institution for the homeless
A shortened form of the dread *workhouse*, which was also known as a *house of industry*.

house man *American* a security guard
Police jargon, and not the *man of the house*.

house of correction a prison
So named in the hope that there will be no recidivism. The American *house of detention* is specific.

house-proud obsessed with domestic cleanliness and tidiness
This tedious affliction may have little to do with pride in the family residence itself.

house-trained no longer given to involuntary urination or defecation
Usually of domestic pets but occasionally of young children. Figurative use of a husband subservient in the home to his wife or of someone nominally in authority, such as a government minister, who is conditioned by subordinates (civil servants, for example) to comply with and support the practices, policies, and abuses which they favour or wish not to be changed.

housecleaning *American* the elimination of undesirable or embarrassing items
The imagery comes from the annual major assault that used to be made in the spring on carpets, curtains, etc. It refers to an investigation and subsequent reorganization in an institution when inefficiency or corruption have reached levels which threaten the security of those in charge; and to the destruction of records which might embarrass them:
    In the afternoon hours of August 8, Ford staff members heard of frantic housecleaning under way at the White

House. (Colodny & Gettlin, 1991, describing the aftermath to Watergate)

housemate *American* a regular sexual partner with whom you cohabit

Not just a fellow lodger or member of the family:

> For the more flip, Americans offer LIL, for live-in lover, or housemate. (Whicker, 1982—he was discussing how to introduce to strangers a woman with whom he shared such a relationship)

Flatmate does not carry the same sexual inference.

how's your father casual copulation or its outcome

A male usage, perhaps from an opening conversational gambit. Where copulation is meant, usually in the phrase, *a bit of how's your father*. Less often of unplanned pregnancy:

> The girl was in the club, knocked up, a bun in the oven—'ow's yer father. (Lyall, 1982)

hulk *obsolete* a floating prison

Originally a ship, and then the hull of a ship no longer seaworthy but deemed good enough for the confinement of convicts. Often in the plural.

human difference a facility below the norm

Not referring to the infinite variety among specimens of *homo sapiens*, nor even to those with acute eyesight or hearing:

> ... many people in the deaf community define their deafness not as a disability, but merely as a 'human difference'. (*Chicago Tribune*, 20 May 1991)

human intelligence the use of spies

Espionage jargon for the acquisition of *intelligence*, or information, by *human* agency rather than the interception of radio signals, satellite photography, etc.

human relations sexual activity

Literally, members of our family or everyone with whom we come in contact:

> She had no idea of elementary human relations. (Fraser, 1969—she was unaware of the process through which babies are conceived)

human remains pouch see BODY

human resources personnel

Pretension rather than euphemism perhaps, although it could mean anything from your muscular development to your bank balance. Often shortened to *HR*.

human rights individual licence beyond that permitted by existing institutions

The phrase comes from the 1948 United Nations' Universal Declaration of Human Rights, a concept to which no exception can be taken by those who consider mankind to be paramount on earth. In practice, *human rights* sometimes provides a slogan for those who wish to overturn an established form of social living acceptable to or tolerated by a majority, using violence if necessary.

human sacrifice the dismissal of employees

Punning on ancient rites to propitiate the gods.

human waste sewage

Not discarded packaging or cans, amputated limbs or corpses, the unemployed, or those without fulfilling lives. Jargon of civil engineers, to distinguish it from surface water and other EFFLUENT.

hump to copulate with

Venerable enough for Grose to note 'once a fashionable word for copulation'. The imagery is from porterage rather than from the *beast with two backs* (see under BEAST). Also as *hump the mutton*.

hung suffering from sub-acute alcoholic poisoning

Not an illiterate use of *hanged* but a shortened version of *hungover*, from HANGOVER, the past and present tenses merging, it would appear.

hung like (of a male) claiming the fabled sexual prowess of

In various clichés. *Hung like a bull*, *horse*, or *stallion* implies large genitalia.

Hung like a rabbit suggests a penchant for frequent copulation.

hunt to seek a homosexual partner in a public place

A male activity:

> Gilbert's given up 'hunting', he says all he ever wanted was love and he's got mine. (I. Murdoch, 1978)

The obsolete American *hunt the brass rail* was to frequent bars, where many offered a brass rail on which you might rest a foot.

The British *hunt the fox down the red lane* was to become drunk, possibly after consuming too many CHASERS, in the days when fox-hunting was a traditional and legal country pursuit.

hush money a bribe to ensure silence

Hush for the ensuing quiet. Less often as *hush payments*.

hustle to cheat, rob, or involve another in a taboo activity

Literally, to push or crowd, whence to sell at an inflated price by skilful banter, to beg with menaces especially for the purchase of narcotics, to pilfer, or to engage in prostitution, from the importuning in a public place. Whence *hustler*, an importunate hawker or a prostitute.

hygiene facilities a lavatory

Hygeia was the Greek goddess of health, which seems quite a step away from lavatories and sanitary towels (see also PERSONAL HYGIENE). A *hygiene break* is a pause in a meeting or stop on a journey to allow those involved to urinate

If a male is seeking the company of a *hygienic* female he is not looking for someone with the virtues of Hygeia but wishing to copulate casually with a partner free of venereal disease.

hygienic treatment *American* the temporary preservation of a corpse

Funeral jargon ignoring the fact that newly dead meat is aseptic.

I

I hear what you say I do not agree with you
A convenient form of words because it avoids the need to enter into discussion or argument.

I must have notice of that question I do not intend to answer you
The response is useful in a broadcast when you may wish to conceal knowledge as much as ignorance. Radio and television are too ephemeral for there to be a risk that your bluff will be called. Those who respond to a question by saying 'I'm glad you asked me that' are usually playing for time rather than expressing gratitude.

ice¹ to kill
The derivation is from lowering the body temperature rather than the ice formerly used in morgues. Also as *put on ice*.

ice² an illegal narcotic
Formerly only cocaine, from the numbing sensation. Also as *ice cream*.

ice box¹ *American* a prison
Originally a cell used for solitary confinement, where you were sent to cool down. Also as *ice-house*.

ice box² *American* a mortuary
This usage has survived the refrigeration of mortuaries.

ice queen a reserved and chaste young woman
Male use, from her supposed frigidity, but not a champion skater.

ideal for modernization dilapidated
In this real estate agents' newspeak, *ideal* means only fit for:
Stone-built detached cottage. Ideal for modernization. (*Western Daily Press*, May 1981)

identification proof of the ability to pay
A passport or driving licence will not suffice. The desk staff in a hotel who ask for *identification* will want to take an imprint of your credit card before handing you the room key.

ideological supervision censorship
In political circles, *supervision* always carries menacing overtones:
Dubcek cracked; he agreed censorship ('ideological supervision') could be restored and accepted the 'temporary stationing' of the invasion forces. (Moynahan, 1994, writing of events in Czechoslovakia in April 1968)

idiosyncrasy homosexuality
Literally, any tendency or unusual preference:
[The Queen] seemed quite comfortable in the company of Anthony Blunt, even after his 'idiosyncrasy' was known. (*Daily Telegraph*, 24 March 1995—Blunt was the Surveyor of the Queen's Pictures, having for years been a Communist spy)

if (or in case) anything should happen (to me) If (I) should be killed or die
Of untimely or unexpected death:
[A wartime pilot in Malta] also sent me written instructions to draw any funds left in his bank account in case 'anything should happen to me'. (Holland, 2003)

ill¹ menstrual
Common female usage:
'When were you ill last?' 'About a fortnight ago,' she replied. (F. Harris, 1925)
Mrs Pepys was *ill of those*:
Thence home and my wife ill of those upon the maid's bed. (Pepys, 1669)

ill² suffering from a taboo disease
Either a venereal disease or AIDS.
'How can you be sure that Étienne knew Eric was ill?' '…you do love euphemisms, don't you?' (P. D. James, 1994—Eric was infected with the AIDS virus)

ill³ drunk
The symptoms of drunkenness can be identical with those of various illnesses:
'Roddy felt ill.' 'Ill,' said Jerry. 'Drunk, you mean.' (Deighton, 1988)

ill⁴ mentally unwell
Now probably obsolete, with our better understanding of mental sickness. Also as *ill-adjusted*:
She had some art treasures which she heaped upon me when she was what we will politely call 'ill', but claimed back again the moment she was well. (Coren, 1995, quoting Dr Conan Doyle writing about a patient)

ill-wished *obsolete* bewitched
The malady might be cured by a visit to the conjuror, or white witch.

illegal operation an induced abortion
In the days before such procedures became legal.

illegitimate born outside wedlock
This is a dog Latin word coined in an age
when people worried a lot about paternity:
  A yearly average of 1,141 illegitimate
  children thrown back on their wretched
  mothers. (Mayhew, 1862)
The meaning unlawful developed later.

illicit pertaining to extramarital copulation
Literally 'unlawful', although English common law saw no criminality in adultery,
leaving jurisdiction to the Church. Usually in
phrases such as *illicit embraces*, *connection*,
commerce, *intercourse*, etc.

illuminated drunk
A rarer form of LIT:
  [The Drones'] euphemisms for 'inebriated'
  include 'awash', 'boiled', 'fried to the
  tonsils', 'full to the back teeth', 'hooched',
  'illuminated' or 'lit up', 'lathered', 'off-
  colour', 'oiled', 'ossified', 'polluted',
  'scrooched', 'squiffy', 'stewed to the gills',
  'stinko', 'tanked', 'tight as an owl', 'under
  the sauce', 'whiffled', and 'woozled'.
  (McCrum, 2004, listing Wodehouse's slang
  expressions)

imaginative   journalism sensationalist
fabrication
It is unwise to call a journalist a liar because
the press has more chances of hurting you
than you have in return.

imbibe to drink intoxicants
Literally, to drink any liquid. Anyone who is
said to *imbibe* is being accused of being an
alcoholic.

immaculate in fair decorative order
No used residence is ever 'spotlessly clean or
neat, perfectly tidy, in perfect condition'
(*SOED*). This is the puffing of estate agents
for a house which looks fit to move into
without immediate attention.

immigrant *British* a non-white citizen of
the United Kingdom
White people who have moved to Britain are
not included in this category in popular
speech, despite the fact that:
  Most 'immigrants' have been here for
  many years, and two of every five of them
  were born in the United Kingdom.
  (Howard, 1977)

immoral associated with prostitution
Literally, contrary to virtue but confined to
sexual behaviour in legal jargon. An *immoral
house* was a brothel where you might find
immoral girls whose *immoral earnings* might be
lived on illegally by a pimp or bawd. The

American Mann Act, also known as the
Immorality Act, makes it illegal to transport
a female across a state line with intent to
'induce, entice or compel her to give herself
up to the practice of prostitution or to give
herself up to debauchery or any other
immoral purpose'.

impaired credit carrying a high risk of
default
The jargon of money-lending:
  Every lender from the most cautious
  building society to the most enthusiastic
  purveyors of 'impaired credit' mortgages
  says how much better than average its risks
  are. (*Daily Telegraph*, 3 December 2003)

impaired hearing deafness.
In standard usage, to *impair* means to damage
or weaken, and while this description is
correct of those who served in the artillery
without the protection of earmuffs, it is
normally not so for the rest of the population
who are so afflicted:
  ... the deaf shall be called 'people with
  impaired hearing'. (*Daily Telegraph*, 1
  October 1990, quoting a memorandum
  issued by Derbyshire County Council's
  Equal Opportunities and Race Relations
  Department)

impairment loss
Financial jargon in a milieu where mention of
loss is taboo:
  Britain's lenders all admit that what they
  coyly call impairments are sharply higher
  this year. (*Daily Telegraph*, 2 March 2006)
An *impairment charge* in a financial statement
is what used to be called a provision.

importune to offer sexual services for
money
Literally, to beseech. Legal jargon of prostitutes who SOLICIT customers in public places.

impotent sexually infertile
Literally, powerless in any respect, but used in
this sense of either sex:
  ... advertisements for doctors who cured
  'all the diseases of love' and promised the
  impotent 'horse-like vigour'. (Manning,
  1977)

improper involving promiscuity
Literally, lacking propriety in any respect. The
obsolete *improper house* was a brothel:
  Neither was the magistracy or the police
  allowed to enter improper or disorderly
  houses, unless to suppress disturbances.
  (Mayhew, 1862—other than in their private
  capacity as customers, we might suppose)
An *improper connection* was adultery:
  I asked him if there was any improper

connection between them—'No, sir, no more than between two statues.' (J. Boswell, 1773)

An improper suggestion is an invitation to a stranger to indulge in a sexual act.

improvement¹ *obsolete Scottish* forcible depopulation
The Scottish Highland Clearances replaced people by sheep in the glens to increase income for the lairds and chiefs.

Many of those evicted emigrated to the American colonies, where they stayed loyal to the crown in the War of Independence and subsequently removed themselves to New Scotland, or Nova Scotia, rather than stay among the successful rebels.

improvement² a reduction in quality or service
Any statement that a change introduced by a manufacturer or provider of services will result in *improvement* for customers should be viewed with suspicion. The only thing it is normally intended to improve is the profitability of the operation:
Improvement means deterioration. (Hutber's Law, propounded by the former City Editor of the *Sunday Telegraph*)

improving knife (the) cosmetic surgery
Some may think that the scalpel might be put to better use in aid of life-threatening ailments.

in imprisoned
Criminal jargon; a shortened form of *in prison* or INSIDE.

in a pig's ear no, or that is nonsense
The *pig's ear* was the receptacle kept on the bridge of a naval vessel into which the watchman and others might urinate without having to leave their post. Non-naval use is always figurative:
'Looking forward to our association, as they say.' In a pig's ear, Lorimer thought, as he trudged the deserted streets looking for a taxi. (Boyd, 1998)

in Abraham's bosom dead
Where Dives reputedly saw Lazarus, although it seems poor recompense for a lifetime of penury and abuse.

in bits suffering from a hangover
Coming apart or very upset:
—That's good. I was in bits meself this mornin'.—Were yeh?
—Yeah. The oul' rum an' blacks, yeh know. (Doyle, 1990)

in calf pregnant

Literally of cows, vulgarly of women. Also as *in foal*, *pig*, *pod*, and *pup*.

in care compulsorily committed to custody in an institution
The fate of children who lack parental presence or discipline and are removed by court order to the control of local government officials. It should not be assumed that other children living normally at home with their parents lack care.

in Carey Street *British* bankrupt
From the location of the London Bankruptcy Court.

in Dutch in trouble
A survival from the maritime antagonism between the English and the men of the Low Counties.
See also DUTCH.

in flagrante (delicto) in the act of copulation
Legal jargon. It may apply to other misconduct:
On one celebrated occasion a soldier was caught in flagrante with a chaplain's goat. (P. McCarthy, 2002)
The French form, *en flagrant délit*, is rare. Also as *in full venery*, a condition in which a boatswain was said by Sydney Smith to have been observed with Queen Caroline.

in for it pregnant
A common use, especially of pregnancy outside marriage.
Both James's Anna and Edward's Elizabeth were ... in the less delicate language of Lord Portsmouth's brother Coulson '*in for it*'. (Tomalin, 1997, quoting from a letter of Jane Austen dated 5 January 1801)

in full fling *obsolete* enjoying an exclusive sexual relationship
A *fling* is a temporary bout of uncharacteristic hedonism.

in heaven dead
Religious use, and by monumental masons. There are many other phrases of the same tendency, such as IN THE ARMS OF JESUS.

in left field *American* eccentric or mentally unstable
A baseball term, with perhaps a hint of the normal *sinister* connection.

in liquor drunk
In fact the LIQUOR is in you.

in my knickers copulating with me
Not just wearing them. Also as *in my pants*:
[Giving a stranger a rose] doesn't get you in my knickers. (Rankin, 2004)

in name only without copulation
Used of a marriage, especially where the parties have continued to live with each other.

in need of modernization derelict
The coded language of the seller of real estate.

in purdah menstruating
But not living apart, as in some Hindu and Muslim societies.

in relation with copulating with
There is no suggestion of consanguinity:
> ...she must have been in relation with both [O'Shea and Parnell]. (Kee, 1993—she was married to one and having children by the other)

in season able to conceive
Standard English of mammals other than humans, for whom the use is a vulgarism.
In rut, the state of excitement of a stag during the mating season, is also vulgarly used of human copulation.

in the altogether naked
Either a shortened form of *altogether without clothes* or from the way we were born, *altogether in sin*. (*John* 9:14) The artist and writer Gerald du Maurier was offered $10,000 by a man from Chicago for a drawing of Trilby *in the altogether*. Also as in *in the raw*, *in your nip*, or *in the skin*. See also BUFF (THE).

in the arms of Jesus dead
Or some other agreeable heavenly embrace.
In the arms of Morpheus means asleep and thought to be dreaming, as his father Hypnos, was the god of sleep.

in the bag[1] taken as a prisoner of war
Sporting imagery, referring to what the hunter shoots and carries away.

in the bag[2] *American* drunk
Like a hunted animal which has no hope of escape.

in the barrel *American* about to be dismissed from employment
Or *fired*, which makes it twice removed from the standard English *discharged*.

in the box *American* copulating
Of a male, from the slang *box*, the vagina.
For the Victorians a *good man in the box* was not an attentive lover but a rousing preacher, that *box* being the pulpit.

in the cart in serious difficulty
An adult male, who was not ill or wounded, would only find himself riding *in the cart* on his way to the scaffold. Apart from degrading the victim (only women and children rode in carts), it was common for the noose to be fixed around his neck and then for the cart to be driven off, leaving him hanging.

in the churchyard dead
And buried.

in the club pregnant
A shortened form of *in the plum(p) pudding club*. Whence to *join the club*, to become pregnant.

in the departure lounge about to be dismissed from employment
The take-off in this case is involuntary:
> Any suggestion that [Stuart Proffitt] was in the departure lounge for reasons of moral or intellectual integrity was simply window-dressing. (*Sunday Telegraph*, 1 March 1998—Proffitt was an editor who had refused to accept a compromise intended to protect his employer's commercial interests in China)

in the family way pregnant
Probably an alteration of *in the way of having a family*, although the phrase is only used of the mother, with a suggestion usually that the pregnancy was unplanned. Also formerly as *in the increasing way* or *in that way*:
> Both James's Anna and Edward's Elizabeth were already 'in the increasing way' as Eliza put it. (Tomalin, 1997, quoting from a letter of Jane Austen dated 5 January 1801)
> Mrs Clement too is in that way again. I am quite tired of so many children. (ibid.—letter dated 13 March 1817)

in the glue in personal difficulty
Unable to move freely.
There are many other figurative expressions meaning the same thing, some vulgarisms, of which *in the nightsoil* is one of the less offensive.

in the hay copulating
Literally, in bed, from the days when a palliasse was filled with hay or straw.
Also as *in the sack*, from a slang word for bed, or *in the saddle*, of a male, with the usual riding imagery.

in the rats suffering from delirium tremens
Army usage. Pink elephants, snakes, and rats are the reputed visitors in the delusions of those so afflicted.

in the red owing or losing money
A survival from the days when bankers and others used red ink for debit balances and black for credits.
In the black is still used to indicate solvency or profitability.

in the ring engaged professionally in cheating at auction

Now used of fraudulent dealers who abstain from bidding against each other at a public auction and hold a private auction later among themselves. The use was formerly of those in a cartel of manufacturers, agreeing minimum prices. In the 19th century the term was used for stealing.

in the soil dead

Usually of those interred.

in the tank *American* drunk

The *drink tank*, or cell, is where inebriates are placed to sober up.

in the trade earning a living from prostitution

Normally of a prostitute but also of a bawd or pimp.

In trade was a derogatory reference by those who thought themselves socially superior to anyone who manufactured or distributed goods, a usage not confined to Britain, as V. S. Naipaul discovered in the Southern States of America in 1989.

in trouble[1] pregnant

A common use where the pregnancy is unintended and the female is unmarried.

in trouble[2] detected by the police in criminal activity

A shortened form of *in trouble with the police* or *with the courts*. Usually only describing the period between detection and sentencing.

in years *obsolete* old

Literally, more than one year old:
[My old friend the widow] was in years and but poor. (Defoe, 1719)
Stricken in years survives in modern speech.

in your cups drunk

You need only one cup, if it is large enough, or refilled sufficiently often.
If you have taken a *cup too many* it means you are drunk.

inamorata a mistress

From the Italian *innamorata*, literally no more than a female with whom someone is in love. *Inamorato* is the male equivalent, although rarer.

incapable *British* very drunk

The legal offence *drunk and incapable* applies to a drunkard who has lost physical control.
The law accused a rowdy or violent drunkard of being *drunk and disorderly*.

incentive a bribe

Literally, a stimulus or reward for extra effort. Thus a drug company may offer an *incentive* to those who specify its products which takes the form of a holiday in an exotic location, described as a conference.
Incentive travel is the provision by an airline of free trips to employees who have previously travelled in their aircraft expensively on business when their employer was paying.

incident a war

Literally, a single occurrence, as a *border incident*, where opponents may loose off a few shots at each other. Many *incidents* have no fixed duration:
... the China 'incident', the cruel war which now had been raging for four years against the Kuomintang government. (Keegan, 1989)

inclusive language changing the former literary convention that the use of the male gender may also imply the female

The purist may find the constant repetition of 'he or she', 'him or her', and 'his or hers' more intrusive than inclusive.

income protection arranging your affairs to avoid tax

Although legal, the practice is looked upon with disfavour by those not in a position to do it themselves.

income support *British* money paid by the state to poorer people

One of a sequence of phrases meant to mask any suggestion of charity in such payments.

inconstancy promiscuity

Used of those with regular sexual partners:
Inconstancy was so much the rule among the British residents in Cairo, the place, she thought, was a bureau of sexual exchange. (Manning, 1978)

incontinent[1] promiscuous

Literally, lacking self-restraint, and the opposite of *continent*, copulating only with your regular partner.
Obedience to the marriage vows is *continence* or *continency*:
In her chamber, making a sermon of continency to her. (Shakespeare, *The Taming of the Shrew*)

incontinent[2] urinating or defecating involuntarily

From the literal meaning, without interval, and again the opposite of *continent*.
Incontinency is the state of being so affected.

incontinent ordnance bombs or shells which miss the target

As indeed most of them do in warfare. The

error is ascribed to the inanimate object rather than to human fallibility.

inconvenienced *mainly American* with permanently impaired faculties
As in *The National Inconvenienced Sportsmen's League* (quoted in Rawson, 1981). The deaf may be described as *aurally inconvenienced*, the blind as *visually inconvenienced*, and so on.

incurable bone-ache *obsolete* syphilis
Not rheumatism or arthritis. Until Fleming's discovery of penicillin, the condition might be arrested but not cured, and mental institutions had many patients suffering from neurosyphilis, or general paralysis of the insane:
> Now the rotten diseases of the
> south . . . incurable bone-ache.
> (Shakespeare, *Troilus and Cressida*)

incursion an unprovoked attack
Literally, a running into, but long used in the military sense:
> The White House describing the invasion
> (or, as it preferred, 'incursion') of
> Granada . . . (McCrum et al., 1986)

indecency an illegal sexual act
Literally, unseemliness of any kind. Males usually *commit indecency* or an *indecent assault* or *offence* against females, except when a female copulates with a boy under the age of sixteen.
Indecent exposure is the display of the penis to strangers in public. See also GROSS INDECENCY.

indescribables *obsolete* trousers
From the vintage years of 19th-century prudery. Also as *inexpressibles* and see also UN-MENTIONABLES[1].

Indian hemp cannabis
A lot of hemp comes out of India other than *Cannabis sativa indica*, the source of marijuana.

indigenous having remote ancestors from the territory where you live
Literally, native, a word which has unacceptable colonial connotations:
> Americans should celebrate 'Columbus
> Day' as *Indigenous People's Day*. (Seitz, 1998)

indiscretion a child born out of wedlock
Literally, an act taken irresponsibly. The mother is supposed to have been indiscreet rather than the father, in the days when these things mattered.
Indiscretions are not siblings so generated but repeated acts of adultery, usually by the husband.

indisposed[1] menstruating

Literally, unwell and used by women of themselves.

indisposed[2] having a hangover
Again from feeling unwell:
> When a rich man gets drunk, he is
> indisposed. (Sanders, 1977)

individual behavior adjustment unit
American a cell for solitary confinement
Circumlocution combined with evasion. It could refer to anything from a dose of medicine to a turnstile.

inducement a bribe
Literally, something which persuades or influences another. The first man to be killed in 1823 in a railway accident, William Huskisson, was so popular that he had been elected to parliament 'without any of the usual inducements', according to *Fraser's Magazine*. (Garfield, 2002)

indulge to drink intoxicants
Literally, to humour or gratify. The term is often used by those who say they *don't* or *won't* *indulge*.
An *indulgence flight* is one made by a private aircraft, often on governmental business or to take a minister and his family on vacation, where the intoxicants are liberally provided to all those aboard, except the pilots.

industrial action *British* a strike
Now standard English for industrial inaction. The plural is not used even when there is more than one strike:
> Khadiq's flight was delayed, successively by
> industrial actions involving luggage
> handlers at Heathrow and air controllers in
> France. (M. Thomas, 1980—the American
> author was misusing British English with
> 'actions' as well as writing 'luggage' for
> 'baggage')

industrializing country a poor and relatively undeveloped state
A coinage based on aspiration rather than reality:
> The term 'developing nations' was to be
> superseded by 'industrialising country'.
> (*Daily Telegraph*, 12 May 1993, quoting a
> directive issued by Leeds Metropolitan
> University)

infamy *obsolete* prostitution
Literally, notoriety:
> Girls sold to infamy. London as centre of
> hideous traffic. (*News of the World* headline,
> quoted in Paxman, 1998)

infantry low-grade prostitutes

Soliciting on foot, unlike the more fortunate CAVALRY.

infidelity adultery
Literally, an absence of faith, whence any dishonest act.
Infidelities imply a consistent pattern of such conduct with different partners.

informal acting illegally or without required permission
Literally, casual or easy-going, which is not one of the properties of a receiver of stolen property, or *informal dealer*.
A British *informal market* is a gathering which is allowed to function in a street or elsewhere despite the lack of an official licence.

information lies, or a selection or suppression of the truth
As provided by the British *Ministry of Information* in the Second World War. Its function has now been taken over by the *Information Research Unit* of the Foreign Office and by ministerial press officers.
Disinformation is the publication of rumours or lies intended to confuse or deceive.

informer a private individual who reports the activity of another surreptitiously to authority
Dr Johnson gives 'One who discovers offenders to the magistrate', but the word is now used mainly of police spies.

initiation the first act of copulation
In standard usage, becoming a member of a club etc., usually with due ceremony. It may be used of either sex. *Initiation into womanhood* is specific.

initiative a reaction to a crisis or blunder
Literally, the first move and the word is used of action initiated by an individual and thus of any proposal to introduce a new policy.
Attempts by successive British governments to suspend the laws of supply and demand by determining wages and prices were labelled *initiatives*.
In America, certain states allow citizens to suggest legislation through *initiatives*.

inner city slum
Used to describe the derelict housing, abandoned shops, etc. which remain when those who can afford to have escaped to the suburbs to avoid noise, smells, and mugging.

innocence virginity
Not having incurred the guilt with which St Paul has surrounded sexual activity:
  The desire to dispense with innocence is said to have become even more desperate

later as the Red Army approached Berlin. (Beevor, 2002)

inoperative untrue
Literally, invalid or not functioning:
  ... the press office that had been damaged by being forced many times to retract earlier statements about Watergate as 'inoperative'. (Colodny & Gettlin, 1991)

Inquiry and Control Section the agency for persecuting Jews
Perhaps the most despicable organization of Vichy France:
  Inside were long trestle tables manned by gendarmes under the supervision of the Inquiry and Control Section, formerly the Police for Jewish Affairs. (Faulks, 1998)

inquisition torture
It would be tempting providence to say that the usage is obsolete. When the 16th-century Spaniards captured heretics, the activity of the men of God went far beyond questioning.

insatiable having a wish for frequent copulation
Literally, not capable of satisfaction in any particular respect. Used of either sex, within or outside marriage.

inseparable forming an exclusive sexual relationship with
Not Siamese twins nor even cohabiting:
  It had long been noticed that Lizzy and Furnivall had been, as Benzie discreetly puts it, 'inseparable' long before they were married. (J. Green, 1996—Furnivall was a 19th-century libertine and philologist without whom the *OED* might not have been produced)

inside in prison
Mainly criminal use. Their associates still at liberty may remain *on the outside* or *on the out*.

inside track an unfair or illegal advantage
19th-century oval racetracks were operated without staggered starts, giving the animal on the inside less far to run than the competition. Now used of unfair promotion, the giving of advance information, and the like.

insider a person using confidential information for private advantage
In standard usage, any person with such knowledge or information, usually of a financial deal, whether or not the confidentiality is abused.
Whence the criminal offence of *insider dealing*.

institutionalize to confine (a person) involuntarily
Especially the mentally ill.

instrument the penis
Viewed sexually and with common imagery:
> I can make my instrument stand whenever
> I please. (F. Harris, 1925, quoting
> Maupassant)

insult to make an unwelcome sexual approach to a female
For the Victorians such as Fitzjames Stephen, an *insult worse than death*.
In modern China, the crime of a foreigner who seeks to make sexual contact with a Chinese woman.

insurance extortion
What criminals may demand from shop-keepers to avoid using the word PROTECTION.

intact still a virgin
Literally, untouched or unimpaired. This specific use may come from the legal jargon for a female virgin, *virgo intacta*.

integrated casting giving black actors roles traditionally taken by white actors
The object is to provide greater opportunities for non-white actors to perform regardless of historical authenticity:
> Referring to cases where blacks have
> undertaken major Shakespearean roles
> hitherto regarded as white...Mr Brown
> said 'This is a victory for integrated
> casting'. (*Daily Telegraph*, 12 August 1996)

intelligence spying
The ability to comprehend has been thus debased since the 16th century.

intemperance regular drunkenness
The converse of *temperance*, moderation, although in an establishment which styles itself a *Temperance Hotel*, alcohol is unavailable.

intentions whether marriage is proposed
In the olden days, when husbands were expected to keep their wives in the manner to which they were accustomed and the rituals of courtship were meant to be observed, a girl's father might, if so minded, ask her suitor what his *intentions* were. To the modern parent, they are usually self-evident.

intercourse copulation
Literally, any verbal or other exchange between people, which is why we should think no ill of Sir Thomas More, nor question his canonization:
> For justifying himself he wrote a full
> account of the intercourse he had with the
> Nun and her complices. (Burnet, 1714)
By the late 18th century *sensual intercourse* meant copulation:

> The conversation today, I know not how,
> turned...upon sensual intercourse
> between the sexes, the delight of which [Dr
> Johnson] ascribed chiefly to the
> imagination. (J. Boswell, 1791)
and *irregular intercourse* was not the spasmodic coupling of spouses but extramarital copulation:
> So then Sir, you would allow of no irregular
> intercourse whatever between the sexes?
> (ibid.—Dr Johnson had been condemning
> the 'licensed stews of Rome')
Now standard English as a shortened form of *sexual intercourse*.

interesting condition see CONDITION[2]

interfere with to assault sexually
Journalistic and forensic jargon for illegal male sexual acts against boys and females:
> They are quite alive and nobody has
> interfered with them, not yet. (N. Mitford,
> 1960, writing about boys who had
> absconded from boarding school)

interim without the security or benefits of full-time employment
Literally, temporary, but some employees, in management positions especially, are so described and engaged, in many cases to facilitate dismissal if the need should arise.

intermission a period of television advertisements
Literally, a temporary cessation which, on some channels, seems more like constant interruption.

internal affairs *American* the investigation by policemen of allegations against the police
Most police forces are reluctant to wash their dirty linen in public, or at all, and complaints against them, sometimes malicious, are the subject of taboo.
The Soviet Russian *Ministry for Internal Affairs* controlled the fearsome MVD, or SECRET (STATE) POLICE.

internal security the repression of dissidents
Its function in a tyranny is to protect the rulers against the ruled.

interpret pragmatically to ignore
The language of politicians, especially in jurisdictions where *tolérance* allows flexibility:
> France, too, now has an ambitious finance
> minister, Nicolas Sarkozy, who says the
> [Growth and Stability] pact should be
> interpreted pragmatically. (*Daily Telegraph*,
> 13 April 2004)

interrogation with prejudice torture

A tactic of the Soviet KGB which used *prejudice* in the same way as the American CIA, as in *terminate with extreme prejudice*, to kill.

intervention¹ a military invasion
Literally, placing yourself between two other parties. The Russian invasion of Afghanistan was so described by Moscow and the BBC. Also used of the Anglo/American invasion of Iraq:
> It is most unlikely that the commander of a Western intervention force [in Iraq] would undertake street battles. (*Daily Telegraph*, 18 March 2003)

intervention² a surgical operation
Also as *medical intervention*:
> The decrepitude of our old age will be attended by ever more expensive NHS interventions. (*Daily Telegraph*, 1 December 2005)

intimacy copulation
Literally, close familiarity. Used more of extramarital copulation than of that within marriage.
An *intimate* is a mistress:
> Edward VII had introduced the resort to golf; a local intimate of his, a dressmaker, had only recently died. (Whicker, 1982—the resort was Carlsbad)
So too as an adjective:
> You also need a bath and a change. Especially if you propose to be intimate with anyone other than myself. (Bradbury, 1975)

intimate sexually taboo
As *intimate part(s)*, the genitalia, or the breasts of a woman, and *intimate person*, the penis.

intrigue a clandestine sexual relationship
In this sense, an *intrigue* is a plot, whence something done surreptitiously. Usually in the plural:
> ...only stipulating for the preservation of secrecy in their intrigues. (Mayhew, 1862)

introduce yourself to a bed to copulate with (someone)
On a single occasion perhaps:
> Jupiter, who was enamoured of her, introduced himself to her bed by changing himself into a shower of gold. (Norfolk, 1991—gold still seems to facilitate this kind of introduction)

introducer's fee a bribe
Literally, a sum paid to a third party who brings the principals together.

introducing house *obsolete* a brothel
Prostitutes frequented it by day.

See also HOUSE¹.

intruder an armed invader
More sinister than merely turning up without an invitation:
> ...so many intruders from across the Pakistan border were killed. (Naipaul, 1990)

invalid coach *American* a hearse
An invalid description.

inventory adjustment a loss caused from prior overvaluation of goods
Usually arising from a failure to write down slow-moving, damaged, or unsaleable stocks and not providing for pilferage. Also as *inventory correction*.

inventory leakage stealing
Not an imperfectly corked bottle in the stores. Trade jargon for routine pilfering by staff and customers.

invert a male homosexual
Figuratively, turned upside down, as seen from a heterosexual's point of view.
Whence *inverted*, homosexual and *inversion*, homosexuality.

investment in prices price reductions
The language was intended, we must assume, not to upset shareholders when used in January 2003 by the Managing Director of Boots, the pharmacist being faced for the first time with competition from supermarkets in the sale of prescription drugs.

investor a gambler
A usage by promoters of football pools and other lotteries to delude subscribers into believing that they are not wasting their money.

invigorating cold
Describing water for swimming, weather for walking, etc. Those who say your participation in the activity to which they are themselves committed would be *invigorating* want you to suffer with them.

inviolate *obsolete* virginal
Literally, free from damage or disturbance but to *violate* a woman has long been standard English for rape:
> ...the young lady's person was inviolate but was it human nature to remain proof against another such fiery trial?
> (Dalrymple, 2002, quoting a letter written in 1799—the 'fiery trial' was nothing more testing than a night-time tryst)

involuntary conversion *American* an aircraft crash

You *convert* an operational aircraft to scrap. True as far as it goes, which is not far enough.

involuntary separation dismissal from employment
In 2002 an American corporation which had reduced its employees by 35,000 in the previous year acknowledged that many had been victims of an 'involuntary separation program'.

involved actively and uncritically committed to an extreme policy
Literally, complex, although those so described are often simple and unthinking. *Involvement* is such devotion to extremism.

involved with enjoying a sexual relationship with
Usually not of a transitory nature but:
    Khan cites the case of one off-duty flight attendant who became 'involved' with two passengers and a crewman on a single flight. (*Daily Telegraph*, 18 April 1995—she had copulated with all three)

Irish illogical or defective
The prefix appears in many offensive and sometimes euphemistic expressions dating from the time when Irish people were deemed to be backward in both Old and New England.

Irish beauty a person with two black eyes
Not necessarily a battered wife.

Irish confetti *American* bricks
Many building workers were Irish and they had a reputation for violence, bricks being handy missiles.

Irish evidence a perjurer
Either because Irish Catholics, forced to swear on a Protestant bible, felt no compunction to tell the truth, or from the denigration of all things Irish by the English:
    The publick shall be acquainted with this, to judge whether you are not fitter to be an Irish Evidence, than to be an Irish peer. (J. Boswell, 1791, quoting a letter from Richard Savage to Lord Tyrconnel)

Irish fever (the) typhus
The disease was endemic in 19th-century Dublin slums, many of which, prior to the forced Union in 1801 with England, Scotland, and Wales, had been town houses of an elegant capital.

Irish hoist *American* a kick in the pants
The way New Englanders treated an Irishman who ignored the warning NINA (the indication on situations vacant notices that No Irish Need Apply).

Irish horse *British* an inedible gobbet of meat
The navy called beef *salt horse*, reserving Irishness for the fat and gristle.

Irish hurricane *British* a calm sea
Another naval usage.

Irish local *American* a wheelbarrow
Because many labourers were Irish and a *local* train moved slowly. Also as an *Irish buggy*.

Irish pennant *American* a loose end
In both the literal and the figurative senses.

Irish promotion a reduction in wages
For doing the same or a similar job.

Irish thing (the) alcoholism
An offensive usage except perhaps when used by an Irish writer:
    Ya father? Well, ya know, he's got the problem, the Irish thing. (McCourt, 1997—father was an habitual drunkard)

Irish toothache[1] being pregnant
Adverting to the supposed confusion of the Irish in English eyes, and the dental troubles of undernourished pregnant women.

Irish toothache[2] an erection of the penis
Although this condition is not unconnected with pregnancy, the connection appears tenuous.

Irish vacation *American* a term in prison
Alluding to the supposed lawlessness of 19th-century Irish immigrants into America, or to a tendency of the authorities to pick on them, or to the preponderance of Irishmen among the jailers.

Irish wedding the emptying of a cesspit
Possibly because people vomited after becoming drunk on what tended to be a riotous and protracted occasion. To have *danced at an Irish wedding* was to have two black eyes.

Irishman's rise a decrease in pay
For doing the same job.

iron[1] a handgun
The metal is inexactly specified.
A *steel* was always a sword or bayonet.

iron[2] a male homosexual
Rhyming slang on *iron hoof*, a POUFF.

iron out to kill
Not from IRON[1] but from the flattening of the victim. Occasionally as *iron off*.

irregular acting in a way which breaks taboos
For Dr Johnson *irregular conduct* was extramarital copulation, to which he 'was very careful not to give encouragement' (J. Boswell, 1791). A sexual relationship between a Roman Catholic priest and his mistress is known by the church as an *irregular situation*.
Irregularities in a person's private life usually refer to promiscuity.
Irregularity can refer to dishonesty or fraud, in individuals or accounts, but is not euphemistic when used in connection with constipation or the menstrual cycle.

irreversible coma death
Used of political leaders such as Franco and Sharon, kept alive by assiduous doctors when ordinary mortals would have been allowed to die.

issue *obsolete* semen
The language of King James's version of the Bible when dealing with 'paramours whose...issue *is like* the issue of horses.' (*Ezekiel* 23:20)

it anything the subject of a taboo
In the 1930s (and the works of Agatha Christie) the sexual attraction of females for males.

Also, depending on the context, copulation, the penis, or the vagina.

Italian vice (the) *obsolete* sodomy
It had to be the practice of one of those depraved foreigners, even in the 18th century.

itch to feel lustful
Usually of a woman, from the supposed aphrodisiac properties of cantharides which, by exciting vaginal itch, is said to stimulate sexual desire:
> A tailor might scratch her where'er she did itch. (Shakespeare, *The Tempest*, with another of his obscure sexual puns)
Less often of men in the same sense.
Itchy feet is the propensity to leave a regular sexual partner for another, as with the SEVEN-YEAR ITCH.

item a continuing sexual partnership between two people outside marriage
Perhaps merely from an *item* of news or gossip.

itinerant *Irish* a gypsy
Even when parked up.

J

jab an act of copulation
From the thrusting. To *jab a vein* is to inject a narcotic illegally.

jack[1] the penis
One of the male names often used. Whence *Jack in the orchard*, copulation, and *jack off*, to masturbate

jack[2] *American* a policeman
The JOHN[2] in familiar speech—many *Johns* are *Jack* for short.

jack it in to die
Literally, to give up an attempt or enterprise.

jack of both sides *obsolete* a male homosexual
Literally, someone who is willing to give his support to either of two opposing sides.

jacket *American* a criminal record
The cover in which the papers are kept:
    ... you don't think people like that have jackets, do you? (Sanders, 1985—referring to people in the learned professions)

jag house *American* a brothel
A *jag* was a load, and used to denote drunkenness just as LOAD[1] does today, and to have a *jag on* was to be drunk. From being an inn, the *jag house* became a brothel and is now used of one which caters for male homosexuals.

jagged *American* drunk
From the roughness rather than the *jag*, or load.

jail bait *American* a sexually mature female below the legal age of copulation
Bait is used of any young person who may attract an older one sexually, and especially of boys attractive to homosexual men. Illegal copulation with a young girl carries a risk of imprisonment.

jakes a lavatory
Just as you visit the JOHN[1] in modern America, so in the past you visited *Jake's place*. Dr Johnson's examples are from Shakespeare, Swift, and Dryden are all lavatorial, although he defines the word as 'a house of office', using another euphemism.
Wits in the 18th and 19th centuries used *Ajax*, punning on the King of Salamis. In modern Irish English, it has been corrupted to *jacks*.

jam rag an absorbent worn during menstruation
Not from the vulgarism *jam*, to copulate, but from the staining.

jane[1] *obsolete* a prostitute
Rhyming slang for *Jane Shore*, a whore, the mistress of King Edward IV.

jane[2] a lavatory
A feminine, or feminist, JOHN[1], although it is not noted in *A Feminist Dictionary* (1985).

jar a drink of an intoxicant
Usually beer, from the container in which it may come.
If you are said to *enjoy a jar*, the implication is that you are a drunkard.

jasper *American* a female homosexual
A variant of JOHN[2] with possible punning on the meaning 'segregated'.

jawbone *American* credit
You talk the seller into parting with the goods without paying for them. Usually in the phrase *on jawbone*.

jerk *American* to fail a pupil
Tugging them out of the class.

jerk off to masturbate
Of a male, and a common vulgarism. Figuratively used as an insult, and also shortened to *jerk* when used in that sense.
In addict slang, to *jerk off* is to inject narcotics slowly.

jerry a pot for urine
Dr Wright says it is a shortened form of 'Jeremiah, a chamber utensil' (*EDD*). There may have been some allusion to the *Jericho*, a lavatory, which was one of the unlikely places to which people said they were going. The German soldier, or *Jerry*, wore a helmet of much the same shape but that is probably only a shortened form of *German*.

jet lag a hangover
In standard use, disruption of the biological clock through time change. On long flights some people drink too much alcohol, but are reluctant to admit that as the cause of their later being off-colour.

jewels the male genitalia
American rather than British use, from their pendulous proclivity.
Also as *crown jewels* or *family jewels*.

Jewish question the killing of all Jews
Mass murder was the answer to the *question* which the Nazis formulated in those parts of

Europe under their control, especially in the later stages of the Second World War:

> Wisliceny had barely returned to Bratislava from Salonika when on 20 September he and three other SD 'specialists in the Jewish question' were transferred to Athens to set up a department for Jewish affairs under Blume. (Mazower, 1993—the Italians, who had controlled the Athens area until September 1943, had refused to implement anti-Jewish policies there)

Jezebel a prostitute

She was the flighty wife of Ahab in the Old Testament.

Until quite recent times, a young woman might be termed a *Jezebel* if she wore make-up on the streets. The epithet was also favoured by the vituperative preacher, John Knox.

jig-a-jig copulation

From the movement involved and in variants such as *jig-jig, jiggy-jig,* and *jig.* The words may be heard when spoken by a pimp or prostitute in the Far East rather than elsewhere.

jiggle (of a male) to masturbate

Literally, to move back and forth:

> 'Nothing of the sort, he lay there jiggling like.' (I guessed what she meant ... frigging himself.) (F. Harris, 1925, writing of Carlyle's behaviour on his wedding night—evidently Mrs Carlyle had more to put up with than the celebrated cup of tea thrown at her by her husband, or less)

Jim Crow *American* the unfair treatment of black people by whites

In early usage, any poor man, from the character in a song in the Negro minstrel show written by Tom Price (1808–60):

> It was my first experience with Jim Crow. I was just five, and I had never ridden in a street car before. (Armstrong, 1955, writing about segregation on public transport in New Orleans)

jimmy an act of urination

Male usage, punning on *Jimmy Riddle,* which may also mean wine. *Jimmy Britts,* less often known as *Edgar Britts,* is diarrhoea, again from rhyming slang.

job an act that is the subject of taboo

In nursery use, used of defecating, and also as BIG JOBS; referring to copulation, a participant is said to be ON THE JOB; of robbery, as in the film title *The Italian Job;* etc.

job action *American* striking or failing to perform an allotted task

The *job inaction* is the equivalent of the equally deceptive British INDUSTRIAL ACTION:

> The pilots' job action in February cost American \$225 million and affected hundreds of thousands of travelers. (*New York Herald Tribune,* 10 August 1999)

job turning *American* reducing the responsibility and pay associated with an appointment

The procedure is adopted by an organization when, to fill a QUOTA or to avoid being sued for DISCRIMINATION, it is obliged to appoint to a situation someone whom it thinks to be of inferior qualifications, ability, or experience.

jock the penis

A vulgarism when used on its own but almost standard English in the description of the genital support garment called a *jock-strap. Jock rash* is a fungal infection of the male genital area.

A *jocker* is a male profligate.

joe a ponce

Rhyming slang on *Joe Ronce,* whose origins and achievements do not seem to have been recorded for posterity.

In the world of espionage fiction, a *Joe* is one of the spies on your side.

john¹ a lavatory

The *cousin John* people said they had to visit as they absented themselves from company.

(I once worked for a manufacturer of casements in Cardiff called 'Jonwindows'. Happily our range was more extensive than the title might have suggested.)

john² a man in a taboo occupation or situation

In America, a woman's unmarried sexual partner, a potential customer for a prostitute, or a policeman.

In homosexual slang, the partner playing the male role, the couple in former times being titled *John and Joan.*

John Barleycorn whisky

The allusion is to its raw material:

> Leeze on thee, John Barleycorn,
> Thou King o' grain. (Burns, 1786)

John Thomas the penis

The commonest given masculine name and without any sexual implications. Less often as *John Peter, John Willie, JP, JT,* or, in America, *Johnson.*

Johnnie's out of jail *American* your trouser zip is undone

The prisoner has not in fact escaped.

johnny a contraceptive sheath

From FRENCH LETTER via *frenchie* and *Johnny Frenchman*.
Also as *Johnnie*.

join¹ *obsolete* to copulate
Of the same tendency as the common COUPLE.

join² to be as dead as
The imagery is of a coming together again in some physical or spiritual existence rather than in the grave. Thus you may *join* your deceased spouse or a variety of others.
If you *join the (great) majority*, you are not just voting for a plausible politician.

joiner a person who seeks popularity or business through insincere involvement with social clubs
Not to be confused with the skilled carpenter. Often in the pejorative phrase *greeter and joiner*.

joint¹ a marijuana cigarette
The derivation is from what was formerly the equipment of an opium user rather than the place in which the smoking may be done.

joint² *American* the penis
With the common MEAT² imagery.
See also UNLIMBER YOUR JOINT.

joint³ *Irish* to incapacitate by shooting
Another type of butchery:
> According to Belfast's grisly argot, he was 'jointed'—shot through both elbows, both knees, and both ankles. (*Sunday Telegraph*, January 1990, reporting on a victim of the IRA)

jolly¹ drunk
An old variant of MERRY.

jolly² an unnecessary treat paid for by a third party
A business use by those attending and by those not asked to attend, but seldom by those who organize and pay for it.

jolt (a) anything taboo which gives you a shock or impetus
For illegal narcotics users, an injection of heroin; for criminals, a time in prison; for drinkers, any intoxicant, but usually whisky.

Jordan *obsolete* a pot for urine
Dr Johnson thought it might have come from the Greek while Onions (1975) favoured a river source:
> They will allow us ne'er a jordan and then we leak in the chimney. (Shakespeare, *1 Henry IV*)

Certainly, if in Edinburgh you heard from above the cry *jordeloo*, you were well advised to avoid the area into which the malodorous liquids were being thrown. *Gardeloo*, *gardez l'eau*, was unpleasant enough, by all accounts.

joy¹ copulation
For male or female, as in *mutual joy(s)*.
Whence the punning *joy ride*, a single act of copulation; *joy-girl* or *joy-boy*, a prostitute; and *joy-house*, a brothel.

joy² heroin
The sensation illegal users seek.
Joy is also used attributively in many compounds, such as *joy popper*, an occasional user; *joy powder*, morphine; *joy flakes*, cocaine; *joy ride*, being under narcotic influence; *joy rider*, a person taking drugs; *joy smoke*, marijuana; *joy stick*, an opium.

joyride to take and drive away a motor vehicle without consent
Under the English Larceny Act, codifying the common law, the offender committed no crime, apart from a possible theft of fuel, because there was no intention 'permanently to deprive the owner thereof'. *Joyriding* is now an offence in its own right.

Judy a prostitute
The derivation is either from the common girls' name which became a name for common girls or, more probably, from *Judith*, the beautiful Jewess who is said to have tricked Nebuchadnezzar's general Holofernes in order to save the town of Bethulia. The general lost his head to her and to the axe.
Then a *Judy* became a mistress.
And now, in Ireland at least, she is an attractive young woman:
> Some great lookin' judies. (Doyle, 1987—the advantages of a public house were being discussed)

jug¹ a prison
From the Scottish *joug*, a pillory rather than the ewer. To *jug* is to imprison.

jug² an intoxicant
Referring to the container:
> I had a way of puttin' in my time with a private jug, on the sly. (Twain, 1884)

jugs a woman's breasts
Probably from their shape and the purpose of producing and holding milk.
Grose tells us that a *double jug* was a man's backside.

juice¹ (the) intoxicants
The common modern use probably came from the literal meaning, liquid of fruit, rather than from the Scottish *juice of the bear*,

whisky. *Juniper juice* was gin but the *juice* can be any spirits.

And as a verb:

> ... would gather after a long day in the IO shop to juice a little. (Herr, 1977—in fact they gathered in the IO shop after a long day elsewhere)

Whence *juiced*, drunk; *juice head*, a drunkard; and *juice joint*, a bar.

juice² *American* a payment made or demanded illegally

What comes in if you squeeze¹:

> The bookie was a big operator and sent his juice money directly to City Hall.
> (Weverka, 1973—I suspect he sent it direct to City Hall, without an intermediary, but not necessarily promptly)

Whence the *juice dealer*, or loan shark, who uses for collection a hoodlum called a *juice man*.

juiced up lustful

Of a female, from the increased sexual secretion. Whence *juicy*, experiencing such arousal and the vulgarism *juicy Lucy*, for a promiscuous woman.

jump¹ to rob

From the pouncing. An English 19th-century use since revived in America:

> Instead of 'jumping' those stores for an average of forty dollars...(Lavine, 1930)

jump² a single act of copulation

Normally a male usage, but he does not literally have to leap on his partner.

To *jump* is to copulate and a *junior jumper* is a youthful rapist.

jump³ to leave in a forbidden or illegal way

Thus to *jump ship* is to stay ashore wrongly, of a sailor, although it may be used of other desertion.

A prisoner not on remand may, if he absconds, *jump bail*; and if you leave somewhere such as a restaurant without paying your bill in America you may be said to *jump a check.*

jump the broomstick to live together as a couple without marrying

This symbolic leap replaced the wedding ceremony.

Whence the *broomstick match*, or common-law marriage.

You might also have been said to *jump the besom.*

jump the last hurdle to die

With steeplechasing in mind.

junk illegal narcotics

Originally, old rope, whence hemp and so to narcotics generally.

A *junkie* is an addict who may be said to have *gone junkyard* and becomes *junked up.*

A *junker* in this milieu is not a Prussian aristocrat but a pedlar of narcotics, or *junkman.*

junket an unnecessary treat provided free by another

Literally, a dessert of flavoured milk curdled by rennet. Now describing an occasion where the provider seeks to obtain a business advantage without overt bribery.

just good friends see FRIEND

justify *obsolete Scottish* to kill by order of a court

It meant to bring to justice, whence either to convict or acquit, which must have been the source of some confusion:

> Our great grand-uncle that was justified at Dumbarton. (W. Scott, 1817—we can only learn great grand-uncle's fate by reading on)

K

kangaroo a prison warder

Convict slang. However a *kangaroo club* is a clique within a jail of long-serving prisoners. A prison is also where someone who has offended the inmates' unofficial code of practice may be hauled before a *kangaroo court*, to be judged and punished by his fellows, whence any such ad hoc investigation and judgement made in an enclosed society such as a terrorist organization, a club, or a trade union.

keel over to die

The capsizing of a boat, or the figurative fall of a bird from its perch.

keelhauled *obsolete* drunk

It was Dutch practice to drag defaulters under the keel of a boat for punishment, and we still use *keelhauling* of a verbal reprimand. If you were very drunk, you might look and feel like the victim of a real *keelhauling*.

keep to maintain a mistress

The usage implies both provision for her upkeep and keeping her sexual activities for your sole use:

> One officer offered to keep me if I would come and live with him. (Mayhew, 1862)

The man was the *keeper* and the woman a *kept mistress*, *wench*, or *woman*:

> Virgins, reporters, housewives, kept wenches. (Longstreet, 1956—which was the oddity in that class?)

The relationship commences when the woman is *taken into keeping*:

> In France, as soon as a man of fashion marries, he takes an opera girl into keeping. (J. Boswell, 1791—there must have been few *men of fashion* or a plethora of artistes)

keep company with to have a sexual relationship with

Literally, to accompany whence, in standard English, to court.

See also COMPANY[1].

keep sheep by moonlight *obsolete* to be killed by hanging

You watch them from the gallows, as did those . . . that shepherded the moonlit sheep a hundred years ago. (Housman, 1896)

keep up with the Joneses to live beyond your means or extravagantly

The *Joneses* are your mythical neighbours who always seem able to afford the new curtains you have coveted or the garden tractor you have been collecting brochures about, and with whom you seek to compete.

keep your legs crossed not to be promiscuous

Of a female who may also be said to *keep her legs together*.

A male who *keeps his pants on* or *zipped* is her counterpart.

kerb-crawling looking for a prostitute

Done by a man who drives slowly in an area known to be frequented by prostitutes:

> [George Wigg] was now fulfilling that function in the Lords, where his self-righteous pomposity would continue until pricked by his arrest for kerb-crawling. (Heffer, 1998—the 'function' was toadying to the then Prime Minister, Harold Wilson)

Whence also to *crawl a kerb*.

Khyber the anus

Rhyming slang for *Khyber Pass*. Sometimes also in the vulgar riposte *up your Khyber*. Less often in full.

kick[1] to die

Probably from the involuntary spasm of a slaughtered animal. Usually as *kick in, it, off* or *up*.

The common *kick the bucket* is supposed by some to come from the *bucket*, or beam, to which a Norfolk pig was tied to facilitate the slitting of its throat and which it kicked in its death throes. It may as well have come from the practice of the victim or suicide standing on a bucket after being strung up to a beam, the bucket then being kicked away.

To *kick the wind* or the punning *kick your heels* was to be killed by hanging.

kick[2] **(the)** summary dismissal from employment

Usually affecting a single employee. The assault is figurative.

An employee *kicked into touch* is retired early or given a less responsible job, with sporting imagery.

kick over the traces to behave in an immoral or an unruly fashion

Like an unschooled horse:

> What about his missus? Does she ever kick over the traces? (Sanders, 1992—an enquiry was being made about her adultery)

kick the habit to cure yourself of an addiction

Usually of those who take narcotics but also of smoking tobacco or alcoholism.

kick the tyres to examine superficially
Business jargon, from the actions of inexpert
buyers of used cars:
> ...a simplistic agrarian vision which the
> war-weary nation had bought without
> kicking the tires. (M. Thomas, 1980)

kick upstairs *British* to deprive of power
or influence
Political jargon for making a politician who is
either a failure or a threat, a member of the
House of Lords. The phrase was first used in
June 1885 when Prime Minister Salisbury so
dealt with and politically emasculated his
House of Commons rival Northcote.

kickback a clandestine illegal payment
The derivation is from the vicious habits of
starting handles in the days before motors
had electric starters. Used of bribery, a share
in the proceeds, and commissions on the
proceeds of illegal activities.

kid an adult
A child since the 16th century, before which
it was only the young of a goat. Untypically
missed by Dr Johnson and his team. As with
MIDDLE-AGE, the usage seeks to minimize age:
> He was still a kid, no more than thirty,
> thirty-two. (M. Thomas, 1980)
In obsolete English to *kid* meant to impregnate or to give birth, of both women and
goats.

kill a snake *Australian* to urinate
Not the usual penis-as-serpent image, but
from going into the bush.

kind promiscuous
Of a female, who is more than friendly or
considerate to the opposite sex.
To *show kindness* to a man is to copulate with
him extramaritally.

kindness *obsolete* bribery
Another form of consideration:
> ...what hath passed between us of
> kindness to hold his tongue. (Pepys, 1668—
> he was worried that the person who had
> bribed him would talk about it)

King Lear *British* a male homosexual
Rhyming slang for QUEER[3], with perhaps an
allusion to the monarch's madness.

king over the water *obsolete British* a
Stuart pretender in exile
Possibly used of Charles II and James II during
their 17th-century absences from the throne,
and certainly much in vogue after the
Hanoverian kings took over after Queen Anne
died in 1714.
Stuart supporters would normally pass their

glass over a glass of water without venturing
verbal amplification. Loyalty to the Stuarts,
especially after 1715, also implied adherence
to Roman Catholicism, which in turn involved civil disabilities if not prosecution.

kingdom come death
Despite society's unsatisfactory experience
with theocracies, we do not demur at the
plea *Thy kingdom come* in the Lord's Prayer.

kinky displaying bizarre sexual tastes
A *kink* is a bend, as in a hosepipe. *Kinky* implies
a number of perverted deviations when
formerly it was applied only to male homosexuality.

kiss *obsolete* to copulate with
This dates to the era when kisses were only
exchanged within the family. If you got that
far with a third party, you might expect to
proceed much further. Whence the euphemistic definition by Dr Wright:
> Obs. To lie with a woman. (*EDD*)

kiss-and-tell the sale of personal memoirs of sexual exploits with a well-
known person
Usually the woman sells the story, doing the
telling (and the selling) when the *kissing* has
stopped, for which she receives *kiss money*:
> ...the television presenter Ulrika Jonsson
> kissed and told of her four-month
> relationship with her fellow Swede [who
> managed the England football team]. (*Daily
> Telegraph*, 22 July 2004)

kiss-off *American* a summary dismissal or
demotion
If a dismissal, those on the west coast will call
it a *New York kiss-off* while those in New
England call it a *Californian kiss-off*, which
shows that the practice of attributing nasty
habits to our rivals still flourishes.
In rare use, or pulp fiction, a *kiss-off* may be a
death. Less often it may refer to a demotion:
> Was Nairobi a sinecure for him? A kiss-off
> at the end of a distinguished career? (le
> Carré, 2001)

kiss St Giles' cup *obsolete* to be killed by
hanging
A victim was traditionally offered a cup of
water at St Giles-in-the-Fields on his last
journey from Newgate to Tyburn.

kiss the ground *obsolete* to die
Referring to the involuntary falling and not in
any way associated with the practice of
kissing the tarmac to express your pleasure
at arrival.

kissed by the maiden *obsolete Scottish* judicially killed

The *maiden* was a guillotine:

> [The Duke of Argyll] was taken to Edinburgh to be kissed by the *Maiden*. (Paterson, 1998—it happened in June 1685)

Kit has come *British* I am menstruating

Kit is a shortened form of Charles which makes this euphemism at a second remove from the common *Charlie's come*.

kitchen-sinking making excessive provision

From the cliché *everything bar the kitchen sink*. It is the practice of those taking control of a business which has been doing badly to ensure that none of the previous losses or managerial errors can be attributed to them.

kite to issue (a negotiable instrument that is not covered by the drawer)

A shortened form of *fly a kite*, an operation which involves launching an object without visible support.

A *kiteman* may still try to issue such paper, but with less success since electronic banking and computerization.

kitty *obsolete* a prison

Common in the northern counties of England in the 19th century.

Note the modern use when, in some communal activity involving expense, we each put something *in the kitty*.

knackers the testicles

A *knack* was a toy or small object, made by a *knacker*, whence a saddler, who bought old or dead beasts for their hides, whence his modern counterpart who disposes of dead cattle. The use may come from the meaning small objects but Dr Wright is persuasive when he gives:

> Two flat pieces of wood or bone... Of unequal length. (*EDD*)

Partridge suggests 'Prob. ex dial knacker, a castanet or other "striker"' (*DSUE*) and the imagery from the small Spanish chestnut is attractive, although unconvincing.

Those who, in their exhaustion, claim to be *knackered* are likely to consider themselves candidates for the *knacker's yard* rather than winded by a blow to the testicles.

knee-trembler a person who copulates while standing up

From the required movement.

kneecap *Irish* to maim by shooting in the knees

A form of punishment used by the IRA in Northern Ireland.

knees up (of a female) copulating

The position sometimes adopted.

A *knees-up* is no more than a party or informal dance.

knight *British* a person associated with any illegal, taboo, or despised occupation

A source of much former wit. A *knight of Hornsey* was a cuckold, punning on the London borough and the horn of cuckoldry; a *knight of the road* was a mounted thief; and a *knight of the Golden Fleece* was a lawyer, although here I fear the preterite may be the wrong tense.

knight starvation *British* excessive and ostentatious zeal in pursuit of a knighthood

An ailment aggravated by conceit. The usage puns on an advertising slogan coined by Horlicks to sell a malted milk product as a nightcap:

> Some might say he deserves the money for taking on such a thankless task, and only the ungracious will mutter about knight starvation. (*Daily Telegraph*, 4 February 1998—a businessman had been appointed Chairman of the Arts Council)

knob the penis

A male vulgarism using the same imagery as KNOCKER. As the word is also used for the head, there can be occasions where misunderstanding occurs.

knobs a woman's breasts

A less common vulgarism than KNOCKERS, but using the same imagery.

knock *obsolete* to copulate

The usage survives in KNOCKING SHOP, a brothel and the slang *knock off*, as a male to copulate on a single occasion promiscuously.

knock back to drink intoxicants

Someone who is said to *knock it back*, is an alcoholic. One may also *knock off* a beer or other long drink.

knock down to kill

Usually of animals, by shooting them. Also as *knock off*, which is not necessarily of a roosting bird, *knock over*, and *knock on the head*, which can be done figuratively by killing humans as well as other animals.

knock off to steal

Usually a minor theft, from the concept of dislodging an object from a counter or barrow. *Knock-off* is also stolen property:

> Car boot sales were clearing houses for knock-off. (Rankin, 1998—they still are)

The *knock-off market* is the criminal disposal of stolen goods.

A *knock-off variety* of goods is manufactured, copying the design, and often using (or making a near copy of) the logo, of a branded product:

> ...soon the Chinese were themselves wearing—not Reeboks but (a sign of things to come) a knock-off variety of sports shoes. (Theroux, 2000)

knock-out a fraudulent auction

Auctioneers' jargon which puns on *knock down*, to register a sale by the fall of the hammer, and the boxing term *knock out*, to end a contest by rendering your opponent unconscious. The phrase is used of cases where there is a conspiracy between the auctioneer and one or more of the bidders to cheat the seller.

knock up to impregnate a female

Usually when it is an unwanted pregnancy:

> ...they told me that seven of the girls were knocked up—well, pregnant. (N. Mitford, 1960)

In the days before alarm clocks, when people lost their jobs if they were late for work, factory workers would be *knocked up* by someone paid to knock on their doors or windows to wake them.

knocker the penis

From the shape of a door knocker and punning on its sexual function.

knockers a woman's breasts

Again from the shape of a door knocker and its movement in a vertical plane when activated.

knocking-shop a brothel

Derived from the obsolete KNOCK but still a common usage.

Formerly also as *knocking-house*, *knocking-joint* or *knocker's shop*.

knot *obsolete* to copulate

From the meaning, to unite or bring together:

> ...a cistern for foul toads
> To knot and gender in. (Shakespeare, *Othello*)

I am not sure about:

> ...young people knotting together, and crying out 'Porridge'. (Pepys, 1662)

know to copulate with

It was a euphemism in Hebrew, Greek, and Latin, which explains why the translators for King James I (of England) found it so useful:

> And he knew her not till she had brought forth her first-born son. (*Matthew* 1:25, of Joseph and Mary)

known to the police having a criminal record or having been suspected of a crime

The usage ignores the fact that the police know many people who are not criminals, not excluding lawyers and politicians.

knuckle sandwich *American* a punch in the face

An equivalent of BUNCH OF FIVES which uses the same imagery.

konk off to die

Presumably what happens if you *konk* (or *conk*) *out*, like a motor:

> I know why you've come to see me. You think I'm going to konk off. (Blessed, 1991—he was visiting a nonagenarian)

Korean tartan *Scottish* an inferior or bogus product

Not made of tweed woven by hand in the Hebrides, or wherever they traditionally do these things:

> He knew someone was selling him a Korean tartan. (Rankin, 2000)

L

labor optimization *American* matching working hours of employees to demand for their services

A feature of the retail industry in which more workers are needed when the stores are busy and employers wish to avoid paying the wages of idle staff despite the inconvenience this may cause them.

labour¹ childbirth

Literally, physical toil, but so long standard English that we do not think about it as a euphemism.

labour² unemployment

A *Labour Exchange* was an office where those without work went to seek a job and claim money, whence being *on the labour* meant being unemployed and in receipt of state cash rather than *labouring*.

labour education arbitrary imprisonment

Usually for political dissenters in China, like the Chinese woman who, in 1981, wished to marry a French diplomat and was sentenced to two years *re-education through labour* for the offence of 'illegally living together with a foreigner'. (*Daily Telegraph*, November 1981)

lack of governance incompetence and peculation

The evasion used by the politicians and officials in Brussels when a scandal is exposed, rules are flouted, funds go missing, and incompetence and corruption are the order of the day.

lack of moral fibre *British* cowardice

Mainly Second World War military use, often as *LMF*.

Under conditions of active service, it is not easy for comrades to distinguish between psychological illness, prudence, and cowardice.

lack of visibility concealment or obfuscation

Financial jargon for opaque or worrying published accounts:
> 'Lack of visibility' is usually code for not liking the view. At Granada, the picture is indeed foggy. (*Financial Times*, 14 June 2001)

lad an exclusive male premarital sexual partner

Literally, a boy or young man, especially in Scotland and the north of England. Elsewhere specifically? one who looks after horses. So too with LASS.

ladder *obsolete* the scaffold

The victim climbed it before being hanged:
> Those who know what it is to have a reprieve brought to them on the ladder...(Defoe, 1719)

laddish antisocial and immature

The adjective describes boisterous behaviour by young men who consider themselves to be *one of the lads*. A *laddish magazine* is a jejune and mildly pornographic publication.

ladies a lavatory exclusively for female use

Usually adjacent to GENTLEMEN. Also as *ladies' convenience, room*, etc.

ladies' fever *obsolete* syphilis

In addition to blaming their condition on foreigners such as the French, the Spanish, and the Neopolitans, it was logical for men also to attribute their infection to those with whom they had copulated domestically.

ladies' man a man who delights in the company of women

A slightly derogatory use by other males who may not share his dress sense or his ability to show interest in every topic of female conversation. He may also be a profligate:
> Blamey was a big 57-year-old who liked to wear a broad-brimmed bush hat and seemed to enjoy his reputation as a ladies' man. (Deighton, 1993—General Blamey commanded the Australian forces in the Middle East between 1940 and 1942)

ladies' medicine *obsolete* a potion to induce an abortion

In the days when abortions were illegal:
> [The doctor] had been crooked once, perhaps in the ladies' medicine line. (Waters, 2002)

ladies' troubles ailments which do not affect males

Those which affect the womb and other taboo parts of the female body but not breast cancer.

lady a prostitute

As in the oldest joke:
> 'Who was that lady I saw you with last night?' 'That was no lady. That was my wife.'

Also as *lady-boarder, lady of a certain description, lady of easy virtue, lady of negotiable affection, lady of no virtue, lady of pleasure, lady of the night, lady of the sisterhood, lady of the stage* (when actresses were considered to work in a lowly and immoral occupation), and *lady of the streets*. A *lady of pleasure* or *ladybird* might also be a mistress. *Ladies of intrigue* were, according to Mayhew, 'married women who have connection with other men than their husbands and unmarried women who gratify their passions secretly'. (1862)

lady bear *American* a policewoman
A version of BEAR².

lady dog a bitch
The very fastidious or prudish use the phrase to avoid confusing the inoffensive quadruped with the spiteful and domineering biped so offensively described.

lady friend a female extramarital sexual partner
She does not have to be a woman of breeding or distinction, but the use implies slightly more acceptability than WOMAN FRIEND.

lady-in-waiting¹ a concubine in the Japanese court
Literally, a female who attends to female royalty:
> A dozen concubines, euphemistically termed ladies-in-waiting, nightly awaited the drop of the imperial handkerchief at their feet to follow him into his quarters. (Behr, 1989, writing about the Emperor Meiji, Hirohito's dissolute father)

lady-in-waiting² a pregnant woman
Mainly humorous use, punning on the court official. The obsolete English *lady in the straw* was a woman in the process of being delivered of a baby.

lady-killer a male profligate
But without murderous intent.

laid out drunk
Either like a boxer who has been floored by his opponent (in this case alcohol) or like a cadaver.

laid to rest dead
A monumental favourite, as in AT REST.
Anyone dying at sea might be *laid in the lockers*, for subsequent burial on land, but if you died beyond the Thames estuary town of Gravesend, your corpse would be disposed of at sea.

lame duck¹ the holder of an office to which he has not been re-elected
His successor will soon hold the reins of power, perhaps with a different policy. The term is often used of an outgoing president of the United States who becomes ineffectual during his last months of office, if not before.

lame duck² a failing enterprise
Peter Pindar described Pitt as 'a duck confounded lame' which may have been mere political abuse. In the 19th century a *lame duck* was 'a stockjobber who speculates beyond his capital, and cannot pay his losses'. (*The Slang Dictionary*, 1874) The phrase was applied to failing companies generally by the British Minister John Davies in 1971, who said they would not receive government funds and then changed his mind.

lamping shooting rabbits at night by dazzling them with light
Either a torch or the headlights of a vehicle are used.

lance (of a male) to copulate with
Literally, to pierce, with the common thrusting imagery.

land of forgetfulness (the) death
Some of us sinners on this ball of clay can hope this is true:
> I was told of a vast number of my acquaintance who were all gone over to the land of forgetfulness. (J. Boswell, 1791)

land of Nod (the) sleep
A pun on Cain's travels when he 'dwelt in the land of Nod' (*Genesis* 4:16):
Mainly nursery use for coaxing children into the frightening dark.

landscaped tidied up
Estate agents' and builders' puff for the garden of a new house from which most of the rubble has been removed or covered with a thin coating of soil.

language swear words
A shortened form of *bad language*:
> I'll have no man usin' language i' my house. (D. Murray, 1886—he was not a Trappist abbot)
In America *language arts* is educational and sociological jargon for the ability to speak coherently.

lard the books dishonestly to increase a claim for repayment
You enrich the mix by adding too much fat.

large¹ pregnant
Occasional female use:
> It was when I was large with our Lizbeth. (*EDD*)

large² small
Or smaller than *jumbo* or *family* in hypermarket hype:
> The smallest tube of toothpaste you can buy is the 'large size'. (Jennings, 1965)

larger obese
Jargon of the clothing industry, without
stating the norm against which the measurement has been made. It may also refer to
females who are taller than the norm.

lass an exclusive extra-marital female
sexual partner
A usage not confined to the Scots. See also
LAD.

last call (the) death
In various other combinations also, sometimes
referring to the dead person's occupation or
interests. Thus the *last call* tends to be taken by
actors or actresses, who make their *last bow*,
although never their last curtsey. Cowboys
head for the *last round-up* but those of us who
pay the *last debt* may in fact die insolvent. The
last trump is not for card players only but for
those who hear the call to the seat of
judgement. The *last end* and the *last resting place*
are specific, at least until the resurrection, as is
the *last voyage* or the *last journey*.

last favour (the) copulation
Granted after other familiarities. Also as *last
intimacies*.
For the diarist, the *last thing*:
I had my full liberty of towsing her and
doing what I would but the last thing.
(Pepys, 1663—to *towse* was to pull or shake
about, whence *towser*, a dog used in bear-
baiting, and then any mastiff)

last shame *obsolete British* a term of imprisonment
A usage at a time when more stigma attached
to criminality.

last waltz *American* the walk to death by
execution
A waltz traditionally ends the ball.

latchkey arriving at an empty home
Of children neither of whose parents is
present when they return from school, with
perhaps unfair implication of maternal neglect.

late¹ dead
Usually in connection with someone recently
deceased. Venerable enough to have been
used by Caxton in 1490 but still sometimes
confused with unpunctuality.

late² failing to menstruate when expected
With fears of unplanned pregnancy.

late booking fraudulently reserving profitable deals for favoured clients
A practice of commodity or money dealers

who defer nominating the beneficiaries of
profitable deals until the end of the trading
session, allocating less successful business or
losses to passive investors. Also known as *late
trading*, which may involve doing deals after
the market has closed but when price movements are known, and allocating the profit
next day.

late developer a poor scholar
Used by parents who have hope rather than
by teachers who have experience.

late disturbances a recent war
Late means former:
The year of 1688 brought to England the
worst turmoil since the 'late disturbances',
as Mr Pepys had once described a brutal
civil war and a royal beheading.
(Monsarrat, 1978)
Also as *late unpleasantness*, describing the
American Civil War and the First World
War. Another version after the Second World
War was *late nastiness*.

latrine a lavatory
As with LAVATORY itself, the derivation is from
the Latin *lavare*, to wash. Usually denoting
primitive and communal structures, as in the
army.

latter end¹ the buttocks
Of the same tendency as BOTTOM. Also in the
form *latter part*.

latter end² death
It should mean no more than our closing
years before death:
I spoke severely, being naturally
indignant (at my time of life) to hear a
young woman of five-and-twenty talking
about her latter end! (W. Collins, 1868—
she was not referring to her anatomy)

laughing academy *American* an institution for the mentally ill
Not a school for comedians. Inappropriate
mirth may be symptom of mental illness.

launder to bring funds dishonestly obtained into apparently legal circulation
or account
Used of money which has been stolen or
which is the proceeds of vice, especially drug
dealing; and of public funds secretly diverted
from the purpose for which they were voted.
A bank permitting such transactions or a
seemingly legal trading company through
which the funds pass is known as a *laundry*.

lavabo a lavatory
'I shall wash', from the Latin Vulgate version
of *Psalms* 26:6—*Lavabo inter innocentes manus*

meas—and still used interchangeably with LAVATORY, but not very often.

lavatory a room set aside for urination and defecation
Originally, a place for washing in, and then the place where you went to wash.

lavender *American* related to male homosexuality
The perfume made from the plant is considered effeminate. A *lavender convention* is a meeting of male homosexuals, or *lavender boys*.

lay[1] to copulate with
The male usually *lays* the female, from his superior attitude or from assisting her to a prone position.
Shakespeare used *lay down*:
   The sly whoresons
   Have got a speeding trick to lay down
   ladies. (*Henry VIII*)
A woman who has copulated is said to have been *laid*.

lay[2] a promiscuous woman
As seen by a man.
It is remarkable that, in malespeak, there are only *good lays* in this context.

lay a child *obsolete British* to apply a cure for rickets
It was necessary to take the child to a smithy where three smiths of the same name worked and there subject it to procedures which are detailed in the *EDD*, none of which we would view with confidence today.

lay a leg on to copulate with
Or *lay a leg over* or *across*, actions taken only by the male, it would seem. Whence a *bit of leg-over*, casual copulation.

lay down your life to be killed in wartime
There are overtones of voluntary sacrifice.

lay hands on to beat
Someone who expresses a wish to *lay his hands on you* is seldom a faith healer or a bishop wishing to confirm you. Occasionally it means to kill, especially in the phrase, *lay hands on yourself*, to commit suicide.

lay off to dismiss from employment
Formerly for a short period only, until business picked up, but now of permanent dismissal.

lay out to prepare (a corpse) for burial
You straighten the limbs before the onset of rigor mortis might make it hard to accommodate the body in the coffin.

lay paper to pass worthless financial instruments
The *paper* is bouncing cheques, forged bank notes, or bogus securities. The imagery is from the 'paper-chase', in which participants followed a trail of torn-up paper dropped by their quarry.

lay pipes *American* to seek election through bribery
The usage comes from elections in New York in 1835 when forged correspondence was produced to suggest that the Whigs described men bribed for their votes as so many yards of the pipe being laid for the Croton water supply project. Now of any unnecessary public works or diversion of government cash to provide employment to potential voters or influence regional opinion.

lay to rest to inter a corpse
The common sleeping imagery:
   But that did not lessen the sadness I felt at not being able to make her life more comfortable, or the pain of not being able to lay her to rest. (Mandela, 1994—he was not allowed to leave prison to attend his mother's funeral)

lead associated with shooting
From the composition of the bullet. The victim might have a *bellyful of lead*, be *filled with lead*, be loaded with *lead ballast*, *eat lead pills*, wear *lead buttons*, or suffer from *lead poisoning*.
Soviet soldiers fought fanatically partly because:
   There seemed little difference between the enemy bullet and that fixed ration from the Soviet state, the NKVD's 'nine ounces of lead'. (Beevor, 1998, of the Second World War)
To be *allergic to lead* is to be a coward:
   Sir Gerald was, to put a fine point on it, allergic to lead. He was very deeply anxious not to get killed—injured even. (Whicker, 1982—after securing a safe billet far behind the lines at Bari, Gerald was killed when an ammunition ship blew up in the harbour)

lead apes in hell *obsolete* (of a woman) to die without having copulated
Alluding to simian sexual vigour:
   I must not dance barefoot on her wedding day
   And for your love for her, lead apes in hell. (Shakespeare, *The Taming of the Shrew*)

lead in your pencil sexual potency

Of a male, *pencil* and *penis* sharing their Latin root. The usage likens the ejaculation of semen to the *pencil's* graphite core.

leak¹ an act of urination
Of obvious derivation. *Leaks* may be *had, done, gone for, needed, sprung, taken*, etc. by either sex in mildly vulgar use.
To *leak* is occasionally used meaning to urinate.

leak² to release information furtively
A habit especially of politicians who wish to sound out public opinion without making a personal commitment, or to use confidential information to their own advantage. A *leak* is the information disclosed, a *leakage* is what has occurred, a *leaker* is the person who makes the disclosure, and a *leak inquiry* is the pretence of looking into the impropriety until the matter is forgotten.

leak³ to sweat
A mainly male slang usage, especially after undue exertion.

leakage the loss of revenue through tax evasion
Treasury jargon, the language of the officials showing more concern about collecting taxation than preventing the greater fiscal seepage which is endemic through waste and inefficiency.

leaky menstruating
Of obvious derivation:
> As leaky as an unstaunch'd wench.
> (Shakespeare, *The Tempest*)
Also used of a person prone to involuntary urination.

lean on to put pressure on (a person) so as to extract a benefit
The benefit may be silence of a witness, money from a victim, etc. and is used of actual or threatened violence.

leaner a cheat at cards
Attempting surreptitiously to see another's hand.

leap in the dark (a) death by hanging
A sack or blindfold covered the victim's eyes. Hobbes is reported to have so described his own imminent (natural) death.

leap on to copulate with
The male is the party thus moving. To *leap into bed* is specific of both sexes, possibly averting to the eagerness with which they move, especially in a promiscuous encounter.

A *leaping-house* was a brothel for Shakespeare (*I Henry IV*), as was a *leaping academy* for the Victorians.

leap the broomstick *obsolete* to live together as a couple without marrying
A variant of JUMP THE BROOMSTICK and also as *leap the besom*. It applied to couples who were by choice cohabiting without being married, or to those without access to a priest.

learn on the pillow to acquire proficiency in a foreign language from a (sexual) mistress who is a native speaker
The expression is used to draw attention to the sexual impropriety rather than the linguistic achievement.

learner a child at school
For some an aspiration rather than an accomplishment:
> ...instructors have to decide whether 'learners', as pupils are now to be known, are taught to eat healthily. (*Daily Telegraph*, 8 October 2005)

learning difficulties a mental illness or incapacity resulting in an inability to keep up with peers in class
The usage describes those with an abnormal mental condition beyond a poor memory or an inability to concentrate. The phrase was first used in the British Warnock Report on education in 1979 and its usefulness as a euphemism was recognized and expanded in the following decade until:
> ...the mentally handicapped shall be defined as 'people with learning difficulties'. (*Daily Telegraph*, 1 October 1990)
Learning disabled, a condition with which those with *learning difficulties* are afflicted, extends into education the DISABILITY theme and a *learning disability* implies more than having difficulty with your homework:
> If someone in your family has a learning disability (mental handicap) he or she needs security. (advertisement for the Royal Society for Mentally Handicapped Children in *Sunday Telegraph*, 30 January 2000)

leather associated with sexual abnormality
From the style of clothing adopted by certain male homosexuals or, in America, *leather queens*, who meet in *leather bars*.

leave to desert (a spouse)
When we use the word, we ignore the fact that married companies part company daily, to come together again in the evening.

leave alone to desist from indulging in a taboo activity

Normally relating to illegal narcotics or taboo sexual activity:

> You remember Philip Haskell, master of foxhounds one year, and the next thing you know—...At least father has been leaving young boys alone. (Flanagan, 1995—Philip chased youths as well as foxes)

leave before the gospel to withdraw from the vagina before ejaculation

Attending church but forgoing the Mass. Especially Roman Catholic use and practice when mechanical and chemical forms of contraception are eschewed.

leave of absence suspension from employment during investigation of a supposed offence

Literally, no more than a vacation, but used by the employer to avoid defamation before an offence is proved.

leave the building to die

The building, I surmise, is the body where your soul resides while you are alive. Also, in America, as *leave town*. To *leave the land of the living* or *leave this life* are circumlocutory rather than euphemistic. Someone who dies is said to *leave* those who survive, the separation being both involuntary and, some would suggest, permanent:

> 'I think,' the maid replied, 'Mr Ford will be leaving us.' (Lacey, 1986—Henry Ford was on his deathbed, not about to visit his workers)

leave the room to go to the lavatory

The request which echoed throughout our schooldays, with the variant *May I leave the class*?

leavings the excreta of animals

Especially from horses in the streets in the days when they pulled carts and carriages:

> The stench of leavings, on a hot week such as this had been was barely tolerable. (Winchester, 2001)

led astray having voluntarily done something for which you later express regret or shame

Men use this as an excuse when they come home drunk, women if they eat fattening food, and both sexes if they commit adultery.

left field *American* crazy or unconventional

The imagery is from baseball, referring to the area less favoured by right-handed hitters.

left-footer a person not conforming to the practices or beliefs of the majority

Someone so described may not play football and, if he does, he may well favour his right boot.

Used of homosexuals, who may be similarly said to be *left-handed* or *to have two left hands*.

In the Royal Navy a *left-footer* might be a Roman Catholic.

left-handed *obsolete* indicating illegitimacy

From the bar sinister on a coat of arms, which is a sign of bastardy.

left-handed wife a woman living with a man to whom she is not married

He takes her left hand, and not her right, in a *left-handed alliance*. (My wife, along with many other virtuous ladies, could be so described, literally but not euphemistically.)

leg it to make an escape

The movement is seldom on foot as the destination is usually remote:

> Collar the cash, send a few wires and leg it to foreign parts. (McCrum, 2004, quoting P. G. Wodehouse)

leg-over an act of copulation

Usually by the male, from the movement involved. *Leg-sliding*, which is less common, may apply to either sex.

legal resident a spy accredited as a diplomat

As different from the *illegal resident* who spies in the host country under cover.

legless very drunk

From your inability to walk steadily, or at all.

lend to lose ownership of

As in the old proverb 'He who lends, gives'. If you *lend* someone a match, or a cigarette, you are unwise to expect repayment. In 1941 the British had exhausted their ability to pay for more supplies from neutral America, which nevertheless wanted the British Empire to be able to continue fighting Germany and Italy on its behalf, all other opponents having been defeated or withdrawn. The US Congress therefore agreed to continue to provide arms to Britain, *leasing* them on credit and *lending* the cost which would be paid after the war, whence the description *lease-lend*. The arrangement was abruptly brought to an end by Harry Truman in 1945. Britain will repay the last instalment of the debt in 2007.

length a term of imprisonment

A rare version of the common STRETCH[1].

lesbian a female homosexual
The poetess Sappho lived on the island.
Lesbianism is female homosexuality, and the
adjectival form is *lesbic*.
You may sometimes hear the corruptions *lez*,
lezzer, or *lizzie*:
> To get into Mortimer's outfit you have to be
> a lizzie or a drunk or an Irishwoman.
> (Manning, 1978—the *outfit* was the First
> Aid Nursing Yeomanry, or FANY, whose
> members were commonly referred to as
> *fannies*)

less lacking a quality in a way which is the
subject of a taboo
Thus *less academic* children are stupid or
unteachable; a *less abled* person lacks mobility
(On 18 January 2004, a sufferer from multiple
sclerosis corrected an interviewer on the BBC
who said *disabled* by insisting on *less abled*); *less
attractive* is ugly, as in Cinderella's two *less
attractive* sisters; *less developed*, of a country, is
poor and backward; *less edited*, of a book or
article, is pornographic; *less enjoyable* is boring,
especially of entertainment; *less gifted* is of
inferior ability or intelligence; *less respectable*
women are prostitutes; etc.

let go to dismiss from employment
The usage seeks to imply that the employee is
being done a favour.
Also, in America, as *let out*, as though those
dismissed were formerly held captive.

let off to fart
A shortened form of *let off wind* rather than
from the firing of a gun.
To *let fly* implies a more violent, noisier,
release.

letterhead appointed other than on
merit
It is used of an attempt to bolster the image or
credibility of an organization through its
association with an eminent person or one
who comes from a MINORITY.
See also STATUTORY and TOKEN.

leveraged involving excessive borrowing
Especially where a predator takes over a
corporation incurring debt which he hopes
to service or repay out of the victim's assets.

liaison an extramarital sexual relationship
Originally, the culinary thickening of a sauce,
whence a close relationship.
Less often the person with whom the relationship is enjoyed, or as the case may be, is so
described:
> ... how she had taken her mother's Visa,
> forged the signature, and bought the
> current 'liaison' from the council houses a
> 500-cc Yamaha. (Seymour, 1995)

libation a drink of an intoxicant
Literally, the ceremonial offering of a drink.

libel chill the censorship or suppression
of news
The wealthy may use the threat of an action
for defamation to deter editors from publishing damaging information, Robert Maxwell
and James Goldsmith being prominent expo-
nents of the technique.

liberal *American* with egalitarian tendencies
The Latin root suggests freedom, a concept
maintained in the British Liberal party tradition, under which members are free to hold
widely diverging or opposing views. Much
pejorative use, especially of a wealthy American Senator, who was described in February
1980 as 'the perfect 24-carat knee-jerk liberal
sap'. Such rich people are also known as
limousine liberals:
> Even now, [Barbara Streisand's] fellow
> limousine liberals insist [California's debt
> and unemployment are] all the fault of the
> 'Bush recession'. (*Sunday Telegraph*, 6 July
> 2003)

For Shakespeare a *liberal* woman was not a
politician but promiscuous. (*I Henry VI*)

liberate[1] to conquer
Literally, to free:
> 'Nehru turned them out in the liberation of
> Goa.' 'Liberation ... did you say *liberation*?'
> (Dalrymple, 1998—Goa was a Portuguese
> enclave in the subcontinent which India
> invaded and annexed)

liberate[2] to steal
Originally, a use by soldiers in the Second
World War, when freeing occupied territories
and looting property whose owner had van-
ished tended to go hand in hand.
Now in general use of thieving.

liberate[3] to permit or encourage to flout
social convention
Again the concept of setting free:
> The custom of keen gardeners who once
> shopped for bedding plants and potting
> compost was replaced by that of cross-
> dressing businessmen and 'liberated
> people' who indulged in group sex in the
> swimming pool. (*Daily Telegraph*, 28
> November 1998—the proprietor of what
> had formerly been a garden centre said
> after his conviction for living off immoral
> earnings—'I did not have sex parties. I had
> liberated parties')

Whence *liberation*, as in WOMEN'S LIBERATION.

liberate[4] peremptorily to dismiss from
employment

The victim is thereby freed from performing the arduous duties of office or employment:

> ... a papal decree was issued by which Dr Errington was 'liberated' from the Co-adjutorship of Westminster, together with the right of succession to the See. (Strachey, 1918—Manning, lately an archdeacon in the Anglican Church, thus cleared the way for his own succession to Wiseman as Roman Catholic Archbishop of Westminster)

lick the dust to die

Usually today after being killed in a Western, from where a corpse lies in dry country, but with a biblical lineage:

> His enemies shall lick the dust. (*Psalms* 72:9)

See also BITE THE DUST.

lid an ounce of marijuana

The quantity which fitted into the lid of a tobacco tin and made about 40 hand-rolled cigarettes.

lie in to await the imminent birth of a child

Greek, Latin, and Teutonic roots of *lie* all mean bed where, in the language of euphemism, you only give birth or copulate.

A *lying-in wife* was a midwife.

Formerly to *lay in* was synonymous:

> When the gal is in the family way, the lads mostly sends them to the workhouse to lay in. (Mayhew, 1851)

lie with to copulate with

It has long been assumed that the adult male and female cannot *lie* in each other's company without copulating, within or outside marriage:

> To tell thee plain, I aim to lie with thee. (Shakespeare, *3 Henry VI*)

Lie on might be more accurate of the male, but is less used:

> Lie with her! lie on her! (Shakespeare, *Othello*)

Lie together implies extramarital copulation.

life[1] **(the)** any taboo way of earning your keep or existing

Prostitutes' jargon for prostitution, thieves' for stealing, and also used by drug addicts, especially when they alternate between scheming to get money to buy illegal narcotics and being under their influence.

life[2] death

As in *life assurance* sold through *life cover* by a *life office* to a *life*, the person whose death will lead to payment. *Life everlasting* is also death, signifying a belief or hope in some form of immortality.

life of infamy prostitution

How the righteous profess to see it. We still may hear talk of a prostitute leading a *life of shame*.

life preserver a cosh

It is not intended to preserve that of the victim.

lifestyle a sexual orientation

The word is used to ask potential blood donors whether they are homosexual as, if they are, there is a greater possibility that they are HIV-positive and it is not worth incurring the expense of checking a sample of their blood.

lift[1] to steal

Usually of pilfering, from the casual removal:

> Billy can lift your jock strap, and you wouldn't feel a thing. (Weverka, 1973—Billy was an adept pickpocket)

Specifically of plagiarism in the 20th century, of picking pockets in the 19th century, and of disinterring corpses for sale in 18th-century Scotland.

A *lifter* is a thief, usually by picking pockets. *Shoplifter*, a thief from a store, has been in use since the 17th century and the verb, to *shoplift*, since the 19th.

lift[2] the feeling after an ingestion of illegal narcotics

Literally, a feeling of well-being or encouragement:

> 'Want a lift?' 'I can use something,' Janette said. She took a small vial from the bag. (Robbins, 1981)

lift[3] an arrest

Mainly police jargon, from removing a suspect from circulation.

Also as a verb in the same sense.

lift[4] a thick sole and heel to enhance height

Only the subject of evasion when worn by a male:

> Beware Greeks wearing lifts. (*Financial Times*, 1988, quoting a quip about the presidential candidate Dukakis who was so shod, the motto being after—long after—Virgil's *timeo danaos et dona ferentes*, 'I fear the Greeks even when they are bearing gifts')

lift a gam *Irish* to fart

A *gam* was a leg in slang. It was also a school of whales but their propensity for blowing does not contribute to the etymology.

lift a leg[1] (of a male) to copulate

Of a male, getting a LEG-OVER.

To *lift a hand to* is to inflict violence on.

lift a leg² to urinate
In standard usage it applies to a dog, which does it literally.

lift the books *obsolete* to withdraw from regular service at a church
A major decision in the days when church attendance was a social necessity, apart from any spiritual benefit.
If you were to *lift your lines*, you would receive a disjunction certificate on changing from one congregation to another.

lift your little finger to drink intoxicants
On a single occasion, from the conveyance of the glass to the mouth, or more often of a drunkard.
In the same sense you may *lift* other parts of your anatomy, including your *arm*, your *elbow*, or your *wrist*.

light promiscuous
Of no moral weight but *light ladies*, *wenches*, or *women* were not successful dieters or those emulating Florence Nightingale but prostitutes:
  Light wenches will burn. Come not near her. (Shakespeare, *The Comedy of Errors*—they were not condemned to the stake but would give you venereal disease)
  Commentators charged that throughout his papacy [Pope John XI] continued committing 'infinite abominations among light women'. (Cawthorne, 1996—he occupied the throne of St Peter from 931 to 936)

light-fingered thieving
It indicates a propensity to lift small objects. An old superstition has passed into oblivion:
  The baby's nails must not be cut till he is a year old, for fear he should grow up a thief, or...'light-fingered'. (W. Henderson, 1879)

light-footed promiscuous
Of a female, who might also be described as *light-heeled*.
A *light skirts* was a prostitute.
An unmarried couple in America cohabiting were said to be *light-housekeeping*, punning on the avocation of the coastguard.

light in the head of low intelligence
Not a turnip on Hallowe'en but supposedly deficient in brain capacity.

light on his toes homosexual
Some homosexual males affect a mincing walk or appear to be walking on tiptoe. Also as *light-footed*.

light the lamp (of a prostitute) to accept customers

The brothel's sign is a RED LAMP:
  She confided in me that she had lit the lamp four hundred times, in one week, in her Casita. (Londres, 1928, in translation)

lightning low-quality spirits
Alluding to the effect when it strikes you. Usually denoting whisky in America and gin in Britain.

like a drink to be addicted to alcohol
Not just the liquid which we enjoy when we are thirsty. We use the phrase of others, in various forms, but not, in the euphemistic sense, of ourselves:
  They say that [Charles Kennedy] likes the odd tipple. (*Daily Telegraph*, 23 March 2004—the party leader was eventually obliged to resign having admitted his alcoholic addiction)
In addict slang, to *like a pipe* is to smoke illegal narcotics, not tobacco.

like that homosexual
Usually of a male.

like the ladies to be a philanderer
Not merely the opposite of being a misogynist.

lily *American* a male homosexual
The derivation is from the woman's name and the pale colouring, despite the flower being the emblem of chastity and innocence.

limb *obsolete* a leg
A classic example of 19th-century prudery, when in America not just humans but dining tables had *limbs*.

limb of the law a policeman
Alluding perhaps to the cliché, the *long arm of the law* and occasionally shortened to *limb*.

limited idle, stupid, or incompetent
Educational jargon of children, to avoid precision or offence. Used of an adult, it means lacking in ability or intelligence. This is one of the sillier euphemisms, as we are all confined within *limits*, of memory, knowledge, experience, common sense, and physical power.

limited action a war
The stronger participant so describes it, especially if his domestic population is not at risk.
An American *limited covert war* is one aided by the CIA without Congress being informed.

limited edition a publication
All *editions* are *limited* in number, however many copies the publisher may decide to print. The pretence, enhanced on occasion by

numbering individual copies, is that the book will soon be scarce, in order to stimulate sales or obtain a higher price.

limp-wrist a male homosexual
From the action of masturbating.
Whence adjectivally as *limp-wristed*:
> His limp-wristed nancy-boy of a son... (*Private Eye*, January 1980)

line¹ to copulate with
Literally, of a dog or wolf, but obsolete of humans:
> Winter garments must be lined,
> So must slender Rosalind. (Shakespeare, *As You Like It*)

Lined, meaning pregnant, is also obsolete.

line² a nasal ingestion of narcotics
From the way it is sprinkled for sniffing:
> Hey, baby, come back to my place, we'll do a couple lines. (Turow, 1999)

line your pocket wrongfully to enrich yourself
The money provides the *lining*.
In America, as *line your vest*:
> I think he's been lining his vest. (Moss, 1987—he was not a tailor but an official suspected of peculation)

An obsolete form was *line your coat*, although Shakespeare's observation of human behaviour is, as ever, timeless:
> And throwing but shows of service on their lords,
> Do well thrive by them, and when they have lin'd their coats,
> Do themselves homage. (*Othello*)

linen *obsolete* a shirt
From the days when legs were BENDERS and cocks became ROOSTERS:
> If such standard English words as 'leg' and 'shirt' were found beyond the pale... (James Gordon Bennett caused a certain frisson when his *New York Herald* refused to print the former as 'limb' and the latter as 'linen')... (J. Green, 1996)

link prices to arrange an illegal cartel
Manufacturers or distributors either divide markets on a geographical basis or agree to quote the same prices as each other.

linked with having a sexual relationship with
A favoured journalistic evasion:
> Since the break-down of her marriage, the Duchess has been linked with a Texan oil executive... and... her financial adviser. (*Daily Telegraph*, 14 December 1994)

liquid consisting of, serving, or containing alcohol
Literally, anything from water to sulphuric acid. Usually in compounds. A *liquid refreshment* is an intoxicant. A *liquid restaurant* serves intoxicants as well as food. A *liquid lunch*, *dinner*, or *supper* is not one with a soup course but where excessive alcohol is drunk with little or no food.

liquidate to kill other than by process of law
Originally, to clear away, whence the implication for ruthless efficiency.
In legal jargon and the commercial world, a *liquidator* kills off failed companies.

liquidity the ability to pay your debts as they fall due
Only euphemistic when you lack it:
> Sir Jeremy came to me saying that he lacked liquidity... that's the delicate way these European aristocrats say in deep shit. (Deighton, 1993/2)

A *liquidity crisis* for a company means that it is insolvent and for a person that he is bankrupt, in each case still staving off the threat or reality.

liquor a spirituous intoxicant
Originally, any liquid, in many spellings.
Liquored means partly drunk and *full of liquor* or *in liquor* mean drunk.

lit drunk or under the influence of narcotics
From the generally exhilarated state rather than the redness of the nose.
Also as *lit up*.

little boys' room a lavatory for exclusive male use
But no smaller than a BOYS' ROOM nor confined to the use of children. A *little girls' room*, providing similar facilities for females, is equally nauseous but less common.

little gentleman in black velvet *obsolete* a mole
King William III, who was hated by the Jacobites (and still is by many of the Irish), was riding a horse which stumbled on a molehill. He fell off, broke his collar bone, and died from complications which ensued. It was treasonable to impugn what Catholics and others saw as the usurping Hanoverian monarchs. If you wished to venerate the mole, you were better to refer to him obliquely.
See also KING OVER THE WATER.

little house a lavatory
It was often a small detached shed in the yard or garden.
Also as *petty house*.

little jobs urination
As different from BIG JOBS, defecation, in nursery use.

little local difficulties a major crisis
The term was used by the British Prime Minister Macmillan in January 1958 when three Treasury ministers resigned. Now used ironically.

little Mary the stomach
This is perhaps the sole survivor in modern speech of the 19th-century evasions about any part of the body which might conceivably have some connection with sex, urination, defecation, or childbirth.

little people the fairies
The fairies were malevolent, unlike their namesakes in Christmas pantomimes, and you had to speak nicely about them. Also as *little folk*.

little something an intoxicant
Usually in an enquiry to a guest.

little stranger an unborn child
Nursery usage, to avoid telling the truth about pregnancy and to prepare a toddler for the arrival of a sibling.

little visitor (a) menstruation
But no less in terms of duration or discomfort than a VISITOR. Common female use, and as *little friend*, which implies a welcome as indicating the woman is not pregnant. *Little sister* is rare.

little woman a mistress
Literally, in ponderous male humour, a wife:
   I think we can take it there's a 'little woman' in the case. (P. D. James, 1962)

live as man and wife to cohabit and regularly copulate without being married
The usage is perhaps as obsolete as the convention that a couple should marry prior to sexual cohabitation. They may also be said to *live in sin* or, even more dastardly, to *live in mortal sin*.
The obsolete *live tally* drew its imagery from the *tally*, or corresponding part, which fitted another.
Live together and *live with* are almost standard English for such an arrangement and may also refer to homosexual cohabitation.
Of a married couple, *not to live as man and wife* means that they no longer copulate with each other despite sharing living accommodation.

live by trade to be a prostitute
Those of us who earn a living in commerce may hope that this usage is obsolete. Also as *live by trading*.

live-in girlfriend a mistress
She resides with a man who is single, or separated or divorced from his wife.
See also GIRLFRIEND.

live it up to behave hedonistically
Often at another's expense:
   The leader [of a post-colonial Caribbean state] lived (or lived it up) on behalf of his people. (Naipaul, 1989)

live on to make a living from sexual services
Descriptive of either a mistress or a pimp. *Live off* means the same thing.

lived-in untidy
You so describe another's house, usually with an implication of untidiness and dirt. A *lived-in face* denotes debauchery on the part of its wearer.

livener an intoxicant taken early in the morning
Either by someone who was drunk the previous evening or by a habitual drunkard.

living space conquered territory
The Nazi German *Lebensraum* to be annexed from Poland, Russia, and others—'to obtain by the German sword sod for the German plough'.
Even more sinister was the Nazi policy of *Lebensborn*, under which fair Polish or Czech children were taken from home and placed with German families to be raised as Germans and thus augment the Teutonic stock.

load¹ the quantity of intoxicants which has made someone drunk
The drunkard *carries a load* or *has a load on*.
Loaded is drunk or under the influence of narcotics, in addition to the slang meaning 'wealthy'.
A *loaded* drink is one which has been laced with intoxicant without the knowledge of the drinker.

load² *American* the genitalia of a male
Homosexual use:
   The long-haired youth entered, came close to Firenza's side, pressed his nylon-sheathed load against the doctor's arm. (Sanders, 1977)

load³ dishonestly to inflate
Of demands for payment which have fictional or inflated items included.

load-shedding a failure of the electricity grid through inability to generate sufficient power

In Britain this was one of the features of the electricity industry when it was owned and operated by the state, whose employees used evasive language to explain inefficiency:

> ... 'load shedding'—the bureaucratic word for power cuts—took place three hours every day. (*Daily Telegraph*, 13 August 1999)

local *British* an inn

Shortened form for *local pub* etc. People do not use the term to describe the village post office or other common amenity in the vicinity.

local bear *American* a police officer attached to a small force

Often looked down on by state or federal law enforcement officers. Also as a *local*, *local boy*, or *local yokel*.

lock out to suspend the provision of work for employees

The jargon of industrial disputes and not referring to thieves and other would-be trespassers who are *locked out* of the premises each evening, or as the case may be.

locked drunk

As in an arm-lock or a prison cell? Probably neither:

> —I was fuckin' locked, said Declan Cuffe. Rum an' blacks, yeh know. (Doyle, 1987—*blacks* is stout)

log-rolling *American* giving selfish or insincere support

Neighbours used to help each other manhandle heavy wood for winter burning, whence figuratively mutual political back-scratching. In modern use, it covers insincere commendation, and any reward for sycophancy.

loins the male genitals in their reproductive role

Literally, the region of your body between your ribs and your hips.

A *surge in the loins* is the ejaculation of semen:

> In no time at all I felt the surge in my loins, and it was as I wrenched with the supreme moment that I awoke. (de Bernières, 1994)

lone love self-masturbation

As different from narcissism.

lone parent a parent living alone with dependent offspring

Usually an unmarried mother or a parent whose spouse lives apart through divorce or other separation, without any suggestion that the child has other than two progenitors.

See also ONE-PARENT FAMILY and SINGLE PARENT.

long acre *Irish* the roadside verge

Where itinerants set up camp and graze their horses.

long-arm inspection *American* a medical inspection of the penis

DAS says the inspection is of the erect penis. See also SHORT-ARM INSPECTION.

long home (your) death

More accurately, perhaps, the grave.

Those who die may also go on their *long journey*.

The *long day* is the Christian Day of Judgement, when a considerable catalogue of offences will come up for simultaneous hearing, requiring a lengthy sitting; whence the admonition:

> Between you and the lang day be it. (Pegge, 1803)

long illness (a) *American* cancer

The language of the obituary notice. A *short illness* may indicate suicide.

long in the tooth old

Horses are aged by the recession of their gums.

long pig human flesh

The language of cannibalism when formerly practised in the South Seas. The flesh of the human and the pig taste much the same.

long-term buy a poor investment

The jargon of the analyst:

> They are required to analyze corporate clients but these pieces of research never say anything negative. The worst phrase you might read is 'neutral' or 'long-term buy'. (*Sunday Telegraph*, 8 August 1999)

long-term relationship an exclusive extra-marital sexual arrangement

The language of the obituary, for both heterosexuals and homosexuals, the other party being a *long-term friend*.

long walk off a short pier (a) death by drowning

Usually murder.

longer-living *American* geriatric

From the moment we are born each of us is longer-living than those younger than ourselves.

loo a lavatory

Probably a corruption of *l'eau*, although this theory does not find favour everywhere.

look after (your) other interests to be peremptorily dismissed from employment
A face-saving reason commonly given for the sudden departure of a manager or director. If the *other interests* are said to be *expanding*, the departure is even more precipitate. The *other interests* may also be *pursued*.

look at the garden to urinate out of doors
Males say they are going to do it. They may also specify which part of the curtilage they intend to examine, such as the *compost heap*, the *roses*, or the *lawn*.

look in a cup to foretell the future
For some, the tea leaves reveal all. Divination has always been the subject of taboo.

look on the wine when it was red to be drunk
Or white, perhaps.

looking glass *obsolete Irish* a pot for urine
I draw your attention to the obvious joke involving the traveller who wished to adjust his tie, and the waitress, in *EDD* vol. iii, p. 635.

loop *obsolete* to kill by hanging
The association is with the noose:
> Like moussie thrappl't in a la',
> Or loon that's loopit by the law. (Ainslie, 1892—the mouse was throttled and a loon was a person of low rank)

looped *American* drunk
From *looping the loop*, acting like a fool (or LOOPY), or the inability to walk in a straight line? We can only guess.

loopy mentally abnormal
The imagery might come from railway shunting practice—see UP THE LOOP. The condition may be anything from severe to eccentric.

loose[1] promiscuous
Used of females rather than males, referring to a relaxation of moral standards.
A *loose woman* was a prostitute, working ON THE LOOSE, either in or out of a *loose house*, or brothel.
In former days she might be described as *loose in the hilts*, punning on a dagger unfit for use (Webster, 1623, quoted in *ODEP*).

loose[2] suffering from diarrhoea
A shortened form of *loose in the bowels* or suffering from the *loose disease*. To *loosen the bowels* is to cause to defecate, as by taking a laxative.

loose cannon a person whose unpredictable conduct may cause difficulties or embarrassment
The imagery is from the gun on a naval vessel which, if not properly secured, fired in another direction than the aimed broadside and caused mayhem on a rolling deck:
> Mr Clinton's policy team … view Mr Carter as a loose cannon. (*Daily Telegraph*, 19 September 1994)

loose in the attic mentally unstable
Attic is a slang word for head.
You may also hear *loose in the head*, or any of the other slang words for head.

Lord of the Flies the devil
Beelzebub, *fly-lord* in Hebrew, was Prince of the Flies in Syrian mythology.

Lord sends for you (the) you are dying
A Christian use, in the expectation of a meeting in heaven.
If *the Lord has you*, you are dead.

lose[1] fraudulently to destroy
What may happen to embarrassing or incriminating files, documents, and tapes:
> It was decided to temporarily lose particularly incriminating correspondence between Derby and the Deputy-Under-Secretary of the India Office. (Stewart, 1999)

lose[2] to dismiss from employment
The essence of this *loss* is that it is involuntary on the part of those dismissed.

lose[3] to be bereaved of
The evasion is used especially when speaking of the death of a relative.
A *loss* is any bereavement, regardless of the esteem in which the deceased was held.

lose hold to become mentally unbalanced
Also as *lose it, lose the plot*, or *lose your grip*.

lose the vital signs to die
Medical jargon which does not mean getting lost on a journey. A dead soldier may *lose the number of the mess* and a sailor may in similar punning fashion *lose the wind*.

lose your (good) character to be discovered in an impropriety
Until recently, the phrase was used of a single woman known to copulate before marriage, who might also be said to *lose her good name* or *lose her reputation*, whether or not she had been previously held in high regard, or to *lose her innocence*. Anyone, male or female, may *lose*

their good character after being convicted of a criminal offence.

lose your cherry (of a woman) to copulate for the first time
The *cherry* is the maidenhead.
The obsolete Scottish *lose your snood* meant the same thing, the silken snood being worn as a symbol of virginity.

lose your lunch to vomit
Usually when drunk or through seasickness. You may also *lose* other meals in this sense.

lose your shirt to be ruined or suffer an excessive financial loss
Figuratively, having nothing left to wear. An American may in the same sense *lose his vest* or *his pants*.

loss of separation flying dangerously close to another aircraft
Air traffic jargon.

loss-shopping taking profits in a jurisdiction with lower taxation
For a multinational, manufacturing or selling in countries with different rates of tax, the object is to show minimal profits or losses in those places where the tax burden is highest. The process is also known as *loss-trafficking*. The commonest mechanism for minimizing cost is through TRANSFER PRICING.

lost[1] engaged in prostitution
Although still aware of their whereabouts.

lost[2] killed
Usually of those engaged in military operations. Drowned sailors are *lost at sea*.

lot a battle in which there were many casualties
A First World War usage which sought to play down the horror of the carnage.

Lothario a male who constantly makes sexual proposals to women
And especially to those who are married. He was a character in Rowe's play of 1703, *The Fair Penitent*.

lotion an intoxicating drink
Originally, the action of washing, whence any liquid applied externally to the body.

love to have a sexual relationship with
Literally, to have affection for but standard English in its sexual senses. Thus a *love affair* may be anything from a formal courtship to a clandestine sexual relationship.

A *love child* is illegitimate, who might also have been said to be *love-born*, *love-begotten*, a *love bird*, or a *lover child*.
The *love muscle*, once romantically the heart, is now vulgarly the penis.
A *love nest* is the accommodation in which a mistress is housed.
Love is also used of homosexual arrangements and the *love that durst not speak its name* was male homosexuality, especially when it was illegal.
To *make love to*, which formerly mean to court, is now explicit of copulation, or *lovemaking*. See also LOVER.

loved one a dead person
Usually describing a member of the family, without regard to the appropriateness of the description, and jargon of the funeral profession.
Evelyn Waugh entitled his 1948 novel about the Californian funeral industry *The Loved One*, dedicating it to the wrong Mitford sister, Nancy instead of Jessica, whose 1963 *The American Way of Death* made a stir and her reputation.

lover a male extramarital sexual partner
Standard English and the masculine of MISTRESS. The plural *lovers* indicates two people involved in a sexual arrangement, either heterosexually or homosexually.

low-budget cheap
The word *budget* is used to avoid the association of cheapness and nastiness, especially in the production of films and television programmes. *Low-cost*, with the same inferences, is more generally used.

low flying speeding in a motor vehicle
As distinct from *flying low* (see also FLY A FLAG). The two are not used interchangeably.

low girls *obsolete* prostitutes
A judgement on their morals and status in their profession rather than on their stature.

low profile with an avoidance of publicity
The imagery is from tank warfare, where you try to keep behind cover to reduce the target. A usage of politicians and other public figures when they do what ought not to be done and leave undone what ought to be done.

lower abdomen the male genitalia
An evasion used by sports commentators when a sportsman has suffered a disabling blow.
The *lower stomach* may refer to the male or female genital regions.

lower ground floor a cellar or basement
To be found in restaurants and shops which seek to maximize their space but wish to avoid any implication of sending customers BELOW STAIRS[1].

lower limbs *obsolete* the legs
Common Victorian usage. The arms never became the *upper limbs*.

lower part anything to do with sexual activity
The location of the genitalia, what some see as the less attractive side of marriage, or a bit of both:

> I believe we shall have a happier union if all that 'perfectly natural but lower' part is eliminated from it. (French, 1995—being so instructed by his fiancée, it is not surprising that Francis Younghusband's later sexual conduct was a trifle bizarre)

lower the boom on to refuse to grant further credit to
The *boom* prevents any entry or exit until it has been raised.
The phrase is also used of an arrest, implying that the victim is being detained in port.

lubricate to bribe or facilitate through bribery
Another form of GREASE or OIL.
To *lubricate your tonsils* is to drink alcohol and *lubrication* is what you drink.

Lucy in the sky with diamonds lysergic acid diethylamide
Or *LSD* and the title of a Lennon/McCartney song of 1967.

lump *American* a corpse
Criminal and police jargon, a shortened form of *lump of meat*.

lunch box the male genitalia
Probably alluding to the shape through tight clothing. Mainly homosexual use.

lunch well to gormandize at midday
Not just eating healthy food. Usually the meal takes a long time and much alcohol is also consumed.

lunchtime engineering bribery
Describing excessive hospitality, where a vendor plies the customer's purchasing agent, clerk, or manager with intoxicants etc.

lungs a woman's breasts
Viewed sexually, but without much anatomical accuracy, by a male:

> '…it's not a bad piece.' 'Good lungs,' Eddie admitted. (Sanders, 1982—the woman so described was not a singer)

lush a drunkard
Literally, succulent:

> He was a lush. He got the sack. (Theroux, 1983—he was dismissed for drunkenness, not given some dry white wine)

Formerly a *lush* was an intoxicant.
Lushy and *lushed* mean drunk.
All these drunken images were once recalled by reference to a London lawyer, *Alderman Lushington*.

Lydford law arbitrary punishment
This is a sample entry of many British local geographical euphemisms. The tin-mining districts of Devonshire and Cornwall, known as the Stannary, made and policed their own laws. On one occasion a judge in the Devon border town of Lydford caused a tin-miner to be hanged in the morning before sitting in judgement on him the same afternoon.

M anything taboo beginning with the letter M
Especially marijuana in addict use.

madam the female keeper of a brothel
The lady of the HOUSE[1] from the days of Shakespeare's *Madam Mitigation* (*Measure for Measure*) onwards:
> 'What can I do for you, Madam?' 'Miss,' she said. 'In my country a lady doesn't like being mistaken for a madam.' (Deighton, 1978)

made at one heat *obsolete Somerset* stolen
When farm tools and household utensils were made in the local smithy, each article was formed by successive reheating and quenching. Only a thief avoided this laborious progression.

Magdalene a prostitute
Christ's disciple, Mary, was supposed to have been one before she changed her ways.

magic word (the) please
Not *abracadabra*, but a reminder to children who may forget their manners.

maid a female domestic servant
Originally, a virgin but standard English of a domestic servant since the 14th century.

mail a letter *American* to defecate
In Britain POST A LETTER uses the same vulgar imagery.

main thing (the) copulation
For Pepys and other males subsequently in their encounters with females:
> ... here finding Mrs Lane, took her over to Lambeth where we were lately, and there did what I would with her but only the main thing, which she would not consent to. (Pepys, 1663, with *but* meaning except)

mainline illegally to inject a narcotic intravenously
With railroad imagery and immediate effect. The *main line* is the vein in the arm.

mainstreaming seeking to favour chosen categories of person
The intention is to give preference to the interests of those other than white males unfairly, especially in employment and promotion (according to critics), or to give others their rightful opportunity in a society dominated by white males:
> Ms Harman's policy of 'mainstreaming', whereby every new government policy was examined for its impact on women, will be diluted. (*Sunday Telegraph*, 4 October 1988)

make[1] to copulate with extramaritally
The male *makes* the female but either sex can *make it with* the other.
A *make* can be the occasion or the female involved and, if the latter, usually embellished adjectivally as, for example, an *easy make*.

make[2] a theft
Criminal jargon:
> 'It's not a make,' I said. 'You're in trouble.' (Chandler, 1939—he was not just being accused of stealing)
In the British army, to *make* an object was to loot or steal it.

make a call to urinate
The CALL OF NATURE, punning on the social visit:
> 'I just want to make a call,' said Willoughby, and he disappeared into the toilet. (Bradbury, 1959)

make a hole in the water to kill yourself by drowning
Plunging from a height, but not of diving.

make a mess to urinate or defecate involuntarily or in an inappropriate place
Nursery and geriatric use when involuntary by humans, indoors by domestic pets.

make a move on to seek to engage sexually
Men do it to women with whom they have had no previous sexual relationship:
> She flinched. She thought he was making a move on her. (Rankin, 2000)
In America, also as *make the moves*, with imagery perhaps from a board game.
To *get a move on* is not to succeed in one's advances but to hurry up in any context.

make a play for *American* to seek to engage sexually
Perhaps from the football tactic and see also PLAY[1].

make a purse for yourself *obsolete* to steal or embezzle
You filled it without having to earn the contents:
> The wife of one of his acquaintance had fraudulently made a purse for herself out of her husband's fortune. (J. Boswell, 1791—the wife died without telling her husband where the money was. He told

Dr Johnson he was more hurt by her lack of confidence in him than by losing the money. The wife's sin was, in the eyes of men and the law, heinous, she not being entitled to own property in her own right)

make a (an improper) suggestion to propose casual copulation
Men do it to women and prostitutes do it to men.

make an honest woman of to marry a woman you have impregnated
Or, in former times, to marry your mistress. Less often as *make a decent woman of*. The usage, and the concept, are now rather dated.

make away with[1] to kill
The victims are usually domestic animals. Of humans, usually reflexive and referring to suicide:
    ... ready to make away with themselves. (Burton, 1621)

make away with[2] to steal
The act of physical removal.

make babies together to copulate with each other
Usually within marriage and not anticipating a multiple birth or using IVF. To *make a child*, which is marginally less cloying and not euphemistic, means to become a parent.

make for the exit to kill yourself
Going out voluntarily:
    As soon as I'm quite sure I have an irreversible terminal condition I shall make for the Exit while I'm still able to walk out unassisted. (Lodge, 2001)

make happy to copulate with promiscuously
The female, not necessarily a prostitute, is normally the person who makes the offer:
    'You've been a good man and I want to make you happy.' He shook his head ... Maybe some other time. (McCall Smith, 1998—a better man than she supposed, perhaps)

make little of *Irish* to copulate with outside marriage
Usually with the woman as the object, after which she is made large by impregnation:
    You let *David Power*, the doctor's son, make little of you, and get you into trouble? (Binchy, 1985)

make love to to copulate with
In gentler times it meant no more than to flirt with or court. Now standard English and also used of homosexual activity.

To *make love to yourself* is to masturbate, especially of a female:
    She sometimes made love to herself on the bath mat. (McCarthy, 1963)

make off with to steal
Standard English. It is never your own property, or wife, that you take with you.

make old bones to live long
Euphemistic in the negative, in which the phrase is normally used:
    I feel I shall never make old bones. (N. Mitford, 1945)

make out with to have a sexual relationship with
Make in with might appear more logical.

make room for tea to urinate
A jocular and almost genteel usage, although based on flawed physiology. You may also claim to be *making room for it, another beer*, etc.

make sheep's eyes at to show sexual interest in (another)
Like the unintelligent staring of the wide-eyed beast. In former times you might *cast sheep's eyes at* the object of your desire:
    I have often seen him cast a sheep's eye out of a calf's head at you. (Swift, 1738—*calf* also implies youthful longing, as in *calf love*)

make the beast with two backs see BEAST

make the (bed) springs creak to copulate
The usual BED[2] imagery. The *springs* may also *squeak* under the same provocation.

make the chick scene *American* to copulate
Of a male but not usually with a CHICK, or prostitute. The phrase may also be used to rebut a suggestion of male homosexuality.

make the supreme sacrifice to be killed on war service
Not necessarily in action.

make time with *American* to seek to engage sexually
The imagery is unclear.

make tracks to escape or leave in a hurry
Most of those about whom this phrase is used are anxious not to *make tracks* which others might follow.

make up to to attempt to court
Either sex can *make up to* the other.

make use of to do something taboo in connection with
Thus to *make use of prostitutes* is not to find them chaste employment but to copulate regularly with them: to *make use of drugs* is not to control your hypertension under medical supervision but to ingest narcotics illegally; so too with firearms, where to *make use of a weapon* is to maim or kill:
> I saw a Jewess climb on to the fence of the ghetto, stick her head through the fence and attempt to steal turnips from a passing cart. I made use of my fire-arm. The Jewess received two fatal shots. (Deighton, 1993/1, quoting from Schoenberner's *Der Gelbe Stern*, translated by Susan Sweet in 1969)

make water to urinate
Discharge would be more accurate. Standard English.
See also WATER.

make way with to have a sexual relationship with
Maritime imagery, perhaps, although to *make way* normally means to allow to pass:
> [He] tried to make way with Oretta, who had him by about thirty years. (Turow, 1999)

make whoopee to copulate
Literally, to celebrate or carouse.

make your bones to kill (someone)
Committing a murder was said to be a prerequisite of full membership of the Mafia. Some figurative use, indicating worthiness for a position of authority or experience:
> The men behind him were old-time spooks who had made their bones on the Berlin Wall when the concrete was not even dry. (Forsyth, 1994)

make yourself available to indicate promiscuity
Not a politician modestly suggesting he be chosen as a candidate but a woman signalling sexual desire to a man.

maladjustment severe mental illness
Literally, faulty adjustment of anything. In educational jargon, *maladjusted*, of children, means that they are naughty or ill-disciplined.

malady of France *obsolete* syphilis
Also known as the FRENCH ACHE:
> My Moll is dead i' th' spital
> Of malady of France. (Shakespeare, *Henry V*—an anachronism as the disease had not been imported from the Americas in 1420)

male homosexual
As in *male videos* or *movies*, for the delectation of those who are *male identified* or *oriented*. But not *tout court* on a lavatory door.

male beast see BIG ANIMAL

male parts the genitalia
Not the beard, manly breast, or other physical indications of masculinity.
See also PRIVATE PARTS.

Malta dog dysentery
Contracted by British servicemen stationed on the island. I cannot explain the canine imagery.

man¹ a woman's male sexual partner
Sometimes her husband; sometimes as different from her husband.
Man friend is explicit in this sense of someone other than her husband.

man² *American* a policeman or warder
Mainly criminal jargon. *The Man* is a prison governor:
> If he went to The Man to complain about it, you got him alone some place, more places to ambush a man in prison.... (McBain, 1981)

man about town a philanderer
Literally, a person often seen in society:
> In his youth, Marcus Sieff had the reputation of being something of a man about town, and he married four times. (*Daily Telegraph*, 24 February 2001)

man cow see BIG ANIMAL

man friend see MAN¹

man of pleasure a profligate
Not just enjoying being alive but also seeking the company of a *lady of pleasure* (see also LADY):
> Talking of London [Dr Johnson] observed...a man of pleasure [thinks of it] as an assemblage of taverns, and the great emporium for ladies of easy virtue. (J. Boswell, 1791)

man-root see ROOT

manage the attrition rate to dismiss from employment
Attrition is natural diminution or wastage:
> Linklaters readily admits to managing the 'attrition rate' of its assistants. (*Financial Times*, 2 June 2003)

management privileges promiscuous copulation with a female employee
A feature, it is said, of the entertainment industry. Also as *managerial privileges*.

manhood the male genitalia
Literally, the state of being an adult male:
> ... tying a handkerchief round the remains
> of his once proud manhood. (Sharpe,
> 1979—he had snagged his penis on a
> rosebush)

To *eliminate manhood* is to castrate.
The *needs of manhood* are copulation.

manure the rotted matter incorporating
the excreta of cattle, has so long been
standard English that we may forget its
origin as a euphemistic corruption of
main d'œuvre. The linguistic progression
went from holding land, to farming it, to
fertilizing it.

many pounds heavier much fatter
Perhaps written more of women, who can be
more sensitive on the subject of weight than
men:
> From time to time, she returned to the
> screen many pounds heavier. (*Daily
> Telegraph*, 19 March 2001, in an obituary of
> the actress Ann Sothern)

marbles the testicles
The association is with the glass spheres, or
alleys, which used to be made of marble.
However, it is not only men who, if mentally
unstable, figuratively *lose their marbles*.

march to a different drummer to be
mentally ill
And out of step.

marching orders dismissal from employment
Not immediately into action but permanently
out of it:
> Sir John Brown said the oil giant ... had
> given 12,000 employees their marching
> orders by the end of July with another
> 2,500 expected by the end of the year.
> (*Daily Telegraph*, 11 August 1999)

margin compression adverse trading conditions
Things which you suggest are beyond your
control are pushing down your gross and net
profit *margins*:
> [Poor results from Zimbabwe due to what]
> the chief executive delicately described as
> 'margin compression'. (*Daily Telegraph*, 9
> August 2005)

marginalized not belonging to a dominant racial or sexual group
Supposedly living on the edge of a society
which does you no favours:
> ... the political drive for 'empowerment' of
> 'marginalised' groups such as blacks,

women and gays. (Mary Kenny in *Sunday
Telegraph*, 30 January 1994)

Maria Monk the male semen
Rhyming slang for SPUNK, from *The Awful
Disclosures of Maria Monk*, a scurrilous anti-
Catholic and pornographic book published in
the 19th century and said to be still in print.
My apologies to the poetess who died in 1715,
and whom I once wrongly associated with this
vulgarism.

marital aid an instrument to use in seeking sexual pleasure
Less likely to feature in any sexual exchange
within wedlock than in solitary activity.

marital rights copulation by a man with
his wife
In the days when this phrase was used
seriously, the sexual meaning transcended
the economic and other *rights* which a
husband acquired over his wife and her
possessions when they married. Both lay and
ecclesiastical law held that it was a woman's
duty to copulate with her husband on request,
even at the risk of dangerous, debilitating,
and unwanted pregnancies. Today the phrase
is used only by husbands with willing wives
and a dated sense of humour.

mark¹ *obsolete Scottish* an invulnerable
spot on the body of a wizard or witch
It played an important role when it came to
unmasking them:
> ... through which mark, when a large
> brass pin was thrust till it was bowed, both
> men and women, neither felt a pain, nor
> did it bleed. (Ritchie, 1883)

mark² a swindler's victim
First watched, or *marked*, for his suitability. He
who *walked penniless in Mark Lane* had been
swindled, although not necessarily in that
London street.

mark a card to register formal dissatisfac-
tion with an employee
The imagery is from golf, where another
player checks your score, but in this usage,
only the bad shots go down:
> I should have shut up and taken the
> bollocking ... I just hoped he hadn't
> marked my card. (McNab, 1995)

market timing dishonestly selecting a favourable price at which to do a deal
As long as the contract has the right date, the
out-of-town client has no chance of telling
when precisely the bargain was made, allowing the broker to take advantage of any
subsequent movement before completing
the record:

Harrington helped Spitzer identify two vicious mutual fund practices, 'late booking' and 'market timing'. (*Sunday Telegraph*, 4 January 2004)

market value adjuster a penalty imposed by the insurer on those who draw their pensions before the specified date
The insurers use the mechanism to deter customers from withdrawing funds:
> ...Market Value Adjusters—the industry euphemism for deducting an arbitrary sum if you take your money out at any time other than on long pre-arranged dates. (*Daily Telegraph*, 10 September 2004)

marriage joys copulation
But what of shared children, companionship, warmed slippers, and cooked meals? Also as the *marriage act*, which is not nuptials.

martyr to (a) suffering from
The death or persecution is only figurative. The *Daily Telegraph* on 7 September 1978 hesitated to call the Prime Minister a liar, a *martyr to selective amnesia* being a more telling and memorable indictment. He who describes himself as *a martyr to indigestion* is merely telling you he has occasional dyspepsia.

Mary marijuana
The abbreviation is used in pop songs for oblique reference to narcotics. Because some English speakers pronounce the J in *marijuana*, sometimes also as *Mary Jane* or *MJ*.

Mary Fivefingers male self-masturbation
The lady is either the same as, or closely related to, the FIVE-FINGERED WIDOW. Also as *Mary Palm*.

masculinity the male genitalia
Or one of the component parts:
> ...lays out his masculinity on the tabletop, where Gasha Rani mistakes it for a Havana cigar. (Dalrymple, 1998)

massage¹ to bribe or flatter
Literally, to apply friction to muscles to loosen them up.

massage² *American* to assault violently
Police jargon for the use of force to obtain information:
> 'Shellacking', 'massaging',... and numerous other phrases are employed by the police... as euphemisms to express how they compel reluctant prisoners to refresh their memories. (Lavine, 1930)

massage³ to overstate or wrongly increase (figures)

It is done by brokers seeking to talk up a stock, or accountants wishing to show profits or assets higher than they really are:
> The massaging of profits came at a 'vital time' for the company, which was floated by Walker in 1985. (*Daily Telegraph*, 3 June 1994—some officers were accused of false accounting)

massage parlour a brothel
The friction applied may indeed be toning up a taboo muscle, for a short while:
> Whether we worked in a Massage Parlour or were rich... we [Indonesians] were all the same too [British soldiers]. Easy women. (Bogarde, 1978)

Whence *massage*, masturbation, by a *masseuse*, a prostitute:
> 'You want a massage,' she says. I says forget it. They don't mean massage. (Theroux, 1975)

mate to copulate
Literally, to pair, of animals and, less often, humans:
> He'll never be able to mate with a woman again. (West, 1979—but what other partner may he have had in mind?)

A *mating* is an act of copulation.

mattress (in compounds and phrases) relating to copulation
The common association of beds and copulating, in such phrases as *mattress drill* and *beating the mattress*. *Mattress extortion* is sexual blackmail or persuasion.

mature old
Literally, fully developed:
> ...the high payers at the front wind up with some of the more mature girls. (Moynahan, 1983—older stewardesses tend to work the first-class section in aircraft)

Matured, less common, is a synonym.
A *mature student* is not necessarily a wise and well-rounded one, but an adult who has rejoined academe as a pupil, usually on a full-time basis.

maturer fatter
The language of those who seek to sell clothes to older women, who generally have put on weight and acquired a *maturer figure*.

maul to caress (a reluctant female)
Literally, to handle roughly, but to an unwilling partner, any male fondling is excessive.

mausoleum crypt *American* a drawer for a corpse facing on to a corridor
The slots which are harder to sell, given the absence of a view.

A far cry from the tomb Mausoleus' widow built at Halicarnassus around 353 BC, with the help of a few thousand slaves.

me-too (of goods and services) exactly copying
Commercial use where a product is launched virtually identical with that of a competitor in an attempt to exploit a market he has developed.

measure for the drop to dismiss from employment
It is one of the duties of the hangman, although weight was more important than height if the job were to be performed properly, and punning on *dropping*, or ceasing to select, a player in a team game.

meat¹ a person viewed sexually
Male or female, heterosexually or homosexually.
A *bit of meat* is a man's sexual partner.
A young prostitute is *fresh meat* and an old one, *stale meat*.

meat² (and two veg) the male penis or genitalia
Usually, as *meat* alone, in a phrase such as *tube of meat* or *hot meat*:
   A lot of [young women] look like they need…a hot meat injection. (Styron, 1976)
Meat and two veg may be used without any sexual overtones:
   …carrying a carving knife with which she planned, she shrieked, 'to cut off his meat and two veg'. (Monkhouse, 1993)

meat³ a human corpse
Although not for consumption.
A *meat wagon* is an ambulance, a hearse, or a police van.

meat rack *American* a meeting place for male homosexuals
Punning on MEAT¹ and the butcher's display. In obsolete British use, a *meat-house* was a brothel.

medal showing a visible undone fly button on trousers
A pre-zip warning from one male to another. Also as an *Abyssinian medal*, from a campaign which lasted from 1893 to 1896 without reflecting much glory on the invaders.

meddle with to have a sexual relationship with
Literally, to interfere with, which may have similar sexual overtones:
   [Cutting the horse's reins] is the crackers' way of warning you not to meddle with their women. (Naipaul, 1989)

medical correctness the avoidance in speech of direct reference to a taboo condition or illness
Not diagnosing patients accurately or treating them wisely:
   Medical Correctness is motivated by compassion, but seized by a dangerous illusion, that if you change words, you change reality. (M. Holman in *Financial Times*, October 1994)
See also POLITICALLY CORRECT.

medicated under narcotic influence
But not prescribed by a medical adviser:
   Court papers said Stopp was 'so intoxicated' or 'medicated' that he was 'unable to sing a single Creed song'. (*Daily Telegraph*, 25 April 2003)

medicine spirituous intoxicants
This substance is seldom ingested to treat disease.
The pretence that we drink SPIRITS for our health is not new, nor does it confound our critics.

medium small
Literally, between little and big, but not in the grocery business or at the coffee shop.

medium machine an atomic bomb
The Soviet Russian equivalent of similar American and British false names intended to deceive, from the *tank* onwards.

meet *obsolete* to engage in a duel
Not just a social coming together, and a *meeting* was the subsequent contest:
   He was so offensive…that I was obliged to ask him whether he would meet me elsewhere. (O'Brian, 1970)
If however your chosen companion says to you 'I've met someone', it refers not to a duel but to the end of your sexual relationship.

meet your Maker to die
This and similar expressions are used even by those with no confidence that the rendezvous will be kept. Similarly, a Muslim might, if so favoured, *meet the Prophet*.

meeting (at/in a) the place where you claim to be when you wish to avoid someone
The standard rebuff to an unwelcome caller in person or on the telephone.

mellow drunk
Literally, ripe, and a euphemism since the 17th century.

melons *American* the breasts of an adult female

Either *tout court*, or as *watermelons*, perhaps for those with a larger bust.

member the penis
Literally, any part of the body.
Also, for classicists, the *membrum virile*.

memorial relating to death
Literally, maintaining a memory or reminder of anything. American, rather than British, usage, and especially the *memorial counsellor*, who may induce you to buy the dearest package for a funeral.
A *memorial house* is a building attached to a cemetery for the placing of tablets recording deaths. The American *memorial society* is the equivalent of the old-fashioned British funeral club in which poor people invested so that they could enjoy a decent interment.

men in sandals unworldly philanthropists
A slighting term for a type of person thought to be unfamiliar with commercial reality:
    Earlier this week we advised Mr Kennedy [the Leader of the Liberal Democrats] to depart with honour before the 'men in sandals' came for him. (*Daily Telegraph*, 16 December 2005—they did and he didn't)

men in suits managers or those in a learned profession other than medicine
A derogatory use by those who produce wealth through skills or physical labour. See also SUITS.

men of respect *American* members of the Mafia
What they call themselves. Others use less flattering appellations.

men's magazine a pornographic publication for male readers
Not *The Economist* or *The Spectator* but equally likely to be kept on the TOP SHELF.

men('s room) a lavatory for male use only
Usually so described in a severe building where nobody is trying to sell you anything. The counterpart of *men* is WOMEN, but you are likely to seek in vain a *women's room*.

ménage à trois three people living together in a sexual relationship
Literally, domestic arrangements for three and sometimes shortened to *à trois*.

menses menstruation
Literally, in Latin, month(s). Formerly standard English in the singular but now always in the plural.

mental suffering from a permanent illness of the mind
Literally, pertaining to any mind, without any suggestion of illness.
Those described as *mentally deficient* do not suffer from a minor loss nor are they suffering from a temporary defect. Also as *mentally challenged*.

mental disease *obsolete* syphilis
A common usage in the days when those with third-degree syphilis, along with dipsomaniacs, formed the majority of those in lunatic asylums:
    ...even in 1966 Winston's son Randolph referred to his grandfather as suffering from a 'severe mental disease'. (R. Massie, 1992—Lord Randolph Churchill had contracted syphilis either from a prostitute at Oxford or from a maid at Blenheim after his wife's confinement with Winston)

mental health day *American* an additional paid holiday
Employees are allowed six a year in addition to their normal allocation, presumably in the hope of keeping them sane.

merchant banker a male term of abuse
Additional to any association with the disrespect in which some hold the calling. Rhyming slang for *wanker*.

mercy death the murder of a patient thought to be terminally ill
And as *mercy killing*.
Also favoured by the Nazis:
    ...the Gestapo is now systematically bumping off the mentally deficient people...the Nazis call them 'mercy deaths'. (Shirer, 1984)

merger accounting the false statement of subsequent profitability
Literally, the creation of provisions against the cost of assimilating an acquisition:
    By the alchemy of merger accounting, some of the 'cost' could be recycled into profits. (*Daily Telegraph*, 16 November 1990—it was suggested that some £60 million were thus shown as profit by Burton after its contested acquisition of the store group Debenhams)

merry drunk
Cheerful, but not offensive. A venerable usage but still current.

merry-begot *obsolete* illegitimate
Conceived in pleasure rather than in drink.

meshugga mentally unstable
From the Yiddish *shagig*, to go astray or wander (*OED*).

mess¹ to act promiscuously
A shortened form of *mess about*, to act in an irresponsible or disorganized manner, which has the same sexual meaning. If you *mess about with* someone, you have a promiscuous relationship with that person:
> ... money to fling around, a girl to mess about with in the back of a car. (Garve, 1963)

To *mess with yourself* is to masturbate.

mess² faeces or urine in an unwanted place
Mainly of household pets, but also of other animals.
To *mess your pants* is to defecate into them involuntarily.

message *American* an advertisement
Television jargon.

Mexican brown *American* marijuana
Not the tan you look for in Cancun.
Also as *Mexican green* or *red*. A *Mexican mushroom* is the hallucinogenic *Psilocybe mexicana*.

Mexican raise *American* a promotion with no increase in pay
Many Mexicans working in the United States without permits are subject to exploitation. A *Mexican promotion* means the same thing.

mickey *Irish* the penis
An example of the common practice of using a masculine name.
In Australian slang a *mickey* is the vagina, but whether this comes from the Shakespearean MOUSE or from seeing things upside down I cannot say.

Mickey (Finn) a drugged intoxicant
Named after a late 19th-century Chicago innkeeper of evil repute. The commonest additive is chlorine, reacting with alcohol with dire effects (which also explains why ex-servicemen who soldiered in remote parts of the globe where all drinking water was heavily chlorinated still tend to drink their spirits neat). Sometimes as *Mickey tout court* or as *MF*.

Mickey Mouse fraudulent
From the cartoon character via the slang meaning, bogus or ineffective:
> It was the revenue who made the first breach of Fleet Street's Spanish practices by exposing the Mickey Mouse payments to printers. (*Daily Telegraph*, 11 August 1994)

middle age the decades prior to becoming a geriatric
Halfway to three score years and ten is 35 but no man under 45 or woman under 50 would

admit to having reached *middle age*:
> Though himself only in early middle-age, the King reminded his listeners that: 'For the second time in the lives of most of us we are at war.' (Kee, 1984—George VI was 44 at the time)

middle-aged spread obesity
A normal function of ageing.

midnight baby *American* an illegitimate child
The time would seem to have been chosen from the supposed moment of conception rather than that of the birth.

midwives' mercy *obsolete* infanticide of an unwanted or deformed baby
A usage in the days of high infant mortality and no antenatal treatment.

migraine a condition blamed for avoiding an obligation or to excuse an indiscretion
Mainly called in aid by women who seek to excuse unwarranted absence from work, or refusal to copulate with their regular sexual partner; or to suggest that they are not drunkards.
Men so afflicted tend to have *bad backs*.

migration forcible deportation as slave labour or for killing
One of the Nazi evasions used in France:
> So 'deportation' was labelled *Abwanderung* (migration), *Evakuierung* (evacuation), *Umseidlung* (resettlement) and, closer to reality but still not that close, *Verschickung zur Zwangarbeit* (sending away for forced labour). (Ousby, 1997)

militant a terrorist
Literally, an aggressive or soldierly person:
> But, inadvertently, the BBC has discovered one bit of truth. If you try to use euphemisms, such as the BBC's preferred word 'militants' for terrorists, the language boomerangs on you. (*Daily Telegraph*, 26 March 2003)

military intelligence spying
It could mean no more than knowing how to fire a gun:
> Foreigners have spies; Britain has military intelligence. (Follett, 1978)

militia an armed body operating outside normal military regulations
Literally, a body supplementing, and under the control of, regular forces.
The French *milice* in the Second World War facilitated the rule of the German occupier,

including rounding up Jews for deportation and murder:

> ... the *Service de l'Ordre Légionnaire*—which is now the Milice—the scum of the scum. (Price, 1978)

milk to cheat or defraud
In general use, to steal small amounts from an inventory or till on a regular basis. Also of stealing fuel from a vehicle by siphoning it into a container. In the racing world, to *milk* means to bet against your own horse which is ridden to lose, or fraudulently to set up an outsider as favourite at short odds.

minor function (the) urination
Defecation is not, however, designated the *major function*.

minor wife a mistress
A Far Eastern usage.

minority those of a different colour, religion, or sex from the majority
The word is only used in connection with taboo or sensitive subjects:

> I used to be coloured, right? Then I was a negro. And then I turned into an Afro-American. After that I was just a member of a Minority Group. Now I'm black. (Theroux, 1982)

Minority issues do not relate, for example, to philatelists, train spotters, or potholers.

minus indicating eccentricity or a lack of common sense
Normally the person is described as being *minus buttons* or *screws* but you come across numerous variants:

> This is one sick jungle-bunny minus one jar on the shelf. (J. Patterson, 2002)

mirror operation a firm formed to continue a previous business while avoiding its liabilities
Not one manufacturing glasses or publishing a type of newspaper daily.

misadventure the consequence of error or negligence
Medical jargon. Elsewhere in life *misadventures* tend to be caused by bad luck. A *therapeutic misadventure* means that the patient died after receiving incorrect treatment and a *surgical misadventure* tells us that the scalpel slipped.

misbehave to engage in sexual activity outside marriage
Either heterosexual or homosexual:

> Elspeth, I have reason to believe, misbehaved in a potting-shed at Windsor Castle with that randy little pig the Prince of Wales. (Fraser, 1994—the holder of that

title was later crowned as Edward VII)

> *The Times* reported: 'They saw two men under a tree misbehaving.' (Parris, 1995—a young soldier and a government minister were masturbating each other in St James's Park, London)

misconduct *obsolete* extramarital copulation
Literally, bad behaviour and usually *committed* in press reports.

misfortune *obsolete* an illegitimate child
Literally, ill-luck, which it was at one time for the mother and child.
An illegitimate child might also be called a *misbegot* or a *mishap*. In its literal sense, an accident, a *mishap* was also the premature delivery of a foetus, in which case the animal or woman was said to *misgo*.

misplace to lose through negligence.
Not just put in the wrong place:

> At the end of the hearing last year [the Financial Services Authority] was forced to admit that it had 'misplaced' (i.e. lost) vital documents. (*Daily Telegraph*, 24 February 2005)

miss[1] *obsolete* a mistress
If a man *kept a miss*, he was not attending to the care and maintenance of his young female offspring.

miss[2] to fail to menstruate at due time
Shortened form of *miss a period* and often with overtones of unwanted pregnancy.
Mis(s) is a common abbreviation for miscarriage.

miss the bus to fail to seize an opportunity
The term was used by Neville Chamberlain when on 6 April 1940 he told the world 'One thing is certain—[Hitler] missed the bus'. Weeks later the Germans overran France and drove the British into the sea.
Also as *miss the boat*.

missing trader *British* a criminal involved in tax fraud
Goods are imported into Britain without paying Value Added Tax, which is collected when the goods are resold. The importer then vanishes without paying the tax to the Inland Revenue in what is known as the *missing trader fraud*. In 2006 the extent of this trade meant that the reported growth of exports had been overstated by around 9%, apart from the unpaid taxation.

missionary position (the) copulation during which the male lies atop the female

Not the status of those who take the Gospel among the heathen but from the practice of missionaries among the Polynesians, who had favoured a quadripedal approach.

misspeak to lie
Originally, to speak evil or to speak incorrectly. One of Richard Nixon's Watergate contributions to linguistics.

mistake[1] a child unintentionally conceived
Usually within marriage but also of illegitimacy.

mistake[2] urination or defecation other than in a prepared place
By young children or domestic pets:
    That was enough to make her father overlook the chewed shoes and occasional mistakes with which the dog was littering the house. (Clancy, 1987)

mistaken developments the loss of Jewish scientific inventiveness
An unintended consequence of Nazi persecution:
    In a euphemism surpassing any Stalinist circumlocution, General Blumentritt referred to the Nazis' anti-semitism as 'the mistaken developments since 1933'. (Beevor, 2002—the General was not worried about the genocide)

mistress a man's regular extramarital sexual partner
Originally, the female head of the household, but now always used in this sense except when shortened to *Mrs* or as the title of a schoolteacher.
Kept mistress is explicit.

misuse to copulate with outside marriage
Literally, to treat wrongly.
See also USE[1].

mitotic disease cancer
Medical jargon but scientifically unspecific, *mitotis* being the process whereby a cell splits into two identical parts.

mixed heritage born to parents of different race
Half-caste and similar phrases are now taboo. The BBC uses *mixed heritage* because *mixed race* is now also thought to be offensive.

mob an association of criminals
From the Latin *mobile vulgis*, the rabble.

mobility impaired crippled
Literally, weakened in strength. Circumlocution which implies that the weakening was

effected by some external agency.
See also IMPAIRED HEARING.

model a prostitute
Shortened form of *model girl*, a mannequin. I am sure that many women so described lead conventional sexual lives. However, prostitutes who advertise their availability through telephone booths and other media often profess to be so employed, as do high-class prostitutes who have no need to advertise:
    Miss Keeler, 20, a freelance model, was visiting Miss Marilyn Rice-Davies, an actress. (*Daily Telegraph*, December 1962)

modern (of weapons) nuclear
A perhaps obsolete military usage, to differentiate from old-fashioned ways of killing people:
    ...the power, range and prospective development of 'modern' weapons—a frequent euphemism—would favour a surprise attack against the United States. (H. Thomas, 1986, quoting US Chiefs of Staff paper of September 1945)

modern conveniences *British* a lavatory and bathroom indoors
Usually shortened in classified advertisements to *(all) mod cons*. The *all* suggests hot running water rather than a jacuzzi.

modernization[1] rendering habitable
Jargon of the estate agent when selling a ramshackle property, in such phrases as *ripe for modernization*.

modernization[2] an expensive change
Political language when a policy is introduced which may cause a deterioration in service but will cost more:
    [Haine announced] he was going to make a speech calling for the 'modernisation' of the tax system. By now we have come to realize that 'modernisation' is code for tax rises. (*Daily Telegraph*, 23 June 2003)

mole a conspirator or spy within an organization
Espionage and labour union jargon, from the habit of the mammal to work underground, and its blackness, but not its blindness.

molest to assault sexually
Originally, to inconvenience, but so pervasive is the euphemism that a female may be reported as having been brutally assaulted but not *molested*, unless the assailant's motives were sexual as well as predatory.
A *child molester* is a paedophile.

moll *obsolete* a prostitute
Originally, a sweetheart, which survives in the

gangster's *moll*. The derivation is from the common girl's name, and a *moll-shop* was a brothel.

Moll Thompson's mark meant nothing more than emptiness, of a bottle, punning on the initials *MT*.

Molotov cocktail a simple petrol bomb
Molotov was Stalin's Foreign Minister in the Second World War. His long and sinister career included making a pact with Hitler in 1939 and organizing the postwar occupation of Eastern European states. The weapon by which he is remembered was in fact invented by the Finns for use against their Russian invaders.

mom-and-pop staid and old fashioned
Like your aged parents and often of a small retail business.
Some figurative use:
> Are you gonna be a mom-and-pop camcorder with Kuralt-ian notions of 'on the road', or are you up to heavyweight digital effects and dazzling graphics? (*Fly Rod and Reel*, March 1991)

Monday morning quarterback *American* a fantasist who judges by hindsight
The spectator who watches the weekend game may take his criticism to work with him on Monday.

money house a paying audience
Not a treasury. Empty seats during a theatrical performance discourage audiences and actors alike, which is why entry may be offered free or at reduced prices. A *good money house* is one where the audience have all paid to be there.

monkey¹ (the) *American* addiction to illegal narcotics
Probably from *having a monkey on your back* which you cannot shake off:
> You think it's the monkey that's killing you. (Macdonald, 1971, writing of a heroin addict, not a zoo-keeper)

monkey² *obsolete British* a mortgage
Again something which it is hard to get free from.

monkey business promiscuity
Literally, any mischief which a monkey might get up to. Used sometimes as a warning to a man to behave decorously towards a young woman.

monosyllable *obsolete* the vagina
The taboo *cunt*.
Grose says 'A woman's commodity'.

Montezuma's revenge diarrhoea
Usually, but not necessarily, contracted in

Mexico by visitors from the United States. Montezuma II was the Aztec emperor when Cortes invaded Mexico, and was killed by his own people in 1520 after he had told them to submit to the invader.
Also as the AZTEC TWO-STEP, *Mexican toothache*, *Mexican two-step*, *Mexican foxtrot*, etc.

monthly period menstruation
Not how many days a month lasts. Standard English, sometimes shortened to *monthlies*:
> Molly was easily excited, especially about the eighth day after her monthlies had ceased. (F. Harris, 1925)

Month's is obsolete.
Monthly courses is also obsolete but a woman my still suffer from *monthly blues*:
> 'You all right?' 'Yes.' 'Monthly blues?' (de Mille, 1988)

mooch *obsolete* to pilfer
Originally, to hang about, whence to beg, and then to steal.
This is an example of a word which has reverted from its euphemistic to its proper use in modern speech.

mood freshener an illicit drug
From the stimulus.

moon to expose the buttocks to others by lowering clothes in public
A *moon-like* expanse of flesh is so revealed:
> ... the Chinese soldiers provoking incidents by dropping their pants and presenting the bare bums northward, mooning the Soviet border. (Theroux, 1988, writing about the Manchurian border)

moon people lunatics
Not lowering their trousers in public or belonging to an eastern cult but from the venerable association of the Latin *luna* with *lunacy*.

moonlight¹ associated with smuggling
It was the weather condition during which the contraband could be taken ashore and hidden or distributed with less chance of detection. Smuggled spirits were known as *moonlight* and smugglers were said to have been *bred in the moonlight*.
A *moonraker* was also a smuggler, from the practice of hiding contraband in a pool for later recovery by trawling for it with a rake.
Moonshine was whisky illegally distilled, but not necessarily at night.

moonlight² *obsolete Irish* to wound
Violence in 19th-century agrarian disturbances tended to take place at night, with warnings about arson and assault being signed *Captain Moonlight*:

He had deposed to his experience of being moonlighted in the thigh. (*Daily Telegraph*, November 1888)

moonlight³ to work at a second job
The work is often done in the evening, without paying tax on the earnings.
The word is also used of those who continue to draw unemployment monies from the state without revealing earnings from casual employment.

moonlight flit the clandestine departure of an absconding debtor
Formerly, a tenant in arrears with his rent, whose chattels could be distrained by the landlord so long as they remained in the rented premises, but not elsewhere.
You might in similar fashion have made a *moonlight flight, march, touch,* or *walk,* or have been said to *bolt* or *shoot the moon.*
The term is also used of avoiding other creditors.
See also FLIT².

moose *American* a prostitute
Neither a corruption of MOUSE nor punning on the deer (or dear), but a Korean War usage from the Japanese *musume*, a girl (*DAS*).

mop up to kill or capture
Military jargon of what happens in the aftermath of a battle or war, when the enemy has been dispersed, with imagery from cleaning spillage.

more than a (good) friend a person with whom you have an extramarital sexual relationship
Another kind of FRIEND.
And in similar phrases, such as *more than just friends.*

morning after (the) a hangover
Shortened form of *the morning after the night before,* when excessive or adulterated alcohol had been consumed.

most precious part the male genitalia
Valued in this usage, by the male at least, for copulation rather than urination:
Corporal Browne was hit in the most precious part of his body. (Farran, 1948)

moth in your wallet (a) stinginess
The *Tineola bisselliella* doesn't normally go for leather, although it favours an undisturbed site for its eggs.

mother¹ *American* an elderly male homosexual
The obsolete British meaning was a bawd.

mother² *American* a term of vulgar abuse

Shortened form of *motherfucker,* but those who use it are unlikely to know that Oedipus was said to have sired four children by Jocasta in a complex saga which includes blinding and suicide as well as incest. Used as an insult, but an inanimate object may also be so castigated.

mother-in-law a mixture of old and bitter ale
Where are the *father-in-law* jokes (if such they be)?

mother's blessing *obsolete* a narcotic administered to a baby
The *blessing* was the peace which came from silencing a crying child:
Give the babies a dose of 'Mother's Blessing' (that's laudanum, sir, or some sich stuff) to sleep 'em when they're squally. (Mayhew, 1862)
The usage and practice continued until after the Second World War.

mother's ruin gin
In the 19th century, cheapness led to wide female addiction and consequent demoralization. Now only humorous use.
Occasionally as the punning *mother's milk.*

motion (a) defecation
Medical jargon, and not just of sitting up in bed but from the movement of the bowels, which result in *motions,* or faeces.

motion discomfort airsickness
Airline jargon, in support of the pretence that any regular passenger actually enjoys flying.
The *motion discomfort bag* you may find on an American airliner is for you to vomit in.

mount to copulate with
Standard English of animals. Occasional use of humans puns on the action of mounting a horse:
Like a full-acorn'd boar, a German one, Cried 'O' and mounted. (Shakespeare, *Cymbeline*)
The punning *mounting drill* was popular among cavalrymen.
A male may describe his complaisant sexual partner as *a good mount*; it remains a mystery where the *bad mounts* get to.

mount a corporal and four (of a male) to masturbate
It puns on the constitution of an army guard and the thumb and four fingers.

mountain chicken the hind legs of a giant toad
A Dominican specialty:
We ate a big dish of 'mountain chicken', a rich white meat fried in batter. Each

succulent serving was revealed, too late, to have been the hindlegs of a giant toad. (Whicker, 1982—and unfortunate for the toad also)

mountain dew whisky
From the process of distillation and the place where it is done.

mountain sickness arrogance
A disease to which politicians, living in a rarefied atmosphere, are especially prone:
Anthony [Eden] lectured his audience, and even the Cabinet. I fear he is showing signs of 'Mountain Sickness.' (Channon, 1993—diary entry of 13 February 1938)

mouse a sexually attractive young woman
Shakespeare suggests that it was more than a pet name:
... tempt you again in bed,
Pinch wanton on your cheek, call you his mouse. (*Hamlet*)
In modern vulgar use, the *mousehole* is the vagina.

move in on to form a sexual relationship with
Which may lead to *moving in with*, or cohabiting extramaritally, with the person concerned.

move on to die
While the corpse might seem incapable of movement, perhaps the spirit will remain mobile:
I want to leave something which might be useful to other people after I move on. (W. F. Deedes in *Daily Telegraph*, 2 March 1998)

move to a more secure camp to retreat
In various phrases replacing *camp* with *location* or *place*:
"[The Italian troops in Nassiarigah, Iraq] did not abandon the camp," said General Kimmitt. "They just moved to a more secure one." (*Daily Telegraph*, 18 May 2004)

move your bowels to defecate
Standard English. The *bowel*, or large intestine, is in constant movement, especially if you eat sufficient roughage.
A *movement*, or act of defecation, is a shortened form of BOWEL MOVEMENT.

movement an institution or collection of institutions
Usually characterized by deep-rooted conservatism to protect the status quo and reluctant to *move* in any direction, exemplified on occasion by the British building society or trade union *movements*.

Mozart drunk

Rhyming slang on *Mozart and Liszt*, pissed. See also BRAHMS.

Mr Big a criminal boss
Despite being possibly of diminutive stature:
'He said you'd tell us about Mr Big.' 'That's what some in the CID called him. Not very original.' (Rankin, 2000)

Mrs Chant *British* a lavatory
Rhyming slang for AUNT[2] in female use.

Mrs Duckett a mild oath
Again rhyming slang.

Mrs Grundy a moralistic bigot and busy-body
From a character in Morton's 1798 play *Speed the Plough*. Whence *Grundyism*, a disease to which politicians of either sex easily fall victim.

muddy *obsolete* tipsy
Not at all clear in the head and not with clothing soiled from falling:
He has an elderly woman ... who lives with him, and jogs his elbow when his glass has stood too long empty ... not that he gets drunk, for he is a very pious man, but he is always muddy. (J. Boswell, 1791)

mudlark *obsolete London* a scavenger or thief
It referred either to those who frequented the exposed banks of the River Thames at low tide to pick up anything of value, or those who picked up stolen goods which an accomplice had tossed over the rail of a ship.

muff the female pubic hair
This usage has survived the practice of using *muffs* to warm the hands when conveyances were unheated.
A *muff-diver* indulges in cunnilingus.

mug to rob by violence in a public place
In obsolete British use to *mug* was to bribe with drink, from the container.
In 19th-century London it came to mean robbery by garrotting, perhaps because the victim was considered a *mug*, or stupid person. Now all too common, and for us the *mugger* is no longer merely 'the broad-nosed crocodile from India' (*SOED*).

muggy drunk
Literally, moist, and usually of the weather. *Muggy* may also mean stupid.

mule a carrier of illegal narcotics in bulk
Like the beast of burden used especially on mountain tracks, and owing nothing to the American slang *mule*, whisky illegally distilled, with its fierce kick.

multicultural embracing people of different skin pigmentation
Multicoloured would be deemed offensive. Whence *multiculturalism*, the integration of non-white people into a mainly white population.

municipal farm *American* a prison
Where convicts are put to work.

Murphy game (the) *American* (of a prostitute) cheating a customer
Perhaps from the simplest of *Murphy's Laws*, that if something can go wrong, it will:
> ...there were rooms for hire above the bar and that Star's specialty was the Murphy game...rolling drunk customers. (Maas, 1986)

muscle to assault criminally
From the force used.
A *muscle man* or *muscle* does the assaulting.
To *muscle in on* something is to seek an undeserved benefit.

mush *obsolete British* to rob from houses
Shortened form of the slang *mushroom*, an umbrella. Itinerants, known as *umbrella* or *mushroom men*, went from house to house offering to mend umbrellas, which provided good cover for crooks and gave the trade a bad name.
Mush is still a mode of male address, importing no ill-will or accusation of dishonesty.

musical *obsolete* (of a male) homosexual
Homosexuals considered themselves to be more artistic than heterosexuals:
> In Harry's estimation they were both homosexual—or 'musical', as the Noel Coward set would say. (Follett, 1991)

muster your bag *British* to be ill

Naval usage, from having to take your kit to the sick bay.

mutilate to castrate
Originally, in this sense, to cut off a limb. Now mainly used of American tomcats.

mutt *British* deaf
From the rhyming slang *Mutt and Jeff*, better known as the First World War service and victory medals than for the comic cartoon characters, but for most people no longer remembered as either.

mutton a person viewed sexually by another
The common MEAT[1] imagery:
> The duke...would eat mutton on Fridays. He's now past it. (Shakespeare, *Measure for Measure*)

A *mutton* was a prostitute, and a *mutton-monger* was a profligate male, illogically it might seem, as he was a buyer, not a seller.
See also COME YOUR MUTTON.

mutton dressed as lamb a woman affecting the dress or style of someone much younger
A derogatory expression:
> 'Youthful excess is one thing,' said the Dean, 'but mutton dressed as lamb is another.' (Sharpe, 1974)

muzzy tipsy
Literally, of the weather, dull and overcast. Quite common female use of themselves.

my word *British* faeces
Rhyming slang for *turd*. Mainly used of canine deposits on pavements etc.

N

N-word the word *nigger*
The usage is offensive unless used by a black person.

nab to steal
Literally, to catch or arrest.
In obsolete use to *nab the snow* was to steal washing from a line, the usage clearly complimenting the laundress.
To *nab the stoop* was to stand in the pillory.

naff off go away
Partridge thought the word derived as back slang for *fan*, a shortened form of FANNY, which is ingenious but improbable. *OED* tells us that it is 'a euphemistic substitution for fuck' which does not explain the adjectival meaning, dated or unfashionable.

nail *American* to copulate with
Perhaps from the slang *nail*, a penis, or from an analogy with SCREW[1]. The rhyming slang *hammer and nail*, TAIL[1], opens yet another line of etymological enquiry:
> Until April [Congressman Gary Condit] was just another horny congressman, nailing—as with many, if not most, of his colleagues—one of the town's vast herd of obliging interns. (*Sunday Telegraph*, 15 July 2001)

nameless crime (the) buggery
A common use when homosexual acts between males were illegal. The charge sheet of an accused would refer to 'the abominable crime of buggery'. Murder and rape earned no such descriptive embellishment.

nancy a male homosexual
The derivation is from the female name. Originally as *Miss Nancy* and also as *nancy boy*.

nanny intrusive and patronizing
When it appears to some that government treats citizens as children in a nursery, in what critics call the *nanny state*:
> What started as a piece of deregulating legislation has turned into a typical piece of nanny Labour law. (*Daily Telegraph*, 6 April 2005)

In obsolete use, a *nanny* was a prostitute, from the female goat rather than her nursing skills, and a *nanny-house* was a brothel.

Napoleon's revenge diarrhoea
As suffered by British tourists in France:
> A lady friend, travelling through France with her family, was stricken with a rather severe attack of 'Napoleon's revenge'. (*At Your Convenience*, 1988)

nappy an infant's towel to contain excreta
A shortened form of *napkin*, a small piece of cloth, and now standard English.

narrow *obsolete* miserly
Not widespread in generosity:
> Archibald, Duke of Argyle, was narrow in his ordinary expenses. (J. Boswell, 1791)

Narrowness was stinginess:
> Dr Johnson said, I ought to write down a collection of the instances of his narrowness, as they almost exceeded belief. (ibid.)

narrow bed a grave
Where we await our summons to the *narrow passageway to the unknown*, perhaps.

nasty a spirituous intoxicant
Unpleasant to a teetotaller, no doubt, and still used humorously by drinkers who, if they imbibe too much, may become *nasty*, or drunk, from the way they behave rather than the liquid which caused their condition.

nasty complaint (a) venereal disease
As indeed may be a rotten cold or an attack of sciatica:
> After a business trip to the Middle East, Brown found he was suffering from a nasty complaint. (*Private Eye*, February 1989)

national assistance *British* monies paid by the state to the poor
Not bankrolling a poorer sovereign state. See also ASSISTANCE.

national emergency *British* the Second World War
It was indeed that, but much more besides before Russia and the United States were attacked and joined the fray:
> When I find this war, in the ninth month of its second phase, still referred to coyly as the 'national emergency' ... (Heffer, 1998, quoting Enoch Powell)

national indoor game (the) copulation
Certainly played by many, and not usually al fresco.

national savings lending to the government
There are many other ways in which citizens may save, contributing to a *national* accumulation of wealth:
> One form of lending to the government is called 'national savings'. This is one of

those maddeningly misleading expressions which summon patriotism to the aid of deception. (Heffer, 1998, quoting Enoch Powell)

national service *British* compulsory conscription into the armed forces
The usage concealed the military nature of the engagement while conscription remained in force after 1945 (prior to which people had simply been *called up*). Others out of uniform may also have thought they were serving the state.

nationalize to expropriate
Standard English for the state compulsorily taking an undertaking out of private ownership, with or without compensation:
    ... a two-hour speech by Colonel Nasser [on 16 July 1956] ... concluding with the announcement that Egypt has 'nationalised', that is to say annexed and confiscated, the Suez Canal. (A. Clark, 1998)

native a non-white person
Literally, as in Dr Johnson's definition, 'an original inhabitant', but extended in the colonial era to all people who were not white.

Native American a person with North American Indian ancestry
For the transatlantic observer, a harsh usage which appears to disparage the greater part of those who were born in the United States and look upon it as their native land, quite apart from what the indigenous inhabitants of other American territories may feel:
    'An Indian,' I said ... 'I mean, a Native American.' (Theroux, 1993)

native elixir (the) *Irish* whiskey
Native certainly to Scotland as well as Ireland, although its properties as an *elixir*, prolonging life or acting as a panacea for all ills, are not universally accepted, especially by the wives of those who happen to appreciate its beneficial nature:
    'Poor Griffith,' Childers said to me, 'a bit too fond of the native elixir, eh?' (Flanagan, 1995—Griffith was the half-English negotiator for Irish independence in 1922 and Erskine Childers was the English supporter of Irish Republicanism, whom they later killed)

natural[1] *obsolete* an idiot
Probably a shortened form of *natural (born) fool*, an expression which antedated this use by a century (*EDD*).

natural[2] (of parentage) illegitimate
Originally, describing a child who was sired by the father of a family as distinct from an adopted child. From the late 16th century until recently, *natural* imputed illegitimacy:
    Edward VII, a most wide-ranging man in his attraction to ladies, was his natural father. (Condon, 1966)
Today it is again used, as long ago, to describe the biological parents of an adopted child.

natural break *British* the intrusion of advertisements in a television broadcast
The licensing authority stipulated that the interruptions for advertising should not spoil the continuity of a programme. Whence also the humorous *natural break* in a meeting, for urination.

natural functions (the) urination and defecation
Eating, sleeping, and breathing are just as *natural*, to name a few. Also as *natural needs* and in former times as *natural necessities*:
    ... severall ... under that relligiouse confynement, wer forced to give way to ther naturall necessities ... bedewing the pavement of churches with other moysture than teares. (R. Paterson, 1998, quoting a 1638 report on the result of lengthy Scottish Covenanting sermons)
Natural vigours in a male are not athleticism but lust.

nature stop *American* a halt on a journey for urination
Not at a viewpoint with a camera but to meet *nature's needs*, a wish to urinate or defecate.

nature's garb nudity
Without even a fig leaf. A naked person was also said to be *in his naturals*.

naturist a nudist
Not someone especially interested in the environment but one with a penchant for wearing NATURE'S GARB, either alone or in the company of like-minded people.

naughty having a reputation for promiscuity
Originally of females only, such conduct being tolerated in males, by other males. Now also of locations:
    Naughty Norfolk [Va] catered [in the Second World War] for those looking for sin before shipping out, notwithstanding the occasional sign that read 'No dogs or sailors'. (Atkinson, 2003)
A *naughty lady* is a prostitute, but we no longer have Shakespearean *naughty houses*, or brothels, as mentioned in *Measure for Measure*.

nautch girl a prostitute
Literally, a professional Indian dancing girl.

Neapolitan bone-ache *obsolete* syphilis
The disease you caught from the Italians, if
not from the French or Spanish:
> Vengeance on the whole camp, or, rather,
> the Neapolitan bone-ache...(Shakespeare,
> *Troilus and Cressida*)

near[1] stingy
A derivative of CLOSE[1].

near[2] imitation
Mencken gave 'near-silk, near-antique, near-
leather, near-mahogany, near-silver and near–
porcelain' (1941). Consumer protection legislation has thinned the list. *Near-beer*,
supposedly with low alcohol content, was
sold in unlicensed premises in Britain until
after the Second World War.

necessary (house) *obsolete* a lavatory
The Italian *necessario* or the French *nécessaire*.
A *necessary woman* was not the TOKEN female
committee member but the emptier of lavatories.

neck to kiss and caress amorously
From the placing of an arm round the other's
neck at some stage:
> ...to copulate, or at least neck, in the
> relative comfort of a parked sedan.
> (Ustinov, 1971)

necklace *South African* to murder by ignit-
ing a rubber tyre placed on the shoulders
of a victim
A method used by black people on other
blacks, for crime or for being of a different
political persuasion.

necktie party a lynching
The *necktie* is the noose.
Also as a *necktie sociable*. The victim might be
measured for a necktie or wear a designated
necktie.
The outcome was to *have his neck stretched*.
After a revolt in the Baltic provinces in 1906,
the Russian Prime Minister Stolypin caused
more than 2,000 rebels to be shot or hanged:
> He followed on with such gusto that the
> noose became known as the 'Stolypin
> necktie'. (Moynahan, 1994—this did not
> stop the British Ambassador in St
> Petersburg naming him as 'the most
> notable figure in Europe')

need help to be incompetent or bankrupt
Each of us *needs* and receives *help* from others
in every aspect of our daily lives:
> It says the NEMC and its chief executive,
> Jennie Page, need help in the running of
> the project. (*Daily Telegraph*, 7 January 2000,
> writing about the New Millennium
> Experience Company, which was

responsible for the ill-fated London
Millennium Dome)

need the bathroom to wish to urinate or
defecate
Or *need* any of the myriad euphemistic
synonyms for *bathroom*.

needle to strengthen (an intoxicant) by
adulteration
Originally, by introducing an electric current
through a rod shaped like a needle, whence
any form of lacing.

negative or negatively are used in the
same way as *less*, to avoid precision or
as an evasion, in many phrasal euphemisms, of which a sample only appears
below.

negative aspect(s) an unacceptable consequence
The usage resurfaced when the media tycoon
Rupert Murdoch objected to the publication
by HarperCollins, one of his subsidiaries, of a
book which he judged might have damaged
his business interests in China:
> Bell, referring to the Patten book, scurried
> to reassure Disney that Murdoch 'has
> outlined to me the negative aspects of
> publication which I fully understand'.
> 'Outlining the negative aspects' is of course
> a recognized Murdochean euphemism for a
> threat of immediate execution. 'Fully
> understanding the negative aspects' is a
> euphemism for the execution itself. (Frank
> Johnson in *Daily Telegraph*, 28 February
> 1998—Disney was an American Murdoch
> employee and Bell the head of
> HarperCollins. The editor of the London
> *Times*, also owned by Murdoch, showed his
> awareness of the *negative aspects* of the
> story, which he ignored, choosing for his
> front page a piece about the late Duke of
> Windsor's handkerchief)

negative cash debt
Or a reduction in liquidity. A *negative cash flow*
means you are spending more than you are
earning or that your payables exceed your
receivables.

negative containment a leak of radiation
from a nuclear reactor
The phrase is used because:
> To report there had been an 'escape' of
> radioactive matter would be alarmist. (*Daily
> Telegraph*, 9 March 1994)

negative contribution a sale at a loss
Commercial jargon. The *contribution* is that
part of the price left after deducting the cost

of labour and materials. A *positive contribution* indicates that some or all of the overhead and selling costs have been recovered. A *negative profit contribution* means that you have lost money after deducting all your costs.

negative coping mechanism being inept or weak-willed
Social scientists' jargon.

negative employee situation *American* the dismissal of staff
Not all those asked to leave can be classified as *negative* in their attitude or demeanour. The introduction of the British minimum wage was expected by the Trade Unions Congress to have 'negative employment effects'. (*Daily Telegraph*, 24 August 1995)

negative equity owing more on an asset than it is worth
Particularly of mortgages on dwellings.

negative growth a decline
Politicians so speak of the national product, businessmen of turnover or profits.

negative incident an event which may cause harm or adverse publicity
A dread event in the world of public relations:
'Will they have a representative on the train?' 'To minimize negative incidents...I'm using their jargon, dammit.' (D. Francis, 1988)

negative (income) tax state payment to the poor
The proposition seems to have been first expounded by Milton Friedman under the title *negative tax*. An object would be to eliminate the present cumbersome methods of individual assessment and distribution of money to the poor and others.

negative investment return a loss
Financial jargon of those for whom *loss* is a taboo word:
The negative investment returns experienced in 2000 and 2001 have still not been fully reflected in present [solvency] levels. (*Daily Telegraph*, 7 March 2002)

negative patient care outcome death
Medical jargon. The phrase could be taken to mean that a test has proved the absence of infection.

negative peer pressure the discouragement of learning
The verbal and physical abuse of keen schoolchildren by those of less ability or discipline:
[Disincentive for black schoolboys to be diligent pupils] was in the news every day:

drugs, crime, street life, 'negative peer pressure' at school. (Naipaul, 1989)

negative pricing selling at a loss
What multinational companies may do to retain a presence in a difficult market:
Competition in the automotive business around the globe remains intense and we're seeing negative pricing in most major markets. (*Daily Telegraph*, 15 October 2004)

negative propaganda the unfair denigration of opponents
Not much different from any other kind of *propaganda*, you might suppose, the word having come far since 1622, when Pope Gregory XV set up a body of cardinals under that title to *propagate* Roman Catholicism:
Denigration—or 'negative propaganda', if you are given to squeamish euphemism—is an essential part of any election, even an internal one. (Cole, 1995)

negative stock-holding orders which cannot be delivered
This is how your computer tells you about empty shelves in the warehouse when you have overdue orders and clamant customers. Normally computers deduct orders or sales from unallocated stocks to throw up reorder or manufacture schedules.

negatively impacted disappointing or loss-making
Bankers, whose existence depends on confidence, adopt linguistic contortions to avoid any word like *loss*:
Last week it revealed a slight downturn in third quarter figures and warned that fourth quarter results would be 'negatively impacted'. (*Daily Telegraph*, 28 September 1998—Goldman Sachs was explaining why its planned flotation had been postponed)

negatively privileged poor
Sociological jargon and a correct statement only of those who have elected to lead a life of monastic asceticism. See also PRIVILEGED and UNDERPRIVILEGED.

negotiable we do not expect to receive the asking price
Estate agents' jargon, often shortened to *neg.* in classified advertisements.

negotiate to yield or appease
The language of diplomacy, where bullies or appeasers are involved:
Halifax...had urged the Polish Foreign Minister, Beck, to negotiate (i.e. yield) upon Hitler's demand to annex Dantzig. (Crossman, 1981—Halifax was in 1939 the British Foreign Secretary)

nelly a homosexual
Either male or female, although a *nelly fag* is
male. A *nelly* is 'a weak-spirited or silly person'
(*SOED*). The derivation might just owe something to the expression *not on your nelly*
(rhyming slang on *Nelly Duff*, or *duffer*), whence
an allusion to the *duff* in FLUFF YOUR DUFF.

Nelson's blood rum
The corpse of the Admiral was returned from
Trafalgar via Gibraltar in 1805 for burial in
London. The preservative in which he was
immersed was probably brandy, not rum.
Tradition has it that the spirit was depleted
on the voyage because sailors siphoned it off
and drank it.

neoplasm a cancer
Literally, a fresh growth. Mainly medical
jargon.

nephew *obsolete* a son
An evasion when the church expected celibacy and clerical errors became cardinal sins:
    He made six of his close relations,
    'nephews' or illegitimate sons, cardinals.
    (Cawthorne, 1996, writing about Pope
    Sixtus IV, 1471–84)

nerve agent a noxious gas
Military jargon. It could mean anything which
excites the senses and so stimulates a nerve,
not excluding a woman's perfume.

nervous breakdown a severe mental illness
Not paralysis, where some of the *nerves* really
do *break down*.
Now standard English covering conditions
varying from depression to madness.

nest *obsolete* the vagina
With visual imagery:
    ... in your daughter's womb I'll bury them:
    Where, in that nest of spicery, they shall
    breed. (Shakespeare, *Richard III*)
The usage persisted in 19th-century slang.

nether parts the genitalia
Literally, the lower parts, but not of the feet
or ankles.
Also as *nether regions*. Shakespeare uses *the
Netherlands*, punning vulgarly on the 'Low
Countries':
    The Netherlands?—O, sir, I did not look so
    low. (*The Comedy of Errors*)

networking using social contacts for political or financial purposes
From the jargon of information technology
rather than the British *old-boy network*, the
mutual support of former schoolfellows.

neutral unfavourable
The coded language of the corporate analyst:
    They are required to analyze corporate
    clients, but these pieces of research never
    say anything negative. The worst phrase
    you might read is 'neutral' or 'long-term
    buy'. (*Sunday Telegraph*, 8 August 1999)

neutralize to kill
Much more than making *neutral* or inert. The
word is favoured by thriller writers, if none
other.

never modest arrogant
The language of the obituary and in similar
phrases such as *never one to hide his light under a
bushel*. The euphemistic device is used to tell
of other unpleasant or taboo characteristics:
    Tennant's never moderate drinking
    became a problem ... (*Daily Telegraph*, 24
    September 2003)

never-never (the) *obsolete* a contract for
hire-purchase
There was a time when people thought it
wrong to buy things which they could not
afford to pay for. Such people would *never*
borrow to finance a purchase of goods
because of the fear that they would *never* be
out of debt.

new is a code word which should alert us
to what is being concealed, as the following examples indicate.

new age the rejection of conventional attitudes
The symptoms may be manifested in dress
and personal appearance, or in an older
person aping the behaviour of the young:
    ... the cream linen suit, the pointy-toed
    black shoes ... the greying pony-tail. 'Gone
    New Age on us, Hugh?' (Rankin, 2000)
New age travellers are itinerants or vagrants.

new Australian *Australian* an immigrant
Not a baby born there. After Australia decided
to accept immigrants who were neither
British nor white, it was necessary to adopt
a phrase which avoided any reference to their
skin pigmentation or country of origin.

New Commonwealth a group of countries in which the majority of people
are not white
After the Second World War *Empire*, even
without the prefix *British*, had too many overtones of conquest and white supremacy, and a
new name was needed for the agglomeration of
former colonies and dependencies which continued to consult with each other, along with
the English-speaking white *Dominions*.

new economic zones the barren places to which opponents were exiled
They were too busy there trying to stay alive to cause trouble, or they starved to death. In this way the victorious Communist Vietnamese sought to eliminate potential dissidents who were unable to get hold of a boat.

New Labour *British* a non-socialist political party
The *Labour Party*, as the political wing of British socialism, had by the 1990s become unelectable unless it discarded its traditional policies which, inter alia, exempted its industrial, or trade union, partner from liability for breaches of contract. It needed however to retain the votes of trade union, or *Labour*, supporters, and their traditional financial support.

new man a male in full employment who also shares domestic chores
No longer just the breadwinner or *my old man*:
  But despite [women-friendly policies] and the rise of "house husbands" and "new men", with their well-publicised commitment to domestic chores [the Economic and Social Research Council] says that many women are physically and emotionally drained. (*Daily Telegraph*, 27 February 2005)

New Order a totalitarian state
As created by the Nazis. The regime also punished any remarks which impugned the *new times* or the *new state*.

new Soviet man a dedicated Communist
The phrase was used by Moscow in 1944 to explain the need to imprison or exile any who had had contact with non-Soviet life, as by having been a prisoner-of-war.

Newgate *obsolete British* a prison
It denoted other prisons than the notorious one in London. There were many compounds to do with jail, crime, or hanging such as *Newgate bird*, a thief, and *Newgate solicitor*, a corrupt lawyer.

news management the suppression of information
For military or political purposes. The *management* embraces delay, obstruction, and manipulation rather than attempts to get lies published.

next door to having taboo features associated with
Usually of criminals or those with mental illness. Thus *next door to a padded cell* implies mental deficiency.

nibble[1] an act of casual copulation
Literally, a small bite.

nibble[2] a theft
Usually taking only a part, in the hope that the depredation will pass unnoticed.

nice time a single act of copulation with a prostitute
Prostitute's jargon when soliciting.

Nick[1] the devil
Named after one of the Nordic evil spirits or monsters
  O thou! Whatever title suit thee,
  Auld Hornie, Satan, Nick, or Clootie.
  (Burns, 1786)
Today usually as *old Nick*; seldom as *Nickie* or *Nicker*.

nick[2] to steal
Literally, to cut an edge, from which the use was originally only of pilfering.

nick[3] a police station or prison
From the slang meaning to catch, the inmate having been caught or *nicked*.

nick[4] a vasectomy
Again from the cutting. In obsolete use, to *nick* was to castrate, used of animals not humans:
  Through mist and fog to nick a sturdy hog.
  (Dickinson, 1866)

nickel and dime *American* to short-change or cheat
Before the Second World War, stores such as Woolworth offered goods to the value of 5c and 10c, giving value but with a sacrifice of quality:
  The kind of guy who'll nickel-and-dime his own mother. (M. Thomas, 1987)

niece[1] *obsolete* a daughter
The medieval Popes tended to be poor genealogists. See also NEPHEW.

niece[2] a mistress
The older male seeks to justify the constant presence of his younger companion:
  The swashbuckling Patton was seldom without comfort—later veiled from the sight back home of the only woman he truly feared, his wife Beatrice, as a visiting 'niece'. (Horne, 1994—Jean Gordon, the *niece* who accompanied him on his campaign in Europe, killed herself two weeks after his death)

night (the) death
The common association with darkness and sleep
  Still there are works which, with God's permission, I would do before the night

cometh. (Strachey, 1918, quoting Dr Arnold in 1842)

night bucket a receptacle for urine
Usually in communal male sleeping quarters, where its use can avoid the ingress of cold air through repeated opening of a door in winter. Less often as the punning *night jar*, which should not be confused with the *Caprimulgus europaeus*.

night games copulation
And in America as *night baseball*, which is often played away from home.

night girl a prostitute
She plies her trade in the dark.
If however she agrees to a *night job*, she will stay with the same customer all night, on an *all-nighter*.

night loss the involuntary emission of semen during sleep
Mainly female use, referring to the soiled sheets. Also as *night emission*.
Night physic, also a male phenomenon, was copulation in the days when some men thought that taking it regularly was a requisite of good health.

night soil human faeces
Soil has meant excrement since the 16th century, and primitive lavatories were cleaned at night, sometimes by a *nightman* in an operation called, in London at least, a *wedding*. Now mainly jocular figurative use, *in the nightsoil* being a synonym for *in the shit*. *Night water*, urine, is obsolete.

night stool a portable lavatory
Not something that passes, or is passed, in the night but a sick-room adjunct which looks like a square seat.

nightcap a drink of intoxicant
Punning on what might be worn in bed. Taken before retiring, it is usually whisky or brandy.

nightclub hostess a prostitute
A *nightclub*, in proper usage, is a place of refreshment and entertainment open to the public until late at night. Some are indeed properly conducted, but not all.

nightingale[1] *obsolete* a police informer
From the *singing* properties of bird and man.

nightingale[2] *obsolete British* a soldier who cried out while being flogged
To show more fortitude, the victim was given a bullet to bite, thus further enriching the language.

nightingale[3] *obsolete* a prostitute
Usually operating in the hours of darkness.

nightwork *obsolete* copulation
As it was in Shakespeare's days and plays.

nil by mouth indicating that a patient should be allowed to die
Normally, an instruction in hospital to starve a patient before an operation.

NINA *American* we do not employ Irish people
The initials in a classified advertisement to be seen frequently not that many decades ago:
> The Irish were never liked up there in New England, and there were signs everywhere saying No Irish Need Apply. (McCourt, 1999)

nineteenth (hole) the bar at a golf club
The first eighteen involve striking a ball and walking after it. Occasionally the *nineteenth* may be where you drink other than in the clubhouse, or what you drink.

nip[1] to steal
Either by *pinching* or by giving short measure.

nip[2] a drink of spirits
Originally, a *nipperkin*, an eighth part of a pint, the quantity normally served.

nip[3] to castrate
From the action of the tool employed.

no (like *non* and *not*) is used as a prefix in many phrases where the statement of the contrary is used as a euphemistic device. Examples follow.

no beauty ugly
Always of a woman, perhaps because comeliness is admired more in females than in males. *No oil painting* may indicate an ill-favoured appearance in either sex.

no better than she should be promiscuous
Usually said of a younger woman by an older. Also as *no better than she ought to be*.

no (spring) chicken old
Of women, usually by younger women.
No longer in the first flush of youth applies to both sexes:
> Although Leeming at 62 is no longer in the first flush of youth ... (*Daily Telegraph*, 17 July 2004)

no Einstein unacademic
Also as *no genius* or *no scholar*.

etc.

no active treatment indicating that a patient should be allowed to die
Hospital code on the notes of a terminally ill patient, sometimes shortened to *NAT*. Also as *no mayday*, from the international distress call, or *m'aider*.

no comment I admit nothing
Political and business use in reply to journalists. It is a defence of those who know that, when scandal is in the air, to be quoted is to be misquoted, and selectively.

no-fly zone a sexually forbidden area
Not as in Saddam Hussein's Iraq but to deter male teachers from copulating with female pupils:
> There was a rigid no-fly zone between faculty and students. (Grisham, 2002)

no heeltaps everyone must drink what is in their glass
A *heeltap* is the layer of leather on the sole of a shoe, hence what is left in the bottom of an unfinished glass.

no longer with us dead
Less common perhaps than *no more*, which may be inaccurate for those who believe in an afterlife.
No longer in service meant that a spy was dead, according to those who write about espionage.
If, as a Soviet prisoner, you had *no right to correspondence*, it was because you were no longer alive to read any letters.

no man's land a lavatory for female use only
Punning on the term for the ground between opponents in trench warfare.

no pot to piss in very poor
The cliché ignores the fact that many wealthy householders with modern sanitation no longer possess these items of furniture.

no show the fraudulent use of a name on a pay sheet
Either the person fails to report for work but, with the connivance of another, continues illegally to collect his pay; or a name is entered on the pay sheet of someone who does not exist or is not employed there, the pay being drawn by a third party.
For the airlines, however, a *no show* is a passenger who books a flight but fails to check in.

nobble *obsolete* to steal
Literally, to tamper with a horse illegally, whence to act dishonestly.
There is an American slang use, meaning to kill.

noble game (the) prostitution
According to Boswell, having paid an actress to participate. See also GAME[2].

nocturnal emission an involuntary ejaculation of semen
Spitting, vomiting, sweating, ejaculation during copulation (or *nocturnal exercise*), and sneezing do not count.

nocturne *obsolete* a prostitute
Literally, a night scene in a painting or a dreamy musical composition. Whence George Sand's apocryphal pun to Chopin: 'One nocturne deserves another.'

noddy *British* a policeman
By translation from PC Plod whose exemplary behaviour graced the *Noddy* books.

noggin an intoxicating drink
Originally, an eighth of a pint of any liquid. Now used of any type of beer or spirits, but not of wine.

non- (like *no* and *not*) is used is a euphemistic device in many phrases where the negative is preferred to the statement of an unpalatable truth. Examples follow.

non-aligned vacillating in allegiance
The representatives of countries which so described themselves met in Belgrade in 1961, claiming with more or less sincerity that they favoured neither Washington nor Moscow. Jennings in 1965 described them as 'no more than potential parasites', as though their approval for either of the then Great Powers might have been obtained by bribery or support for an autocrat. Perish the thought!

non-Aryan Jewish
One of the Nazi obsessions, along with their hatred of gypsies and Slavs. See also ARYAN.

non-heart beating donor a corpse
It sounds better to the recipient of a transplanted organ, or his relatives:
> [Transplant surgeons] proposed alternative for dead ... 'non-heart beating donor'. (*Daily Telegraph*, 12 May 1993, quoting the *British Medical Journal*)

non-industrial poor and relatively uncivilized
One of the long line of euphemisms adopted to avoid offending post-colonial rulers:
> 'Civilized' and 'primitive' were to be replaced by 'industrial' and 'non-industrial'. (*Daily Telegraph*, 12 May 1993, quoting a document issued by Leeds Metropolitan University)

non-performing loss making
Of financial dealings. Sometimes *tout court*:
> Hundreds of billions of dollars of
> borrowing [by Latin American countries]
> was in 1982 'non-performing'. (A. Clark,
> 1998—giving one of the reasons for
> Washington's vacillation concerning the
> invasion of the Falkland Islands)

Usually as a *non-performing asset*, from which
no income is derived, or a *non-performing loan*,
on which interest is not being paid and the
return of capital is uncertain.

non-person a person without civil rights
A Communist appellation of those, not being
supporters or advocates of Communism,
whose fame or achievements embarrassed
the current oligarchy.

non-profit *American* avoiding taxation
Not any old loss-making enterprise, but one
set up in such a way that the eventual
beneficiary avoids tax through a tax-exempt
charity:
> The profits that are now extracted by the
> promoters of 'non-profit' cemeteries are
> spectacular. (J. Mitford, 1963)

non-self material foreign matter present
in a human body
A pusillanimous linguistic distortion introduced by the British Open University:
> Among [the words and phrases proscribed]
> was the phrase "foreign body" in health
> and disease issues, which must be replaced
> by "non-self material" lest we offend
> anyone from overseas. (*Sunday Telegraph*, 27
> May 2004)

non-strategic loss making
Financial jargon. Literally, not in accord with
long-term objectives, one of which, for a
bank, is making profits and recovering loans:
> Desdner [Bank] classifies one-eighth of its
> advances as 'non-strategic', which it denies
> is a euphemism for 'we won't get our
> money back'. (*Daily Telegraph*, 21 March
> 2000)

non-traditional (casting) using a black
actor in a role written for a white
Stage jargon:
> ...the term 'non-traditional' is inadequate.
> What we have is theatrical PC. (*Daily
> Telegraph*, 6 February 1993—a black actor
> without make-up had been cast to play the
> part of a white New Englander)

non-white not a Caucasian
A usage in press reports of a crime involving a
black person:
> He said the driver of the [stolen] car which
> killed Mr Evans was non-white. (*Daily
> Telegraph*, 23 January 2004)

nonsense promiscuous sexual activity
Literally, an absurdity:
> [The proprietor of an erotic photographic
> studio] was a calm, down-to-earth creature,
> who brooked no kind of 'nonsense'.
> (Bogarde, 1981)

normalization the suppression of rebellion or protest
The *normality* sought is the state desired by
those who do the suppression:
> The so-called policy of 'normalization' ... was
> just an abdication of responsibility that
> would be dearly paid for in blood. (McCrum,
> 1991)

North to prison
Not as fatal as being sent EAST by the Nazis,
but the direction of some of the Gulags if you
lived in Moscow:
> When his five years were up he went back
> to Moscow and immediately telephoned
> Svetlana, was arrested again and sent
> 'north' for another five years. (Muir, 1997—
> say what you will, Stalin had style when it
> came to damping the ardour of what he
> considered an unsuitable prospective son-
> in-law)

North Britain *obsolete* Scotland
Common and acceptable enough, in the days
when the Scots still considered themselves to
be British, for *North British* to be chosen as a
title of a Scottish railway company. A *North
Briton* was a Scot, although John Wilkes, who
chose it as a nom de plume, was English.

nose job (a) cosmetic surgery on the nose
Women seem to be less content with their
natural noses than men.
To *have a nose*, in addict circles, is to sniff
cocaine.

nose open lustful
Bulls and stallions flare their nostrils when
sexually excited. Of humans, the phrase is
used figuratively.

not (like *no* and *non-*) is used in many
phrases where understatement or contradiction is used as a euphemistic device. A sample follows.

not a great reader illiterate
Still heard among old country folk in south-
west England, and probably elsewhere,

not all she should be sexually promiscuous

More common when chastity was more fashionable.
Also as *not all she ought to be*.

not all there stupid or confused
It describes a mental state, not that of an amputee.
Atypically, *all there* means keenly intelligent.

not as young as I was old
None of us is as young as we were, even as the eye crosses the page.
Not in the first flush of youth also means old, but is not used of geriatrics.

not inconsolable promiscuous in the absence of a regular sexual partner
See also CONSOLE:
> It is feared she waited for [Kim Philby] in vain. Not that the Lady Francis, a creature of some resilience, proved inconsolable. (Boyle, 1979)

not interested in the opposite sex homosexual

not known for having a specified unpleasant characteristic
A usage favoured by obituarists. Thus someone *not known for suffering fools gladly* may be an intolerant bully and a person *not known for his intemperance*, a drunkard:
> Crompton-Bell...was an inveterate party animal who was not known for his intemperance. (*Daily Telegraph*, obituary 23 September 2004)

not long for this world about to die
> Mrs Finucane...says she's not long for this world and the more Masses said for her soul the better she'll feel. (McCourt, 1997)

not rocket science simple
Usually of a technological theory or a mechanical problem.

not sixteen annas to the rupee of low intelligence
Before its abolition, there were sixteen annas to a rupee and see also TWELVE ANNAS TO THE RUPEE. Despite decimalization, you may still hear that someone is *not sixteen ounces in the pound* or *not the full shilling*.

not very well very ill
Hospital and valetudinarian jargon, which ignores the presumption that *very well* implies perfect health. Also as *not at all well*, which may indicate a fatal condition.

not with it mentally ill or absent-minded
Of a temporary lapse or a permanent condition.

etc.

not at home at home but unwilling to talk
The converse of *at home*, a formal invitation to visit at a certain time. Also as *not in*.

not available (to comment) unwilling to be publicly compromised or shown up
The coded language of those who do not wish to be interviewed and of the journalists who wish to interview them.

not dead but gone before dead
Also as *not lost but gone before*, *before* meaning ahead, to await the arrival of a survivor, it would seem.

not invented here we reject and denigrate all other ideas than our own
A defensive mechanism of those who are employed to think and innovate, whose position is threatened if a third party achieves what they are being paid to do:
> They didn't think of it, so they'll piss all over it. *Not invented here*! (M. Thomas, 1980)
Often abbreviated to *NIH*.

not return calls to avoid being interviewed
Journalese for saying that an allegation is correct but they can't prove it yet:
> A spokesman...declined to comment [about split-trust operations]. Framlington did not return calls. (*Daily Telegraph*, 17 May 2002)

not seeing anybody not involved in any sexual relationship
Despite enjoying 20/20 vision.

nothing intrusive indicating that a patient should be allowed to die
> Medical direction in the case of a terminally ill patient.

notice dismissal from employment
Shortened form of *notice of dismissal*, which is given or received. *Notice* as a verb is obsolete:
> Notice me as much as ye like, I'll not clean them pigs out. (M. Francis, 1901)

nouvelle cuisine small portions of food sold at high prices
The presentation on the plate may be attractive, the shortage of edible matter providing ample space for the artistic pretensions of the chef.
See also HAUTE CUISINE.

nullification killing
One form of cancelling out.

number is up (your) you are about to be killed

First World War usage, from the game of House, where each player has a numbered card, and punning on a soldier's individual army number. It indicates the fatalism of the trenches, where death appeared to come on a chance basis.

number nine *British* a laxative
The standard army purgative. A laggard soldier might be told that he needed a *dose of number nines*, which was not a medical diagnosis.
In obsolete use *Number Nine* was the Fleet prison in London.

number one(s)¹ urination
Mainly nursery usage.

number one² self-interest
Perhaps from the adage *Number one comes first*:
... he believes trade policy should be founded on protection. Look after Number One. (A. Clark, 1993)

number two(s) defecation
Mainly of small children. Adult usage is rare.

nun *obsolete* a prostitute
There seemed to be an assumption, among men at least, that religious houses were not occupied by chaste females, the dissolution of the monasteries in the 1530s being survived by the dissolution of their occupants.
Thus an *abbess* was a bawd and a *nunnery* a brothel, while *Convent*, or COVENT GARDEN, had its own euphemistic associations.

nurse to suckle (a baby)
Perhaps from the *wet nurse*, who suckled another's child, or from the cradling of the child as it feeds.

The obsolete *nurse-child* was illegitimate, brought up away from its mother.

nursing home an institution for geriatrics
Literally, a hospital for any sick person.

nut a mentally ill person
Nut is slang for a human head and this is a shortened form of *gone in the nut*, or some such expression.
A *nut college, farm, hutch*, or *house* is an institution for the insane.
A *nut-coat* is a straitjacket.
The FBI list of mad or unstable people likely to attack a public figure is called the *nut-box*.
A *nutter* is anything from an irrational person to a madman, described as *nutty, nuts*, or *off his nut*.

nuts the testicles
Also as, and perhaps a shortened form of, *nutmegs*; and see also COBS.

nymph *obsolete* a prostitute
In standard usage, a mythical semi-divine and beautiful maiden. More explicitly as *nymph of darkness, of delight, of the pavement*, etc.

NYR an airman lost in action
Second World War usage, as an abbreviation of *not yet returned* from a mission over enemy territory:
'We've got a lot of NYRs, Lester.' 'Not yet returned doesn't mean dead.' (Deighton, 1982—but it meant shot down or crashed, with death a probability)

O

o opium
Addict use, and not of oxygen.

oats copulation
Usually by a male, within or outside marriage, with an implication of regular need, as in the daily nourishment of horses.
An *oat opera* is pornography:
> 'Whatever you think is best, Percy,' Harry said, turning the page of the oat opera he was reading. (King, 1996)

obligatory appointed other than on merit
Describing membership of committees, boards, etc. where it may be thought expedient or politically necessary to have other than those chosen from a male dominant group.
See also STATUTORY and TOKEN.

oblige *British* to work for someone as a domestic servant
The employee, always female and often elderly, is shown to be conferring a favour on her employer by undertaking a menial task for money.

oblique not heterosexual
Diverging from the straight, if not narrow, path.

obtain to acquire illegally
Usually of stealing but also of acquiring forbidden or other embargoed goods.

occupied defeated and annexed
The fate of Tibet, which is no longer *occupied* only by native Tibetans.
Soviet officers in *occupied* Germany after the Second World War, who had taken women with them while on the move as *campaign wives*, called their German mistresses *occupation wives*. (Beevor, 2002)

occupy to copulate with
From the physical entry rather than gaining her attention:
> These villains will make the word as odious as the word 'occupy', which was an excellent good word before it was ill sorted. (Shakespeare, *2 Henry IV*)
And in modern use:
> Karl was not ready, having been occupied with a Negro girl in his tent. (F. Harris, 1925)

odd homosexual
Literally, out of the ordinary.

odorously challenged smelly
An ingenious extension of those before whom that traditional symbol, the gauntlet, is thrown down—see also CHALLENGED for other examples:
> The list of minority victim-groups with special rights [in the United States] is growing longer every year, and now includes Hispanics, Asian-Americans, women (all 51 per cent of the population), the obese, and finally the smelly (odorously challenged). (*Sunday Telegraph*, 20 November 1994)

of mature years old
The phrase indicates not full development but incipient decline.
See also MATURE.

off[1] *American* to kill
Perhaps a shortened form of BUMP[4] (OFF).
To *off yourself* is to commit suicide.

off[2] with its implications of departure and decay precedes many phrases indicating types of mental illness, as follows:
Off at the side, of a mild condition, is obsolete. *Off your head* covers anything from a temporary forgetfulness to lunacy, with many slang variants for *head*, such as *chump*, *gourd*, *napper*, *nut*, *onion*, and *turnip*.
Another group of phrases comes from malfunctioning transport, with the vehicle figuratively leaving the *rails*, its *tree* (or axle), or the *rocker* or *trolley* which picks up the overhead electric supply of a tram or trolley bus.
The American *off the wall*, from the unpredictable bounce off the fence in baseball, can be used of mental illness or figuratively.

off-colour[1] vulgar or offensive
The colour is not necessarily BLUE[2]:
> I don't want any of your off-colour stuff from the Drones' smoking-room. (Wodehouse, 1934)

off-colour[2] ill
It may describe a temporary affliction, which may make the victim paler than usual. Also used of menstruation.

off duty menstruating
A female use, inferring also that she is unavailable for copulation. Also as *off games*, punning on SPORT and a pupil's minor indisposition.

off-line *American* dead
From the meaning, no longer connected:

'She was off-line, Judge. Clearly.' Dead, in other words. The cops are always at their toughest when the subject is dying. They have a thousand euphemisms. (Turow, 1996)

Off-line is also a synonym for *out of line*, meaning behaving improperly or illegally.

off the chandelier bogus

It describes bids at an auction, where the auctioneer is trying to run up the bidding by pretending there is another active bidder in the hall.

Depending on the décor, such bids may also come *off the ceiling*, *wall*, or whatever else catches the auctioneer's eye, other than a genuine bid.

off the payroll dismissed from employment

Joining the rest of humanity who were never on that particular payroll in the first place.

The phrase may also be used to explain the absence of an employee who has joined a competitor.

off the peg inferior or ill-cut

In standard usage, this describes garments which are bought ready-made rather than individually tailored:

In an off-the-peg dress...she did not look her best. (Ellman, 1988)

off the rails engaged in reprehensible conduct

Criminal or sexual, of someone hitherto considered above reproach, and implying a continued pattern of bad behaviour:

Johnny Depp is a dream as the bad boy tempting a nice girl off the rails. (*TV Quick*, 9 December 1992)

off the reservation acting beyond your authority

Moving outside the RESERVATION where you are meant to live:

B'ai B'rith raced to condemn the off-the-reservation rabbi. (Clancy, 1991—the rabbi had been expressing extremist views)

off the voting list dead

Not necessarily applicable to Northern Ireland, Cook County, or parts of Florida, it might appear, where the dead may inadvertently remain on the *voting* or *voters' list* and express their preference from beyond the grave.

off the wagon habitually drinking alcohol after a period of abstinence

After having been ON THE WAGON.

off the wall *American* mentally ill

Sporting imagery, but I'm not sure which sport.

off-white wedding the marriage of a pregnant bride

She may or may not eschew the pleasure of wearing a virginal white dress.

off your face drunk

The etymology is unclear:

Off their faces on happy hour cocktails...(Rankin, 1999)

offer yourself to ask a man to copulate with you

Usually promiscuously:

She tracked me down to my rooms in Oxford and offered herself to me. (Amis, 1978)

The obsolete *offer kindness* was at the gift of either sex.

oil a bribe

A form of GREASE. More often as the punning *palm oil* and sometimes as *old oil*, which may also mean flattery.

oiled drunk

Things may for a time seem to run more smoothly.

The commonest cliché, whatever the state of inebriation, is *well oiled*.

The obsolete British *oil the wig* was to become drunk, and in Scotland *oil of malt* was whisky.

old or auld is a prefix to numerous *nicknames*, or names for NICK[1], the devil, who was liable to appear if you spoke about him directly: whence our expression *talk of the devil*, if a person about whom we have been speaking in his absence comes into view. Instead of using the word *devil*, people spoke of (the) *old* or *auld bendy*, *blazes*, *bogey*, *boots*, *boy*, *chap*, *child*, *cloot*, *clootie*, *dad*, *Davy*, *driver*, *gentleman*, *gooseberry*, *Harry*, *hornie*, *lad*, *mahoon*, *man*, *Nick*, *one*, *poger*, *poker*, *Roger*, *ruffin*, *Sandy*, *scratch*, *serpent*, *smoker*, *sooty*, *thief*, *toast*, etc. Some of these names are dealt with elsewhere, without the prefix. It was not uncommon for a farmer to leave a patch of ground untilled for the devil's use (today Brussels calls it set-aside), in the hope that he might be induced to leave the rest of the farm alone.

See also *clootie's croft* under CLOOT.

old Adam a man's lust

Referring to the unregenerate character of our common ancestor before life became complicated for him and he passed on to us, with St Paul's help, our sexual complexes.

old Bill see BILL

old faithful menstruation
By coming back regularly, it lifts anxiety about unwanted pregnancy.

old-fashioned derelict
Real-estate jargon:
> When applied to houses old-fashioned means a draughty ruin. When applied to clubs it means bad food and no women. (Theroux, 1982)

old maid an unmarried woman who is unlikely to marry
From the meaning, a virgin, (a usage we still see in the cattle category *maiden heifer*, for example) a *maid* became an unmarried girl and then any female who had not been married. As Shakespeare pointed out, the devil had no use for such people: Beatrice imagines him greeting her at the gates of hell with the words 'get you to heaven, here's no place for you maids'. (*Much Ado About Nothing*)

old man the penis
Possibly adverting to the *old man*, the devil, and the libidinous behaviour he may encourage, although the phrase is generally used by men of the penis in its flaccid state.

old man's friend pneumonia
It is an illness which allows the elderly to die quickly and without much pain. Penicillin may now preserve them for more lingering, painful, and degrading deaths.

Old Sparky *America* judicial killing by electrocution
The chair in which the victim sits when the current is turned on.

older woman an elderly female
Advertising jargon which omits to state what her age is compared with. Similarly, the advertisers' 'larger woman' is not merely bigger than a midget, but unusually tall or fat.

oldest profession (the) prostitution
With its biblical references:
> It was maybe the oldest profession ... but New Orleans was proud and ashamed of its cathouses. (Longstreet, 1956)
See also PROFESSION (THE).

on[1] drunk
In a mild state.
This use is obsolete except in the expression *half on*, where, as usual with drunkenness, the half equals the whole.

on[2] pregnant
Today in a phrase, such as *four months on*. In former use, *tout court*:
> I doubt she's on again, poor lass. (*EDD—doubt* means suspect)

on[3] habitually ingesting illegal narcotics
A shortened form of *on drugs*.
Those *on the needle* inject the drug. They may feel then from the sensation of floating that they are *on a cloud*, normally *cloud nine*, the cumulonimbus which may reach an altitude of 40,000 ft.

on[4] potentially promiscuous
On in the sense, happening or going ahead.

on health grounds through incompetence
A face-saving formula, implying that the health of the dismissed employee is at risk rather than that of the company.

on heat[1] able to conceive
Standard English of mammals other than humans, from the increased bodily temperature associated with the condition.

on heat[2] lustful
Of either sex:
> Are you on heat for her, Reverend? (B. Cornwell, 1993)
In heat is less common:
> 'I'm no bitch in heat,' she said between tight teeth. 'Take your paws off me.' (Chandler, 1958)
In the heat means copulating:
> ... make love to her afterwards. Would you like to hear tapes [of] Mike Santos in the heat? (M. West, 1979—Mr Santos was not a sprinter)

on her way *obsolete* pregnant
The destination is unstated:
> She's two months on her way. (Shakespeare, *Love's Labour's Lost*)

on ice in prison
Stored like edible provisions.

on-message uncritically obedient to a party line
Not just receiving the *message* but endorsing it without question:
> The on-message columnists in other newspapers have been deployed [by Ministers] to pour scorn on those who suggest that pensions are something to worry about. (*Daily Telegraph*, 24 October 2004—nor indeed do Ministers or government employees have any such worries)
The phrase may also refer to other sycophantic behaviour:
> Successful politicians were ventriloquists'

dummies, their clothes chosen for them by others, colour-coordinated and 'on message'. (Rankin, 2000)

on the beach dismissed from employment
It is used of sailors, especially if they have been discharged in a foreign port.

on the black working without paying tax
Probably a development of *black market*.

on the bottle see BOTTLE[1]

on the box *obsolete Scottish* ill and needy
The *box* was the Poor Box kept in church, in which donations for the poor were left.

on the club *British* ill and absent from work
From the days when employees might join a benefit society, paying weekly subscriptions against possible ill health.

on the couch engaged in casual copulation
This mythical article of furniture is put to the same use as the CASTING COUCH:
> My wife thinks I have endless lines of big-titted girls trying to get me on the couch. (Deighton, 1972)

on the cross engaged in robbery as a prostitute
The victim is figuratively crucified, or *double-crossed*, in circumstances in which he may decline to make a complaint, by a *cross-girl*, who may in fact be rather pleased with the outcome.

on the dole see DOLE

on the fly without paying tax
From the verbal meaning to disappear quickly or from the adjectival meaning, cunning:
> ... they'd asked him if he needed any work doing. 'On the fly, like. Cheaper that way.' (Rankin, 1993)
It may also refer to services performed for a third party by someone keeping the payment and not informing an employer.

on the gallop *Irish* (of a criminal) evading capture
A variant of the standard English ON THE RUN:
> Apart from six months spent 'on the gallop' in Eire, he's been away for eighteen years. (Stamp, 1994, writing about a terrorist bomb-maker who had spent much of his life in prison)

on the game working as a prostitute
Standard English:
> [The writer William Donaldson] returned to London where he learnt his former

girlfriend had gone on the game, moved in to her Chelsea brothel as a 'ponce' and used his experiences as the basis of his first book. (*Daily Telegraph*, 27 June 2005)
On the grind uses more appropriate imagery but is less common.
On the stroll, on the town, or *on the street* suggest that the prostitute solicits on public.
On the loose is obsolete.

on the job copulating
Literally, being involved in work of some kind. Common male usage.

on the labour see LABOUR[2]

on the lam *American* as a fugitive evading arrest
Literally, to *lam* is to beat whence, in slang, to beat it or run away.

on the left *American* operating illegally
The usual sinister connection, usually of operating without a licence:
> ... a small shop whose manager made more money selling drink 'on the left' than he did by dry-cleaning. (Clancy, 1988)
In Britain it means being able to enjoy reading editorials in the *Guardian*.

on the make seeking a sexual relationship
Literally, overly ambitious or greedy in an impatient way. Of either sex.

on the nest *American* pregnant
From the sedentary behaviour of a broody hen.

on the pad *American* in receipt of regular bribes
Police jargon, from the notebook in which the transactions may be recorded, albeit usually in coded form.

on the panel *British* absent from work through illness
Prior to the provision of free medical care for all, a list, or *panel*, of medical advisers was published telling the sick where they could get treatment on a charitable basis.
The obsolete Scottish *upon the panel* was being charged with a criminal offence before the *panel* of magistrates:
> Mr James Mitchel was upon the panell at the criminal court for shutting at the Archbishop of St Andrews. (Kirkton, 1817—shouting at bishops being then illegal, it would appear)

on the parish *obsolete British* destitute
Money needed for communal use was levied by means of a *parish* or *parochial rate* on property. Part of it went towards providing for the homeless and destitute. Also as *on the parochial*.

on the pill see PILL[2]

on the piss engaged in a drunken carouse
Usually from drinking beer, where the volume requires frequent urination. The phrase does not mean that, like the former Indian premier, Desai, you drink your urine for medicinal purposes.

on the pull see PULL[2]

on the ribs indigent
The ribs of an undernourished person are prominent. Also as *on your bones*, with the same derivation.

on the roof *American* engaged in a carouse
Where a tomcat may spend the night.
Also generally as *on the tiles*.

on the run (of a fugitive) trying to avoid capture
Standard English, and not of taking part in a marathon. Less often as *on the trot*.

on the seat in the lavatory
Not in an armchair, and often as an explanation for a delayed response.

on the shelf (of a female) unmarried and unlikely to marry
The imagery is from slow-moving inventory in retailing.
A synonym, *on the peg*, is obsolete.

on the side enjoyed illegally or immorally
From the *side* dish additional to the main plate. The phrase may indicate a bribe or earnings on which tax is not paid.
A *bit on the side* is promiscuous copulation, usually by the male, or the person with whom it takes place, either on a transitory or permanent basis.

on the skids failing
A *skid* is a piece of wood on which an object is placed to facilitate unstoppable movement, such as the launching of a ship:
  His current affairs flagship World in Action is on the skids. (*Private Eye*, May 1981)

on the square living honestly
Criminal jargon in a society where it is reprehensible to be law-abiding.
The Freemasons so describe their participation in their secret society, not because they lead honest lives but from the set-square used in building.

on the take accepting bribes
It may describe a pattern of conduct rather than a single payment.

on the town engaged in a carouse
Literally, a visit to the attractions of a city such as a theatre.

on the trot suffering from diarrhoea
Making hurried visits to the lavatory.

on the wagon refraining from drinking intoxicants
Taking potable fluids only from the *water wagon*. It may describe a single case of abstinence, as with someone about to drive a car, or a former alcoholic who is trying to cure himself of the addiction.

on vacation *American* in prison
The common black humour.
Also as *on the wall*, although *within* might seem a more appropriate preposition.

on your back (of a female) copulating
The posture commonly adopted:
  One way to travel. On my back. (L. Thomas, 1977—she had not booked a *wagon-lit*)

on your shield dead
The shield doubled for a stretcher if you were killed in battle.

on your way out dying
The common imagery of departure.
The phrase is also used of someone about to lose his job or his place in a team.

onanism masturbation
Onan spilled his seed on the ground, for which he was slain by the Lord (*Genesis* 38:9, 10). The expression is used of males and, illogically, of females:
  Those poor girls, he went on, were dying by the thousand from consumption, but really from self-abuse or onanism, as it was often called. Masturbation would also arrest growth, distort the pelvis, and prevent the development of the breasts. (Pearsall, 1969, quoting MacFadden's *The Power and Beauty of Superb Womanhood*, 1901—and what about blindness?)

one-armed bandit a mechanical gambling device
You pull the lever and barrels with coloured pictures on them spin to tell you that you have lost.

one bubble left of level mentally abnormal
On a single occasion or permanently, but not of severe mental illness. There are many similar phrases such as *one brick short of a load*.

one foot in the grave near death
Through old age or terminal disease.

one for the road an extra drink of intoxi-cant before leaving company
The warming, or stirrup, cup formerly taken before cold winter journeys on horseback or in an unheated coach.

one-night stand a single night of copula-tion with a chance partner
Punning on a travelling show, which plays a single performance before moving on.
A *one-nighter* means either the same thing, or the partner with whom the night is enjoyed (or as the case may be).

one o'clock at the waterworks *American* your trouser zip is undone
The hour at which an employee might leave his office and appear in public.

one of those a homosexual
Usually of a male.
In former use among sober and godly ma-trons, *one of those* might be a prostitute.

one of us a person with similar tastes and manners
Euphemistic only in the negative when imply-ing that someone is not your social equal:
    ... he's not what Aunt Fenny calls one of us. (P. Scott, 1968, referring to a policeman commissioned into the army)

one over the eight an excessive intake of intoxicants on a single occasion
There are eight pints in the gallon, which was considered a sufficient amount of beer or cider for a regular drinker in an evening.

one-parent family a parent living alone with dependent offspring
There are normally two parents still alive, of whom one is permanently absent from the home, or, in the case of many young women, was never there at all.
See also LONE PARENT and SINGLE PARENT.

one thing copulation
It is a commonly held belief among adult females that a man's interest in them is solely sexually based:
    I'd really—only—wanted—one—thing. She told me so this morning. (Amis, 1978)

one too many an intoxicant taken to ex-cess
Whence *had one too many*, became drunk.

one-way ride *American* an abduction and murder
Criminal jargon. Mr Luciano was called *Lucky* because he managed to make the return journey.

open access needing minimal qualifica-tions
A device adopted by some institutes of higher education to facilitate entry for those from selected categories who would not normally qualify academically, thus achieving higher enrolment and making tertiary education more widely available.

open housing *American* the banning of restrictions on ownership
Not providing hospitality to all but stopping white Christian residents preventing Jews or black people from buying houses on the estate.

open legged promiscuous
Of a woman and to *open your legs* is to copulate.

open marriage a marriage in which nei-ther spouse hides extramarital copula-tion
The *openness* consists in not lying to the other about lying with others.
An *open relationship* is a similar arrangement, without the prior wedding bells.

open palm see PALM[1]

open your bowels to defecate
A *bowel* is an intestine, whence any internal organ, as when Cromwell in a 1643 letter wrote 'The enemy will be in our bowels in ten days.'
Opening medicine is a laxative.

operation (an) surgery
Literally, a work, deed, or action. Standard English.

Operation Defensive Shield an invasion
The name chosen by the Israeli Defense Force for its onslaught on its Palestinian neighbour in 2002.

operational difficulties the ostensible reason why your journey will be delayed
The excuse given by transport operators, especially of trains and aircraft, to cover up breakdowns or incompetence. Also as *operat-ing difficulties*.

operator a swindler
Literally, anyone who carries out an opera-tion, but beware of so describing a surgeon in his hearing.
The word is also used of politicians and businessmen who use unconventional or questionable tactics to achieve their ends, and of dealers in illicit drugs.

Oppositional Defiant Disorder bad be-haviour

Educational jargon in a world where there are no naughty children but only medical conditions, one of which is called *ODD*.

optically challenged having defective eyesight

The usage covers anything from poor eyesight to blindness. Also as *optically handicapped*, *inconvenienced*, or *marginalized*.

oral sex cunnilingus or fellatio

Passionate kissing is not so described.

In the same sense, *oral service* is not what your dentist provides.

orchestras the testicles

Rhyming slang on *orchestra stalls*, BALLS.

order of the boot *British* summary dismissal from employment

After the ancient *Orders* of chivalry. Also as the *order of the push*.

orderly making illegal arrangements with regard to pricing

Thus an *orderly market* is one in which manufacturers collude to maintain higher profitability, either in a cartel, through establishing a monopoly, or by other price fixing. *Orderly progress* for a politician or government official is the maintenance of a monopoly which provides a justification for their continued control:

> Last week [a minister opposing the sale of a
> , state monopoly] sang of 'orderly progress'
> as preferable to the dangers of unbridled
> competition. (*Sunday Express*, May 1981—in
> this instance 'unbridled' was tautological)

ordure faeces

This is one of the venerable words of which it is difficult to say whether it meant dirt before or after it came to be used of faeces, vomit, and other human excreta.

organ the penis

Literally, an instrument and specifically the type played in churches. A shortened form of *sexual organ* or *organ of sex*.

The *organ of bliss* is the vagina.

Organs are the male genitalia. A factory in Taunton where church *organs* were manufactured displayed a prominent sign announcing 'Osmond's Organ Works'. Before its removal some accused Mr Osmond of boasting.

organic more expensive

All foodstuffs are *organic*, being derived from living plants or animals. The World Health Organization reported in 2002 that food sold as *organic*, i.e. produced without the use of chemicals, is no more nutritious than any other.

organize to induce to join a trade union

In the jargon, a company which is not obliged to negotiate with a trade union is not *organized*, however well its affairs may be managed.

In underworld slang the *organization* is an association of criminals.

orientation homosexuality

We have moved a long way from the Christian desire to site a building so that it faces towards the east, or *Orient*. In this use, a shortened form of *sexual orientation*.

orphan-hugging seeking publicity through a display of compassion

A practice of western politicians in poor countries when photographers are present:

> [Hillary Clinton's] stately progression on
> the orphan-hugging circuit through various
> third world capitals. (*Sunday Telegraph*, 8
> June 2003)

Oscar a male homosexual

Not an actor receiving a coveted award but from the late Mr Wilde. The use is more common in America and Australia than in his native Ireland or Britain.

other (the) promiscuous copulation

Usually in the phrase *a bit of the other*.

If indulged in by a married man with a specific partner or regular mistress, she is known as the *other woman*.

The *other thing* may be copulation within marriage:

> Won't drink with me, won't eat with me,
> won't look me in the eye. Won't do the
> other thing. (le Carré, 2001)

other side (the) death

For spiritualists, across the barrier between this world and the next. For some others, the far bank of the Styx or Jordan, on the way to the Elysian Fields or life eternal.

other side of the tracks *American* the poor section of town

When the railroad arrived, it was often located on the edge of town where property was cheaper, and it could be placed downwind of houses to minimize smoke, noise, and fire hazards. Eventually the town would develop around the station, with the richer inhabitants staying in the more salubrious quarter and the poorer living *on the other side of the tracks*. Now also some figurative use.

other way (the) homosexual

The phrase applies to either sex:

> He wouldn't look at his servants. His
> inclinations, if she knew it, are all the
> other way. (G. Greene, 1932—female

servants sometimes caught the eye of the master of the house)

others *Irish* menstruation
The etymology is unclear:
> —I told him I thought I was pregnint.— GOOD JAYSIS! Jimmy roared laughing.— Yeh fuckin' didn't!—I did, Jimmy....Me others were late. (Doyle, 1987)

out¹ available for marriage
A shortened form of *out in society*, when girls approaching marriageable age had their season in which they met bachelors, among others. Despite the attraction of linking matrimony with the chase, I fear that we cannot call in aid the hunting jargon *out*, engaged on horseback chasing fox or deer.

out² overtly homosexual
Having come *out of the closet*. Whence the verb, meaning publicly to expose another's homosexuality:
> Militant activists claim that they are now 'negotiating' with five other bishops (who, it is said, are being urged to admit to homosexuality or be 'outed'). (*Sunday Telegraph*, 12 March 1995)

In this context an *outing* is not a Sunday School treat but such involuntary exposure.

out³ *obsolete* involved in a duel
The venue was generally in the open air.

out of a position *obsolete* involuntarily unemployed
In the days when there was a stigma attached to idleness, unless you were rich:
> They included bankrupts, hypochondriacs, persons who were 'out of a position'...(Hardy, 1886)

out of circulation menstruating
Female usage, often to a male, with imagery from the lending library.

out of context said inadvisedly
A use by politicians when they have forgotten what exactly they may have said, wish they had never said it, or were unaware that anyone was recording it. As journalists are known to be selective in their quotations, this defensive manoeuvre is often effective.

out of the envelope acting eccentrically or without authority
Pilots' jargon, the *envelope* being the parameters within which an aircraft is designed to perform, as to rates of climb, stall, turn, etc.

out of town *American* in prison
Suggesting the convict may be away on business. Some humorous use.

out of your skull mentally unwell
You may also be described as being *out of your gourd, head, senses, tree*, etc.:
> Lady Macbeth was...clearly out of her tree. (N. Evans, 1995—and not after hiding in Birnham Wood)

out to lunch *American* mentally unstable
The imagery is of a short absence from home, whence indicating a mild and perhaps temporary affliction.

outdoor plumbing *American* a primitive lavatory
A humorous use of a shed with a seat, a hole, but no water or drainage.

outhouse a lavatory
In a courtyard or down the garden, away from the dwelling house. It was the place you visited if you said you were going *out the back*.

outplace to dismiss from employment
Not being sent to work away from the plant or office:
> ...despite the fact that your company is doing rather well, you have been sacked or, rather, 're-engineered', 'downsized', 'unassigned', 'proactively outplaced' or 'put in the mobility pool'. (*Sunday Telegraph*, 27 October 1996)

outrage to copulate with a woman against her will
Literally, to offend in any way:
> She complained that...some British soldiers had assaulted and outraged her...She could have identified at least forty men who had outraged her. (Richards, 1933—she was a French prostitute)

outsourcing *British* handing management over to or buying services from the private sector
It is embarrassing for a socialist to concede that state or municipal ownership is often not compatible with economy or efficiency:
> Estelle Morris, the schools minister, announced that...some at least of Leeds' functions would be privatised, though she preferred to call it 'outsourcing'. (*Daily Telegraph*, 3 February 2000)

oval office *American* the vagina viewed sexually
Punning on the personal office of the President of the United States, without any implication that the holder of that position would ever be guilty of sexual impropriety.

over-civilized decadent
Nazi dysphemism in a culture where to appreciate beauty was to be effete:

They are nearer to France, Europe's most over-civilized country. (Goebbels, 1945, in translation, writing about his native Rhinelanders who did not resist the Anglo-American invaders)

over-familiar making an unwanted sexual approach to a female
Literally, being too affable. See also FAMILIAR.

over-fond of the bottle an alcoholic
The contents rather than the container. An evasion used in obituaries.

over-gallant see GALLANT

over-geared insolvent
Gearing is the relationship between assets and debt. Unless you are its banker, to imply that a company is insolvent is taboo as well as being actionable.

over-invoicing the payment of money additional to the agreed price in a place selected by the recipient
In markets where corruption is rife and taxation heavy, a customer may ask a foreign supplier to inflate the price of imports, with the difference being paid as a bribe or as a return of the excess in another country. See also UNDER-INVOICING.

over-privileged rich
But no more *privileged* than PRIVILEGED.

over-refreshed drunk
Not much different from *refreshed*. *Over-sedated* still means, and *over-excited* used to mean, the same thing.

over the broomstick *obsolete* cohabiting and copulating outside marriage
The outcome if you decided to JUMP THE BROOMSTICK.

over the Jordan dead
What happens when you reach the OTHER SIDE.

over the top achieving a sexual orgasm
Usually of a female, from the cliché meaning excessive:
   She made love to herself on the bath mat... She always felt awful afterwards... especially when she took herself... over the top. (M. McCarthy, 1963)

over the wall escaping from prison
Of obvious imagery and by whatever means egress is obtained. In British naval use, *over the wall* had the opposite meaning, the *wall* being the side of the ship over which the prisoner passed on his way to a prison on shore:

The Court Martial sentenced him to six months over the wall and he got dismissed the Service as well. (Jolly, 1988)

over there engaged in warfare on foreign soil
For the British, France in the First World War. For the American military *over there* meant service in Europe in both World Wars.

overactive naughty
An excuse or delusion of parents whose lack of discipline may have caused the problem.

overdo the Dionysian rites to become drunk
Dionysus discovered the art of wine-making. Being of catholic tastes, the god sought pleasure also in sexual orgies, plays, human sacrifice, and flagellation.

overdose an attempt at suicide by self-poisoning with drugs
Literally, an excessive ingestion, especially of medicine. Medical jargon, sometimes shortened to *OD*, applied both to the attempt and to the person who does it:
   William sold all his possessions from his Exeter townhouse; and on 22 August he overdosed on laudanum. (Dalrymple, 2002)
   She's a person, not a goddamned *OD*. (Clancy, 1989)

overdue[1] pregnant
Failing to menstruate at the expected time but not necessarily denoting an unwanted pregnancy.

overdue[2] in difficulty or crashed
Aviation jargon, of an aircraft which has failed to report routinely during flight, or has not landed as expected:
   Overdue connoted something quite different from late in airline parlance. (Block, 1979)

overflight a spying mission
Literally, crossing a country in the course of a commercial flight by a recognized and agreed path. The American government in May 1960 so described the mission of Gary Powers, who was shot down over Russia in a U2 aircraft. In 1962 the Russians exchanged Powers for their spy Rudolf Abel.

overfriendly involving sexual impropriety
The excess of amity is usually shown by a male:
   Verity makes no secret of having had an overfriendly involvement with a pupil's mother in Leeds, where he was headmaster of the grammar school for ten years. (*Daily Telegraph*, 18 August 1998)

overhaul a dismissal of employees
Literally, an act of repairing or improving something, but in business an *overhaul* implies staff reduction to save costs:
   ...520 jobs are to be chopped out of the company's portfolio of regional newspaper titles. The headline of the press release: 'Overhaul of profit margins at Westminster Press.' (*Daily Telegraph*, 1 July 1995)
In 1934 the Nazis introduced an annual four-week *national political overhaul*, a period set aside for indoctrination. (Klemperer, 1998, in translation)

overhear *American* a clandestine listening device
Evasions are necessary because of sensitivity about illegal eavesdropping:
   I asked if there was an 'overhear', the feds' delicate term for a bug. (Turow, 1999)

overindulge to drink intoxicants to excess
On a single occasion or habitually.
See also INDULGE.

oversee *obsolete* to bewitch
Literally, to inspect or supervise, but one glance was enough for a true witch. Also as to *overlook* or *overshadow*.

overtired drunk
Alcohol makes you sleepy, or TIRED[2], and *overtiredness* is drunkenness:
   [The Deputy Prime Minister, George Brown] turned up to the first production meeting—in the morning—in an advanced state of over-tiredness. (*Private Eye*, 1980)

owl a prostitute
A predatory bird which hunts by night.

owned second-hand
A refinement of the PRE-OWNED theme. In 1999 prospective customers were being invited in advertisements to buy *owned Rolls-Royce* motor cars, as though there were also a store of abandoned vehicles from which to draw, if they so chose.

own goal an accusation or campaign which damages the originator
The result for a soccer player of inadvertently scoring against his own side:
   Occasionally there was an 'own goal'. Usually there was a warning. (McCrum, 1991, describing terrorists attempting to blow up others but killing themselves)

P

P urine
The initial letter of *piss*. Also, as a verb, to urinate and in the vulgar expression *p off*. See also PEE.

PC see POLITICALLY CORRECT

pacify to conduct military operations in foreign territory
Literally, to bring peace to, which tends to be the stated objective. Whence *pacification*, such behaviour, as reportedly practised by the Americans in Vietnam, their opponents, if caught, being held in a *pacification camp* or *center*. For the British in sub-Saharan Africa, their colonial rule was the *era of pacification*, which, in retrospect, may not have been not a misnomer. (Allen, 1970)

pack it in to die
Literally, to desist.

package on (a) drunkenness
Carrying a LOAD and owing nothing to the obsolete English *pack*, rum, named after the English general Pakenham who had the misfortune of being killed in the battle of New Orleans two months after the signing in Europe of the peace treaty between the combatants.

package store American a place which sells intoxicants
A survival from the days when buying liquor to drink at home was taboo.

packet¹ a serious wound or death
Literally, a small pack, hence an article sent by post, as in the *packet boat* which carried the mail. See also CATCH A PACKET¹.

packet² a venereal disease
Another unwelcome small pack for soldiers in the Second World War—see CATCH A PACKET². Today, if you *catch a packet*, it may mean no more than having a number of bills descend on you at once.

pad dishonestly to inflate
Used of claims and accounts, from *padding* clothing to cause an apparent increase in size. There is no etymological link with the obsolete *pad*, to rob, as in *footpad* (see HIGHWAYMAN), which came from *pad*, a path.

Paddington obsolete relating to hanging
The geographical location in London of the gallows:

Tyburn being in the parish of Paddington, execution day was known as Paddington Fair, the hood drawn over one's head was the Paddington spectacles, and in dying one danced the Paddington frisk. (Hughes, 1987)

paddy wagon American a police vehicle
There was a preponderance of those of Irish origin in New England police departments but not necessarily among those incarcerated.

pagan obsolete a prostitute
Prostitution was no occupation for the upright:
> Prince Henry What pagan may that be?
> Page A proper gentlewoman. (Shakespeare, 1 Henry IV)

paint the tape American fraudulently to record deals at fictitious prices
From the *ticker tape* once used for the dissemination of market information.
To *paint a picture* means to tell a lie.

paint the town red to carouse
Usually of a single session of celebratory drunken debauchery. It has been suggested, somewhat improbably, that the phrase originated in the American west, where a drunken spree might start in a brothel area and then move uptown, although a reverse itinerary would have seemed more likely.

painted woman obsolete a prostitute
Not an artist's model but someone who used cosmetics before the practice became in succession permitted, normal, and then obligatory.

painters are in (the) I am menstruating
From the disruption and discoloration. Dated female use.

palm¹ an indication of bribery
The hand of the recipient is upturned. Their *palm* may also be *slippery*, and *tickled* when the bribe is paid. Shakespeare writes of an *itching palm* in *Julius Caesar*. To *anoint a palm* is to bribe, and punning terms for bribery include *palm grease*, *oil*, *soap*, or *palmistry*, which puns on divination.
An *open palm* indicates a desire to be bribed or excessively tipped, although that is not why *Palm Beach* is so called, despite the reputation of its hotel and restaurant staff.

palm² to cheat by prestidigitation
The cards are concealed in the *palm* of the hand. Used figuratively of other forms of cheating and sharp practice, as in the phrase *palm off with*, to give (someone) something

which is worthless or of less value than had been agreed.

pan a pedestal-type lavatory
Literally, any bowl. Whence the figurative *down the pan*, irretrievably lost.
A *bedpan* is used for defecation and urination, not for eating from or washing in.

pancake the faeces of cows
From the shape on the grass.
Whence also to *pancake*, to land an aircraft with the undercarriage retracted.

panel¹ (the) *obsolete British* the list of doctors available to treat the poor
Those whom poor sick people consulted prior to the National Health Service.
To be ON THE PANEL meant to be absent from work due to illness.

panel² *obsolete* a prostitute
There seems to be no link between this *panel* and the American *panel-house* or *panel–joint*, a brothel, where the rooms were divided into wooden cubicles.

panhandle *American* to beg in a public place
From the receptacle thrust at the victim.
A *panhandler* is such a beggar, often using menaces, and may also be a thief, and not necessarily an inhabitant of the Panhandle in Western Florida.

pansy a male homosexual
Like the delicate flower, *Viola tricolour*.

panther sweat *American* whisky
DAS suggests: May have originally been a euphemism for 'panther piss'.
But where did *panther piss* come from, in the absence of panthers?

paper aeroplane a project to construct a new aircraft
Usually drawn in outline with a draft specification in the hope of securing backing for development costs from a potential customer or government. The pun is less obvious with *paper helicopter*.

paper-hanger¹ *American* a policeman punishing a motorist for speeding
Referring to the *ticket* which may be handed out on such occasions. With similar punning humour, the officer may be described as *doing his paperwork*.

paper-hanger² a person who passes false negotiable instruments
Usually of cheques which have been stolen or are not covered by deposits.

paper (out) on having a commercial agreement to murder
Criminal slang. It is unlikely that such a CONTRACT will have been written down.

paper the house to fill seats in a theatre by giving tickets away
Punning theatrical jargon, the *house* being the audience. The phrase is also used of ensuring that politicians have a sympathetic crowd at public meetings, with supporters being conveyed to the venue, especially if television cameras are about.

Paphian associated with prostitution
Paphos, or Cyprus, was sacred to Venus, the goddess of love.

parallel importing illegally or breach of contract
Keeping pace with, but a distance from, a legitimate operation.
A *parallel importer* smuggles commodities, such as cigarettes and alcohol into Britain from Europe, or prescription drugs from Canada to the United States, buying where prices are lower due to tax or other factors.
A *parallel trader* sells branded goods at prices below those stipulated by the manufacturer, having perhaps bought them abroad at a discount.
Parallel pricing is where two suppliers operate a cartel.
In the Spanish Civil War, when the government became ineffective and control in some areas passed to anarchists, a system of *parallel justice* was enforced by *parallel police*. (Mitchell, 1982)

parallel parking *American* having a mistress
One vehicle legally at the kerb and another beside it in the street.

paralysed very drunk
And immobile. Also as *paralytic*.

paramour a person with whom you have a regular extramarital sexual relationship
Originally a suitor, acting 'through love', and of both sexes, although latterly women have acquired more *paramours* than men.

parboiled drunk
Literally, thoroughly boiled, whence overheated. The common culinary imagery.

Paris Mean Time Greenwich Mean Time adapted to French chauvinism
The preferred French locution for Greenwich Mean Time was 'Paris Mean Time retarded by nine minutes and twenty-nine seconds'. (Sobel,

1996—it was, for the French, both unjust and unacceptable that the meridian was judged to have been centred in an observatory in England).

parity the achievement of the best in any aspect of employment
Trade union jargon. The equality you seek is always better in terms of wages, hours of work, holidays, pensions, paternity leave, or whatever.

park to transfer (stocks) to an accomplice so as to conceal ownership
Using the same imagery as WAREHOUSE.

park women *obsolete* prostitutes
As found in 19th-century London, where a plethora of open spaces offered convenient locations.

parliament[1] *obsolete British* a lavatory
An excruciating Victorian pun on sitting.

parliament[2] *obsolete* smuggled or illegally distilled spirits
Because no excise duty had been paid on it.

parlor house *American* a brothel
The room in which you might be expected to meet a female visitor.

parsley bed *obsolete* the place where new girl babies are found
EDD defines it as 'A euphemism for the uterus' but the ensuing quotation and dissertation do not support the definition (vol. iv, p. 427). Parsley seeds itself and, like the GOOSEBERRY BUSHes which provided similar antenatal accommodation for boys, thrives without weeding, resulting in unkempt areas in many Victorian gardens where the stork might discreetly drop its bundle.

part to die
Usually of a spouse, in the hope of being united later, perhaps:
    She told me, that to part was the greatest pain she had ever felt, and that we would meet again in a better place. (J. Boswell, 1791)

part with patrick *obsolete Scottish* to abort a foetus prematurely
A version of the former standard English, *part with child*.

partake to drink alcohol
Really no more than to share in, in this case sharing a drink.

partially sighted nearly blind
There are more taboos about blindness than about deafness, possibly because the blind are

at a greater disadvantage in society than the deaf. Thus if people are *partially sighted*, it does not mean that you have had but a fleeting glimpse of them.

partner a person having a regular unmarried sexual relationship with another
Usually they also cohabit. The word is used of homosexuals and heterosexuals:
    Maternity nurses at the Royal United Hospital in Bath have been told to call fathers of newborn babies 'partners' rather than 'husbands', so as not to upset single mothers. (*Sunday Telegraph*, 20 March 1994)

parts the human genitalia
A shortened form of PRIVATE PARTS.
The former meaning, virtues, might lead to misunderstanding today:
    I think highly of Campbell. In the first place, he has very good parts. (J. Boswell, 1773)

party a battle
A Second World War version of the First World War SHOW[2], understating the danger and the unpleasantness.

party girl *American* a prostitute
Literally, a girl who attends parties, whence one who is invited to be available for male guests, or one who attends in the hope of meeting a customer.

party member a Communist
The usage dates from the period prior to the Second World War when you kept quiet about being a Communist because many would consider you to be a traitor with revolutionary tendencies.

pash a homosexual desire
A shortened version of *passion*. Formerly much used to denote such feelings between schoolgirls for each other, or for a female teacher:
    Are you getting a pash for that little thing? (G. Greene, 1932—but people normally had *pashes on* not *pashes for*)
Less often of one-sided heterosexual feeling.

pass[1] to die
The passage from this world to the next.
We are all also destined, in due time, to *pass away, beyond the veil, into the next world*, or *in our checks*, the last when we stop gambling or return to the surface after a shift in the mine. We may also *pass over, tout court*, without saying what is being crossed, or we may *pass to the other side of the Great Divide, of the Jordan, of the Styx*, or some other obstacle of our choice.
Whichever route we select, our *passing* is death.

pass² an unsolicited sexual approach
Usually by a male to a female he does not know well, from the reconnaissance before attacking.
Occasionally of homosexuals.
Although normally *made*, it seems that *passes* can also be *thrown*, as in football.

pass air *American* to fart
You may also, if so minded, *pass gas* or *wind*.

pass water to urinate
The phrase is so common that we do not confuse it with driving by a river or handing someone a jug at table.

past its sell-by date outmoded or useless
A cliché from the dating of food sold by retail, which is intended to convince the customer of its freshness.

past (your) something shameful or secret about your past life
It usually refers to criminal activity or to adultery, the latter in the days when it was not socially accepted, especially in a woman:
    'Part of your past, I presume?' 'No. At least, not as you mean it.' (Manning, 1965)

patriotic reticence the suppression of bad news
The phrase was coined by the British Prime Minister Asquith in 1914 to justify suppressing news of the extent of the German advance. (Tuchman, 1962)

patron *obsolete* a man who keeps a mistress
Originally, he who stands in the relationship of a father, whence the concept of endorsing or protecting.
Patron is widely, and pretentiously, used to mean customer in an attempt to add a non-commercial gloss to a business arrangement.

pause¹ the natural cessation of menstruation
Literally, a cessation of something which will be resumed but, in this usage, a shortened form of *menopause*.

pause² a statutory restriction on increases in pay
One of a series of terms used by politicians of attempts to hold down wages as a supposed cure for inflation brought about in part by their ill-conceived fiscal policies.

pavement girl *American* a prostitute
Standing on roadside at which her trucker customers pull up rather than in any old STREET.
Also as *pavement princess*.

pavement people beggars
The place where they beg and where some of them sleep. For the POLITICALLY CORRECT, the word 'vagrant' is taboo.

paw to fondle sexually
Perhaps punning on *paw*, the hand, and on the vigour with which an impatient stallion strikes the ground with his hoof.

pay a visit to urinate
Shortened form of *pay a visit to the lavatory* and punning on making a social call. Very common of urination but seldom of defecation.

pay lip service insincerely to say you agree with or support
Not kissing but saying rather than doing.

pay nature's (last) debt to die of natural causes
From the necessity of death in the natural order. To *pay the supreme sacrifice* or *price* is to be killed in the course of duty or, less often, judicially.
To *pay the price* (when not *supreme*) or *pay your debt to society* is to be killed judicially.

pay with the roll of a drum *obsolete British* to avoid payment
It was illegal to seek to arrest a soldier for debt while he was on the march.

paying guest see GUEST²

payoff a bribe or illegal reward
Not what you receive when leaving lawful employment. If however you are *paid off*, you lose your job.

payroll adjustment the summary dismissal of staff
Not merely correcting an error in a previous computation.

peace a preparation for violence
First noted in Hitler's notorious *peace speech* of 17 May 1933, which heralded his assaults upon his neighbours. The concept and language were adopted by Communists and other aggressors, with *peace councils*, *offensives*, and the like:
    Its official name was Operation Peace for Galilee, even though the siege of Beirut, far to the north of Galilee, had been going on for weeks. (Simpson, 1998, writing of the 1982 invasion of Lebanon by Israel)
Peace-keeping action is an invasion of another's territory, the units taking part being described as a *peace-keeping force*.

peace at last death
A tombstone and obituary favourite, referring to the dead person and not to the survivors.

pear-shaped unsuccessful
Probably from the form of an analyst's graph, the use having started as jargon in financial circles. As with the fruit, the weight is at the lower end.

pecker *American* the penis
Literally, an instrument for making a hole by pecking.
The British *pecker* was the nose, whence the expression *keep your pecker up*, keep cheerful, an exhortation which an American might find impracticable as well as impertinent.

peculiar homosexual
A variant of QUEER³.
In obsolete British use a *peculiar* was a mistress, someone you kept for your own exclusive use.
For Webster in 1833 the *peculiar members* were the testicles.

peculiar institution (the) *obsolete American* slavery
19th-century usage, when slavery was thought to be an integral part of the economy of the South. It also continued in some Unionist states for much of the Civil War:
   ...it was unthinkable that the American flag should impose the South's 'peculiar institution' on new lands won by Americans from every part of the country. (Ward, 1990—dispossessing American Indians was all right, it seems)

peddle your arse to be a prostitute
From *peddle*, to offer for sale, and *ass* in America. Heterosexual and homosexual use.

pee to urinate
The first letter of *piss*, and the usual spelling of P.
A *pee* is an act of urination.
Pee-pee for urination is rare in English (although common in colloquial French).

peel a banana *American* to copulate
Of a male, presumably from the movement of the prepuce, with the common *banana* imagery of an erect penis.

peeler a policeman
After the original BOBBY, Sir Robert Peel. Whence perhaps the American slang *peel*, to arrest.

peeper *American* a private detective
Employed commonly, but not exclusively, to provide evidence of adultery. Also a *voyeur*, as a shortened form of PEEPING TOM.

Peeping Tom a sexual voyeur
Leofric, the Anglo-Saxon Lord of Coventry,

agreed to postpone an increase in taxes if his wife, Godiva, rode naked through the streets. The townspeople were forbidden to watch, and how anybody would have known if Tom hadn't peeped is a matter for conjecture.

peg *obsolete* to be a drunkard
From the communal drinking bowl in which each participant's share was marked with a *peg*. In Anglo-Indian use, a *peg* was a drink of spirits, being a shortened form of CHOTA PEG.

peg out to die
Not necessarily of drink but from the scoring at cribbage, where the first to finish moves his *peg* to the end of a row of holes on a board and *pegs out*.

pencil¹ the penis
From the shape and construction rather than the shared Latin ancestry. Now only as LEAD IN YOUR PENCIL, although Partridge gave *pencil and tassel* as a child's penis and scrotum (*DSUE*).

pencil² not legally binding
Attributive use, from the ability to erase what is written in pencil.
A busy or self-important person who *pencils* an appointment in a diary is likely to cancel it or fail to keep it.

penetrate¹ to copulate with
Of a male, with *penetration* or *full penetration* being the legal jargon for copulation. The imagery is from the entry, although the words share an etymological ancestry with penis.

penetrate² to effect access without consent
The language of espionage. You may *penetrate* a building to steal documents or install listening devices; or you may *penetrate* an organization of which you disapprove in order to monitor the activities of its members.

penitentiary *American* a prison
Some of the inmates may indeed be *penitent*, but probably not the majority. Shortened to *pen*. Standard American English.

penman a forger
Literally, a skilled writer with a pen. Criminal jargon.

penny short of a pound (a) simple-minded
239 out of 240 in the old imperial coinage, using the common imagery as in NOT SIXTEEN ANNAS TO THE RUPEE and similar phrases which imply that someone is NOT ALL THERE.

people cuts the dismissal of employees
Industrial jargon. The term is not used by surgeons.

people of/with those having a particular characteristic

POLITICALLY CORRECT language adopted by those so described. Thus *people of colour* are black.

People with impaired hearing are deaf and *people with learning difficulties* are those who are unable to keep up with their peers in class.

People of size, which might be thought to include all of us and not just interior decorators fixing wallpaper, does not refer to stature but to girth.

The usage was to be found before 1939:

Among those not allowed to emigrate to Britain, Palestine or the colonies were the infirm, anyone with a criminal record, those who could not support themselves and 'people with unacceptable politics'—a euphemism for communists. (M. Smith, 1999)

We can only rejoice with Mr B. F. Freeman, who won $50,000 in a 'Create a New Word' competition by suggesting *people with differing abilities* to describe those suffering from a physical disability (Beard & Cerf, 1990). Now we know at last why Arnold Palmer or Tiger Woods routinely turn in lower scores on the golf course than ourselves.

people's imposed by autocracy

The language of totalitarianism, or contempt. Less often, in modern use, seeking to imply disinterested benevolence. In various compounds, as follows:

people's army an army pledged to the support of a regime when the former non-political or professional army has been disbanded

As in Communist China and other totalitarian regimes. In July 1944, having abandoned those involved in the Warsaw uprising to the Germans and ignoring the Polish troops still fighting elsewhere in Europe, the puppet Lublin Committee renamed its military wing the *People's Army*.

people's car a device for financing Nazi re-armament

In 1938 any German who had paid 750 marks at a rate of not less than 5 marks a week received an order number, but none received a car. Today *Volkswagen* has long shaken off its dubious beginnings.

people's court a tribunal supporting the regime without trained judges or juries, and without justice or mercy

There is a certain irony in the fact that the three Communists acquitted by a properly constituted court in 1934 of involvement in the Reichstag fire should have been the first victims of the Nazi *Volksgerichtshof*.

people's democracy an autocracy

Usually Communist, and newspeak at its best, since its citizens are denied effective voting rights or access to a free press.

people's government a totalitarian tyranny

One so named was proposed by the Malayan Communist Hor Lung in a 'Liberated Area' which he controlled. The local inhabitants were subjected to violent intimidation and summary execution until British-led forces ousted the rebels. (Barber, 1971)

people's justice summary killing without trial

Without even the legalistic routine of a PEOPLE'S COURT to delay the process.

people's lottery a national lottery operated by a licensee

people's militia an armed force supporting those who have seized power

It may be institutionalized to keep a watch over and counterbalance what remains of a professional army.

people's palace a mansion for the exclusive use of an autocrat

As in Syria:

And it was he who told me that his palace in Damascus, built at a cost of 120 million dollars—and of course no one but the Commander was allowed to enter it—was called Kasr el Sharb, the People's Palace. (Theroux, 1995—the 'Commander' (of the Nation) was the autocrat Assad)

people's party a political grouping

Not a gathering in the village hall or a political organization where membership is confined to human beings. *People's parties*, such as the *British People's Party*, usually advocate extreme policies.

people's republic an autocracy

Usually Communist and slightly less offensive than PEOPLE'S DEMOCRACY, although the *people* are unlikely to notice any difference.

people's tribunal a political court

Operating on the lines of a PEOPLE'S COURT. The first public news of a hearing by the *People's Tribunal* operated by the Nazis in 1939 was a placard announcing that an accused had been guillotined. (Kee, 1984)

perform to defecate or urinate when required

A shortened form of *perform a natural function* or some such expression.

Common nursery usage to describe a child

being trained to control urination or defecation:

> On the rare occasions when by pure chance—he 'performed', she moderated her pantomime of approval. (M. McCarthy, 1963)

Also used of domestic pets.

period¹ the time of menstruation
Shortened form of MONTHLY PERIOD of menstrual flow.

period² old and dilapidated
Literally, a passage of time, but for this attributive use the estate agent is unlikely to go into historical detail, having given the impression that the property is venerable.

periodic rest a term in prison
Usually of a habitual criminal. The phrase was used of the incarceration of Jimmy Hoffa, the former boss of the Teamsters' Union, who was jailed through the efforts of Robert Kennedy and released by Richard Nixon in 1971.

permissive less constrained by custom in personal conduct
Formerly meaning not obligatory, and then relaxed or lenient, as in the British *permissive society* resulting in part from reforms initiated by Roy Jenkins in the 1960s, which decriminalized acts of homosexual behaviour between consenting adults and generally led to a less censorious attitude to promiscuity.

person the male genitalia
A shortened form of *personal parts*, the full term also being used for the vagina. Specifically of the penis, also shortened to *Percy*, punning on the male name.
In obsolete use, a *person* was a body viewed sexually, as in a report from the British Embassy in Paris dated 16 April 1749 which stated that Louis XV had a 'grave affection for the *person* of Madame de Pompadour'. (Tombs & Tombs, 2006)

person of/with someone having a particular characteristic
Used in much the same way as PEOPLE OF/WITH. Thus a *person of colour* is a black person, and a *person with AIDS* becomes a *PWA*, an abbreviation not usually accorded to the victims of other diseases. To avoid mentioning sex, the bedroom, or unmarried copulation we have to turn to an American circumlocutory bureaucrat:

> At the other end of the scale, the US Census Bureau came up with 'Person of the opposite sex sharing living quarters'. As an introduction it seemed a mite unromantic. (Whicker, 1982—he was pondering how to describe his mistress)

persona non grata someone caught spying
Literally, any unwelcome person, but used specifically of a diplomat accused of spying on a host nation. Sometimes abbreviated to *PNG*.

personal correction *obsolete* flogging
As practised in 19th-century English boarding schools by even so reputedly enlightened a pedagogue as Thomas Arnold.

personal hygiene the paraphernalia of menstruation
Hygiene originally meant knowledge and practice that relates to the maintenance of health, and menstruation is not an illness but a natural process.
Also as *feminine hygiene*, as seen on containers in lavatories for the disposal of sanitary towels and tampons.
On a spacecraft a *personal hygiene station* is a lavatory.

personal parts see PERSON

personal relations sexual activity with another
In literal terms, you have *personal relations* with everyone you meet. Of copulation and, less often, of homosexuality:

> [The homosexual traitor] Burgess had ample opportunities to indulge his fetish for 'personal relations' under cover of the rigidly enforced nightly blackout. (Boyle, 1979)

Personal services means willingness to copulate in a coded advertisement by a prostitute or MASSAGE PARLOUR.

personal representatives those who administer the estate of a person who dies intestate or without a living executor
The *person* whom they supposedly *represent* is dead.

personality a nonentity
Literally, the fact of being a person, with individual characteristics. Jargon of the entertainment industry:

> He wouldn't allow the *TV Times* to describe him as a TV personality. That's just for jokeless comics wishing they could sing and dance. (Deighton, 1972)

personnel ceiling reduction *American* the dismissal of employees
It does not mean that they continue to work in an office with a lower headroom.

persuade to compel through violence or threats

Literally, to convince by argument.
Criminal jargon and a *persuader* is a weapon so used.

pet¹ to caress physically during courtship
Probably from the stroking of the domestic animal.

pet² *American* a mistress
The imagery is of the domestic animal kept for its owner's pleasure, or pleasuring.

peter *American* the penis
One of the common male names so used, but not, as has been suggested, from *petard*, a mine, or from blowing up a safe.

petite very small
Not merely describing a young girl. Jargon of the garment trade.

petite amie a mistress
The little female friend but not necessarily either small or French. Also as *petite femme*.
A *petit ami* is the partner of a male homosexual playing the female role.

petrified *American* drunk
Showing no sign of movement, as if turned into stone. The imagery is the same as the common STONED.

petticoat dominated by a female
For the Victorians a *petticoat* was a female, without expressly sexual overtones.
It is not necessary to dilate further to sufferers on what is meant by *petticoat government*.

petting-stone *obsolete Northern England* a stone at the church gate at which a bride supposedly renounced her ill humours
Such were unfortunately to be found only in Northumberland and Durham. A bride, after leaving the marriage service, had to jump, stride, or be carried across the stone. If she failed to do so, the marriage was doomed. The ritual was later commuted for a cash payment before being abandoned.

petty house SEE LITTLE HOUSE

phantom *American* a person paid while not working or a nonexistent employee whose wage is drawn by another
The victim is usually a public-sector employer. Either the person named on the payroll exists but, as a friend of a politician or a supervisor, gets paid while not working; or the payroll numbers are inflated by the name of a person who has no connection with the enterprise or does not exist, with someone stealing the wages.

pharmaceuticals illegal narcotics
Literally, relating to drugs but not used in addict circles of aspirin or penicillin.
For such people, a *pharmacy* is their personal stock of narcotics.

phoenix seeking to avoid the payment of liabilities
Usually in the phrase *phoenix company* which, like the fabulous bird, rises from the ashes of an administration, receivership, liquidation, or life under *Chapter Eleven* (under GO²) with the same proprietors, the same assets, and a trail of unpaid suppliers and cheated investors. To *do a phoenix* is to conduct your business in this manner.

physic a laxative
Literally, any medical treatment.

physical involvement a sexual relationship
Not just shaking hands, which is all the words might imply:
> Her solicitors have been instructed to sue any hack who dares to suggest a physical involvement. (*Private Eye*, March 1981)

pick to steal
OED notes a use in 1300, which makes it one of the oldest euphemisms in the language, and in regular use since then.
To *pick a pocket* is explicit, and we are still plagued with *pickpockets* who steal articles from our clothing.
The obsolete forms of *pickle* and the Scottish *pike* also meant to steal.

pick a daisy to urinate
A punning female use, perhaps from the bending down and the *daisy*, or chamber pot, so called from the common floral decorative motif of the rim. To *pick a pea* punned with less subtlety. To *pick a rose* brought to mind a nozzle producing a fine spray. These, and other flowers, might also be *gathered*, *plucked*, or *pulled* by a woman wishing to urinate.

pick-me-up a drink of an intoxicant
Literally, a medicine taken as a tonic, whence jokingly used of spirits.

pick off to kill
From a distance, selecting your target, either of humans or other animals.

pick up to acquire a sexual partner casually
Not literally raising the other from the ground. Of either sex, the other person being a *pick-up*, even if not selected in a *pick-up joint*

frequented by prostitutes and other promiscuous people.

pick up a knife *obsolete* to fall off a horse
An object of shame in the days when most people could ride. The pretence was that the loss of your seat was intentional. Much humorous use.

pick up a nail to contract gonorrhea
The discomfort felt by the male when urinating or undergoing a pre-penicillin cure was akin to the lameness of a horse.

pickled drunk
The common culinary imagery but this time also alluding to the preservation of anatomical specimens in alcohol.

pie-eyed drunk
Unable to focus rather than with eyes like pies.

piece¹ a female viewed sexually by a male
Literally, a part of something and a synonym of BIT¹.
More often as a *piece of arse* or *ass, crackling, crumpet, goods*, or *skirt*. *Piece of buttered bun, muslin, on a fork*, or *of trade* (a prostitute) are obsolete. A *piece of gash, spare*, or *rump* is a woman considered readily available for promiscuous copulation.
A *piece on the side* is a mistress.
A *piece of work* is a smart or clever woman with other than sexual attributes in male eyes.

piece² a handgun
Used of both cannons and personal weapons since the 16th century, and of crossbows before that. It is a shortened form of *fowling-piece* or *carrying piece*.

piece of the action a share in the proceeds or enjoyment of vice, illegality, or any taboo activity
Usually prostitution, narcotics, or gambling. Occasionally also of someone trying to benefit from the enterprise or initiative of another.

piece off *American* to bribe
From the actual or figurative peeling of bills from a bankroll, to buy silence or a favour, and especially of bribing a foreman to give you a job in return for part of your wage.

pig's ear see IN A PIG'S EAR

pigeon the dupe of a criminal
Venerable enough to be noted by Grose but still in modern criminal use, and to *pluck the pigeon* is to swindle a victim.
In America, to *pigeon* is to steal, after the habit of the voracious birds.

The *pigeon-drop* is the trick whereby the victim pays money to thieves for a share in a bogus bankroll which they profess to have found.

piggyback to use another's reputation for your financial or social ends
Apart from the basic meaning, a *piggyback* is a ride given to a child on the back of an adult.

pigment black skin colour
Literally, a substance providing colour, without which we would all be albinos:
    And that's your fate too, Henry. He's
    makin' good use of your pigment.
    (Anonymous, 1996—the black Henry was
    supporting a white candidate)

piled with French velvet *obsolete* infected with syphilis
A complex pun on the *pile* of shorn cloth and the FRENCH ACHE. Shakespeare has 'Thou art piled, for a French velvet'. (*Measure for Measure*)

pill¹ *obsolete* the penis
This Scottish/northern English use, from Norwegian dialect, survives in the word *pillock*, which is commonly used figuratively (and usually in ignorance) as a mild insult.

pill² a contraceptive taken orally by females
Not just any medicament prepared for swallowing.
Whence *on the pill*, taking such a contraceptive regularly and by implication able to copulate without impregnation.

pill³ *obsolete* to blackball from membership of a club
From the slang meaning, a ball:
    After someone he had put up for the
    Kildare Street Club had been pilled, he
    never entered the doors of the Club
    again. (Fingall, 1977—the Kildare Street
    Club in Dublin was habituated by the
    Protestant gentry, especially prior to
    1914)

pillow partner a person with whom you copulate
Of either sex, but not a spouse.

pills the testicles
From *pill*, a ball, rather than from likeness to medical tablets, and see also BALLS.

pin the penis
Of the same tendency as PRICK but much less common.

pin-up an erotic picture
Or its subject. In the Second World War

titillating and sometimes crude pictures of women were displayed in barrack rooms etc. using drawing pins. The same description is now also given to representations of males similarly displayed in offices etc., and to those pictured.

pinch¹ to steal
Literally, to nip between the fingers.

pinch² to arrest
From the grasping of the subject.
In American use a *pinch* is also an arrest.

pine overcoat a coffin
Accorded, it would seem, to those who die of violence rather than naturally. See also WOODEN BOX.

ping-ponging passing a rich client from one specialist to another
A medical version of the long rallies in table tennis.

pink associated with male homosexuality
From the traditional colour of the boudoir.
In America a *pink district* is one habituated by homosexual men.
The *pink pound* is used to identify the specific purchasing power of homosexuals, reflecting also the greater disposable income of those without families to support.

pink slip *American* a notice of dismissal
From the actual or figurative colour of the paper on which the news is given. The term may also be used for retirement. To be *pink-slipped* is to be dismissed summarily.
In 19th-century England a *yellow cover* meant dismissal from government employment, the usage, like the possibility of the dismissal of any public employee, now being obsolete.

pioneer¹ a soldier sent to intervene in a foreign war
Originally, one who clears the way for his own following troops, although in the Second World War the British *Pioneer Corps* usually handed that privilege to the infantry or Royal Engineers.

pioneer² *Irish* a person who has forsworn intoxicants
Showing the way to others.

pipe an illegal narcotic
The instrument used for ingestion.

piran *Cornish* drunk
Cornwall was the county where tin was mined from Roman times until recently:
St Piran is the patron saint of tinners, popularly supposed to have died drunk. (*EDD*)

piss pins and needles to be infected with gonorrhoea
From the sensation in a male when urinating.
Also as *piss pure cream*.
Shakespeare's *piss your tallow* meant to ejaculate prematurely. (*The Merry Wives of Windsor*)

pissed drunk
Referring perhaps to the need to dispose of beer, sometimes referred to as the *piss*, drunk to excess, but you can become *pissed* on wine or spirits.
The American *pissed* can also, like the British *pissed off*, mean dejected, although Maureen Reagan in March 1987 referred to her father Ronald as being *P.O.'d*.

pistol *obsolete* the penis
Of obvious imagery. Whence Shakespeare's punning character.

pit-stop an occasion for leaving company for a short taboo activity
Normally the need is for urination. With somewhat inverted logic, the derivation is from the replenishment and repair of a car during a race. Less often, but more logically, the desire is to ingest narcotics.

place a lavatory
Only heard in the male enquiry *Where's the place?* in a restaurant or similar establishment.

place-man a spy
Originally, someone who holds a responsible *place* in government service. In this use punning on having been *placed* there by his masters.

place of correction *obsolete* a prison
Named for an honest, but usually unfulfilled, aspiration.

place of ill fame a brothel
Whether or not it has a good reputation with its clients.

place of safety an inhumane prison
Himmler's favoured term for his CONCENTRATION CAMPS.

planned unexpected and unwelcome
A common usage when we prefer not to admit that we have been wrong or lacking in foresight:
    Surprise and mobility, coupled with overwhelming air support, turned 'planned withdrawals' into creeping rout. (Boyle, 1979)

The appearance of *as planned* in any corporate statement should always be greeted with scepticism and invite further enquiry.

planned parenthood *American* the abortion of a foetus
The antithesis of *planning*, it might seem.
The abortion is a *planned termination*, a phrase also used of suicide.

planning the restriction of development
A reactive rather than proactive process seeking to regulate the use of land and buildings, carried out by *planning officials* or *planners*.

plant¹ to bury a corpse
The imagery of horticulture, without the crop.

plant² falsely to place incriminating evidence
Again with horticultural imagery.

plant³ an item introduced editorially into a periodical for promotional or political purposes
Journalistic jargon. The story is not necessarily false or misleading.

plasma an intoxicant
Literally, the substance in the blood in which other elements are suspended.

plastered drunk
Literally, covered with a substance that sticks to a surface, as does the smell of intoxicants, but perhaps only referring to the immobility of a limb in plaster.

plastic chicken circuit (the) dinners organized by institutions
Usually on an annual basis with speeches and obligatory attendance for some functionaries. As Chamberlain's Second Law teaches us, 'Everything tastes more or less like chicken', especially in the world of mass catering.

play¹ to indulge in sexual activity
The common sporting imagery, as in Shakespeare's homophobic lines 'As well a woman with a eunuch play'd As with a woman.' (*Antony and Cleopatra*). *Play* appears in many compounds referring to copulation or masturbation, some of which follow:

play about to copulate with other than your regular sexual partner

play around to be promiscuous, usually of a male

play at hot cockles to masturbate

Of a female, the *cockles* being the vulva.

play away (from home) to commit adultery
Punning on the team game played on the opponents' ground.

play-fellow a sexual partner
Of Shakespearean antiquity but not your spouse:
    To seek her as a bed-fellow,
    In marriage pleasures play-fellow. (*Pericles*):

play games to be promiscuous
Usually of a woman, with a single extramarital partner:
    She was playing games with Vannier.
    (Chandler, 1943)

play hookie to commit adultery
Of either sex, with the imagery of playing truant from school.

play house *obsolete* a brothel
Not a theatre.

play in the hay to copulate
But not necessarily al fresco; and see also IN THE HAY.

play mothers and fathers to copulate
Usually outside marriage. Also as *play mummies and daddies* or *mums and dads*.

play on your back to copulate
Of a female, from the posture adopted.

play Onan to withdraw before ejaculation
A method of seeking to avoid impregnation, like Onan who 'spilt his seed upon the ground'. Also of male masturbation.

play the beast with two backs to copulate
From the position normally adopted.

play the field to be sexually promiscuous
Of either sex, from betting on several runners in the same race.

play the goat to be promiscuous
Of a male, from the animal's reputation and that of the god Pan, whose upper half was man and lower half was goat.

play the organ to copulate or masturbate
Of either sex, punning on the musical instrument.

play the pink oboe to engage in sodomy or be a male homosexual

The *pink* is from the colour of the boudoir and the vulgar *oboe* is a penis. Also as *play the skin flute*.

play tricks to copulate with other than your regular sexual partner
Usually of a female, punning perhaps on the prostitute's jargon TRICK.

play with to excite sexually
Usually heterosexually. To *play with yourself* is to masturbate.
etc.

play² to gamble
With the activity looked upon as a *game* rather than a potentially addictive disease. To *play the dogs* or *horses* is habitually to bet on greyhounds or racehorses. To be *addicted to play* is to be an obsessive gambler.

play a card to deploy an argument based on prejudice or emotion
The imagery suggests trumping your opponents with a CARD² of higher value. Those which are often seen in circulation are the *race card*, and the *sexual discrimination card*.
To *play with a full deck* means to be mentally alert, being euphemistic only in the negative.

play back to provide false information through an enemy spy
The spy may either be observed and left at liberty, or detained and subverted. Information is channelled to or through him to mislead the enemy. The device was used successfully in England in the Second World War when false information was passed through captured German agents as to where V-2 rockets were falling, resulting in most falling short of London.

playboy *obsolete* the devil
Not the modern wealthy hedonist.

player *American* a non-critical or sycophantic supporter
The person who partakes in a team game became in standard American English a constructive member of an organization.

pleasure to copulate with
Either sex may do the *pleasuring*, the *pleasure* presumably being given or received or both. A *pleasure house* was a brothel where *pleasure(s)*, or copulation, might be enjoyed, or as the case might be.
Shakespeare used *please yourself on* (Pericles), of male activity, in the days when some supposed the female enjoyed copulation less than males, if at all.

pledge an undertaking never to drink intoxicants

Signed, taken, kept, or *broken* by those who have, usually as a member of a church, forsworn the 'demon drink'.

plod a policeman
At second remove from the measured gait when one such might be seen patrolling on foot, perhaps via *Mr Plod*, Enid Blyton's character and Noddy's friend.

plotcock *obsolete* the devil
To *plot* was to 'scald in boiling water' in northern English and Scottish dialect, as a chicken before plucking, and the *cock* was a symbol of the occult powers:
Seven times does her prayers backwards pray, Till Plotcock comes with lumps of Lapland clay. (Ramsay, 1800—all genuine witches pray backwards, and Lapland was their fabled homeland before being taken over by Father Christmas)

plough¹ to copulate with
Of a male, with imagery from a share going into a furrow and the chance of issue. For Shakespeare 'He plough'd her and she crop'd'. (*Antony and Cleopatra*)

plough² to fail a candidate in an examination
Of uncertain origin. Possibly the American *plowed*, drunk, comes from the inability of the subject to pass a test of sobriety.

plough under SEE PLOW UNDER

ploughman's (a) *British* bread and cheese
A shortened form of *ploughman's lunch*, from a campaign initiated in 1961 on the part of cheesemakers to promote the consumption of cheese in pubs. Thereafter innkeepers were progressively able to charge more for what had previously been a cheap snack, especially if GARNISHED by a lettuce leaf and a slice of tomato.

plow under *American* needlessly to cause the death of
The way a farmer disposes of an unwanted crop. Wendell Willkie, opposing Roosevelt's third term as President, appealed to isolationists and pacifists in the electorate by accusing Roosevelt of being a warmonger determined to 'plow under every fourth American boy'. Because Willkie lost, we forget how close he came to winning.

pluck a rose to copulate with a virgin
Of a male, with obvious imagery. *Pluck, tout court*, of copulation, is rare.

plucked *obsolete British* not awarded a degree at a graduation ceremony

In universities an unpaid tradesman had the right to *pluck* the gown of the chancellor awarding the degree if he were owed money by the candidate. The degree would not then be conferred until the debt had been paid.

plug¹ to kill by shooting
Literally, to stop a hole, which I suppose the bullet may do, after making it.

plug² to have penetrative sex with
Of a male, heterosexually or homosexually, a vulgarism with common thrusting imagery.

plug³ to give unwarranted publicity to
Disk jockeys thus advertise popular music on radio etc., sometimes in return for a bribe. Also as a noun.

Plum Book *American* a list of the patronage at the disposal of an incoming president
An election campaign can only be financed if there is an expectation of supporters receiving a success fee, usually in the form of a *plum*, or desirable, even if quite unsuitable, post.

plum(p) pudding club see IN THE CLUB

plumb to copulate with
Of a male, or in vulgar speech, *plumber*, from the literal meaning, to sound a depth.

plumber *American* a presidential staff member acting improperly
His function, after the Ellsberg disclosures in 1971, was to trace or stop any LEAK².

plumbing¹ a lavatory
Referring to the ancillary piping:
    Unless you've shifted the plumbing around here, I can find it. (M. McCarthy, 1963)

plumbing² the parts of the body concerned with urination and defecation
A genteel and rather coy use, likening the body to an aspect of domestic construction.

pocket to steal
Normally of trifles small enough to go into it, without premeditation but now also of embezzlement.

pocket job (a) male masturbation
By himself or another. Also as *pocket pool* or, in Britain, *pocket billiards*, from the *pockets*, balls, and cue used in the game.
Pocket the red is a vulgarism meaning to copulate.

poetic truth lies
A translation of an expression used by

Goebbels, who was appointed Minister of Advertising by Hitler in 1933.

point Percy at the porcelain to urinate
Of a male, from the material used in urinals and the slang *Percy*, a corruption of PERSON, the penis.

point shaving *American* fraudulently reducing the margin of victory
One of the ways in which players contrive to beat the bookies and help the gamblers. A Boston College player received 10 years in prison after being convicted of this offence in 1981.

poison a preferred intoxicant
A jocular reference to the possible harmful effects.

poison pill the deliberate assumption of corporate liabilities to deter or repel an unwanted predator
A tactic of the defended bid, with success perhaps leaving a sour taste in the mouth and failure a similar discomfort for the winner.

poke¹ (the) *obsolete* summary dismissal from employment
Punning on the meaning to *push*, and a *poke* is also a sack, as in the phrase *buy a pig in a poke*, to be deceived or cheated.

poke² to copulate with
Of a male, with common thrusting imagery. A *poke* is a single act of copulation or the female participant, as seen by the male, and usually with a laudatory adjectival endorsement, there being, it might seem, no *bad pokes*.
Some male homosexual use.
The American *pogey bait*, candy, was the 'inducement held out by old sailors for the favours of fat-cheeked smooth-bottomed young cabin boys'. (Styron, 1976)

poke³ a prison
Possibly from the meaning sack, and as *pokey*.

pole an erect penis
An obvious vulgarism. In archaic use, to *pole* was to copulate with, of a male.

police action a war
First noted in September 1948, when the fledgling Indian state conquered Hyderabad:
    In a remarkably successful manoeuvre
    against Hyderabad's state forces
    (codenamed 'Operation Polo' and referred
    to euphemistically as 'police action'),
    Indian troops destroyed their rivals within
    four days. (French, 1997)
The phrase became notorious in the Korean War:

Truman agreed with a reporter who asked 'Would it be correct to call it a police action under the United Nations?' This was a phrase which would later haunt Truman. (M. Hastings, 1987)

polish the mahogany to urinate
The allusion is to the wooden lavatory seat. I thought this was obsolete until I heard it on television in February 1994.

political change a humiliating defeat
Kissinger's contemporary description of the conquest of South Vietnam by the North and the final American withdrawal.

political (re-)education the arbitrary imprisonment of dissidents
A Communist phrase to describe and justify internal repression.

political engineering *American* using government patronage to engender political support
Specifically, describing awarding defence procurement projects to provide work in as many congressional districts as possible, regardless of expense or efficiency.

politically correct conforming in behaviour or language to dogmatic opinions
The subject is wittily and provocatively examined in *The Official Politically Correct Dictionary and Handbook* (Beard & Cerf, 1992). For those who espouse *political correctness*, every topic the subject of taboo must be referred to by euphemism or circumlocution, or ignored, while the conduct of its devotees can rival fascism in its rigour.
Sometimes shortened to *PC*.

pollute to affect in a taboo manner
Literally, to corrupt or make dirty. To *pollute yourself* is to masturbate, while to *pollute* a female was to copulate with her extramaritally. *Polluted* may describe being drunk or under illegal narcotic influence.

polygraph a lie detector
Literally, a machine giving a number of simultaneous read-outs.

pony an act of defecation
Rhyming slang on *pony and trap*, a crap. Some figurative use:
　　The voice must have realized I was giving him a lot of old pony. (McNab, 1993—he was lying during interrogation by the Iraqis)

poodle a sycophant
Literally, a type of lapdog:
　　Last week Jacques Chirac nominated Jean-Claude Trichet...who has a long line of

form as a trained poodle. (*Daily Telegraph*, 12 November 1997—the nomination was as head of a European bank where, as a good European, he could promote French interests)

poontang *American* casual copulation
A corruption of the French *putain*, a prostitute, and formerly used in the Southern states of copulation by a white male with a black female. Also, in the Second World War, as *poontan*.

poop¹ to defecate
An onomatopoeic usage, used in the nursery and of animals.
Poop is faeces and a *pooper-scooper* the shovel you are meant to use for picking it up after your pet has defecated in a public place.

poop² to fart
More onomatopoeia. Some figurative use as an insult.

pooped drunk
Originally, flooded by the sea coming over the stern, but not only of sailors.

poor-mouth to ignore or refer to in unfavourable terms
A more consistent practice than the occasional denigration implied when you BAD-MOUTH:
　　Naturally the Chinese have always poor-mouthed the foreign-built railways' contribution to their economic well-being. (Faith, 1990)

poorly¹ very seriously ill
Hospital jargon, replacing the normal meaning, unwell, and seeking to comfort the family of the patient.

poorly² menstruating
Again unwell, and often in the phrase *my poorly time*.

pop¹ to ingest narcotics illegally
Either from *popping* them into your mouth as a pill or into vein by injection. Whence *popper*, such a pill or injection.

pop² an act of copulation
Possibly from the sensation of orgasm, but more likely because *pop* can be a synonym of go, meaning a single occasion.
To *pop* is to copulate, of a male.

pop³ to pawn
Perhaps from *popping in* to effect the transaction with UNCLE¹.
And in the old song:
　　Up and down the City Road,
　　In and out the Eagle.

That's the way the money goes.
Pop goes the weasel.

The Eagle was a London public house of which a former landlord was the father of one of my aunts by marriage, a shameful connection of which other family members were long kept unaware. The *weasel* was the *weasel and stoat*, overcoat.

pop⁴ to kill
Not necessary with a *popgun* although normally by shooting.

pop off to die
Literally, in slang, to depart, rather than from a cork leaving a bottle.
Also as *pop your clogs*, when you no longer need any shoes.
You end up *popping up the daisies*, the common churchyard flower, even if cremated or buried at sea.

popsy a woman available for casual copulation
Originally, and still used as, a term of endearment to a girl, whence an attractive young female. The euphemistic use is usually generic and not of prostitutes.

population transfer forcible resettlement
Not the natural movements which take place on a surprising scale in a civilized country but the language used for the forcible uprooting of a racial group for political reasons, as practised by the Germans under Hitler, the Russians under Stalin, the South Africans under apartheid, etc.

porch climber *American* a thief who steals from houses
A convenient mode of access to an upstairs window.
A *porch climber* may also be an illegal narcotic, presumably because those who ingest may be tempted to do something rash.

pork¹ *American* Federal or State funds diverted to local political purposes
From the richness of the meat.
A *pork barrel* is the allocation of such bounty, in Britain as in America. Also as a verb:
America's production of space
centres...symbolise[s] an ancient
discipline which lies at the heart of politics
here: pork-barrelling. (*Private Eye*, July 1983)
The punning *pork chopper*, often a professional politician, receives a sinecure from government.

pork² to copulate with
Of a male, using the *pork*, or *pork sword*, the penis. Pork also means to sodomize.

pork pies lies
Rhyming slang. Also as *porkie pies* or *porkies*.

porridge *British* prison
Partridge suggests a pun on STIR but the dish is also a staple item of food in prisons.

position to display in a favourable or deceptive light
The language of those for whom presentation matters more than substance. Thus facts and issues must be *positioned* before the media are briefed and the public is hoodwinked.

positive militaristic and aggressive
How tyrants like to see and describe themselves:
...was in tune with Japan's increasingly
aggressive or, to use the euphemistic Japanese
term, 'positive' foreign policy. (Behr, 1989)

possess to copulate with
Historically the male *possessed* the female, despite the physical contradiction:
I have bought the mansion of a love,
But not possess'd it. (Shakespeare, *Romeo and Juliet*)
And explicitly:
We find men who have violated the best
principles of society, and ruined their fame and
their fortune, that they might possess a woman
of rank. (J. Boswell, 1791—Johnson had
suggested that copulation with a duchess was
more pleasurable than with a chambermaid)

post a letter to defecate
Punning on an excuse for absenting yourself from company and the process of defecation. In America as *mail a letter*.

post-war credit *British* a tax
Levied in addition to income- and super-tax. It was repaid in a much depreciated currency many years later.

postal *American* mentally unstable
The imagery escapes me.

posted dismissed by being sent to another unit
Military usage, of those who are unsatisfactory or ill-disciplined, not of civilians moved on promotion:
Four had been killed in action, two were
POWs, and the rest were injured or
found wanting in some way and 'posted'.
(Clayton & Craig, 2000)
The threat of *posting* a troublemaker away from his unit, and possibly to a more active theatre, was a potent disciplinary weapon in the Second World War.

posterior(s) the buttocks

Posterior originally meant late in time, whence
BEHIND.

In homosexual use, a *posterior assault* is
sodomy.

pot¹ to kill by shooting
Referring to hunting for the cooking *pot*, but
now also used of attempts to kill or wound.
A *potshot* is one taken without premeditation.

pot² a habitual drunkard
From the drinking vessel rather than the
slang for a belly. *Pot-valour* is drunken courage
and *potted*, rarely, drunk.

A *pot-walloper* was also a drunkard, punning
on the suffrage under the British Reform Act
of 1832 which gave the vote to any adult male
householder who had *walloped his pot*, or
cooked food in his house, for a period of six
months previously. Women probably did the
cooking, but they didn't get the vote.

pot³ a receptacle for urine
Literally, any receptacle for liquids. Sometimes as *po* or *potty* and *potty-training* is
teaching small children to control day-time
urination and defecation.

pot⁴ marijuana
Either derived from the American Indian
potaguya or from the container in which the
leaves and stalks are cooked or brewed.
The shortening of *pot liquor* to *pot* favours
the latter:
   ... to graduate to student parties to smoke
   pot. (Bradbury, 1976)

pot hunter an egoist seeking public recognition
Not an archaeologist or drunkard but literally
or figuratively after a *pot*, a cup or trophy
given to a winner.

potation an alcoholic drink
Literally, the act of drinking, whence anything drunk.

potboiler a repetitive or facile work by an
established artist or author
In primitive societies where earthenware did
not stand heat, the *potboiler* was a stone
heated in the fire and plunged into water in
a jar. Before the electric kettle, a hob on open
fires was used for placing a kettle or *pot* to
simmer away as a source of hot water. The
imagery is from the latter practice rather than
the hot stone.

To *keep the pot boiling* is to publish such
mediocre work, or republish in a new format
what has been published previously.

potentially ineffective care not allowing
the mortally ill to die

Medical jargon, there being in fact no *potential*
that it will restore to health:
   The rich and the famous are particularly
   vulnerable to what is known
   euphemistically as Potentially Ineffective
   Care ... Last week Israeli surgeons' seven
   hour operation [on] Ariel Sharon's brain
   was pure PIC. (James le Fanu in *Sunday
   Telegraph*, 15 January 2006)

Potomac fever *American* a desire to be
elected to high Federal office
Not an ague caught from the river flowing
through the nation's capital.

Potsdam *obsolete British* a prison for captured soldiers
Where the Kaiser had a palace. In the First
World War capture was referred to as dining
there with him.

potty mad or eccentric
Perhaps from having *gone to pot* or using the
same imagery as *crackpot*, meaning unwise or
bizarre.

pouch to steal
Originally Scottish but now widely used as a
synonym of POCKET:
   I had given Master Boy Scout a fair amount
   of money ... doubtless he had merely
   pouched it. (Fergusson, 1945—he had paid
   a tribesman for help behind the lines in
   Burma in the Second World War)

pouff a male homosexual
Not from the English dialect meaning 'a big
stupid person' (*EDD*) but probably from the
exclamation, implying, in those who use the
term, a lack of substance or value. Also as
pooftah. The usage has caused us to use circumlocution when we describe a padded footstool.

pound salt *American* go away and leave
me alone
A shortened form of *go pound salt up your ass*.
Less often as *pound sand*.

pourboire a bribe
Significantly more has to change hands than
would pay for a drink.

powder a narcotic taken illegally
The form in which it may be marketed.
A *powdered lunch* is one where narcotics are
ingested illegally in addition to or instead of
food.
The punning *powder your nose* is to snort
cocaine.
You do not have to be a drug addict to *take a
powder*, which means to depart in a hurry, the
imagery coming perhaps from having taken a
laxative.

powder room a lavatory for the exclusive use of females
It used to be that part of a warship where the gunpowder was stored. To minimize danger from flashbacks, the size of the passage to the gun deck was restricted and children were used to pass the powder to the guns. Today the *powder* is scented talc which women put on their faces.

powder your nose to urinate
A female use, cosmetics usually being applied in a place to which men have no access. A vulgar variant is *powder your puff*, punning on the cosmetic device.

pox (the) syphilis
Literally, any disease that brings pustules on the skin but, as Dr Johnson reminds us, 'This is the sense when it has no epithet'.

prairie-dogging *American* unnecessarily standing up to look over the partition of a work station
The derivation is from the animal's behaviour on emerging from its hole.

prairie oyster[1] the testicle of a calf
Eaten as a delicacy, especially in America.

prairie oyster[2] a pungent alcoholic drink with a raw egg in it
Perhaps because the egg is swallowed whole, as is an *oyster*. The American *prairie dew* is an illegally distilled spirit.

pre-arrangement *American* the payment for a funeral before death
Funeral jargon for selling burials and their trappings to the living, especially those who are morbid or lonely. Also as *pre-need*.

pre-dawn vertical insertion an invasion by parachutists
Neither inserting your card for clocking on an early shift nor starting the day with copulation but how the American invaders of Grenada on 27 October 1983 described their mission.

pre-driven *American* not new
Anything to avoid saying the car is 'second-hand' but how did the vehicle reach the forecourt? Also as *pre-used*.
Previously owned is more flummery than euphemism.

pre-emptive unprovoked and without warning
Used of warfare or violence. *Pre-emption* is buying first, whence denying the purchase to others. In the phrases *pre-emptive strike* and *pre-emptive offensive*.
A *pre-emptive action* or *pre-emptive self-defence* may be no more than killing one person.

precautions contraception
Shortened form of *precautions* against pregnancy or disease.

precocious spoilt and ill-mannered
Originally, developing early. Used of children other than your own, out of earshot of their parents.

predilection (a) homosexuality
Literally, a tendency or preference for anything.

preference (a) being homosexual
Shortened form of *sexual preference*, but not used about heterosexuals.

pregnancy interruption an induced abortion
An *interruption* is a disturbance with an assumption of resumption. This medical jargon is sometimes enlarged to *voluntary pregnancy interruption* or *VPI*.

preliterate uncivilized
Anthropological and social science jargon to describe primitive societies which remain illiterate, denoting concern on behalf of those who cannot read what they would be concerned about.

premature *obsolete* conceived before marriage
How couples used to explain a birth before they had been married the requisite nine months.

premium costing more
An attributive use of a noun, which originally meant an award or prize, whence something worth more than its face value. Advertising jargon.

prepare *American* to embalm
For viewing by survivors rather than awaiting resurrection.
A morgue may, in the jargon, be called a *preparation room*.

prepared biography *American* a draft obituary of a living person
A delicate expression masking the inevitability of death.

preparedness *American* the military help given by the United States to Britain in the Second World War before Pearl Harbor

Isolationism was so widely supported that Roosevelt and his supporters had to conceal their actions in euphemism:

> [Henry Ford] had financed an expensive advertising campaign in the country's largest newspapers savagely attacking 'preparedness'. (Lacey, 1986—Ford's anti-Jewish paranoia attracted him to elements of Nazism)

present a bribe

The gift is a payment for a service which should be provided free:

> I stood behind Nazir as he discussed the 'present' necessary to 'reopen' the border. (Dalrymple, 1989, writing about entering Pakistan—the border had been wrongly closed so that the guards could extract bribes from travellers)

present arms to have an erect penis

Punning on the military drill in which the rifle is held vertically in front of the body.

presentation the distortion or suppression of news

A feature of modern democratic government where it is considered necessary to mislead voters in order to retain power:

> ... the constant theme, through all the paperwork and all the computer trail; of urgent missives, of posturing and feints, of slight of hand and repeatedly of 'presentation', that modern euphemism for saleable deceit. (*Sunday Telegraph*, 23 August 2003)

preserved *American* drunk

A variant of the more common PICKLED, with alcohol the preservative agent.

press *obsolete* to kidnap for service in the navy

By a *press gang*, which seized men in public places.

press your attentions on to copulate with

Usually extramaritally. It might literally mean no more, for example, than the concentration of a dentist filling a patient's tooth.

To *press conjugal rights on* is to copulate with a reluctant wife, although those married owe each other many other rights, and duties, apart from copulation.

pressure torture

Exerted on a prisoner.

Pressure is also much used, or over-used, by professional athletes and commentators about the desire to win. The immortal Keith Miller reminded other sportsmen that, in his experience, *pressure* was flying a Spitfire

and having a Messerschmitt on your tail at 20,000 feet.

pressure of work an excuse for neglect, inefficiency, or discourtesy

The phrase is seldom used by businesslike people:

> I feel an awful worm, not having written to you for so long, but a genuine pressure of work stopped me. (P. G. Wodehouse in a letter of 1930, in Donaldson 1990—note the qualification *genuine*)

prestige expensive

A word much loved by the developers of real estate.

Also as *prestigious*, which used to mean using prestidigitation, and often figuratively still does.

preventable diseases *American* syphilis and gonorrhoea

Army usage from the Second World War. They were to prove insidious enemies.

preventative a contraceptive sheath

Preventing, it was hoped, disease and impregnation but not necessarily worn by the former British *preventative man*, a coastguard.

preventive detention arbitrary imprisonment

Literally, a long sentence for a dangerous or hardened criminal. In a totalitarian state the phrase describes the incarceration of critics, without process of law.

prey to (a) suffering from

The victimization is in most cases figurative, as with those who describe themselves as being a *prey to dyspepsia*, for example.

Not so the obsolete British *prey to the bicorn*, a cuckold. The *bicorn* was a mythical two-horned beast which devoured men whose wives dominated or deceived them. Its counterpart, the *chichevache*, which ate obedient wives, was reputed to feed but rarely.

priapus an erect penis

Priapus was the Pan of Mysia, usually depicted in such a condition. Whence *priapism*, such an erection.

In America *Priapus* may be used as a mild insult between men.

price crowding a price increase not authorized by the proprietor

Mainly supermarket jargon, for a practice under which a manager seeks to create a reserve which can be used to make good losses for which he might be held responsible.

prick a penis

Once standard English but now a vulgarism.

Also used figuratively as a term of mild abuse or rebuke among males.

pride an erect penis
Shortened form of *pride of the morning*, an erection of the penis on waking, which comes from the proper meaning, a mist or shower heralding a fine day.
Somewhat irrationally, a man's *pride and joy* may be the penis in its flaccid state and his *prides* may mean the penis and testicles.

prima donna *obsolete* a prostitute
A Victorian usage (Mayhew, 1862) from the principal female singer or dancer in an opera or ballet. Outside the theatrical world, in modern use, a *prima donna* is a temperamental or self-important person, from the reputed behaviour of some artistes.

prime saleable
Literally, first, whence implying of first quality. Commonly used of perishable food-stuff, especially meat.

prime the pump deliberately to cause inflation by excessive government spending
The fiscal theory, now largely discredited, is that higher taxation or borrowing spent on more public works will lead to economic growth without inflation or depreciating the value of the currency.

primed *obsolete* drunk
Like a pump and perhaps also alluding to an explosive charge.

Prince of Darkness the devil
Not the eldest son of King Edward III, the *Black Prince*, but another evasive way of talking of the devil.

prince has come (the) *obsolete* I am menstruating
A phrase used by Georgiana, Duchess of Devonshire, in a letter written to her mother in October 1779, possibly because of the distinguished VISITOR being welcome. (Foreman, 1998)

princess an expensive prostitute
From the meaning, a classy type of female or one who affects airs.
Also as *pavement princess*.

private enterprise illegal trading by an employee
Literally, trade or industry not financed by or under the direct control of the state. A *private sale* may be such a transaction, on a larger scale:

A 'private' sale [of an illegal cargo], as it is euphemistically called, was agreed while the boat was still at sea. (Clover, 2004)

private office *obsolete* a lavatory
What was once also called a *house of office*. Today only rather grand or self-important people run *private offices*, with individual secretarial help and lots of potted plants.

private parts the human genitalia
Those not normally exposed to the public gaze.
Also as *privates*, *privities*, or *privy parts*.

private patient *British* a person paying for specific medical care
Not waiting to be treated under the National Health Service which, as a relic of command economy theory, cannot plan to have immediate resources available free and on demand for each of some sixty million people whose needs are random. The usage ignores the fact that each *patient* is *private*, whether the bills are paid through taxes, insurance, income, or savings.

privileged rich
Sociological jargon not really implying that those so described have honourable distinctions; in the eyes of those who use this dysphemism, the opposite is true. See also UNDERPRIVILEGED.

privy a lavatory
From the privacy of the closed door. A *privy-stool* was a lavatory seat and bucket below.

PRN *British* administer diamorphine
Perhaps from the Latin, *pro re nata*, 'for the affair born', used by doctors to mean 'as required', of any medication. It may be used as a coded message in a hospital for euthanasia of a patient in pain and mortally afflicted.

pro a prostitute
A shortened form of *professional woman*, or of prostitute, or of both.
A *pro-pack*, the contraceptive kit issued to soldiers in the Second World War, came from PROPHYLACTIC, not from the woman with whom it might be associated.
A PRO is no more than a public relations officer whose *pro-pack* may include tendentious or misleading matter which you may find irrelevant, but no contraceptives.

pro bono *American* without payment
Legal jargon for the good deed of defending a pauper free of charge.

pro-choice *American* in favour of abortion on demand
Not the selection of a PRO, or even suggesting that those not wanting children should remain celibate.
Pro-life means opposing such abortion.

probe to copulate with
Of a male, but not with a blunt-ended exploratory surgical instrument.

problem an unwanted and often irreversible condition
The word is used in many phrases to conceal truth or inadequacy. Thus a *cash problem* in an individual is a shortage of money, and not a superfluity or a lack of pockets to put it in. In a company a *cash flow problem* means that it is overtrading or insolvent. A *communication problem* means that nobody understands us or we don't understand them. A *crossword problem* means we cannot complete the crossword (a *problem problem*?) although a *problem crossword* is one we may expect to solve. A *drink problem* is alcoholic addiction by a *problem drinker*. However, a *drinks problem* at a party would indicate only that you might be running out of supplies. A *heart problem* is a malfunction of that organ, with other organs or bodily parts similarly identified according to your disability. The onset of menstruation may herald a woman's *problem days*, but if she suffers from a *women's problem* she may have a disorder of the womb or of some other part exclusive to her sex. Staying with health, the obese may have a *weight problem*.
A society which includes many races may face a *colour problem*, while a black person may be said offensively to have a *pigmentation problem*. Politicians profess to face innumerable *problems*, not all of their own making. Thus Hitler was tested by a so-called *Austrian problem*, which he resolved by having Austria's chancellor murdered and then by invading the country.

procedure any taboo or unpleasant act
Literally, a method of behaving. In medical jargon, as a shortened form of *medical procedure*, it is something which will involve pain, discomfort, or danger for the patient and an *aesthetic procedure* is cosmetic surgery. For police and lawyers, a *procedure* is a civil or criminal legal action. For the Nazis it meant mass murder:
> Schindler had heard rumours that 'procedures in the ghetto' were getting more intense. (Keneally, 1982)

proclivities unconventional sexual preferences

Literally, any personal choice:
> Shaleen had never made any secret about her proclivities. She had a wild thing going for a make-up girl. (Turow, 1999)

procure to arrange (prostitution) on behalf of another
Literally, to obtain, of anything, but legal jargon in this sense.
Whence a *procurer*, a pimp, and *procuress*, a bawd.

product a service
Jargon of bankers and other financial institutions which seeks to suggest that their activities actually *produce* something.

product placement securing media exposure of an article on sale
The *product* is *placed* on the television screen, or seen in use by a well-known person, as well as on shop shelves or the car dealer's forecourt.

product shrinkage the supply of a lesser quantity at the previous price
Not settlement in a package.

production difficulties strikes
The universal code words used by British national newspapers prior to the taming of the print unions and the introduction of new technology which reduced their power to disrupt:
> On at least one day this week, our readers will be deprived of copies of this newspaper...The failure to deliver will be due, not in the language of our trade to 'production difficulties' but to the decisions of the TUC to stage a day of action ostensibly in support of hospital workers. (Deedes, 1997, writing about the 1970s)

profession (the) female prostitution
Prostitutes' jargon, in which *professional women* ply their trade. See also the OLDEST PROFESSION.

professional unsporting
The behaviour of those paid for playing a sport and for whom winning is no longer a game.
A *professional foul* is a cynical infringement of the rules to deny an advantage to an opponent.

professional car *American* a hearse
Funeral jargon. *Processional* would be more appropriate.

progressive opposed to conventional manners or methods
Literally, moving towards improvement, so long as it is to the left in political terms.

Euphemistic only when used by political doubters or opponents.

proletarian Communist

The *proletariat*, from the Latin *proletarius*, 'the lowest class in the Servian arrangement' (W. M. Smith, 1933) first described those in feudal service and then anyone who worked for a wage, among whom middle-class revolutionaries traditionally seek support. Whence a *proletarian democracy*, a Communist autocracy; *proletarian internationalism*, Soviet Russian imperialism; etc.

promised *obsolete* engaged to be married

From the days when a man (and very occasionally a woman) might be sued for *breach of promise* if an engagement were broken off and it was considered shameful for a woman to remain unmarried and so become an OLD MAID.

promoted to Glory dead

A usage of the Salvation Army, whose members live as closely as any may get to the Christian ethic, and deserve any glory that may be going.

pronounce *American* to confirm the death of

Police jargon, and not just getting the name right:

Rifle shot to the head. Single shot, we think. He's already been pronounced. (J. Patterson, 2002)

proper *obsolete* chaste

From the days when only men were free to indulge in *improper* sexual conduct:

I am not a—proper woman. (Hardy, 1891)

prophylactic a contraceptive sheath

Literally, associated with the prevention of any disease. Used in the Second World War to describe any process to reduce the incidence of venereal disease.

proposition to suggest engaging in a sexual act

Made to other than a regular sexual partner, of both heterosexuals and homosexuals.

A *proposition* is such a suggestion.

proposition selling the use of misleading hypotheses to confuse a buyer

The commercial use of leading questions:

His technique is old-style American 'proposition selling'. The salesman puts forward a series of numbskull propositions with which you have *no choice but to agree*. (*Daily Telegraph*, August 1989, reporting on a time-sharing scam)

protect to reunite by force

The language of Hitlerism, especially with regard to Sudeten Germans and those living in Polish Danzig. He and other tyrants *protect their territory* by attacking their neighbours which are then ruled as colonies or *protectorates*. The 1940 Winter Games organized by the Nazis included teams from Italy, Hungary, Yugoslavia, Slovakia, and the *Protectorate* (the Czech Republic), as well as Germany.

For the Americans in Vietnam, a *protective reaction* was dropping bombs on the Vietcong and others. (Commager, 1972)

A *protectorate* was also formerly a European colony in Africa, the occupying power being more anxious to *protect* it from being grabbed by a rival than to safeguard the well-being of the indigenous population.

For the Nazis, *protected* Jews were those they elected not to kill for economic reasons:

Six months later Frenkel writes again from the 'Jewish Home' in Barneveld, a country estate where seven hundred 'protected' Jews were staying. (Kuper, 2003)

protected sex copulation or sodomy using a condom

Not girls looked after by chaperones but seeking to *protect* against the transfer of disease, by wearing a *protector*, or contraceptive sheath.

protection extortion

The practice of selling immunity from your own depredations is well documented, from Anglo-Saxon payment of *Danegeld* in England to the Mafia in America and Italy.

Being *in* or *into protection* is engaging is such extortion.

protective custody arbitrary imprisonment

The pretence is that the victims are incarcerated to prevent any harm befalling them.

provision an arbitrary adjustment in figures to be publicly reported

Literally, a reserve made against contingencies, to avoid a misleading statement of assets or profits. A *provision* is normally made on a subjective basis by managers, who may wish, by using a high figure, to reduce what appears as profit and therefore become subject to tax or, by understatement, to seek to show a stronger financial position than is the reality.

pruned *American* drunk

Probably from feeling like a tree or plant which has had its appendages or extremities removed rather than from *prune juice*, a spirituous intoxicant.

psycho a mentally ill person who is prone to violence

From the Greek, it means relating to the breath, whence of the soul or mind. *Psycho* is probably no more than a shortened form of *psychopath*.

psychological warfare the dissemination of lies and half-truths
From 1939 until the end of the Second World War, the phrase also included truthful broadcasting from Britain to Germany and to countries occupied by Germany.

psychologically disadvantaged under the influence of narcotics
An interesting variant of the DISADVANTAGED theme:

> Wilson, who won a lawsuit in 1992 claiming that his father, Murray Wilson, had bullied him into giving away the publishing rights to his songs while he was 'psychologically disadvantaged' (spaced out on drugs)...(*Daily Telegraph*, 7 October 1994—Wilson was one of The Beach Boys)

public assistance money paid regularly by the state to the needy
Not just helping an old lady to cross the road.

public convenience a lavatory
If in the plural, there may be separate lavatories for the general use of males and females, and also possibly one with wheelchair access.

public house an establishment where intoxicants may be sold and drunk
A *house* open at times to the *public*. Indeed, it used to be called a *public* but is now referred to, even in France, as a *pub*.

public ownership control and management by politicians and bureaucrats
The use of the phrase is normally confined to commercial businesses, utilities, etc. No member of the public should be so rash as to try to assert ownership rights over them:

> Various failings, real or imaginary, in state-run undertakings created the need for fresh euphemism, and 'public ownership' was promptly produced. (S. Hoggart, in Enright, 1985)

public–private partnership *Britain* accepting private finance and management for a public service
Having long opposed privatization when out of office, Labour needed a new term for it when elected.

public sector borrowing requirement government overspending

The *public sector* is that part of a mixed economy which is controlled, financed, and managed by government, the activities of its components not being subject to commercial pressures such as the need to generate cash or make profits, while losses can be met by further borrowing.

puddle the result of involuntary urination
Literally, a shallow and temporary pool of rainwater. The usage is of small children and domestic pets.

pull[1] to cause a horse to lose a race
Racing jargon, from the jockey's handling of the reins. To *pull up* means, in racing circles as in motoring, to cause to come to a standstill.

pull[2] to seek to strike up an acquaintance with a member of the opposite sex
Commonly known as going *on the pull*. The word is also used of casual copulation:

> If someone does recognize me, word will go back that the brigadier's pulling outside duty. (Ludlum, 1984—he was meeting a woman in a truck stop)

pull a Benedict Arnold *American* to renege on a deal
From the rebel who changed his mind about rebelling. Judge Leo E. Strine in February 2004 used the phrase to describe a proposal to the Barclay brothers by Conrad Black concerning the sale of the *Daily Telegraph*. (The lexicographer Noah Webster was later to acquire Arnold's desirable residence in New Haven.)

pull his trigger to cause to ejaculate semen
The PISTOL imagery:

> I know how to pull his trigger. His wife doesn't. (Sanders, 1981)

pull in (for a chat) to arrest
Police jargon, the CHAT being an interrogation.

pull off *American* to refrain improperly from investigating a crime or prosecuting a criminal
From the meaning, to draw back from:

> The detectives who were offered all kinds of inducements to pull off...(Lavine, 1930)

pull out of a hat to produce irresponsibly
As the conjurer produces the rabbit:

> The *Veterinary Journal* said he 'pulled figures out of a hat to fit his arguments'. (*Private Eye*, May 1981)

Pull out of the air has the same meaning.

pull rank to use seniority to secure an unfair advantage

It applies to those in hierarchical employment, such a sailors or public officials, and is euphemistic only when not used of normal commands and orders.

pull the pin *American* to retire from employment
The imagery is from uncoupling of rolling stock on a railroad, allowing the engine to run free, and not from activating the primer on a hand grenade.
The phrase is also used of a man deserting his wife, with the same imagery.

pull the plug on to kill by withdrawing mechanical life support
Punning on the electrical connection to life support machinery and the flushing of a lavatory. Whence also a meaning, to murder.

pull the pud(ding) to masturbate
Of a male. Also as *pull your rod* or *pull yourself off*.

pull the rug to render bankrupt
The imagery is from causing a person standing on a mat to fall when you jerk it. The use is of a banker who declines to give more credit or a creditor who obtains judgement for a debt. Whence figuratively or unilateral action by another precipitating a crisis.

pump *American* fraudulently to recommend a security
Inflating its worth to gullible investors. The procedure is known as *pump and dump*, especially if it involves a public offering of stock at an inflated price.

pump bilges to urinate
Of a male who, with similar maritime imagery, may also *pump ship*.

pump up to copulate with
Presumably from the motion involved, likened to inflating a tyre:
> If you work for a big corporation, the head of the firm is always pumping up the secretary. (*Sunday Telegraph*, 20 March 1994—to say *always* is to put rather a fine point on it)

pump your shaft to masturbate
Of a male, from the motion involved. Also as *pump your pickle*, alluding to the shape of a gherkin.

punish the bottle to drink wine to excess
In former times, *jars* or *pots* could suffer similar abuse.

punk[1] *American* a male homosexual

From the meaning, rotten, of wood, whence worthless or of low quality. The word also came into general use of adolescent exuberance or excess.
In obsolete use, and in *Measure for Measure*, a *punk* was a prostitute, from a Worcestershire dialect meaning 'Trash: an article of inferior quality.' (*EDD*)

punk[2] low-quality marijuana
Again from the meaning, of low quality. *Punk pills* may be any narcotic illegally taken orally.

punter *British* an inexperienced visitor who can be overcharged or robbed
Literally, someone who bets on horses or greyhounds, whence a habitual loser.

pup to impregnate a woman
Canine imagery, without any suggestion of bitchiness.
In coarse speech, to *pup* is also to be delivered of a child and *in pup* means pregnant, of a woman as, in standard English, of a dog.

puppy fat obesity in a child
Usually of a young female, with the implication that the plumpness will vanish as the child grows up, without any dietary change or regular exercise.

purge[1] beer
From its effect as a laxative. Porter was especially recommended for its 'gentle purgative effect'. (Tombs & Tombs, 2006)

purge[2] to attack violently
Another form of cleaning out:
> The next day what the [Israelis] euphemistically call a 'purging operation' was effected. In this instance they 'purged' Fatah. (Price, 1971)

purification of the race the systematic killing of gypsies, Jews, and mentally or physically subnormal Germans
How the Nazis sought to justify mass murder.

purpose(s) of nature urination and defecation
One among many, we might suppose:
> ...the gendarme...walked down the slipway for the purposes of nature and discovered the body. (Higgins, 1989)

pursue to court
What a follower used to do:
> Gaston Palewski, Nancy Mitford's great love, also pursued [Hermione, Countess of Ranfurly]. (*Daily Telegraph*, 13 February 2001, in an obituary of the Countess, whose fascinating diaries were published as *To War With Whitaker*)

pursue other interests to be peremptorily dismissed from employment

One of the many face-saving expressions used when senior managers are dismissed. The person departing may also be said to be pursuing *another career, other opportunities,* or various anodyne expressions in the same sense.

push¹ to copulate with

Of a male, with the usual thrusting imagery and also from the rhyming slang, *a push in a truck.*

In West Africa, *push* means copulation.

In obsolete use a *pushing academy* or *shop* was a brothel.

push² (the) peremptory dismissal from employment

Given by the employer. Seldom of an employee leaving of his own volition.

push³ a sustained attack in war

Jargon from the Second World War.

push⁴ to distribute (narcotics) illegally

Literally, to sell energetically or fraudulently, as with a *share pusher* who sells securities at false values. A *pusher* is an illegal distributor of narcotics.

push the button on *American* to kill or cause to be killed

Criminal jargon, or of those who write crime novels, with imagery from operating a machine or extinguishing a light.

push the envelope to act in a reckless or extravagant manner

Over-inflating the container. Figurative use:

Shell...had begun to push the envelope, and went on pushing it until it burst. (*Daily Telegraph,* 31 August 2004—the oil company had consistently overstated its hydro-carbon reserves)

push up the daisies to be dead

Referring to the supposed nourishment of the common churchyard flower. Less often as *push up the weeds.*

pussy the vagina

A commoner version of CAT².

Pussy-whipped means besotted, of a male.

A *pussy hound* is not a dog which chases felines but a human male philanderer.

In America, a *pussy lift* is an operation to tighten the vagina, and so enhance sexual enjoyment. Whence also the generic *pussy,* females thought by males to be available for promiscuous copulation.

put *American* to copulate

The imagery is uncertain and probably has nothing to do with holing out at golf.

A *put,* a single act of copulation, may be *had* or *done* by a male.

In obsolete use, to *put to* came from the meaning, to start work:

As rank as any wench that puts-to, Before her troth-plight. (Shakespeare, *The Winter's Tale*)

To *put it in,* or *up* are explicit of male copulation.

To *put it about* is to copulate promiscuously, of either sex, although it seems that only females *put out* in this sense.

put a move on *American* to make a sexual approach

Usually to a stranger by a male. Occasionally in the plural, despite only one target being in view:

He doesn't seem to understand the etiquette of putting the moves on a woman. (de Mille, 1988)

put (a person's) lights out to kill

Lights are eyes, but the phrase also puns on extinguishing a lamp:

All men who were lucky at gambling very soon had their lights put out. (Richards, 1933, writing of First World War trench life)

put against a wall to kill

The classic form of execution by shooting in a prison yard:

They will put anyone that answers back against a wall. (A. Clark, 1995, quoting Bormann's instructions to the Nazi Home Army in 1945)

put away¹ to kill

Especially of old, diseased, or unwanted pets. To *put yourself away* is to commit suicide.

put away² *obsolete* to bury

From the days when the poor were anxious that a proper burial in hallowed ground should give them as good a chance of resurrection as the better-off might anticipate:

Some poor comrades undertook to see her put away. (Hartley, 1870)

put away³ to confine involuntarily to an institution

Referring to criminals and those with severe mental illness.

put (it) away⁴ to consume (intoxicants)

Not merely returning the bottle to its rack, and usually to excess.

put daylight through to kill by shooting

Mainly First World War usage but with common imagery.

put down to kill
Normally of old, diseased, or unwanted domestic pets and less often as *put off*. *Put down* is seldom used of murdering people although formerly it might imply judicial killing.
Today if someone *puts you down*, you may be denigrated or insulted but not killed.

put in the mobility pool summarily dismissed from employment
The jargon of management consultants who see employees as units of output, possessing job *mobility* just as those in a *typing pool* might sometimes have been competent stenographers.

put in your ticket to die
A ship's officer surrenders his *ticket* on retirement.

put on file rejected for employment
An excuse by a prospective employer where he fears there might be a claim for unlawful discrimination if the candidate were rejected outright or given the true reason for rejection:
Photos are demanded—if you're ugly you are 'put on file'. (*Sunday Telegraph*, 14 January 1996—the applicants wished to be employed as showgirls)

put on the spot to kill
From the slang meaning, to accuse or embarrass.

put out of your troubles to kill
Or *put out of your misery*, as the case may be:
Shore's you're born, he'll turn State's evidence...I'm for putting him out of his troubles. (Twain, 1884)

put out to grass to cause to retire from work prematurely
The imagery is from the horse which escapes the knacker. Also as *put out to pasture*.

put the arm on to attempt to compel to do what you wish through a threat of violence
Usually seeking to extort money. The imagery is from wrestling. Also as *put the black on*, from BLACKMAIL, *put the burn on*, *put the muscle on*, *put the scissors on*, or *put the squeeze on*.

put the boot in to disrupt or upset through offensive behaviour or the threat of violence

Literally, what a ruffian may do when he has knocked you down. Figuratively of any harmful or dishonest action, or of deliberately making a hurtful remark.

put the clock back fraudulently to alter the reading of a milometer
Motor trade jargon; and see also CLOCK.

put the clog in deliberately to injure an opposing player
In the game of soccer, where the players wear boots rather than wooden footwear.
To *clog* is to attempt to maim.

put the juice to *American* to kill by electrocution
The *juice* is the electric current used in the CHAIR.

put the skids under wilfully to cause to fail
The imagery is from the way of launching a ship or getting tree trunks to a mill. Once on the *skids*, the motion cannot be voluntarily arrested.

put to to cause to mate with
Standard English of mares and other cattle in season and left with stallions, bulls, etc.

put to rest dead
When the dead person is said to be AT REST.

put to sleep to kill
The fate of old, ill, or unwanted domestic pets.

put to the question *obsolete* to torture
The language of the Inquisition, but also a common method of medieval criminal investigation elsewhere.

put to the sword to kill
Usually of a large number of helpless victims, by any form of violence.

put under the sod dead
And presumably buried.
To suggest *putting someone underground* is a threat to murder them.

put yourself about to be promiscuous
Mainly of males, from circulating freely.

Q

quail *obsolete* a prostitute
Not from the Celtic *caile*, a young girl, but the common avian imagery, this time from the reputedly amorous game bird:

> Agamemnon, an honest fellow enough, and one that loves quails. (Shakespeare, *Troilus and Cressida*)

Quaker gun *American* a decoy cannon
A usage from the Civil War because, like the *Quakers*, it wouldn't fire in anger.

qualify accounts to throw doubt on published figures
Literally, to *qualify* means to modify in some respect, and there are some technical *qualifications* in auditors' reports which do not indicate that the directors are suspect and the company is headed for receivership, but not many.

quality time a period sacrificed to being with your young child or children
The parent who uses the expression would usually rather be doing something else, apart from housework.

quantitatively challenged obese
Another variant of the CHALLENGED theme and not describing a contest between sumo wrestlers.

quarantine a military blockade
Originally, the period of forty (*quarante*) days in which a widow might stay in her deceased husband's house, whence any period of isolation against disease etc. J. F. Kennedy used the phrase of the 1962 blockade of Cuba.

queen¹ *obsolete* a prostitute
Probably from the old meaning a female animal, punning on CAT. A *queen-house* was a brothel, not a palace.

queen² a male homosexual
Usually an older man playing the female role or affecting effeminate mannerisms or dress.

Queen's evidence *British* betraying a fellow malefactor
Or *King's evidence*, depending on the occupant of the throne. The derivation is from the convention that the crown prosecutes in British criminal cases.

queer¹ drunk
Originally, not in your normal state of health,

and still occasionally used of a drunkard, with a suggestion that his condition may have been caused by something else. The meaning to make drunk is obsolete.

queer² of unsound mind
A shortened form of *queer in the head*. For Hardy (1886), *queer* meant 'idiotic simplicity'. Today it indicates a harmless or mild aberration.

queer³ homosexual
Almost always of males. It is used adjectivally and as a noun.

queer⁴ (the) *American* forged banknotes
Criminal usage.

quench your thirst to drink alcohol to excess
Not necessarily imbibing a long drink:

> [Members of Parliament] quenched their thirst in the Smoking Room and when they returned to hear the PM's statement, many of them were full of 'Dutch Courage'. (Channon, 1993—diary entry of 2 September 1939)

question¹ to arrest
Police jargon, much used when publicizing particulars of a suspect to avoid the legal implications of a direct assertion of guilt. If the police announce that they would like to *question* someone corresponding with your description, you should take an overnight bag to the interview.

question² a persistent problem to which there appears to be no answer
Common political usage:

> I have always expressed my belief that the present Parliament and Government would fail to settle the Irish land question. (Kee, 1993, quoting Parnell from 1881)

Such a *question*, in German and French as well as English, may also concern matters to which allusive reference may be thought preferable, especially during the Second World War:

> One of [Mitterrand's] friends ... held a leading position in the Paris office of the *Commissariat-Général aux Questions Juives*, the Vichy agency charged with hunting down Jews, listing them for deportation and, in due course, looting their property. (*Sunday Telegraph*, 2 October 1994)

questionable immoral or illegal
Literally, something which should be inquired into, but now almost always in a derogatory or euphemistic sense. A *questionable motive* is concealed or dishonest, a *questionable act* offends the law or propriety, a *questionable*

remark or *joke* is one in bad taste, and a *questionable payment* is a bribe.

quick (with child) pregnant
Quick, tout court, as used by Shakespeare in *Love's Labours Lost*, is obsolete. From the standard English meaning animate, and used after the foetus has started kicking.

quick one a drink of intoxicant
Not necessarily imbibed by an addict. Also as a *quickie*.

quick time a single act of copulation with a prostitute
The jargon of prostitutes who have a time-based tariff.

A *quickie* may be had with any casual sexual partner.

quiescent in a flaccid state
Literally, dormant, of the penis. The Victorian explorer, Richard Burton, who had a keen interest in sexual matters, noted that one man 'when quiescent, numbered nearly six inches'. (Theroux, 2002)

quietus death
Literally, a legal discharge from an obligation, whence removal from an office. A *quietus* was *made*, according to Shakespeare in *Hamlet*, but *got* in more recent use. (Christie, 1939)

quit to die
From the departure and as *quit the scene*. To *quit cold* or *quit breathing* is to be killed.

quod prison
It was formerly spelt *quad*, a shortened form of *quadrangle*, the area in which students were confined for punishment.

To *quod*, to send to prison, is obsolete.

quota appointed to meet an arbitrary target for types of employee rather than on suitability, aptitude, or qualification
Originally an American phenomenon where employers of more than fifteen people were required to reflect in their workforce the local mix of race to a minimum ratio of 80%.

R

R-word (the) recession
Not to be said in financial circles.

RD see REFER TO DRAWER

rabbit an incompetent performer in sport
The allusion is to the timid creature *Oryctola-gus cuniculus*, which was known as a *coney* for two centuries after its introduction to England by the Normans. As *coney* and *cunny* sound much the same, prudery required another appellation for the long-eared, fecund, burrowing animal.

race defilement sexual relations between a non-Jewish German and a Jew
An early manifestation of Nazi persecution:
Gunter Powitzer had been arrested at the beginning of 1937 for 'race defilement', after getting his non-Jewish girlfriend Friedl pregnant. (M. Smith, 1999)
Late in the Second World War, even friendship between a Jew and a non-Jew became a Nazi crime.

race-norming *American* setting different pass standards in examinations for blacks and whites
A method of achieving a QUOTA.

race relations the reality within a community of differing racial descent or nationality
Not international diplomacy but relating to any attempt in a community to combat prejudice against and conflict between people of different race, colour, or nationality. Whence the *race relations officer*, who monitors conduct and offers advice, particularly in mixed communities; *race relations laws*, which decree individual or institutional behaviour; the *race relations board*, which seeks out and sponsors litigation against alleged offenders; and the pejorative *race relations industry*, which, in the eyes of its critics, has an obsessive attitude to matters which they feel would be better left to individual choice.

racial displaying prejudice against or hostility towards an ethnic group
Originally, referring to humanity in its entirety, as when Dr Marie Stopes was president of the *Society for Constructive Birth Control and Racial Progress*. The Nazis adopted and fostered a nascent tendency to intolerance, with their doctrines of the Nordic German master race, their spurious *racial science*, and their *racial purity*, for which to qualify it was necessary to prove that there was no gypsy, Jew, or Slav among your ancestors since 1750. That led to *racial purification*, the killing of gypsies and Jews especially, but also of other mentally ill and physically deformed Germans.
The 1941 German invasion of Russia was, for the Nazis, a *racial war*:
The idea of *rassenkampf*, or 'race war', gave the Russian campaign its unprecedented character. (Beevor, 1998)

racism intolerance towards or illtreatment of those of a different race or nationality
Literally, a belief that people from different races may have inherent qualities and differences, as that Armenians and Parsees tend to be very intelligent, and Kenyans better long-distance runners. Now much pejorative use of prejudice, DISCRIMINATION, and conflict towards a MINORITY.
Also as *racialism*.

racist an intolerant bigot in matters of race and nationality
Originally, one who perceived or studied differences between races but now only used in a pejorative sense. Also as *racialist*.

racked *American* drunk or under the influence of illegal narcotics
Not tortured on a *rack*, but otherwise laid out, it would seem.

racy immoral or pornographic
Literally, lively, whence reckless, of sexual behaviour, and lewd, of humour:
[King George V] had a racy mind and liked a vulgar joke. (Channon, 1993)

radical accepting or advocating extreme political policies
Literally, going back to the roots.
The word is now used pejoratively:
...avid, punitive, radical ladies...enlisting my support for experimental sex-play in the nursery schools. (Bradbury, 1976)
In obsolete English dialect a *radical* was an impudent, idle, dissipated fellow; but do not assume that there was any connection with academia. In the 1930s the New York police *Radical Squad* existed mainly to break up Communist rallies.

rag (the) *British* a brothel
British Indian Army use, perhaps from the slang name of the London Army and Navy Club.

rag(s) on menstruating
Usually *had* or *got*.

Rag week, punning on the university fund-raising occasion, and *ragtime*, punning on the music, are the duration of menstruation.

ragged drunk
The way you may feel later.

railroad to pressurize or treat unfairly
The imagery is from involuntary movement in a fixed direction. In America, it may refer to falsely committing to prison or summary dismissal from employment; and in general use, to hustling a prospective customer:
Emilio, stop trying to railroad me. We don't even know the asking price. (Lambert, 2000)

railroad bible *American* a pack of playing cards
Gambling was prevalent on long train journeys:
In the United States a pack of cards became known as a 'railroad bible'. Some 300 card sharks operated the Union Pacific. (Faith, 1990—for the sake of passenger safety, I hope he meant 'operated on the Union Pacific')

rainbow fascist an intolerant person obsessed with ecological matters
Dysphemism rather than euphemism, but descriptive of those who ignore or break the law in their pursuit of environmental or animal issues.

raincoat[1] *American* a male contraceptive sheath
Punning on the RUBBER and the avoidance of getting wet.

raincoat[2] a private investigator
The clothing they wear in a job which exposes them to the elements.

rainmaker a person valued in an organization primarily for his contacts
He attracts clients or voters as his African namesake generates precipitation.

raise a beat to have an erection of the penis
From the observable pulse. Also as *have a beat on* or *raise a gallop*. Some figurative use, as when an exhausted man may declare that he *could not raise a beat*, without any suggestion that he might be required to indulge in sexual activity.

raisin a male homosexual
I suspect from the French meaning, lipstick; FRUIT[1] may have come later.

rake-off a payment made under bribery or extortion
Usually on a regular basis, with imagery probably from the roulette table.

ram a promiscuous male
Like the fecund animal.
Whence, as a verb, to copulate, of a male, referring also to the common thrusting imagery.

ram-riding (a) *obsolete* public humiliation
An adulterous wife or a henpecked husband might be compelled to mount a sheep in this venerable ceremony.
Also as a *riding*:
I found the stairs full of people, there being a great Riding there today for a man, the constable of the town, whose wife beat him. (Pepys, 1667)

ramp to rob, cheat, or overcharge
Originally, to snatch. The overcharging use may owe something to the upward inclination. A *ramp* usually refers to cheating or overcharging, not robbery.

ramps (the) *obsolete British* a brothel
Army use, possibly because you paid dearly for your pleasure, then or later.

randy *British* eager for copulation
The *ran-dan* is a carouse, perhaps more in Scotland than elsewhere (Rankin, 1999), and *randy* is a corruption of it. A century ago 'A randy sort o' a 'ooman' was one who enjoyed a good party (*EDD*). American men called Randolph who use the shortened version of their name may be greeted with some misgiving when introducing themselves to British females.

Rangoon itch a fungal infection of the penis
Burmese prostitutes were notoriously disease-ridden.
The *Rangoon runs* were not journeys to and from the city, but diarrhoea.

rap the accusation of a criminal offence
Literally, a rebuke or slap.
A *rap sheet* is a list of previous convictions.

rap club *American* a brothel
To *rap* is to talk or chatter, or to perform *rap music*.
Also as *rap parlor* or *studio*.

raspberry[1] a fart
Rhyming slang on *raspberry tart*. To *blow a raspberry* is to simulate the sound orally through pursed lips. Much figurative use indicating a mild admonition, refusal, or reproach:
...popped question to Dutch girl and got raspberry. So that is that, eh. Stiff upper lip and dropped cock. (E. Waugh, July 1936, quoted in S. Hastings, 1994)

raspberry² a lame person
Rhyming slang on *raspberry ripple*, a cripple.

rat-arsed drunk
A vulgar and possibly ephemeral expression of which the etymology escapes me.

rather exceedingly
Many expressions introduced by *rather* are on the borderline of understatement and euphemism. Thus a *rather naughty child* is almost certainly a spoilt and undisciplined brat, and a hospital patient who is described as being *rather poorly* is very ill.

rational agreeing with a prejudice
Literally, using logic or reason. The language of a bigot:
> A rational debate for their purposes is one which reached the approved conclusions. (*Daily Telegraph*, 26 June 2001)

rationalize arbitrarily to reduce
Literally, to think in a *rational* manner, whence to deal sensibly with a problem. To *rationalize* a workforce is summarily to dismiss employees. So too with other resources:
> Every time the Government... encouraged local authorities to 'rationalise' their recreational areas, school pitches have been lucratively sacrificed for houses and supermarkets as a way of keeping down the rates. (*Daily Telegraph*, 3 March 1994)

rattle¹ to copulate with
Of a male, from the shaking about that may be involved.
Also of the act and the female participant.

rattle² *American* to urinate
Rhyming slang on *rattle and hiss*, perhaps with the usual serpentine imagery in mind.

rattled *mainly American* drunk
I suspect, from the antiquity, that the derivation is from the Scottish meaning, to beat, with the common violent imagery.

raunchy lustful or pornographic
It originally meant sloppy, whence, with an unusual rapidity of progression, poor, then cheap, then drunken.
Now almost entirely used in its sexual sense.

ravish to copulate with a woman against her will
Originally, to seize or carry off anything:
> The ravish'd Helen, Menelaus' wife,
> With wanton Paris sleeps. (Shakespeare, *Troilus and Cressida*)
and in more modern use:
> I don't know why, but that ravishing of Lily made her dear to me. (F. Harris, 1925)

The dated female expression of delight *How ravishing!* came from the meaning 'ecstatic' rather than from any Freudian fantasies.

raw naked
The undressed state and usually referring to a man who does not use pyjamas but *sleeps raw*. Often as *in the raw*.

razor to maim or kill by cutting
Here the cut-throat open blade is not used for shaving.

re-educate to seek to subvert an allegiance while in prison
As practised by the Americans in Vietnam. For the Nazis and Communists, *re-education* meant the imprisonment of malcontents or those whom they distrusted, usually accompanied by brutality.

re-emigration *obsolete* encouraging black immigrants to Britain to return to their place of birth
A usage after repatriation had become a dirty word:
> ...[Enoch Powell] repeating that repatriation (which he called 're-emigration') was also a vital part of Conservative policy. (Cosgrave, 1989)

read out of *American* to dismiss from
The treatment accorded by the devout to sinners:
> My father was read out of the United Methodist Church in Meridian, Mississippi, in 1931—when he was seventeen—because he went to a dance. (Naipaul, 1998)

reading Geneva print *obsolete* drunk
This is a sample entry of several literary puns on the city noted for its piety and its printing, and on *gin*, which was also then called *Geneva*, from the French *genièvre*, the juniper berry:
> You have been reading Geneva print this morning already. (W. Scott, 1816)

realign to devalue
Of currency. *Realignments* by politicians always seem to be downwards.

ream to sodomize
Literally, the engineering term for enlarging a hole by inserting a metal tool.

Reaper (the) death
Father Time, also known as the GRIM REAPER, carries a scythe as well as an hourglass:
> Worked for my daddy two year before the Reaper cut him down. (Proulx, 2002)

rear to defecate
The etymology suggested elsewhere based on soldiers falling out *to the rear* seems

implausible. The derivation was more probably from REAR (END) and REARS.

rear end the buttocks
Not the shoulder blades or the heels. Occasionally as *rear*, *tout court*:
> Don't tell *me* about rears and vices. I have been in the navy all my life. (O'Brian, 1970)

rears lavatories
Those in a communal block are usually situated behind the dwellings whose occupants used them.

reasonable submissive to coercion or the threat of force
The language of bullies and tyrants:
> My official did not see why it should not be a peaceful [settlement] if, as he said, the Poles were 'reasonable'. (Shirer, 1999, quoting a broadcast on 22 August 1939, nine days before Germany invaded Poland: as Klemperer reminds us, Hitler and Stalin had already agreed to divide Poland between themselves—diary entry 7 June 1939)

reasons of health see FOR REASONS OF HEALTH

rebalance to increase
Of prices, when the *balance* is always heavier rather than lighter:
> Royal Mail is discussing with Postcomm over whether it should rebalance its prices. It is suggested that this could put 2p on the price of a first class stamp. (*Daily Telegraph*, 19 November 2004)

However to *rebalance stock* is to sell excess inventory, the phrase being used in November 2003 when the failing manufacturer MG-Rover closed its production line for three days to stop assembling too many cars too few people wished to buy.

rebase to reduce
Financial jargon, especially when dividends are lowered. The *base* could with equal logic be raised, but never is.

rebuilding costs reparations on a defeated foe
The language of Nazi Germany:
> Hitler...preferred to call the financial burden the Reich imposed on defeated nations, not *Beatzungcosten* (occupation costs) but *Aufbaucosten* (rebuilding costs). (Ousby, 1997)

receding (hairline) baldness
Among men, baldness is always a delicate subject, except in other men.

receiver a dealer in stolen property
From his willingness to 'receive anything bought' (Mayhew, 1862). Now standard English, and not to be confused with the official charged with winding up the affairs of a bankrupt business.

receiver-general *obsolete* a prostitute
Punning on the officer appointed by the court in a case of insolvency and her *reception* of men *generally*.

recent unpleasantness a war
A version of *late unpleasantness* and its variant, LATE DISTURBANCES, seeking to play down or forget the horror.

recognition *British* the receipt of a honorific title
Not just knowing a likeness but the use of government patronage in awarding HONOURS:
> ...someone who hopes that it may result at some future date in their recognition. (A. Clark, 1993—he was as caustic about those who through flattery or bribery (political donations) seek such 'awards', as he was anxious to secure for himself the appointment as a Privy Counsellor)

record the evidence of a criminal conviction
We all have *records* of a sort, although we modestly prefer to use the French *résumé* or the Latin *curriculum vitae* when we talk about them.

recreational drug an illegal narcotic
As opposed to one taken for medical purposes.

recreational sex promiscuous copulation
Re-creation might, incorrectly, seem to imply a desire to achieve impregnation of the female.

rectification of frontiers the annexation of territory by force
The party which seeks the putting right, from Hitler onwards, is never minded in turn to divest itself of territory.

red an allusion to menstruation
From the bleeding. Also as *the reds*.
A woman may speak of wearing a *red rag*, punning on the cliché about the bull, or of having a *red-haired visitor*.
Another female evasion, *the red flag is up*, alludes not to political allegiance but to the signal warning people to keep away.
The Red Sea is in refers to the adventures of Moses and others in Egypt and the flow which covered the channel of their escape.

red card to dismiss or deny entry to
From the action of the referee at soccer sending a player off who *shows a red card*. Here the noun becomes a verb:

Or what? You'll red card me again. (Rankin, 2004—he was threatened with being banned from a pub)

red cross morphine
Addict jargon. It can be stolen from a first aid kit. A *red devil* is a barbiturate, from the colour of the pill.

red eye *American* poor-quality potable alcohol
Usually whisky, from one of its effects on the drinker, and not to be confused with the *red-eye (special)*, the overnight flight from the Pacific to the East coast in which travellers lose four hours and a good night's sleep.

red ink an indication of loss
In the olden days, black ink on a bank statement indicated a credit balance and *red ink* a debit. Now common commercial use:
Is it any wonder Carlton is struggling. [Its major investment] ITV Digital is awash with red ink. (*Sunday Telegraph*, 9 December 2001)

red lamp a brothel
The traditional sign displayed outside. Less often as *red light*.
A *red light precinct* or *district* is a brothel area where you would expect to find more than one *red-lighted number*.

redeployed dismissed from employment
Not transferred to another assignment:
...these are probably one or two disgruntled 'redeployed' employees who know enough about the 'funny' accounting to get us in trouble. (*Sunday Telegraph*, 20 January 2002, quoting a prophetic letter from Sharon Watkins to Kenneth Lay, the Chairman of Enron)

redistribution of property looting
Not penal taxation of the rich but Second World War use of soldiers in Europe:
He didn't call it stealing though, 'redistribution of property' he called it. (Price, 1978)

redistribution of wealth punitive taxation
A stated objective of some high-minded politicians who nonetheless seldom appear anxious to share their salaries, expenses, pension entitlements, and other benefits with the indigent. As Abe Lincoln observed, making the rich poor doesn't make the poor rich.

redlining *American* refusing credit solely because of the place of residence of the applicant
The address is highlighted in a list, figuratively or in fact.

redneck *American* a poorly educated and bigoted white man
Dysphemism rather than euphemism describing a person who works in the open, perhaps at an unskilled job, but not someone who used to be called a *Red Indian*.

reduce the headcount to dismiss employees
It is the bodies, not the *headcount*, who suffer the *reduction*.
A *headcount reduction* is what happens.

reduce your commitments involuntarily to leave employment
Not just paying off your debts or moving to a cheaper house:
...a former finance director of Mirror Group Newspapers facing charges of false accounting and conspiring with Robert and Kevin Maxwell, has reduced his commitments...(*Daily Telegraph*, 2 March 1995)

reduction in force *American* the summary dismissal of an employee or employees
Whence the acronym *riff*, used as noun and verb.

redundant dismissed from employment
Originally meaning, in superabundance, which an individual *made redundant* can hardly be.

reefer a marijuana cigarette
Possibly from the method of hand-rolling the cigarettes.

reengineer summarily to dismiss employees
It is people who are thrown away, rather than parts of the product:
In a reengineering, a number of people get reengineered out of a job. (*Sunday Telegraph*, 6 May 1995, quoting a lawyer in a London legal firm which had just 'released' eleven partners)

refer to drawer this cheque is unpaid through lack of funds
Banks use this evasion because it is dangerous to dishonour a cheque by mistake and thereby imply that the drawer has acted fraudulently. Commonly abbreviated to *RD*.

referred *British* failed
Originally, put back. University jargon.

refresh your memory to correct previous perjury
What happens when a witness is recalled to the stand after giving misleading or false

evidence.A prisoner in police custody may also *refresh his memory* by making a confession or implicating others under threat or receipt of violence.

refresher a drink of an intoxicant
From the supposed bracing effect. Also as *refreshment*. Someone described as *refreshed* is drunk.

refuse nothing to copulate
Pepys preferred to use the Latin—*nulla puella negat*. (Tomalin, 2002)

regroup to fail to advance
Military jargon for failing to advance in the face or uncertainty or danger, or for an attempt to reconstitute a beaten formation.

regular¹ in the habit of daily defecation
Laxative advertisements enshrined this use.

regular² menstruating at a predictable time
There is a danger of confusion with REGULAR¹:
'What are you talking about?' 'She was a regular girl.' (R. Harris, 1998—she was perhaps pregnant)

regular³ small
In the jargon of packet sizes, this comes after ECONOMY, *jumbo*, *family*, MEDIUM, etc.

regularize to invade and conquer
The intended implication is that the political situation is being returned to normal. It took one Polish, one East German, and twelve Russian divisions to *regularize* the position in Czechoslovakia in 1968.

relations have come (my) I am menstruating
From the limited duration and inconvenience of the visitation, or, in some cases, the relief at seeing them. The kinship is sometimes identified as being with *country cousins*, from their ruddy complexion.

relationship an extramarital sexual involvement with another
In fact, we have a *relationship* with everyone we meet, as buyer or seller, friend or enemy. Often with adjectival embellishment such as *close*, *long-term*, *special*, or as the case may be.

relaxation services masturbation by a third party
Available in Chinese barbers' shops for 50 yuan. (Theroux, 2000)

release¹ to dismiss from employment
The employee has not hitherto been held against his will.
Also as a noun.

release² death

Normally after a painful terminal illness, as in the cliché a HAPPY RELEASE:
Winston [Churchill]'s distaste for what is left of him in life makes him yearn for release; he wants to die. (Moran, 1966)

release³ sexual activity
The theory is that unrelieved sexual tension is unhealthy, especially for an adult male:
...indulged in this pastime night after night as much to give him some 'release' (she actually used the odious word). (Styron, 1976, writing about masturbation)

relief¹ public aid given to the indigent
Originally, a feudal payment to an overlord on coming into an estate.

relief² urination
You usually *need* or *obtain* it.
Whence the American *relief-station*, a lavatory.

relief³ sexual activity
From the supposed effect of relieving tension. It may describe mainly male copulation or masturbation by either sex.

relieve *American* to dismiss from employment
The use suggests that the employer is doing the employee a kindness. The British *relieve of duties* is usually of an official for misbehaviour or dereliction of duty, pending a full enquiry and dismissal.

relieved of your sufferings dead
After a prolonged period of illness.

relieve yourself to urinate
Obtaining RELIEF² and as *relieve your bladder*. To *relieve your bowels* is to defecate.

relinquish to leave after being dismissed
Normally of a senior manager, with a face-saving suggestion that the parting was voluntary:
Mr Barker 'relinquished' these roles in May last year on the same day that Hartstone issued its second profits warning. (*Daily Telegraph*, 16 July 1994)

relocate *American* to dismiss from employment
The victim does not necessarily have to move house to find another job although there will certainly be a change of working environment. For the Nazis *relocation* meant rounding up Jews to send them to extermination camps. For the Americans in the Second World War, a *relocation camp* was where they imprisoned enemy aliens, and specifically those of Japanese descent living on the West Coast, who, despite their incarceration, remained loyal to their adopted country.

reluctant to depart suggesting that the verdict of dismissal was wrong
A cricket usage, where unwillingness immediately to accept the decision of the umpire is considered unsporting.

remain above ground not to die
I include this entry to illustrate the dangers and risks confronting those who use euphemisms:

> Mrs Van Butchell's marriage settlement stipulated that her husband should have control of her fortune 'as long as she remained above ground'. The embalming was a great success. (J. Mitford, 1963— Mr Van Butchell showed more enterprise than taste)

remainder to dispose of (surplus stock of a book) by selling cheaply
The jargon of the publishing trade and the humiliation of an author.

remains a corpse
Funeral jargon:

> Today though, 'body' is Out and 'remains' or 'Mr Jones' is In. (J. Mitford, 1963)

remedial applicable to the dull, the lazy, and the badly taught
Literally, helping to cure something, but not, in common educational jargon, used to describe special instruction to overcome a specific weakness in an otherwise normal child.
As with mental illness, the use of euphemism to mask levels of disability is no kindness for those who require long-term help.

remittance man *obsolete* an unsuccessful, embarrassing, or improvident member of a wealthy family sent to reside in a distant country
He received, rather than sent, the *remittance* so long as he stayed away.

removal[1] a murder
But not necessarily making off with the body. *DSUE* says: 'Ex a witness's euphemism in the Phoenix Park assassination case.' (On 6 May 1882 Burke and Cavendish, the Permanent Under-Secretary for Ireland and the Chief Secretary, were hacked to pieces with surgical knives in Phoenix Park, Dublin. Five of the murderers were hanged, but the killings led to a harsh Prevention of Crimes Act, the abolition of trial by jury, and a worsening of relations between England and Ireland.)

removal[2] dismissal from employment
Venerable enough to be noted by Dr Johnson in 1755.

removal[3] *American* a burial
Moving the corpse for the last time before its resurrection perhaps.
In obsolete Scottish use, *removed* meant dead. (*EDD*)

remunerated balances credit accounts on which interest is paid
Pompous circumlocution more than euphemism except when used by the Old Lady of Threadneedle Street:

> Now [the Bank of England] is thinking of offering [depositors] what it delicately calls remunerated balances. (*Daily Telegraph*, 22 May 2004)

renegotiate to renege on
The language of sovereign governments when they wish to extract more revenue from foreign operators:

> They may not nationalise oil and gas fields, but they are keen to 'renegotiate' (i.e. repudiate) existing contracts with foreign companies. (*Sunday Telegraph*, 12 February 2006)

In Britain, a *renegotiation* may be no more than a bribe or subsidy illegally given to a contractor whose employees live near parliamentary seats Ministers wish to retain in a forthcoming general election:

> The MoD insisted that the [parliamentary] reply was in order. Increasing the contract value [by £82m] was not 'financial support—that's renegotiating a contract'. (*Daily Telegraph*, 10 February 2005—with the election won, the contract was cancelled, the work was moved elsewhere, and the lie to the House of Commons was forgotten)

rent boy a young male homosexual prostitute
Not from the old meaning of *rent*, a payment in respect of an illegal transaction, but payment for temporary use, or abuse.
A *renter* is any prostitute working on a part-time basis.

répos de guerrier copulation with a wartime mistress
The Iron Duke seems not to have been fastidious about where he took his rest:

> Except in the case of [the Duke of Wellington's] own indiscreet *répos de gerrier* with Napoleon's ex-mistress the singer Grassini... (Tombs & Tombs, 2006)

repose *American* to be dead and buried
The common imagery of the corpse being asleep:

> The companions will repose one above the other in a single grave space. (J. Mitford, 1963)

In funeral jargon, a *reposing room* is a morgue.

repositioning the dismissal of staff
A usage first noted in America in 1996 but too
useful to be confined to one side of the water:
> Following dismal news on repositioning
> from two of the UK's three largest legacy
> retailers, Boots and Sainsbury, we admit to
> some trepidation that Marks & Spencer will
> administer the same unpleasant medicine.
> (*Daily Telegraph*, 9 April 2004—a *legacy retailer*
> does not sell bequests, unfortunately)

reproductive freedom *American* the right
to abort a healthy foetus
Not the right to multiple parenthood, which
Chinese citizens do not enjoy. The phrase is
also used to denote the effect on a woman's
life of the availability of contraceptives.

requisition to steal
Literally, to take over on a temporary basis for
military or urgent purposes:
> Captain Martin...suggested we 'requisition'
> the...drum kit to prevent it falling into
> German hands. (Milligan, 1971—the drums
> were taken from the Old Town Church Hall
> of Bexhill-on-Sea in 1940)

reservation an area of land not taken
from American Indians by white settlers
The HOMELANDS of South Africa were not an
original idea.

resettle to carry away and kill
The Nazi *Unsiedlung*. Whence *resettlement*, such
systematic killing:
> ...the huge 'resettlements' from the
> Warsaw ghetto...were coincident with the
> establishment of...Treblika and its gas
> chambers. (Styron, 1976)

resettlement the forcible eviction of
white farmers in Zimbabwe
A feature of the autocratic Mugabe's regime,
leading to hardship and starvation for most of
the population.

reshape to instigate multiple changes
True as far as it goes, but an evasion far from the
whole truth. The Beeching Report of 1963,
which led to multiple line closures and huge
job losses, was entitled 'The Reshaping of
Britain's Railways'.

reshuffle to dismiss from employment
In the case of governments, the numbers of
cards in the pack remain the same, as in a
ministerial *reshuffle*, where the head of government dismisses ministers and appoints
others to their place. In an industrial *reshuffle*
many of the cards no longer remain in the
pack.

residential provision *British* a place in a
boarding institution
More than mere inelegance or circumlocution
because sociological jargon must avoid the
taboo *board school*, a prison for young criminals,
and the equally abhorrent *boarding school*,
attended by fee-paying pupils outside the state
system. The *resident* may be a homeless geriatric,
a lunatic, a chronic invalid, or a prisoner.

resign to be dismissed from employment
The word is used by and of the employee to
save face:
> I worked as a personal secretary in London
> until I was fi...until I resigned. (Bradbury,
> 1976)

resign your spirit *obsolete* to die
The usage seems to discount the prospect of
reincarnation.

resistance any dissent or divergence
from the standards of an autocracy
Those Germans who were not Nazis were
deemed to be against them and so characterized, without having to emulate the courage
of the Poles, Dutch, and other nationals living
under German occupation:
> People who are mad or had epileptic fits
> were shot for 'resistance'. (Burleigh, 2000,
> describing Buchenwald concentration
> camp in 1938)

resisting arrest while in custody
Police usage to explain the wrongful wounding or killing of a prisoner.

resolved without trial *American* involving the acceptance of a guilty plea
Part of the process of plea bargaining, but not
implying that the accused was acquitted for
want of prosecution.

resources employees
A shortened form of HUMAN RESOURCES and
even more dehumanizing. A *resources director*
is not concerned with raw materials or the
supply of gas.
For the Americans in Vietnam, *resources control*
was the destruction of crops in an attempt to
starve the Vietcong and its supporters.

rest home an institution for the aged or
mentally ill
Not punning on the fact that its residents will
spend the *rest of their lives* there. For geriatrics
and for those with mental illness.

rest room *American* a lavatory
Wide use by both sexes:
> ...asked where the bathroom was. The
> restroom was filthy. (Diehl, 1978—but in
> what state was the lavatory?)

An attempt by the funeral industry to use *restroom* for morgue not surprisingly found few takers.

resting unemployed
Theatrical jargon which seeks to imply that the idleness is voluntary.

restorative a drink of intoxicant
Making good the tensions and easing the weariness occasioned by the daily grind, perhaps. In Edwardian slang, a drinker might *restore the tissues*.

restorative art *American* embalming
Funeral jargon.

restore order to invade and conquer (a country)
The excuse of the Russians in Hungary and Czechoslovakia, and of others elsewhere.

restraint[1] an attempt to limit wage increases
One of a series of euphemisms used by governments which seek to curb the inflation generated in part by their own profligacy or incompetence, by limiting wages and salaries.

restraint[2] a recession
A usage of politicians who wish to avoid the dread word 'recession' and to imply that the economic mess is caused other than through their own policies:
> The country [under Harold Wilson] was going through a period of severe economic restraint. (Mantle, 1988)

restricted growth dwarfishness
Restricted comes from a Latin verb meaning to hold back deliberately, and the only true human *restricted growth* was among the hapless Chinese women whose feet had been bound to keep them small.

restructure to dismiss from employment
Not altogether misleading, as the new *structure* will be different from the old, with fewer folk to pay:
> The men (and one woman) are unemployed, swept from their jobs by a deadly combination of recession and 'restructuring'. (*Telegraph Magazine*, 1 July 1995)

restructured presented in a dishonest or misleading way
It applies to financial reports and the like.

restructuring managing after a financial failure
An evasion used by accountants to avoid saying receivership and to imply that all will be well.

result a satisfactory outcome
Of a sexual encounter, a business transaction, etc.

Euphemistic only in the negative in British soccer jargon, where *not to get a result* means to lose, a loss not being a *result* even when it is.

resurrection man *obsolete Scottish* a stealer of corpses
When it was widely supposed that those who died in Christian belief would in due course undergo a *resurrection* of the body, few wished to risk having their corpses dissected in pursuit of medical knowledge for a fear of a dismembered or partial return to earth. In the 19th century the pre-eminent medical school was in Edinburgh, and the demand for bodies led to suppliers raiding churchyards.
This punning usage may first have been applied to Burke and Hare, who carried the business a stage further by murdering chance victims when a paucity of natural deaths caused fresh corpses to be in short supply.
Also as *resurrection cove* and *resurrectionist*.

retainer a series of payments made to an extortionist
Literally, a sum paid to retain the services of a lawyer, when some may consider the definition to be doubly apt.

retard a simpleton
Literally, anything delayed or held back.
In educational jargon, *retarded* is used to describe a person with a congenital inability to learn.

retire[1] to go to urinate
When the monarch *retires* on a public occasion, she does not abdicate. Whence a *retiring-room*, a lavatory, which may be any old lavatory in America but, if so described in Britain, is reserved for royalty or honoured guests.

retire[2] to dismiss from employment
The victim does not cease to work in that post voluntarily:
> George Owen was 'retired' from Mercury by Lord Young, C & W's well-rewarded chairman. (*Daily Telegraph*, 6 December 1994)

retread a single woman who has previously lived with a man in a sexual relationship
The imagery is from a tyre, suggesting that the previous owner has had the better use when the article was pristine.

retrenched dismissed from employment
Literally, reduced in the interests of economy, but illogically used of those who have gone rather than those who remain in the workforce.

return fire to attack without warning
The Goebbels propaganda ministry announced that the German troops invading Poland on 1 September 1939 were 'merely returning Polish fire'. The same wording was used again about

the 1940 invasion of Holland and has become a stand-by of other aggressors.

return to to die
The destination is normally specified, such as to *ashes*, *dust*, etc.:
> Great travail is created for all men...from the day that they go out of their mother's womb, unto that day when they return to the mother of all things. (R. Burton, 1621)

returned empty *British obsolete* unable to find a husband
The unkind phrase was used of single women sent out to India, supposedly on social visits, who failed to receive a proposal of marriage from the British bachelors stationed or working there. (Dalrymple, 2002)

returned to unit *British* failed
Army usage, often abbreviated to *RTU*, to describe those who fail to complete a course to qualify for an elite corps, to become an officer, etc.

revenue enhancement raising taxes
What is *enhancement* for the tax collector is the opposite for his victims. Less often as *revenue emolument*, an *emolument* being originally the fee you paid to a miller for grinding your corn. A *revenue protection officer* is someone charged with the collection of fines.

reverse discrimination a failure to appoint the more suitable candidate
DISCRIMINATION, *tout court*, might seem sufficient to have covered the concept:
> White men have scored two major victories in reverse discrimination rulings by the US Supreme Court, confirming that the mood in America is turning sharply against race-based 'affirmative action'. (*Daily Telegraph*, 19 April 1995)

reverse engineering unauthorized copying
Not the gear which propels backwards. You obtain your competitor's product, take it apart, and then incorporate the technical improvements in your own.

reviver a drink of an intoxicant
Referring to its supposed ability to liven up the drinker, but not used only, as you might suppose, of the first potation.

revolutionary Communist
You might have thought that things would stop revolving after the Communists had attained power, but you would have been wrong.
Such power, if threatened, has to be met with *revolutionary firmness*.
Revolutionary elections are those rigged by the Communists.

revolving-door[1] unduly lenient and ineffective
It describes the treatment of criminals who, soon after capture, are released to continue their former activities, figuratively entering (and leaving) the police station, court, or jail through such an access:
> The people of California are sick of revolving-door justice. (*Daily Telegraph*, 4 March 1995)

revolving-door[2] involving excessive change of management
Those appointed come and go, figuratively without having entered the building.

rib joint *American* a brothel
Probably from the obsolete *rib*, a woman, after the manner of Eve's creation. *DAS* says 'from 'tenderloin' reinforced by 'crib joint', which might be right, although most sexual euphemisms have less complex ancestry.

rich friend a man with a much younger mistress
Not just someone of either sex who happens to be better off than we are.

Richard a turd
Rhyming slang on *Richard the Third*. This English king had a bad press from the Tudors and Shakespeare, which is why he is commonly considered more of a shit than Edward, William, Henry, or George, of whom there were also more than three.

richness of stock an excess inventory
Retailers' jargon, not alluding to the merchandise offered by a jeweller:
> Mr Rose [of Marks & Spencer] admitted to a 'richness of stock I'd rather not have'. (*Daily Telegraph*, 15 December 2004)

ride to copulate with
Usually of a *male*, with the common equine imagery. A *ride* may be the act, or the other party involved. To *ride St George* was to copulate with 'The woman uppermost in the amorous congress, that is, the dragon upon St George. (Grose) It was said to be the most reliable way of begetting a bishop.
To *ride abroad with St George but at home with St Michael* was merely to be a hen-pecked braggart, with no episcopal connotations. A *riding academy* is a brothel, the name being specifically given by American troops of the 34th Division to the Belgravia Hotel when stationed in Belfast in 1942. (Atkinson, 2003)
In obsolete use, a *riding master* was a woman's extramarital sexual partner and *riding time* was the season for tupping sheep, an expression used figuratively of human copulation by Burns in 1786.

ride backwards *obsolete* to be taken to your execution

The way in which the victim was made to sit in the cart. Men did not usually *ride* in carts unless they were unfit or being taken to the gallows.

Also as *ride up Holborn Hill*, which was on the way from Newgate prison to the Tyburn gallows.

ride-by carried out from a moving motor vehicle

It is used of a crime, such as shooting someone from a car or snatching a handbag from the pillion of a scooter:

In nine months, she has mastered all the terminology: 'ride-by' (shooting on the move); 'drive-up' (firing from a stop); 'drive-through' (the car is the weapon); 'chase-aways' (the enemy flees). (Turow, 1996)

ride the red horse to menstruate

In America the horse may be white, from the colour of the absorbent cloth. Also as *ride the rag*.

ride the wooden horse *obsolete* to be flogged

From the *horse*, or stool, to which the victim was strapped.

right-on conforming to fashionable dogma

The usage suggests a lack of independent thought coupled with toadyism:

...to the horror of the BBC's right-on staff a proposal to allow householders to attack burglars topped a *Today* programme poll. (*Daily Telegraph*, 9 December 2004—there are those who think burglars more sinned against than sinning)

right-sizing the dismissal of employees

Right for the management or owners, perhaps:

'We enter 1995 with the bulk of our right-sizing behind us,' Lou Gerstner, chairman of IBM, on last year's 35,000 redundancies. (*Daily Telegraph*, 20 January 1995)

rights at work the legal imposition of additional costs and obligations on employers

Not just the entitlement to wages, holidays, overtime pay, safe working conditions, and other normal arrangements between employer and employee.

ring[1] the vagina or anus

Viewed sexually. Heterosexual use:

...I'll fear no other thing

So sore as keeping safe Nerissa's ring. (Shakespeare, *The Merchant of Venice*)

and homosexual:

Listen, Ted—he's you know, after yer ring! (Parris, 1995—a boy was warning another

about his friendship with a homosexual British Member of Parliament)

ring[2] a cartel

The concept is of meeting in, and making complete, a circle.

Apart from commercial use, dealers at auctions are reputed to operate in *rings*.

ring eight bells to die

The watch is over. Jolly (1988) draws our attention to the punning Alastair Maclean novel title, *When Eight Bells Toll*.

ring the bell to impregnate a woman

Normally intentionally, from the fairground trial of strength which involves a blow with a sledgehammer to drive an object up a vertical column. If the object reaches the top, the bell placed there will ring.

ringer a racehorse etc. fraudulently substituted for another

In early 20th-century slang, a *ringer* was a person who closely resembled someone else. The cliché a *dead ringer* does not denote that the substitute is deceased, but that the likeness is perfect. It is just possible that the usage came from *ringing the changes* in campanology.

rinse[1] a dye applied to the hair

Literally, a cleaning with water. Mainly female hairdressing jargon, although the *blue rinse* seems to have gone out of fashion.

rinse[2] to bring funds dishonestly obtained into apparently legal circulation or account

The word, as with LAUNDER, is widely used of the proceeds of dealing in illegal narcotics.

Rio trade *British* a desperate financial gamble

The action of a commodity dealer or broker trying to recover prior trading losses. There is no extradition treaty between Brazil and Britain.

rip off to cheat or steal from

The imagery is from tearing paper off a pad or banknotes off a roll. Of cheating and, as a noun, of stealing.

To *rip off a piece of arse* or *ass* is to copulate with a female, when you may CHEAT perhaps, but are not stealing.

ripe *American* drunk

And ready to fall.

ripped *American* drunk or under the influence of illegal narcotics

Feeling torn by alcohol or drugs.

ripple to experience a series of orgasms

A female experience and usage, for some, with aquatic imagery.

ripples on (have) *obsolete* to be mildly drunk
Ripples are the attachments to the side of a cart to enable it to carry more than its normal load.

rise an erection of the penis
In America you call an increase in pay a *raise*, to avoid misunderstanding.

riser a thick sole and heel to enhance the appearance of height
Worn by a man: women are not ashamed of wearing *high heels*.

rivet to copulate with
Of a male, from the engineering meaning, to pass a rigid metal fastener through a hole.

roach *American* a cockroach
The usage displayed a prudish anxiety to avoid any mention of *cock*. *Rooster-roach* was found unsatisfactory, as well as being ridiculous. Now standard American English.
Why a *roach* should also mean the butt of a marijuana cigarette I do not know.

road apples *American* horse turds in the street
From the way they pile up naturally, as a fruiterer may display his wares.

road is up for repair (the) I am menstruating
A pun on the red warning light, the restriction of the passage, and the temporary nature of the affliction.

roast *British* to copulate with while engaged in a sexual orgy
By a male, with the female as the culinary dish to be enjoyed by those present. A court case in March 2004, in which well-paid but undisciplined young professional footballers were accused of various offences against females, including rape, added a number of jargon words to the lexicon of sexual depravity.

rob the cradle to form a sexual attachment with a much younger person
The *robber* may be male or female.

rocks the testicles
Of no greater size, it would seem, than a man's STONES. Usually in the phrase *get your rocks off*, to copulate, not be castrated.

rocky[1] of unsound mind
Unstable, like an unbalanced chair.

rocky[2] *American* drunk

Again from the lack of balance.

rod a handgun
Literally, a straight piece of wood.
To be *rodded* is to be armed with a pistol.

roger to copulate with
Originally from the name shepherds gave to a ram. The suggestion that the derivation might be from the piracy of the *Jolly Roger* seems an allusion too far. In August 1945, the code name for the aborted or unsuccessful invasion of Phuket by the British/Indian 14th Army was *Operation Roger*.

roll[1] to copulate with
Of either sex, from the movement. A *roll* is copulation and a female who *rolls over* is promiscuous. A *roll in the hay* does not necessarily imply copulation in an agrarian setting.

roll[2] *American* to rob with violence
Often applied to a drunkard who is knocked, or *rolled*, over before being robbed. Also in general use of street theft.

roll[3] to kill
After violent assault.

roll over (of a criminal) to give information against other criminals
Another form of submission:
> The ATF likes to work with criminal defendants who have 'rolled over' to avoid prosecution. (Evans-Pritchard, 1998)

roller-coaster involving past impropriety
Journalistic jargon of a business manager or financier whose career includes episodes the detailed reporting of which might lead to an action for defamation. The imagery is from the fairground ride.

rollocked drunk
It is difficult to work out what the device for holding an oar on a rowing boat has to do with inebriation.

Roman *American* sexually orgiastic
From the fabled orgies of the ancient Romans rather than any depravities of the modern city or its church. Now found in advertisements offering access to sexual depravity, such as *Roman culture* or the *Roman way*.

Roman candle a failure of a parachute
Failing to open fully, it resembles the firework.

Roman spring (a) lust in the elderly
It attempts to do for geriatrics what an Indian summer does for the climate.

romance a sexual relationship outside
marriage
In standard use, a courtship, from the
romance, or tale of chivalry, which was set
down in a vernacular tongue rather than in
Latin. Also as a verb:
> Stanford Court, where he'd romanced
> another highly recognisable blonde star,
> Frances Day. (Monkhouse, 1993)

A *romantic affair*, *attachment*, or *relationship* is
what the parties are engaged in, often more
sordid than *romantic* in its standard English
sense. They may also be described as *romantically linked*. A *romantic indiscretion* is such an
event when detection causes embarrassment:
> [Sarah Ferguson's] father became a public
> figure in his own right, his every activity—
> and in particular his occasional romantic
> indiscretions—of consuming interest to the
> tabloid press. (*Daily Telegraph*, 18 March 2003)

romp to copulate
Literally, to frolic or play boisterously.
A *romp* may be an act of extramarital
copulation, or the person with whom it is
undertaken.

roof rabbit a cat
Eaten in that part of Holland denied food by
Hitler in the winter of 1944–5 in retaliation
for the strike by Dutch railway workers.
Before its Second World War siege was raised,
Maltese people also ate cats, described as
rabbits. (Holland, 2003)

room and board with Uncle Sam *American* imprisonment
In a Federal penitentiary, from the shared
letters U and S.

rooster a cock
A survival from 19th-century American prudery, when any mention of a *cock* was taboo.

root a penis
The source of procreation or the shape of a
vegetable. Also as *man-root*.
A *root* or *root rat* is a profligate male and to
root, or more often to *root about*, is to copulate,
punning on porcine behaviour.

rootless Jewish
The language of Nazi Germany and Communist Russia, where Jews were seen as a threat
because of their intelligence, their independence, and their shared religion and culture:
> Nine Kremlin doctors were said to be
> plotting to kill the leadership. Seven of
> them were described as 'rootless
> cosmopolitans', Sovspeak for Jews.
> (Moynahan, 1994, writing about the
> paranoid Stalin's 'Doctor's Plot' in January
> 1953)

> And a couple of hundred rootless
> internationalists—interruption: 'Jews'—
> want to set nations of millions at one
> another's throats. (Hitler speech reported
> in Klemperer, 1998, in translation—diary
> entry of 11 November 1933)

rope (the) death by hanging
Noose and all.

roses menstruation
The usual reference to the colour of blood.

rosy drunk
Referring to the facial glow. The meaning
wine may have been merely the anglicizing of
rosé:
> ...fetched the rosy, and applied himself
> to...another glassful. (Dickens, 1840)

rough trade an uncouth male in a sexual
role
Aggressive and often badly dressed or un-
washed, he may be the consort, with whom
she regularly copulates, of a wealthy or
cultured woman.
Much homosexual use, both of an uncouth
person and of consorting with him.

round the bend mentally unbalanced
Going out of sight. Less often as *around the
bend* or *round the twist*.
See also HARPIC.

round-trip dishonestly inflating turnover
Jargon of reciprocal trading in specialist markets such as energy where an increase in
declared volume can influence the stock price.
The parties buy and sell each other the same
amount of product in a *round-trip trade*.

roundheels *American* a promiscuous woman
Like the unsuccessful boxer, the shape of
whose *heels* facilitates a quick descent to the
canvas.

routine (nursing) care only allow to die
Hospital jargon for the procedure where extra
medication or resuscitation would only pro-
long suffering.

roving eye a tendency towards promiscuity
Usually, but not exclusively, an ocular affliction of males and not referring to the
ceaseless vigilance of a mariner on watch.
A male who so behaves may be known as a
rover, although not often, because of a
possible canine confusion.

rub off to masturbate
Usually of a male. Also as *rub up* or *rub yourself*.

To *rub the bacon* or *rub the pork* is to copulate, describing the action of either or both parties.

rub out to kill
The act of erasing.

rubber *American* a contraceptive sheath
A usage for what in the British Isles used to be an inoffensive article of stationery.
The synonym *rubber johnny* is common but *rubber cookie* is rare.
A merchant advertising *rubber goods* may sell sexual apparatus as well as contraceptives.

rubber cheque a cheque which is dishonoured
It is liable to BOUNCE².

rubber heel *American* a detective
From their habit of walking around quietly.

ruddy a mild oath
Literally, glowing with a pink hue. Used in place of the once taboo bloody.

rude noise a belch or fart
Which a child may say it has made, or be reprimanded for making.

rug a wig worn by a male
The covering of a bare area.
Whence the figurative use of exasperation, to *pull your rug out in handfuls* etc.

ruin *obsolete* to copulate with (a female) outside marriage
The implication was that her marriageable worth had been lowered.
Such a female would have been said to have been *ruined in character*.

rum-johnny *obsolete* the Indian mistress of a white man
She didn't drink alcohol but was so called through a corruption of *ramjani*, a dancing girl in Hindi, or *rama-jani* in Sanskrit.
Do not confuse this meaning with the similar corruption of *Ramazami* (a common Muslim name) to *rum-johnny*, which referred to Indian servants seeking work from new European arrivals in the port of Calcutta.

rumble to steal
Probably from the name of the improvised seat at the back of the carriage, a hackney coach or *rumbler*, from which servants might pass purloined goods to an accomplice, or *running rumbler*, in the street. *Rumble* is still used of casual thefts of inventory by an employee.

run¹ to smuggle
From the meaning, a single trip or excursion. We still have to live with *gunrunners*.

run² to desert or flee from a field of battle
The direction is always away from perceived danger:
    What? Do they run already? Then I die happy. (General Wolfe, 1759, as Montcalm's troops fled from the Heights of Abraham in Quebec)
To be ON THE RUN is to be fugitive.

run³ an unexpected and sustained series of demands on a bank for repayment
The phenomenon occurs when depositors fear for their savings.

run⁴ (the) peremptory dismissal from employment
A mordant wit may also give you your *running shoes*.

run⁵ deliberately to ignore
When we disobey traffic signals:
    She ran a red light and turned a corner. (Follett, 1996—the lady was not a bawd who repented of her ways)

run (a)round the Horn *American* repeatedly to mislead, frustrate, or deceive
The fluctuating winds of the Cape so hindered the progress of sailing ships.
There is a specific use when the police move a suspect under arrest from one police station to another to frustrate a lawyer trying to gain access. Also as *waltz around the Horn*.

run around with to have a sexual relationship with
Not just jogging in the park. In normal use, to comport with socially on a regular basis.

run away permanently to leave the matrimonial home
The action usually of a wife, but not necessarily with or for another man.
Husbands are more likely to *run off*.

run off an act of urination
Like emptying a tub.

run on (a) menstruation
Common female usage.

runner¹ *obsolete* a policeman
Today they all ride around in pairs and cars, although the Victorian *runners* were not renowned for their youth or celerity. (As with RUN¹, there are many euphemistic meanings for *runner*, including smuggler, fugitive, conveyor of illegal bets, etc.)

runner² an escape
From *running away*. Thus to *do a runner* is not to repair a curtain or assault an athlete, but to make yourself scarce.

runner³ a person who introduces business surreptitiously

Perhaps from the old-fashioned *bookies' runner*, who collected illegal bets. This *runner* however may remain stationary:

> He knew the guys on the rigs, and when there was a death or injury he'd get the case. I'd give him a nice percentage. Gotta take care of your runners. (Grisham, 2002)

runny nose an addiction to cocaine

From sniffing it and the consequent damage to the nasal tissue.

runny tummy (a) diarrhoea

Referring to the looseness of the stool rather than *running* to a lavatory. Also as the *runs*.

rush job the marriage of a pregnant bride

The hastily arranged wedding used to be to the putative father.

rush the growler *American* to send for beer to drink at home

A *growler* is a large pitcher. If you dallied on the return journey, the beer might become warm.

rusticate to banish

Standard English of dismissing British students from university for a while because of idleness or misconduct, even if they continue to reside in a town. The Chinese Communists take things more literally:

> His parents had been rusticated—sent shovelling. (Theroux, 1988—they were city dwellers banished to the countryside)

S

sack (the) dismissal from employment
In the days when workmen had to provide
their own tools, they were kept in a bag or
sack at the employer's workshop, or carried in
them to work. To be given it, or *sacked*, by
your master meant you were dismissed.
An unsatisfactory member of the Sultan of
Turkey's harem who *got the sack* received
more peremptory and drastic treatment: she
was stitched up in one and thrown into the
Bosporus.

sacrifice your honour (of a female) to
copulate outside marriage
The usage, and the concept which led to it,
may well be obsolete in western society.

saddle soap flattery
Its quality is to make the seat more comfortable by softening it.

saddle up with (of a male) to copulate
with
The common equine imagery. Also as *get in the
saddle*.

safe house a refuge
Not merely one which is unlikely to collapse.

safe sex sexual activity with another in
which a protective sheath is used
No longer merely worrying about an unwanted pregnancy or a curable disease.
Safer sex means the same thing.

safety *American* a contraceptive sheath
The use pre-dates SAFE SEX. Also called a *safe*.

safety camera a roadside radar camera
recording vehicle speed
The *speed camera* is unpopular with motorists
who suspect it is used as a device for raising
taxes rather than achieving road safety:
> In a bid to make speed cameras more
> 'consumer friendly', the Department of
> Transport is intending to rebrand them
> 'safety cameras' in its official documents.
> (*Sunday Telegraph*, 5 May 2002)

St Colman's girdle has lost its virtue
obsolete there has been extramarital
copulation
The mythical but magical garment encircled
only those who were chaste. The euphemism
was used in 1890 when Parnell's adultery
with Katie O'Shea, which had been widely
known in political circles but not publicized,

was exposed in open court, thereby ruining
his career.

salami achieving an unpopular or deceitful result by small increments
Cutting into the sausage slice by slice, as with
the Communist *salami tactics* in Hungary after
the Second World War; or stealing regularly
from another in small amounts; or overcharging by deducting more than one fee:
> ... the salami shares of costs which have
> stood between the policyholder and the
> value of assets his money has bought. (*Daily
> Telegraph*, 30 May 2003)

salt to cheat by improper addition
Normally, to add salt to food, to improve or
disguise its taste. The common euphemistic
use is in mining, where valuable ores or
minerals are introduced into samples to
deceive assayers and investors.
Accounts may also be *salted*, with non-existent
deliveries being charged or excessive prices
claimed.

salvage to steal
Mainly Second World War usage, when
advancing troops came across a lot of abandoned property.

Sam *American* a policeman
Especially if on counter-narcotic duties for
Uncle Sam.

same gender oriented *American* homosexual
SGO for short, and not just referring to those
who prefer the social company of others of
their own sex.

sample a quantity of urine
Medical jargon. If a nurse asks you to provide
a *sample*, it might as well be of saliva or blood
or just about anything, but it isn't.

sand rat *British* a cheap prostitute
Army use in the Far East, from the prevalent
rodent in bashas, or sleeping huts.

Sandy McNabs *British* crab lice
Army rhyming slang on crabs, or *Phthirus
pubis*, the proper name indicating where the
infection, usually sexually transmitted, is to
be found.

sanitary man a cleaner of lavatories
Sanitary means pertaining to health. For the
avoidance of doubt, the British *sanitary inspector* is now styled a Public Health Inspector.
The American *sanitation man* collects garbage.

sanitary stop an opportunity to urinate
A phrase used by Montgomery to Churchill:
> After we had been dwiving for an hour,
> I said to [Churchill], Pwime Minister, would

you like a sanitary stop? (Attenborough, 2002—Churchill decided to wait 40 minutes so that he could piss on the Siegfried Line)

sanitary towel an absorbent padding worn during menstruation
Once again health and cleanliness are confused.
Also as *ST* and, in America, as *sanitary napkin*.

sanitized cleaned or rendered harmless
You read it on the irritating paper strips across lavatory bowls and toothmugs in certain types of hotel which need to convince you that they clean the rooms between customers.
Also of files etc. from which damaging evidence has been eliminated:
Erlichman says he never received that material, and doesn't know whether he got all of what Welander had turned over to Haig, or if the batch was sanitized by either man. (Colodny & Gettlin, 1991)

Sappho a homosexual female
From the poetess who lived on Lesbos, thus twice enriching the language.
Sapphic is used as a noun and as an adjective.

Sarah *American* a wealthy divorced woman
Having had a rich husband and a good lawyer:
... Sarahs (Single, [and] rich and happy) who have made their cash through clever wrangling in the divorce courts. (*Daily Telegraph*, 22 April 2005)

sartorially challenged badly dressed
An extension of the CHALLENGED theme which has added a new dimension to the world of euphemism:
The sartorially-challenged Sir John Harvey-Jones ... (*Daily Telegraph*, 30 March 1994—Sir John was not considered a snappy dresser)

satisfaction *obsolete* the acceptance of a challenge to a duel
Whatever the outcome:
My first impulse was to ask him for an explanation, and for satisfaction. (O'Brian, 1970)

sauce (the) intoxicants
Usually spirits and implying excess. Someone *on the sauce* is either an alcoholic or has been on a carouse.
See also GRAVY.

sauna a brothel
Since antiquity public wash houses have catered for other masculine needs than cleanliness:
... more magazines restrict advertisements for 'saunas' or 'escorts' to a few pages. (*Sunday Telegraph*, 28 August 1994,

reporting on attempts to curtail advertising by prostitutes)
You are, however, more likely to be offered a sauna in a sauna parlour than a massage in a MASSAGE PARLOUR.

save to spend
A commercial inducement to buy something you don't need because of a supposed reduction in price. The British *saver fare* on railways was a cheaper one offering less comfort and convenience.
A single woman who *saved it*, refused to copulate before marriage:
A wet tongue kiss, a few minutes in their arms ... but ... she was saving it for her husband. (Longstreet, 1956)

say a few words to make a speech
Would that they were only a few on most occasions.

say goodbye to to dismiss from employment
Not just parting for the day:
This will leave the streamlined Corus, which has also said goodbye to 10,000 workers, ready to take advantage of the rising price of steel. (*Daily Telegraph*, 2 July 2002)

scald *obsolete* to infect with a venereal disease
From the burning sensation, especially in the male, who might have been infected in a *scalding-house*, or brothel.

scalp to kill
Originally the scalp was the skull, as in the American *scalp dolly*, or wig, and thence the hair on the head. The verb form arose from the practice of the American Indians, in which the skin and hair were removed from their victims both to prove their success and to retain as a trophy.
To *scalp* is also used figuratively meaning to cheat, in a commercial transaction:
... her air of innocence made her seem like a tout; and yet she did not scalp me, but asked for the exact price that was printed on the ticket. (Theroux, 1995)

scandal sheet a form on which expenses are claimed
Because of the outrageous greed of some of the items included.
A *scandal sheet* is, in common use, a newspaper which features lurid or sensational stories.
For the Red Army in Berlin in 1945 *scandalous events* included the rape and murder of German civilians:
On 3 August, three months after the surrender of Berlin, Zhukov had to issue even tougher regulations to control

'robbery', 'physical violence', and 'scandalous events'. (Beevor, 2002)

scarlet woman a prostitute
The woman 'arrayed in purple and scarlet colour... THE MOTHER OF HARLOTS' (*Revelations* 17:4/5), whence any adulteress.
Our Protestant ancestors found it a useful abusive epithet for the Church of Rome.
Whence the obsolete *scarlet fever*, or lust for soldiers, involving a treble pun—on the disease, on the colour of their uniform, and on the activities of the *scarlet woman*.

scheduled classes those condemned by birth to menial employment
Indian society retains gradations which would provide endless occupation for those whose function it is to seize upon and punish any form of DISCRIMINATION:
... the Dulits (or scheduled classes or harijans or untouchables, to take the wounding nomenclature back through its earlier stages)... (Naipaul, 1990)

school *American* a prison
The *big school* is for men and the *little school* for women and children.

scissor-and-paste job a book or article not based on original research
The author figuratively clips and inserts material from published sources.

scoop an alcoholic drink
This was the method of taking potable liquid for sale from a large container in the days before environmental health officers were invented and the public lost much of its gastric immunity to a measure of impurity in foodstuffs:
They did this every Christmas, went to one of their houses and had a few scoops before the dinner. (Doyle, 1991)

scope for modernization ramshackle
One of the coded phrases used by estate agents when selling a property in a bad state of repair.

scorch eliminator a fire extinguisher
Early Xerox copying machines had a tendency to catch fire. Implicit admission of the fault by incorporating a fire extinguisher would have damaged sales in a way that the *scorch eliminator* did not.

scorched *American* drunk or under the influence of illegal narcotics
After you BURN WITH A (LOW) BLUE FLAME? A bit far-fetched, but the imagery is the same.

score[1] succeed in copulating with a female
Usually of a single episode on a casual basis without payment:
Brunton was all set to score with a Moral Philosophy student in his rooms—a female student. (Price, 1979—but clearly not that moral)
The punning *know the score* is to be sexually experienced, of both men and women.

score[2] to commit a crime successfully
Mainly of theft carried out to buy illegal narcotics.
To *score* can also mean to buy or to ingest such narcotics.

score adjustment *American* giving higher marks to non-whites
A device to conceal lower scholastic achievement or to compensate for inadequate schooling etc.:
The little-known practice is also referred to in certain government and employment circles as 'within-group norming' or 'score adjustment strategy'. (*Chicago Times*, 14 May 1991)

Scotch mist *British* drunk
Rhyming slang on PISSED, punning on the drizzle which blots out the landscape, and on the whisky.

scour to administer a laxative to
Literally, to clean thoroughly the inside of anything. A beast with *scour* has diarrhoea, which humans also caught from bad beer, or *scour-the-gate*.
The *scours* is diarrhoea.

scrag to kill
From the meaning, neck, whence death by throttling or garrotting.

scratch[1] *obsolete* the devil
Because of his propensity to 'seize rapaciously' (*OED*). Usually as *old scratch*.

scratch[2] a wound
A brave soldier seeks to minimize the extent of his injury:
She gave a little scream. 'You are wounded! Your arm!' 'It's a scratch, nothing more.' (Fraser, 1970)

scratch[3] *American* to kill
Literally, to retire from a contest by eliminating your name from a list.

screw[1] (of a male) to copulate with
Referring to the entry into a reciprocal aperture.

Either sex may be said to *screw around*, to copulate indiscriminately.

A *screw* is a female sexual partner, always with a laudatory adjective. As I note elsewhere, in male vanity or fantasy, there are no bad *screws*. Also figurative use as an expletive:

> She was drowned out by a chorus of 'Screw the profiteers'. (Hailey, 1979)

screw² a prison warder

Not from turning the key in the lock so much as from tightening the screw on the apparatus on which a prisoner underwent forced exercise, or hard labour.

screw³ to cheat

A venerable standard English usage, from the accentuated application of force implicit in the *screwing* process. It is the victim who usually so refers to his plight in the passive sense:

> Your chance of being screwed by a Canadian factory owner then were as good as your chance of being screwed by an American factory owner. (*Sunday Night Toronto*, 12 February 1974)

screw loose (a) mental instability

The imagery is from falling apart.

Whence *screwy*, having an abnormal mental condition or behaving in an eccentric manner. The American *screw factory* is an institution for the mentally ill.

To be *screwed up* is to be confused or upset, while to *screw up* is to handle a situation badly.

screwed drunk

Probably a pun on TIGHT¹.

To be *half-screwed* is to be no more sober.

screwed down dead

As the coffin is sealed after a last peep at the corpse:

> Then don't talk as if I'd been screwed down. (Cookson, 1967)

scrubber a prostitute

Of the meaner sort, perhaps from the status and posture of the floor cleaner.

A London *Times* 1972 headline 'Heath's Whitehall Scrubbers' Party' was changed in the second edition to 'Celebrating a Whiter Whitehall', without giving the office cleaners time to consult their lawyers.

scuttered *Irish* drunk

The *EDD* gives thirteen definitions of dialect meanings for *scutter*, including to make short runs or have diarrhoea, which have some association with the symptoms of drunkenness:

> Having one of those beside the bed would have been very handy for when you come home scuttered at night. (Doyle, 1991, referring to a machine to help those with bad eyesight)

sea food *obsolete American* whisky

A Prohibition use 'to mislead the police or strangers' (*DAS*). Most bootleg liquor came by sea or over the Great Lakes.

sea-lawyer see BARRACK-ROOM LAWYER

season (the) the annual period in which upper-class marriageable girls were put on display

In the days when COME OUT meant no more than to appear in society:

> 'The Season' being a sort of ritual marriage market to which every parent then subscribed anxiously. (Blanch, 1954—not every parent, only the rich ones)

seasonal ownership an entitlement to occupy for a limited period

TIME-SHARE having become no longer acceptable as a term to describe the sale of limited rights to occupy premises subject to the payment of uncertain annual charges, the marketing teams have to come up with phrases less redolent of thievery:

> A spectacular Scottish second home with en suite 5 star hotel...Select your chosen week (or weeks)...Gleneagles Seasonal Ownership. (advertisement in *Daily Telegraph*, 6 February 2004—most of us would be content with an en suite bathroom)

seat the buttocks

A transference from the thing you sit upon to the part of the body on which you sit. As with BOTTOM, a familiar coy evasion.

The American *seat cover* is a nubile female in a car:

> Lay an eyeball on that seat cover comin' up in that show-off lane. (Dills, 1976)

and to *check the seat covers* in Citizens' Band slang is to look for or at an attractive woman in a car.

secluded inconveniently isolated

Estate agent's jargon to describe a house with limited or no access to public transport, utilities, shops, etc.

Seclusion, for a violent criminal or lunatic, is involuntary solitary confinement.

second eye see BRONZE EYE

second strike retaliation

Nuclear warfare jargon, and not a further blow from the party making the FIRST STRIKE. A *second-strike capability* is your ability to reply in kind to a nuclear attack, inflicting *second-strike destruction*.

secret parts the human genitalia

Those not generally revealed in company rather than the subject of ignorance:

Hamlet Then you live about her waist, or in the middle of her favours?
Guildenstern Faith, her privates we.
Hamlet In the secret parts of fortune? O, most true, she is a strumpet. (Shakespeare, *Hamlet*)

secret (state) police an instrument of civil repression
The full phrase is a literal translation of *Geheime Staatspolizei*, which we all recognize in its shortened form, *Gestapo*. Every tyranny needs its *secret police* if it is to survive.

secret vice (the) masturbation
Of either sex, but usually a male.
Also as the *secret sin* or *secret indulgence*.

section *British* to detain involuntarily in a mental hospital
Social service jargon, from *sections two* and *three* of the Act which empowers such confinement:
Should she be sectioned under the Mental Health Act and forced back into hospital? (*London Times*, 19 October 1991)
Under American service regulations during the Second World War, the equivalent section was numbered eight:
You hold on... Or you get shipped home on a Section Eight. (Deighton, 1982, writing about American wartime fliers)

security an excuse for aggression, espionage, or repression
For Hitler, the invasion of neighbouring states.
For Senator Joseph McCarthy, a *security risk* was anyone he disagreed with. For despots, a *security service* concerns itself with the survival of the rulers and not the safety of the ruled. The system was exported by Soviet Russia to client states through *security advisers*:
Shehu made the way easy for the rapid growth at the end of 1945 of a Soviet military mission [to Albania] to which 'security advisers'—dull euphemism for torturers...—were already attached. (H. Thomas, 1986)
A *security service*, even in a democracy, is likely to act illegally.
During the Second World War, the Nazis made much use of *security battalions*, which were recruited from those they had conquered, to enforce their rule. These often acted with more ruthlessness and sadism than soldiers from the Wehrmacht.

seduce to persuade a woman to copulate with you extramaritally
Originally, to persuade a vassal to break his vows of loyalty:
By long and vehement suit I was seduced

To make room for him in my husband's bed. (Shakespeare, *King John*)
In modern use, there seems to be less long and vehement suit.

see[1] to have a sexual relationship with
Of either sex, and in the sense 'to visit' rather than 'to observe'. A woman who is *seeing* a man is doing more than merely looking at him. A prostitute who *sees* a man copulates with him:
Thousands of women... from eastern Europe... are kept as slaves, raped, beaten and forced to see up to 30 clients a day. (*Sunday Telegraph*, 1 January 2006)

see[2] to satisfy by bribery
As in the American *see the cops*:
... doing business without seeing the cops. (Lavine, 1930)
Lavine also uses *see* for sharing a bribe with a superior:
Woe to the cop who collects anything... and doesn't 'see the sergeant'. (ibid.)

see a man about a dog to go to any place that is the subject of taboo or embarrassment
Dog fancying is a sport which might call you away unexpectedly. The dog's location depends on the company you keep—a lavatory, in mixed society; an inn, in the presence of your family at home; home, if you are with friends in an inn; and so on.

see the rosebed (of a male) to urinate out of doors
Usually in mixed company, when the indoor lavatory is reserved for use by the females. He may elect to see many other outdoor locations, such as *the view* or the *compost heap*.
To *see your aunt*, normally in female use, involves a visit to the lavatory, or AUNT[2], indoors.

see to to inflict on or provide a taboo service for
Literally, to attend to. Of criminal violence and sexual activity:
There's something melancholy about her though, she looks to me as if she hasn't had a good seeing to, I shouldn't think she's had it since her husband died. (Lodge, 2001)

seed the male semen
That which is sown:
She that sets seeds and roots of shame and iniquity. (Shakespeare, *Pericles*—involving two vulgar puns)
In the days of Victorian prudery, the American *seed-ox* was a bull.

seek fresh challenges to be summarily dismissed from employment
One of the excuses given when senior managers are dismissed. Their main challenge is often to find another job.

seen better days poor
It describes people who have fallen on hard times or machinery which is worn out.

seepage the amount stolen from a retail store
Literally, the liquid which has slowly escaped from a container.

segregation the availability of inferior facilities for a minority ethnic group
Literally, no more than separating one thing from another. A dysphemism in America and South Africa for giving whites better conditions than blacks.
A *segregation unit*, in American prison jargon, is a cell for the solitary confinement of a prisoner.

select capable of being offered for sale
Shopkeepers' puff for perishable commodities which are unsaleable when rotten. Things so described are unlikely to have been subjected to any process of *selection*. For an estate agent, *select* means no more than better than average—you can reject any implication that there has been any discrimination in their choice of what they will try to sell.

selected out dismissed from employment
Sam Goldwyn, famous for such contradictory catchphrases as 'include me out', would have been proud of it.

selective indiscriminate
It denotes various military activities, where you wish to play down the horror.
Selective ordnance is usually napalm, less widely destructive than a nuclear blast but hardly discriminating in its victims.
A *selective strike* or *response* is one where you don't intentionally wipe out civilians as well as soldiers.
Selective facts are lies.
Selective distribution, conversely, is a policy whereby a manufacturer sells only to the retail outlets which keep the prices high.

self-abuse[1] masturbation
Usually by a male, from the supposition that he may be damaging his body or soul—or go blind. Also as *self-gratification*, *self-indulgence*, or *self-manipulation*.
Self-pollution and *self-pleasuring* are obsolete. *Self-love* usually refers to female masturbation, but without any implication of narcissism.

self-abuse[2] inflicting injury on yourself
To attract attention or through mental illness:
Self-abuse is often one of the reasons they move offenders so quickly. It's not unknown for a prisoner who is kept in lock-up overnight to cut his wrists. (Archer, 2004)

self-defence an unannounced military attack
Specifically, the explanation given by Iraq for its September 1980 unprovoked assault on Iran.

self-deliverance suicide
Deliverance is the preferred usage of those who advocate euthanasia.
You may also hear of *self-destruction*, *-execution*, *-immolation*, or *-violence*.

sell out to betray
But not necessarily for cash.
A *sell-out* is such betrayal, or any agreement of which you happen to disapprove, such as the settlement of a trade dispute.

sell yourself to be a prostitute
Correctly viewed, the transaction is at best one of hire, lease, or licence. Also as *sell your back*, *body*, or *desires*:
A housewife that, by selling her desires,
Buys herself bread and clothes.
(Shakespeare, *Othello*)
A politician or candidate who *sells himself* does no more than to try to convince others of his worth.

semi-detached (of a house) sharing a party wall
The standard English usage avoids direct mention of the fact that the house is not separate from its neighbour:
And the novel's title was the first recorded use (in 1859) of the word 'semi-detached'. 'Double cottages' built with a shared party wall had been common in the eighteenth century. (Muir, 1990)

send ashore to dismiss from the navy
A figurative use, covering misconduct on land or at sea.

send away to commit involuntarily to an institution
Not going on holiday:
You can stay with the firm... assuming the IRS doesn't send you away. (Grisham, 1999—he had been evading tax)

send down to dismiss
Of students expelled from a British university, and the opposite of *go up*, to take up residence.

Also of prisoners in the dock after being sentenced, the cells usually being below the courtroom.

Send down the road, to dismiss from employment, is probably obsolete.

send in your papers *British* (of an officer) to retire prematurely

From the figurative return to the sovereign of the commission addressed individually to each officer. The act describes voluntary as well as unplanned retirement.

send to heaven to kill

The destination depends on your religion and nationality. Thus a Christian might also be *sent home, to his last* or *long account*, etc. An American Indian, in a Western at least, might be *sent to his happy hunting grounds* while a Chinese person might be *sent to the happy land* or *to the land of the lotus blossom*.

send to the showers *American* to dismiss from a game

By the referee for foul play or the coach for indifferent performance. British players so treated TAKE AN EARLY BATH.

send up to pass a prison sentence upon

The prisons of New York and New Orleans were upstream of the cities, and convicts were *sent up the river* or *line* of which this is a shortened, and confusing, form, meaning the same as SEND DOWN.

senior citizen an old person

As *senior* comes from the Latin *senex*, this is arguably not a euphemism, merely a cloying evasion. Also shortened to *seniors*.

senior moment (a) temporary forgetfulness

When Memory Lane runs into Amnesia Avenue.

sensible unfashionable but practical

It is used to describe women's shoes and clothes, perhaps with supposed transference from the wearer.

sensitive payment a bribe

So described because of its impropriety and probable illegality in the hands of the recipient, if others find out about it. If the person paying the bribe is American or British, the payment is illegal for him as well.

sent drunk or under the influence of illegal narcotics

The subject has passed to another stage of consciousness, if not unconsciousness.

sent home in a body bag *American* killed

How American dead service personnel are returned for burial in the United States. The phrase is used emotionally by those Americans opposed to military involvement abroad.

separate¹ to dismiss from employment

Literally, to cause to part. Now rare.

separate² to cease living together as man and wife

As distinct from what happens when they go about their respective daily business. Those who are *separated* in this sense are living apart from their spouses without the intention of resuming cohabitation in future, but not, or not yet, divorced. Their condition, *separation*, has a precise legal meaning.

separate but equal *American* subject to inferior and humiliating treatment

An interim stage in the relaxation of laws enforcing the supremacy of white people over black:

> ...the case of Brown v the Board of Education, a test case of 'separate but equal' development that would . demonstrate what Negro lives were really worth in the Delta. (Faulks, 2001)

separate development *South African* the suppression of a black majority by a white minority

The unfair and discredited *apartheid* which, although professing that black citizens should be SEPARATE BUT EQUAL, ensured that they were not.

separation death

Usually spoken of a spouse, although it might refer to the body and the soul going their different ways:

> The dreadful shock of separation took place in the night. (J. Boswell, 1791—Dr Johnson's wife had died)

seraglio a brothel

Originally, the palace of the Turkish sultan in the Golden Horn, of which a part only was the harem, or secret spot.

serpent a penis

The imagery is obvious. A girl STUNG BY A SERPENT has received an unwanted, though perhaps not unexpected, shock.

servant *obsolete American* a slave

An antebellum usage in the Southern states.

serve to copulate with

In standard usage, of male animals, and a fruitful ground for innuendo, as in the television comedy series set in a store and entitled *Are You Being Served?*
Specifically as *serve your lust*:

I would we had a thousand Roman dames
At such a bay; by turn to serve our lust.
(Shakespeare, *Titus Andronicus*)

service¹ to engage in a sexual act with
another
Standard English for arranged copulation by a
bull or stallion with a cow or mare. In vulgar
speech of humans:
> Aldo had walked in while he was servicing
> the cigarette girl over his desk. (J. Collins,
> 1981)

The punning American *service station* is a brothel.
Services are acts performed by prostitutes:
> Will would leave him next day—leave him
> to take up with another man who would
> want his 'services' and pay handsomely for
> them. (Tremain, 2003)

service² a charge additional to the cost of
the goods supplied
As levied in some restaurants regardless of the
quality of the attendance. The roadside *service
station* is a misnomer, as the motorist is
usually expected to attend to his own needs
and get his hands stinking of fuel, except
where he finds the tautological announcement *Attended Service*.

service lawyer *American* a clerk in a law
office
Not unlike what the English used to call
managing clerks (before status deprivation
changed them into legal executives):
> He is what they call a 'service lawyer', like
> me, somebody who does the work that one
> of our hotshot partners has been hired for.
> (Turow, 1993)

services no longer required dismissed
from employment
The blow is perhaps softened by the implication that the function no longer exists:
> I was given a discharge, ostensibly on the
> grounds that my services 'were no longer
> required', this being a curious euphemism.
> (Jones, 1978—Jones was the outstanding
> British scientist of the Second World War)

set aside *American* the reservation of jobs
or contracts for those who are not white
males
Thus, for example, the City of San Francisco
ordained that four-fifths of its legal services
must be conducted by Asians, Latins, blacks, or
women. There were however escape routes:
> A white who claimed to be five-eighths
> Indian could not be easily convicted of
> fraud even if he did it to get a set-aside
> contract. (P. Johnson, 1997)

set back to cause (a person) to pay a cost
that cannot easily be afforded
Literally, to cause a reverse or relapse.

set up¹ to provide accommodation for (a
mistress)
From the meaning, to establish. The object of
the setter-up is to keep her away from others,
if he can:
> When Christine refused to leave Ward and
> be set up in a flat, [Profumo] refused to
> meet her. (S. Green, 1979)

set up² to incriminate falsely
As with skittles, for the purpose of knocking
them down again:
> They 'set up' MacLennan in an attempt to
> discredit him. (*Private Eye*, July 1980)

set up shop on Goodwin Sands *obsolete* to
be shipwrecked off the Kent coast
A low-lying island of some 4,000 acres in the
English Channel was taken from (and named
after) the Anglo-Saxon Earl Godwin by the
Norman conquerors and handed over to
clerics who neglected the sea walls. A great
storm overwhelmed it in 1100. Since then the
land has remained a hazard to shipping,
emerging above the waves to a varying extent
at each low tide.

settle¹ to kill
Literally, to reach a conclusion.
To *settle someone's hash* may mean no more
than to repay an injury or disservice.

settle² to conquer and appropriate
The language of aggression and imperialism.
Whence the *settler*, who goes to live in
conquered territory:
> Rubin resists calls to evict settlers. (*Daily
> Telegraph*, 7 March 1994, writing about Jews
> who had taken over part of the city of
> Hebron)

Such communities living among or replacing
the indigenous population are called *settle-
ments*:
> The settlements are usually built on
> hilltops outside Arab towns and villages.
> (ibid.)

settled *Irish* unlikely ever to marry
A use in a community where remoteness,
differences in religion, and tribalism often
combined to limit the catchment area, especially for a bride:
> Being generally regarded as 'settled' in the
> expressive Irish phrase, into single
> blessedness, he sprang it on all of us that
> was going to be married to a schoolteacher.
> (Fingall, 1977)

seven-year itch a wish for extramarital
sexual variety
Seven years is the classic cycle of change.
See also ITCH.

severance dismissal from employment
A kind of cutting:

> She would call her lawyer about the tedious
> details of her severance. (Evans, 1995—she had
> not lost a husband or a limb, but been dismissed)

Whence *severance pay*, the compensation for
losing the job.

sewage a noxious domestic discharge
Originally, no more than a draining of water.
Standard English for centuries.

sewn up[1] pregnant
Perhaps from the meaning, stitched up, being
placed in a compromising or difficult position; or from the meaning, finally arranged;
or even from the distended appearance.

sewn up[2] *American* drunk
A variant of STITCHED.

sex[1] copulation
Literally, the classifications male and female,
although the euphemistic use has long been
standard English. Heterosexually or homo
sexually.

Sex love is obsolete:

> Katie told [Parnell] in 1891 ... that 'sex love'
> between herself and Willie was 'long-since
> dead'. (Kee, 1993—Katie was Mrs O'Shea
> and Willie was her husband)

The American *sex worker* is a prostitute,
although I prefer, etymologically speaking,
the alternative form *sex care provider*, whose
therapy is strictly non-medical.

sex[2] the penis or vagina
Referring to their reproductive function.

sex and travel alluding to a vulgar riposte
A variant of the common vulgarism *fuck off*:

> Bert's reply was always related to sex and
> travel. (Rowlands, 1990)

sexual ambiguity having bisexual tastes
Ambiguity here does not usually imply doubt or
uncertainty—rather it indicates over-catholic
tastes.

sexual assault *obsolete* an unsuccessful
attempt at rape
Nowadays no longer a euphemism but:

> 'Sexual assault' is the euphemism for the
> rape that fails ... Sexual assault depended
> on the time and place. (Pearsall, 1969,
> writing about 19th-century usage)

sexual intercourse copulation

Not just dealings or conversation between
individuals. Now standard English.

Sexual commerce is archaic, and there was no
suggestion in the phrase that anybody was
getting paid for their services.

Sexual congress does not refer to goings-on on
or around Capitol Hill.

Sexual conjunction sounds more like differentiating grammatically between the masculine
and feminine cases.

Sexual knowledge, which is usually had by an
adult male with an under-age girl, does not
mean simply that she has been told about the
birds and the bees.

Sexual relations may also imply familiarities
short of copulation, and *sexual relief* refers to
what the male obtains, implying that his
health might suffer from an excess of celibacy. *Sexual liaison* in this sense is rare:

> [Mao] believed, as some Chinese emperors
> had believed, that sexual liaison with
> young virgins enhanced the chance of
> longevity in an old man. (Cheng, 1984—or
> it made a convenient excuse)

These concepts are further explored at COM-
MERCE, CONGRESS, INTERCOURSE, KNOW, etc.

sexual preference homosexuality
Not *preference* in the heterosexual sense,
whereby gentlemen may prefer blondes and
ladies relish moustaches:

> ... impossible to ask questions about (as
> they said on the current affairs
> programmes) Ron's 'sexual preference'.
> (Keneally, 1985)

Also as *sexual irregularity, orientation, proclivity,* or
tropism—the last being normally a vegetable
rather than an animal reaction to a stimulus.
To be *sexually non-conformist* is to be homosexual
or bisexual, but not abstinent, and the notorious Cambridge traitors Blunt, Philby, McLean,
Burgess, and Cairncross were so described
(*Daily Telegraph*, 5 April 1998).

Sexual variety may mean no more than
promiscuity.

shack up (with) to cohabit in an extramarital sexual relationship
A *shack* is a rudely built rural residence, but
the arrangement so described usually has a
degree of permanence.

shade[1] to reduce in price
Commercial jargon, for making the price a
shade less than it was. A genteel usage in a shop
where overt haggling is frowned upon.

shade[2] *American* to influence illegally
It describes an act done out of the glare of full
light:

> My guess is they think your buddy Orleans
> there has been shading games. (Turow,
> 1993—Orleans was a basketball referee)

A *shade* is also a dealer in stolen goods, working in the shadows.

shaft¹ (of a male) to copulate with
The imagery is from the insertion of a spindle into a bore. Also as a noun:
> ...the old thing had no trouble, even across the dividing decades, in spotting him as a king of shaft. (Amis, 1988)

To confuse matters, in vulgar speech the *shaft* may be either the penis, from the handle of a tool or other rigid object; or the vagina, a space into which an object may be inserted and move smoothly up and down, as in an elevator shaft.

shaft² to deceive or betray
Originally an American slang meaning, presumably from being struck by such an object.

shag¹ to copulate with
The derivation is perhaps from the old meanings, to shake or to wrestle with—the cormorant is certainly not a renowned sexual performer. Men usually do the *shagging*.
The main use of females is in the cliché *She shags like a rattlesnake*, using daunting imagery.

shag² to masturbate yourself
Usually of boys, again from the shaking.

shake¹ to rob
By violence or trickery:
> How much you shake him for? (Chandler, 1953)

To *shake down* is to rob or cheat through trickery rather than violence, and a *shakedown* is a fraudulent scheme.

shake² *American* an arrest
Police jargon, usually on trivial grounds to show activity, generate income, or fill a quota.

shake hands with the bishop (of a male) to urinate
An uncircumcised penis may resemble the chess piece:
> Help me to the toilet...I have to go and shake the bishop's hand. (Theroux, 1979, quoting Borges)

Others may *shake hands with their best friend, their wife's best friend*, or, with melancholy humour, *the unemployed* or *the unemployable*. In modern use, a female may *shake the lettuce*.

shake the pagoda tree *obsolete* to make a rapid fortune in India
Punning on the *pagoda*, an Indian gold coin.

shame extramarital copulation by a woman
What disgraced the female was thought less reprehensible in the male:

> Is't not a kind of incest, to take life
> From thine own sister's shame?
> (Shakespeare, *Measure for Measure*)

The *shame* was also one of the devil's names.

shanghai forcibly to abduct a person
Originally to replace a missing crew member in the crime-ridden city with another sailor rendered senseless and carried aboard ship before sailing, whence any forcible abduction.

share (someone's) affections to have an open adulterous relationship
Not just talking about the common love a parent will have for siblings:
> The mistress even suggested that his wife should contemporaneously share his affections. (*Daily Telegraph*, 1979)

To *share someone's bed* is to copulate with someone, the phrase not being used of married couples. An assumption is made that such proximity outside marriage will always overcome chastity or disinclination.

shared freehold an entitlement to occupy property for a limited period
Freeholds are only *shared* by joint tenants, tenants-in-common, and others named in the Land Registry as joint owners. This is another evasion thought up by an advertising agency to avoid referring to *time-share*:
> Fully furnished quality apartments from £17,000 shared freehold. (*Daily Telegraph*, 10 September 2005)

sharp elbows inconsiderate selfishness
Those so endowed thrust themselves forward in a throng:
> Things were not helped by Brian Redhead who had, shall we say, sharp elbows for a cuddly-looking man. (*Daily Telegraph*, 20 March 2001)

sharpen your pencil to alter your stance in bargaining
An injunction to the prospective seller to lower the price or the buyer to raise it:
> I am disappointed that we didn't get another [franchise]. But I did not want to sharpen my pencil as hard as some of the others have done...(*Sunday Telegraph*, 23 February 1997)

To be *sharp with the pencil* or *pen* is to be inclined to charge excessively and may be used to describe rapacious lawyers, although for some the use of the adjective may be thought tautological.

sharpener an intoxicating drink
Usually whisky or gin, which are supposed to liven you up:
> I managed to escape from Colditz for a sharpener or twain with the Major at the

RAC Club. (*Private Eye*, May 1981—*Colditz* was Number 10, Downing Street, where Denis Thatcher then lived)

shattered drunk
Now also used of narcotic addiction.

sheath a contraceptive worn by a male
Literally, the covering in which a blade is kept.
The rare *sheathe the sword* meant to copulate, using obvious imagery. In literal use, it meant to cease to fight.

sheep buck *obsolete American* a ram
Another example of 19th-century prudery about farm animals. Although a *buck* is a correct usage for the male of several quadrupeds, it is not of the genus *Ovis aries*. See also BIG ANIMAL for similar pruderies.

sheep's eyes (make) to indicate sexual attraction in a look
The derivation is from the ophthalmic dilation of those seeking to attract the attention of a potential mate, which makes them look ovine.

sheet in the wind (a) mildly drunk
A *sheet* is a rope tying a sail to a spar, not the sail itself as landlubbers sometimes assume. If one or more breaks loose, the vessel is in some disarray.
A drunkard may also be *three, four* or *several sheets in* or *to the wind*, but not, it seems, *two*.

sheets an allusion to copulation
Blankets and *mattresses*, but not yet *duvets* it would seem, are associated with the BED[2] of copulation:
    Happiness to their sheets. (Shakespeare, *Othello*)
In vulgar speech, *pressing the sheets* is not the action of a laundress going about her normal business.

shellacked *mainly American* very drunk
Literally, covered with shellac, a varnish which is stoved to give a glazed appearance. To be *shellacked* may also mean to be utterly defeated (*WCND*).

sheltered for those unable to look after themselves
It is used of accommodation where invalids or geriatrics can be watched over and helped, although it is no less likely to let in wind or water than the normal home.

shelved dismissed from employment
Normally describing those asked to retire early or overlooked for promotion because of their declining powers, from storing objects on a shelf:

... so that men who lack drive and imagination can, without undue cruelty, be shelved. (Colville, 1976)

sheriff's hotel *American* a prison
And in the old days to *dance at a sheriff's ball* used to mean you were killed by hanging.

shield *American* a policeman
From the badge.

shift(a) defecation
In the male vulgarism, *do a shift*, from the MOVEMENT.

shift expenses improperly seek to avoid the payment of higher taxes or interest charges
A widespread practice of multinational companies, including the most reputable, to conserve cash by paying the lowest possible sums in taxes, interest charges, licence fees, agents' commissions, and royalties through the manipulation of transfer prices between wholly owned subsidiaries operating in different jurisdictions:
    Investigators from a powerful Congressional committee investigating the WorldCom collapse are probing allegations of suspect practices in a British subsidiary. These include 'shifting expenses' totalling $33.6m, according to Washington officials. (*Sunday Telegraph*, 14 July 2002)

ship *American* to dismiss from employment
Likening the departure to the dispatch of goods from a warehouse. Sometimes also referring to the dismissal of a student from a college.

ship's lawyer see BARRACK-ROOM LAWYER

shirtlifter a male homosexual
The usage ignores the occasions on which heterosexual men lift their shirts and shirttails in the normal course of dressing and undressing. Also shortened to *lifter*.
Shirtlifting is sodomy.

shoo-in a favoured successor
Originally, in America, it described a horse chosen to win a race fraudulently, which was *shooed into* the winning post. Now only figurative use, occasionally mis-spelt as *shoe-in*:
    The old guard preferred Chernenko, but they had run out of options even before Chernenko died of emphysema in 1985. By the time Gorbachev came to London he was a shoe-in. (Simpson, 1998)

shoot[1] to kill or wound by a firearm
Literally, to discharge a projectile. This

standard use implies an accurate aim by the person who does the shooting.

shoot² (the) peremptory dismissal from employment

An unusual version of the FIRE theme.

shoot³ to inject an illegal narcotic intravenously

It has a direct passage into a vein.

shoot a line to boast

The imagery is probably not from whaling. Nowadays you are as likely, if so inclined, to *shoot the bull*, of which more under BULL²:

No-one lingers, no-one sits down and shoots the bull. (Theroux, 1988, writing of the aftermath of a Chinese banquet, not of a Spanish *corrida*)

Shooting the breeze is usually of male flirtation:

Inside, oblivious of all this, are the two highway policemen, sitting at the counter and shooting the breeze with the waitress. (Bryson, 1989)

The obsolete Scottish *shoot among the doves*, again meaning to boast, referred to the ease with which tame birds might be hit:

A lady...had heard her husband mention...that such a gentleman...was thought to shoot among the doves. She immediately took the alarm and said to him with great eagerness...'My husband says ye shoot among the doves. Now as I am very fond of my pigeons, I beg you winna meddle wi' them.' (*EDD*)

shoot a lion (of a male) to urinate

Usually he goes out of doors to do it. In America you are more likely to say that you are going to *shoot a dog*.

shoot off to ejaculate semen

Usually prematurely, under intense sexual excitement. To *shoot your load* or *shoot your roe* refers to any ejaculation. To *shoot over the stubble* was to ejaculate semen in a woman's pubic hair.

To *shoot between wind and water* was to infect with venereal disease, punning on the crippling shot to a sailing ship.

To *shoot blanks* is not to fire a starting pistol but, of a male, to be sexually impotent.

shoot the agate *American* to seek out a woman for sexual purposes

Derived from the name of an affected form of strutting seen in some parades by black people.

shoot the cat to become drunk

Originally, to vomit, from a similar tendency in cats.

shoot the moon see MOONLIGHT FLIT

shoot with a silver gun *obsolete* to be unable to provide meat by hunting

In those far-off days when a gentleman was supposed to keep the household supplied with fresh game birds in season by shooting them, and a lady was content to pluck, draw, hang, and cook them, it was thought demeaning if he had to go out and buy what he should have shot:

Shooting with a *silver gun* is a saying among game eaters. That is to say, *purchasing* the game. (Cobbett, 1830)

See also CATCH FISH WITH A SILVER HOOK.

shop¹ *American* to dismiss summarily from employment

This usage may be obsolete and the etymology is uncertain.

shop² to give information leading to arrest

You might suppose that, with the commercial imagery, the information would be sold, but most *shopping* occurs through malice or self-protection.

This criminal slang usage has nothing to do with the *cop-shop*, or police station.

shop door is open (the) your trousers are unfastened

An oblique warning, usually to another male, of an undone zip. If a portion of shirt-tail protrudes, you may be told you are *flying a flag*.

shoplift to pilfer from a shop

A prevalent variety of LIFT¹ and now standard English.

short¹ a measure of spirits

Shortened from *short drink* as different from a *long drink* like beer or cider.

short² a handgun

As different from a *long*, a rifle. Army jargon.

short-arm inspection an examination of servicemen for venereal disease

Punning on the regular rifle, or *small arm*, inspection and *short-arm*, the penis:

The mandatory 'short-arm inspections' for venereal disease gave many a Lothario his comeuppance. (Atkinson, 2003)

short arms an indication of stinginess

Showing a reluctance to reach for your wallet:

Ken [Thomson's pockets] were matched by remarkably short arms. (*Daily Telegraph*, 16 June 2006)

short hairs the pubic hair

Even though they may be more luxuriant than those on other parts of the body. The use is almost always in the figurative cliché:

I think I've got them by the short hairs.
(Sharpe, 1974)
The *short and curlies* is specific.

short illness (a) *American* suicide
A coded notice in an obituary.

short-shipped lost in transit
Airlines do not like talking about the luggage
which goes astray:
    'It's not lost,' said a BA spokesman, 'it's
    short-shipped.' (*Daily Telegraph*, 25
    September 1999)

short time a single act of copulation
Prostitutes' jargon for a contact with few pre-
liminaries and no sequel. Also as *short session(s)*.
If the hotel receptionist asks you whether you
need the room for *short-time* occupation, he
concludes you will be using the room for such
activity and you will be charged accordingly.
Short-term carries the same implication.

shorten the front (line)[1] to retreat under
pressure
Soldiers and their apologists thus explain a
defeat by implying that a salient is being
voluntarily abandoned:
    He was painfully familiar with the
    Fuehrer's attitude to 'shortening the front'
    under enemy pressure. (A. Clark, 1995)

shorten the front (line)[2] to lose weight
Punning on the military euphemism and
usually of men.

shortism the pursuit of quick profit
Financial jargon, especially of investors and
hedge funds who are unwilling to await
growth over the longer term and wish to cash
in regardless of the interests of other parties
such as employees.
Shortism, prejudice against people below normal height, is not a euphemism.

shorts (the) indigence
Usually of a temporary nature, being *short* of
cash until the next pay cheque.

shot[1] a measure of spirits
Probably from the way it is discharged into
the glass. In the British Isles it is usually
measured with an excess of caution, a
reprehensible habit that now seems to have
spread to America.

shot[2] a narcotic taken illegally
Usually by injection.

shot in the tail pregnant
A rather tasteless multiple pun on *shot*,
semen, and TAIL[1].

shot while trying to escape murdered in
custody
A favoured excuse of the Nazis and other
tyrants. Also as *shot while fleeing*.

shotgun marriage the marriage of a pregnant bride to the putative father
The man is supposed to have come to the altar
or register office under duress. Also as *shotgun
wedding*:
    Princess Caroline of Monaco is finding it
    impossible to secure an annulment of her
    1978 marriage ... made even more difficult
    following a shotgun marriage last
    December to Italian Stefano Casiraghi.
    (*Private Eye*, August 1984)
Shotgun is used of other precipitate action
taken under duress:
    He understood only too well that my father
    was acting against all his personal
    inclination under the duress of a shot-gun
    Coalition caused by Lord Fisher's desertion.
    (V. B. Carter, 1965—her father was the
    British prime minister, H. H. Asquith)

shout[1] **(the)** peremptory dismissal from
employment
Dismissed employees may say they have *had the
shout*, even if dismissed *sotto voce* or in writing.

shout[2] an obligation to pay for a round of
drinks in a bar
Only euphemistic when someone is said not
to pay his *shout*, implying parsimony.
To *shout yourself hoarse* is to drink in public to
excess.
To *shout a beer*, meaning to order it, is rare:
    Come into the bar. I'll shout you a beer.
    (Garve, 1969)

shove (the) peremptory dismissal from
employment
No physical rejection or ejection is involved.

shove over *American* to kill
Not necessarily involving a cliff but into
another state of existence, perhaps.

shovelled under dead
But not necessarily buried:
    My last day in the Fourteenth Army will
    be the day they shovel me under.
    (Fraser, 1992—the British/Indian 14th
    Army, which fought in the Far East in
    the Second World War under General
    Bill Slim, was known as the *Forgotten
    Army* because of the lack of publicity, the
    paucity of supplies, and the absence of
    home leave for its minority British soldiers.
    It is also forgotten that it was the most
    successful of all allied formations fighting
    on land against the Japanese, killing more
    than in all the other Pacific campaigns
    combined.)

show¹ to menstruate
Usually of animals and especially of mares when breeding is planned. In women, the noun a *show* indicates vaginal bleeding at the onset of menstruation or childbirth.

show² a battle
Mainly First World War usage, minimizing the danger by referring to a theatrical production or a pyrotechnic display.

show the door to dismiss peremptorily from employment
The exit, not the entrance. The phrase may also be used when an unwelcome visitor is asked to leave.

showers¹ deviant sexual activity
A code word in prostitutes' advertisements, from the penchant of some males for sexual antics involving the urine of another or, in the jargon, a *golden shower*:
    The gangs control drugs. Hooking, that's mostly for oddball stuff now, golden showers, Greek, not straight sex. (Turow, 1993)
A *brown shower* is offered for customers who prefer faeces. A *showercap* in this company is either a contraceptive sheath or a diaphragm.

showers² gas chambers
Part of the Nazi pretence that prisoners arriving at an extermination camp were merely being disinfected. Also as *shower baths*:
    His first job was to work in one of the ante-rooms where prisoners had to remove their clothes before going through a door to the 'showers'. (C. Booker in *Sunday Telegraph*, 29 January 1995, writing about Auschwitz)
    But it might be acceptable to evacuate the children and the old people (presumably to 'shower baths'). (A. Clark, 1995, describing German policy planned for Leningrad in 1942)

shrink see HEADSHRINKER

shrinkage the amount stolen from retail stores
Literally, a reduction in weight or volume of packed goods due to settlement or dehydration. Retailers' jargon.

shroud waving a tactic for safeguarding or augmenting expenditure on medical projects or the salaries of those employed in the industry
The sponsor is threatened, usually with more publicity than veracity, that deaths will result if the funds are not forthcoming.
A *shroud waver* is a doctor or politician, or frequently a combination of the two, who so acts.

shuffle off (this mortal coil) to die
Shakespeare said it first in *Hamlet*. The shortened form, to *shuffle off*, may also be alluding to the way old people walk:
    [Chlorofluorocarbons] will almost certainly be around and devouring ozone long after you and I have shuffled off. (Bryson, 2003)

sick menstruating
A rarer version of ILL¹.

sick-out a strike by public service employees
Those forbidden by law or contract from going on strike may absent themselves due to pretended illness. The usage is mainly found in the aircraft business, as with British Airways cabin attendants in 1998, and in America:
    The dispute over Reno... led to a sick-out by pilots. (*New York Herald Tribune*, 10 August 1999)

sick through negligence *American obsolete* suffering from venereal disease
A usage from the First World War, where the US army suffered 60,000 such casualties in 1918.

sickie an unauthorized absence from work
The employee pretends to be unwell. The affliction affects twice as many employed in the public sector than those with less complaisant employers:
    Common sense suggests that if people are worried about losing their jobs, they tend to take fewer 'sickies'. (*Sunday Telegraph*, 20 April 2003)

side orders sexual practices of an unusual or depraved nature
Like the dishes available additional to the main course, although the phrase may also refer to plain adultery.

sides pads worn to accentuate a woman's figure
From the days when men seemed to be attracted to big hips:
    She pulled off a pair of 'sides', artificial hips she wore to give herself a good figure. (Armstrong, 1955)

sight-deprived blind
It should literally mean blinded.

sigma phi syphilis
Medical jargon from the Greek letters used as shorthand, which also conceals the diagnosis from the less-educated patient.

sign the pledge see PLEDGE

significant other a regular sexual companion without marriage
Normally heterosexual, but sometimes homosexual, as:

I started the yacht upholstery, you know, after my friend died. In 1979. What these days they'd call a 'significant other'. (Proulx, 1993—they were both female)

silk (the) a parachute
Euphemistic only in the phrase *on the silk*, referring to a military air crew obliged to abandon an aircraft in flight.
Whence the figurative *hit the silk*, to seek to escape from or avoid a calamity, as by using a parachute:
    In markets like this, if that happens, everyone'll hit the silk at once and no one'll get out the door. (M. Thomas, 1987)

simple of small intelligence
Not just lacking knowledge or experience, as in Simple Simon's commercial exchange with the Pieman. *Simple* is now widely used of those of limited mental powers considered fit to remain in society.

sin to copulate extramaritally
Literally, to commit a forbidden act but, since St Paul's obsession with that particular wrongdoing, used of any activity which is taboo sexually:
    Most dangerous
    In that temptation that doth goad us on
    To sin in loving virtue. (Shakespeare, *Measure for Measure*)
Sinful means relating to such copulation, as in *sinful commerce*, which is not trading in stolen goods To *live in sin* implies unmarried cohabitation.

sing (of a criminal) to give information to the police
The imagery is from the songbird in a cage, and may relate to your own misdeeds or those of other criminals.

sing a different tune to change your story, attitude, or opinion
The same imagery recurs in various phrases. Thus the musical British politician Edward Heath, not especially renowned for the consistency of his policies, was once said to *sing from a different song sheet*.
Those said to *sing from the same hymn sheet* or to *sing the same tune* are taking the same line or expressing publicly the same opinion.

single parent a parent living with dependent offspring without an adult partner
A variant of LONE PARENT and seldom referring to a widow or widower. As most such people are female, *single mother* is a common specific description. The cloying *single mum* seeks to avoid any thought that the children's plight has been caused by either, or both, of their parents' irresponsibility.

singles describing a place where individuals can meet strangers for companionship or sexual relations
From *single*, unmarried, although you will observe that females who frequent such places tend to hunt in pairs. Whence *singles bars*, *nights*, *joints*, etc.

sink[1] a lavatory
Originally, a drain or cesspit and now perhaps obsolete.

sink[2] to be terminally ill
But not liable to drown:
    'How is Grandad?' Her voice dropped as if she were reluctant to ask. 'He's being himself. But he's sinking'. (L. Thomas, 1994—Grandad died soon afterwards)

sip a drink of intoxicant
Literally, anything drunk in small quantities:
    By the time they had had a few sips there was damned little left for us. (Richards, 1933, describing a rum ration)
The Scottish and northern English *siper*, a drunkard, came from a dialect verb meaning to soak.

siphon off to steal
Usually by embezzlement and not necessarily of liquids.
Siphon is specific of stealing fuel from the tanks of motor vehicles.

siphon the python (of a male) to urinate
The common serpentine/penis imagery.

sissy *American* a male homosexual
An alternative spelling of CISSY, with the same derivation, and also used of effeminate heterosexuals.

sister a prostitute
Asian pimps sometimes claim this relationship. When they offer to introduce you to their *sister, very white, very clean*, they make three assertions in which little confidence should be placed. A western prostitute may be known as a *sister of mercy* or *of charity*, punning on those who follow a more devout calling.
In the American black community, a *sister* may be a black woman.

sit-in a trespass to draw attention to a grievance
By a body of people, often without violence, sometimes in the course of a trade dispute. A *sleep-in* continues overnight, and during a *love-in* the participants may while the hours promiscuously away.

sit-upon the buttocks
More common in Great Britain than in America, where *sit-upons* were trousers, not bottoms, the equivalent of the contemporary

British *sit-in-'ems*. Also as a *sit-down-upon* or as a *sitting*:

> She had a tumour going from her sitting.
> (*EDD*, from 1887)

sitting by the window underemployed
A phenomenon of Japanese industrial society, where paternalistic attitudes deterred the dismissal of employees for whom there was no longer a job.

six feet of earth death
The length of an average grave rather than its depth:

> Six feet of earth make all men equal.
> (Proverb)

Six feet underground emphasizes the depth rather than the length:

> I'm glad his father's six feet underground.
> (G. Greene, 1978)

six o'clock swill *Australian/New Zealand* an excessive drinking of beer
An Antipodean phenomenon arising from aridity, machismo, thirst, and unhelpful licensing laws.
In New Zealand, for five decades until 1967, all bars closed at six in the afternoon.

sixty-nine see SOIXANTE-NEUF

sizzle *American* to be killed by electrocution
One of several culinary images for the process.

skidmarks the stains of excrement on underpants
Normally linear, like rubber on the road from excessive braking.

skim to embezzle or extort
Taking a little on a regular basis, like cream from milk. An American usage relates to removing some of the cash in a casino before an assessment of tax on gambling revenue has been made.
A *skim* is a bribe or the amount stolen.

skin¹ *American* a male contraceptive sheath
Whence the punning *skin-diver* who uses that form of contraception.

skin² pornographic
From the implication of nudity. Thus a *skin flick* is a pornographic film, which used to be shown in a *skin house*, a cinema specializing in pornography, before becoming freely available to young and old alike in every video shop. A *skin magazine*, often shortened to *skin mag*, contains erotic pictures, mainly for male edification or whatever. The *skin business* is operating such ventures.

skin off all dead horses to marry your mistress
A *dead horse* is something of small value, which it is not worth flogging, although at one time it had had its uses. In obsolete Irish use, to *work on a dead horse* was to have to complete a job for which you had already been paid, and when the task was done, you were said to have *skinned a dead horse*.

skinful an excessive quantity of intoxicating drink
Usually of beer, which suggests derivation from a distended bladder rather than from a wine skin.

skinny-dip to bathe in the nude
Originally American, nakedness in public being a matter of greater taboo in the US than in Britain. *Skinny-dipping* is not done only by excessively thin people.

skippy *American* a male homosexual taking the female role.
Using an affected walk. Black slang.

skirt a woman viewed sexually by a male
The garment is worn normally only by females. Men call them kilts:

> He's got a nice skirt all right... I wouldn't say pretty, but a good figure. (G. Greene, 1932)

A *bit* or *piece of skirt* may be a woman viewed sexually, a man's sexual partner, or the act of copulation in general:

> He enjoyed nothing better in the world than a nice bit of skirt. (Richards, 1933)

skivvy a prostitute
In standard use, a female domestic servant. The American *skivvie-house* is a brothel.

sky-piece a wig
It used to mean a hat. Only of those worn by males, which an American may also call a *sky-rug*.

slack (of a male) to urinate
Sometimes as *slack off*, which indicates a relieving of pressure.

slack fill delivering less than the customer thinks has been sold
Commercial jargon for the design and manufacture of bottles and cartons which look as if they hold more than they do. Sometimes too of only partly filling them, with packing or air taking up the empty space.

slag a promiscuous woman
Usually young. Partridge (*DSUE*) suggested 'perhaps ex slagger', which was an old term used for a bawd but I just wonder if it is not simply back slang for *gals*, as *yob* is for *boy*.

slake your lust (of a male) to copulate
Usually extramaritally, from *slake*, to quench or satisfy. A man may also *slake his (base) passion*.
In obsolete Westmorland dialect, a *sleck-trough* was a prostitute, the cooling place into which a smith plunged his red-hot iron.

slammer a prison
Either from the *slamming* of the door as you are admitted or the rough treatment you receive once inside. Also shortened to *slam*.

slang *American* to sell illegal narcotics
A black usage of uncertain derivation:
> 'And how, sir, did you make a living prior to your incarceration?' 'Slanging.' 'Slanging?' 'Slanging dope.' 'Hanging, banging and slanging' is the motto of gang life, in that street doggerel. Slang, which originally meant to talk the talk, now is the term for selling drugs. (Turow, 1996)

slap and tickle sexual play
Literally, no more than what might occur in any courtship, which is all this phrase normally implies.

slapper a prostitute
Not just catering for those with a fetish for sado-masochism, but she may be no more than a promiscuous female. A *slapper sweep* is a police action arresting prostitutes on the streets.

slash an act of urination
Originally, a splashing or bespattering. Of both sexes.
Slash and burn is gonorrhoea in a male, from the pain while urinating.

slash and burn asset stripping and ruthless cost-cutting
Financial jargon copied from primitive agriculture:
> One analyst said: 'We like slash-and-burn deals. The more people who get fired the better.' (*Daily Telegraph*, 9 May 2001)

slate-off a person with low intelligence or lacking common sense
Like an incomplete house roof.
Such a person is still said to *have a slate loose*.

sledge unsportingly to harass (an opponent)
Jargon of professional cricket where the rewards become more important than the game. *OED* suggests the origin may have been *sledgehammer*, but I prefer the imagery of what was once used to pull a man to his execution. The practice seems to have originated in Australia and is definitely not cricket, as they say.

sleep to be dead
While you await the resurrection of the body. Often in compounds according to the circumstance. Thus to *sleep in your leaden hammock* or in *Davy Jones's locker* was to have died and been buried at sea.
To *sleep in your shoes* was to be killed in battle. When F. D. Roosevelt died, the official White House statement said he had *slept away*, which did not refer to yet another overnight absence from Eleanor with his mistress at Mount David:
> The four Roosevelt boys in the services have been sent a message by their mother which said, 'President slept away this afternoon'. (Ranfurly, 1994—1945 diary entry)
Sleep is death.

sleep around to copulate promiscuously
Of either sex, supposedly in various beds.

sleep-in see SIT-IN

sleep over to stay overnight for extramarital sexual activity
Not involving the occupation of bunk beds:
> He wanted to sleep over that night. (Sanders, 1982)

sleep together (of a couple) to copulate
Usually extramaritally on a regular basis, and also of homosexuals. *Not to sleep together*, of spouses, means that they have ceased to copulate with each other, even though they may continue to share the same bed or room.

sleep with to copulate with
Perhaps the commonest use, normally of extramarital copulation by either sex, or both, and now standard English.
A *sleeping dictionary* is a native-speaking mistress from whom you hope to learn the language.
A *sleeping partner*, with whom you regularly copulate, puns on the part-owner who plays no active part in the running of the business. Also rarely as *sleepy time girl*, who can be a mistress or a prostitute.

slewed drunk
Not going straight.
Also as *half-slewed*, where as usual the half equals the whole.

slice to cheat (a customer)
Retailer's jargon for overcharging by removing a sliver of cheese etc. from what has been weighed and priced. I cherish the punning phrase *slice the gentry*, to cheat the better-off.

slice of the action see ACTION[1]

slight chill a pretext for not keeping an engagement
An indisposition which the draughts of royal palaces seem to induce:
> 'What shall I tell them? A slight chill?'
> 'That sounds a deal too much like Buckingham Palace. Just say I'm out.'
> (Ustinov, 1971)

Royal personages are also martyrs to *slight colds* and *indispositions*. However, the phrases can also be used, as with geriatric Russian leaders, to try to conceal the gravity of an illness:
> Every other paper reported that Attlee is now getting better from a slight indisposition. (Crossman, 1981—when Prime Minister Attlee had had an attack of cerebral thrombosis)

slip[1] to give premature birth to
Usually of domestic animals:
> Cows slipped their calves, horses fell lame. (Hunt, 1865)

but not for the great diarist:
> Fraizer is so great with my Lady Castlemain and Steward and all the ladies at Court, in helping them slip their calfes when there is occasion. (Pepys, 1664—Fraizer was a court physician and royal abortionist, without whom there might have been many more royal dukedoms)

To *slip a foot* or *slip a girth* was to give birth to an illegitimate child, both with imagery from a fall whilst riding.

slip[2] to die
The concept of gliding easily away and usually in compounds. To *slip away* is to die painlessly, usually in old age or after long illness.
Old people may also *slip off*. With nautical imagery you may *slip your breath*, *cable*, *grip* or *wind*.
I don't think people *slip to Nod* any more:
> He the bizzy roun' hath trod,
> An' quietly wants to slip to Nod. (W. Taylor, 1787—later in the verse his fate is to 'trudge on Pluto's gloomy shore')

slippage mental illness or decline
Not the ability to skate, nor used to denote physical deterioration:
> I learned all this much later from my mother who, after my father's death, had begun to show signs of slippage. (Desai, 1988)

slippery palm see PALM[1]

slops the police
Punning back slang indicating disrespect.

sloshed drunk

To *slosh* is to be a glutton but there is also the imagery of an over-full container.
Usually as *half-sloshed*, which means no less drunk.

slot to kill
The imagery of piercing perhaps, or from the slang *slot away*, to place an object in an aperture, as scoring a goal at football.

slow stupid
Mainly educational jargon of children, but also of adults of low mental capacity. *Slow upstairs* is used only of adults:
> He's the Irish version of a street hood, very good with weapons but a little slow upstairs. (Clancy, 1987—repeating a common but fallacious myth about the intelligence of the Irish)

slowdown[1] *American* a deliberate failure to do work for which you are being paid
A variant of the British GO SLOW whereby employees exert pressure on their employer in a labour dispute, especially when, as in the case of Federal workers, striking might be illegal:
> ... air controllers or postal workers staged 'slowdowns'. (*Daily Telegraph*, August 1981—Reagan was soon to turn the air controllers' *slowdown* into a full stop by dismissing them all)

See also SICK-OUT.

slowdown[2] a recession
One of the soothing words used by politicians when referring to an economic collapse for which they may bear some blame.

slug[1] a bullet
In the olden days leaden bullets had much the same shape and colour as the gastropod.
To *get a slug* means to be killed or wounded by a bullet, but *slugged* means being hit by any agency, including a fist, a baseball bat, or an excess of alcohol.

slug[2] a quantity of spirits
Probably punning on SHOT[1], although there is a rare meaning, to swallow:
> Jackie sighed and took a slug from her glass. (Doyle, 1990)

Usually in the cliché a *slug of whisky* and *slugged* means drunk, from the hitting, the swallowing, and the measure.

sluice[1] to copulate with
Literally, to flush:
> ... she has been sluic'd in's absence,
> And his pond fish'd by his next neighbour. (Shakespeare, *The Winter's Tale*)

This may be a spurious entry based on a single metaphorical use, but it is still more worthy of notice than the American *sluice*, to shoot eagles from a helicopter.

sluice² a lavatory
From the controlled flow of water in a flush system.

slumber *American* death
The common imagery of SLEEP but this usage is mainly the jargon of the mortician. Thus a *slumber cot* or *box* is a coffin, a *slumber robe* is a shroud, and a *slumber room* is a morgue.

slush bribery
Originally, a mixture of grease and oil and still so used of waste cooking fat aboard ship, which used to (or may still) be sold to create a *slush fund*, to be shared among the favoured few. For landlubbers the phrase means only cash which may be used for corporate bribery.

smack illegal heroin
A corruption of the Yiddish *schmeck*, to sniff, rather than what it does for you. Derivation from the nickname of a bandleader who died in 1952 is implausible.

small folk (the) the fairies
Alluding to their stature in the days when they were real to West Country folk and, with their vicious natures, not to be trifled with or talked about directly. Also as the *small men* or the *small people*:
    The small people are believed by some to be the spirits of the people who inhabited Cornwall many thousands of years ago. (Hunt, 1865)

small print onerous conditions in a contract which are not given prominence
A smaller typeface is chosen for that part of the document to discourage the buyer from reading it. Some figurative use:
    Ministers say the [Pensions Protection Fund] will guarantee people's pensions but the small print says pensions may be cut. (*Daily Telegraph*, 3 March 2005)

smallest room (the) the lavatory
Even if, by geometric computation, it isn't: smallest room, the The bathroom; restroom. *A facetious euphem.* (*DAS*, which contrives to define one euphemism by two others)

smalls underpants and brassières
A shortened form of *small clothes*.

smashed drunk or under the influence of illegal narcotics
Or, in these depraved times, both, your consciousness having been destroyed by what you have ingested.

To *smash the teapot* was to resume regular drinking of alcohol after a period of abstinence.

smear¹ to bribe
Literally, to spread:
    A little smearing of the right palm...
    (Longstreet, 1956—not implying that the left palm would not have done equally well)
The American spelling *schmear* comes from the German *schmieren* via Yiddish to mean the same thing as a verb or a noun.

smear² a test for cervical cancer
The usage avoids any reference to the dread disease or the place from which the sample is taken.

smear³ to attempt to bring into disrepute
Spreading what the subject prefers to keep hidden. The tabloid press often regales its readership with *smear campaigns* against persons known to the public, and politicians who adopt the same tactics also know that mud sticks.

smear out to kill
A variant of *wipe out*.

smeared *American* drunk
Using the same imagery as the slang *blotto*? Or just unable to see things in focus.

smell of to be tainted with
What you are said to *smell of* is something taboo. Thus to *smell of the counting-house* was, among the landed gentry, to be contaminated by having actually earned your wealth:
    If she thought that any of her newcomers smelt of the counting-house, she would tell her friends 'Have nothing to do with them'. (Bence-Jones, 1987, writing about Anglo-Irish protestants in the 19th century)

Smithfield bargain *British obsolete* a marriage to secure wealth
From the London meat market in the days when husbands took over their wives' assets, and ignoring the old adage 'Don't marry for money but marry where money is'.

smoke¹ (the) opium
From the method of ingestion.

smoke² to murder
Presumably from the discharge of burnt powder.
To *smoke it* is to kill yourself, from putting the barrel of a handgun in your mouth.

smoke and mirrors deception
From the technique of the stage magician:
    [The stock market IT boom] was a period one analyst remembers for 'smoke and mirrors'. (*Daily Telegraph*, 9 September 2005)

smoker the devil
With his emissions of fire and brimstone.

smokey *American* a policeman
The *DAS* suggests this comes from *Smokey the Bear*, the US Forestry Service symbol, and see also BEAR[2].
Whence many compounds: *smokey beaver*, a policewoman; *smokey on four legs*, a policeman on horseback; *smokey with camera*, police with radar; *smokey on rubber*, police in a car; *smokey with ears*, police listening or able to listen to CB; and so on.

smoking gun (a) conclusive evidence of guilt
From the emission from the barrel immediately after a shot has been fired:
> ...the tape is a 'smoking gun', that is, in police and prosecutional slang, direct evidence of criminal guilt. (Colodny & Gettlin, 1991, writing of a White House tape dated June 1973)

smooth to distort (published accounts)
You conceal, or try to even out, fluctuations by carrying forward exceptional movements up or down, of cash and inventory, but especially of profit and loss. This keeps stockholders and analysts quiet, for a time.

smut house *American* a place where pornographic programmes are screened.
Smut as in DIRTY, and nothing to do with an old-fashioned boiler-room.

snaffle to steal
Originally, to saunter, as many chance thieves do.

snag to pilfer
The allusion is to the involuntary catching, as a garment on a nail:
> He snagged my Texas toast when he thought no one was looking. (Anonymous, 1996)

snake oil *American* something worthless or deceitful
What confidence tricksters, *snake-oil sellers* or *merchants*, sell to gullible people.

snake pit a mental hospital
Probably from one of the common delusions of the mentally ill, but also a place where the sane hope not to find themselves.
The less common *snake ranch* is a brothel, punning on the SERPENT imagery.

snapper an ampoule of amyl nitrite
The drug, used in the treatment of heart disease, is popularly supposed to be an aphrodisiac and is therefore sought after for illegal use. It is ingested by *snapping* the cap off an ampoule, and sniffing.

snatch[1] a single act of copulation
Usually extramaritally. The derivation might be from any of several standard English meanings of *snatch*—a snare, an entanglement, a hasty meal, a sudden jerk—or merely from SNATCH[2], the vagina. Shakespeare could have been using the word in either sexual sense:
> ...it seems some certain snatch or so
> Would serve your turns. (*Titus Andronicus*)
but there is no equivocation in:
> I could not abide marriage, but as a rambler I took a snatch when I could get it. (Burton, 1621)

snatch[2] the vagina
Perhaps from the meaning, a portion of hair, or merely from its association with SNATCH[1]. A *snatch mouse* is a tampon in American slang.

snatch[3] to steal
From the seizing. A *snatch* is the event rather than the proceeds.

snatch[4] to kidnap or arrest
Seizing a person. An army or police *snatch squad* is a formation trained to arrest ringleaders in a riot.

snatched from us dead
The figurative kidnapping is done by the deity. Also as *snatched away*:
> The depth and reality of his religious faith, coupled with his practical wisdom, was what supported us both when our only son and then our only daughter were snatched from us. (Wright, 1932—the children of Joseph Wright, who gave us the *EDD*, died respectively of septicaemia and peritonitis)
> ...a routine operation went wrong and she was snatched away. Her death was a terrible shock. (Major, 1999)

sneak to steal
In standard English, to move furtively, whence, in the children's use, to inform against. In the 19th century it applied particularly to thefts from private houses.
Today we only meet (but far too often) the tautological *sneak thief*.

sneezer *American* a prison
Possibly a corruption of FREEZER. I thought it might have come into the language because a typist couldn't read Chandler's handwriting until I found Runyon using the same word in the 1930s.

sniff to inhale narcotics or stimulants illegally

Either cocaine, or glue, especially by juveniles. To be *on the sniff* is habitually to inhale in this way.

sniff out to kill
Perhaps a corruption of SNUFF (OUT), because it means literally no more than to detect.
To *take a long (deep) sniff* indicates that you are about to BREATHE YOUR LAST.

snifter a drink of spirits
Literally, a sniff, whence a small portion of brandy etc. offered so that the aroma can be sampled, and then any spirits.

snip a vasectomy
Medical jargon which has passed into standard use. (The Kent trading standards officer, dealing with a complaint that a surgeon's fee for a vasectomy was too high, dismissed the charge, remarking that it was a snip, for which he found himself reported to the chief executive.) *Snib* and *snick* were dialect words for the castration of domestic and farm animals.

snort[1] a drink of spirits
Also as a *snorter*, perhaps because it makes you exhale noisily.

snort[2] to ingest an illegal narcotic
By taking a big SNIFF. It also may mean the substance ingested.

snout[1] a police informer
Underworld slang from the nose of the PIG.

snout[2] tobacco
As this was a 19th-century usage, it may have been derived from the sniffing of snuff. Now British prison jargon, especially of tobacco used as a currency inside a jail.

snow[1] cocaine
In its crystalline or powdered form, from the colour and coldness.
Whence many derivatives. A *snowball* is a quantity or derivative of cocaine or heroin. A *snowbird* is a person addicted to cocaine; *snowed in, under,* or *up,* is under the influence of narcotics; a *snow-storm* is a gathering where cocaine is taken illegally. To be *snow-blind* is to become addicted to cocaine:
> But Renzo got snow-blind real bad. He began to deal, and deal heavily enough to draw attention. (Anonymous, 1996—Renzo was not an arctic explorer or a card player)
An addict will turn into a *snowman*.

snow[2] deliberately to obfuscate (an issue) or deceive (a person)
As a landscape may be obscured by a snowfall. To *snow* a person is to produce masses of documentation which will make it hard for the recipient to pick out and understand the relevant points.
Such an operation is known as a *snow-job*.

snow-capping establishing an organization where whites are managers and blacks do the menial tasks
Perhaps also known to politicians as controlling 'the commanding heights of the economy':
> ...the NHS was a prime example of the phenomenon he called 'snow-capping' where the organizational pyramid is white at the top and black at the bottom. (*Daily Telegraph*, 30 April 2004)

snowdrop *American* a military policeman
They wore white spats in the Second World War.

snowing down south *American obsolete?* the hem of your petticoat is showing
An oblique warning when women wore white petticoats and modestly preferred to conceal underwear.

snuff (out) to kill
Like extinguishing a candle. To *snuff it* is to die, whence the nickname of the Kent and Sussex Hospital in Tunbridge Wells—the *Kent and Snuff it*. (Fortunately my short stay as an emergency patient had a happier outcome.)

snug inconveniently small
The language of the estate agent seeking to convey an impression of cosiness.

so in a condition the subject of a taboo
Pregnant:
> A euphemism for pregnant...Mrs Brown is so. (*EDD*)
or homosexual (*SOED*). Both uses may be obsolete.

so-and-so a mild insult
Each *so* being a substitute for the abusive epithet, as in the expression, *He's a right so-and-so.*

so-so in a physical condition which differs from the normal
In common speech, it indicates mediocrity. It is used of pregnancy and mild indisposition.

soak a drunkard
Formerly, it meant to drink alcohol to excess:
> A 'slug for the drink' is a man who soaks and never succumbs. (Douglas, 1901)
Soaked means drunk.

social used in many evasive or misleading phrases. In some it has the advantage of imprecision; in others it may imply that the condition to which it refers is the fault or concern of society rather than the individual. In either case the whiskers of the euphemism-hunter start to twitch whenever the adjective appears.

social agenda an attempt to impose conformity
The phrase allows politicians to rationalize their wish or duty to control the lives of others:
> ...a 'new EU Social Agenda' in welfare harmonisation...Angela Merkel [the German Chancellor] has similarly called for the constitution to be preserved...by adding a 'social dimension'. (*Daily Telegraph*, 16 January 2006)

Social Area Council *British* a discussion group sponsored and paid for by the British government
In 2005 an inquiry was started to investigate what its remit and purpose might have been.

social cohesion the absence of hostility between ethnic groups
Cohesion implies sticking together:
> The think-tank says that the trend [whereby white and non-white people gravitate to separate locations in Britain] has serious consequences for 'social cohesion'. (*Daily Telegraph*, 19 February 2005)

social dimension see SOCIAL AGENDA

social disease a venereal disease
Mainly 19th-century usage, and also as *social infection*:
> 'He has contracted a social disease, which makes it impossible that he marry.' 'You mean he's got a dose of clap?' (Fraser, 1970—writing in 19th-century style)
> ...contracting certain indelicate social infections from—hem, hem—female camp-followers. (Fraser, 1975—again in 19th-century style)

social dumping the unwillingness of manufacturers to base their businesses in countries where taxes and labour costs are higher:
> ...regulations which are intended to prevent 'social dumping'...an EU concept whereby business shifts from expensive and heavily regulated regions to less costly and more lightly regulated regions. (*Daily Telegraph*, 16 January 2006)

social education arbitrary imprisonment
A pretext given by the Nazis for imprisoning Jews:
> Jews were given two years labour in

concentration camps where we would receive 'appropriate social education'. (Szpilman in translation, 1998)

social evil (the) *obsolete* prostitution
So considered in Victorian times, which may be why Gladstone was so interested in meeting its practitioners.

social fairness giving favourable treatment to the poor
An objective of government provided that the cost is borne by others:
> At the time of the [National Minimum Wage's] introduction one of the main concerns was that the Government would ratchet up the rate in the name of 'social fairness' at no cost to itself. (Ruth Lea in *Daily Telegraph*, 9 October 2006)

social housing accommodation built with the aid of subsidy for poor people
Those able to afford to make their own arrangements are not necessary antisocial:
> Certain non-profit sectors seem to work better than others...and I suspect that social housing is one. Social landlords seem better at collecting rents, maintaining buildings and evicting antisocial tenants than local authorities. (*Sunday Telegraph*, 6 February 2005)

social inclusion giving special advantages to selected groups of people
The jargon of social science. See also SOCIALLY EXCLUDED:
> The University [Lincolnshire at Humberside] performs well in the Government's social inclusion scale. More than 90 per cent of the 12,000 students come from state schools or colleges. (*Sunday Telegraph*, 3 February 2001—unfortunately its academic performance was less noteworthy)

social justice an imprecise dogma based on a wish to improve the situation of the poor rather than on the rule of law
Some see it as being based on envy:
> The robbery of the rich is called social justice. (M. Roberts, 1951)
For others, like those who set the courses at Haverford College in Pennsylvania, the phrase may refer to what is seen to be morally right:
> ...students must complete a 'Social Justice Requirement' in order to graduate. This means taking courses in Feminist Political Theory. (*Daily Telegraph*, 23 February 1991)
Goebbels saw *social justice* in January 1945 as one of the Nazi war aims. (A. Clark, 1995)
And so, as Alice discovered in Wonderland, the phrase tends to mean what you want it to mean.

social landlord see SOCIAL HOUSING

social model conservative protectionism
Not a comely maiden with an active lifestyle:
    All this [restriction on trade] has been done
    in the name of protecting the European
    'social model' from the scourge of 'Anglo-
    Saxon' competition. (*Daily Telegraph*, 17
    February 2006)

social ownership control by politicians
and bureaucrats
The control is achieved by expropriation, with
or without compensation. In 1986 the British
Labour Party needed another word than
NATIONALIZE to describe a process in which
much of the electorate had ceased to have
confidence:
    ... the substitution of phrases like 'social
    ownership' for nasty brutal words like
    'nationalization'. (*Daily Telegraph*, August
    1986)

social rented home a house let at less
than the market price
A variant of SOCIAL HOUSING:
    An increase in the average house price ...
    coupled with a 7 per cent decrease in the
    number of social rented homes has caused
    the problem [that young people were moving
    away from St Briavels in the Forest of Dean
    because they could not afford to live there].
    (*Daily Telegraph*, 13 November 2004)

social security the payment of money by
the state to the poor
A durable phrase among the many with
which we have sought to mask the plight of,
and charity to, fellow citizens. Sometimes
shortened to *the social*.

social services *British* an institution of
the state for dealing with the young,
old, ill, and poor members of society
Not the provision of food, transport, or many
other services needed to sustain life.

social worker a public employee concerned with the poor, sick, old, and criminal elements of society
The usage should not be taken to suggest that
other workers are antisocial. (For cryptic crossword enthusiasts, a *social worker* is an ant.)

socialist justice arbitrary punishment
The Russian Communist euphemism for
legalistic tyranny:
    [Gorbachev] read law; an unusual choice in
    a country where 'socialist justice'—the
    Gulag, the execution cellar—had for so
    long taken precedence over juridical
    nicety. (Moynahan, 1994)

socially excluded poor
Not denied the vote, refused free education,
or forbidden to participate in public functions
but unable to afford what others can buy or to
have access to credit.

sodden habitually drunk
Permanently soaked, but with the wrong kind
of liquid.

soft¹ of low intelligence
A shortened form of *soft in the head*.

soft² inflicting less harm than an alternative
The opposite to HARD in pornography, illegal
narcotics, etc. A *soft drink* is non-alcoholic, and
will harm your teeth more than your liver. For
the military, a *soft target* is one which you can
attack with relative impunity. A *soft option* is a
simple solution, with overtones of laziness or
cowardice if you take it.

soft commission a bribe
Either a reciprocal favour commensurate to
the business transacted, such as a paid
vacation, or a level of payment above what
would be negotiated on a commercial basis in
a process known as *softing*:
    You may not know much about soft
    commissions. That's the way the brokers
    like it ... The FSA calculate that 40% of
    today's dealing costs are actually the cost of
    softing. (*Daily Telegraph*, 8 March 2003)

soft-shoe a clandestine or indirect approach
From the silence of the tread and the association with shuffling:
    Doing the same soft-shoe as you, talking to
    me about something else, then trying to
    slide this Litiplex name in so I wouldn't
    notice. (Turow, 1993)

soft skills application and discipline
If not taught in the home, hardest of all to
acquire at school:
    There are also problems with many basic
    skills such as literacy and numeracy and
    there are difficulties with 'soft skills' such
    as the ability to communicate with, or
    work in a team or show initiative. (*Daily
    Telegraph*, 14 March 2001, writing about
    unemployed young people)

soft soap flattery
Originally, what we now call *shampoo*, a word
borrowed from the Hindi.
Also as a verb.
See also SADDLE SOAP.

softness in the economy a recession
When it would seem, conversely, that times
are hard.

soil excrement
With EARTH CLOSETS, solid matter had to be regularly removed, an operation usually carried out at night, whence NIGHT SOIL. Professional window cleaners call bird droppings on glass *impacted soilage*.
To *soil yourself* or *your pants* is to defecate or urinate involuntarily before getting your clothing out of the way.

soiled dove *obsolete* a prostitute
Not the smutty birds in London's Trafalgar Square:
> Society [Salisbury] argued, had closed its eyes to the way that 'soiled doves' had become a 'formidable nuisance' in central London. (A. Roberts, 1999)

A woman who *soiled her reputation* had engaged in extramarital copulation.

soixante-neuf simultaneous fellatio and cunnilingus
The reversible numbers 6 and 9, indicating the position adopted by the participants. This French form is normal in the British Isles—I speak etymologically—with *six-à-neuf* being rare:
Another usage, more direct or less Francophone, is *sixty-nine*.
The participants may also be described as *sixty-nining*.

solace extramarital copulation
Supposedly consolation during the absence or disinterestedness of a spouse:
> [Lloyd George] was hardly the first or the last politician to find solace in a woman more clever and attractive than his own wife. (G. Stewart, 1999)

solicit to offer sexual services for money
Literally, to request or entreat in any context, as does the British *solicitor*, a lawyer who pleads for you in court, or the American *solicitor* who calls on customers seeking orders, often ignoring a notice ordering him to stay away.

solid waste human excrement
Civil engineering jargon. The term does not include empty tins or potato peelings. Sometimes simply as *solids*, as in the cliché *when the solids hit the fan*.

solidarity participating in a strike on behalf of others
The word was used, as in modern Poland, for the coming together of workers in a single bargaining unit, whence support for other employees in dispute with their employer.

solitary sex masturbation

Not hermaphroditism. Also as *solitary sin* or *solitary vice*:
> Carter had seen 'young unmarried women, of the middle-class of society reduced, by the constant use of the speculum, to the mental and moral condition of prostitutes; seeking to give themselves the same indulgence by the practice of solitary vice'. (Pearsall, 1969, quoting from a document of 1853)

something[1] an alcoholic drink
The *little something* your host offers you may turn out to be quite substantial. Also as *something damp, for the thirst* or *throat, helpful, moist,* or *short*.

something[2] an expletive
Of the same tendency as BLANK[1] and, similarly, seldom used today.
You may also hear *something-something* used in the same sense, in polite circles.

something for the weekend a contraceptive sheath
Or a packet of contraceptives, from the days when the main purveyors were barbers, and men had their hair cut more often.

something on you a damaging piece of knowledge about you
Not the clothes you are wearing. In this usage, *on* means against.

somewhere in . . . the location is secret
A usage in time of war, to conceal information about where specific regiments were located:
> As it was, most already had their soldier 'somewhere in France'—that delightful euphemism of the censors. (Horne, 1969)

You may still hear an embattled war correspondent be similarly evasive about a location.

somewhere where he (or she) can be looked after off our hands
Used of aged, ill, or burdensome dependants, implying that they, not you, will benefit from the impersonal care of paid attendants.

son of a bitch an illegitimate child
Once a deadly insult to both mother and child, but now a mild insult or expletive, often abbreviated to *S.O.B*. For a dissertation on *son of a gun* see also GUNNER'S DAUGHTER. The synonymous *son of a bachelor* is obsolete.

sop a drunkard
Literally, something dipped in liquid or the liquid in which it is dipped. It may just be confused with the common SOT.

sore a carcinoma
The symptom, in this case an ulcer, is used for the dread affliction.

sot a drunkard

The original meaning was a fool:

> If ony Whiggish whingin sot,
> To blame poor Matthew dare. (Burns, 1786)

whence to act foolishly in association with drunkenness.

sought after expensive

Estate agents' puff, when they want to imply that a buyer will have plenty of competition. Any property, however humble, is likely to be *sought after*, if the price is right.

sound bite a spoken phrase or sentence short and pithy enough to be broadcast in its entirety

An art form developed by politicians who know that any fuller statement is likely to be truncated or distorted prior to or on being broadcast:

> We are in the age of the satellite image, the spin-doctor, and the three-second sound bite. (McCrum, 1991)

souper *Irish* a Roman Catholic coerced into joining the Protestant Church of Ireland or someone attempting to bring about such conversion

In the recurrent periods of 19th-century famine some Protestant churches in Ireland provided food exclusively for members of their congregation, which was augmented on occasion by starving former Roman Catholics. (In 2006 French anti-Semitic extremists opposed to North African immigration established free feeding centres for the poor, the food incorporating pork so that it would not be consumed by Jews or Muslims.)

source an associate briefed to give confidential information

The origin of the LEAK[2]. A *well-informed source* indicates that the revelation has official blessing.

souse a drunkard

The common culinary imagery, this time from soaking in vinegar or the like. *Soused* means drunk.

south[1] the poorer or less industrialized countries

The geographical location of many of them relative to western Europe and North America, although you are unlikely to use the term of or in the Antipodes. The usage seeks to avoid other patronizing or offensive language.

south[2] a person's reproductive parts

The trunk would be to the north of them, if you were a cartographer.

The *south pole* is a vulgarism for the penis.

south[3] **(going or moving)** deteriorating

Alluding to business and share prices, from the direction taken on the wall charts. An improvement does not, however, lead to the comment that prices are *going north*.

South Chelsea Battersea

An example of what the snobs and estate agents do to upgrade an address in cities where a fashionable area is bounded by an unfashionable.

souvenir an illegitimate child

Certainly a lasting memory for the mother. For most wartime soldiers, *souvenirs* were things they stole.

sow your wild oats to behave wildly or irresponsibly

With extravagance or with promiscuous seminal distribution, like the persistent weed *Avena fatua*.

sozzle to drink to excess

Originally, to splash and in America, to soak or dowse.

The past participle, *sozzled* meaning drunk, is more common.

space *American* a grave

Funeral jargon.

A *space and bronze deal* was what you got if you bought your plot and casket in advance.

spaced out under the influence of illegal drugs

Referring to the floating sensation, especially after ingesting a hallucinogen. A *space-head* is someone who habitually takes such drugs.

spam[1] a penis

The common MEAT[2] imagery, from the proprietary brand of processed sweet pork (which is said to taste like human flesh).

In many vulgarisms such as *spam alley* or *chasm*, the vagina; *spam sceptre* or *javelin*, the penis viewed sexually.

spam[2] the malicious violation of computer security by overloading with messages

The derivation is uncertain. As noun and verb.

Spanish gout syphilis

Honest British tarts thought that Spanish girls must have infected them, if not French, Italian, or other 'foreign' prostitutes.

Spanish practices regular cheating by employees

A feature of the old Fleet Street newspaper industry in London, where overmanning, falsification of time sheets, paid absenteeism, and other similar goings-on were endemic.

Spanish tummy diarrhoea
The British holidaymaker's equivalent of the
American TOURISTAS.

spare promiscuous
Not merely unaccompanied and available for
companionship:
> Yanks are so frightfully overbearing and
> boastful when they go with a lot of 'spare'
> women. (Garfield, 2004, diary entry 1946)

The modern male vulgarism a *bit of spare*
means a sexually complaisant female companion.

spare tyre obesity at the waistline
Usually of a male, from the roll of fat
overhanging his belt.
In America, sometimes as *rubber tire*.

spared still alive
The deity doesn't require your company just
yet.

speak to *obsolete* to propose marriage to
This is a reminder of 19th-century reticence
about marriage:
> When Jamie 'spoke to' Janet Carson, who
> told her people at once, having no
> opposition to expect...(Strain, 1900)

Also as the Scottish *speak for* and *speak till*.

speak with forked tongue to dissimulate
Serpents want to have a word with animal
rights enthusiasts about this usage, without
which writers of screenplays for Westerns
would have had to dream up another cliché.

special one of those words which makes
the ears of a collector of euphemisms
prick up. Whatever is so qualified is *especially* bad or suspect in some respect.

special action the rounding up and murdering of Jews
A Nazi usage and practice.

special area *British* a region of economic
decline and relative poverty
So designated in the 1930s and, when the title
no longer masked their situation, they became *Development Areas*.

Special Branch *British/Irish* police dealing
with subversion and terrorism
Less liable to public scrutiny and more
ruthless than other police officers.

special camp a place for the arbitrary imprisonment of potential enemies
A feature of all totalitarian regimes:
> [A prison system] at first known as the
> system of 'special camps' or 'extraordinary

camps'. From the start the 'special prison
system' was meant to deal with special
prisoners, priests, former tsarist officials,
bourgeois speculators, [and] enemies of the
new order [who] merited special treatment.
(Applebaum, 2003)

special care the nursing of the mentally
ill
It may take place in a *special home* or *hospital*.
A *special care unit* in America is an institution
for the insane.

special class a form for children unable to
be taught by conventional means
Those so educated may suffer from mental
illness or be exceedingly ill-disciplined. Also
as *special school* where they receive *special
education*.

special clinic a hospital reserved for the
families of politicians and senior officials
A feature of the Soviet Union and other
Communist and totalitarian regimes. They
also ate *special food* bought in *special stores*, and
took holidays in *special resorts*.

special constable *British* an ancillary and
voluntary police officer
Pillars of society except in Northern Ireland
where the *B-specials*, Protestant to a man, were
notorious for oppressing the Roman Catholic
minority. They were also detested by the
terrorists because of their local knowledge.

special court a tribunal with extra-legal
powers and procedures
The Nazi *Sondergericht* set up in March 1933 to
overrule and supersede the independent
judiciary was a good example:
> Dr Bergshasser...—an aryan by the way—
> was sentenced to ten months by the special
> court. (Klemperer, 1998, in translation,
> diary entry of 13 January 1934—the doctor
> had been overheard repeating a joke about
> Hitler)

special detachment an army or police unit
established to terrorize dissidents etc.
> Even the Jews of the Special Detachment
> were reluctant to pick the children up.
> (Styron, 1976, writing of Poland in the
> Second World War, where the Nazis so
> named a police force consisting of Jews
> working for the SS, mainly responsible for
> controlling other Jews)

special duty illegal or inhuman activity
sanctioned by the state
> 'Special duty groups' is a close translation
> [of *Einsatzgruppen*]. But the amorphous

word 'Einsatz' had another shade of meaning—knightliness. (Keneally, 1982, writing about Nazi gangs appointed to harass and round up Jews)
Other tyrannies employ the same language, methods, and concepts.

special friend a sexual partner to whom you are not married
Heterosexual or homosexual.

special investigations unit malefactors for political purposes
... the work of the Special Investigations Unit (Plumbers). (Colodny & Gettlin, 1991, writing about Watergate)

special needs requiring extra facilities and attention
Of children suffering from physical or mental illness, or otherwise not teachable among their age group:
Mrs Evans was attacked by ... the special needs pupil who suffers from Attention Deficit Disorder after he was told he was not allowed to go swimming. (*Daily Telegraph*, 2 September 2000—Mrs Evans was then suspended and prosecuted)

special operations something illegal or secret
Often authorized by government:
Sirven ... knows more political secrets than any one man in France as a result of his position in charge of Elf's 'special operations', a euphemism for wholesale bribery and political manipulation. (*(Daily Telegraph*, 8 February 2001—ministers used the state-owned company to pay bribes on their behalf)

special police police seconded from normal duties to control subversion and political disorder
A London variant, the *special patrol group*, was a riot squad which sometimes used excessive violence and unauthorized weaponry. In underworld slang, as *special fuzz*.

special regime a treatment intended to kill, or destroy the health of, a prisoner
The most severe of the four categories of Russian treatment of prisoners; the others were *general* (the mildest), *intensified*, and *strict*. If you were classed as *special*, you would be required to do heavy manual work for long hours under harsh conditions on 800 calories of food a day, so long as you survived. The Chinese Communists call such treatment *special education*.

special services and investigations the covert monitoring of law-abiding citizens
Caulfield had been a member of the NYPD and its undercover unit, the Bureau of Special Services and Investigations (BUSSI) ... known for its ability to penetrate and keep track of left-wing and black groups. (Colodny and Gettlin, 1991)

special squad a unit set up by an autocracy to harass or eliminate its opponents
So named by many tyrants, especially in Latin America. The Nazis used their *Sonderkommandos* for this duty.

special task force an extra-legal police group
Another instrument of tyranny or religious bigotry:
Their attempts at non-violent protests were brutally put down by the Special Task Force, a kind of Buddhist Gestapo. (Dalrymple, 1998, writing about Sri Lankan Tamils)

special treatment the torture and killing of your opponents
[He knows] ... what Sonderbehandlung means, that though it says *Special Treatment*, it means pyramids of cyanosed corpses. (Keneally, 1982)
A 1983 British Airways advertisement in Germany relied on a literal translation of 'You fly frequently. Don't you deserve a little special treatment?' Many travellers felt the use of *Sonderbehandlung* was a Freudian slip.

special weapons missiles with nuclear explosive warheads
Also known, especially in the navy, as *special stores*.

specimen a sample of urine
Medical jargon, sometimes confusing to patients.

spectral writing a book to be published in another's name
Acting as a GHOST[2]:
... Davies, the most skilful spectral author around. (*Daily Telegraph*, 19 August 2006)

speed[1] an illegal stimulant
Usually amphetamine. To *speed*, punning on driving a car above the legal limit, is to take such a substance illegally.
A *speedball* may be a cocktail of illegal narcotics.

speed[2] to drive a vehicle faster than the legal speed
And hope not to be caught by a *speed camera*.

speed money bribes
As demanded by officials and others in Bangladesh, and paid if you want service.

spend (seed) to ejaculate (semen)
Or for Shakespeare, *spend his manly marrow*. (*All's Well That Ends Well*)
Standard English and *spent* is a male's post-coital state.

spend a penny to urinate
Normally referring to urination by either sex, although only women were required, for the purpose of urination, to produce that particular coin needed to operate the lock of a British public lavatory turnstile or cubicle.

spend more time with your family to be dismissed from employment
Usually of a senior employee who has been peremptorily dismissed:
   ...he has not resigned...He will be preparing for the trial and 'would like to spend some time with [his] family'. (*Daily Telegraph*, 2 March 1995—as he was accused of false accounting there was some risk of his seeing his family only on permitted visiting days)

spend the night with to copulate with
Of either sex, usually in a transient relationship.
There is a legal presumption that adult males and females cannot spend a night in each other's company without copulating, if they are not married to each other.

spicy pornographic
Literally, highly flavoured, whence salacious.

spifflicated drunk
Originally, beaten up, although the *EDD* gives dialect meanings which include to confound or kill, which are the more normal imageries of intoxication. The slang shortened form is *spiffed*.

spike[1] to adulterate or introduce an intoxicant to (a drink)
Perhaps from *spiking*, or destroying, a gun by driving a metal object through the touch hole, or merely from the practice of inserting a hot piece of metal into a fluid. It is used of the addition of alcohol surreptitiously to a non-alcoholic drink or, these days, of the adulteration of a drink by the addition of narcotics.

spike[2] to reject for publication
Editorial jargon, from the metal *spike* on which rejects were once impaled.

spill to give information of a criminal or damaging nature

A shortened form of the common *spill the beans*, to reveal a secret.

spin the editing, suppression, or correction of a public statement
First noted in the *Washington Post* in 1977. Whether the derivation is from the twisting or from the entrapment techniques of the spider will never be known.
The activity is carried out by aides known as *spin doctors* or *spinners*.

spin a line to boast
A less common variant of SHOOT A LINE, but with the same fishing imagery, as some anglers favour *spinners* to attract a bite.

spirits[1] a man's semen
In obsolete use, the essence of maleness, whence the symbol of courage:
   Much use of Venus doth dim the light...The cause of dimness is the expense of spirits. (Bacon, 1627)
The modern SPUNK has the same duality of meaning.

spirits[2] spirituous intoxicant
Literally, no more than any liquid in the form of a distillation or essence.
Now generically of whisky, gin, rum, vodka, brandy, schnapps, etc.

splash to crash into the sea
Of aircraft, and also used transitively, meaning to force down into the sea:
   So, if Bronco...does have to splash the inbound druggie, nobody'll know about it. (Clancy, 1989—Bronco was a fighter pilot)

splash your boots to urinate
Usually of a male, but not necessarily out of doors or even wetting your footwear.

splice the mainbrace to drink intoxicants
The *mainbrace* was the rope which held the mainsail in position, and a vessel was in peril if it broke. In rough weather *splicing* it, or mending it by joining up the severed parts, was a hazardous operation and the seamen received as a reward a large tot of rum. The custom continues under the same style in the modern navy, to celebrate some national event. For the rest of us, *splicing the mainbrace* is more likely to involve whisky or gin and tonic than rum.

spoken for retained as an exclusive mistress
Literally, engaged to be married:
   You can spot these spoken for girls in the public trucks, sitting and smiling a lovely white smile. (Theroux, 1992—of the French colonial South Pacific where white soldiers

provided their gummy mistresses with
dentures, which they repossess to retain
title when they go back to their wives and
families on leave)

sponge a habitual drunkard
Punning perhaps on the soaking up of liquid
and his willingness to accept free refills,
sponging on others.
The British *sponging-house* was not an inn but a
temporary prison for debtors, where they
might be relieved, or *sponged*, of their cash
and valuables before passing into a long-stay
debtors' prison.

sponsor an advertiser
Originally, a godparent, whence one who supports a candidate or public performance.
Now standard use of paying for publicity by
financing another activity, especially in American television programming:
> Sponsors didn't write the programmes any
> more, but they did impose a firm control
> on the contents. (Bryson, 1994)
And the sickening introduction to an advertising break—'A word from our sponsor'.

spoon to caress heterosexually
A boon to songwriters from having, for once,
a whole series of unforced rhymes like *moon*,
June, *swoon*, and so on. There was once a
phrase to *lie spoons*, to nestle closely with the
convex side of one against the concave side of
the other. The Welsh too used to give their
sweethearts suitably carved wooden spoons,
as a token of their amorous interest. In the
19th century it referred also to homosexual
relationships between males:
> 'Spooning' between master and boy was a
> subject for cruel jest. (Pearsall, 1969, writing
> of Victorian boarding schools for boys)

sport (the) copulation
For Shakespeare *tout court*:
> He had some feeling for the sport, he knew
> the service. (*Measure for Measure*—he was
> not a tennis player)
Also as the *sport for Jove* and the *amorous sport*. A
sport-trap or punning *sporting section* was
the brothel area of an American city where
you might find the *sporting-houses*, or
brothels, staffed by *sporting girls*, or prostitutes.
In a modern *sports bar* you may not find anything
more titillating than a TOPLESS waitress:
> If nothing else [a soya-oil breast implant]
> means the topless waitress in your local
> sports bar can double as a salad-dressing
> dispenser. (M. Steyn in *Daily Telegraph*, 5
> December 1998)

sports medicine illegal drugs
Although prevalent among professional athletes on an individual basis, the practice and

language reflected state policy in Communist
East Germany:
> ... in order to win, everything possible
> must be done, and ... sports medicine had
> its part to play. (*Sunday Telegraph*, 27
> February 1994)
Cheating, or acting with exceptions (*mit
Abstrichen*), also had its official part to play,
and the use of drugs was called *laufende
Versuche*, or continuing experiments.

sportsman a gambler
The modern equivalent of GAMESTER[2]. Usually
it refers to regular or spectacular punters on
the results of horse or dog racing.

spot[1] a drink of spirituous intoxicant
I suppose a shortened form of a *spot of* whisky
etc.

spot[2] to kill
From the entry mark of the bullet, from
noting the victim, or merely a shortened form
of PUT ON THE SPOT:
> That's enough to spot a guy for. (Chandler,
> 1939)

spot[3] a tubercular infection
Usually referring to pulmonary tuberculosis,
when there is a hole in the lining of the lung
which appears as a spot on the X-ray plate. In
the days when the disease was prevalent and
difficult to cure, a *spot on the lung* sounded
better than a clinical description.

sprain your ankle *obsolete* to copulate
with a man before marriage
Usually in the past tense, especially if the
woman was pregnant. British women might
also suffer similar injuries to their knees,
elbows, and *thighs*, of which more at BREAK
YOUR ELBOW.

spread for (of a female) to copulate with
Usually willingly, once, and outside marriage.
Explicitly as *spread your legs*.

spring to secure the release of (someone)
Either referring to a legal pardon, to an
escape, or occasionally to bail before conviction, from the unexpected and positive action
of a released coil.

spring-loading *American* fraudulently
awarding stock options
The board rewards employees, including
themselves, when good news is on the way,
knowing that the price of the stock will jump
up shortly.

sprung slightly drunk
Like a ship which leaks but hasn't sunk.
Half-sprung is no more drunk or less sober.

spunk a man's semen
Originally, courage, and still used in that sense by the innocent or naïve.
As with SPIRITS[1], there were originally three associated meanings—semen, courage, and distilled intoxicants:
> Spunkie ance to make us mellow. (Burns, of whisky in an undated letter)

spur of the moment passion unpremeditated extramarital copulation
Not momentary anger or other forms of suffering:
> ... spur of the moment passion with a married woman ... (*Daily Telegraph*, April 1980)

spurious illegitimate
From the days when birth other than to married parents was viewed differently. Literally, it meant not real, although the resultant human beings certainly existed:
> He would not have spurious children to get any share of the family inheritance.
> (J. Boswell, 1791—Johnson was saying that adultery by a wife should be reported to her father-in-law)

Specifically as *spurious issue*:
> She only argues that she may indulge herself in gallantries with equal freedom as her husband does, provided she takes care not to introduce a spurious issue into his family. (ibid.)

squash to kill
Slang, from the way we kill insects.
Squashed means drunk.

squat[1] to defecate
The posture adopted and perhaps referring to the dialect meaning, to SQUIRT.
For females, a *squat* may mean urination only. Some figurative use, as:
> ... the 52 has told me squat about the enemy now facing me. (Coyle, 1987—the 52 is an American staff officer responsible for obtaining and disseminating information about the enemy)

A *squatter* is a lavatory without a pedestal seat.

squat[2] to occupy (a building or land) by trespass
Squatters' rights is an English legal concept dating from the social and economic need in the Middle Ages to see land and buildings, vacated and ownerless through plague, brought back into productive use. The verb is used both transitively and intransitively.
A *squat* is such a trespass, or the property in which it happens.
A *squatter* is someone who so trespasses except in New Zealand, where it meant a sheep farmer (Sinclair, 1991).

squeal (of a criminal) to give information to the police
There is an implication of duress, with the *squeal* indicating pain. It is used of informing on others or confessing your own guilt.

squeeze[1] to extort from illegally
Of all forms of extortion, especially in the Far East. Also as a noun, where it may mean no more than a tip to a servant, which is extortion of a sort I suppose.

squeeze[2] an attempted deflationary measure
A shortened form of *credit squeeze* in the days when politicians thought that a cure for governmental profligacy and incompetence might be to try to control wages and prices:
> Credit? An overdraft? Not much chance of that while the current squeeze was on. (Garve, 1968)

squiffy drunk
Literally, uneven or lopsided.

squirrel *American* the patient of a psychiatrist
The animal has a penchant for a NUT. A *squirrel tank* is an institution for the insane.

squirt to defecate
Normally of diarrhoea.
As a noun, always in the plural as *the squirts*, although a singular *squirt* is a relatively mild insult. *Skeet*, *skitters*, *squit*, and *squitters* are also diarrhoea.

stab (of a male) to copulate with
The common imagery of violence and pushing:
> He'd stabb'd me in mine own house ... he will foin like any devil. (Shakespeare, *2 Henry IV*—foin means thrust)

Being *stabbed with a Bridport dagger* was not copulating with a native of the Dorset town but suffering death by hanging, Bridport being famous for rope-making because of a climate in which flax flourished.

stabilization price control by government
Another political attempt to replace the law of supply and demand by statute:
> It cost then $888 a month, rent-stabilized. If it hadn't been for the rent-stabilization law, it would probably have cost $1,500. (Wolfe, 1987)

stable horse *obsolete American* a stallion
Another example of prudery about male animals kept for breeding: see also BIG ANIMAL. A *stable boss* does not keep stallions but is a pimp running more than one prostitute.

stacked having large breasts
Like the heavy loading of shelves etc. A male usage by those who see this as a desirable feature in a female.

stag pornographic
It is incorrectly assumed that all-male parties favour such titillation.
For *stag month* see STEG MONTH.

stain¹ *obsolete* (of a male) to copulate with outside marriage
He pollutes the female morally rather than seminally:
    Give up your body to such sweet
    uncleanness,
    As she that he hath stain'd. (Shakespeare,
    Measure for Measure)

stain² **(the)** *obsolete Australian* descent from a convict
A matter of shame for some Australians until after the Second World War:
    John Pilger...writes that in his Sydney
    boyhood in the 1950s even among the
    family one never made reference to 'The
    Stain'. (Bryson, 2000)

staining bleeding
Medical jargon, from the seepage of blood through a bandage.

stake (the) killing by burning
The victim was tied to a pole. The significance of this form of death for heretics was that nothing remained to reappear and cause trouble at the Resurrection.

stake-out a police trap where a crime is anticipated
There has been a previous survey of the location.

stale¹ *obsolete* a prostitute
Her freshness having been already destroyed by others.
Stale meat was a more experienced prostitute.

stale² *obsolete* urine
From its retention in former times for laundry and other use.

stale prices lower and more favourable prices than those currently quoted
A privilege accorded by some brokers to major customers is to allow them to deal after hours at prices which had been quoted earlier or when the exchange officially closed but had since changed, the loser being the private or overseas investor:
    Large sophisticated hedge fund clients were
    accorded privileges that were not offered to other
    investors, such as trading after hours at 'stale
    prices'. (*Sunday Telegraph*, 4 January 2004)

stalk to harass obsessively
Hunting game, but not on a single occasion with a view of photographing it or killing it. Men usually stalk women but:
    Is that how you saw it—she was 'stalking'
    him? (R. N. Patterson, 1996)

stand¹ an erection of the penis
In modern use, a noun, but Shakespeare used it as a verb in one of his lewd puns:
    When it stands well with him, it stands
    well with her. (*The Comedy of Errors*)
The penis may also be said to *stand to attention*, punning on the military drill.

stand² to be available for breeding
Standard English of a male quadruped, although MOUNT is more appropriate.

stand before your Maker to die
It would be presumptuous to sit. In various forms:
    ...none should accept Gratitude until it is
    his time to stand before the Father of us all.
    (le Carré, 1986)

stand by not to part from despite provocation
Normally of a wife who stays with her husband despite his adultery or disgrace:
    ...forced to resign...because of his
    'association' with a woman he met at an
    alcohol dependency clinic, even though his
    wife is 'standing by' him. (A. Clark, 2002)

stand down to be dismissed or prematurely retired from employment
Literally, to end a tour of duty or to revert to a lower state of preparedness after an alert. The term is used to protect the self-esteem of a departing, and usually senior, employee.

stand up¹ without notice or apology to fail to keep a date with (someone)
Usually in the past tense:
    Cannot believe it. Am stood up. Entire
    waste of whole day's effort. (Helen Fielding,
    1996)
To *stand up and be counted* is to express in cliché form your support in public for an unpopular or minority cause.

stand-up² *American* a person paid to make an instant comment on television
What others may call a *talking head*—see under TALKING. Perhaps from the *stand-up comedian*, who *stands* alone before an audience to perform his act.

standard small or poor quality
No longer the level of size, quality, etc. against which judgement of other similar products can be made. You will find that a *standard pack*

is small and a *standard* model of anything is the cheapest version without any refinements.

standstill an attempt by government to restrict pay increases
Another, but equally ineffective, version of FREEZE[1] and PAUSE[2] in the days when British politicians still revered King Canute:
> Thus, in the House of Commons on 6 November, 1972, when Heath announced a standstill on wages and prices, thereby introducing the kind of incomes policy which he had always sworn to eschew…(Cosgrave, 1989)

star in the east (a) an undone fly-button
An oblique warning from one male to another which seems not to have survived the zip age.

stark naked
Stark in this sense means completely, and this is probably merely a shortened form of the idiom *stark naked*.
The obsolete meaning, dead, came from a dialect meaning, stiff, often found in the tautological *stiff and stark*.

start bleeding to menstruate for the first time
The female concerned will certainly have bled from her nose or a wound on previous occasions:
> Yes, I matured early…I started bleeding at eleven. (Sanders, 1970)

starter (home) a small house
Not *you remember, you remember, the house where you were born* (with apologies to Thomas Hood) but the first you may be induced to buy. Less often as *starter house* or *starter*.

stash a supply of illegal narcotics
Or the place where the hoard is hidden, as in *stash pad*, a room or apartment used for that purpose.
To *stash* is to put such drugs in a hidden place, whence the addict adage *Never carry when you can stash*.

state farm *American* an institution where people are detained involuntarily
Where you consign forlorn children and geriatrics as well as criminals and lunatics. Also as *state home, hospital, training school*, etc.

state of armed conflict a war
This is how Prime Minister Eden described the position when he asserted, at the time of the Suez fiasco, that Britain was not at war with Egypt.

state of excitement having an erection of the penis
Not just enjoying a thrilling game:
> The picture allegedly shows Fr -------, the Anglican vicar of Burnham-on-Crouch, Essex, in a state of excitement. (*Daily Telegraph* 18 February 2004)

state of nature (a) nudity
Not that being clothed is unnatural, but using the imagery of NATURE'S GARB.

state protection the preservation of tyranny
As in the *Department of State Protection*, which controlled political prisons and all forms of publication as well as routinely spying on citizens in Communist Russia. In Amin's Uganda the body charged with similar functions was called the *State Research Bureau*.

statement *British* to assess for corrective treatment
A bureaucratic shortening of *prepare a statement* for consideration:
> …the mother of a child who was dyslexic and slightly deaf, describing how her daughter had been 'statemented' by the local authority. (P. D. James, 2001)

status deprivation being thought badly of
Educational jargon for a child who is objectionable or does badly at school and is not therefore respected or liked by teachers and fellow pupils.

statutory appointed other than on merit
It is used of membership of committees, boards, etc. where those perceived as being oppressed or the subject of prejudice secure appointment regardless of merit:
> I realised that the government would wish to include certain 'statutory members' such as representatives of the trade unions and the Co-operative movements—though not, to my regret, a Statutory Lady. (Cork, 1988)

See also OBLIGATORY and TOKEN.

statutory offense *American* the rape of a female
Legal jargon. A *statutory rape* is copulation with a female below an age chosen by law rather than by her physical development—see also JAIL BAIT.

steady company a person with whom you have regular extramarital sexual relationship
Usually in the phrase *keep steady company (with)*.
See also COMPANY[1] and KEEP COMPANY WITH.

steal privately to *obsolete* to copulate with extramaritally
From the surreptitious approach within a household:
> If, for instance, from mere wantonness of appetite, [a husband] steals privately to her chambermaid, Sir, a wife ought not greatly to resent this. (J. Boswell, 1791—Dr Johnson's views would find less favour today, but then there are fewer chambermaids about)

steer dishonestly to influence the placing of business
By pretending to give disinterested counsel in the selection of an adviser, vendor, or service when you are receiving a bribe, commission, or reciprocal benefit.

steg month *obsolete* the period around childbirth when a husband might copulate extramaritally with relative impunity
From being a gander in northern English dialect, wandering about while the goose was hatching the goslings, a *steg* became an aimless male. The wife who was unavailable for copulation was known as a *steg-widow*. See also GANDER-MOONER. *Stag month* and *stag widow*, which you may find in other works of reference, are mistaken corruptions.
In modern, probably ephemeral, slang, a *steg*, a shortened form of *stegosaurus*, is a sexually unattractive woman.

step away *obsolete Scottish* to die
Also as *step off*.

step down to be dismissed from employment
Used of retiring of your own volition, but also of when you are pushed:
> Sanders must step down. (*London Standard* headline, January 1987—the story was about a company chairman who was later dismissed, prosecuted, convicted, incarcerated, and then released from prison on account of an incurable disease from which he was to make a miraculous recovery)

step-ins *American* women's underpants
Not a bath tub or a pair of slippers. This usage has survived most of the evasions used for nether garments—see also UNMENTIONABLES[1].

step on *American* to kill
As we might squash an insect.
The obsolete Scottish *step on* meant to grow old, being a shortened form of *step on in years*.

step out on to have a sexual relationship with other than your regular partner
The phrase does not necessarily imply an end to cohabitation. To *step out with* someone is to be courting, or *stepping out together*.

stepney *obsolete* a pimp's favourite prostitute
I include this for the pleasure of explaining the derivation. A *stepney* was the spare wheel, carried on the step, or running-board, of a car, and only brought into use when one of the other four wheels was unserviceable.

sterilize to destroy
Literally, to render barren, whence to purify or make clean. It may refer to obliterating tapes or removing documents from files if they might prove embarrassing. In Vietnam military jargon, it meant dropping bombs and trying to kill or drive out the Vietcong.

stern the buttocks
Naval imagery in general use. The punning *stern-chaser* may have heterosexual or homosexual preferences.

stewed drunk
The common culinary imagery:
> ...most of the time in camp...poor old Abel was stewed. (Kenneally, 1979—Abel was not in the hands of cannibals)
You are no less drunk if *half-stewed*.
Sometimes also of being under the influence of narcotics:
> They kept piling the old hashish into the shisheh...He's totally stewed. (Deighton, 1991—a *shisheh* is a bowl made of shisham wood, or *Dalbergia sissoo*)

stews (the) *obsolete* a brothel
Originally a bathhouse, and we know what the other use of those places usually was:
> An I could get me but a wife in the stews. (Shakespeare, *2 Henry IV*)

stick[1] to kill
Of cattle in an abattoir and wild boars while hunting, or *pig-sticking*.
Of humans it means to kill or to wound, not necessarily using a slang *stick*, or pistol.

stick[2] a marijuana cigarette
Also known as a *stick of tea*, *dream stick*, or punning *joy-stick*.
To *stick a drink* is to add spirits to it.

stick it into to extort from
From wounding figuratively, I suppose. However, a man who *sticks it into a woman* is more likely to be copulating with her, the phrase owing nothing to the vulgar *stick*, a penis.

stick up to rob with a threat of, or actual, violence
From the command to *stick up your hands* rather than the use of a *stick* or hand-gun. A *stick-up* is such a robbery:
'You'll hold me up, I suppose?' ... 'I'm a stick-up artist now, am I?' (Chandler, 1939)

sticky a spirituous intoxicant
Usually a liqueur, from its tacky properties.

sticky-fingered thieving or corrupt
Other people's property adheres to the *sticky fingers*:
... during the two-year operation three hundred [and] fifty thousand was sneaked across the bench into the judge's sticky fingers. (Grisham, 2002)

sticky floor a low-paid job in which certain categories of employee may remain indefinitely
They are glued to their lowly positions:
Campaigners for equal pay say women face either a 'glass ceiling' because they are passed over for senior positions or a 'sticky floor' because they are stuck in menial jobs. (*Daily Telegraph*, 17 October 2003—a list of women 'barrier breakers' prepared in 2006 by the Equal Opportunities Commission chose the Labour politician Betty Boothroyd, who became the first woman Speaker of the House of Commons, for their Politics category, rather than the Conservative Margaret Thatcher, the first woman Prime Minister)

sticky stranger a clandestine electronic listening device
Espionage jargon—the device incorporates some form of glue or magnet for rapid deployment.

stiff¹(one) a corpse
Referring to the rigor mortis.
In vulgar slang it may also refer to an erection of the penis, or *stiffy*.

stiff² (out) to fail to honour a commitment
Criminal jargon, especially concerning narcotics:
'Suppose', she asked, 'he was in trouble over drugs. Stiffed his supplier, somehow.' (R. N. Patterson, 1996)

stiff-arm to compel through threats or violence
From a disabling hold in wrestling:
One more attempt to stiff-arm him occurred at 8.30 p.m. (Colodny & Gettlin, 1991—the White House was seeking to make the Attorney-General suppress the Nixon tapes)

stiff one a drink of spirits

The alcohol so described may be diluted by water, soda water, or tonic but will be a generous measure.
Also as a *stiffener*, from the supposed effect on the drinker.
Stiff, meaning drunk, may be the result of having imbibed too many *stiff ones*, but probably refers rather to the corpse-like condition of the inebriated.

stimulant (a) spirits or an illegal narcotic
Not a bribe, a kiss, a gift, an encouraging word, or any of the other things you might find stimulating:
... if ever there was a man who needed a snappy stimulant, it was he. (Wodehouse, 1934)
Their main source of revenue is from trafficking in stimulants, especially crystal methamphetamine (known as ice). (*Economist*, 29 February 1992)

sting to deprive by trickery
It refers to robbery, overcharging, cheating, or any other form of knavery.
The sting is the ultimate coup in an elaborate confidence trick or a complex police operation set up to catch criminals.

stinking very drunk
Not just *stinking of drink* but from the meaning, exceedingly, whence also the slang *stinko*.
The American *stink on* means to betray or deceive, possibly a variant of the vulgarism, to shit on someone.

stir a prison
Probably from the Romany and not what you do to your breakfast PORRIDGE.
To be *stir-wise* is to be experienced in prison life.
To *stir the porridge* is not to be incarcerated but to copulate with a woman shortly after she has copulated with another.

stitch up to fabricate evidence against
The imagery is from the securing of a canvas bag.

stitched drunk
Probably derived from the slang *stitched up*, embarrassed or compromised, rather than being sent home in a body bag. A *stitch in your wig* meant being mildly drunk in the days when a wig might be worn askew by those not totally sober, and to *stitch* meant to rumple.

stoat a libertine
It is unclear why the European ermine should have acquired such a reputation.
Forster in 1971 used the same animal to represent homosexual lust.

stock beast see BIG ANIMAL

stockade *American* a military prison
Literally, a strong fence forming an enclosure.
See also CHOKEY, which uses the same
imagery. (Conversely, the imagery is also used
in the word *paradise*, which comes from
ancient Persian meaning a wall around, via
Greek and Latin, being originally the description of the magnificent gardens built by (or
for) the Emperor Cyrus at Sardis.)

Stoke-on-Trent *British* homosexual
Not from the inhabitants of that worthy town
but cockney rhyming slang for BENT².

stomach (a) obesity around the waist
Usually of a male and incorrectly specifying
the internal chamber through which food
passes in the process of digestion. A *bit of a
stomach* also implies obesity rather than post-
surgical deprivation.

stoned drunk or under the influence of
illegal narcotics
It is hard to see what the discomfort of St
Stephen and others had to do with this
common use.
> He did his best work half-stoned. When
> you stare at motels for a living, you need to
> be stoned. (Grisham, 1992—referring to an
> investigator who habitually smoked
> cannabis. Here, as usual in this context, the
> half equals the whole.)

stones the testicles
On man and other mammals:
> A philosopher, with two stones more
> than's artificial one. (Shakespeare, *Timon of
> Athens*)
The obsolete *stoned horse man* was not a heroin
addict but the groom who took a stallion—
stony—around farms to impregnate mares.

stool pigeon a police informer
Pigeons were tied to stools to lure other
pigeons for capture.
To *stool* is to inform against.

stoop your body to pollution *obsolete* (of
a female) to copulate extramaritally
She is more likely to be recumbent than
bending down:
> Before her sister should her body stoop
> To such abhorred pollution
> Then, Isabel, live chaste. (Shakespeare,
> *Measure for Measure*)

stop a mouth to kill
Not necessarily by suffocation:
> 'That's all right,' I said, 'but their mouths
> must be stopped...They mustn't be
> allowed to talk.' (A. Massie, 1986)

stop one to be killed or wounded

A common First World War usage.
To *stop a slug* is more specific:
> I wasn't hired to kill people. Until Frisky
> stopped that slug I didn't have no such
> ideas. (Chandler, 1939—Frisky was a
> gunman, not a gardener)
To *stop the big one* is to be killed.

stoppage¹ an inability to defecate
Medical jargon and also used of nasal and
other physical blockages.

stoppage² a strike by employees
Trade union jargon which is still used despite
the fact that the organization affected continues to function. If the employer stops
people working it is called a LOCK OUT.

story a lie
Nursery usage, although the punning *story-
teller* may also be used of an adult. A *tall story*
implies exaggeration, and a *cock-and-bull story*
(ROOSTER and BIG ANIMAL story in 19th-century
America?) is an improbable fabrication.

straddle (of a male) to copulate with
Using the common riding imagery.

straighten out to bribe
You induce another to follow the line which
you indicate. We also use the phrase of our
forceful, but usually unavailing, correction of
someone with a different opinion to our own.

straighten the line to retreat under pressure
A military evasion:
> Forrest in the *News Chronicle* called the
> Catalonian retreat 'a straightening of the
> Government line'. (Kee, 1984—it was the
> start of the final collapse)

strain credulity to be considered un-
truthful
Members of Parliament are credited with
telling the truth even when few believe them:
> Mr Blair's decision to clear [Jowell] on the
> grounds that she had been ignorant of the
> money's existence—and Miss Jowell's
> further admission that she was unaware
> for several years that the mortgage had
> been paid off [by her husband]—strained
> credulity at Westminster. (*Daily Telegraph*,
> 3 March 2006)

strain your greens (of a female) to urinate
Referring to the colour of the urine and
perhaps its mode of egress.

stranger to the truth a habitual liar
Not more than circumlocution perhaps, but
people still don't like being called liars outright.

strangle to cause (a horse) to run badly in a race
You figuratively throttle it by tugging on the bridle.

strap a handgun
The etymology is obscure, except that *strapped* means carrying a gun in a harness.
To be *strapped for cash* is not to act as a mercenary but to be short of money.

strategic is an adjective which should always put us on the alert. It means according to a plan but more often seeks to indicate failure or an action taken under compulsion.

strategic differences arguments between managers or politicians
More often over personalities than plans:
   The official announcement referred to strategic differences between Pearson and Gowers...that classic example of euphemistic PR-speak. (*Daily Telegraph*, 4 November 2005)

strategic movement to the rear a defeat in battle
If the words 'in good order' are added, it may not have been a complete rout.

strategic premium an overpayment
The pretence is that synergy will justify the purchase:
   [The] Chief Executive admits the group paid a 'strategic premium' (too much) for Inter-Continental. (Daily Telegraph, 5 April 2001)

strategic review a commercial inquest
An exercise when managers try to discover why they are in difficulty and whom they can blame:
   The Chief Executive was ditched...the fine words were eaten, and a 'strategic review' (Cityspeak for U-turn) announced. (*Daily Telegraph*, 20 June 2004)

strategic targets any part of Germany
Mentioned nightly in news bulletins in the Second World War, explaining where the Allied airmen dropped their bombs.

strategic withdrawal a retreat
A commonplace of the military bulletins when things are going badly.

stray to copulate extramaritally
The *lust* in wanderlust. On its own:
   She's lonely—as well she might be, married to the sodden and straying major. (Atwood, 1996)
And in phrases like *stray your affection* or *stray from the hearth*:
   Stray'd his affection in unlawful love. (Shakespeare, *The Comedy of Errors*)

stray off the reservation to diverge from an agreed line
This is another contribution to the language from the Watergate conspirators:
   ...if Jeb 'strayed off the reservation'—the phrase had come to be used in the Nixon inner elite to mean refusing to adhere to the approved story of the burglary and the cover-up—Dean would not have remained at liberty himself. (Colodny & Gettlin, 1991)

streak to run naked in a public place
In this practice, which started in the mid-1970s, the speed was meant to restrict the visibility as well as to postpone capture. A *streaker* so behaves.

streamline to dismiss
Making things run smoother, it is hoped:
   She said the decision [to dismiss a senior employee] was taken to streamline the management. (*Daily Telegraph*, 17 October 2003)
Whence *streamlining*, making dismissals.

street a venue for taboo or criminal activity
The place where a prostitute, a *street girl* or *streetwalker*, may go *street tricking* to pick up customers, her occupation being *on the street*.
Street bets were wagers placed illegally through bookmakers' runners in the days when off-course gambling was illegal.
Street drugs are bought from illegal dealers and not through a pharmacy.
The American *street tax* is what may be regularly paid to a criminal to stop him disrupting your business, perhaps not too different to *street money*, the proceeds of vice or, on occasion, bribes to electors:
   He claimed Mrs Whitman's campaign paid what is known as 'street money' to black clergy and elected officials to dissuade them from getting out the black vote. (*Daily Telegraph*, 23 November 1993)

stretch¹ a period of imprisonment
A shortened form of *stretch of years*. In America a *three stretch* is a term of three years, or as the case may be.

stretch² a shortage of liquidity or assets
The jargon of businessmen who are short of cash, are unwilling to admit it outright, and would like published figures to enjoy the property of elasticity:
   A deal with Keebler, whether it is sold or we find a joint venture partner, will substantially resolve the stretch in our

balance sheet and leave us in a much more favourable cash position. (*Daily Telegraph*, 18 July 1998)

stretch the hemp to kill by hanging
From the material of the noose. The victim may be said to have effected the expansion:
Molly Maguire stretching the hemp in the last act. (*Pearson's Magazine*, October 1900)
More practically as *stretch the neck*:
At home it ran full tilt into the autocracy; into ... provincial governors with powers to stretch a neck at whim. (Moynahan, 1994, writing of Russia under the Czars)

stretch your legs to urinate
Why we say we have breaks in meetings or stops on long journeys.

stretcher a lie or exaggeration
Stretching the truth and those who do it are punning *stretcher cases*. If anyone is said to have *stretched credibility*, there is a question about their veracity, and if it has been *stretched to the limit*, the answer is self-evident:
Miss Hughes had stretched her credibility to the limit when ... she had said that she was unaware of the alleged abuses. (*Sunday Telegraph*, 4 April 2004)

strike out *American* to die
As in baseball.

string up to kill by hanging
Usually of lynching, on a conveniently placed branch which always seems to be to hand in cowboy films.

stripper *American* a thief
Especially of radios etc. from cars.
In standard English, a *stripper* removes clothes for sexual titillation.

stroke to attempt to persuade by flattery
As you might comfort a pet:
He asked himself over a glass of vodka whether Pokryshkin had handled—he didn't know the Western expression 'stroked'—him enough to create a false impression. (Clancy, 1988)
and the Watergate team reported:
We are giving him a lot of stroking. (Colodny & Gettlin, 1991—they were trying to persuade a witness to keep quiet)
A *stroke job* is such flattery.
(*Stroke* is a word which occupies several pages in the *OED*. Inevitably it has had a number of euphemistic uses, including copulation (Grose) and death, as well as being the standard English for a cerebral haemorrhage.)

stroke off to masturbate
Usually of the male. Sundry vulgar compounds also as *stroke the bishop, dummy, lizard,*

etc. A *stroke-mag* is a pornographic publication for males.

stroller *Irish* a habitual itinerant
But not *on the stroll* working as a prostitute.

strong-arm to steal
With the use or a threat of force:
If he had not strong-armed that money out of me I would have given him lots more. (Armstrong, 1955—his own surname originated from the English/Scottish borders where for centuries such activities were endemic)

strong waters spirituous intoxicants
Not a fast-flowing stream.
In Ireland the delightful *strong weakness* was dipsomania.

strop your beak (of a male) to copulate or masturbate
The allusion is to the movements in sharpening an open razor and punning on the slang *beak*, the penis.

structural changes the onset of cancer
True as far as it goes, but not the whole truth:
Why, [Churchill] asked, had the doctors used the words 'structural changes'? 'Because ... they were anxious to avoid talking about cancer.' (Moran, 1966—Moran was Churchill's physician)

structured arranged as a cartel
The imagery is the same as in *orderly market*—see under ORDERLY. The American *structured competition* describes attempts to disguise illegal agreements on price, market share, and so on.

struggle a political campaign
Fighting against the status quo but not necessarily using violence or engaging in an ARMED STRUGGLE.
For the Nazis, the *struggle for national existence* was the extermination of Jews, gypsies, and the chronically ill, a matter of such urgency that Himmler and the fanatics in the SS accorded the fight against the Anglo-Americans and the Russians a lower priority, until it was too late.

strung out addicted to illegal narcotics
From the haggard appearance? Also of anyone under their influence.

stuck cheated
Probably a shortened form of *stuck with a poor bargain*:
I experienced that peculiar sinking that accompanies the birth of the conviction that one has been stuck. (Somerville & Ross, 1897, telling of a horse deal)

stuck on infatuated with
No doubt from the desire to enjoy propin-
quity.

stud a male viewed sexually
The imagery is from the place where stallions
are kept for breeding, rather than a projecting
lug. Of heterosexuals or homosexuals.
The punning *stud farm* is a place where
homosexuals congregate.

studio a garret
How an estate agent may describe an attic
being sold as an apartment, investing it with
spurious artistic associations.

study tour a vacation at another's expense
Enjoyed by politicians and public employees,
and not just in poor countries:
    These [third world government] officials
    enjoy other essential items: luxury office
    furniture, mobile phones, laptops, Toyota
    Land Cruisers and 'study tours' (i.e.
    junkets). (*Daily Telegraph*, 13 October 2004)

stuff[1] any taboo or forbidden substance
Literally, any substance or material. Among
other things, it may refer to semen, to
contraband spirits, or to illegal drugs:
    ... put stuff
    To some she-beggar. (Shakespeare, *Timon of
    Athens*)
    A considerable amount of 'stuff' finds its
    way to the consumers without the formality
    of the Custom House. (Stoker, 1895)
    ... he smokes too much, and 'stuff'.
    (Bogarde, 1981)

stuff[2] to copulate with
From the physical entry rather than impregnation, despite:
    A maid, and stuff'd! there's goodly catching
    of cold. (Shakespeare, *Much Ado About
    Nothing*)
There is much figurative use:
    As for the flute, he knew where he could
    stuff that. (Davidson, 1978)
and in abusive phrases like *get stuffed* and *stuff
that*.

stuff the channel to show profit on sales
which have not been made
Either by over-delivering, delivering in advance of the date requested by the customer,
or taking revenue yet to be earned:
    Analysts accused AIT of prematurely
    booking sales, known within the software
    industry as 'stuffing the channel'. (*Daily
    Telegraph*, 14 June 2002)

stump liquor *American* illegal spirits
Probably made by a *stump-jumper*, or hillbilly.

stung by a serpent pregnant
The common imagery of the penis as a snake,
in this instance leaving an unwanted mark.
Stung may also mean drunk.

stunned *American* drunk
Common slang, with obvious imagery.

stunt a limited battle
Much more than just a trick, but soldiers in
the First World War understated the horrors:
    If he don't get the Victoria Cross for this
    stunt I'm a bloody Dutchman. (Richards,
    1933)

stunted hare a rabbit
For seamen, the mention of rabbit is taboo
although it is a long time since chandlers
substituted salted rabbit meat, which decays
quickly, for the conventional salted pork. See
also FURRY THING.

stupid drunk
Derived from the drunkard's behaviour rather
than from the folly of getting like it. Common
still in Scotland as *stupid-fou*.

subdue to your will to copulate with
extramaritally
Males do it, overcoming, so it suggests, female
fears or scruples. The woman has to be royal
or rich to reciprocate:
    ... the queen has only two uses for foreign
    men—first to subdue them to her will, if
    you follow me ... (Fraser, 1977)

submit to to copulate with
It is usually the female who *submits* to a man's
will or *pleasure*, with a suggestion that she is a
reluctant participant.

subnormal suffering from mental illness
or disability
Statistically, half the population is below the
norm. Standard English for those in society
with very low intelligence.

sub-prime not creditworthy
Prime suggests the highest quality below
which most of us can be found, but not in
the world of banking:
    Household specialises in what are known
    euphemistically as 'sub-prime' borrowers—
    those people the other banks wouldn't
    touch. (*Daily Telegraph*, 30 May 2003)

subsidy publishing the publication of a
book at the author's expense
VANITY PUBLISHING, which means the same
thing, is nearer to the truth.

substance an illegal narcotic
Literally, any matter. Normally in compounds
like *illegal substance*, which could just as well
mean Semtex in the hands of a terrorist.
Substance abuse is the ingestion of illegal
narcotics, or sniffing glue or solvents.

succubus a prostitute
Originally, a female demon who copulates with men in their sleep, thus for the fastidious providing an excuse for involuntary nocturnal seminal ejaculation:
> 'Yes, thou barbarian,' said she, turning to Wagtail, 'thou tiger, thou succubus!' (Smollett, 1748)

Succuba would seem the correct gender, but is wrong.

succumb¹ to die
Literally, to give way to anything, and usually of natural death.

succumb² to copulate outside marriage
Another form of giving way, or something, by either sex:
> I'm willing to bet you five dollars she doesn't succumb even to the charms of William. (Archer, 1979)

suck off to practise fellatio or cunnilingus on
Of obvious derivation.
Sucker, a dupe, came from the supposed gullibility of a 19th-century American piglet rather than any sexual association.

suck the monkey *British* to steal rum
A naval practice, by inserting a straw surreptitiously in a cask. It also referred to the practice of filling a coconut with rum to drink on board ship. The obsolete *suck the daisy roots* meant to be dead.

suffer to be killed
An obsolete use, as in the Apostles' Creed, which tells us 'He suffered and was buried':
> In it is a pyramid erected to the memory of Thomas Lord Lovat, by his son Lord Simon, who suffered on Tower-hill. (J. Boswell, 1792—Thomas, not Simon, had sided with the Stuart Prince Charles and had his head chopped off as a result)

To *suffer the supreme penalty* is explicit.

suffer fools gladly to tolerate incompetence
Euphemistic only in the negative, especially of impatient people:
> I could not easily forgive the mistakes of others, what is euphemistically called not suffering fools gladly. (Lomax, 1995)

sugar¹ a bribe
The common imagery when you SWEETEN¹ a deal.

sugar² a mild oath
Common genteel use, for the taboo *shit*.

sugar³ an illegal narcotic
It describes any white narcotic in crystalline form, or LSD deposited on a lump of sugar to make it palatable.

sugar daddy a man with a mistress much younger than himself
Daddy from the generation gap and *sugar* from the sweet things of life which she may expect of him.
Sometimes shortened to *daddy*.

suggestion the unauthorized disclosure of privileged or confidential information
How an INSIDER tips off his friends:
> He'll get a commission of five percent of all profits generated by his 'suggestions'. (Erdman, 1987, writing about share dealing)

Although to make such a *suggestion* may be improper, an *improper suggestion* is specifically making a sexual proposal to someone who resents receiving it.

suits (the) men in professional or managerial jobs
A derogatory term used by those over whom they think they can exercise authority and who may be less formally attired.

sun has been hot today *obsolete* there are signs of drunkenness
At harvest time, cider or small beer was provided for the workers in the fields, who would become progressively more tipsy as they slaked their thirst. A drunkard might also be said to *have the sun in his eyes* or to *have been in the sunshine*.

sun is over the yardarm let us drink some alcohol
By naval tradition, you might start drinking alcohol when the sun had fallen below the *yardarm*, a horizontal spar from the mast. Landlubbers may use the phrase at the end of a day's work.

Sunday incompetent or amateur
As different from those who perform functions during the week for a living. Thus a *Sunday driver* may try your patience by dawdling or threaten your life by incompetence. It can, however, mean no more than doing something as a hobby:
> [Ira Gershwin] was an enthusiastic, gently gifted, Sunday painter. (Muir, 1997)

Sunday traveller *obsolete Irish* an illegal drinker of intoxicants at an inn
At one time only a bona fide traveller could legally be served with intoxicants on Sundays in Ireland.

sundowner a drink of intoxicants
From the habit of drinking alcohol in the tropics after the risk of dehydration is lessened.

sunset years old age
Those who appreciate the beauty of sunset normally do not relish the darkness which must follow. Less sickly however than the GOLDEN YEARS.

supplier discount *British* a preferential price
The penalty suppliers may have to pay for having supermarkets as their customers and a reason why other shopkeepers shall have to charge more or go out of business:
> A quarter of M&S's sourcing comes directly from factories and these supplier discounts are moving from 5% to 10.5%. (*Daily Telegraph*, 3 March 2006)

supporters' club investors who act in concert
Often following the lead or career of a successful investor or manager, forming a FAN CLUB which skirts the fringes of the law. Less often it may refer to the employees of a potential customer who favour a specific vendor, from whom they may receive bribes.

supportive obsessive
Literally, ready to support, but the use may imply a deep commitment to, and obsession with, a cause, and contempt for those who may not share the same opinions or emotions:
> ... if the caring and supportive wanted a political focus, it was necessary to drive ... to meet others with similar ambitions for the use of the planet. (*Daily Telegraph*, May 1990—the ecological point might have been better made by leaving the car in the garage)

supreme measure of punishment death by execution
Not suffered voluntarily by those who MAKE THE SUPREME SACRIFICE. Also as *the supreme penalty*:
> With an affectionate pat, he assured the historian Yuri Staklov that he was safe; the NKVD came for Staklov that night. The scribbled letters SMP, Supreme Measure of Punishment, filled the margins of his lists. (Moynahan, 1994, writing of Stalin and his terror)

sure thing a promiscuous woman
And considered likely by male acquaintants to be so. The derivation is from the racehorse so described by a tipster, although there are no certainties in either sport:
> ... hardly at all like someone who in her time had been one of the surest things between Bridgend and Carmarthen. (Amis, 1986)

surgical appliance see APPLIANCE

surgical strike a bombing raid
Supposedly as accurate as the first incision of the scalpel:
> ... precision bombing is 'surgical strikes'. (Commager, 1972, writing about Vietnam, where carpet bombing was liable to be classified as *precision*)

surplus[1] *American* to dismiss from employment
Discharging the excess quantity:
> IBM has reportedly 'surplused' 25,000 jobs corporate-wide. (*Computer Shopper*, July 1993)
Perhaps less euphemistic as a noun:
> BT expects no significant job losses from the tie-up but AT&T president John Zeglis admitted his company might find some 'pockets of potential surplus'. (*Daily Telegraph*, 27 July 1998)

surplus[2] a profit
An evasion used by an organization which purports to be charitable rather than commercial:
> In the old days [building] societies never used to talk about profits, preferring the euphemism 'surplus'. (*Daily Telegraph*, 19 November 2004)

surprising fraudulent
Code word for racing journalists when the outsider wins at long odds, which have shortened rapidly just before the off. Thus a *surprising change of form* or *of staying power* in a report indicates that this was the race the insiders, or a corrupt trainer, had fixed.

surrender to (of a female) to copulate with
The common imagery of male aggression and dominance.

surrendered personnel Japanese prisoners of war
In September 1945, the British/Indian 14th Army, having driven the Japanese out of Burma in a crushing victory, was faced with rounding up superior numbers of Japanese troops in Malaya, Siam, Indo-China, and the Dutch East Indies. As a salve to Japanese pride, and to discourage any from heroics, the victors were instructed not to refer to their captives as prisoners of war.

surveillance spying
Literally, no more than keeping a watch over. Police and espionage jargon for clandestine observation. *Electronic* or *technical surveillance* is the use of hidden microphones, wiretaps, or other gadgetry of spying.

suspect cigarette an illegal narcotic
Normally marijuana, smoked as you would legal tobacco:
> An unsuccessful party to welcome Mrs Neville culminated in a black saxophonist,

playing with the blatant inspiration of a suspect cigarette, strolling overboard into the Thames. (*Daily Telegraph*, 13 June 1997—the party was being held on a houseboat)

swallow the anchor to retire from a career at sea
Originally a British naval use but also adopted by yachtsmen and others.

swallow the Bible *American* to perjure yourself
From swearing on the Bible when you take the oath in court:
    They will stick together, stretch conscience and at times 'swallow the Bible'. (Lavine, 1930)
See also EAT THE BIBLE and SWITCH THE PRIMER.

swaps matched business dealings between two parties aimed at deceiving investors
Each purports to sell to the other the same goods or services as are bought, thereby reporting higher sales and demand:
    Yesterday's deal was seen as good news for the ailing telecoms sector, most of which is facing investigations for curious accounting methods such as 'swaps'. This saw major players sell access to each other's networks, often at identical prices, in an attempt to boost reported income. (*Daily Telegraph*, 21 August 2002)

sweat it out of to obtain information from by coercion
Police jargon, sometimes shortened to *sweat*. The coercion usually takes place in a cell named a *sweat-box*, which, significantly, used to be 19th-century criminal slang for any cell in a British police station.

Sweeney see FLYING SQUAD

sweet equity shares issued to favoured parties at below their value
As a reward for those on the inside arranging a deal or to satisfy the greed of their advisers and other associates:
    ...those ubiquitous buy-out teams with their dazzling 'sweet equity' incentive packages. (*Daily Telegraph*, 8 April 1999)

sweet man *American* a woman's regular extramarital sexual partner
Mainly black usage. A *sweet woman* is a black man's black mistress and a *sweet boy* is a catamite.

sweet tooth an addiction to illegal narcotics
A fondness for CANDY.

sweetbreads animal glands used for food
Literally, the thymus or pancreas, but also the testicles. See also VARIETY MEATS and PRAIRIE OYSTER[1].

sweeten[1] to bribe
Using the common imagery of making something more toothsome:
    Now-a-days ane canna' phraise,
    An' sooth, an' lie, an' sweeten,
    An' palm, an' sconse. (Lauderdale, 1796—
    referring to flattery, bribery, and trickery)
And in modern use of an improper inducement. A *sweetener* is such a bribe, not necessarily in cash.

sweeten[2] to attempt to improve by deception
Of an auctioneer who purports to accept spurious bids or, in show business, describing the practice of interposing canned laughter in a recorded programme so that, when broadcast, it appears that the studio audience found the show funnier than it had, or was.

sweetheart indicative of an arrangement which improperly benefits two parties at the expense of a third
It may describe deals between an employer and union officials, like channelling pension funds through the union with the officials taking a commission, at the expense of the wages paid to the workforce; or insiders cheating stockholders on a share deal.

swell to be pregnant
Of obvious imagery, and not used of male or female obesity:
    Unless it swell past hiding, and then it's past watching. (Shakespeare, *Troilus and Cressida*)

swill to be a habitual drunkard
Literally, to rinse out, but long standard English for drunkenness. The usual stream of derivatives—*swilled*, *swiller*, *swill-pot*, and the like—seem to have passed into disuse. See also SIX O'CLOCK SWILL.

swim for a wizard *obsolete Lancashire* to test for magical powers of evil
Witchcraft was a fruitful subject for taboo and euphemism. I include this sample entry to remind us of the social behaviour and beliefs of our recent ancestors, which were not confined to Salem:
    So late as 1863, an old man was flung into a mill-stream...being what was called 'swimming for a wizard'. (Harland & Wilkinson, 1867—presumably, he drowned if he was human and you killed him if he proved himself a wizard by not drowning)
See also WAKE A WITCH.

swing[1] to be killed by hanging

The motion of a suspended corpse. Now used figuratively after an error in the phrase *I'll swing for this*.

To *swing off* is to die by other means.

swing² to engage in any taboo act
From the meaning, to act in a modern or unrestrained fashion. It is used of ingesting illegal drugs, extramarital copulation, and any other conduct which may offend conventional mores, including homosexuality.

Married couples jointly participating in a taboo activity may be said to *swing together*:

> One couple we know are Godparents of the other couple's children—but they swing together. It's just a friendly way of showing friendship. (Whicker, 1982, quoting a wife who, like her husband, regularly copulated with third parties)

To *swing both ways* is to have both heterosexual and homosexual tastes.

swing around the buoy *British* to have an easy job
Naval imagery, from a ship at anchor moving with the tides, and the consequent inactivity for the crew.

swing the lamp *British* to boast
Naval usage and imagery, probably from the action of a signaller passing a message between ships at night rather than from the movement of a suspended lamp below decks.

swing the lead to pretend unfitness to avoid work or duty
The association with the function of the leadsman is unclear.

swipe to steal
The *SOED* observes that it was originally an American use of the word, but an old English dialect use meant to take possession of:

> When awd man deed, Bob swipet all bit o' brass he had. (*EDD*, mid-19th century)

swish *American* (of a male) to flaunt your homosexuality
He conducts himself in a manner recognized by fellow homosexuals, possibly from the slang meaning, smart. A *swish* is a homosexual male.

switch-hitter a person with both homosexual and heterosexual tastes
From the American ambidextrous baseball player.

In obsolete British use, to *switch* was to copulate, along with to *swinge* and to *swive* (Grose).

To *switch on* means to excite sexually, being a variant of TURN ON.

switch-selling dishonest advertising of cheap goods designed to induce a customer to buy something dearer

Not offering for sale whips or false hair but a scam outlawed in 1962 by the British Code of Advertising Practices.

switch the primer *Irish* to perjure yourself
The *primer* was a prayer book, and a Roman Catholic would have small regard for the mana of the Protestant Bible produced in court for him to swear upon.

sword the penis
Viewed sexually as in the male vulgarism *pork sword*. A *sword-swallower* is the patient in fellatio. A *swordsman* is a male profligate.

sympathetic ear a self-righteous person forcing his attention on those suffering a misfortune
Literally, someone prepared to listen with sympathy:

> No tragedy is too immense and no personal anxiety too insignificant to be absorbed by Britain's vast emotional sponge of psychotherapists, social workers, trauma experts, do-gooders, and assorted sympathetic ears. (*Daily Telegraph*, 31 March 1994—what about the omnipresent *counsellor*?)

syndicate *American* an association of powerful criminals
Literally, any group of business associates.

syndrome any taboo medical condition
Originally, a set of symptoms of which the cause was conjectural or unknown, but now denoting established afflictions like DOWN'S SYNDROME, *Acquired Immune Deficiency Syndrome* (AIDS), *Korsakoff's Syndrome* (delirium tremens) and the deadly *School Phobia Syndrome*, which makes the life of an EDUCATION WELFARE MANAGER so stressful.

synergy benefit the dismissal of employees
An advantage of coming together, except for those who lose their jobs:

> Aviva, like so many large companies, has been a job-shredding machine for years and the much-vaunted 'synergy benefits' of this deal consist of just that—redundancies. (*Sunday Telegraph*, 20 March 2005)

syrup a wig
Rhyming slang on *syrup of figs*. Usually of one worn by a male, against which the taboo remains stronger in Britain than in America:

> ...a hairline down to his eyebrows... It can't be an iffy syrup, because he's too drunk to put it on. (P. McCarthy, 2000)

T

tackle the male genitalia
Literally, equipment.
Also as *marriage* or *wedding tackle*, which does not refer to the buttonhole or morning coat, the veil, the bouquet, or bridal gown.

tactical done involuntarily under pressure
Originally, relating to the deployment of troops, but something announced as a *tactical regrouping* is a forced retreat. A *tactical nuclear weapon*, for use against troops, is correctly described.

tagged¹ hit by a bullet
Literally, labelled, from the old superstition among soldiers that the bullet which hits you *has your name on it.*

tagged² *American* detected in the commission of a crime
Being caught and named.

tail¹ a woman or women viewed sexually by a male
Not from following someone but probably from her physical attributes. A *flash-tail*, in obsolete use, was a prostitute. Often in the vulgarism a *bit* or *piece of tail*. The punning *tail-gunner* is a male homosexual.

tail² to follow surreptitiously
Staying close behind. Whence a *tail*, who does the following, and a *tail-job*, such an operation.

tail-pulling the publication of a book at the author's expense
Publishers' punning usage, from the meaning, teasing.

take¹ to steal
OED gives a first use in this sense in 1200, since when it had been standard English. In modern use it may refer to being bribed.

take² to copulate with
Usually the male *takes* the female, although the converse would be more logical.
To *take a bit from*, *take advantage of*, or *take pleasure with* is to copulate with promiscuously.
To *take a liberty with* is to make an unsolicited physical sexual approach, by a male.

take³ to kill
The victims are usually animals, culled or hunted. If you *take someone with you*, you kill

another while being killed yourself. Humans may be *taken off*:
> ...he called pneumonia 'the old man's friend'...because it takes them off so quickly. (Moran, 1966)

Those who are *taken away*, *taken home*, *taken to God's bosom* (or to a place of similar comfort), or who *take leave of life* may be assumed to have died of natural causes. To *take your life* is to kill yourself.

take⁴ to succeed in a competitive or illegal venture
An omnibus usage which covers anything from aggressively passing another vehicle on the highway to robbery or assault:
> [The cracksman] had no doubt he could 'take' the apartment at Fontenoy House. (Forsyth, 1984)

take a bath to suffer a heavy financial loss
Your boat is capsized.

take a break to allow the intrusion of advertisements
Television jargon, especially when the same programme will be resumed.

take a drink to be an alcoholic
The liquid is not water and the noun would be more correctly used in the plural. Also as *take too much*.
To *take (a little) something* does not imply alcoholic excess.
To *take needle* is to inject drugs illegally.

take a hike to leave in a hurry
The departure may be involuntarily from employment, as a synonym of the more common TAKE A WALK; a disappearance to avoid your creditors; or becoming a fugitive for any other reason. Also as *take a powder*, as with the rapid movement after taking a laxative.

take a leap to kill yourself by jumping off a high place
This is an example of many similar expressions for suicide. Thus he who *takes a long walk off a short pier* is assumed to be a non-swimmer, and the water deep.

take a turn in the stubble *obsolete* (of a male) to copulate
One of many vulgar puns of which our forefathers were so fond, a *turn*, being a stroll or outing, and the *stubble*, pubic hair. To *shoot over the stubble* was to suffer premature ejaculation or the withdrawal method of contraception. Grose tells us that a man might take many other similar *turns*, in *Cupid's Corner*, *Love Lane*, *Mount Pleasant*, and other punning addresses in

London. A female might *take a turn on her back* in any part of the Kingdom.

take a walk to leave involuntarily or under taboo circumstances
In American use, it means to be summarily dismissed from employment or courtship.
A spouse who *takes a walk* is not just going to the shops or exercising the dog. In espionage fiction, it means to defect.
Inanimate objects which *take a walk* have been stolen.

take a wheel off the cart to force another into bankruptcy
Bankers' jargon. Also as *take the wheels off the wagon*.

take an early bath to be dismissed for foul play or poor performance
Sporting jargon, but some figurative use also of dismissal from employment:
　　The week started with the farce of Sunday newspaper stories about...the chairman taking an early bath. (*Daily Telegraph*, 7 October 2000)

take care of to deal with in a taboo or illegal fashion
For a criminal or soldier, injuring or killing. For a tomcat it implies castration rather than tender loving care.
An official or politician who has been *taken care of* has been bribed.

take electricity *American* to be judicially killed
In the *electric chair*. In the jargon of death row, also as *take the walk*.

take for a ride to murder
You bundled your victim into a car and killed him in a secluded place.
Whence the current figurative meaning, to cheat.

take in your coals *American* to contract venereal disease
Naval usage, punning on the burning sensation.

take little interest in the opposite sex to be a homosexual
The case of the British naval spy Vassall highlighted the danger of using euphemism instead of direct speech. One of Vassall's referees, when he was being considered for a job which involved access to secret material, instead of warning of his homosexuality (and, at that time, the possibility of his being blackmailed), merely said that:...he took very little interest in the opposite sex. (N. West, 1982)

Also as *take no interest in the opposite sex*. See also NOT INTERESTED IN THE OPPOSITE SEX.

take out[1] (of a male) to court a female
The action may take place in the front room, if secluded enough.

take out[2] to render ineffective
By killing or other violent action.

take refuge in a better world by your own hand to kill yourself
How John Major (1999) described the suicide of a fellow politician.

take someone's (good or dear) name away to copulate with casually
The male takes the *dear* or *good name* by altering the female's reputation rather than her form of address through marriage.

take the air to absent yourself for a taboo reason
In the days when outside lavatories were common, for urination.
Those who *take the air abroad* seek relief from their creditors or arrest rather than a health cure.

take the can back to be held responsible
See also CARRY THE CAN for a dissertation on this usage.

take the drop to be killed by hanging from the scaffold
The hangman would first MEASURE FOR THE DROP, although weight was a more important factor in calculating how far the body should be allowed to fall.
Also as *take the high walk*.
To *take a drop* is merely to drink alcohol, not necessarily to excess.

take the Fifth *American* to decline to testify in court
The Fifth Amendment to the Constitution of the United States provides that witnesses cannot be forced to give testimony which may incriminate themselves.

take the mick(e)y to taunt or mimic
Rhyming slang on *Michael*, *Mick*, or *Micky Bliss* and *piss*, in the phrase, *take the piss*, an expression which is not used in nursing circles when a catheter is inserted. Seldom *tout court* as *micky*.

take the pants off *American* to reduce to penury
Figurative use of a financial rather than a sexual episode. Also as *take the shirt off*.

take the pledge see PLEDGE

take the soup *Irish* to convert under duress to Protestantism
See also SOUPER for an explanation.

take the wall *obsolete* to be socially superior
Those who walked closer to the buildings were less likely to be splashed or jostled. It therefore became a status symbol to occupy that space:
> When I returned to Lichfield, after having been in London, my mother asked me whether I was one of those who gave the wall, or those who took it. *Now* it is fixed that every man keeps to the right; or, if one is taking the wall, another yields it; and it is never a dispute. (J. Boswell, 1791, quoting Dr Johnson)

take the wind *American* to be summarily dismissed from employment or courtship
Usually of the person dismissed but occasionally of the one who rejects.
Also as *take the breeze*.

take to bed to copulate with
Of either sex, and see also BED².

take to the cleaners to rob or cheat
The process thoroughly removes all surplus matter.

take to the hills to escape or absent yourself for a taboo reason
Literally, mountains are the refuge of fugitives. Figurative use of errant spouses or absconding debtors.

take up with to have an extramarital sexual relationship with
Literally, no more than to consort with or support.

take your end *American* to accept bribes regularly
Your *end* of the bargain:
> Chicago was a right town then. The fix was in. The dicks took their end without a beef. (Weverka, 1973)

take your trousers off (of a male) to copulate
Not just retiring for the night:
> The belief... that they were 'the best people in the world' did not stop them taking their trousers off. (Paxman, 1998—writing of British colonial administrators)

taken (hence) dead
Not being killed but conducted by a beneficent deity from this world to another, or as the case may be. Also as *took*.

A *taking* or *taking hence* is such a death.

taken short needing to urinate at an inconvenient time or place
From the days when coaches, and trains without corridors, made no intermediate stops between staging posts or stations.

talent a stranger viewed as a possible sexual partner
Singly or collectively, by females of males and vice versa.
The punning *talent-spotting* is a male searching for such females.

talk to to bribe
More than verbal persuasion is involved:
> Pincus handled all arrangements with the lawyers who 'talked' to the judge. (Turow, 1999)

talking pretentious and boring
The adjective is applied to those summoned to a television studio to pontificate about and make judgement upon a current issue, filling airtime although seldom contributing much to the stock of human knowledge.
Usually as a *talking head*, even if rather more of the subject appears on camera.
A *talking cardigan* may be expected to adopt a staid or conventional approach, in line with the old-style attire.

Tampax time the period of menstruation
Of obvious derivation.

tank deliberately to lose a sporting contest
From the American *tank fight*, a boxing match in which one of the contestants took a dive into a figurative *tank* of water, punning on a contest between armoured vehicles. Whence *tanking*, such behaviour.

tanked (up) under the influence of alcohol or narcotics
Motoring imagery perhaps, which may owe something to the German *tanken*, to fill with fuel, although an association with the American *drink tank*, or police cell for inebriates, is more likely.

tanquem sororem without any copulation
Legal jargon in British divorce pleas when an annulment was sought on the grounds of non-consummation, the wife living 'as a sister'.

tap¹ to drink intoxicants
From piercing a cask to draw off liquid through a *tap*.

tap² to obtain an advantageous loan or other finance from
Again the imagery of the faucet, with a suggestion that repayment may be uncertain.

tap³ the constant availability of stock from willing sellers
Whence the market adage, *Where there's a tip, there's a tap.*

tap⁴ see DO-LALLY-TAP

taps (the) *American* death
Military use, from the roll of a drum at a funeral.

tarbrush (the) partial descent from a non-white ancestor
If a brush is used for tarring, it will retain dark streaks when you seek to use it later for a lighter colour. The genes controlling dark skin pigmentation are also dominant.
The use, once prevalent, especially among the British in India, is offensive.

target of opportunity (a) random bombing
The common instruction to bomber crews in the Second World War, giving them an excuse to jettison their bombs if they failed to reach or identify their designated target.

tart a prostitute or promiscuous person
The derivation is from *jam tart*, rhyming slang for sweetheart.
Now used of both sexes. One of my granddaughters used the word of a philanderer in January 2001.

Tartans (the) *Macbeth*
It is taboo among actors to mention that particular tragedy.

taskforce a committee hastily summoned to deflect attention from previous incompetence
A political ploy, and jargon, referring to the function of the specialist military unit which is truly a *force* and sometimes receives a *task*.

taste for the bottle an addiction to alcohol
See also BOTTLE. A *taste of something* is a single alcoholic drink:
   . . . they were proud if they wouldn't have a little taste of something. (Dickens, 1841)

tax *American* to steal with a threat of violence
Our contributions to central and municipal funds, involuntary and onerous though they may be, are not made under threat to our persons:

The principle of 'taxing'—mugging to steal shoes—is well established in the tough cauldrons of America's inner cities. (*Daily Telegraph*, June 1990)

tea *American* marijuana
From its likeness, when chopped, to tea leaves. Also as *tea-sticks* or *sticks of tea*.
Thus *tea-heads* may smoke marijuana at a punning *tea party*.

tea leaf *British* a thief
Rhyming slang.

tea money *British* a bribe or tip
A non-alcoholic DRINK². Sometimes, more expensively, as *beer money*.

team player *American* a non-critical supporter
Even if it involves condoning illegality:
   The case had been closed long before. Hickman Ewing was a team player. (Evans-Pritchard, 1997—Ewing had shown little enthusiasm for re-opening an enquiry into the mysterious death of Vincent Foster)
See also PLAYER.

tearoom *American* a public lavatory frequented by homosexuals
Another sort of meeting place frequented for refreshment and gossip. Whence the *tearoom trade*, those who frequent such haunts.
A Japanese *teahouse* is something else again:
   A teahouse isn't for tea, you see; it's the place the men go to be entertained by geisha. (Golden, 1997)

technical adjustment a sudden fall in stock market prices
The phrase seeks to imply that market-makers are merely covering their positions without anything so worrying as an absence of buyers or bad news. Be equally wary of a *technical correction* or a *technical reaction*.

technicolor yawn (a) vomiting due to drunkenness
Of obvious imagery.

teflon able to avoid responsibility
From the non-stick material serendipitously invented in America. Thus he who evades blame may be called a *teflon man*.

tell me about it I am already aware of that unfortunate fact
You are likely to get a withering look if you accept the invitation.

temperance see INTEMPERANCE

temporary permanent and embarrassing
A common evasion of politicians, soldiers, businessmen, and others seeking to mask the severity of a situation.

Major American defeats in Vietnam were described as *temporary*.
In commerce, a *temporary liquidity problem* indicates insolvency.

ten commandments (the) scratches by a woman's fingernails
When she says to a man 'Thou shalt not':
    Could I come near your beauty with my nails,
    I'd set my ten commandments in your face.
    (Shakespeare, *2 Henry VI*)
In occasional modern use it may refer to punches by either sex.

ten one hundred *American* stopping at the roadside to urinate
CB code which I have not unravelled. A *ten two thousand* is a seller of illegal narcotics.

tender a fool *obsolete* to give birth to an illegitimate child
To *tender* is to attend or wait upon, whence to offer or present. So spoke the punning Polonius to Ophelia:
    Tender yourself more dearly;
    Or—not to crack the wind of the poor phrase,
    Running it thus—you'll tender me a fool.
    (Shakespeare, *Hamlet*)

tender loving care *used in the context of* allowing someone to die
Hospital jargon of those mortally ill without hope of recovery. If you see the initials *TLC* on the charts at the foot of your bed, put your affairs in order.

tenderloin *American* associated with promiscuity and other illegality
Alluding to the choice cuts which the police might take in bribery.
A *tenderloin district* is the precinct where prostitution, illegal gambling, and other rackets are rife.

tenure a job for life
University jargon for security of employment until retirement of a teacher confirmed in his post, to encourage and ensure academic freedom but sometimes providing for the idle, the ageing, the tired, and the incompetent at the expense of their fellows, their students, and research.

term the duration of a taboo condition
Normally describing a prison sentence.
Formerly, in the plural, of menstruation:
    My wife, after absence of her terms for seven weeks...(Pepys, 1660)

terminate¹ to kill
Literally, to end.
When killing illegally, the CIA *terminated with extreme prejudice*.

terminate² to dismiss from employment
Another form of ending.

termination an induced abortion
Either referring to an unwanted pregnancy or on medical advice:
    A nice girl from a nice home...the thought of termination was unthinkable. (Seymour, 1980)

terminological inexactitude a lie
The term was coined by Winston Churchill in a speech quoted by Hansard on 22 February 1906, meaning inaccuracy rather than untruth:
    [Chinese labour in South Africa] cannot in the opinion of His Majesty's Government be classified as slavery in the extreme acceptance of the word without some risk of terminological inexactitude.
    (V. B. Carter, 1965)
But clearly too elegant a phrase to countenance desuetude:
    ...half lies, or as Erskine May finds more acceptable, terminological inexactitudes. (Howard, 1977)

testing unfavourable
Literally, no more than problematic. Commercial jargon when trade is poor and the figures are bad.

Thai stick a cigarette composed of an illegal narcotic
Usually marijuana but also of heroin.

thank to bribe
In many places, verbal appreciation is not sufficient.

that side of marriage copulation
What brides-to-be were warned about in the days when they were still virgins.

that way¹ homosexual
Of either sex.

that way² pregnant
Female use, normally of an unexpected or unwanted pregnancy.

the worse drunk
A shortened form of *the worse for drink* or *liquor*.

thick of hearing *obsolete* deaf
Now replaced by HARD OF HEARING.
Thick on its own means stupid, a shortened form of *thick in the head*.

thief (of the world) *mainly Irish* the devil
Often further particularized as *old* or *black*.

thin out the team to dismiss employees
Usually of a reduction in management staff rather than less senior workers.

thing any taboo object to which you refer allusively

In former times, a ghost. Now the penis or, less often, the vagina:

> Uncle trying to find Aunty Joan's 'thing' and giving it to her in the bum. (Sharpe, 2004)

To have a *thing about* is to have a sexual feeling towards, and a *thing going* is an extramarital sexual arrangement between two people.

third age (the) senescence

As in the *University of the Third Age*, a British lecture and discussion group for elderly people.

third degree police violence to extract information

Probably from the scale of seriousness of burns, of which the *third degree* is the worst. Also as *third*.

third leg the penis

Also vulgarly as the *middle leg*.

third party payment a bribe

The favourite commercial euphemism of the 1990s. A *third party* is someone with a casual connection to the matter in hand.

third world poor

As different from the FIRST WORLD, rich countries, and the former *second* (Communist) *world*.

thirst an addiction to alcohol

Not dehydrated. *Thirsty* means so addicted:

> Tony Blair's thirsty father-in-law, actor Tony Booth, 71,...has withdrawn from starring in Humble Boy...saying his fourth wife, Stephanie, is unwell. (*Daily Mail*, 30 September 2003)

those days menstruation

A common female usage:

> Girls were separated off from the boys so they could be told about the curse. Not that the word was used. 'Those days' was the accepted, official phrase. (Atwood, 1988)

three-legged stool *obsolete* the gallows

Also known as the *triple stool*, from the method of construction.

three-letter man[1] *obsolete* a swindler or cheat

From the Latin *fur*, a thief.

three-letter man[2] *American* a male homosexual

The letters are, or perhaps were, f-a-g; and see also FAG.

three-point play *American* the recruitment of a non-white woman

The imagery is from basketball. The employer got a point for taking on another worker, a second point if the worker was a female, to show that he was not prejudiced about employing women, and a third point when he contributed to his quota of non-white employees. He hit the jackpot only if the recruit had American-Indian ancestry.

three sheets in the wind see SHEET IN THE WIND

threepennies (the) *British* diarrhoea

Rhyming slang on the duodecimal *three-penny bits* (for shits), useful as currency apart from their insertion in Christmas puddings to be prodded for eagerly on Christmas Day before you swallowed them or broke a tooth. Now obsolete apart from among those ancient enough to remember the ritual prodding.

throat a wish to drink intoxicants

Possibly a shortened form of *dry throat*, which makes you thirsty:

> I'd go to bed with yeh only I've a throat on me. (Doyle, 1987—he preferred to go to the pub)

throne a pedestal lavatory

From the shape, elevation, and solitary location. A person sitting on it is said to be *enthroned*.

throw[1] to give premature birth to

Usually of cattle, and still used in western England.

throw[2] to lose deliberately

Usually involving gambling fraud, and a shortened form of *throw away*.

To *throw in the towel* is to concede defeat in any endeavour, with imagery from boxing, where the second so indicates to the referee that his man concedes the bout.

throw down *obsolete* to copulate with

The common violent imagery, or the Bard's wordplay:

> And better would it fit Achilles much
> To throw down Hector than Polyxena.
> (Shakespeare, *Troilus and Cressida*)

Today a male may in vulgar speech *throw a leg over* or *throw a bop into* his sexual partner.

throw the book at to charge with every feasible offence

Mainly police jargon, the *book* being the manual setting out criminal offences.

throw the switches to become mentally unbalanced
The imagery is probably from electric power, although it might just refer to some sporting manoeuvre.

throw up to vomit
The oral expulsion, often due to drunkenness, is usually directed downwards.
An Australian may claim to *throw a map*. To *throw up your toenails* is to vomit excessively.

thump (of a male) to copulate with
Then and now, with the usual violent imagery:
> Jump her and thump her. (Shakespeare, *The Winter's Tale*)
> Well, if I'd had my way, he'd still have been thumping her every night. (Fraser, 1973)

thunderbox a portable lavatory
The sitter produces the sounds overhead. The Second World War American military *thunder-mug*, for urination, was not to be found in less lavishly equipped armies.

tick a person clandestinely following another
Espionage writers' jargon, referring to the parasitic arachnid, which sticks to your skin. In common use, a *tick* is merely a tedious or boring person.

ticker the heart
You only refer to it in this way if you have a fear it will shortly wind down, and cease *ticking*.

tickle to caress sexually
Of a male, and not necessarily touching the *tickler*, or clitoris.
A *French tickler* is not an ardent Parisian but a contraceptive sheath.

tiddly slightly drunk
Rhyming and punning slang on *tiddly-wink*, a drink, which was an unlicensed inn or pawnshop before it came to mean the game played in pubs with counters.

tie a can on *American* to dismiss from employment
Punning on CAN² and the cruel practice of tying an old can to the tail of a stray cat to drive it away.

tie one on *American* to go on a carouse
The etymology of this phrase is unexplained:
> We could tie one good one on, two days, three days, five empty bottles at the foot of the bed. (Mailer, 1965)

tied up unwilling to see or speak to a caller
The phrase has no connection with the old meaning, constipated, or with a fetish for bondage:
> Wouldn't it be better to say 'I'm tied up' or 'in a meeting'? (P. D. James, 1994)

tiger-sweat *American* an impure intoxicant
It may be beer or spirits, with no aspersions being cast at very potable *Tiger* beer from Singapore.
Also as *tiger juice*, *milk*, or *piss*. See also PANTHER SWEAT.

tight¹ drunk
Perhaps a pun on SCREWED, as the *OED* suggests, but I am not sure which usage came first.

tight² stingy
Tight with the purse strings and *tight-fisted*. A *tightwad* is a miser.

time the occurrence or duration of something the subject of a taboo
Of death or of childbirth, as in 'Elizabeth's full time came that she should be delivered and she brought forth a son'. (*Luke* 1:52).
For a convict it means a stay in prison.
The *time of the month* or *time of blood* is menstruation.

tin ear (a) arrogant disregard
It hears only what you want it to hear:
> Since leaving the White House, Mrs Clinton has displayed a tin ear to public opinion. (*Daily Telegraph*, 20 March 2001)

tin handshake a derisory payment on dismissal from employment
He who leaves would prefer it to be GOLDEN.

tincture¹ a partial descent from other than white ancestry
Literally, a pigment, and used offensively of those whose dark skin pigmentation indicates a non-white ancestor.

tincture² an intoxicant
Literally, in pharmacy, a medical solution in alcohol.

tinker *Irish* a gypsy or itinerant
At one time he made a living travelling from door to door mending pans. Mainly derogatory use.

tinkle to urinate
Onomatopoeic nursery usage, from the noise of urinating into a mild steel (not tin)

receptacle:
> Then that stopped…as a punishment for 'tinkling' behind the cupboard on the top floor. (A. Clark, 2000)

tinpot pretentiously assuming the trappings and manner of authority
The usage arose because a TINKER was loath to use expensive *tin* when repairing a *pot*. The substitute, prior to the availability of aluminium, was mild steel, which rusted and did not make a good repair.

tint to dye (hair)
Literally, to colour slightly.

tip¹ to copulate with
In former Scottish use, the rams *tipped* the ewes, whence the proverb:
> Tip where you will, you shall lamb with the leave.
In modern American use, to *tip* means to copulate with other than your regular sexual partner.

tip² (the bottle) to drink intoxicants to excess
From the motion of *tipping* the container.
Tipped and *tipsy* mean drunk.
A *tiper* or *tipper* was a drunkard; and see also TIPPLE.

tip off *obsolete* to die
The common avian imagery, being a shortened form of *tip off the perch*.
The slang *tip off*, meaning to warn or inform against, is not euphemistic.
If however you *tip off your trolley*, you are mentally ill, no longer figuratively connected to your overhead power supply.

tip over¹ to rob
Originally, from upsetting a stall and stealing some of the goods in the ensuing confusion, rather than from knocking over the victim. In modern American use it can apply to any theft.

tip over² *American* (of the police) to make a thorough search
After an unannounced raid, when the place is turned upside down looking for evidence.

tipple an intoxicating drink
Probably, despite its venerable ancestry, from *tip*, which meant beer.
A *tippler*, who today drinks alcohol to excess, used to be an innkeeper, who kept a *tippling-house*:
> No vyattler nor tipler to sell any ale or beer brewed out of town. (*Lincoln Corporation Records*, 1575)

tired¹ unwilling to copulate with your regular partner
A female explanation or excuse which may or may not have to do with weariness.

tired² drunk
The symptoms of weariness and intoxication can be the same:
> Mr Brown had been tired and overwrought on many occasions. (*Private Eye*, 29 September 1967—George Brown was a drunken British Cabinet minister; the more common phrase to describe his condition was *tired and emotional*)

to one side of the truth untrue
A Victorian evasion used in the British House of Commons where nobody must be called a liar regardless of their veracity.

to the knuckle devoid of resources
All the meat has gone.

together having a permanent sexual relationship with each other
Not meeting for a morning coffee or the companionship of wedlock. American more than British use.

toilet a lavatory
Originally, a towel, whence washing and the place where the washing was done. *Toilet paper* is used for wiping rather than washing.

token appointed other than on merit
The female or black member of the committee etc. whose presence is POLITICALLY CORRECT.
Whence *tokenism*, making such an appointment.

tolbooth *obsolete Scottish* a prison
Originally, the Town Hall, where tolls were paid. The jail was often in the same building.

Tom¹ (Tit) an act of defecation
Rhyming slang, always of defecation and never used as an insult.

Tom² *American* a black man who defers unduly to whites
A shortened form of UNCLE TOM.

tomboy *obsolete* a prostitute
From the reputation of male felines, perhaps, and also punning on TUMBLE¹:
> A lady
> So fair…to be partner'd
> With tomboys. (Shakespeare, *Cymbeline*)
Today it means no more than a girl who enjoys the athletic and other traditional pursuits of a boy.

tomcatting sexual excess
The reference is to the lustful feline:
> The tomcatting made history in the form of songs. (Longstreet, 1956, of New Orleans)

Tommy the penis
Rarer than DICK[1], commoner than *Harry*.

tongue an enemy prisoner captured for interrogation
In the Stalingrad campaign neither side was content with limiting a captive's speech to what the Geneva Convention stipulated, namely name, rank, and number:
> NVD officers and interpreters worked late into the night interrogating German prisoners, including the first deserters, as well as 'tongues' captured by reconnaissance companies. (Beevor, 1998)

too busy to take/return calls unwilling to speak to a journalist
The common excuse given when scandal is in the air, journalists are on the rampage, and heads need to be kept below the parapet.

tool the penis
Literally, any instrument:
> 'Draw thy tool.'...'My naked weapon is out.' (Shakespeare, *Romeo and Juliet*—another of the Bard's vulgar puns)
Grose has:
> *Tools*. the private parts of a man.

toot indulgence in a taboo activity
Down the centuries *toot* meant the devil and then, as noun and verb, has given us a wide choice, including farting, mental illness, defecation, the ingestion of illegal narcotics, and a drunken carouse. Some of these meanings at least must be associated with the onomatopoeic sense, a loud noise.
To *toot your own whistle* is to boast:
> 'Timbrell', said one contemporary, 'was a non-fuss sort of fellow who never tooted his own whistle.' (*Daily Telegraph*, 27 April 2006, in the obituary of a Canadian who, aged 20 and armed with an old pistol, had taken a motor yacht to Dunkirk and rescued some 900 men from the beaches)

top[1] *obsolete* to copulate with
Either a corruption of the standard English TUP, or from the position adopted by the male, or from his supposed dominance:
> Behold her top'd? (Shakespeare, *Othello*)

top[2] to kill
Illegally or legally, but not necessarily by beheading.
The obsolete *topping fellow* was a public hangman and a gruesome pun.

top and tail to clean up a baby
Nursery usage, with imagery from preparing gooseberries or root crops for cooking. The baby may have vomited as well as defecated.

top floor (the) senior management
Not necessarily sinister, as are the *boys upstairs*, under BOY[1], but occupying the best offices, wielding the power, and best spoken of obliquely.

top-heavy drunk
Unable to stand up without swaying.

top line visibility an inability to forecast profit or loss
Financial gobbledegook in a milieu where ignorance must never be admitted:
> ABM Amro would like its clients to know that 'top line visibility remains limited'. (*Daily Telegraph*, 10 April 2002—and were the clients any the wiser after this communication?)

top shelf pornographic
The publications so described are displayed there in newsagents, supposedly out of the reach of children.

top up to conceal inferior goods below those of higher quality
Usually of fruit sold by weight, where only part of the purchase is visible.

topless exposing your breasts in public
Beach, bar, and entertainment usage:
> As one of the show-girls who had to strut around the stage topless...(S. Green, 1979)
Thus a *topless bar* is not one which is open to the skies, and it is no longer prudent to use the adjective of a bare-headed man.

torch to set light to as an arsonist
Matches are more commonly used to start the fire.

torch of Hymen (the) copulation only within marriage
Hymen, the god of marriage, was depicted carrying a torch:
> The torch of Hymen burns less brightly than of yore. (Mayhew, 1862—and has by now probably gone out)

toss[1] to search (another's property)
Usually without consent and throwing things carelessly into the air as you rummage through drawers etc.

toss[2] summarily to dismiss
As might a bull.

toss down to drink (an intoxicant)
Not hay from a stack but alcohol down the

throat, from the movement of the glass.

A *toss-pot* is an alcoholic:

> The curate of Madras in 1666, for example, was described as 'a drunken toss-pot' (Dalrymple, 2002)

toss in the hay an act of copulation

The normal hay and BED[2] association which is noted at IN THE HAY.

Whence the common vulgarism *I don't give a toss*.

toss off (of a male) to masturbate

The imagery is obvious.

The figurative *tosser* is a term of male abuse:

> What would they know? Bunch of tossers. (C. Thomas, 1993)

tot a drink of sprits

Literally, anything small, whence a small drinking vessel or measure, which used to be from quarter to half a pint. Formerly, to *tot* was to drink intoxicants.

totty a sexually available young woman

DSUE suggests it is a corruption of the name *Dorothy* but *totty* as an adjective used to mean of bad character, whence a prostitute.

Now also of young females generically.

touch[1] to copulate with

Of the male only, despite the mutuality of the encounter and ignoring frequent previous handshakes and other physical contact by women with men:

> You have touch'd his queen forbiddenly ... (Shakespeare, *The Winter's Tale*)
>
> How do you know that [he] is an 'artist of love' ... if he is the only man who ever touched you? (Tremain, 2003)

Grose gives *touch up* in the same sense.

To *touch yourself* is to masturbate.

touch[2] an act of cadging

Normally described by the recipient as a loan, but do not expect repayment:

> A quick ten or twenty dollar *touch*, which of course was never intended to be returned. (Lavine, 1930)

In former use, to *touch* was to steal, usually from a pocket, except in a *touch-crib*, or low brothel, where the loot was taken from the victim's clothing.

touch signature a fingerprint

Bankers' jargon, when they want positively to identify their customers without using the language of criminal investigation.

touch up[1] digitally to excite the genitals (of another)

Usually the male does it to the female.

touch up[2] to dye (hair)

Barbers' jargon, implying a partial application where in fact the whole is treated.

touched[1] *obsolete* drunk

A shortened form of *touched with liquor* and usually of mild drunkenness:

> In respect of her liquor-traffic, she was seen 'touched' about once a week. (Tweeddale, 1896)

touched[2] **(in the head)** mentally ill

Not suffering from sunstroke but with a mind affected by some alien influence.

touchy-feely demonstrating insincere expressions of sympathy, or bonhomie

A politician or businessman so described does not need to make physical contact with those he seeks to impress.

tourist inferior

The jargon of air transport. Richer-sounding names are thought up for those who pay more, such as *club*, *sovereign*, *executive*, or *clipper*.

touristas (the) *American* diarrhoea

Suffered by many a tourist, or *turista* (including myself), on a Mexican vacation.

tout *Irish* a police informer

Terrorist jargon, from the tipster who covertly watches horses in training. Also as a verb.

town bike a promiscuous woman

The common *bicycle* who all men can RIDE. Not necessarily a prostitute.

toy boy a man consorting sexually with a much older woman

Not necessarily a gigolo, but often lavished with gifts.

tracks the scars left by repeated injections of illegal narcotics

Like railroad lines.

Track-marks seems tautological.

trade (the) prostitution

Or PROFESSION.

The *trade* can also refer to the customer:

> She doesn't like the trade, she packs it in and goes home. (Diehl, 1978)

traditionally built obese

In those parts of the world where men are supposed to prefer plump females.

trail to release information without attribution

The train of a garment which can be followed without seeing the source and another way to LEAK[2]:

> Mr Campbell's rules [as Tony Blair's Press

secretary] now require 'trailing' (the euphemism for leaking) to 'position' issues. (*Sunday Telegraph*, 9 July 2000)

trainspotter a boring person
Derogatory use of those who have non-intellectual hobbies, such as watching railway operations.

tramp a prostitute or promiscuous woman
Originally, from her walking the streets.

transfer the forcible deportation of a population
Those made to move do not go voluntarily to another place:
    Ze'evi, 62, is an advocate of transfer, the euphemism employed by the supporters for the removal from Israel and the Occupied Territories of the Arab population. (*Daily Telegraph*, October 1988)
The same euphemism was used for the forced movement of Jews by the Nazis and the Vichy French.

transfer pricing the fraudulent adjustment of prices between connected companies in different jurisdictions so as to reduce outgoings
Literally, the price one subsidiary charges another. Corporations seek improperly to minimize liability for tax, commission, royalties, and other payments by adjusting sales prices between associated companies to take profit in the most advantageous location and reduce commitments to third parties.

transfusion an alcoholic drink
Ingested, not injected.

translated *obsolete* drunk
Literally, transferred from one state or place to another, as from life to death or, in the jargon of the church, from one clerical living to another:
    Bless thee, Bottom, bless thee! thou art translated. (Shakespeare, *A Midsummer Night's Dream*)

translocation a surgical error
Literally, a rearrangement of genes or a movement from one place to another. Medical jargon for failure to locate correctly an implant or other device.

transported *obsolete British* sentenced to exile for a criminal offence
Not merely carried from one place to another:
    One old offender, who stole the Duke of Beaufort's dog, was transported, not for selling the dog, but his collar. (Mayhew, 1851—under English Common Law there

was no property in dogs or corpses)

travel agent a dealer in illegal narcotics
He allows his customers to go on a TRIP.

travel expenses bribes or money claimed dishonestly
Paid for trips which were not made, or for first class when you rode second:
    Owen, a former miner, had been recruited during a 1957 visit to Czechoslovakia and had been supplied with his 'travel expenses'. Thereafter he received regular cash payments from the Czechs. (N. West, 1982—Owen, a British Member of Parliament, was named by the defector Forlik as being in the pay of the Communists. Nobody was more surprised than the accused when he was later acquitted of charges of spying.)

traveller *Irish* a habitual itinerant
Often gypsies, although it is also a way of life for many families without Romany blood. Also as *travelling community* or *people*:
    ...there must have been fifty or sixty travellers crammed in the back of the close, malodorous cave. (O'Donoghue, 1988)
    Up to 100 members of the travelling community were involved in the fracas. (*Daily Telegraph*, 25 June 2001—six people were stabbed at a wedding reception)
    News was passed on with the speed of Morse among the travelling people. (O'Donoghue, 1988)
See also *new age travellers* under NEW AGE.

tread to copulate
It is used of birds, from their foot movements.

treasonable activity losing a battle or retreating
What Russian generals were guilty of in the Second World War, however gallant or out-gunned:
    General Rychagov...was under sentence of death for 'treasonable activity' (that is to say having been defeated). (A. Clark, 1995)

treat to bribe
Literally, to pay for another's enjoyment of an outing etc. In the 19th century, it was specific of bribing voters:
    ...the emollience with which the established Radical election agent offers treating at the polls. (R. F. Foster, 1993—a limited franchise allowed for individual bribery, a practice economically less harmful perhaps than today's pre-electoral governmental profligacy)

treatment the use of violence to extract information
Far removed from the medication which cures sickness.

tree-hugger a person thought to be unduly obsessed with preservation of the environment
Mainly pejorative use, especially when trespass or violence is used to prevent legally sanctioned development.

tree rat a prostitute
The small mammal infests the bashas used by troops as billets in India:
. . . any man who availed himself of the 'tree rats' or 'grass bidis' was properly dealt with. (Allen, 1975—a *grass bidi* was also a prostitute)

triangular where two people wish to enjoy an exclusive sexual relationship with a third
The *eternal triangle*, as different from a MÉNAGE À TROIS:
. . . not only was much left intentionally unsolved on the political scene, but also much in the triangular situation at Eltham. (Kee, 1993—reporting a conversation between Parnell and Mrs O'Shea)

triangular trade (the) trading in slaves
On the first leg, manufactured goods went from England to Africa; on the second leg, slaves went from Africa to America; on the third leg, commodities went from America to Europe. It was also known as the *African Trade*.

tribute a regular payment to an extortionist
The Latin *tributum* was what the tribes paid the Romans to leave them in peace, whence taxation, and then merely acknowledging the virtues of another. When demanded from shopkeepers or manufacturers by terrorists such as the Spanish ETA or the IRA, the word has come full circle.

trick *American* a prostitute's customer
From the limited turn of duty rather than any deception.
Whence to *trick*, as a prostitute to copulate with a customer.
See also the punning CALL THE TRICKS.

trim (your wick) to copulate
Seldom *tout court*. The imagery is from what was once done to candles to make them burn evenly.

trip a condition induced by the ingestion of illegal hallucinogens
What your TRAVEL AGENT may arrange for you. To *trip* is to hallucinate as a result of taking a drug.

triple a sexual act involving three people
Usually, of one man with two women:
Oh, and they don't do triples. As a rule. These are respectable girls. (R. Harris, 1998—but not that respectable, it would seem)

triple entry fraudulent
It refers to book-keeping; and see also DOUBLE ENTRY.
In France, it means having separate sets of accounts for your wife, your mistress, and the taxman.

troll to seek a casual sexual partner
From a car or on foot, homosexual or heterosexual, paid or free. The imagery is from dangling a lure in the water while fishing.

trollop a prostitute
Originally, an untidy or slatternly woman and to *trollop* was to work in a slovenly manner. The euphemism dates from the 18th century:
That impudent trollop, who is with child by you. (Henry Fielding, 1742)

trophy advertising your wealth and status
Something which can be flaunted to indicate great wealth or fame.
A man may thus marry a younger attractive woman, known as a *trophy wife* or *model*, whom he may take to live in a *trophy home*.

trot *obsolete* a prostitute
The common equine imagery, whence the punning:
Marry him to . . . an old trot . . . though she have as many diseases as two and fifty horses. (Shakespeare, *The Taming of the Shrew*)

trots (the) diarrhoea
The need is too immediate for walking.
A sufferer is said to be *on the trot*.

trouble any unpleasant, taboo, or unwanted experience
Of physical conditions, known often as *my trouble*, such as varicose veins, piles, and menstruation.
A criminal, if caught, *gets into trouble*, as does a single woman unwillingly impregnated.
If a man is described as *having trouble with his flies*, he is not finding the salmon hard to catch but has a tendency to be sexually licentious.

troubles (the) *Irish* fighting or violence against the British or between rival communities
The differences between those participating are frequently more tribal than religious:
> The 'troubles'—that quaint...word for murder and mayhem. (Theroux, 1983)

trouser to appropriate improperly
The garment which has the pocket into which the proceeds of bribery or theft are figuratively deposited:
> [Livingstone] summed up the national mood when he asked why the Labour Party had trousered £1 million from the head of Formula One. (*Daily Telegraph*, 13 November 1997—the government thereupon fortuitously exempted racing cars from regulations forbidding the advertisement of tobacco)
> [Lord] Black and his cronies had trousered more than $400m disguised as fees, bonuses and expenses. (*Daily Telegraph*, 2 December 2005, writing of its former proprietor)

trouser test the forced inspection of a prepuce to determine religion
A feature of the horrendous events which followed the partition of India in 1947:
> Muslims in Mumbai were given the 'trouser test' by mobs of Sena activists, a euphemism which refers to the ripping off of a man's trousers in search of a foreskin. If he lacks one, he is drenched in kerosene and lit. (French, 1997—Mumbai was then called, as it still is by many, Bombay)

truant with your bed *obsolete* to copulate extramaritally
A *truant* was a professional beggar, whence an absconder, and so a child absenting himself from school:
> The double wrong to truant with your bed, And let her read it in thy looks at board. (Shakespeare, *The Comedy of Errors*)

true not copulating with other than your regular sexual partner
The opposite of FALSE and UNTRUE.

trunk *American* falsely to conceal
Referring to the hiding of evidence etc. and the place where it might be hidden.

trustee *American* a placid prisoner
Not to be confused with those charged with looking after an estate for a third party. In Britain spelt *trusty*. He is *trusted* by the warders not to step out of line.

truth-shader *American* a liar
To *shade* is to discolour or darken slightly:
> The second Republican choice, businessman John Laklan, has shown himself to be a truth-shader impressive even by the generous standards of Massachusetts. (*Sunday Telegraph*, 14 August 1994)

tub of grease *American* a place or situation where corruption is endemic
GREASE and bribery have been long associated.

tube *American* sodomy
In prison jargon, *have* or *lay tube*, with obvious imagery and involving the vulgarism, *tube of meat*, or penis.

tuck the cosmetic removal of surplus fat or flesh by surgery
The imagery is from adjusting clothing, whence also to *tuck*, to perform such a procedure.

tuck away to kill or inter
With imagery perhaps from bedtime.
The synonym, *tuck under*, suggests burial.

tuft-hunter a sycophant
From seeking the company of wealthier Oxford undergraduates sporting gold tassels on their mortar boards rather than black.

tumble¹ to copulate with
Of either sex, from the alacrity of the move into the prone position:
> Quoth she, before you tumbled me,
> You promised me to wed. (Shakespeare, *Hamlet*)
Modern use can be intransitive, or, as a noun, of a single act.

tumble² (down the sink) a drink of an intoxicant
From the rhyming slang, and occasionally used in full.

tumescent having an erection of the penis
Literally, swelling, of anything:
> I don't in the least mind letting girls see my penis. I suppose it's because I fear ...becoming lightly, or indeed heavily, tumescent and attracting the attention of other men. (A. Clark, 1993—explaining why he was reluctant that men also should be so favoured)

tumour (a) cancer
Originally, any swelling, as with Dryden's *tender tumour*, or erect penis.

tup to copulate with
Dr Johnson coyly says 'To but like a ram'. The use in connection with ovine behaviour remains standard English, being euphemistic only when applied to humans.

turf accountant a person who accepts bets for a living

Standard English which sounds grander than BOOKMAKER.

turkey shoot *American* a business easily concluded
Based on the ease with which the bird can be hunted. Figurative use of swindling a dupe or winning an easy victory.
A *turkey farmer* does not enjoy such good fortune but is an unsuccessful businessman, from the slang *turkey*, an enterprise such as a film or play, which is a failure.

Turkish ally an unreliable supporter
From their supposed cowardice and treachery, although etymologically the Greeks fare little better.

Turkish medal *obsolete British* an inadvertently exposed trouser fly-button
A warning in the pre-zip days from one male to another, from the casual way in which some Turks wear Western-style dress:
> Their flybuttons were undone, and now I could understand why these buttons were called 'Turkish medals' by British soldiers in the First World War. (Theroux, 1975)

turn[1] an act of copulation
The imagery is from the stage:
> To obtain lodgings she fell prey to a Jamaican pimp whose girls worked Wilberforce Road in Finsbury Park at £5 a turn. (Fiennes, 1996)

turn[2] **(round/around)** to subvert from allegiance
Espionage jargon, facing the opposite direction.
To *turn your coat* is dishonourably to desert a cause, from the days when livery denoted allegiance on and off the battlefield.

turn[3] a sudden illness
Anything from dizziness to a cerebral haemorrhage. Perhaps a shortened form of a *turn for the worse*.

turn[4] *American* to alter the ethnic balance of a community
Usually where white Christians have permitted, or been obliged to permit, the ingress of householders of other colours and religions.

turn away to dismiss summarily from employment
Not refusing a job to those who apply:
> She said that as soon as it was known what sort of trouble she was in, she would be turned away. (Atwood, 1996—a housemaid was pregnant)

turn in to betray to authority
Also, in America, as *turn up*.

turn off[1] to kill
Usually judicially by hanging, with imagery from a lamp rather than the *turning tree*, the gallows on which a corpse rotated.

turn off[2] not to excite sexually
As we might expect, the converse of TURN ON.

turn off[3] *obsolete* to dismiss from employment or courtship
The imagery of the faucet:
> He can turn a poor gal off, as soon as he tires of her. (Mayhew, 1851)

turn on to excite
Something is set in motion. Apart from non-euphemistic uses, specifically of the ingestion of illegal narcotics and of sexual attraction.

turn over to steal from
Possibly from upsetting a stall so that the contents can be gathered in the confusion:
> Maybe [the car] was stolen for a job, turn over a petrol station. (Rankin, 1989)

turn to to have sexual relations with
Relying on, as much as moving towards, another. To *turn to yourself* is to masturbate:
> In the last hour of the day ... Sonny turns to him, as formerly she turned to herself. (Turow, 1996)

turn up your little finger to be a habitual drunkard
From the way of holding a glass, although many hold a teacup in the same fashion. Also in Scotland as *turn up pinkie*.

turn up your tail *obsolete* to defecate or (of a woman) to urinate
Al fresco:
> ... it being very pleasant to see how everyone turns up his tail, here one and there another, in a bush, and the women in their Quarters the like. (Pepys, 1663—the lavatory facilities at Epsom for race-goers were clearly insufficient for those moved by the spectacle and the famous salts)

turn up your toes to die
Most people die in bed and are buried on their back.
Also as *turn your face to the wall*, from the privacy sought by a mortally ill person.

twelve annas to the rupee of mixed Indian and white ancestry
British Indian derogatory use of those of mixed race, especially if they pretended to be white. There were sixteen annas to the

rupee.
See also NOT SIXTEEN ANNAS TO THE RUPEE.

twenty-four-hour service we have a telephone recording device
A misleading advertisement, and not much
help when you have a burst pipe in the early
hours.

twilight home an institution for the geriatric
Not a summer house facing the west but from
the cliché *twilight of your life*.

twin-tracking *British* sinecures recipro-
cally given to each other by sympathetic
politicians in neighbouring administra-
tions
Thus the councillors of one district are paid,
albeit absent, employees of another, to the
councillors of which they provide similar
situations, leaving both of them able to devote
their energies to retaining office without the
distraction of having to earn a living.

twisted *obsolete* killed by hanging
Referring to the rotation of the corpse on the
gibbet.

two-backed beast see BEAST

two-by-four *British* a prostitute
Rhyming slang for whore, punning on the rag
used as a pull-through to clean the barrel of
a .303 rifle, although soldiers in the Second
World War called it *four-by-two*.

two-fingered involving a vulgar gesture

The Latins use a single digit.

two-on-one two people sexually using a
third
Two prostitutes with a single man, or three
male homosexuals.

two-time contemporaneously to have a
sexual relationship with two people
Literally, in slang, to CHEAT:
> Lonsdale...who is the latest escort of the
> gracious Princess Margaret, is reputed to be
> still two-timing with his old flame. (*Private
> Eye*, December 1981)

Tyburn *obsolete* appertaining to death by
hanging
The London gallows were located in the
parish named after two *burns*, or streams,
but now called St Marylebone. The *Tyburn
dance*, *hornpipe*, or *jig* was a hanging, by the
Tyburn tippet, the noose, on the *Tyburn tree* or
triple tree, the gallows. The *King of Tyburn*, the
hangman, used to conduct a *Tyburn scragging*,
a ceremony, at which he would hang a *Tyburn
blossom*, a young convict, who would be said to
preach at Tyburn Cross. A *Tyburn ticket* was a
certificate of exemption from payment of all
taxes in the parish in which a felony had been
committed (or other reward) given to an
informer who secured a conviction and
hanging. A *Tyburn top* was a wig worn 'in a
knowing style...by the gentlemen pads,
scamps, divers, and other knowing hands'
(Grose), all of whom might expect to be
sentenced to death in the fullness of time.

U

U-turn a fundamental change of policy
Political use, usually where a previous policy
has failed.

Uganda a promiscuous sexual relationship
A long-running *Private Eye* in-joke based on an
alleged incident in which an African princess,
found in compromising circumstances, said
that she had been discussing *Ugandan affairs*
with the man involved. It is used of heterosexual or homosexual behaviour.

ultimate (the) copulation
The final act of courtship and specifically as
the *ultimate connection*.

ultimate intentions the killing of all Jews
The Nazis' FINAL SOLUTION after 1943.

unaddressed sent as unsolicited advertising matter
Of junk mail delivered to a household without
naming the recipient:
    TNT also controls a chunk of the German
    unaddressed (that is, junk) market. (*Daily
    Telegraph*, 21 October 2005)

un-American *American* differing from an
accepted or assumed standard
Originally, in 1844, used to deride the Know
Nothing movement. Subsequent political use
of any opponent with whose philosophy you
disagree, especially by Senator Joseph
McCarthy.

unassigned *American* dismissed from employment
Not awaiting another *assignment* in the same
organization:
    ...despite the fact that your company is
    doing rather well, you have just been
    sacked ... 'unassigned'. (*Sunday Telegraph*,
    27 October 1996)

unavailable avoiding contact
Business, social, and political jargon, whether
the approach is in person or by telephone.
Specifically as *unavailable for comment*, especially when scandal is suspected.
Unavailable is also police and criminal jargon
for someone evading arrest.

unbalanced of unsound mind
Not just dizziness.

unbiblical sex *American* incest
It is certainly frowned on in the Scriptures,
although the Tables of Consanguinity, which

allow first cousins to marry but bar in-laws,
might have benefited from the advice of a
geneticist.

uncertain economically depressed
The future is always *uncertain*. This is the
jargon of economists who fear that to talk of
recession will bring it about.

uncertain sexual preferences homosexual tendencies
The phrase is only used when there is a high
degree of certainty. Also as *uncertain proclivities*.

uncle[1] a pawnbroker
Punning on the Latin *uncus*, the hook on his
scales, and the supposed benevolence of your
relative. This does not explain why the French
call a pawnbroker an aunt.

uncle[2] *Indian* a tiger
As with the devil, it is bad luck to name the
evil one explicitly.

Uncle Tom a black person who defers unduly to whites
From the character in *Uncle Tom's Cabin, or, Life
among the Lowly*, published in 1851.

uncontaminated free from sexual activity
Literally, not subjected to impurity or pollution:
    Every mother must be yearning that her
    own son should keep himself
    uncontaminated. (French, 1995)

uncoordinated withdrawal a rout
The phrase was used to describe the defeat of
the American troops at the Kasserine Pass
when inexperienced soldiers came up against
German veterans.

uncover nakedness *obsolete* to copulate
An evasion favoured by the translators of the
Authorized Version of the Bible:
    Frequently the words used to cover the sex
    act are 'uncover nakedness' (another
    example of the literal translation of a
    Hebrew metaphor). (Peter Mullen in
    Enright, 1985—and see his essay 'The
    Religious Speak-Easy' for further
    enlightenment and linguistic delight)

under-invoicing a fraudulent device to
avoid import duties
The practice is found where the importing
country imposes high tariffs and the buyer
has access to external funds. The documentation shows a lower price than that agreed
between the parties, on which duty is levied,
the balance being paid free of duty offshore.
See also OVER-INVOICING.

under the counter illegal
The physical reality with many scarce goods
in war-torn countries.
Now used figuratively of transactions involving stolen goods, wages paid without deduc-
tion of tax, etc.

under the daisies dead
And buried. Also as *under the sod, under the
grass, underground,* or *undersod.*

under the influence drunk
Shortened form of the legal jargon *under the
influence of drink or drugs. Half under* is no less
drunk.

under the knife having undergone cosmetic surgery
In normal use, having been subjected to any
other surgical procedure, in which case the
patient is normally keen to show you the scar
rather than be coy about the operation.

under the table¹ very drunk
You are supposed to end up there after a
drinking bout. The phrase is normally used
when one person claims to be able to drink
more alcohol than another without becoming
inebriated.

under the table² illicit
Of business transactions, where it is a synonym of UNDER THE COUNTER, and of cash
payments made avoiding the payment of tax:
  [He] had bought the house with under-the-
  table money while still on welfare.
  (Hosseini, 2003)

under the weather unwell
Standard English, despite it being the condition of all other than mountaineers, aviators,
and astronauts. The phrase is also used of
those recovering from drunkenness or of
women menstruating.

under water showing a loss or worthless
Financial jargon when no gains can be seen or
projected above the surface. The phrase is
specifically used of share options granted at a
figure higher than the current share price and
so valueless.

underachiever an idle or stupid child
Literally, a child capable of doing better,
especially in examinations, but failing
through nervousness or ill-health. As educational jargon, it seeks to excuse wilfulness
under a cloak of misfortune.

underdeveloped poor
The inference is that a greater degree of
development was or is attainable and desirable.
It may describe sovereign states or regions.

underground railroad *American* the escape route for antebellum slaves from
the South to the North
The line was organized by philanthropists in
the North with assistance from some Confed-
erates.

underprivileged poor
Literally, lacking honourable distinction, a
description which applies to the mass of the
population. Sociological jargon which threatens to become standard English.

undertaker a professional arranger of
funerals
Standard English since the late 17th century.
Literally, someone who takes on an obligation
for or helps another, which meant, among
other things at different times, settling Crown
lands in Ireland or publishing books.

undisciplined neglected and overgrown
Estate agent speak for a garden which is in a
mess.

undiscovered country (the) death
The
  Undiscover'd country, from whose bourn
  No traveller returns. (Shakespeare, *Hamlet*)
and in later use:
  I shall have entered the great 'Perhaps', as
  Danton I think called the 'undiscovered
  country'. (F. Harris, 1925)

undo to copulate with a female outside
marriage
From the loss of reputation rather than
clothing:
  Weeks later the Jervases told Pepys that
  Jane was 'undone'...She had been sleeping
  with her fiddler. (Tomalin, 2002—the
  'fiddler' was also a musician)

undocumented *American* arriving without proper authority
The word is used of illegal immigrants into
the United States, mainly from China and
Mexico.

uneven bad
A code message in financial statements,. of
which the cypher was broken long ago.

unfair economically embarrassing
Protectionists use the adjective to describe
competition from lower cost or more efficient
producers:
  [French] small businessmen and
  farmers... have long practice in forcing
  politicians to pay heed to their wishes,
  which usually include protection against
  'unfair' competition. (Tombs & Tombs,
  2006)

unfaithful having had a sexual relationship with other than your regular sexual partner

Of either sex, within marriage or of other heterosexual and homosexual arrangements.

unfortified not having drunk alcohol

Describing those whose courage is less when sober.

unfortunate *obsolete* engaged in prostitution

A common 18th- and 19th-century use, especially by women who earned their living in other ways, or not at all.

unglued *American* mentally ill

Your mind had become unstuck.

unhealthy homosexual

The objection of those who use the term is to moral rather than physical damage:

Hattie heard one of the mistresses, talking about her and Pearl, say 'It's an unhealthy relationship'. (I. Murdoch, 1983)

unheard presence someone dismissed from employment

Television and radio jargon of a character WRITTEN OUT OF THE SCRIPT.

unhinged mad

The common *gate* imagery.

uniform a police officer

Jargon of criminals and their associates or admirers:

Some kids had decided that the uniforms should be the focus of their own complaints. (Rankin, 2004—the children were referring to the police, not to their compulsory school garb)

union¹ copulation

Venerable use, making two into one, or three:

The union of your bed... (Shakespeare, *The Tempest*)

union² *obsolete British* an institution for the homeless poor

Shortened form of *union house*, set up by a Poor Law Union (of parishes) which had an obligation to provide food and shelter to the indigent.

uniquely *American* suffering from a particular defect

In phrases such as *uniquely abled*, crippled; *uniquely coordinated*, pathologically clumsy; *uniquely proficient*, incompetent; and so on, for all the world as if each person so described were the only such case.

united dead

You have joined, or rejoined, your Maker, or a spouse who has predeceased you. Monumental usage.

university a political prison

Where Napoleon III developed his economic theory, alongside a romantic attachment, and, on Robben Island, where Nelson Mandela studied:

At the height of his career as Emperor, he was fond of saying... 'I took my honours at the University of Ham.' (Corley, 1961)

unknown to men a virgin

And, less often, a man might be *unknown to woman*:

I am yet
Unknown to woman. (Shakespeare, *Macbeth*)

unlawful *obsolete* illegitimate

Of children, when it was a matter of great concern to our ancestors because, especially with primogeniture, it was vital that the heir should be his father's son. Whence Shakespeare's *unlawful bed* (*Richard III*), *unlawful purpose* (*All's Well That Ends Well*), and *unlawfully born* (*Measure for Measure*).

Unlawfulness was promiscuity:

You see he might have gone the bad road and given his eyes to unlawfulness entirely. (Hardy, 1874—he removed his wedding ring when with another woman)

unlimber your joint to urinate

Of a male, from the American JOINT², a penis.

unmarried homosexual

Most bachelors are not homosexual, and, as ever, the euphemistic use depends on the context:

Neighbours of unmarried Mr Hamilton contacted police six months ago...a male model and a tenant at Mr Hamilton's house...is acting as Mr Hamilton's agent. (*Sunday Telegraph*, December 1986)

The phrase *He was unmarried* at the end of an obituary sometimes indicates that the subject was homosexual.

unmentionable crime (the) buggery or sodomy

Once one of the great taboos.

The *unmentionable disease* was syphilis.

unmentionables¹ *obsolete* trousers or undergarments

19th-century prudery forbade the mention of anything to do with legs:

She had vowed never to change her unmentionables until her husband, Archduke Albert, took the city of Ostend by siege. (Jennings, 1965—as it held out for three years, she must have kept her vow at the expense of her friends and her marriage)

Also as *unexpressibles, unspeakables, unwhisperables, ineffables, indescribables,* and *inexpressibles.*

unmentionables² haemorrhoids
A female evasion. Men seem to suffer from FARMER GILES.

unnatural not heterosexual
Legal jargon in the phrases *unnatural crime, practice, vice,* etc. Formerly of buggery as well as sodomy:
... seeing a Turk severely whipped and his beard singed for attempting unnatural vice. (Ollard, 1974)

unofficial action a strike in breach of an agreement
The *action* is inaction, especially where the strike, if officially sanctioned by a trade union, might involve legal penalties.

unofficial relations corrupt practices
Not your illegitimate offspring but the way business was conducted in Communist Russia:
Economic ties were entangled in a dense network of 'unofficial relations' (extortions and gifts, bribery, exaggeration of results, embezzlement). (Gorbachev, 1995, in translation)

unplugged mentally ill
The supply of electricity for the light has been removed.

unpredictable potentially less profitable
Financial jargon. The future is always *unpredictable:*
The US market remains 'unpredictable', which is worrying for investors.
(G. Wimpey Report, 6 July 2006)

unprotected sex copulation without a condom
Where SEX¹ means copulation. The phrase could equally apply to a cricketer batting without wearing a shield or to the Sabine women. Also as *unsafe sex:*
Except that [Congressman Condit is] into unsafe sex, according to another mistress. (*Sunday Telegraph,* 15 July 2001—
Congressman appears not to have been a deliberate pun)

unscheduled caused by accident or necessity
Airline jargon, which seeks to avoid any implication of loss of reliability or safety.

unscrewed mad
What happens after you have a SCREW LOOSE.

unsighted blind
Literally, prevented from seeing by an intervening obstruction.

unslated *obsolete* of unsound mind
The outcome if you have a SLATE-OFF.

unsociable performing a taboo act
Such as farting in public or urinating elsewhere than is acceptable by convention:
... [a dog] biting a property company chairman on the ear, or being unsociable on the carpet. (Muir, 1997)

unsound not to be trusted
More from a faulty ship than from the legal jargon for mental illness, *of unsound mind.* Among bureaucrats, of judgement rather than honesty. Among autocrats, *unsoundness* indicates unwelcome independence of thought or action.

untoward incident an avoidable illness
Medical jargon. From its original meaning, awkward or perverse, *untoward* now means inauspicious or unfortunate:
... surgical link infections and 'untoward incidents associated with infections' are part of mandatory surveillance programmes. (*Daily Telegraph,* 23 June 2005)

untrimmed *obsolete* (of a woman) virgin
The imagery is from a wick rather than from the meaning, to put in order:
In likeness of a new untrimmed bride. (Shakespeare, *King John*)

untrue having copulated outside marriage
The reverse of TRUE, and also applicable to those who have eschewed the trip up the aisle.

unwaged involuntarily unemployed
Not the war which was averted but the pay which is not earned.

unwell¹ menstruating
Being ILL¹:
... all's well that ends unwell. (F. Harris, 1925—he feared he had impregnated a woman)

unwell² drunk
Covering up the taboo condition with one of its symptoms:
'Our Mr Fellowes had been 'very unwell' at the time of the move.' 'He wasn't unwell,' said my sister. 'He was drunk.' (Bogarde, 1983)

unwired mentally unbalanced
Like an electrical device which is not connected to a power supply.

up¹ (of a male) copulating with
Tout court and in a variety of vulgar phrases:
'When you're up who, Barbara's down on whom?' asks Flora. 'Flora, you're coarse,' says Howard. (Bradbury, 1975)

up² under the influence of illegal narcotics
The result of getting HIGH. *Ups* or *uppers* are the drugs, usually amphetamine.

up along old
Shortened form of *up along in years* and still common in English West Country dialect. The Scottish *up in life* is obsolete:
Though up in life, I'll get a wife.
(A. Boswell, 1871)

up-and-coming run-down and less central
Estate agents' jargon of unfashionable districts on the periphery of a city where houses are older, prices are lower, and crime is higher.

up for it agreeable to casual copulation
Literally, prepared for what is coming:
A thuggish, dim young man with a short fuse and a lot of aggression is going to expect that a pretty girl who visits his hotel bedroom in the small hours is up for it. (Mary Kenny, in *Sunday Telegraph*, 16 January 2000)

up the creek in severe difficulties
The British army waterway, in which you might find yourself *without a paddle*, was *shit creek*, a vulgarism for the anus. Today most people who use the phrase figuratively are unaware of its provenance, and the association with sodomy:
...telling them that if they'd followed this far up shit creek it's a long way to walk back. (*Private Eye*, July 1981, with some choice mixing of metaphors)

up the loop mad
The imagery was from railway shunting practices, where a wagon might be misdirected on to the wrong *loop*, or siding.

up the pole pregnant
Usually of unwanted pregnancy, from the place where the monkey is said to find itself, as also with *up the stick*. *Up the duff*, where the pregnancy is not necessarily unplanned, uses the common pudding imagery. *Up the spout* comes from a shell rammed into a rifled barrel from which, the copper band having

been engaged in the steel groove, it can only be extracted with danger and difficulty. Apart from *up the duff*, these phrases are also used of financial difficulties.

upstairs¹ an allusion to a taboo act or place
In former times, *she's gone upstairs* meant that a birth was imminent. An invalid who *has been upstairs for two months* indicates the duration of his infirmity. Socially, *Would you like to go upstairs?* invites urination. *Upstairs* is also where the bedrooms are, for copulation.

upstairs² death
Where God lives and heaven is to be found. However, to *go upstairs out of this world* was to be hanged, punning on the climb up the scaffold.

upstairs³ in authority
The senior staff occupy the higher floors. And see also *boys upstairs* under BOY¹.

Uranian a male homosexual
From *Urania*, another name for Aphrodite, and not, as some suppose, a pun on the planet and a part of the body. Also as *child of Uranus* or *Uranist*.

use¹ (of a male) to copulate with
Normally outside marriage:
Be a whore still: they love thee not that use thee. (Shakespeare, *Timon of Athens*)

use² to be addicted to illegal narcotics
A shortened form of *use drugs* or, in the jargon *use some help*. A *user* is an addict.

use³ (in) capable of conception
It is used of those mammals which indicate their readiness by bleeding.

use a wheelchair to be physically incapable of walking
The word *cripple* is taboo:
You should not say that someone 'cannot walk'. Instead say 'uses a wheelchair'. (M. Holman, in *Financial Times*, October 1994)

use paper to defecate
Hospital jargon in an enquiry to a patient from a nurse, but not about writing a letter. Less often as *use the bathroom*.

use your tin *American* to identify yourself as a policeman
From the badge;
I'd be in civilian clothes...Could I use my tin? (Sanders, 1973)

used second-hand
To remove the stigma of prior ownership, especially of cars.

useful expenditure a bribe

True, we might suppose, if it lands you the contract:

> A German who bribes a French official in an EU-wide open tender procedure cannot be prosecuted in Germany and the bribe can be written off against tax. Such costs on the tax form are called *nuetzliche Ausgaben*—'useful expenditures'. (*Sunday Telegraph*, 20 January 1997)

useful fool a dupe of the Communists

Lenin's phrase for the shallow thinkers in the West whom the Communists manipulated. Also as *useful idiot*:

> It had taken courage to write his kind of books, thirty years ago, on the Famine and the Terror, when every other useful idiot in academia was screeching for détente. (R. Harris, 1998)

useful girl *?obsolete American* a domestic servant

The phrase avoids any implication of subservience.

useless eaters people to be killed

Those who could not contribute economically to German production in the Second World War:

> Himmler issued orders that were to resolve the question of those Jews who were considered 'useless eaters' by the Nazis. (Rees, 2005)

V

vacation *American* a prison sentence
Literally, a holiday which involves any absence from home:
> ...won a twenty years' vacation in the Big House. (Lavine, 1930)

vacuum to destroy incriminating evidence
Sucking the information away. In his notes from a White House meeting on 5 November 1993 Associate Counsel William H. Kennedy unwisely wrote 'Vacuum Rose Law files'.

valentine *American* a warning or notice of dismissal
Punning on the CARDS received by some on 14 February.

vanity publishing the publication of a book or article at the author's expense
Where the venture is not commercially attractive to a professional publisher.
A *vanity plate* is a personalized number plate for a vehicle.

variety meats *American* offal
Lungs, liver, testicles, and all the bits you would rather not spell out with precision. See also SWEETBREADS.

Vatican roulette the use of the safe period method of contraception
Punning on the Roman Catholic dogma against contraception and Russian roulette. In either case you cannot be quite sure there isn't one *up the spout*, as it were.

vault¹ *obsolete* (of a male) to copulate with
Pre-dating the modern JUMP²:
> While he is vaulting variable ramps. (Shakespeare, *Cymbeline*)
The punning *vaulting-school* was a brothel.

vault² *American* a cupboard for the storage of a corpse
Literally, any structure with an arched roof, which is how many early tombs were built.

vehicle incident a car or truck crash
An *incident* is no more than an event. In January 2003 the oil company BP reported that 'vehicle incidents' averaged six a month in its Alaskan operations.

velvet obtained gratuitously
From the luxurious fabric and the cliché *in velvet*, having an easy time.

Thus *velvet* may be a bribe deposited in a *velvet-lined drawer* or *pocket*.

ventilate to kill
Army slang, and another way to FILL FULL OF HOLES.

Venus appertaining to copulation
The Roman goddess of Love has enriched the language in several compounds and derivative words or phrases, as with Shakespeare's 'heart Inflam'd with Venus' (*Troilus and Cressida*). In 1627 Bacon wrote 'Much use of Venus doth dim the sight' shortly before collecting snow to stuff a dead chicken, from which he contracted pneumonia and died. In obsolete use the *venerous act* was copulation and *venery* was pursuing women rather than deer. *Venereal disease* is standard English.

verbal *British* an oral admission of guilt
Police jargon, for something which may or may not have been given voluntarily. To *verbal* an accused is falsely to record such an alleged admission.

verbally deficient unable to read
Not merely having a restricted vocabulary. Jennings (1965) pointed out how odd it is that those who cannot read need a written euphemism to conceal their ignorance, but that was before we became POLITICALLY CORRECT.

vertically challenged of short stature
But not a mountaineer. See also CHALLENGED:
> A better deal for the vertically challenged was urged yesterday by Dr David Weeks, a consultant psychiatrist, who said that 'shortism' was as pernicious as sexism and racism. (*Daily Telegraph*, 12 April 1994—the doctor should know, being himself 5ft 2in tall)

vicar of Bray a cowardly or opportunistic trimmer
A cleric held this living in the 16th century during the reign of four English monarchs, two of whom were Roman Catholic and three Protestant, Henry VIII being both. Other incumbents were replaced as the state religion altered, as can be seen from the records of incumbents displayed in many English parish churches. When he was accused of being of a changeable turn, he replied:
> No, I am steadfast, however other folk change I remain Vicar of Bray. (reported by Alleyn, Bishop of Exeter)

victualler *obsolete* the keeper of a brothel
He provided the MEAT¹:

Falstaff... suffering flesh to be eaten in thy house contrary to the law; for the which I think thou wilt howl.
Hostess All victuallers do so. (Shakespeare, *2 Henry IV*—note the two sexual puns)
A *victualling-house* was a brothel.

vigorous promiscuous
With energy expended sexually:
Cabinet ministers were (or claimed to be) so disgusted by Birkenhead's vigorous private life. (A. Clark, 1998—especially when he took his daughter's school friend as a mistress)

violate (of a male) to copulate with extra-maritally
The common violent imagery, although the word is also used where there have been blandishments and no force:
With unchaste purpose, and with oath to violate
My lady's honour. (Shakespeare, *Cymbeline*)

virtue the property of not having copulated extramaritally
Literally, conformity with all moral standards, but in this use of women since the 16th century, and in the centuries subsequently when wives were expected to be *virtuous*:
Betimes in the morning I will beseech the virtuous Desdemona. (Shakespeare, *Othello*)

visible not white-skinned
It must not be assumed that white people have become invisible in communities where they form a majority of the population. In June 1999 the London Metropolitan Police suggested its officers refer to those of Indian or African descent as *visible minority ethnic groups*, while in 1992 Concorde University in Montreal claimed especially to encourage applications from women, 'visible minorities', and the disabled. For the POLITICALLY CORRECT but philologically inept, the *visible community* does not include white people:
The BBC does not attract as many people as it should from the 'visible community'. (*Daily Telegraph*, 10 January 2001)

visiting card traces of urine or faeces left in a public place
Left by domestic pets.
See also PAY A VISIT.

visiting fireman a troubleshooter
Usually sent from or by the senior management to investigate and sort out a poorly performing subsidiary. Sometimes *tout court* as *fireman*.
In America a *visiting fireman* may also be someone behaving boorishly at a convention.

visitor (a) menstruation
Common female usage. In America she may come from a place called *Redbank*.

visually challenged ugly
Not by a sentry but an extension of the CHALLENGED theme. The phrase was used by Auberon Waugh in the *Daily Telegraph* on 4 October 1993 when describing a politician.

visually impaired blind or with very poor eyesight
Literally, *impaired* means damaged or weakened:
Two more blind magistrates have been appointed to establish whether the visually impaired should become JPs. (*Daily Telegraph*, 7 August 1999)

vital statistics the measurement of a woman's chest, waist, and buttocks
As so often, here *vital* means no more than interesting or important, which the information seems to be in the world of entertainment.

vitals the testicles
Literally, the parts of the body essential to the continuation of life, whence usually the organs located in the trunk:
... him so bad with the mumps and all, so that his poor vitals were swelled to pumpkin size. (Graves, 1941)

voice risk analysis lie detection
Insurance companies and banks would prefer not to suggest that their clients are not telling the truth:
... motor insurer Admiral said a quarter of policyholders have withdrawn claims that their vehicle has been stolen after 'voice risk analysis' software was introduced last year. (*Daily Telegraph*, 19 January 2004)

void water *obsolete* to urinate
Not spitting or sweating. To *void your bowels* was to defecate.

voluntary done under duress or compulsion
Admission of guilt may be made in a *voluntary statement* after the subject has been detained and aggressively questioned by the police. In the Second World War, before Russia and the United States were attacked, British forces were frequently subject to *voluntary withdrawal* from the Germans.
A *voluntary patient* is a person in a psychiatric hospital who is not present under a court order and therefore, in theory, free to leave.
A *voluntary pregnancy interruption* is an abortion.

volunteer a person instructed to fight for a third party

Used originally of those who intervened in military formations for the Nazis, Fascists, and Communists during the Spanish Civil War. Now of any organized military interference where you wish to influence events without a declaration of war.

voyeur a person who enjoys watching the sexual activity of others

Literally, a watcher of anything:

> Hamilton had been an enthusiastic voyeur...In one home, microphones had been installed throughout the bedrooms.

(S. Green, 1979—an ÉCOUTEUR also, it would seem)

Vulcan's badge *literary* an indication of cuckoldry

Worn by *Vulcan*, and countless husbands since, when his wife Venus copulated with Mars.

vulnerable poor or inadequate

None of us is exempt from the possibility of being wounded:

> Large supermarket chains [are] letting down customers, especially the vulnerable in society. (*Daily Telegraph*, 15 February 2006—by not fitting brakes on the trolleys, perhaps)

W

W/WC see WATER CLOSET

wages of sin (the) death
The venerable inducement to leading a virtuous life as suggested in *Romans* 6:23.

wake a death
From the verbal form, which meant to stay awake to watch over a corpse, to prevent anyone trying to take it for sale.
To *wake the churchyard* was not to sound the last trump but to keep an eye out for grave-robbers.

wake a witch *obsolete Scottish* to force a woman to confess to witchcraft
As with SWIM FOR A WIZARD, this entry illustrates the behaviour of our recent ancestors. In this procedure an iron hoop was placed over the victim's face, with four prongs in her mouth. Chained to a wall so that she could not lie down, she was kept awake by relays of men until she admitted she was a witch, after which she might be ducked or burnt to death.

walk¹ (the streets) to be a prostitute
Seldom *tout court*, but if so used, the confusion may be considerable. In 1891 Daisy Hopkins was sentenced to fourteen days in prison by the University Court of Cambridge after being accused of *walking with a member of the university*. A higher court on appeal, perhaps unversed in euphemism, held this to have been no offence.

walk² to be dismissed from employment or courtship
Seldom a voluntary departure.
Those dismissed are said to have received their *walking papers*.
In the jargon of the travel business, a customer is *walked* if involuntarily directed to another hotel than that for which the booking was made.

walk³ to be stolen
Normally of small tools or army kit, attributing powers of locomotion to inanimate objects rather than accusing one of your mates of theft. Such objects may also *go for a walk*.

walk⁴ to acknowledge dismissal before an umpire's adjudication
Euphemistic only in the negative, where *not to walk* is unsporting behaviour by a batsman at

cricket who knows that he should be given out:
> [E. W. Swanton] could be guilty of the most appalling gamesmanship, even refusing to walk when he had hit an obvious catch. (*Sunday Telegraph*, 8 August 2004)

To *walk* an opponent in baseball is for the pitcher deliberately to throw wide balls so that the batter has a free saunter to first base but no chance to score.

walk⁵ to be wrongly acquitted of an offence
The accused is free to leave. Also of early release from a prison sentence:
> ...the most they'll get is twenty years, walk in seven or eight. (Clancy, 1989)

walk out to go on strike
Not just the departure of workers on foot at the end of a shift. Also, as a noun, to describe concerted strike action, usually taken at short notice.

walk out with to court
The usage has just about survived from the days when courtship was a pedestrian affair:
> Donald Campbell...for many years has walked out with Julie Christie, the actress...(*Daily Telegraph*, 28 December 2000)

Also as *walk along with* or *walk with*.
A *walker* is a male engaged by a female to accompany her on a social occasion, with imagery from someone paid to exercise a dog, but without the lead.

walk the plank to be killed by drowning
Favoured by pirates for the disposal of their captives. Some figurative use:
> A 15-year-old daughter broke out upon sexual adventures [on a cruise] and a singer with the ship's band was only saved from walking the plank by some polaroid pictures of her performance in other cabins. (Whicker, 1982)

To *walk the golden gangplank* implies departure from employment with a generous payoff.

wall-eyed drunk
Literally, strabismic, with difficulty in focusing, and drunkenness can cause that too.

wallflower a young woman who is failing to attract a male companion
From the far-off days when girls sat around the periphery of dance halls, waiting for a male partner to ask them to take the floor with him.
Wallflower week is the time of menstruation.

wander to philander within marriage
It is the male who tends to STRAY.

wandered *Scottish* mentally confused
From the inability to concentrate.

wandering eye a tendency to promiscuity
An affliction of husbands rather than wives:
No wonder Bill has a wandering eye.
(Michael Sheldon in *Sunday Telegraph*, 3
March 1996, reviewing a book by Hillary
Clinton)

wang-house *American* a brothel
Possibly a corruption of WANK, and not from a
Chinese dialect.

wank to masturbate
Literally, to beat or thrash and not from the
Irish *wank*, a penis. Also as *wank off*.
Wankery is erotic literature for men.

want¹ (a) low mental ability
A shortened form of *want of understanding* or
sense.
Wanting means slow-witted or imbecile and
such people may be described in a cliché such
as *want some pence in a shilling*.

want² to lust after
This kind of *want* is not for social intercourse:
Yet he wanted my mother, his half-sister,
and in trying to get his way with her caused
her untold agony of mind. (Cookson, 1969)
Specifically, as *want sex, a body, intercourse, it,
love, relations*, etc.

want out to wish to kill yourself
Literally, to wish to extract yourself from a
deal or arrangement:
'Does the letter signify anything to you?'
'Only that he wanted out.' (B. Forbes,
1983—it was a suicide note)

ward off invasion to launch a pre-emptive
strike
The language of Nazism, and one of the
excuses given for the German invasion of
Poland in August 1939, and of Holland and
Belgium in May 1940:
Naturally a 'counter-attack' to 'ward off the
hostile invasion'. (Klemperer, 1998, in
translation—diary entry of 11 May 1940,
noting the reason given for the attack on
the Low Countries)

wardrobe malfunction *American* the public exposure of a woman's breasts
The phrase was used after the 2004 Super
Bowl when the singer Janet Jackson bared a
breast to the assembled multitude.

warehouse to hold (securities) for a principal to conceal his interest
Stock exchange jargon when the arrangement is clandestine or illegal.

warm¹ sexually aroused
And not noticeably cooler than HOT¹:
The warm effects which she in him finds
missing. (Shakespeare, *Venus and Adonis*)
In obsolete use, a *warm one* was a prostitute,
whom you might find in a *warm shop*, or
brothel.

warm² (with wine) tipsy
Rum or whisky *warm* better:
Col's bowl was finished; and by that time
we were well warmed. (J. Boswell, 1773—
he himself felt far from well the next
morning)
Addison wrote some of his best papers
in *The Spectator* when warm with wine.
(J. Boswell, 1791)

warm a bed to copulate with someone
promiscuously
Not by using a hot-water bottle or electric
blanket:
It was equally possible she was warming
another man's bed. (Moss, 1987)

warm up old porridge to renew a discontinued sexual relationship
It never tastes the same, so they say.

warn off to expel from participation in
horse-racing for dishonesty
A shortened form of *warn off the turf*:
[He] realized that he might be warned-off.
Might suffer the ultimate disgrace.
(D. Francis, 1998)

warning *obsolete* a notice of termination
of employment
Usually, but not always, given by the employer
to the employee:
If respectable young girls are set picking
grass out of your gravel, in place of their
proper work, they will give warning.
(Somerville & Ross, 1897)

warpaint facial cosmetics
Punning jocular female usage (although the
process of application and its purpose are
serious).

wash¹ *obsolete* stale urine
As once commonly used in laundry:
Dochter, here is a bottle o' my father's
wash. (Graham, 1883—it was for medical
examination)
A *wash-mug* was a piss-pot.

wash² *British* to deal unnecessarily in
securities to obtain commission
Stock exchange jargon. It is one way in which
the broker can TAKE TO THE CLEANERS a
trusting client. See also CHURN.

wash³ to bring into open circulation
It indicates money or assets obtained illegally, and a less common version of LAUNDER.

wash and brush up *American* a lavatory
You are unlikely to find anyone to do the *brushing up* in one these days.

wash out to destroy or bankrupt
Literally, to cause an event to be abandoned because of rain and a *wash-out* is the result. Whence *washed up*, finished or bankrupted. A venture or investment which *washes its face* is one which does not lose money.

wash the baby's head to drink intoxicants in celebration of a birth
A less common variant of *wet the baby's head*, given under WET².

wash your hands to urinate
Arriving guests may be invited to do this, not because their hands are dirty but because the lavatory is beside a hand basin. Whence the American *washroom*, a lavatory not a laundry. When Pilate 'took water and washed his hands before the multitude' (*Matthew* 27:24) he was seeking to absolve himself from blame for the murder or Jesus.

waste¹ *American* to kill
Literally, to destroy or use up:
  You wanted a photo of Roger Kope, the cop who got wasted. (Sanders, 1973—British cops are only *wasted* by excessive bureaucracy)

waste² *American* urine or faeces
Canine faeces on the sidewalk or *house waste*, from an earth closet. A spacecraft is said to have no lavatory but it will boast a *waste management compartment*. In Britain a *waste management centre*, in Oxford and elsewhere, is a rubbish dump.

wasted *American* drunk
Not from spilling the liquid or resultant bodily emaciation.

watch *Irish* to sit with a corpse
The tradition of the WAKE persists in Ireland, where mourners visit the house to view the body, being suitably refreshed, before subsequently attending the funeral.

water urine
Used in this sense since the 14th century even though urine differs significantly from the clear and potable compound of hydrogen and oxygen:
  Sirrah, you giant, what says the doctor to my water? (Shakespeare, *2 Henry IV*)

To *water* something, such as *the garden, the roses*, or whatever, is to urinate on it:
  Then the officer excused himself to Jean-Marie, turned away, undid a fly, watered a rock…(Furst, 1995)

water closet a lavatory with a flush mechanism
Standard English, abbreviated to *WC*, and occasionally in Britain to *W*.
This is a euphemism we have passed on to the French, as *le water* or *le water-closet*.

water cure a form of torture
Much different from attending a spa to cure your rheumatism. The *water* is applied in persistent drips externally, or in excessive quantities orally.

water gardener someone who improperly releases confidential information to the media
Cultivating the press, preparing the ground for policy changes, and the source of many a LEAK².

water of life (the) *Scottish/Irish* whisky
The Gaelic *usquebaugh* (and in various spellings) rather than the French *eau de vie*.

water stock *American* to render securities less valuable by constant dilution
As a drover, Daniel Drew, as was usual, fed salt to cattle as they were being driven to market, so that they drank a lot and put on weight, making up for the flesh they lost during the drive. He adopted the same principle when he started financing railroads, especially the Erie. (Faith, 1990)

watering hole a place licensed to sell intoxicants
Punning jocular usage, although there would be no smiles if only water was on offer.

watermelon *American* an indication of pregnancy
In phrases such as *have a watermelon on the vine* or *swallow a watermelon seed*. *Watermelons*, in vulgar male talk, may be female breasts.

waterworks¹ the human urinary system
The pun is only used in the case of malfunction, to avoid mentioning a taboo condition.

waterworks² tears
Especially those of a woman or child thought to be producing them to obtain sympathy:
  It's impossible to reason with Ma; she just turns on the waterworks. (Seth, 1993)

wax¹ to remove unwanted hair from (a part of the body)
Mainly female usage and practice.

wax² *American* to kill
Perhaps only in the past participle, from the appearance of a corpse rather than the immobility of a dummy in a *waxworks*:

> After you saw Sophie Millstein get waxed...(Katzenbach, 1995—Sophie had not had cosmetic treatment but was murdered)

way of all flesh (the) death
From the Douay Bible:

> I am going the way of all flesh. (*Joshua* 23:14)

Made a cliché by Samuel Butler's novel of the same title, published posthumously in 1903.

way out under the influence of illegal narcotics
In standard usage, showing any wide deviance from a norm, whence a drug-induced elation in which some instrumentalists consider they work best.

weaker half (the) females
Euphemism, dysphemism, chauvinist insult, assessment of physical strength, or merely how our male ancestors, and many female ones also, regarded the comparison between the sexes. A shortened form of *weaker half of the human family* or *race*:

> At this latter proceeding, the weaker half of the human family went distracted on the spot. (W. Collins, 1868—he might have written 'the women became excited')

weakness a tendency towards self-indulgence
Often *tout court* of drunkenness, and in phrases such as a *weakness for the drink*, a *weakness for men* or *women* (profligacy), a *weakness for boys* (homosexuality in men), a *weakness for the horses* (addiction to gambling), etc.
See also the delightful Irish *strong weakness* under STRONG WATERS.

wear a bullet to be killed or wounded by shooting
It is unlikely to be visible on the outer garment. Also as *wear lead buttons*.

wear a fork *obsolete* to be cuckolded
The *fork*, or antlers, was a traditional indication of cuckoldry. Also as *wear horns*:

> I wondered how many sets of horns Griswald III was wearing. (Sanders, 1994—he had just added one more himself)

See also FORKED PLAGUE (THE).

wear a pad to be menstruating
The phrase is not used of female hockey players.

wear away *obsolete* to die a lingering death

Usually of pulmonary tuberculosis, commonly called CONSUMPTION because of the debilitating effect of the disease.
To *wear down* was merely to grow old.

wear Dick's hatband see DICK¹

wear green garters *obsolete Scottish* to remain unmarried after a younger sister's wedding
By tradition, the unmarried elder sister wore green or yellow garters at the wedding of a younger. The taboos surrounding spinsterhood arose from the plight of those women who failed to obtain the support of a husband and were forbidden by convention to seek work to support themselves.

wear lead boots *American* to be ineligible for promotion
As worn by the deep-sea diver, to keep him down.

wear the breeches to be the dominant partner in a relationship between a man and a woman
Usually of the woman, from the days when only men wore *the breech, breeches, trousers*, or (in America) *pants*:

> That you might still have worn the petticoat,
> And ne'er have stol'n the breech from Lancaster. (Shakespeare, *3 Henry IV*)

wear your heart upon your sleeve to fail to conceal heterosexual longing
At one time men might advertise their intentions or desires by displaying some keepsake from the woman:

> But I will wear my heart upon my sleeve
> For daws to peck at. (Shakespeare, *Othello*—a *daw* was a jackdaw)

wee drop *mainly Irish/Scottish* a drink of whisky
As a with a LITTLE SOMETHING, the volume is seldom small. Also as *wee dram* or *wee half*.

wee folk *obsolete mainly Irish* the fairies
Malevolent creatures of whom you had to speak nicely to appease them. Also as the *wee people*.

wee(-wee) to urinate
The derivation is from *little* as in LITTLE JOBS, or is a corruption of *eau*, with the common WATER imagery. The repetition of *wee* does not indicate a double effusion.

weed a taboo substance which is smoked
Formerly tobacco, while *weeds* were cigars: in Victorian times, it was considered antisocial

to smoke indoors except in a Smoking Room. Now used of marijuana.

weekend dishonestly to use a customer's money after the close of business on Friday

Banking jargon and practice. By delaying the transfer of funds, the banker earns, on the customer's credit balance or transfer, interest which is accrued on a daily business. For some banks, this kind of *weekend* starts on a Thursday and ends on a Tuesday.

weenie *American* a penis

Possibly from the German *wienerworst*, Vienna sausage, whence *wienie*, and the Anglicized *weenie*, a frankfurter, and the common *sausage* imagery. To *step on* or *shoot your weenie* is a variant of the cliché, to shoot yourself in the foot.

weigh the thumb deliberately to overcharge

From the practice of surreptitiously depressing the scales to give a heavier reading, but now used figuratively of any overcharging.

weight watcher a fat person

But at least conscious of the condition and perhaps seeking to alleviate it. Obese people rather than anorexics are said to have a *weight problem*.

welfare state aid to the poor

It originally meant prosperity, which is not how all the recipients today see it.

The British *Welfare State*, a Utopian concept introduced after the Second World War, had the laudable intention of providing all citizens with free medical care, free schooling, and provision for adequate shelter, food, and clothing, regardless of whether they were in employment or paid taxes.

well away drunk

Also as *well bottled, in the way, corned, oiled, sprung*, etc.:

The Colonel... overcomes his resistance to vodka to such an extent that he is soon well away and sings songs of Old Kentucky. (A. Carter, 1984)

Some forms are obsolete.

well built fat

Used of men and women, and of children also, because manufacturers know better than to describe somebody's little darling as obese. Less often as *well fleshed*.

well endowed having large genitals or breasts

Nature's dowry rather than a parental marriage settlement.

Such a male may be also said to be *well hung* while a busty female may claim, or be said, to have a *large endowment*:

Exceptionally good-looking, personable, muscular athlete is available. Her bottom plus large endowment equals a good time. (*Sunday Telegraph*, September 1989, quoting an advertisement to which Representative Frank responded, appointing the prostitute as his personal aide in Congress)

well-informed sources the person involved

Political usage when the passer of the information wishes to remain anonymous, to influence public opinion without making a direct statement, or to reveal confidential details. As the attribution no longer deceives many people, the information now tends to come from *friends* of the politician in question.

well rewarded overpaid

It is better not to be seen to accuse the beneficiary of greed:

...Lord Young, C & W's well-rewarded chairman. (*Daily Telegraph*, 6 December 1994)

welly a contraceptive sheath

A shortened form of *Wellington boot*, which is also made of rubber and has protective properties:

Wellies from the Queen are condoms held by the QM at the brow during foreign port visits. (Jolly, 1988—the *brow* is the gangway)

wench *archaic* a prostitute

Originally, a girl, whence a promiscuous woman.

He who *wenches* is a womanizer.

West Briton *Irish* an Anglicized Irishman

Often Protestant, educated in England, and affecting the speech and manners of the British professional classes. Used derogatively by some other Irish people:

Those on the other side, he said, were mere 'West Britons'. (Kee, 1993—this was rather rich coming from C. S. Parnell, a Protestant cricket-lover educated at Cambridge who spoke with a British upper-class accent)

Whence the obsolete *West Britonism*, the policy of advocating the continuation of the union with Great Britain.

And the adjectival *West British*:

After a short time the paper's policy could no longer with any justice be called 'West British'. (Fleming, 1965—of the *Irish Times*, which maintained a Unionist stance for some time after the creation of the Irish Free State)

wet¹ (the bed) to urinate in an inappropriate place
And in various other phrases, such as *wet yourself*, to urinate in your clothing; *wet your pants*, to urinate in your trousers, etc.

wet² a drink of an intoxicant
Seldom on its own but in phrases such as *wet goods* or *wet stuff*.
A *wetting* used to be an alcoholic drink. Intoxicants are still served in a *wet canteen*.
A *wet hand* was a drunkard who might be said to *wet his beard, mouth, quill*, or *whistle*.
To *wet a bargain* was to seal it with a shared alcoholic drink and to *wet the baby's head* is to drink intoxicants to celebrate its birth.

wet³ lustful
Of a female, from the secretion of vaginal fluid:
    . . . he coolly proposed that we should go upstairs and, as he put it, 'very pleasantly fuck'. Oh dear, just writing those words makes me wet. (Lodge, 2001)
Also as *wet your drawers, knickers, pants*, or *yourself*.
To *wet for* is to lust after a specific male.
A *wet hen* was a prostitute and a *wet deck* copulation with a woman who had recently copulated with another.

wet-back *American* an illegal Mexican immigrant into the United States
At one time many swam across the border.

wet dream an involuntary seminal ejaculation while asleep
The experience may be accompanied by an erotic dream.
Figurative use only of female lust.

wet job a murder
But not necessarily by drowning. Also as *wet operations* or *work*.

wet nurse a woman paid to suckle another's baby
Once a common practice, from the breast feeding. Standard English.

wet weekend *Australian* a period of menstruation
Weather during which the opportunity for SPORT is curtailed.

wetness sweat
Female usage and advertising jargon, often as *underarm wetness*.

whack to kill
The common hitting imagery. Also as *whack out*.

whack off to masturbate
To *whack* is to pull, among other meanings.

whacked drunk
From the slang meaning, exhausted. The symptoms can be the same.

wham (of a male) to copulate with
The usual violent imagery, and also in the phrase *wham, bang, and thank you ma'am*, of a selfish philanderer.

what the traffic will bear an excessive but obtainable price
The imagery is from transport pricing policy. The cliché is most used by lawyers, merchant bankers, etc. when setting fee levels for corporate, careless, or care-worn customers.

what you may call it any taboo object
The lavatory for many females, or a part of the body associated with sex or urination. Often shortened to *whatsit*, less often to *whatzis*.

whelp to give birth to a child
A *whelp* is literally the cub of a bitch, a lioness, or a tigress.

whiff of an association with something illegal or taboo
From the smell:
    . . . we got a definite whiff of march hare. (Monkhouse, 1993—somebody was acting strangely)
Carlyle's *whiff of grapeshot* was the firing on the Paris mob by Napoleon which established order and his personal authority.

whiffled drunk
To *whiffle* was to be unsteady, as drunkards often are.

whip to steal
Usually of small objects, perhaps from the moving of a distant article with the use of a *whip*. Common slang use.

whip the cat to be drunk
Cats are associated with vomiting and vomiting with drunkenness, although that does not explain the *whipping*.

whistle the penis
Nursery usage, from the shape in a young boy.

whistleblower a person who reveals damaging confidential information
The position of a referee, who stops the game when he detects foul play.
See also BLOW⁵.

whistled *?obsolete* drunk
A *whistle* in slang is a mouth, which we still WET². A *whistle-shop* was an unlicensed inn, operated by a *whistler*.

white elephant an unwanted or onerous possession
The King of Siam, also titled 'the King of the White Elephant', was said to present such a beast to any courtier he wished to ruin. Unable to sell or work the animal, the recipient had to provide for it with no return.

white feather cowardice
Such a feather in the plumage of a fighting cock was said to indicate poor breeding whence less aggressive behaviour.

white girl heroin or cocaine
Addict jargon. Also as *white lady*, *line*, *powder*, or *stuff*.
White lightning is LSD.

white flight *American* the loss of residential exclusivity
A phenomenon following the relocation of white householders from a locality following the ingress of less affluent non-whites.

white knight an industrial predator
In normal commercial jargon, a third party offering to save a company from an unwanted takeover:
> ...they are rightly sending 'white knights' packing when they show up with a flick knife up their sleeve. (*Daily Telegraph*, 19 April 2006)

white-knuckler *American* a small aircraft on a scheduled service
Alluding to the anxious grip of the passengers on the arms of the seats, especially in bad weather.
Various local carriers are called the *White-Knuckle Line* by their regular passengers.

white marriage a marriage in which the parties do not copulate
The traditional virginal colour, so often seen inappropriately in the bridal gown, remains appropriate here.

white meat[1] the breast of cooked poultry
As with DARK MEAT[1] now standard English, with Victorian prudery forgotten:
> When she offered [Winston Churchill] some cold chicken, he asked if he could have a breast...his hostess informed him genteelly that 'we Southern ladies use the term "white meat".' (D. Enright, 2002—the next day Churchill sent her a corsage, suggesting she pin it to her white meat)

white meat[2] a white woman viewed sexually

The converse of DARK MEAT[2], but also used of the aspirations of a white man living among black people:
> If it's white meat you want, ji, you won't find-o much on her. (Rushdie, 1995—it was suggested that Jawaharlal Nehru would find Edwina, Countess Mountbatten, an unsatisfactory sexual partner)

white plague (the) *obsolete* pulmonary tuberculosis
The illness attracted much euphemism because it killed many young adults.

white rabbit scut cowardice
The *scut* is the short white erect tail, the sign of the fleeing rabbit.

white sale an occasion when concessions are freely given
There is recurrent heavy discounting by retailers of *white goods*, bedlinen, and domestic appliances. Some figurative use:
> I got him everything. It was a white sale at the U.S. Attorney's office. (Turow, 1990)

white satin gin or vodka
If distilled illegally, also as *white lightning* or *stuff*.

white slave a prostitute under the control of a pimp
Formerly, a white female forced into prostitution outside Europe, and especially in Argentina or the Middle East.
The phrase is now used of Asian, Mexican, and South American women, as well as those from Eastern Europe, who are bought and sold for the purpose of prostitution.

white tail a completed but unsold new aircraft
The manufacturer leaves it in a white finish until the buyer stipulates the livery. *White tails* are a treble disaster for the maker: his finance charges continue, his cash flow is interrupted, and the presence of unsold aircraft spoils the market.

white top a geriatric
A man so described may be bald, and a woman may have BLUE HAIR.

white van man a trader who does not observe the law
The unmarked *white van* provides anonymity, especially when it comes to declaring activities to the Revenue:
> It is uneconomic to set taxes and duties so high that evading them pays. White Van Man could tell Gordon Brown that. (*Daily Telegraph*, 21 December 2002)

Whitehall warrior *British* a military officer given a routine desk job in London
The armed services in peacetime find themselves with an excessive number of officers for whom there are no ships, aircraft, or soldiers. Giving them a clerical role has replaced the former practice of putting them on half-pay until they might again be needed for active service or reach retirement age.

whitewash an attempt to hush up an embarrassing or shameful event
The compound of lime and water, or similar non-permanent materials, easily and liberally applied to a surface, provides temporary cover for the blemishes underneath. In February 2001 a fiscal scandal involving the British government granting accelerated citizenship to generous Indians led to a report considered so insipid that, rather than use the term *whitewash*, the press dubbed its author *Dulux*, after a brand of paint.

whizz *American* an act of urination
Onomatopoeic use.

wholesome *obsolete* not suffering from venereal disease
Literally, no more than healthy:
> The woman, indeed, is a most lovely woman; but I had no courage to meddle with her, for fear of her not being wholesome. (Pepys, 1664—perhaps too he was feeling weary, having already 'had his pleasure of' Mrs Lane twice that day)

wick the penis
A unique example of both parts of a rhyming slang phrase being used individually, although, unlike HAMPTON, *wick* is also used figuratively, in the phrase *it gets on my wick*, expressing annoyance.
To *wet your wick* is to copulate.

wicked way (your) copulation
It is the male who seeks this path, which is not to be confused with Jermyn Street or the Reeperbahn. The phrase is mostly used humorously, and as *wicked design, purposes*, etc.

widening access making a facility available on grounds other than merit
Not enlarging the doors but making the criteria for admission less demanding for selected classes of people.

wiener *American* a penis
From *wienerworst* and see also WEENIE

will *obsolete* a homosexual
Widespread dialect use of either sex. *EDD* says 'an effeminate man; a mannish woman', which is as close to defining homosexuality

as Dr Wright would venture. It is a shortened form of *will-o-the-wisp*, the *ignis fatuus*, of which first appearances are deceptive.

will there be anything else? *obsolete* do you wish to buy condoms?
The question was asked of adult males by their barber, when condoms were not sold openly in places to which women went and were freely available through barbers' shops.

willie-waught *obsolete Scottish* a drink of intoxicant
Good willie meant hospitable and *waught* meant to drink deeply:
> 'And we'll take a right guid willie-waught' was changed to, 'We'll give a right guid hearty shake', in deference to temperance principles. (E. Murray, 1977, writing of Sir James Murray, the creator of the *OED* and domestically the bowdlerizer of Robert Burns. He also omitted from the *OED* the common vulgarisms noted by Grose, and other taboo words)

willy a penis
Or *willie*, in nursery and adult use:
> There are almost as many names for a man's most intimate possession as there are for himself... from Tom, Dick and Harry to Jean-Claude, Giorgio and Fritz. The villain of this book is called Willie. (Joliffe & Mayle, 1984)
A *willie-puller*, a masturbator, is a term of vulgar abuse.

win¹ to steal
Old general use and still current among soldiers:
> In the army it is always considered more excusable to 'win' or 'borrow' things from men belonging to other companies. (Richards, 1936)

win² to copulate with
In a bygone age, to *win* a woman was to secure her consent to marriage. It now refers to extramarital sexual conquest:
> I resolved to win her altogether. (F. Harris, 1925—but not with a proposal of wedlock)

win home *obsolete Scottish* to die
Christian devout use of the death of another, although the speaker seldom seemed anxious to secure a similar victory for himself. Also as *win your way* or *win to rest*.

wind¹ a belch or fart
In genteel use, only of belching, about which there are fewer taboos than farting. *Windy* means suffering from, or liable to cause, flatulence or flatus.

wind² (the) *American* dismissal from employment, courtship, or occupancy
Something which you may be *given*.
If *taken*, it implied voluntary departure.

wind up (the) cowardice
Fearful of being blown away, perhaps.
Windy means apprehensive more than cowardly. In the trench warfare of the First World War, a position where an occupant was likely to be shot was called *Windy Corner*.

winded (of a male) incapacitated by a blow to the genitalia
Supposedly, having received a blow in the stomach.
The evasion is much favoured by sports commentators.

windfall a bribe
Fruit which fell to the ground used to be given to whomsoever wished to gather it. Thus a *windfall* was something of value for which you did not have to pay, including a legacy or other unexpected benefit:
> The cop and those higher up share in the windfall. (Lavine, 1930—describing bribery, not apples)

window dressing falsely or fraudulently issuing figures or statements relating to a business
Commercial and banking jargon, using imagery from retail trading:
> The cheques were part of the 'window dressing' of the balance sheet at London and County Securities. (*Private Eye*, September 1981—beware always the words *security* or *trust* in any financial organization which asks you to invest)

winged wounded
Second World War use of humans, from the shooting of birds which, if hit in the wing, fall to the ground alive.

winkle a penis
Nursery usage, perhaps from the *Willie* in *Wee Willie Winkie*. Occasionally also as *winkie*.

wipe off to kill
The imagery is from erasing chalk from a blackboard
Also as *wipe out*, which has in addition the figurative meaning to impoverish or bring into disrepute.

wire to render ineffective a tachograph (on a commercial vehicle)
The tachograph records the times when the vehicle is moving, thus providing evidence that statutory rest periods are taken by the driver.
See also HOT-WIRE.

wire-pulling the covert use of influence or pressure
Like the actuation of a puppet:
> ...promises were held out of 'wire-pulling tactics in high political circles'. (R. F. Foster, 1993, referring to the advance publicity for Mrs Parnell's 1914 autobiography)

wired¹ drunk or under the influence of narcotics
Of the same tendency as LIT and more of drug-taking than alcohol.

wired² (up) subject to clandestine surveillance
This espionage and police jargon has survived the introduction of devices which are almost always *wire-less*.
An investigator or person seeking evidence clandestinely may be said to *wear a wire*.
A *wireman* is an expert in the technology.

wise woman *obsolete* a witch
And a *wise man* was a wizard.

with child pregnant
Standard English, and not just somebody left holding the baby.

with respect you are wrong
Used in polite discussion and jargon of the courts where an advocate wishes to contradict a judge without prejudicing his case:
> There is high authority for the view that (with respect) means 'You are wrong' ...just as 'with great respect' means 'you are utterly wrong' and 'with the utmost respect' equals 'send for the men in white coats'. (Mr Justice Staughton, quoted in *Daily Telegraph*, February 1987)

with your Maker dead
Christian usage in various forms, from the posthumous heavenly gathering of the righteous and others, who may also aspire to *meet God, Jesus, the Lord*, etc. Muslims may expect to *meet the Prophet*.
Those who are *with us no more* are no less dead, although perhaps unsure who is waiting to meet them.

withdraw from life to kill yourself
The destination is unspecified:
> Due to the hopelessness of the state of her health, she decided to withdraw from life. (*Daily Telegraph*, 6 July 2001—reporting a statement about the suicide of Hannelore, the wife of Helmut Kohl)

withdraw your labour to go on strike
Trade union jargon. It could simply mean to go home or to change your employment.

withdrawal to prepared positions a forced retreat
One way in which the defeated seek to play down or mitigate failure. A *withdrawal in good order* is probably a rout.

withdrawn from the roll of the living dead
Lord Salisbury used this evasive circumlocution to tell the House of Lords that a politician had died.

within-group norming *American* giving lower marks to white candidates than to blacks
An attempt to meet a QUOTA in employment ratios by penalizing those who are likely to have had better educational opportunities.
See also RACE-NORMING.

without a head *obsolete Scottish* unmarried
This expression refers to the time when many unmarried women had little security outside their parents' house, few opportunities to maintain themselves, and almost no protection in law:
    It's no easy thing...for a woman to go through the world without a head. (Miller, 1879)
(Males who are vexed by the antics of modern feminists should remember that this pendulum once swung the other way.)

without baggage *obsolete* to execution
One of the coded phrases used by the Russians under Communism for prisoners taken out of jail to be killed. Also as *without the right to correspondence*, which at least acknowledged that dead people can't read:
    From time to time someone would depart from the camp 'without baggage'. Those were sinister words—we all knew what they meant. (Horrocks, 1960—he was imprisoned in Moscow in 1920 after serving with the White Russian forces)

without domestic bliss denied copulation
In a plea for mitigation in the trial of a Lambeth labourer convicted of copulation with a child of 13, Counsel told the judge that, although married, he had for many years been *without domestic bliss*. Although it might be thought that there were other forms of felicity in the home than his wife's willingness to copulate with him, the euphemism needed no further elaboration.

without the highest IQ in the world slow-witted
A sample entry to cover many similar phrases,

which logically might refer to all of us, bar one.

woman a female viewed lustfully by a man
He who says *I feel like a woman tonight* does not postulate an incipient sex change.
A *womanizer* is a male profligate.

woman friend a mistress
As distinct from a FRIEND who is a *woman*:
    Somoza, his woman friend...and four of his five children. (*Daily Telegraph*, August 1979)

woman in a gilded cage a mistress
In the 19th-century she might be provided with separate accommodation by her wealthy keeper.
In modern America, she may be the young (second or subsequent) bride of a much older wealthy man.

woman named *British* a woman accused by the wife of an adulterous association with her husband
Legal jargon in a divorce suit. A man accused by the husband of a similar involvement with his wife might be joined in the proceedings as a CO-RESPONDENT, thereby making him liable for damages and costs. *Naming* the woman brought nothing worse than unwelcome publicity.

woman of intrigue *obsolete* a dissolute woman
As different from an *intriguing woman*:
    Praise me...for my good qualities—you know them; but tell also how odd, how constant, how impetuous, how much accustomed to women of intrigue. (Lynd, 1946—Boswell was instructing Temple about approaching Miss Blair on his behalf)

woman of the town a prostitute
Not just someone who does not live in the country:
    It is ordered that hereafter when any female shall...show contempt for any officer or soldier of the United States, she shall be regarded and held liable as a woman of the town, plying her avocation. (Ward, 1990, quoting an order by the Yankee military governor of New Orleans in 1862)
Also as a *woman of the world*, although to be a *man of the world* implies knowledge of, rather than participation in, shameful activities.

woman's thing (the) female homosexuality
Homosexual jargon.

women a lavatory for exclusively female use
Not generally less salubrious than a lavatory marked LADIES. Also as *women's room* etc.

women's liberation aggressive feminism
For most men, and many women, a dysphemism, especially when shortened to *women's lib*. An enthusiast may be called a *women's libber* or *libber*, which latter was once the job title of a castrator of pigs—further comment seems inappropriate.

women's movement an association of committed feminists
Nothing to do with calisthenics; and see also MOVEMENT.

women's rights the claim to or enjoyment of economic and social conditions historically exclusive to or awarded in priority to men
As different from the normal rights of females as citizens.

women's things any taboo matter or article exclusive to women
Usually the phrase refers to a medical condition exclusive to females, or to absorbent matter worn during menstruation:
    For the Curse—you know. Women's things. (W. Smith, 1979)

wooden box a coffin
A current usage. *Wooden breeches*, *breeks*, *coat*, *overcoat*, etc. are obsolete.
Whence figurative use of death:
    The Winston treatment when it finally comes to the wooden box. (*Private Eye*, June 1981—Churchill had an elaborate state funeral)

wooden hill the staircase
Nursery usage. Children may be told to *climb* it when reluctant to go to bed or, in the hallowed punning phrase, *to Bedfordshire*.

wooden log a human used involuntarily for medical research
The phrase was used by the Japanese General Ishii, commanding Unit 731, which subjected prisoners of war to medical experimentation until the end of the Second World War. Ishii also tried to send plague-bearing fleas by submarine to Saipan to infect American troops, although the submarine was sunk. Neither he nor his master, Hirohito, was charged as a war criminal.

word from our sponsor (a) *American* an advertisement on television
Would that it were only one.

word to the wise a warning or threat
There is a suggestion that it would be unwise to ignore the message:
    When questions of the legitimacy of the Zogoiby children began to be hinted at...the editors of all the major newspapers...had a word-to-the-wise in their ears; and after that the press campaign stopped instantly. (Rushdie, 1995)

words *American* an advertisement on television
Another way of covering up the intrusion.

work both sides of the street to serve people with conflicting interests
To *work a street* was to attempt to sell goods from door to door, not always honestly, as different from to WORK THE STREETS.

work off *obsolete* to kill
Victorian slang used by Charles Dickens (1841).

work on[1] to extract information from through violence
Literally, to have an effect on physically: 'Shellacking', 'massaging', 'breaking the news', 'working on the——'...'giving him the works'...express how [the NYC police] compel reluctant prisoners to refresh their memories. (Lavine, 1930)

work on[2] (of a male) to copulate with
The concept is of rough handling rather than referring to the posture assumed:
    We could...give you an examination too, and see if you've been working on her tonight. (Mailer, 1965)

work the streets to be a prostitute
From her public solicitation.

work to rule *British* to behave in a way calculated to obstruct and cause loss
Not what the Queen does but, as an employee, consulting an actual or notional *Rule Book* and observing the minutiae so that the business cannot operate efficiently. In this way, the employee still gets paid, the employer loses money, and the customers suffer. Also as a noun.

work with writers as an author to employ someone else to write the book or article
It was suggested that this would be the procedure for a young actress and model not renowned for literary prowess who received a six-figure advance from the publisher Random House in 2005 to write an autobiography and two novels.

workers' control the oppressive rule by an oligarchy
Communist jargon which implied that the populace controlled the ruling and self-perpetuating oligarchs, rather than the contrary:
> Within the Leninist model... 'Worker's control' here means control of the workers. (*Sunday Telegraph*, August 1980, referring to Poland where before long the *workers* did take *control*)

workhouse an institution for the homeless indigent
The intention was that the unfortunate inmates should work to pay for their keep, although the name outlived the concept.

working capital shortfall an insolvency
Evasive circumlocution in a sphere of activity where a suggestion of failure must be avoided:
> Without the transaction, the group said, it 'would incur a working capital shortfall this month'. (*Daily Telegraph*, 21 December 2002)

working dictionary a mistress taken by an expatriate from the indigenous community
There must be, for a young man, less congenial ways of learning a new language.

working girl a prostitute
But hoping not, as a consequence, to go into labour.

working party a committee
Usually appointed by politicians to postpone public judgement on a fiasco caused by their incompetence until such time as another tragedy or scandal is in the headlines granting them a 'good day to bury bad news'.

working people *British* industrial workers not self-employed or in management
Those who once claimed to belong to the *working class*, but the people who use the phrase tend to ignore others who also work for a living. Also as *working men*:
> I doubt whether working people will be willing to go on making sacrifices of this nature for much longer. (*Daily Telegraph*, January 1977—the *sacrifice* was not to receive a wage increase much exceeding the rate of inflation)

workshop a discussion group
Those involved seek to justify the activity by association with a productive enterprise:
> 'Excuse me, I've got a series of meetings.'

'There's a panel this afternoon' was another line I heard. Yet another: 'We're having a workshop.' (Theroux, 2002 reporting on his attempts to talk to Western aid workers in Africa about their activities)

World Peace Council an instrument of Soviet foreign policy
A weapon of the Cold War; and see also PEACE: World Peace Council, see under *front organization*. (Bullock & Stallybrass, 1977—a magisterially dismissive comment)

worry to make sexual advances to an unwilling partner
Originally, of dogs and animals, to kill by gripping the throat, whence, by transference, mental distress in, or harassment of, humans:
> It is perfectly dreadful that Wifie should be so worried at night. (Kee, 1993—Parnell was writing to his mistress Katie O'Shea, commiserating with her on the fact that her husband wished to copulate with her)

worship at the shrine of to be unhealthily addicted to
Usually of alcohol, illegal narcotics, or sexual excess:
> Among newspapermen, most of whom worshipped more frequently at the shrine of Bacchus than Ariadne... (Deighton, 1991—Bacchus was the god of wine. Ariadne was of an enquiring mind, helping Theseus to escape from the maze devised by Daedalus, from which subsequently Daedalus himself and his son Icarus made their aerial escape)

wrack *obsolete* to deflower a woman
Literally, to destroy. Used as a verb by Shakespeare in *Hamlet* and as the *wrack of maidenhead* in *All's Well That Ends Well*.

wreak your passion on to copulate with
Passion, originally the suffering of pain, has been used of lust, especially in males, since the 16th century.

wrecked drunk or under the influence of illegal narcotics
The way you may feel and look.

wretched calendar (the) I am menstruating
Referring to the practice of noting the date of the expected onset.

wrinkly an old person
Used by the young, mindless of 'time's wingéd chariot'.

wrist job (a) masturbation
Referring to the act and, figuratively as an insult, the actor.

write off to kill or destroy
The imagery is from the removal of an unserviceable item from an inventory.

written out of the script dismissed from employment
Literally, in the case of a television serial and figuratively of those not in show business.

wrong[1] to copulate with extramaritally
The *wrong* was done by the man, even if the woman said it was all right:

Ravish'd and wrong'd, as Philomena was. (Shakespeare, *Titus Andronicus*)

Also as *do wrong (to)*:

As man to man, I solemnly swear that I did her no wrong. (Hardy, 1886)

wrong[2] homosexual
Possibly obsolete, with the change in attitudes to homosexuality.

Specifically as *wrong sexual preference* etc.

wrong side of the blanket an allusion to illegitimacy
The impregnation supposedly took place on or out of the marital bed, rather than in it. The painter Augustus John was said to have fathered various children in and out of wedlock, or *from both sides of the blanket*. (*Daily Telegraph*, 24 September 2003)

wrong time of the month the period of menstruation
Mainly female usage, from the inconvenience and discomfort rather than the suspension of copulation. See also TIME.

Y

yak *American* a human carrier of illegal narcotics in bulk
See also MULE—different continent, same concept.

yard *obsolete* a penis
I hesitate to suggest a derivation or allude to imperial measurements:
> 'Leave her by the foot.' 'He may not by the yard.' (Shakespeare, *Love's Labour's Lost*)
> He put his yard up my backside and told me not to say anything. (L. James, 2001, reporting a naval Court Martial in 1807)

yardbird *American* a convict
He uses the exercise *yard* in a penitentiary.

year of progress *American* a period of irreversible decline
Progress, in the statements of politicians or company chairman, usually indicates that things have gone badly:
> In the year leading up to the Tet Offensive ('1987—Year of progress' was the name of the official year-end report)...(Herr, 1977)

yellow¹ cowardly
From the pallor of fright. In many phrases such as *yellow belly*, a coward, who might show a *yellow streak* or *stripe*.
For Shakespeare however, in *Twelfth Night*, *yellow stockings* were an indication of jealousy.

yellow² *American* of mixed black and white ancestry
Originally describing a light-skinned female slave, often used as a house servant. Also as *high-yellow*.
In China the *yellow trade* is not prostitution but any kind of illegality or vice.

yellow page common or inferior
The implication is that those offering high-quality goods or services do not have to advertise in the popular directory, *Yellow Pages*:

> They followed Wally Bright, their yellow page lawyer. (Grisham, 1999)

yield to copulate with a man outside marriage
Literally, to submit, and of venerable ancestry:
> There is no woman, Eupheus, but she will yield in time. (Lely, 1579, quoted in *ODEP*)
The female may also *yield to ardour, desire, solicitation*, etc. *yielding her body, person*, or (less probably) *virginity*.

yob see SLAG

you-know-what any taboo matter within the context
Normally a lavatory, when its location is being indicated.
A *bit of you-know-what* is promiscuous copulation.

young not over 45 years old
Mainly journalistic use, often to describe public figures who have achieved prominence at an earlier age than most of their contemporaries:
> Nick was very young, still in his early thirties. (M. Thomas, 1982)

young lady a man's premarital sexual partner
As with the more severe *young woman*, it may imply no more than courtship:
> The marriage has been annulled by the papal courts and it would be very painful to me & my young lady to have it referred to. (S. Hastings, 1994, quoting a letter written by E. Waugh in January 1937)

younger brother *obsolete* an indigenous Indonesian male
A usage of the Dutch colonists who considered themselves their *elders*, regardless of age or ability.

youth (guidance) center *American* an institution for the punishment of young offenders
Unlike the British *youth centre*, which provides leisure facilities, it may require a young criminal to attend on a daily or permanent basis.

Z

zero grazing intensive farming of cattle
The animals are confined to a barn or yard instead of being put out to pasture.

zipper a male profligate
One who readily un*zips* his trousers other than to urinate or retire for the night.
He may also be said to have a *zipper problem*:
   I knew all about the President's alleged attractiveness. His 'zipper problem' had provided hours of dinner-party amusement for his friends and me. (Nina Burleigh, in *Daily Telegraph*, 3 August 1998—it is to be hoped that the amusement was confined to the dinner parties)

zoned out *American* drunk or under the influence of illegal narcotics
The imagery is from a defensive play in football and basketball.

zoning *American* the restriction of construction or development
Supposedly for the protection of the environment but see also BANANA.

zonked *American* drunk or under the influence of illegal drugs
Literally in slang, hit:
   ...he should be banging women zonked out of their gourds on high-quality coke. (Sanders, 1990)

zoo *American* a brothel
A variety of creatures are available to the visitor.